The New Introduction to Geographic

Geographical economics starts from the observation that, clearly, economic activity is not randomly distributed across space. This revised and updated introduction to geographical economics uses the modern tools of economic theory to explain the who, why, and where of the location of economic activity.

Key features:

- Provides an integrated, first-principles introduction to geographical economics for advanced undergraduate students and first-year graduate students
- Thoroughly revised and updated to reflect important recent developments in the field, including new chapters on alternative core models and policy implications
- Presents a truly global analysis of issues in geographical economics using case studies from all over the world, including North America, Europe, Africa, and Australasia
- Contains many computer simulations and end-of chapter exercises to encourage learning and understanding through application

A companion website is available at www.cambridge.org/geog-econ.

Steven Brakman is Professor of International Economics at the University of Groningen, the Netherlands.

Harry Garretsen is Professor of International Economics and Business at the University of Groningen, the Netherlands.

Charles van Marrewijk is Professor of International Economics at Utrecht University, the Netherlands.

The New Introduction to Geographical Economics

New edition

Steven Brakman, **Harry Garretsen**, and

Charles van Marrewijk

CAMBRIDGE
UNIVERSITY PRESS

CAMBRIDGE
UNIVERSITY PRESS

University Printing House, Cambridge CB2 8BS, United Kingdom

Cambridge University Press is part of the University of Cambridge.

It furthers the University's mission by disseminating knowledge in the pursuit of education, learning and research at the highest international levels of excellence.

www.cambridge.org
Information on this title: www.cambridge.org/9780521698030

First published 2001
Second Edition 2009
Reprinted with corrections 2011

A catalogue record for this publication is available from the British Library

Library of Congress Cataloguing in Publication data
Brakman, Steven.
  The new introduction to geographical economics / Steven Brakman, Harry Garretsen, Charles van Marrewijk. – New ed.
    p.   cm.
  Rev. ed. of: An introduction to geographical economics. 2001
  Includes bibliographical references and index.
  ISBN 978-0-521-87532-5 (hardback)   1. Economic geography.   I. Garretsen, Harry.
  II. Marrewijk, Charles van.   III. Brakman, Steven. An introduction to geographical economics.
  IV. Title.
  HF1025.B68 2009
  330.9–dc22
  2009000058

ISBN 978-0-521-87532-5 Hardback
ISBN 978-0-521-69803-0 Paperback

Cambridge University Press has no responsibility for the persistence or accuracy of URLs for external or third-party internet websites referred to in this publication, and does not guarantee that any content on such websites is, or will remain, accurate or appropriate.

Contents

Figures

Tables

Boxes

Technical notes

Symbols and Parameters

Symbols

Indices	r,s for regions
	i,j for varieties
B	break point
S	sustain point or stable equilibrium
U	utility
L	labor force
K	(human) capital stock
C	consumption
H	housing stock
HI	Herfindahl index
$H(N)$	cost of living curve
T	transport costs; units to be shipped to ensure one unit arrives
T_{rs}	transport costs; units to be shipped from region r to ensure one unit arrives in region s
t	time index or iteration index
l_{ir}	labor required to produce variety i in region r
R	number of regions ro rank
N	number of varieties or labor force
N_r, n_r	number of varieties of manufactures produced in region r
x_{ir}	amount of variety i produced in region r
x_r	total production of manufactures of a representative producer in region r
P_r	locally charged price for a variety of manufactures in region r
W_r	nominal wage in region r
w_r	real wage in region r
r_s	reward to (human) capital in region s

$\overline{w}$	average real wage
Y	income
y	real income
q	slope of rank size rule
F	food
M	manufactures
I	exact price index of manufactures
c_i	consumption of manufacturing variety i
E_{rs}	expenditures in region r on goods from region s
D_{rs}	distance from region r to region s
D_J	intermediate good for sector $J = A,B$

Parameters

α	fixed cost or econometric coefficient
β	marginal cost or econometric coefficient
γ	share of labor force in manufactures or econometric coefficient, Cobb–Douglas parameter
ε	elasticity of substitution $= 1/(1-\rho)$
δ	share of income spent on manufactured goods or stable equilibrium
λ_r	share of manufacturing labor force working in region r
σ	threshold value for real wage differences in simulations
τ	congestion parameter
ϕ_r	fraction of food labor in region r
φ	freeness of trade $= T^{1-\varepsilon}$
θ	miscellaneous parameter
η	speed of adjustment, intersectoral labor mobility, or elasticity of labor supply
ρ	substitution parameter (love-of-variety), relative indirect utility, or shock persistence
π	extent of comparative advantage or profits
κ	miscellaneous parameter (for econometric equations and knowledge spillovers)
μ	intermediate input share or capital intensity of sector A (factor abundance)
Ω	initial city size

Preface to the new edition

Positioning of the book

The purpose of this book is to offer an *introduction* to an important field in economics, entitled *geographical economics*, which sets out to explain the distribution of economic activity across space. In doing so, it endeavors to bring together and apply insights from various fields of economics. The book will therefore be of interest to students and scholars from international economics and business, as well as from economic geography, regional economics, and urban economics. The fact that we offer an "introduction" does not mean that we avoid models or shy away from difficult concepts; it indicates that we have attempted to write a book that is accessible to readers and students who are new to the field of geographical economics.

Although we introduce and discuss various modeling approaches, we keep the required technicalities to a minimum. Whenever possible we draw attention to important concepts and applications in *special interest boxes*, making ample use of examples and diagrams to explain the workings of the models. Chapter 3, which explains the structure of the core model of geographical economics, gives background derivations in *technical notes*. Throughout the book the required level of mathematical competence required does not go beyond simple optimization techniques that should be familiar to upper-level undergraduate and first-year graduate students, both in economics and in other fields of social sciences. The target audience of our book is not limited to these students, however, but includes professionals working at government agencies, banks, international organizations, and private research firms, as well as students and scholars of international business and economic geography. The latter category may find the book of interest if only to get to know what they disagree with when it comes to the analysis of the location of economic activity!

To help the reader in developing his or her intuition for different aspects important in determining the interaction between location decisions and economic performance, and to get a better feel for the modeling structure and empirical relevance of geographical economics, we include discussions of many real-world examples, and present and evaluate the currently available empirical evidence. In addition, we explain in detail an important but often neglected aspect of the geographical economics approach: *computer simulations.* We discuss their advantages and disadvantages, what is needed to actually perform such simulations, and give the reader access to a few user-friendly simple simulations (see below). The emphasis on examples, diagrams, and empirical evidence, together with the introductory nature of the book, the limited technical requirements in our analysis, and our concern to include explanatory simulation exercises, sets our book clearly apart from, and makes it a suitable introduction to, *The Spatial Economy*, the seminal contribution of Masahisa Fujita, Paul Krugman, and Anthony Venables (1999) that was the first major book to appear on geographical economics and that caters to the needs of the academic world (PhD students and fellow researchers).

There is a special *website* available for our book, for several reasons. First, it gives brief general background information on the structure of the book. Second, it deals with some aspects of the exercises to be found in the *problem set* at the end of every chapter. Not only do the exercises test the reader's knowledge of the contents of the chapter but they are also used to introduce some additional material. Third, the website provides illustrations and data material on economic location. Fourth, it provides some simple and user-friendly simulation models, which can familiarize the reader with this aspect of the geographical economics approach. Fifth, for the interested reader the website provides some additional derivations of technical details not dealt with in the book itself, as well as some more advanced (working) papers. Sixth, the website is a source of information for links to relevant researchers and institutions. Finally, it provides some background information on the authors.

Geographical economics: what's in a name?

In our view, the approach in this book is best characterized as an attempt to put more geography into economics. It is the main reason for us to prefer the term "geographical economics" rather than alternatives, such as "new regional science" or the widely used term; "*new economic geography.*" Not only does the label "new" inevitably wear off after some time, but the latter term also has the disadvantage that it suggests that the theory was developed by economic geographers. This is not the case. Instead, geographical economics has its roots firmly in international economics, and modern international trade and economic growth theory. It adds the location of economic activity to these theories.

In the end a label is just a label, and what really matters, of course, are the topics covered in geographical economics. In 1933 the Swedish economist Bertil Ohlin published a book called *Interregional and International Trade,* in which he strongly advocated a closer collaboration between what is now called international economics and regional economics, as they share, in Ohlin's view, the same research objective. To a large extent, geographical economics can be looked upon as a (somewhat belated) reply to Ohlin's call, originating from within international economics. As Krugman puts it (1991b: 7), it is an attempt "to resurrect economic geography as a major field within economics." An attempt in which the modern tools of mainstream economic theory are used to explain the *who, why, and where* of the location of economic activity. As to the scientific recognition of geographical economics, the Nobel Prize in economics was awarded to Paul Krugman for his work on international trade and economic geography on October 13, 2008.

Geographical economics takes as its starting point the empirical fact that economic activity is, clearly, not distributed randomly across space. A quick look at any map suffices to show that the clustering of people and firms is the rule and not the exception. Geographical economics seeks to give a microeconomic foundation for this fact using a general equilibrium framework. Geographical economics models are often hard to solve analytically, such that the approach relies to a large extent on *computer simulations* to determine the distribution of economic activity across space and build intuition for the strength of the powers involved. Throughout our book we will also often use computer simulations.

Given the target audience, a considerable part of our book explains in detail the structure and main results of the so-called core models of geographical economics in chapters 3 and 4 of the book, after an introduction to the topic in chapter 1 and a discussion of the antecedents of geographical economics in chapter 2. Chapters 3 and 4, together with chapters 5 and 6 on empirical research and evidence, constitute the heart of the book. Chapters 7–10 deal with a variety of extensions to and modified empirical applications of the core model. In our selection of these extensions we deliberately chose applications requiring only relatively small modifications of the core model. Topics covered by chapters 7–10 are urban economics and city-size distributions, foreign direct investment (FDI) and multinationals, the theory and empirics of international trade, and dynamics and economic growth. The final two chapters deal with policy implications (chapter 11) and an evaluation of geographical economics (chapter 12).

What's new?

The first edition of this book, called *An Introduction to Geographical Economics*, was published in December 2001. At that time the only other book around on geographical economics was the *The Spatial Economy* by Fujita, Krugman, and Venables (1999). Since the turn of the century research in geographical economics has boomed, and this has resulted not only in many important new papers but also in a number of books and surveys that bring together and summarize the latest developments and insights. In particular, three additional books on geographical economics should be mentioned here: *Economics of Agglomeration*, by Fujita and Jacques-François Thisse (2002); *Economic Geography and Public Policy*, by Richard Baldwin, Richard Forslid, Philippe Martin, Gianmarco Ottaviano, and Frederic Robert-Nicoud (2003); and *Economic Geography*, by Pierre-Philippe Combes, Thierry Mayer, and Thisse (2006, 2008). Besides these new books, there are also very good (and critical) surveys of geographical economics available (such as that by Peter Neary, 2001), and, last but not least, in *The Handbook of Regional and Urban Economics*, vol. IV (Vernon Henderson and Thisse, 2004), geographical economics is the central topic. Various chapters in this handbook (e.g. Gilles Duranton and Diego Puga, 2004, Ottaviano and Thisse, 2004, and Keith Head and Mayer, 2004a) do a great job in summarizing and synthesizing this field of research. All the same, just as with the first edition of our book, we still feel that there is a clear need for a book that can serve as an introduction to geographical economics.

Based on the feedback and encouragement we received for the first edition from fellow researchers and students, and inspired by the many developments that have taken place in the literature since 2001, we started to work on a second edition of the book. The initial idea was to merely update and expand the previous version, but as we sat down to work on the new edition it quickly became clear that a more substantial revision was called for in order to do justice to the latest developments in the field. In the end, and while still sticking to the basic set-up of the first edition, the present edition covers a lot of new ground, and the slight change in the title of the book signals these changes.

So, what are the main changes? Besides updating the empirical material throughout the book, adjusting references (about 50 percent of the references postdate the first edition of the book), making numerous smaller changes, and the like, the most important changes are:

- The discussion and set-up of the core model of geographical economics (Krugman, 1991a) is now concentrated in a single chapter, chapter 3, whereas chapter 4 is largely new and discusses three other core models at length: an intermediate goods model, a model that may give rise to the so-called bell-shaped curve, and a solvable model.
- Given the surge of empirical research in geographical economics in the first decade of the twenty-first century, the empirical evidence is now discussed in two chapters (chapters 5 and 6) instead of a single chapter. Inspired by Head and Mayer's (2004a) list of five testable hypotheses, the second part of chapter 5 has been rewritten, and chapter 6 is wholly new.
- In the first edition of the book, the discussion of urban economics in chapter 7 focused rather strongly on city-size distributions and Zipf's Law. Interesting though this is, we have decided this time to trim down this part of the analysis and instead include more material on the main ingredients of modern urban economics. Based on the paper by Combes, Duranton, and Henry Overman (2005), this chapter now also uses a diagrammatic (non-formal) analysis of the core urban and geographical economics models, as initially developed by Henderson (1974) and Krugman (1991a) respectively.
- In international economics two burgeoning fields of research have been those on FDI (and firm heterogeneity) and gravity models. In chapters 8 and 9 we have included some of these new insights in order to illustrate their relevance for geographical economics.
- Chapter 10 still deals with dynamics and growth. Apart from a wholly new section on stylized facts, the main change considers the inclusion of a new section on the role of (first-nature) geography and institutions, as well as a discussion on the importance of (both first-nature and second-nature) geography and institutions as the "deep" determinants of economic development.
- Chapter 11 in the first edition discussed policy implications and provided a critical evaluation of the contributions of geographical economics.

In the new edition, these issues are separated in a largely extended discussion. Inspired by the Baldwin *et al.* (2003) book, the new Chapter 11 analyzes the policy implications of geographical economics. Chapter 12 evaluates the contributions of geographical economics and deals simultaneously with the critical remarks raised by, for example, economic geographers.

The *website of the book* (at www.cambridge.org/geog-econ) has been extensively updated and provides a lot of new material. Some supporting material that was part of the first edition but for which we did not have enough space in the second edition is also posted on the website.

As building blocks for the revisions and extensions, we not only made use of the new books and papers (see above), but also included our own research efforts, when appropriate. Our main consideration in this respect was always whether or not our own research was a fair representation of a wider body of work (it does not signal a preference for our own research relative to related research!).

Acknowledgments

In addition to the colleagues and institutions mentioned in the preface of the first edition, and also in addition to the numerous fellow researchers who commented on our own papers that we somehow (re-)used for the new edition, we want to single out and thank the following colleagues for joint research efforts, discussions, and suggestions, or comments on draft versions: Gilles Duranton, Ron Martin, Bernard Fingleton, Xavier Gabaix, Joeri Gorter, Jeroen Hinloopen, Ron Boschma, Koen Frenken, Henri de Groot, Herman de Jong, Albert van der Horst, Jolanda Peeters, Mark van den Brom, Till von Viersen, and, above all, Marc Schramm and Maarten Bosker. The intellectual debt to all our fellow researchers on geographical economics is obvious. We also want to thank our publisher, Cambridge University Press (CUP), for giving us the opportunity to produce a new edition of our book, and in particular we would like to thank the social sciences editor at CUP, Chris Harrison, for his patience and support. We are also very grateful to Mike Richardson, who went through the whole manuscript and corrected many mistakes and also considerably improved the use of English. Herma van der Vleuten was of great help in compiling and updating the list of references. Finally, we want to thank our respective families for their continued support.

Steven Brakman, Harry Garretsen, and Charles van Marrewijk
November 2008

Part I

Introduction

1   A first look at geography, trade, and development

1.1 Introduction

It happened on October 12, 1999 – at least, according to the United Nations (UN).[1] That was the day the human population of planet Earth officially reached 6 billion. Of course, given the inaccuracy of the data, the UN could have been off by 100 million people or so. Every day some 100 million billion sperm are released[2] and 400,000 babies are born, whereas "only" 140,000 persons die. Consequently, the world population is growing rapidly, especially since the second half of the twentieth century.

Given the average population density in the world, of about fifty people per square kilometer (Km^2), if you are part of a family with two children, your family could have about eight hectares (or twenty acres) at its disposal. The great majority of our readers will probably look around in amazement as they realize that they do not own an area close to this size. The reason is simple: the world population is unevenly distributed. But why?

There may be many reasons why people cluster together. Sociological: you like to interact with other human beings. Psychological: you are afraid of being alone. Historical: your grandfather used to live where you live now. Cultural: the atmosphere here is unlike anywhere else in the world. Geographical: the scenery is breathtaking and the beach is wonderful. We will at best cursorily discuss the above reasons for clustering. Instead, we focus attention in this book on the economic rationale behind clustering, known technically as agglomeration.

---

[1] The data in the first paragraph are from www.popexpo.net/english.html. Unless otherwise specified, all other empirical information in chapter 1 is based on our own calculations using data from the World Bank (WDI online) for 2005.

[2] Apparently, the UN is familiar with our sex habits.

In a sense, an economic motive behind population clustering might be a prerequisite for other motives. Psychological, sociological, cultural, and historical motives may have developed largely in response to an economic motive that brought people together to live in villages and cities. In this Chapter we briefly describe some of the characteristics of clustering of economies in space and their interactions.

1.2 Clustering and the world economy

In describing clustering, it is useful to distinguish between various levels of aggregation at which clustering occurs:

- the global level (section 1.2.1: the worldwide distribution of activity of resources);
- the continental level (section 1.2.2: production distribution in Europe); and
- the country level (section 1.2.3: urban agglomeration in India).

The main reason for looking at these different levels of aggregation is that, in understanding clustering, geographical economics shows that to a large extent the same basic forces apply to all levels of aggregation.

1.2.1 The global view

The World Bank collects and processes statistical information from virtually all countries in the world. To characterize various regions at a global scale, the World Bank aggregates country data to the seven groups illustrated in figure 1.1: (i) east Asia and the Pacific (EAP; including China and Indonesia); (ii) (east) Europe and central Asia (ECA; including Russia and Turkey); (iii) Latin America and the Caribbean (LAC; including Brazil and Mexico); (iv) the Middle East and north Africa (MNA; including Egypt); (v) south Asia (SAS; including India); (vi) sub-Saharan Africa (SSA; including Nigeria and South Africa); and (vii) the high-income countries (High; including the United States, the countries of the European Union, and Japan). We use this grouping to describe regional diversity at the global level.

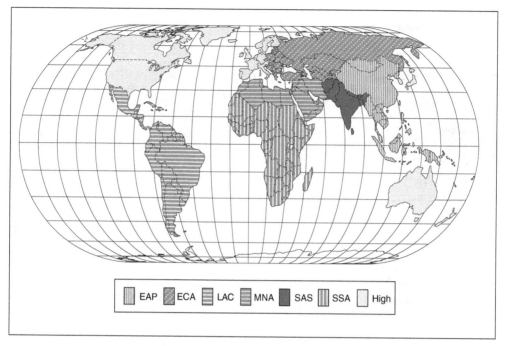

Figure 1.1   World Bank regional classification
EAP = East Asia and Pacific; ECA = Europe and Central Asia; LAC = Latin America and Caribbean; MNA = Middle East and North Africa; SAS = South Asia; SSA = Sub-Saharan Africa; High = High-income countries.

Figures 1.2 and 1.3 illustrate some key economic data for the above global regional classification. Further details of these data, as used in the rest of this chapter, are summarized in the appendix to this chapter (table A1.1). There is considerable variation in land area (figure 1.2a), from 4.8 million km² (4 percent of the world total) for south Asia to 33 million km² (26 percent of the world total) for the high-income countries. This may, of course, simply be an artifact of the classification method. The same holds, necessary changes being made, for the large differences in population size (figure 1.2b), ranging from 305 million people (5 percent) for north Africa to 1,885 million people (28 percent) for east Asia. The variation becomes more striking when we investigate the ratio of these two measures – that is, the population density (figure 1.3c). The number of persons per square kilometer varies from twenty for Europe and central Asia to 307 for South Asia, which is about fifteen times

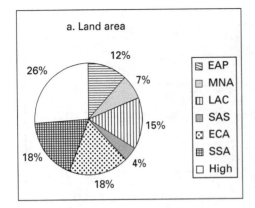

a. Land area

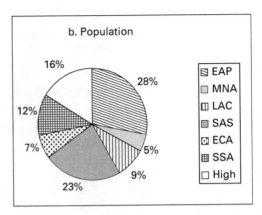

b. Population

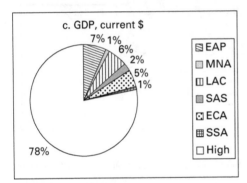

c. GDP, current $

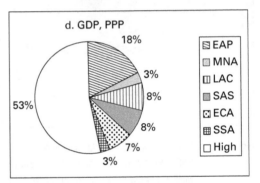

d. GDP, PPP

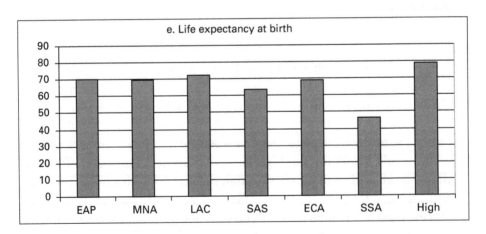

e. Life expectancy at birth

Figure 1.2   Life expectancy and regional shares of population, land, and income, 2005
Source: WDI online. GDP = gross domestic product; PPP = purchasing power parity.

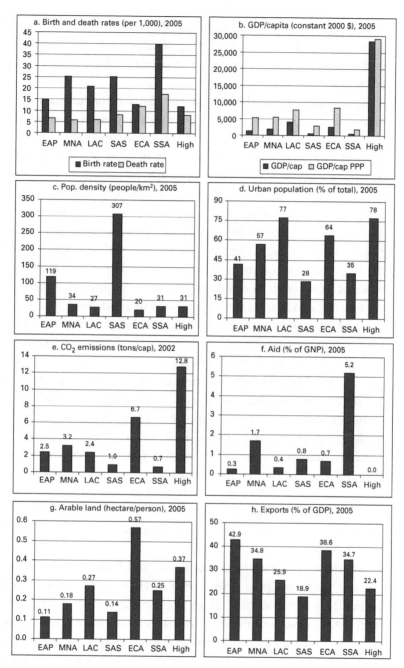

Figure 1.3 Characteristics of global regions
Source: WDI online. GNP = gross national product.

higher. There is thus an enormous difference in the distribution of the population, even at a high level of aggregation. We return to this issue in the next section. For now, we concentrate on some of the other characteristics of the World Bank regions.

Figure 1.2c clearly shows that the distribution of economic mass, as measured by the total value of all goods and services produced in each global region, is very skewed: the gross domestic product of the high-income countries accounts for 78 percent of world production calculated in current US dollars, using only 16 percent of the world population. Measured similarly, sub-Saharan Africa accounts for 1 percent of world production using 12 percent of the world population. These production levels translate into enormous differences in per capita income, ranging from $745 per year in sub-Saharan Africa to $35,130 per year for the high-income countries. A word of caution is in order at this point, however. If we want to compare gross national product – that is, GDP plus the value of goods and services produced by residents of a country abroad – in different countries we have to express this in a common unit of measurement, usually the US dollar. Since the exchange rates tend to fluctuate strongly, the World Bank calculates an average over three years for conversion (the "Atlas" method). These are the statistics reported above. Price levels for non-tradable goods and services differ considerably between countries however. Going to a movie in the United States may cost you $8, while going to the same movie in Tanzania may cost you less than $1. Getting a haircut in Amsterdam will cost you at least $10, rather than the $2 you will pay in Manila. To correct for these differences in "purchasing power," the United Nations spends a lot of time and effort gathering data on the prices of thousands of goods and services in virtually all countries, so as to calculate as accurately as possible "purchasing power parity" exchange rates.

A better estimate of the economic size of a region is therefore given when we use PPP exchange rates rather than current dollars (or the Atlas method). It turns out that $1 in China or India will deliver you approximately the same consumption basket as $4 in the United States or more than $6 in Japan. Figure 1.2d shows that, even after correction for PPP, the high-income countries still produce most goods and services (roughly 53 percent of world production), leading to somewhat smaller, but still sizable, differences in per capita income (figure 1.3b).

Most other characteristics are correlated with income per capita; see table A1.2 in the appendix. People with higher incomes tend to live longer

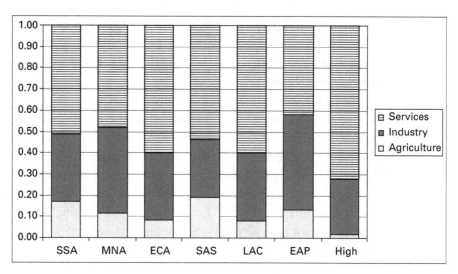

Figure 1.4   Sectoral distribution of GDP, global regions (value added, share of total), 2005
Source: WDI online. Regions are ordered from left to right in increasing GDP/cap, PPP.

(figure 1.2a), have more arable land at their disposal (figure 1.3g), have fewer children (figure 1.3a), live in cities (figure 1.3d), receive little foreign aid (figure 1.3f), and pollute more, especially greenhouse gases (figure 1.3e). Of course, there are some noteworthy exceptions. For example, (east) Europe and central Asia has (relative to PPP income per capita) a lot of arable land available (figure 1.3g), is highly urbanized (figure 1.3d), and is a heavy CO_2 emitter (figure 1.3e). Similarly, Latin America, north Africa, and the Middle East are also highly urbanized.

Other variables are only weakly correlated with per capita income. Although death rates, for example, are particularly high in poor sub-Saharan Africa (in part as a result of the AIDS epidemic, which also causes a low life expectancy), they are lower in Latin America, north Africa and the Middle East than in the high-income countries, which are confronted with a rapidly aging population. Remarkably, perhaps, the openness of the global regions, as measured by the percentage of GDP exported, is hardly correlated with income per capita. We return to this issue later in the chapter. Figure 1.4 illustrates the main sectoral composition of output in the various regions, with respect to agriculture, industry, and services. The share of output generated in the agricultural sector clearly declines, and in the services sector clearly increases, as the per capita income level increases. Regarding industry, the development is less clear-cut, as the share of output generated by industry tends to be low for low-income *and* high-income countries.

This subsection shows, *inter alia,* that the world population is very unevenly distributed when viewed at a large scale, identifying only seven regions in the world. Economic activity is even more unevenly distributed than population, whether measured using current dollars (and the Atlas method) or using purchasing power parity. Moreover, we indicated that at this large scale there is a strong correlation between the degree of urbanization and per capita income (see table A1.2). The next two subsections "zoom in" on the distribution of activity in two steps, first at the continental level for nations and then at the level for cities. It concludes the latter by drawing attention to a remarkable empirical regularity known as the rank size distribution.

1.2.2 Production distribution in Europe[3]

Figure 1.5 illustrates the first "zooming in" step, for which we picked the continent of Europe as an example. In terms of the regional classification of section 1.2, about a half of the countries in the figure, mainly in the west, belong to the region of high-income countries, while the other half is part of the (east) Europe and central Asia (ECA) region. Regional economists have long felt a need to measure the unevenness of the distribution of economic activity, and subsequently to identify and analyze core–periphery structures. Chapter 2 explains this "market potential" approach in more detail, but the general procedure is to calculate an indicator of market potential at the regional level, taking into consideration the size of economic markets in the vicinity of this region, corrected for distance to this market.

Andrew Copus (1999) studies 1,105 European regions, where he defines a "center" (usually the largest city, but sometimes the geometric center) and calculates detailed travel times to other centers, taking into consideration the type of road, ferries, waiting times for ferries and crossing a border, driving speeds in mountains and urban areas, rest times for drivers, etc.[4] Copus uses this and the market potential approach to construct a periphery index, ranging from zero for the most central region (with the highest potential) to 100 for the peripheral region (with the lowest potential).

---

[3] This subsection is based on Jeroen Hinloopen and Charles van Marrewijk (2005).
[4] The distance of a region to itself equals one-third of the axis of the smallest rectangle containing the region.

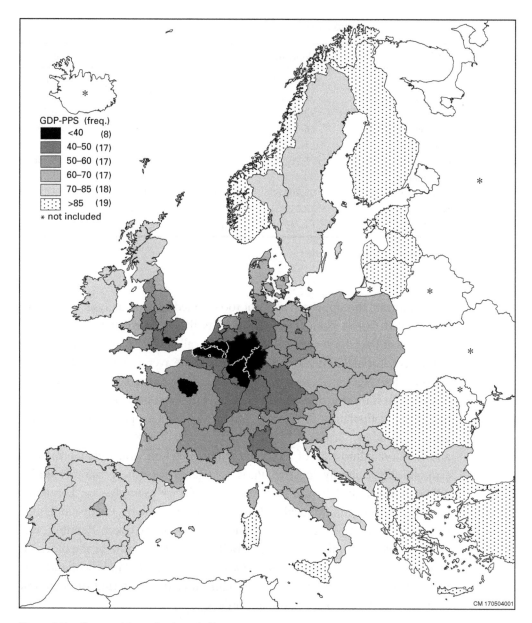

Figure 1.5 Core–periphery structures in Europe
Note: GDP-PPS = gross domestic product corrected for purchasing power.
Source: Hinloopen and van Marrewijk (2005); GDP-PPS = gross domestic product corrected for
purchasing power.

Table 1.1 Ten largest urban agglomerations in India, 2001

Agglomeration	Population	Rank	ln(rank − ½)	ln(size)
Mumbai (Bombay)	16,434,386	1	−0.693	16.615
Kolkata (Calcutta)	13,211,853	2	0.405	16.397
Delhi	12,877,470	3	0.916	16.371
Chennai (Madras)	6,560,242	4	1.253	15.697
Hyderābād	5,742,036	5	1.504	15.563
Bangalore	5,701,456	6	1.705	15.556
Ahmadābād	4,518,240	7	1.872	15.324
Pune (Poona)	3,760,636	8	2.015	15.140
Sūrat	2,811,614	9	2.140	14.849
Kānpur	2,715,555	10	2.251	14.815

Source: www.citypopulation.de.

To illustrate this approach at a not too detailed level of analysis while using the detailed Copus data, figure 1.5 depicts the European core – periphery structures at the largest regional level (the so-called NUTS [Nomenclature des Unités Territoriales Statistiques] I level) using the average score of the smaller regions (the NUTS III components) with GDP corrected for purchasing power as an indicator of economic mass. At the European level, the southern half of the Netherlands, for example is part of a big European core, consisting also of Flanders, Brussels, Nordrhein-Westfalen, Hessen, Rheinland-Palts, and London. Almost all of the Netherlands, Belgium, and west Germany is economically centrally located. Paris is a fairly separate economic entity, although still linked to the European core. Other examples are Lombardy (Milan), Berlin, and Madrid. Clearly, some of the new European Union members entering on May 1, 2004, such as Poland, the Czech Republic, and Slovakia, are economically more centrally located than some of the older EU members, such as Greece, Finland, Sweden, Portugal, Ireland, Scotland, and parts of Italy. It is evident from the figure that the clustering of economic activity in Europe crosses national borders.

1.2.3 Urban agglomeration in India

Table 1.1 illustrates the second "zooming in" step, for which we take the urban agglomerations in India as an example. Table 1.1 lists just the ten largest urban agglomerations in India, but figure 1.6 is based on the 165 largest agglomerations. Even if we restrict our attention to the ten largest

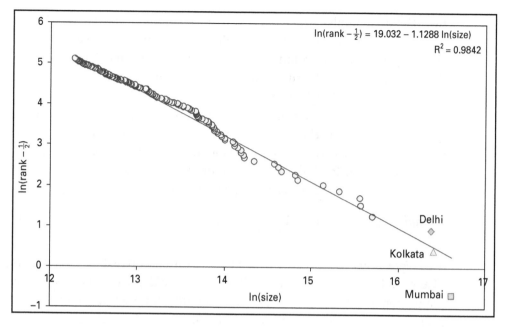

Figure 1.6   The rank size distribution for India (urban agglomerations), 2001
Source: www.citypopulation.de.

agglomerations of table 1.1, we are again confronted with a considerable variation in size, and thus of population density at the national level, ranging from about 16.4 million people in Mumbai (Bombay), the largest agglomeration, to about 2.7 million in Kānpur, the tenth largest agglomeration.

We have now illustrated the large variation in density of population and economic activity at the global, continental, and national levels. It appears that the highly uneven distribution of economic activity across space has a fractal dimension – that is, it repeats itself at different levels of aggregation. An important question is whether the spatial similarities between different levels of aggregation imply that (to some extent) the same clustering mechanisms are at work at the city, national, or global level. Another crucial question that we address in this book is why there is clustering of economic activity to begin with. Finally, we address the *regularity* of the distribution of economic activity, mainly in chapter 7. In fact, it follows a remarkable pattern throughout the world. We illustrate this using the city size distribution in India. Table 1.1 orders the ten largest urban agglomerations, first Mumbai, then Kolkata (Calcutta), then Delhi, etc. We now rank the agglomerations in order of size. Mumbai is number one, Kolkata is number two, Delhi is number three, etc. Next, in columns 5 and 6, we take the natural logarithm of both the rank (minus ½) and the size.[5] We do this for all 165 agglomerations in India with at least 100,000 people. Finally, we plot the log of the rank − ½ and the log of the size in figure 1.6. The outcome is an almost perfect straight line.

Obviously, there is a negative relationship between size and rank by construction. The puzzling feature is why this is an almost perfect log-linear straight line. If, based on the data plotted in figure 1.6, one performs a simple regression for India the estimation results yield the following rank size distribution (standard error in parentheses):

$$\ln(rank - \tfrac{1}{2}) = 19.032 - \underset{(0.1243)}{1.1288} \cdot \ln(size) \tag{1.1}$$

This regression explains 98.42 percent of the variance. Based on this estimate of the rank size distribution for India, we would predict the size of the population of urban agglomeration number fifty, for example, to be 662,000 people. This is very close to the actual size of number fifty (Hubli-Dharwar), which consists of 648,000 people. By far the largest deviation between predicted and actual size, as evident from figure 1.6, is for the largest urban agglomeration − Mumbai. The fact that the largest agglomeration, the so-called "primate city," usually does not perform well for the rank-size distribution is a well-known problem, which is investigated further in chapter 7. All in all, the empirical success of the rank-size distribution for many countries, indicating a well-ordered pattern underlying the distribution of economic activity, poses an economic modeler with the formidable task of constructing a coherent model in accordance with this empirical regularity.

1.3 Economic interaction

The uneven distribution of economic activity, and the apparent regularity in this distribution, tempts us to have a look first at the structure of the interaction between different economic centers. Clearly, such interaction takes place in many different ways, most notably in the form of trade, whether of goods or services, but also in the shape of capital and labor flows, or via the various means of modern communication, the exchange of ideas,

---

[5] The "minus ½" for the rank is based on Xavier Gabaix and Rustam Ibragimov's (2007) elegant new procedure for estimating power exponents. See chapter 7 and Hinloopen and van Marrewijk (2006) for details.

and the exposure to other cultural influences, etc. Again, we give two suggestive examples, to which we will return later in this book. We start with a mini-case study of the hard disk drive (HDD) industry, and then focus on the structure of German trade with respect to geographic distance.

1.3.1 An example at the firm level: hard disk drives[6]

The manufacture of hard disk drives, an essential component for the computer industry, is a very dynamic industry, with revenues of more than $30 billion, product life cycles of less than eighteen months, and prices falling at a rate of more than 40 percent per annum for more than a decade. Fifteen years ago not only was 80 percent of all HDD production carried out by US firms but the same was true for the assembly activities. As we will see, the pressure of globalization has rapidly changed the structure of doing business, as measured by the value chain, in this high-tech industry dominated by multinationals (see chapter 8).

Figure 1.7 gives a simplified picture of the main steps in the HDD value chain, the sequence and range of activities that go into making a final product. Ignoring research and development (R&D), there are four major steps in the value chain: (i) electronics – including semiconductors, printed circuit boards (PCBs) and their assembly; (ii) heads – devices that read and write the data, which are manufactured in stages with labor-intensive sub-assembly activities, such as head gimbal assembly (HGA) and head-stack assembly (HSA); (iii) media – the material on which the information is stored;[7] and (iv) motors, which spin the media with extreme precision.[8] Producers locate the production of the many discrete steps in the value chain around the world for a variety of reasons. The final assembly of the disk, which gives it the "Made in Singapore" or "Made in Taiwan" label, is only one – and not necessarily the most important – aspect in this process. As Gourevitch, Bohn, and McKendrick (2000: 304–5), discussing the structure of Seagate, the world's largest manufacturer of HDDs, put it:

Although Seagate has kept control over almost all production, it has globally dispersed its operations to an extraordinary degree. A single component may be worked on in five countries and cross two oceans while Seagate is building it up

---

[6] This subsection is based on Peter Gourevitch, Roger Bohn, and David McKendrick (2000).

[7] According to Gourevitch, Bohn, and Mc Kendrick (2000: 304): "Typically, aluminum blank substrates are nickel-plated and polished before the platters are sputtered and finished. As with heads, media are a very high-technology aspect of HDD production."

[8] The Japanese Nippon Densan company has about a 75 percent share of the worldwide market in motors.

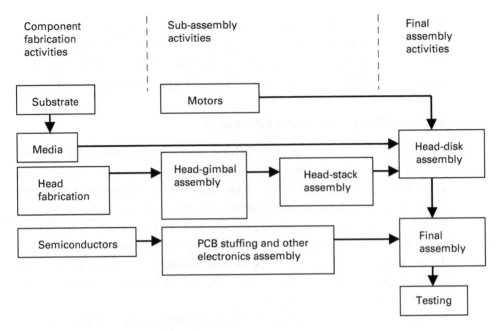

Figure 1.7   The hard disk drive value chain
Simplified version of Gourevitch et al. (2000), Figure 1.

through its value chain. Seagate develops new products (and processes) at seven locations in the United States and Singapore. It assembles disk drives in Singapore, Malaysia, Thailand, and China. In heads, the company fabricates its wafers in the United States and Northern Ireland, and cuts them into bars and assembles them into HGAs in Thailand, Malaysia, and the Philippines. It makes media in Singapore and motors in Thailand. It manufactures printed circuit cables in Thailand and assembles the electronics onto printed circuit boards in Indonesia, Malaysia, and Singapore. It is the largest nongovernment employer in Thailand and Singapore.

Table 1.2 gives four different indicators of the nationality of production for the HDD industry. The great majority (88.4 percent per unit of output) of HDDs are made by US firms. In sharp contrast to fifteen years ago, however, only 4.6 percent of the final assembly of HDDs is done in the United States. Most final assembly of disks now takes place in south-east Asia (64.2 percent), which means in turn that the bulk of employment is in south-east Asia (44 percent) rather than in the United States (19.3 per-cent), even though the value of the wages paid is much higher in the United States (39.5 percent) than in south-east Asia (12.9 percent). Essentially, the HDD industry currently has two concentration clusters. The first is Silicon

Table 1.2 Hard disk drives: indicators of the nationality of production, 1995

Measure	United States	Japan	South-east Asia	Other Asia	Europe	Other
Nationality of firm	88.4	9.4	0	2.2	0	0
Final assembly	4.6	15.5	64.2	5.7	10.0	0
Employment	19.3	8.3	44.0	17.1	4.7	6.5
Wages paid	39.5	29.7	12.9	3.3	8.5	6.1

Notes: All numbers as percentage of world total. "Nationality of firm" relates to the percentage of unit output. The remaining three variables relate to the location of final assembly, employment in the value chain, and wages paid in value chain, respectively. *Source:* Gourevitch, Bohn, and McKendrick (2000: tab. 2).

Valley in the United States, with a substantial share of research, design, development, marketing, and management (with a smaller counterpart in Japan). The second is in south-east Asia, which dominates final assembly, most labor-intensive sub-assemblies, and low-tech components, such as baseplates. The question of why we have clustering is a central theme of this book. At the industry level, this phenomenon is known as concentration (see chapters 5, 6, and 8). The hard disk drive industry discussed here is only an example; similar concentration and globalization results hold for other industries, such as automobiles, entertainment, the clothing industry, etc. Clearly, this is an aspect of modern production with a distinct geographical flavor.

1.3.2 Germany, trade, and distance

To illustrate the structure of the interaction between economic centers at the national level, we focus on Germany, the largest European economy. Germany is located right in the center of the European population agglomeration (see figure 1.5), and it is also the largest European exporter of goods and services. Table 1.3, listing the fifteen largest German export markets, gives two additional pieces of information, namely the GDP of those export markets and the "distance to Germany." The latter variable is explained in detail below.

A respectable €79 billion of German exports go to France, a neighbor of Germany and its largest export market. Remarkably, German exports to France are 14 percent higher than German exports to the United States, *the economic giant in the world*, with a GDP that is almost eight times as large

Table 1.3 Germany: fifteen largest export markets, 2005

	Country	Exports from Germany (€ million)	Distance to Germany (km)	GDP (constant 2000 $ billion)
1	France	79,039	883	1,436
2	United States	69,299	7,097	11,141
3	United Kingdom	60,394	930	1,607
4	Italy	53,855	1,182	1,114
5	Netherlands	49,033	579	384
6	Belgium	43,613	650	245
7	Austria	43,305	518	207
8	Spain	40,018	1,869	677
9	Switzerland	29,629	672	259
10	Poland	22,349	516	198
11	China	21,235	7,366	1,885
12	Czech Republic	19,161	278	66
13	Russia	17,278	1,610	350
14	Sweden	17,238	808	266
15	Hungary	13,646	688	57

Source: World Bank (GDP) and www.destatis.de (exports).

as that of France. Similarly, German exports to France are six times higher than German exports to Japan (not shown in the table), the other economic giant. In fact, Japan only ranks sixteenth on the German export market list, far behind the Netherlands, another neighbor of Germany, which ranks fifth and imports almost four times as much from Germany as Japan with an economy that is only 8 percent the size of Japan's. Both the United States and Japan are much further away from Germany than either France or the Netherlands. It would appear that there is a strong local flavor to the German top export markets: the top fifteen list includes seven of the eight German neighbors,[9] the majority of which are rather small countries.

The export of goods and services from one country to another involves time and effort, and hence costs. Goods have to be physically loaded and unloaded, transported by truck, train, ship, or plane, and packed, insured, traced, etc., before they even reach their destination. There they have to be unpacked, checked, assembled, and displayed before they can be sold to the consumer or an intermediate firm. A distribution and maintenance network

---

[9] France, the Netherlands, Belgium (which includes Luxembourg in the trade statistics), Austria, Switzerland, Poland, and the Czech Republic.

has to be established, and the exporter will have to familiarize him- or herself with the (legal) rules and procedures in another country, usually in another language and embedded in a different culture. All this involves costs, which tend to increase with "distance." As indicated above, this can be either physical distance, which may be hampered or alleviated by geographical phenomena such as mountain ranges or easy access to good waterways, or political, cultural, or social distance, which also require time and effort before one can successfully engage in international business. Throughout this book we use the term "transport costs" as shorthand notation for both types of distance described above. The presumption is, of course, that as transport costs rise it becomes more difficult to trade goods and services between nations. The nature of transport costs is discussed further in chapters 3 and 5.

Table 1.3 gives a first impression of the relationship between transport costs and trade flows. As an initial and rather crude proxy for transport costs we calculated the "distance to Germany" for all German export markets. We took the coordinates of the main economic center of each nation as the hypothetical center of economic activity. We then act as if all German export flows are simply from the German economic center to each respective nation's economic center. To confirm the impression on the negative relationship between distance and trade flows given by table 1.3 we plotted the natural logarithm of German exports against the natural logarithm of the distance to Germany for 149 German trading partners in figure 1.8a. This relationship is known as the "gravity equation."

A simple regression (t-value in parentheses) already gives a better impression:

$$\ln(export) = 18.33 - \underset{(-8.01)}{1.48} \cdot \ln(distance); \qquad R^2 = 0.304 \qquad (1.2)$$

This is a first confirmation of the negative relationship between distance and trade flows. Distance is, obviously, not the only determinant of trade flows. As table 1.3 indicates, for example, exports from Germany to Italy are larger than those from Germany to the Netherlands, even though Italy is about twice as far away using our measure of distance. Italy, however, is a much larger country (with a higher population and larger GDP) than the Netherlands, such that the potential demand for German goods is, other things being equal, larger in Italy than in the Netherlands. Figure 1.8b corrects the German export flows for this demand effect, by dividing exports by a country's GDP, and then portrays again the impact of

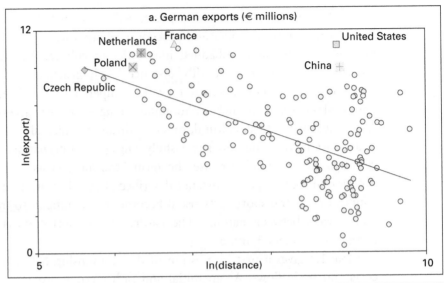

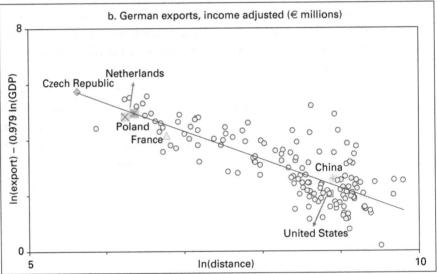

Figure 1.8   Gravity equation: German exports and distance, 2005
Sources: World Bank (GDP, constant 2000 $), www.destatis.de (exports), and Maddison, 2003 (GDP of Afghanistan, Cuba, Qatar, and Taiwan, calibrated based on US data).

distance on trade flows. The relationship is clearly "tighter" this way (closer to the regression line). The various example countries (close by or with large GDP) identified in figure 1.8a (which tend to be above the regression line) are all close to the regression line in figure 1.8b. A simple regression including both the impact of income and distance on export flows gives (t-value in parentheses):

$$\text{In}(export) = 11.49 + \underset{32.42}{0.98} \cdot \text{In}(GDP) - \underset{(-15.49)}{1.02} \cdot \text{In}(distance);$$
$$R^2 = 0.915 \tag{1.3}$$

It appears that about 91.5 percent of the variation in German export flows can be explained this way. Since the estimated coefficient on distance can be interpreted as an elasticity, it indicates that, other things equal, a 10 percent increase in the distance to the German economic center results in a 10 percent drop in export flows from Germany. More details on this so-called "gravity" analysis are given in chapters 2 and 9.

1.4 Rapid change in the distribution of production and population

So far, we have seen several examples of the uneven distribution across space of population and economic activity, as well as regularity in this distribution, and two examples of interaction between economic centers. As these were all relatively recent examples, the question may arise as to whether economic activity was always unevenly distributed. The answer is "yes and no."

The answer is "yes" in the sense that cities, for example, were already beginning to emerge after the Neolithic revolution as a consequence of an increase in agricultural surplus (see Huriot and Thisse, 2000). Although the nature of cities has changed over time, from the early cities of Mesopotamia, China, and India, through the city states of ancient Greece to the large metropoles of our time, as a dense concentration of people they have always represented centers of economic, political, cultural, sociological, military, and scientific power. As such, cities have to a large extent dominated the chain of events and the decisions taken in many different areas of human interest over the course of history. The balance of power between these economic centers has, of course, changed drastically over time. The cities of Egypt and Greece, for example, no longer exert the same influence they once did. Nor do the cities of England, China, Spain, and so many other nations. The phenomenon of the "city" as such, however, as a representation of the uneven distribution of activity, has already been with us for a long time.

The answer is "no" in the sense that the skewness or "unevenness" of the distribution of economic activity has changed over time. The clearest

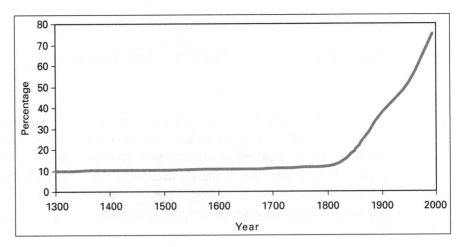

Figure 1.9   Percentage of urbanized population in Europe, 1300–2000
Source: Huriot and Thisse (2000: ix).

example in this respect is perhaps the degree of urbanization in Europe (see Bairoch, 1988). Figure 1.9 shows the share of the European population in cities from 1300 to the present. The most striking feature about the figure is how rapidly such a fundamental phenomenon as the degree of urbanization can change over time when put in the proper historical perspective.[10] Until the beginning of the nineteenth century the percentage of the population that was urbanized had increased very slowly, rising from about 10 percent to 12 percent. Around 1800 the *urban revolution*, fueled by the Industrial Revolution (Huriot and Thisse, 2000: ix), drastically increased the attractiveness of the city as a place to live and work, such that the percentage of the population that was urbanized increased rapidly over the next 200 years to its current level of around 75 percent. This confronts the geographic economic modeler with yet another challenge: the model must in principle be able to explain rapid changes in the distribution of economic activity across space.

The challenge of explaining rapid changes exists not only for the (changes in the) distribution of economic activity at the city level, but also at a global level. Figure 1.10 shows the evolution of the share in world production (in constant dollars and corrected for PPP), measured as a nation's GDP relative to world GDP, for four "Asian miracle" countries (China,

---

[10] Chapter 7 argues that the degree of urbanization affects the distribution of economic activity across space, as measured by the rank size distribution, but not the regularity in this distribution.

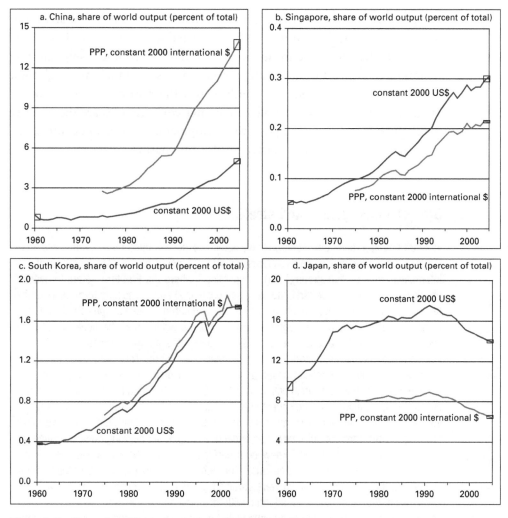

Figure 1.10 Share of world output, selected countries, 1960–2005
Source: WDI online; country GDP/world GDP (%) in constant 2000 US $ and in PPP, constant 2000 international $.

Singapore, South Korea, and Japan) in the period 1960–2005. Measured in constant dollars, the increase is striking for China since about 1980, for Singapore since about 1965, for South Korea from about 1965 until 2000, and for Japan until about 1970. Note that these impressive increases in the share of world production indicates that output in these countries increased substantially faster than world output in those periods. Moreover, the changes occurred very rapidly.

Figure 1.10 also shows that a country's share of world income can decline for the Asian miracle countries, as has occurred for Japan since about 1990. Moreover, the difference in developments and perceptions using constant dollars or corrected for purchasing power can be substantial. Although these indicators largely coincide for South Korea, the positive developments in Singapore are mitigated to some extent after correction, as are the negative developments in Japan. The positive developments in China, in contrast, are even more impressive after correction for purchasing power.

Box 1.1 Guns, germs, and steel

In a fascinating, broad, and yet surprisingly detailed exposé entitled *Guns, Germs, and Steel* (1997), Jared Diamond explains various important aspects of the consequences of the interaction between "geography" and "economics," where the first term refers to general physical circumstances (or "first nature" – see chapter 2) and the second term refers to the forces associated with human interaction (or "second nature" – see chapter 2). Despite the extensive period covered, as suggested by Diamond's writing that the book provides "a short history of everybody for the last 13,000 years," the author provides detailed information on plants, germs, history, animals, language, and so on. This information is needed to answer the central question posed at the beginning of the book by Yali, an eminent, intelligent, and charismatic local politician in New Guinea. Referring to all sorts of amenities developed by mankind over the course of history as "cargo," Yali asked (14): "Why is it that you white people developed so much cargo and brought it to New Guinea, but we black people had little cargo of our own?" It is, indeed, a simple, but puzzling question, since, as Diamond notes (14), "He and I knew both perfectly well that New Guineans are on the average at least as smart as Europeans." The book essentially explains how the circumstances on the Eurasian continent were particularly favorable compared to other places on Earth, such that the ability to interact with neighboring people and benefit from the knowledge created elsewhere and accumulated in the past translated into large economic advantages over time.

A vital step in the economic accumulation process is the movement from a hunter-gathering lifestyle to a sedentary lifestyle based on food production, which is enabled by the domestication of plants and animals, as it allows for the accumulation of non-portable possessions, greater population densities, and the development of cities with non-food-producing specialists. As indicated in table 1.4, independent domestication first occurred in the Fertile Crescent in south-west Asia in about 8500 BC and some thousand years later in China. Similar developments occurred much later in Mesoamerica, the Andes and Amazonia, and what is now the eastern United States. Diamond argues quite convincingly that these earlier developments are likely caused by the abundance of available species to choose from for experimentation. For example, of the world's fifty-six heaviest-seeded wild grass species that are potentially suitable candidates for domestication, thirty-three can be found in west Asia, Europe, and north Africa (thirty-two of them in the Mediterranean zone),

Box 1.1 (cont.)

Table 1.4 Independent origins of domestication

Area	Domesticated Plants	Animals	Earliest date of domestication
South-west Asia	Wheat, pea, olive	Sheep, goat	8500 BC
China	Rice, millet	Pig, silkworm	by 7500 BC
Mesoamerica	Corn, beans, squash	Turkey	by 3500 BC
Andes and Amazonia	Potato, manioc	Llama, guinea pig	by 3500 BC
Eastern United States	Sunflower, goosefoot	None	2500 BC

Source: Based on Diamond (1997: tab. 5.1).

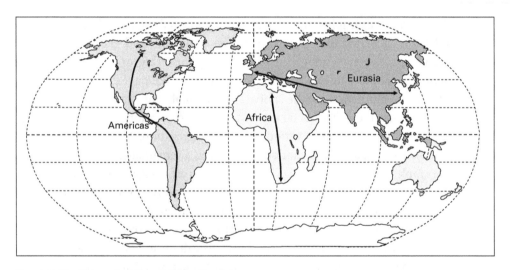

Figure 1.11   Major orientation of the continents

compared to only four in sub-Sahara Africa, four in North America, five in Mesoamerica, and two in South America. The distribution of large mammalian animals is even more favorable to the Eurasian continent, which was able to domesticate thirteen species, compared to only one in the Americas. Despite the abundance of large mammalian animals in sub-Saharan Africa, none turned out to be suitable for domestication.

Another important advantage of the Eurasian continent (including north Africa) is its main orientation from west to east rather than from north to south, as is the case in the Americas and Africa (see figure 1.11). Areas of the same latitude share the same day length

> ### Box 1.1 (cont.)
>
> and seasonal variation, and to some extent similar diseases, temperatures, and rainfall. This greatly facilitated the spread of knowledge regarding food production from west to east or vice versa, rather than from north to south. For that reason, western Europe, the Indus valley, and Egypt were able to enjoy the benefits of domesticated plants and animals by assimilation rather than by invention thousands of years before their invention in the Americas. Over the course of history the accumulation of the benefits of economic inter-action and knowledge spillovers on the Eurasian continent brought it to its dominant position in about 1500, paving the way for the subsequent expansion of the peoples of that continent into the rest of the world.

1.5 Overview of the book

The various examples and discussions presented in this chapter paint a relatively clear picture. The distribution of people and economic activity across space is very uneven, with a strong clustering or agglomeration of economic activity in various important centers. We have given illustrations of this phenomenon at the global, continental, and national levels. This suggests that there is a fractal aspect to these observations – that is, the phenomenon repeats itself at various levels of aggregation. Moreover, the distribution across space is not random but follows a remarkable pattern, known as the rank size distribution. These observations suggest that similar, but not necessarily identical, economic forces may be relevant in explaining the clustering phenomenon and its regularities at different levels of aggregation.[11]

We have also discussed the interaction between economic centers. First, we used a mini-case study of the hard disk drive industry, which is dominated by multinationals trying to use the location advantages of different nations in the production process. We found essentially two global concentration clusters for this industry, namely in Silicon Valley and in southeast Asia. Second, we briefly investigated the relationship between German exports and the distance of the export market to Germany. After correcting for the size of the destination market, this relationship was clearly negative – a phenomenon known as a gravity equation. Finally, we showed that the uneven distribution of activity across space could very rapidly change over

---

[11] There have been studies of the rank size distribution at the firm level as well (see Sutton, 1997).

time, for example as measured by the percentage of the urbanized population in Europe.

The remainder of this book does, of course, get back to the issues raised in this chapter in more detail. The question at this point is: how to proceed? The empirical phenomena touched upon above have been studied thoroughly from many different angles, based on different theoretical frameworks, for a long time. From what is primarily a location perspective there is urban economics, economic geography, regional economics, and regional science. The interaction between economic centers is addressed by international economics, development economics, and industrial organization. One way to proceed is to investigate each empirical phenomenon separately, using the insights of those of the above fields in- or outside economics, which are thought to be relevant for the issue at hand. Clearly, the rest of the book would be rather fragmentary if we were to proceed in this way.

Instead, we proceed differently. We have already mentioned that the fractal nature of the location phenomena described in this chapter suggests that similar economic forces might be relevant to explain them. We therefore use throughout this book a common structural approach to help understand the phenomena that are introduced in this chapter. In fact, finding a common framework to get a better grip on a plethora of (economic) data is what makes economic models useful. That being said, the common framework should not become a straitjacket. As we will see time and again in the chapters to come, if we want to explain a particular economic phenomenon we have to be flexible in adapting the common framework to better suit the problem at hand. In each of those instances we draw inspiration from the various fields of research mentioned above.[12] As explained in the preface of our book, we follow the suggestions of, inter alia, Ron Martin (1999: 67) and Fujita and Thisse (2000: 6) in labeling this approach *geographical economics*, which in our view is better suited than the more often used phrase "new economic geography." The size of this book, or any other book, for that matter, does not allow us to take full advantage of all the insights from all the contributing fields. We therefore have to be eclectic in what we do and do not use, and hope that we make the right choices most of the time. We are, however, selective in our choices in the sense that we use insights from different fields that we can relate to the core geographical economics model.

---

[12] These include, *inter alia*, urban economics, economic geography, spatial economics, regional science, international economics, development economics, and industrial organization.

Our book is in four parts. Besides the present introductory chapter, Part I also includes chapter 2, in which we give an overview of the role of geography or location in economic theory. In doing so, we focus on the contributions of urban and regional economics, economic geography, international trade theory, economic growth theory, and development economics. The goal of this chapter is not to survey all these (sub-)fields in detail but merely to provide a benchmark to better understand the relevance of geographical economics.

Part II (chapters 3 to 6) constitutes the backbone of the book. Chapter 3 introduces and analyzes the core model of geographical economics as first developed by Krugman (1991a), which is adapted to our particular needs in chapters to come. Chapter 4 further discusses the core model and extends the theoretical analysis through the introduction of three additional "core" models. Chapters 5 and 6 provide a systematic overview of the available empirical evidence to assess the relevance of geographical economics. Following Head and Mayer (2004a), we list five testable hypotheses derived from the theoretical models in chapters 3 and 4.

In part III (chapters 7 to 10), the key models and insights from geographical economics are applied to more specific topics: urban economics and city-size distributions (chapter 7), foreign direct investment and multinationals (chapter 8), international trade (chapter 9), and dynamics and growth (chapter 10).

Part IV first discusses the policy implications of geographical economics (chapter 11), and then evaluates geographical economics by discussing its main pros and cons and suggesting some possible avenues for further research (chapter 12).

Appendix

The table below summarizes the information on global regional characteristics illustrated graphically in section 1.2.

Table A1.1 Global regional characteristics, 2005

Variable[#]	EAP	ECA	High	LAC	MNA	SAS	SSA	World
Land area	15.9	23.4	33.0	20.1	9.0	4.8	23.6	129.6
Population	1,885	473	1,011	551	305	1,470	741	6,462
Population density	119	20	31	27	34	307	31	50
GNP	3,033	2,191	34,466	2,456	633	996	615	45,054
GNP (PPP)	9,962	3,972	29,370	4,177	1,682	4,153	1,371	41,431
GNP/capita (Atlas)	1,352	2,604	28,304	4,037	1,790	562	560	5,659
GNP/capita (PPP)	5,284	8,398	29,041	7,575	5,506	2,825	1,849	6,415
Birth rate	14.8	12.8	12.0	20.8	25.1	25.1	39.9	20.2
Death rate	6.7	12.0	8.2	6.1	5.9	8.2	17.6	8.5
Arable/capita	0.11	0.57	0.37	0.27	0.18	0.14	0.25	0.24
CO_2/capita	2.5	7.4	12.1	2.5	3.9	0.9	0.8	4
Exports (%)	42.9	38.6	22.4	25.9	34.8	18.9	34.7	27.0
Aid (%)	0.3	0.7	-	0.4	1.7	0.8	5.2	0.2
Life expectancy	70.3	68.8	78.7	72.2	69.4	63.4	46.2	68.0
Urban (%)	41.5	63.7	77.6	77.2	57.1	28.5	35.2	48.7

Data source: WDI online. EAP = East Asia and Pacific; ECA = Europe and Central Asia; High = High-income countries; LAC = Latin America and Caribbean; MNA = Middle East and North Africa; SAS = South Asia; SSA = Sub-Saharan Africa.

[#] Respectively: land area (million sq. km); population (millions); population density (people per sq. km); GNP at market prices (current billion US $); GNP PPP (constant int. 2000 $, billion); GNP per capita (current US$); GNP per capita, PPP (constant int. 2000 $); birth rate, crude (per 1,000 people); death rate, crude (per 1,000 people); arable land (hectares per person); CO^2 emissions, industrial (metric tons per capita, 1996); exports of goods and services (% of GDP); aid (% of GNP); life expectancy at birth, total (years); urban population (% of total).

The next table provides the correlation coefficients for the variables in table A1.1.

Table A1.2 Correlation coefficients

	LA	POP	DEN	YAT	YPP	YAc	YPc	BIR	DEA	LAc	CO$_2$	EXP	AID	LIF	URB
LA	1.00														
POP	−0.20	1.00													
DEN	−0.68	0.66	1.00												
YAT	0.69	0.10	−0.22	1.00											
YPP	0.63	0.29	−0.13	0.97	1.00										
YAc	0.70	0.01	−0.27	0.99	0.95	1.00									
YPc	0.71	−0.03	−0.33	0.98	0.94	0.99	1.00								
BIR	−0.28	−0.20	0.09	−0.48	−0.58	−0.48	−0.60	1.00							
DEA	0.37	−0.18	−0.20	−0.13	−0.22	−0.15	−0.21	0.57	1.00						
LAc	0.64	−0.53	−0.53	0.29	0.19	0.33	0.42	−0.39	0.35	1.00					
CO$_2$	0.69	−0.19	−0.44	0.85	0.80	0.86	0.92	−0.69	−0.13	0.65	1.00				
EXP	0.04	−0.02	−0.43	−0.41	−0.33	−0.43	−0.36	−0.04	0.20	0.08	−0.13	1.00			
AID	0.02	−0.28	−0.19	−0.36	−0.46	−0.37	−0.46	0.91	0.80	−0.11	−0.46	0.22	1.00		
LIF	0.17	0.05	−0.12	0.55	0.60	0.57	0.66	−0.90	−0.81	0.19	0.66	−0.18	−0.92	1.00	
URB	0.60	−0.52	−0.68	0.54	0.47	0.61	0.69	−0.57	−0.36	0.57	0.71	−0.14	−0.48	0.71	1.00

Notes: LA = land area, POP = population, DEN = population density, YAT = GNP (Atlas), YPP = GNP (PPP), YAc = GNP/capita (Atlas), YPc = GNP/capita (PPP), BIR = birth rate, DEA = death rate, LAc = arable/capita, CO$_2$ = CO$_2$/capita, EXP = export percentage of GDP, AID = aid percentage of GNP, LIF = life expentancy, and URB = urban percentage; see table A1.1 for further details.

Exercises[13]

1.1 The website to this book gives additional information on the rank size distribution of cities for many countries, as illustrated in figure 1.6 for India. This remarkable phenomenon is further investigated in chapter 7. Go to the website and look up the q value (the slope of the line in figure 1.6) and the R^2 for the column "city proper" in the graphs of the following countries: Egypt, South Africa, France, the United Kingdom, Poland, Japan, South Korea, Russia, Turkey, the United States, and Brazil. Comment on your general findings.

1.2 Table 1.3 and figure 1.8 show and illustrate a negative relationship between the size of the export market and the distance to those markets for Germany. Does a similar relationship hold for your country? Do the following.
 (i) Find the ten or fifteen largest export markets for your country.
 (ii) Determine the "distance" from your country to those markets, for example using the number of kilometers between the capital cities, or another, perhaps more appropriate, measure.
(iii) Make a plot of your findings and give comments on the results
(note: do this exercise for France if "your country" is Germany).

1.3 Finish exercise 1.2 along the lines of the analysis in section 1.4.
 (i) Gather export data for as many export markets for your country as you can.
 (ii) Determine the distance to those markets and look up the GDP of those markets.
(iii) Perform a simple regression: ln(export) = constant + ln(distance); similar to equation (1.2).
(iv) Correct your estimate for market size – that is, perform a regression similar to equation (1.3), namely: ln(export) = constant + ln(distance) + ln(GDP).
 (v) Comment on your findings.

---

[13] Throughout the book, exercises marked with an asterisk are more advanced.

2 Geography and economic theory

2.1 Introduction

The central message of chapter 1 is that geography is important. Economic activity is not evenly distributed across space. On the contrary, clustering of economic activities can be found at various levels of aggregation: the considerable variation in economic size of cities or regions at the national level, or the uneven distribution of wealth and production at the global level. The question arises, of course, as to why location seems to be so important for economic activities. To answer this question, we need an analytical framework in which geography plays a part one way or another. In particular, we would like to show that the decisions of economic agents are partly determined by geography, and that they provide a framework in which the geography of the economy itself can be derived from the behavior of economic agents. This, in a nutshell, is what the approach developed in this book tries to do. We want to make absolutely clear from the start that this approach, referred to throughout this book as geographical economics but also known as new economic geography (see the preface), is by no means the first theory to address location issues. There is a long tradition that deals with the questions to be discussed in this chapter. The novelty of geographical economics as such is mainly in the way it tackles the relationship between economics and geography.

Before we turn to the core model of geographical economics in chapters 3 and 4, this chapter discusses the role of geography in economic theory. Clearly, it is beyond the scope of our book to try to give a complete survey of the literature. Instead, we highlight the role of geography in some important fields of economics. As we will see, though with some notable exceptions, economic theory either has not much to say on our subject matter or, when it does, it typically assumes as given what has to be explained from the underlying behavior of economic agents, namely the spatial structure of economic activity. Cities and regions vary in size and relevance (see chapter 1). This is a prime topic for regional and urban economics and also for economic geography proper, which traditionally deal with the theoretical analysis of the interdependencies between cities and regions within a country. Section 2.2 discusses the main ingredients of the rather heterogeneous approaches in these fields. Section 2.3 investigates the geographical components in international trade theory. The data on trade flows between nations clearly indicate a local concentration, in the sense that many countries predominantly trade with neighboring countries (see section 1.4). Moreover, most trade takes place within the OECD area. This suggests that geographical variables should be part of trade theory.

Surprisingly, this is not the case, which has provided a strong impetus for the development of geographical economics. At a global scale, economic development is very uneven (recall figures 1.2 and 1.3). Economic growth and wealth are certainly not evenly distributed across the world economy, but largely confined to a few parts of the map. It is evident from the history of economic development that spurs to economic growth are often geographically concentrated (see section 1.4). We argue that the relevance of geography for economic growth has long been recognized in development economics (see also Krugman, 1995a). Section 2.4 discusses the main ingredients of neoclassical and new growth theory, focusing on the role of geography. Section 2.5 concludes and evaluates the contributions from various fields of economics.

This chapter covers a considerable amount of ground, and introduces many important concepts that are discussed more thoroughly in the remainder of the book. Our approach for the overview of each field is as follows. We start with a summary of the main arguments involved, which then serves as background information for a discussion of the main question: what does each theory have to say about the role of geography?

It walks like a survey, it talks like a survey, so surely it must be ...

What this chapter does *not* offer is a full-fledged survey of urban and regional economics, economic geography, international trade theory, or growth theory. Instead, we introduce the bare essentials of these theoretical approaches, to be used as a benchmark for our subsequent discussion of geographical economics and to enable the reader to grasp the main differences between geographical economics and the alternative theories. For anyone interested in learning more about the theories discussed in this chapter, there is a wide array of very good introductory as well as advanced textbooks and surveys available for each of the (sub-)fields concerned.[1]

2.2 Geography in regional and urban economics

According to Peter Nijkamp and Edwin Mills (1986), the editors of the *Handbook of Regional and Urban Economics*, regional economics analyzes the "spatial dispersion and coherence of economic activity." When this is compared to the definition of economic geography used in the textbook of Peter Dicken and Peter Lloyd (1990) as the study of "the spatial organization of economic systems," one would be inclined to think that regional economics and economic geography are two different labels for the same field of research. This is not the case, however. Or, more accurately, it is no longer the case. Although both fields have their roots in the German-based tradition of Johann von Thünen, Walter Christaller, Alfred Weber, and August Lösch (see below) and still basically address the same research question, regional economics and economic geography now differ quite considerably.

Regional economics (also known as regional science) is based on neo-classical economic theory and is, in effect, "the formalized successor to the German 'location economics' tradition" (Martin, 1999: 61). Economic geography, on the other hand, is more eclectic and empirically oriented. It gets its inspiration from heterodox economic theories and, increasingly, from outside economics, areas such as sociology, political science, and regulation theory (see Storper, 1997, Scott, 2000, or Peck, 2000). We return to this division in chapter 12. Despite their differences, our main observations in subsection 2.2.2 apply to a large extent to both fields. We start, however, in subsection 2.2.1 with an overview of a younger field of study, namely urban economics, which studies the spatial structure of urban areas. Like regional economics, urban economics is based heavily on the tools of neoclassical analysis, such that the division between regional and urban economics is not always clear. Our objective is simply to show that the concepts and ideas used in geographical economics have been studied

---

[1] Some suggestions at the introductory as well as the advanced level are as follows: for urban and regional economics, McCann (2002) and Fujita and Thisse (2002); for economic geography, McCann (2002) and Armstrong and Taylor (2000); for international trade, van Marrewijk (2007) and Feenstra (2004); and, for growth theory, Helpman (2004) and Barro and Sala-i-Martin (2004). The major books on geographical economics to date are Fujita, Krugman, and Venables (1999), Fujita and Thisse (2002), Baldwin *et al.* (2003), and Combes, Mayer, and Thisse (2008).

before. In addition, we propose that geographical economics has something to add to these analyses. The "proof" of this suggestion starts in chapter 3.

2.2.1 Urban economics

The uneven distribution of economic activity within every country is the starting point for urban economics. The modern analysis of the agglomeration of firms and people in cities or metropolitan areas relies strongly on "the economics of agglomeration, a term which refers to the decline in average costs as more production occurs within a specified geographical area" (Anas, Arnott, and Small, 1998: 1427). In other words, it relies on increasing returns to scale.[2] Before we go into the relevance of scale economies for cities and other forms of agglomeration, we first discuss a model in which there are no increasing returns to scale whatsoever. This model, the *monocentric city* model, originates with von Thünen (1826) and remains a benchmark model for urban (and regional) economics to this day. A brief discussion is justified if only to be able to note the differences with the geographical economics approach and to make clear that, in the end the analysis of cities will remain rather limited so long as there are no increasing returns to scale.

The monocentric city model

The monocentric city model assumes the existence of a featureless plane, perfectly flat and homogeneous in all respects. In the midst of this plane there is a single city. Outside the city farmers grow crops, which they must sell in the city. There are positive transportation costs associated with getting the farming products to the city, which differ for the various crops, as do the prices for these crops. Von Thünen analyzes how the farmers locate themselves across the plane. Each farmer wants to be as close to the city as possible to minimize his or her transport costs. This incentive to be close to the city results in higher land rents near the city than at the edge of the plane. Each farmer thus faces a trade-off between land rents and transport costs.

Von Thünen showed that competition for locations ensures that the resulting equilibrium allocation of land among the farmers will be efficient. For every type of crop there is a bid–rent curve that indicates, depending on

---

[2] This formulation of increasing returns to scale does not say how the decline in a firm's average costs comes about. See box 2.1 for a discussion of external and internal economies of scale.

the distance to the city, how much the farmers are willing to pay for the land (see figure 2.1a). Since the bid–rent curves differ per crop, as a result of different prices for those crops in the city and different transport costs, the farmers of a particular type of crop are able to outbid their competitors (that is, they are willing to pay more) for any given distance to the city. As we move away from the city center in figure 2.1a, we see that, first, the flower producers outbid the other two groups of farmers, then that between points A and B the vegetable producers are willing to pay the highest rents, and that to the right of point B (and thus the farthest removed from the city center) the grain producers will pay the highest rent. This results in a concentric circle pattern of land use around the city, every ring consisting of farms that grow the same crop; in sequence: flowers, vegetables, and grain (see figure 2.1b).

Urban economics probably started as a separate discipline with William Alonso (1964), who took the von Thünen model and, essentially, replaced the city by a central business center and the farmers by commuters. The commuters travel back and forth to their work at the business center, and each commuter derives utility from his or her space for living but also faces transportation costs. Again, land rents are the highest near the city and fall with distance. The bid–rent approach can thus be applied, and competition for land between the commuters implies an efficient allocation of land. The efficiency of land allocation in the monocentric model hinges on the assumption that there are no externalities of location (see below).[3] Combined with the work of Richard Muth (1969) and Mills (1967), the model by Alonso (1964) is still the backbone of modern urban economics; for an excellent non-technical introduction to the Alonso–Muth–Mills model, and urban economics in general, see Edward Glaeser (2007).

As Alex Anas, Richard Arnott, and Kenneth Small (1998: 1435) point out, a number of stylized facts about urban spatial structure are in accordance with the monocentric model. First, the population density declines with distance from central business centers. Second, almost every major city in the Western world decentralized in the twentieth century (as people started to locate further away from the city center), which can be linked to a fall in transport costs. The monocentric model also has some serious limitations. We mention just two. First, the model does not account for any interaction between cities; it cannot deal with urban systems. Second, the model takes the existence and location of the city as given and focuses on the location of

---

[3] If there are externalities there will not be a Pareto-efficient allocation of land; see Fujita (1989, part II).

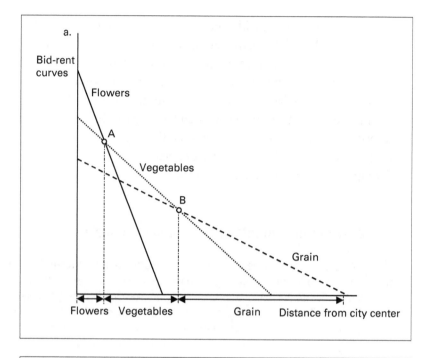

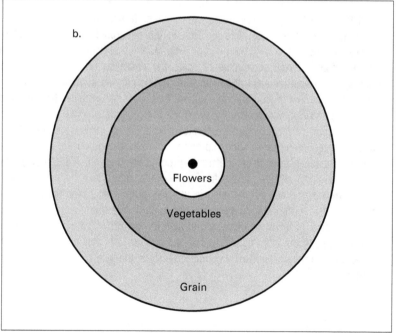

Figure 2.1   The von Thünen model

farmers/commuters outside the city. The question of why there is a city to begin with is left unanswered. To deal with these limitations, urban economists have long recognized that a theory of cities cannot do without the introduction and theoretical foundation of some type of increasing returns to scale (Glaeser, 2007: 15–16; Duranton, 2008).[4] These can occur at the firm level or at a more aggregated level (the industry level or the national level). We will see in this book that the type of increasing returns may matter a great deal. Box 2.1 therefore elaborates upon the terminology used for various forms of scale economies.

Box 2.1 External and internal economies of scale

The term "economies of scale," or "increasing returns to scale," refers to a situation in which an increase in the level of output produced implies a decrease in the average costs per unit of output for the firm. It translates itself to a downward-sloping average cost curve (see figure 2.2). To identify the source of the fall in average costs, Tibor Scitovsky (1954) distinguishes between *internal* and *external* economies of scale. With internal economies of scale the decrease in average costs is brought about by an increase in the production level of the firm itself. The more the firm produces the better it can profit from scale economies, and the higher its cost advantage over smaller firms. The market structure underlying internal scale economies, typically used in the geographical economics literature, must necessarily be one of *im*perfect competition, as internal economies of scale imply market power. With external economies of scale the decrease in average costs comes about through an output increase at the level of the industry as a whole, making average costs per unit a function of industry-wide output. Scitovsky distinguishes here between *pure* and *pecuniary* external economies.

With *pure* (or *technological*) external economies an increase in industry-wide output alters the technological relationship between inputs and output for each individual firm. It therefore has an impact on the firm's production function. A frequently used example (dating back to Alfred Marshall; see also the main text below this box) concerns information spillovers. An increase in industry output increases the stock of knowledge through positive information spillovers for each firm, leading to an increase in output at the firm level. In urban economics, but also in new growth theory (section 2.4) and new trade theory (box 2.5), pure external economies are assumed to exist. The market structure can then be perfectly competitive since the size of the *individual* firm does not matter.

---

[4] As Glaeser (2007) explains, the Alonso–Muth–Mills model essentially helps in understanding the location choice of individuals by assuming constant income and amenities and analyzing whether or not housing costs and low transport costs offset each other. Applied to Boston, it explains that an extra mile from the center results in a $1,100 drop in housing prices. A drawback of the model is that it assumes monocentric cities, which is often at odds with reality.

Box 2.1 (cont.)

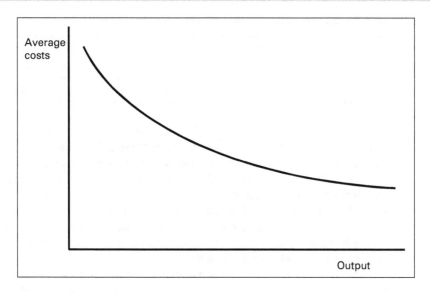

Figure 2.2   Average costs under increasing returns to scale

Pecuniary external economies are transmitted by the market through price effects for the individual firm, which may alter its output decision. Two examples, again based on Marshall, are the existence of a large local market for specialized inputs and labor market pooling. A large industry can support a market for specialized intermediate inputs and a pool of industry-specific skilled workers, which benefits the individual firm. Contrary to pure external economies, these spillovers do not affect the technological relationship between inputs and output (the production function). Pecuniary externalities exist in the geographical economics literature through a love-of-variety effect in a large local market. Each consumer's utility depends positively on the number of varieties that he or she can buy of a manufactured good. The price effects crucial to pecuniary externalities can come about only with imperfect competition. This is consistent with the imperfect competition requirement for internal economies of scale, also used in the geographical economics literature.

Some concluding remarks are in order. First, spillovers or externalities are crucial for external economies. The concept of spillovers is sometimes used only for pure external economies, referring to pecuniary external economies as a case of market interdependence. We stick to the use of spillovers or externalities when we refer to external economies of scale in general. Similarly, the term "increasing returns" is sometimes used for internal economies of scale only. We also use the phrase "increasing returns" when discussing external economies. From the context it will be clear if we are referring to the firm or the industry level.

Box 2.1 (cont.)

Table 2.1 Regional (location-specific) spillovers/externalities typology

Marshall–Arrow–Romer (MAR) externalities	Localization economics	Sector-specific spillovers
Jacobs externalities	Urbanization economics	City-specific spillovers

Second, external economies can apply at a higher level of aggregation than the firm. This is often the industry level, but in modern trade theory and modern growth theory it can also be the economy as a whole. Third, the external economies in the models are static, whereas the literature also considers dynamic external economies. In that case the average costs per unit of output are a negative function of the *cumulative* output of the industry. Again, if this is relevant it will be clear whether we refer to static or dynamic external economies. Fourth, the external economies discussed above are positive. They can, as we will see in chapter 7, also be negative – that is, an increase in a firm's production leads to an increase in per unit costs for other firms.

Finally, a remark on the somewhat confusing terminology regarding *regional* economic externalities or spillovers. It is customary to distinguish between Marshall–Arrow–Romer (MAR) externalities and Jacobs externalities. In both cases, the emphasis is on regional (location-specific) spillovers – that is, firms have to be located closely enough together to benefit from these externalities. The MAR externalities focus on sector-specific spillovers and are also referred to as "localization economics." The Jacobs externalities focus on city-specific spillovers that cross the boundaries between individual sectors. These are also known as "urbanization economics" (see the overview in table 2.1). Since the distinction between MAR and Jacobs externalities as such is non-descriptive (and hence not informative) and the localization/urbanization distinction may be confusing (since both are location-specific), it is perhaps best to talk of sector-specific and city-specific spillovers. We discuss these issues further in chapter 7.

Urban economics and increasing returns

We now turn to a prime example of modern urban economics in which, as opposed to the monocentric city model, increasing returns to scale are included. Specifically *external* economies to scale are crucial in the important strand of work initiated by Henderson (1974, 1977, 1988), following the writings of Mills (1967) and Muth (1969), on cities – or, more precisely, a *system of cities*. The starting point is quite different from the monocentric model. There are no transport costs and the *hinterland* of a city is no longer part of the analysis. In a sense, it is an analysis of cities in which space, – that is, space outside the cities – has no role to play. The justification for this geographical neglect of non-city space is that, in modern industrialized countries a large part of the overall economic activity and population is situated in urban areas (see chapters 1 and 7), such that the relevance of urban versus non-urban transactions is assumed to be limited. Instead, the analysis focuses on the forces determining the size of cities and the interactions between them. The agglomerating forces in the Henderson model are positive external economies of scale that are industry-specific. The latter means that there are positive spillovers when a firm of a particular industry locates in a city where other firms from the same industry are located. Using a well-known categorization that can be traced back to the works of Marshall, these may be due to (i) the sharing of information, (ii) the existence of a large pool of labor, or (iii) the existence of specialized suppliers (see also box 2.1). The external economies may therefore in principle involve either pure external economies (as in the original Henderson approach) or pecuniary external economies.[5]

The spreading forces are negative external economies of scale within the city, such as congestion, which is a function of the overall size of the city. A large city implies relatively high commuting costs and land rents. The diseconomies of scale do not depend on the type of production taking place in the city, such that they depend only on the overall size of a city. Together with the industry-specific external economies, this has two important implications. First, it can rationalize systems of cities (different city sizes catering to the needs of different industries). Based on the assumption that the positive spillovers of location are industry-specific, each industry has its own optimum size.[6] Second, by explicitly giving a microeconomic foundation for increasing returns, it provides a rationale for specialization, and thus an urban system in which cities of different sizes trade with each other. Compared with the framework of von Thünen or Alonso, modern urban economics is far less ad-hoc because it can give a theoretical foundation for the increasing returns that drive the existence of cities, and it yields

---

[5] Recently (see Henderson, 2000, or Duranton and Puga, 2004, for surveys) research in urban economics has increasingly used pecuniary externalities and hence imperfect competition. See Takatoshi Tabuchi (1998) for an attempt to synthesize urban economics *à la* Alonso/Henderson with geographical economics. Duranton and Puga (2004) summarize Marshall's famous categorization of the mechanisms for increasing returns by the trilogy *sharing, matching*, and *learning*; see section 7.2.

[6] As a consequence, in equilibrium each city is also of an optimal size, maximizing the utility of the inhabitants. The reasoning is as follows. Suppose a city is not of an optimum size. This creates a profit opportunity. If the city is too large, moving people out of the city would be welfare-improving, and vice versa if it is too small. Henderson (1988) introduces the city entrepreneur, who, in view of this profit opportunity, organizes enough people to move into a city that is too small, or out of a city that is too large. These entrepreneurs are necessary, because an individual in a city of non-optimal size has no incentive to move on his or her own; see also Randy Becker and Henderson (2000).

insights as to urban systems. In chapter 7 we discuss at some length how urban economics "Henderson style" differs from geographical economics "Krugman style."

Which type of external economies of scale?

There is ample empirical support for the idea that industry-specific spillovers are important for cities (see Henderson, Kuncoro, and Turner, 1995, Beardsell and Henderson, 1999, and Black and Henderson, 1999a; for a survey, see Abdel-Rahman and Anas, 2004). These industry-specific external economies are known as *localization* economies, as opposed to *urbanization* economies. The latter are external economies that apply to firms across industries and capture the notion of positive spillovers for a firm as a result of the total economic activity in a city. Both types of external economies often relate to the location of cities in a static sense, but they are also applied in a dynamic context (how do cities develop over time?). With respect to the growth of cities in the United States, Glaeser, Hedi Kallal, José Scheinkman, and Andrei Shleifer (1992) find no support for the hypothesis that cities specializing in certain industries grow more rapidly on average. Instead, they conclude that if external economies are important it is probably more important to have a variety of diversified industries in a city.[7] If the latter is the case, the question arises as to why so many cities are specialized in particular industries. Glaeser *et al.* (1992: 1148–50) suggest that both localization and urbanization economies are relevant (though they favor urbanization economies in the end), while Duncan Black and Henderson (1999a) argue that in a dynamic context localization economies are more relevant.[8] We return to these empirical concerns in chapters 5 and 7. In chapter 7 we put the above brief discussion on the empirical findings about the sources and scope for scale economies into a wider perspective; see also Stuart Rosenthal and William Strange (2004).

---

[7] Using the terminology of Glaeser *et al.* (1992), their study is an attempt to test for the relevance of three externalities (see also box 2.1): (i) the Marshall–Arrow–Romer externality, in which knowledge spillovers occur between firms that belong to the same industry and in which local monopoly is better suited than local competition to foster these spillovers; (ii) the Porter externality (based on Porter, 1990; see chapter 8), in which knowledge spillovers are also industry-specific but the preferred market structure is local competition; and (iii) the Jacobs externality (based on Jacobs, 1969), in which the knowledge spillovers are not industry-specific but between firms of different industries and in which local competition stimulates these spillovers. The empirical evidence in Glaeser *et al.* (1992) is relatively favorable for the Jacobs externality. Henderson, Kuncoro, and Turner (1995) and Black and Henderson (1999a) are two examples of empirical studies that conclude that localization economies and hence, in a dynamic context, MAR externalities are far more important than, for instance, the Glaeser study suggests. We return to this issue in chapter 7.

[8] When applied to cities, external economies are typically urbanization economies in the geographical economics approach; see also chapter 7.

From a theoretical point of view, it should be stressed that Henderson's urban systems approach does not take the existence of the city for granted, as did the monocentric model. It also provides for a theory of the inter-actions between cities. The problem with the approach is that the space outside the cities is (deliberately) not part of the analysis. This is trouble-some if one wants to be able to say where cities are located relative to one another and the "non-city" part of the geography: "The systems of cities literature has emphasized urban space but neglected national space" (Dobkins and Ioannides, 2001).[9] As we will see, the location of manufacturing activity and the relationship between these locations and the rest of space is a key issue in geographical economics. To analyze this relationship, transportation costs have to be part of the analysis, since they are crucial in determining the balance between agglomeration and spreading forces (Fujita, Krugman, and Venables, 1999: 23). Chapter 7 returns to the topic of urban economics and *inter alia*, discusses – using the city-size distribution as an example – how geographical economics may add to our theoretical and empirical under-standing of urban systems and their evolution over time.

In their surveys of theories of agglomeration, which includes urban economics, Fujita and Thisse (1996, 2002) discuss three basic approaches: increasing returns, externalities, and spatial competition. In the terminology of box 2.1, their use of increasing returns and externalities corresponds to our definition of pure external economies and pecuniary external econ-omies respectively. Both types of external economies are important in our book. This leaves spatial competition, by which is meant that competition among firms is almost automatically of an oligopolistic nature when space is taken into consideration. Competition is restricted by distance; a firm typically is thought to compete only with its neighboring firms. Spatial competition is, therefore, intrinsically linked with strategic behavior by firms. In the remainder of the book we do not deal with spatial competition. The reason is simply that in geographical economics and in particular in the Avinash Dixit and Joseph Stiglitz (1977) version of monopolistic compe-tition (see section 2.3 and chapter 3), which characterizes the market structure in our core geographical economics model, strategic behavior is not taken into account. Firms take each other's (pricing) behavior as given. In addition to the three approaches mentioned by Fujita and Thisse (1996),

---

[9] In contrast to central place theory; see subsection 2.2.2. This is not to say that modern urban economics denies, for instance, the importance of transport costs between cities in explaining urban growth; see Glaeser and Kohlhase (2004) for a very instructive paper on transport costs and urban development.

Anas, Arnott, and Small (1998) give two additional reasons for (urban) agglomeration: the existence of non-homogeneous space and *internal* economies of scale in a production process. With the former one can rationalize agglomeration without any form of increasing returns to scale (think about the differences in the actual physical geography giving rise, for example to a natural harbor and the corresponding agglomeration). Non-homogeneous space or non-neutral space is discussed at various instances in the remainder of this chapter, and more extensively in chapter 6.

2.2.2 Regional economics

Regional economics analyzes the spatial organization of economic systems (and not just of cities) and must somehow also account for the uneven distribution across space. It has its roots in a research tradition going back to von Thünen (1826), Wilhelm Launhardt (1885), Weber (1909), Christaller (1933), and Lösch (1940). All these German contributions take the national or economy-wide space into consideration to analyze where economic activities are located. This is a relevant question as the movement of goods and people is not costless and production is typically subject to some form of increasing returns. The founding fathers of regional economics focus on different aspects of the location of economic activity, however. As we saw, von Thünen, for example, emphasized the location decisions made by farmers, while Weber analyzed the optimal location and plant size for manufacturing firms. This subsection focuses on the ideas first put forward (and tested) by Christaller and Lösch, who tried not only to explain the location of cities but also to differentiate cities by the various functions they perform and to deal with relationships between cities and the "non-cities." This approach is known as the *central place theory*, which shows "that different points or locations on the economic landscape have different levels of *centrality* and that goods and services are efficiently provided on a *hierarchical* basis" (Mulligan, 1984: 4; emphasis in original).[10]

Central place theory

Given an even distribution of identical consumers across a homogeneous plane, the central place theory argues that locations differ in centrality, and

---

[10] Note the difference with the analysis of urban systems mentioned in subsection 2.2.1. Central place theory analyzes not only the connections between cities, but also the hierarchy of cities, and the interaction between cities and the rural area. This is also true for recent models of urban growth (see Black and Henderson, 1999b, and chapter 7 of this volume).

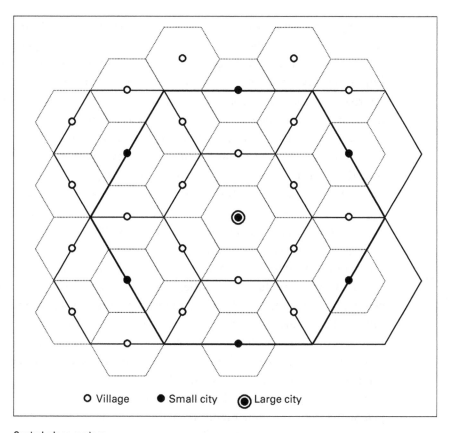

Figure 2.3   Central place system

that this centrality determines the type of goods the location provides. The provision of these goods is determined by internal increasing returns to scale, while the location is relevant because consumers incur transportation costs. To minimize these costs, consumers want access to nearby suppliers of goods. For some types of goods, such as bread, this is easier than for others, such as television sets, because the increasing returns to scale are relatively limited. Thus, the economy can support many relatively small locations (villages) where bakers are active to supply bread. In contrast, there can only be relatively few locations (small cities, the central places) where electronics firms sell television sets, which people buy less frequently. To minimize transport costs both these types of locations are rather evenly distributed across space. Moreover, we get a hierarchy of locations where the city performs all functions (sells bread and television sets), while the village performs only some functions (sells only bread). This is illustrated in figure 2.3, where the equidistant central place is surrounded by six equidistant smaller cities, which together form a hexagon. Each small city in turn is surrounded by six equidistant villages (see box 2.2 for an application).

The fact that it deals explicitly with the location of economic activity is an important advantage of central place theory. The main problem with the approach is that the economic rationale behind consumers' and firms' decisions remains unclear. What kind of behavior of individual agents leads to a central place outcome? Increasing returns at the firm level require some form of imperfect competition – an analysis that is lacking. Consequently, central place theory, especially the graphical version still found in most introductory textbooks on economic geography, is indeed more a descriptive story – or an exercise in geometry, as figure 2.3 depicts – than a causal model (Fujita, Krugman, and Venables, 1999: 27).

Regional scientists and economic geographers have, of course, also been aware of the limitations of this version of central place theory, which during the last thirty years has received less interest, particularly within economic geography (Martin, 1999). For a theoretical foundation, economic geographers have started to look elsewhere. We deal with this "turn" in economic geography in chapter 12, and also explain why modern economic geographers are rather critical of the work done by geographical economists (and vice versa). Following Walter Isard (1956, 1960), regional scientists have, however, tried to build on the basic ideas of central place theory, to give a theoretical (often highly formalized) economic foundation for this theory (see Mulligan, 1984). These models are mostly of a partial equilibrium nature, explaining some aspects of the central place system while ignoring others. A model in this tradition typically does not deal with individual firms or consumers, but essentially formalizes the geometric pattern of a central place system, as illustrated in figure 2.3, (see Nijkamp and Mills, 1986).[11] The central place outcome is therefore merely rationalized and not explained by the underlying behavior of consumers and producers, nor by their decisions and (market) interactions. For example, the demand curve facing a firm at a particular location is not derived from first principles but simply assumed. Geographical economics attempts to fill this gap in the literature by giving a microeconomic foundation to the hierarchy of central places (Fujita, Krugman, and Mori, 1999; Fujita, Krugman, and Venables, 1999: chap. 9; and chapter 7 of this volume).

---

[11] It is beyond the scope of this chapter to survey the modern contributions to regional science/regional economics, and we therefore pay no attention to important earlier building blocks of this approach, such as the work of François Perroux (1955); see the contributions in Nijkamp and Mills (1986), however.

Box 2.2 Central place theory in a Dutch polder

Between 1937 and 1942 an area of 48,000 hectares (120,000 acres) was reclaimed from the sea and turned into a polder in the center of the Netherlands. The new polder, called the *Noord-Oost Polder* (North-east Polder), was and still is used mainly for agriculture. The Dutch authorities also planned the establishment of a number of (small) towns and villages in this polder, and their planning was explicitly influenced by the work of Christaller and Lösch on central places. The polder clearly met some of the assumptions of central place theory: the land is extremely flat and almost perfectly homogeneous in all other respects. The initial settlers in the polder (the farmers) were also evenly distributed across the polder, and it was not too far-fetched to assume that these farmers had identical preferences.

   The outlay of the new locations in the polder, given in figure 2.4, therefore looked very much like the central place outlay shown in figure 2.3. There was one central place (the city of *Emmeloord*), which became surrounded over a period of ten years by a number of smaller (almost) equidistant locations. These smaller locations were explicitly devised to supply only lower-order goods, whereas Emmeloord was designed to supply the

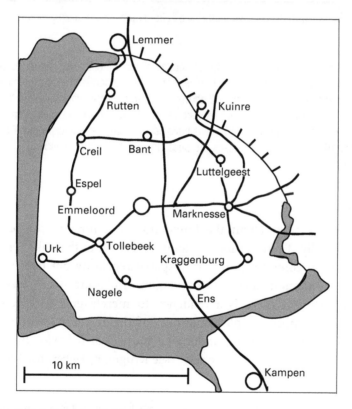

Figure 2.4   Central places in a Dutch polder

Box 2.2 (cont.)

Table 2.2 Population of locations in the Noord-Oost Polder

Location	Start	Planned population	Population in 2007
Emmeloord	1946	10,000	24,743
Marknesse	1946	2,000	3,847
Ens	1948	2,000	3,129
Kraggenburg	1948	2,000	1,465
Luttelgeest	1950	2,000	2,396
Bant	1951	2,000	1,357
Rutten	1952	2,000	1,752
Creil	1953	2,000	1,665
Nagele	1954	2,000	1,959
Espel	1956	2,000	1,340
Tollebeek	1956	2,000	2,073

Source: Dorpen in de Noordoostpolder Gemeente Noordoostpolder/Bevolking per dorp, 2007.

higher-order goods (see figure 2.4 for the outlay of the various locations in the polder).[12] Based on this core idea from central place theory, the authorities made projections about the size of each location. As table 2.2 shows, these projections were removed from reality after sixty years. The central place had become much larger than predicted, some locations are just about correct, and some locations have become smaller than expected. Exercise 2.2 at the end of this chapter addresses the possible explanations for this result.

Market potential

The above remarks about the foundation of central place theory apply more generally. There are more examples of theories that, like central place theory, try to come to grips with a spatial regularity but that lack a convincing economic-theoretical foundation. In contrast to (neoclassical) economic theory, there is a tendency to merely give a representation, using, for example, simple equations, of the regularity without a connection to a model of the underlying individual behavior by economic agents. Other examples of "models" (see Krugman, 1995a) used to describe

---

[12] The outlay of the various villages and towns was such that it took each farmer at most ten minutes, travel time (by bike!) to reach a lower-order good store. Moreover, in their planning frenzy the Dutch authorities decided that locations should also be equal with respect to the religion of their inhabitants. So they tried to make sure that every location had a proportional share of Catholic and Protestant people.

or mimic particular empirical spatial regularities are (i) the equations underlying the rank-size distribution (chapter 7), (ii) the gravity model of trade (chapter 9), and (iii) the market potential analysis (chapter 5). The latter, due to Chauncy Harris (1954), is widely used in regional economics. For the case of the United States, and using the value of retail sales per US county, Harris finds that the market potential of any location can be described by

$$MP_i = \sum_{j=1}^{n} \left(\frac{M_j}{D_{ij}} \right) \tag{2.1}$$

in which MP_i is the market potential of location i, M_j is the demand by location j for goods from location i, and D_{ij} is the distance between locations i and j.

The market potential equation therefore provides an indication of the general proximity of a location (in his study: a US county) in relation to total demand. Harris (1954), and many regional economists since then, have found that the market potential (and hence demand) is typically high in those areas where production is also actually located. This gives support to the notion of the clustering of economic activity, and indicates that the agglomeration and location decisions on which it is based are not only a supply-side issue, but that demand also plays its part. In fact, the idea that production takes place where demand is high can also be reversed. Demand is high where production is located as a result of the purchasing power of the workers making production at that location possible. Though convincing from an empirical point of view, the market potential analysis lacks a theoretical foundation (and thereby it also lacks content: what does MP_i represent?). As we will see in sections 2.3 and 2.4, this is not very surprising, because economic trade and growth theory have great difficulties in explaining any phenomenon in which geography plays a part. In particular, the distance variable D_{ij} is difficult to reconcile with economic theory (in box 2.4 we argue that the same is true for the gravity model of international trade). The ideas behind the market potential analysis play a prominent role in geographical economics, however. As will be argued in chapter 3 the core model of geographical economics can be interpreted as an attempt to provide a theoretical foundation for equation (2.1). Empirical work in geographical economics also uses the market potential approach, as we will see at length in section 5.5 of chapter 5.

Both examples (central place theory and the market potential approach) illustrate some points that apply more generally.[13] The theoretical approaches, like central place theory, and the more empirically inspired approaches, like the market potential analysis, deal with important aspects of the spatial organization of economic activity. The framework of analysis by and large does not, however, meet the standards of mainstream economic theory, which requires the conclusions to be based on the actions and interactions of individual economic agents in the market place. This calls for the analysis of individual consumer and producer behavior, market structure, and the resulting equilibria. Such a microeconomic foundation of geography does not exist (or was simply not considered to be useful to begin with) in some corners of regional economics (Fujita and Thisse, 1996, 2000).[14] Different strands of existing economic theory may provide such a microeconomic foundation, but, as we will see in the remainder of this chapter, they are lacking in geographical content.

2.2.3 Is geographical economics new? The view from urban and regional economics

Geographical economics can be seen as *new* economic geography to the extent that it combines well-established spatial insights from regional and urban economics *with the general equilibrium framework of mainstream economic theory*. It tries not just to put more economic theory into

---

[13] Another early approach influential in regional economics and relevant here is the so-called *export base multiplier approach*. The main idea is a restatement of the Keynesian income multiplier. Suppose that total regional income I consists of income earned in the non-tradable sector I_n and income earned by the tradable sector with exports I_e. Also assume that the income earned locally (I_n) is a constant fraction a of the (exogenous) income earned with exports (with $0 < a < 1$). Then, an increase in exports will set in motion a more than proportional increase in total regional income using the income multiplier, leading to a total increase $I = I_e / (1-a)$. The conclusion is that the economic development of a region depends on the expansion of its tradable sector and the size of the income multiplier. Further developments in this approach focused on the role of the non-tradable sector, emphasizing that the share of income earned locally was not a simple function of export income but related to the characteristics of the regional economy, thus endogenizing regional economic development. As Fujita, Krugman, and Venables (1999: 28) argue, this means that a is no longer fixed but increases if, through a process of endogenous growth, the non-tradable sector expands. The main proponent of this approach, Pred (1966), envisages a growth process for the regional economy similar to the process of circular and cumulative growth discussed in section 2.4.

[14] Even though there are considerable differences within economic geography itself as to the proper method and framework, it seems safe to say that in modern versions of economic geography (Martin, 1999; Scott, 2000; Peck, 2000; Boschma and Frenken, 2006) the search for such a microeconomic foundation provided by geographical economics is rejected. Preferred instead is an alternative foundation of economic geography, based not on neoclassical economics but on alternative economic approaches such as evolutionary economics, or even on explicitly "non-economic" theories such as regulation theory. We return to this matter and the relationship between geographical economics and economic geography in chapter 12.

geography but, above all, more geography into mainstream economics, while using the toolkit of mainstream economics. Whether this attempt yields new insights into the relationships between geography and economics or only grounds existing (and, for some economic geographers, outdated) work on a different analytical framework is a different question. This question cannot be addressed until chapter 12, by which time the reader will have gained a thorough knowledge of geographical economics in chapters 3–11. Before we turn to mainstream economic trade and growth theory and their analysis (or lack thereof) of geography in the remainder of this chapter, it is useful to make the following two observations about the "legacy" of urban and regional economics for geographical economics and its attempt to ground the analysis of the allocation of economic activity across space on a general equilibrium framework.

The first observation is that the standard general equilibrium framework will not work if we want geography or space to matter. As David Starrett (1978) has shown, the existence of positive transportation or trade costs will result in an equilibrium within which no transportation or trade of goods will take place (see box 2.3)!

Box 2.3 The spatial impossibility theorem

The spatial impossibility theorem states that in an economy with a finite number of locations and a finite number of consumers and firms, in which space is homogeneous and transport is costly, no perfectly competitive equilibrium exists in which actual transport takes place. This is intuitively easy to understand, as in such an economy transport costs can always be avoided because production and consumption can take place at an arbitrarily small level, without additional costs (a situation referred to as "backyard capitalism" in the literature). In such a hypothetical world of perfect divisibility, it would be impossible to explain why clustering or agglomeration of activities occurs (as we observe in reality). Only if there are indivisibilities, or extra costs involved if production is split, does the location of economic activities become important; Starrett (1978: 27) states: "[A]s long as there are some indivisibilities in the system (so that individual operations must take up space) then a sufficiently complicated set of interrelated activities will generate transport costs." This principle is know as *Starrett's spatial impossibility theorem*; see chapter 2 in Fujita and Thisse (2002) for a formal analysis and summary.

It is interesting to note that Tjalling Koopmans pointed out half a century ago that we can only begin to understand the importance of location or geography for economics if we recognize the fact that economic activities are not infinitely divisible; or, in Koopmans' words (1957: 154; emphasis in original), "Without recognizing indivisibilities – in human person, in residences, plants, equipment, and in transportation – ... location patterns, down to those of the smallest village, *cannot* be understood."

Box 2.3 (cont.)

Each location will prefer autarky to save on transportation costs, and, if every economic activity is perfectly (and costlessly) divisible across space, autarky or *backyard capitalism* with self-producing consumers/workers is the only feasible outcome. This runs, of course, counter to the most basic facts – namely that we do indeed observe trade between locations and the absence of backyard capitalism. Duranton (2008) therefore concludes: "If one takes transport costs as an unavoidable fact of life, one must assume either some non-homogeneity of space or some non-convexity of production sets."

As we will see in the next section, the non-homogeneity of space option is the route traditionally taken by international trade theory. The theories on urban and regional economics discussed in the present section take the second route. With von Thünen, the friction or non-divisibility called upon to arrive at a meaningful equilibrium outcome in a world of positive transport costs is the assumption that output must be sold at the central market. In modern urban and regional economics, it is usually the introduction of some form of increasing returns that performs this role. Fujita and Thisse (2002: chap. 4) refer to the economic forces increasing returns – transport costs as the *fundamental trade-off for a spatial economy*. As we will see in chapters 3 and 4, this also holds for geographical economics. With increasing returns but without transport costs, firms may find it profitable to produce at a single plant, but they do not care about the location of this plant. As we argued above, in the absence of increasing returns (or non-homogeneous space) but with transport costs, we will thus end up in a situation of backyard capitalism.

The second, related, observation is that, because it turned out to be difficult to combine transportation costs, increasing returns to scale, and imperfect competition in a general equilibrium framework, it took quite some time from Koopmans (1957), via Starrett (1978) to arrive at the first geographical economics model, by Krugman (1991a). Having said this, it is also clear that many of the ingredients of geographical economics are not new and were already well known in 1991, when Krugman published his model in *The Journal of Political Economy*. In their survey of the theory of agglomeration, Ottaviano and Thisse (2004) ask the question "Where did we stand in 1990?," which is prior to Krugman (1991a). They observe that, with one crucial exception, all the important elements were already floating around in the existing location theory. More specifically, the legacy of location theory can be summed up in the following five points (Ottaviano and Thisse, 2004: 2576; emphasis in original):

(i) [T]he economic space is the outcome of a trade-off between various forms of increasing returns and different types of mobility costs;

(ii) price competition, high transport costs and land use foster the dispersion of production and consumption; therefore

(iii) firms are likely to cluster within large metropolitan areas when they sell differentiated products and transport costs are low;

(iv) cities provide a wide array of final goods and specialized labor markets that make them attractive to consumer/workers; and

(v) agglomerations are the outcome of cumulative processes involving both the supply and demand sides.

Consequently, *the space economy has to be understood as the outcome of the interplay between agglomeration and dispersion forces*, an idea put forward by geographers and regional scientists long ago, *within a general equilibrium framework accounting explicitly for market failures.*

As will become clear after reading chapters 3 and 4, these five points are also at the heart of geographical economics, which raises the question as to the key difference between geographical economics Krugman-style (1991a) and the existing location theories from urban and regional economics. The answer is indeed that (Ottaviano and Thisse, 2004: 2576) "what was missing was a general equilibrium framework with imperfect competition connecting these various insights and allowing for a detailed study of their interactions." The main contribution of geographical economics, is therefore, to combine the existing elements into one single analytical framework, even though Krugman himself at the time remained somewhat silent on these antecedents (see chapter 12).

2.3 International trade theory

This section discusses the role of geography in the theory of international trade. We are more specific here than in sections 2.2 and 2.4 because the core model of geographical economics has its roots firmly in international trade theory. In many ways it is an extension of the so-called new trade theory, specifically of Krugman (1979, 1980). These two articles, together with Krugman (1991a) – the core geographical economics model-earned him the Nobel Prize in economics in 2008. Subsection 2.3.2 therefore focuses on the geographical content of these two seminal papers by

Krugman, rather than giving a survey of new trade theory.[15] Subsection 2.3.1 briefly discusses its "predecessor," neoclassical trade theory. Here we must point out that the discussion of trade theory in this section only touches upon issues such as the (Dixit–Stiglitz) modeling of imperfect competition, transportation costs, or the determination of different equilibria. These issues (and the technicalities that go along with them) are addressed in more detail in chapter 3.

2.3.1 Neoclassical trade theory

The label "neoclassical trade theory" refers to theories in which the trade flows between nations is based on comparative advantage, resulting from technological differences (David Ricardo) or from factor abundance. In the factor abundance model, developed by Eli Heckscher, Ohlin, and Paul Samuelson, comparative advantage is determined – as the name suggests – by cross-country differences in the relative abundance of factor endowments. It suffices to think of the simple $2 \times 2 \times 2$ (two goods, two countries, and two factors of production) factor abundance model, which is still the backbone of any introductory course in international trade. It was widely used, for example, in the debate on the effects of globalization for the Organisation for Economic Co-operation and Development (OECD) labor markets; see box 2.4.

Assume that there are two countries, (North and South), two tradable goods (apparel and machinery), and two factors of production (high-skilled labor and low-skilled labor). Suppose that North is relatively well endowed with high-skilled labor, and South with low-skilled labor. The production of both sets of goods requires both inputs, but the production of machinery is relatively highly skill-intensive. Consumers in North and South have identical preferences and consume both goods. In the absence of trade, North, which is abundant in high-skilled labor, can more easily make machinery than South, because machinery production is highly skill-intensive. In autarky, this results in a relatively low price for machinery in North and apparel in South. Once North and South start to trade, prices will be equalized, resulting in a higher price for machinery in North and a higher price for apparel in South. As a consequence, North will have an

---

[15] In the new trade theory, trade is analyzed in models in a world of increasing returns to scale and monopolistic competition. Neary (2004) provides a survey of the basic models, of which Krugman (1979, 1980) are prime (but not the only) examples.

incentive to (partially) specialize in the production of machinery. A similar reasoning holds for South with respect to apparel. The resulting trade flows are of the inter-industry type (trade of machinery for apparel). Furthermore, factor prices will be equalized between North and South as a result of trade.

The factor abundance model uses some additional specific assumptions, such as perfect competition, homogeneous goods, production with constant returns to scale, no transport costs associated with the trade of goods, and mobility of the factors of production between industries, but not between countries. It is clear (see section 2.2) that a number of these assumptions are at odds with key assumptions in regional and urban economics, in which we have external and/or internal increasing returns to scale, imperfect competition, positive transportation costs, and mobility of the factors of production (and firms). We concluded in section 2.2 that these ingredients are required to account for spatial economic patterns. Does this mean that geography or the location of economic activity is a non-issue in neoclassical trade theory? Well, yes and no.

To explain this answer, it is useful to distinguish between the first nature and the second nature of the economics of location (see Krugman, 1993b). The location of economic activity is relevant in the factor abundance model so far as the uneven distribution of factor endowments is concerned. This distribution is given, and thus a first-nature determinant of location in Krugman's terminology. In our example, North specializes in machinery and South in apparel as a result of the geographic distribution of endowments, which translates into an uneven distribution of economic activity across global space. In this restricted sense geography matters.

We would like to reach this conclusion in another way, however, namely by showing how the relevance of location follows from the decisions made by economic agents and their interactions and not (only) from some exogenous difference in factor endowments. In other words, the location of production should be an endogenous variable, a second-nature determinant of location in Krugman's terminology. This second-nature is clearly lacking in factor abundance theory. As argued in chapter 3, the endogenization of location decisions is needed to produce agglomeration of economic activity. Differences in factor endowments cannot imply a core–periphery pattern of production; they just lead to specialization (as opposed to agglomeration). Trade between countries cannot lead to inequality in the sense that machinery and apparel cannot both agglomerate in North.

The factor abundance model leads to the equalization of high-skilled wages between North and South (and similarly for low-skilled wages). This has been used to analyze a phenomenon with an obvious geographical component: globalization and its alleged impact on the allocation of production and income in the Western industrialized economies (North) (see Venables, 1998, and box 2.4). Globalization can be defined as the growing interdependence between countries through increased trade and/or increased factor mobility.

Box 2.4 Globalization, factor abundance, and clustering

Suppose the world can be characterized with a factor abundance model with two countries (North and South), two manufacturing goods (machines and apparel), and one non-tradable, non-manufacturing good. North is relatively well endowed with high-skilled labor, South with low-skilled labor. Both factors of production are needed for the production of all goods, but machine production is relatively highly-skill-intensive. North thus has a comparative advantage in the production of machines. Both countries produce both tradable goods, there is perfect competition, technology is fixed, and there is no cross-border labor mobility. Suppose that initially, due to very high transaction costs, both countries do not trade at all. Now, the transaction costs decrease, and trade opens up. The fall in transaction costs (which serves as a proxy for globalization) can be policy-driven (lowering of tariffs and the like) or technology-driven (improved transport and communication technologies). What are the main effects of trade for North? It will specialize in the production of machinery and start to import apparel – that is, the machinery sector expands and the apparel sector contracts. This has the following implications for North.

(1) There will be one high-skilled wage and one low-skilled wage (the *factor price equalization theorem*). Since wages are determined on the world market, changes in national factor supplies do not have any impact anymore on wages.

(2) North is confronted with an increase in the world production of apparel, which results in a fall in the relative price of apparel. This will hurt low-skilled labor in North, used intensively in the production of apparel, by lowering their real wage (*Stolper–Samuelson theorem*).

(3) The expansion of the machinery sector in North increases the relative demand for high-skilled labor, thus raising high-skilled wages relative to low-skilled wages in North. This induces firms in North to substitute away from high-skilled labor, and *de*creases the skill intensity of manufacturing production in North.

(4) The contraction of the apparel sector in North not only changes the mix of manufacturing production in North, it also implies a contraction of the manufacturing sector as a whole, because some of the labor released from the apparel sector will be employed in the non-tradable services sector. Consequently, the non-manufacturing sector expands and North is confronted with *deindustrialization*.

The factor abundance model can thus be called upon to give a theoretical foundation for the idea that globalization (increased imports by North of low-skilled intensive goods from South) may hurt low-skilled workers, by lowering their relative wages, and may lead to

Box 2.4 (cont.)

deindustrialization. The main geographical dimension of this analysis of globalization is the implication that North (the OECD countries) specializes in highly skill–intensive production, while South specializes in low skill–intensive production (south-east Asia, Latin America, or the transition economies in eastern Europe).

An important question for this version of the globalization debate is, of course, whether there is any empirical evidence to support the factor abundance model in general so as to validate implications 1–4 above. The factor abundance model has recently been the subject of an impressive amount of empirical research (see, for example, Davis and Weinstein, 2001, 2003, and, for a survey, Feenstra, 2004). Although there is some disagreement, the general consensus seems to be that relatively strong *additional* assumptions are needed to close the gap between the neoclassical theory and the data. In any event, the four implications of the factor abundance model are not convincingly substantiated by the empirical evidence. It is doubtful therefore whether the factor abundance model (alone) can explain the worsening of the position of low-skilled labor in North.

Relative differences in factor endowments can thus be used to give a theoretical justification for the differences in specialization patterns between countries. Other versions of neoclassical trade theory have similar implications as far as the relevance of geography is concerned. In the Ricardian model, comparative advantage, and hence the trade pattern, is determined by exogenous cross-country differences in technology. Countries specialize in the production of those goods in which they have a comparatively high productivity, which determines the location of production. Our main objection to the factor abundance model also holds for the Ricardian model: to the limited extent that geography matters, this relevance is given exogenously. Naturally, differences in factor endowment or technology can be the result of differences in geography. Consider, for example, land as a factor of production, as in the von Thünen tradition in urban economics. The availability of (fertile) land shapes comparative advantage. Similarly, the physical geography of a country (access to the sea, altitude, climate, etc.) can also be an underlying determinant of comparative advantage, which certainly holds for the stock of natural resources. John Gallup, Jeffrey Sachs and Andrew Mellinger (1998) and Sachs (2003) show that such cross-country differences in geography do indeed help to explain differences in economic development. We return to this issue in section 2.4, and in chapter 10, where we discuss the relevance of first-nature geography in explaining cross-country income differences when set against competing explanations.

The limited role for geography in neoclassical trade theory is perhaps best illustrated by the so-called specific factors model. Part of a country's factor endowments (labor, for example) is then internationally mobile, whereas other parts (land and capital, for example) are not. Production of a certain good requires inputs from the mobile factor as well as one particular or *specific* immobile factor (that is, usually land or sector-specific capital). Differences in the endowment of the specific factors thus influence the production and trade pattern, with a country specializing, *ceteris paribus*, in the production of the good requiring the input of the specific factor with which the country is relatively well endowed. There is a geographical link to the extent that the distribution of the immobile endowments is determined by geographical conditions. Again, such a connection is indirect at best, and the impact of geography is determined outside the trade model.[16]

To summarize, Anas, Arnott, and Small (1998: 1445) correctly state that non-homogeneous space, also known as non-neutral space, has traditionally been invoked to explain the uneven distribution of economic activity in international economics. These give rise to different sources of comparative advantage, which make the spreading of economic activity impossible. The location relevance therefore exists only by assumption, and there is no interdependence between geography and economics. In particular, the equilibrium location of economic activity is not the result of the underlying behavior of economic agents. The (trade) equilibrium is usually unique and fully determined by exogenous forces. More importantly, neoclassical trade theory does not allow for the establishment of a core–periphery equilibrium, which presents a problem in view of the many examples given in chapter 1. To permit the agglomeration of economic activity some of the assumptions underlying neoclassical trade theory have to be changed. An obvious candidate is the introduction of internal increasing returns to scale, and hence of imperfect competition (see subsection 2.3.2).

A final remark on the relationship between geography and neoclassical trade theory is that, without an uneven distribution of resources, and thus without comparative advantage, there is *ceteris paribus* no longer a rationale for trade, and geography ceases to be an issue.[17] Introducing positive

---

[16] Paul Courant and Alan Deardorff (1992) provide a factor abundance model in which the factors of production are unevenly distributed within a country. They show that if a country is "lumpy" enough the trade pattern can deviate from the trade pattern that would arise if the factors of production were evenly spread over the country; the country tends to export the good that uses intensively the most "lumpy" production factor. It is also the case, though, that in this model "geography" is exogenous.

[17] We reach a similar conclusion for the relevance of geography in neoclassical growth theory (section 2.4)

transportation costs, a similar conclusion can be reached even if comparative advantages exist. If these costs are high enough, the production of goods will be perfectly dispersed across space (Ottaviano and Puga, 1997). The economy will then consist of many small firms, producing for their own consumption – *backyard capitalism* again. This relates directly to the discussion of the *spatial impossibility theorem* in subsection 2.2.3, where we concluded that one way out was to introduce non-homogeneous space (the route traditionally taken in international trade theory) and another way out was to introduce "non-convexities in production," of which increasing returns to scale is the prime example. In this respect, the new trade theory below has more in common with urban and regional economics than with neoclassical trade theory.

2.3.2 New trade theory

From the late 1970s onwards the neoclassical trade theory has been challenged by the development of the new trade theory, which is now complementary to neoclassical trade theory and part of almost every textbook on international trade. The reason for trade between countries in new trade theory does not depend on comparative advantage. In fact, Krugman (1979, 1980) has developed a (by now standard) model in which countries engage in welfare-enhancing trade even when there is no comparative advantage whatsoever. The starting point for new trade theory was the stylized fact that a very large part of international trade takes place between countries with very similar factor endowments (see the German example in subsection 1.3.2). This trade is not, as the neoclassical trade theory would predict, inter-industry trade (exporting cereal in exchange for cars) but intra-industry trade (exporting cars in exchange for cars). The empirical relevance of intra-industry trade was, of course, well known but the theoretical foundation of this type of trade called for a class of models in which some of the building blocks of the neoclassical trade theory had to be overturned.

Krugman (1979)

The basic insights from Krugman (1979) can be illustrated as follows. Suppose there are two countries of equal market size, West and East, which have the same endowments, use the same technology, and both have one (immobile) car-producing firm. In the factor abundance model these countries would not trade. Both firms make various types of cars under increasing returns to scale for each type. In autarky, the firms produce three types of cars, namely types X, Y, and Z in West and types A, B, and C in East. Thus there is one industry that produces six types or *varieties* of cars. The consumers (workers) in West and East are immobile, evenly distributed, and have identical preferences. The varieties are imperfect substitutes and preferences are such that consumers always prefer more varieties of a car to fewer (this is the "love-of-variety" effect; see also chapter 3). The key to understanding the rationale for trade in this model is the combination of increasing returns to scale at the firm level (*internal* economies of scale; see box 2.1) and the love-of-variety effect in consumers' preferences, which is an externality not taken into account by firms. Moving from autarky to free trade these two assumptions ensure that trade will take place and is welfare-improving.

The extent to which each firm can exploit the increasing returns to scale is determined by the size of the market. The opening up of trade enlarges the market size for each type of car. Since each variety is produced under increasing returns to scale, this larger market enables the firms to better exploit the increasing returns.[18] The opening up of trade means that the car production *per variety* can increase as the larger market makes it profitable to expand the scale of production. In doing so, the prices per variety will decrease. To make this possible in the integrated market of West and East the total number of varieties produced must decrease. To see this, note that the total (West + East) endowments and the total market size are fixed, such that it is not possible to simultaneously increase the production of all six varieties. In free trade, the two countries together produce fewer than six varieties, say four (X, Y, A, and B). There are then two positive welfare effects. First, the decrease in prices brought about by the increased scale of production implies that workers/consumers end up with a higher real wage. Second, after trade, consumers are able to consume four rather than three varieties,[19] and this increases welfare through the love-of-variety effect.

Although the basic insights of Krugman (1979) are easy to understand, the introduction of increasing returns to scale implies a market structure of imperfect competition. The theoretical challenge was, therefore, to provide a trade model with imperfect competition – a real challenge in view of the discussion on urban and regional economics (section 2.2). Fortunately,

---

[18] "The effect [of trade] will be the same as if *each* country had experienced an increase in its labor force" (Krugman, 1979: 474).

[19] Note that, in autarky, the world as a whole produces six varieties, but each country produces and consumes only three varieties.

Krugman could build on a model of monopolistic competition that had just been published: Dixit and Stiglitz (1977). The Dixit–Stiglitz approach is now widely used in many fields, including geographical economics. In chapter 3 (see also box 3.2), we discuss and explain the main features of the Dixit–Stiglitz model. In view of the difficulty of dealing with imperfect competition it is not surprising that the new trade theory also includes models with pure external, instead of internal, economies of scale (Helpman, 1984; Helpman and Krugman, 1985), as it allows geographical economists to stick to a market structure of perfect competition; see box 2.5.

Box 2.5 New trade theory and external economies

Suppose an industry, say the personal computer (PC) industry, is characterized by pure external economies of scale, arising, for example, from information spillovers when the increase in the production of a single firm increases the production knowledge for all firms in the PC industry. This implies not only that average costs per PC for each firm are a decreasing function of the *industry* output, but also that we can still use perfect competition (box 2.1). There is no advantage for a firm in being large (in view of the external economies of scale), so typically the economy now consists of many small firms. Under perfect competition, price equals average cost for each firm. Finally, suppose there are two countries, A and B, and that consumers in both countries have identical preferences.

As in the case of internal economies of scale, intra-industry trade may develop between the two countries, with both countries producing and exporting PC varieties. With external economies, however, we can also have an equilibrium in which one country produces the total world demand for PCs. If, for some historical reason, the PC industry initially establishes itself in country A, the external economies may turn this initial distribution of production into a lasting equilibrium even if the PC industry in country B would be more efficient (*lock-in effect*). Two issues, also part of geographical economics, are relevant in this case. First, initial conditions can determine the (stable) equilibrium outcome. Depending on which firm enters the market first, either country could end up being the world producer of PCs. Second, the resulting trade equilibrium may be inefficient.

A simple example illustrates the possibility of a "bad" equilibrium. Suppose country A is the first to set up a PC industry and produces 500,000 PCs. At this level of *industry* output a price (equal to average cost) of $1,000 per PC can be charged to meet world demand, which is fixed at 500,000 units for simplicity. Suppose that the PC industry in country B could produce 500,000 PCs more efficiently, say for $750 per unit of output. This does not imply that country B will start producing PCs, since these costs apply for the whole *industry*. In the absence of a PC industry in country B, and thus in the absence of positive external economies, a single firm in country B may be able to produce 500 PCs only for a price above $1,000 – that is, at a higher cost than in country A, thus not making it worthwhile to set up shop in country B. This is illustrated in figure 2.5.

Box 2.5 (cont.)

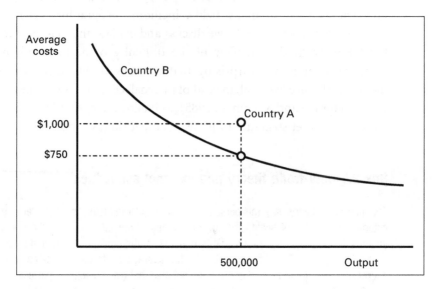

Figure 2.5   Example of the lock-in effect

External economies of scale are important in this example. Given that world demand is met by the industry in country A at an average cost of $1,000, the individual firm in country B can produce only at a higher average cost. This is true for all firms in country B. It is only when all firms in B *jointly* decide to start producing PCs that they can take over the PC market, as this brings average cost down below $1,000 as a result of external economies of scale. There's nothing that induces firms in B to make such a decision, however, because the individual firm is confronted only with the fact that its average costs exceed the prevailing market price. This problem would not occur with *internal* economies of scale, in which the average costs for a firm fall as the firm produces more output.[20]

The question is now whether new trade theory has something to say on the role of geography. In the Krugman (1979) model, the answer is simple. The location of economic activity is not really an issue. Trade costs are zero, so firms are indifferent with regard to the location of their production sites. Even if there are positive trade costs the (exogenous) market size is evenly distributed between the two countries, which precludes any agglomeration

---

[20] For further reading on external economies and trade, we refer to Elhanan Helpman and Krugman (1985: chap. 2), and the surveys in the *Handbook of International Economics* by Helpman (1984b) and Krugman (1995b). For a similar example, see Krugman and Maurice Obstfeld's *International Economics*, fifth edition (2000: 150–1).

of economic activity. It is indeterminate which country ends up producing which varieties. All one can say is that countries produce different varieties and the pattern of trade is indeterminate. Nevertheless, this model is important as the basis of the core model of geographical economics, for example with respect to the analysis of producer and consumer behavior. With external economies of scale the location of economic activity is also not addressed. One could argue that the lock-in effects in some of these models allow initial conditions to play a role in determining the allocation of production. As with neoclassical trade theory, this role for geography is determined outside the model.

Krugman (1980)

Krugman (1980) is a crucial step from the initial new trade model in Krugman (1979) to the core model of geographical economics. The rationale for intra-industry trade is the same as in the 1979 model, with a few notable differences. First, in the 1980 model the opening up of trade, and hence the increase of the market size, does *not* lead to an increase in the scale of production, despite increasing returns to scale at the firm level. Instead, the volume of production of each variety (at the firm level) is the same under autarky and trade, and prices do not change.[21] The gains from trade are now completely due to the love-of-variety effect, as consumers can choose between more varieties under trade than autarky. The core model of geographical economics coincides with Krugman (1980) on this important issue. Second, in the 1980 model trade between nations incurs transport costs – which, obviously, is relevant from a geographical point of view. Third, in the 1980 model, demand per variety is no longer symmetric as countries differ in market size.

This uneven distribution of market size becomes important when combined with positive transportation costs, because a country will produce those varieties for which the demand in the country is relatively high. In this sense, the location of production matters and a concentration of economic activity can be an outcome of the model. The reasoning is simple: given the uneven distribution of demand, firms, which are still immobile, minimize transportation costs if they produce those varieties for which home demand is relatively strong. Moreover, and in contrast to the model without

---

[21] If the number of firms (and hence the number of varieties) is large, the elasticity of demand will be constant (Dixit and Norman, 1980). In chapter 3 we will see that this feature, which follows from the Dixit-Stiglitz (1977) formulation of monopolistic competition, is also a crucial element of the geographical economics models. This assumption is not undisputed; Holmes (1999) criticizes new trade and geographical economics for this assumption.

transport costs, the direction of trade is no longer indeterminate, because the concentration of production implies that countries will be net exporters of those varieties for which home demand is relatively high. As Krugman (1980: 955) puts it: "Countries will tend to export those kind of products for which they have relatively large home demand. Notice that this argument is wholly dependent on increasing returns; in a world of diminishing returns, strong domestic demand for a good will tend to make it an import rather than an export." This phenomenon is known as the *home market effect*.[22]

In an attempt to test for the home market effect, Donald Davis and David Weinstein (1999) refer to Krugman (1980) as a model of economic geography (see chapter 5). This suggests that there is no fundamental difference between this model and the core model in chapter 3. We do not agree with that view, however, for three reasons. First, neither firms nor workers decide anything about location in Krugman (1980). There is no mobility of firms or the factors of production. Given their (exogenous) location, firms make a decision only about the varieties they want to produce. Second, the concentration of production of varieties (and, by assumption, of demand) does not allow for the agglomeration of economic activity. Core–periphery equilibria are not possible because the concentration of demand in the first country, say for X varieties, is mirrored by a similar concentration of demand for the $(1 - X)$ varieties in the other country. In this sense, both countries are characterized by a geographic concentration of industry. Third, the allocation of the market size for the varieties is not an outcome of the model but is simply given (income is therefore also given). This is closely linked to the immobility of workers (who demand the goods produced) and firms. In these respects, location in Krugman (1980) is still determined outside the model.

Krugman and Venables (1990)

The consequences of Krugman (1980) are analyzed in Krugman and Venables (1990). They allow *countries* (!) to differ in size, thereby developing a model

---

[22] Donald Davis (1998) shows that the home market effect is not very robust (see also section 5.4). The effect occurs in Krugman (1980) because a larger market for a good in a country (and thus higher demand for this good) implies a more than proportional change in employment for and the production of that good, which in turn means that the country must be a net exporter of the good. In general, the extent to which relatively large home demand leads to exports depends on the elasticity of the labor supply. If this is not perfectly elastic, as in the core model of chapter 3, the relatively high demand will also result in higher wages (see equation (3.27) in section 3.9 for a derivation of the home market effect).

that looks very similar to the core model of geographical economics one year before this core model was published by Krugman in 1991. It is a two-country model, in which country 1 is large: it has more factor endowments (capital and labor) and a larger market than country 2.[23] In the main part of their study, the relative endowments are the same between the two countries, so there is no comparative advantage and trade is of the intra-industry type. There are two sectors in both countries, one perfectly competitive and one imperfectly competitive (manufactures), both producing tradable goods. Country 1 also has a larger number of firms in the manufacturing sector. This sector produces differentiated products under increasing returns to scale and monopolistic competition. The entry and exit of firms is allowed, but firms cannot move between countries. The latter also holds for the factors of production. Both for firms and the factors of production, there is only inter-sectoral mobility. The central question is how an increase in the degree of economic integration (using a fall in transportation costs as a proxy) affects the core (country 1) and periphery (country 2).

In autarky (when high transport costs prohibit trade), both countries have a share in the manufacturing sector equal to their share in world endowments. The difference in endowments is given by segments A and B in figure 2.6. It turns out that, for an intermediate range of transportation costs, economic integration strengthens the core: the core's share of world industry, S_1, gets larger than its share of world endowments (the latter is 0.6), and vice versa for the periphery ($S_2 < 0.4$). New firms enter the manufacturing sector in country 1, while some firms exit this sector in country 2. Given the larger market in country 1 and the minimization of transportation costs, new firms prefer country 1 even though wages are higher. As transportation costs continue to fall, the core's share of world industry eventually starts to decrease again. At very low transport costs the advantage of producing in the country with the larger market becomes small, which, combined with the stiffer labor market competition in country 1 (more firms compete for the country's production factors, which raises factor prices), implies that new firms find it profitable to start production in country 2, where wages are lower. At the extreme case of zero transport costs, wages will be equal and each country's share of manufactures will return to its share in world endowments. There is thus a non-linear

---

[23] Our discussion of Krugman and Venables (1990), including figure 2.6, is based on Ottaviano and Puga (1997).

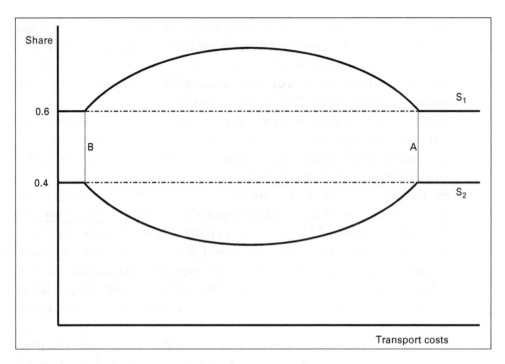

Figure 2.6   Share of world production in manufactures

relationship between a country's share in world industry and transportation costs; in figure 2.6, the shares always sum to one.

Why is the analysis underlying figure 2.6 interesting? First, it deals with the agglomeration of economic activity, because it allows for an uneven overall distribution of manufacturing activity. Recall that this is not the case in the Krugman (1980) model, in which there is a geographic concentration of a single industry but there is no concentration of manufacturing production as a whole. Second, as will become clear in chapters 3 to 5, the U-shaped pattern in figure 2.6 foreshadows important theoretical and empirical results in the geographical economics literature. Third, figure 2.6 is based on numerical examples, and they are used to analyze the effects of economic integration on the core and periphery. This resembles the strategy in geographical economics to use computer simulations to analyze the agglomeration of economic activity. The question therefore arises, *is this a full-fledged geographical economics model?* The answer is that it goes a long way, but in the end it is not. The main reason is that the existence of core and periphery is not derived from the model itself. The assumption that the market sizes differ begs the question of why there should be a core and periphery to start with. Along with fixing the market size goes the assumption that workers are immobile. Mobility of workers, and hence of demand, would run counter to the idea that one could a priori fix the relative market size of the two countries. The core model of chapters 3 and 4 adds endogenization of market size (and mobility of consumers/workers, who determine the market size) to the Krugman and Venables (1990) model.

In the introduction to their book, Fujita, Krugman, and Venables (1999) list four main features of geographical economics. Two of these features (Dixit–Stiglitz monopolistic competition and transportation costs of the iceberg type) are also present in Krugman (1980). The Krugman and Venables (1990) model adds a (crude) attempt to use simulations. In our view, the real novelty of geographical economics is to be found in the fourth feature, dynamics, which tackles the question of how to deal with the mobility of economic agents (notably firms and workers), which *endogenizes the size of the market*. The emphasis underlines the fact that this is the key difference between new trade theory and geographical economics. As in our discussion in subsection 2.2.3 regarding the similarities between urban and regional economics, on the one hand, and geographical economics, on the other hand, we have come to the conclusion that, in addition to one crucial element: dynamics, new trade theory in 1990 was very similar to the geographical economics of Krugman (1991a). From the perspective of new trade theory, this is aptly summarized by Head and Mayer (2004a). They list the five following essential ingredients of geographical economics (2613–4):

   (i)   increasing returns to scale that are internal to the firm;
   (ii) imperfect competition;
   (iii) positive transportation or trade costs;
   (iv) endogenous firm locations; and
   (v)   the *endogenous location* of demand, through either mobile workers (Krugman, 1991; see chapter 3) or firms using their sector output as intermediate inputs (Venables, 1996, and Krugman and Venables, 1995; see chapter 4).

Head and Mayer (2004a: 2614; emphasis in original) conclude that

ingredients [1–4] all appeared in the new trade literature, and in particular gave rise to the *home market effects* identified by Krugman (1980). With these assumptions, agglomeration can arise but only through the magnification of initial region size asymmetries. The key innovation of new economic geography relative to new trade is assumption [5]. Without [5] symmetric initial conditions can be expected to lead to symmetric outcomes. With all five assumptions, initial symmetry can be broken and agglomerations can form through a process of circular causation.

How the introduction of condition (5) is able to set in motion a process of circular causation will become clear after reading chapters 3 and 4; the point to stress here is the important legacy of new trade theory for geographical economics.

Before we turn to the core model in which all the features come together, we round up chapter 2 with a discussion of the role of geography in theories of economic growth and development. This serves as an introduction to chapter 10.

2.4 Economic growth and development

Trade theory deals, above all, with the question of how international trade determines the allocation of economic activity between countries. As such, it does not deal with the dynamic issue of economic growth and development over time. A geographical neglect of economic growth would not be a problem in the context of our study if countries experienced a more or less similar process of economic growth and converged to roughly the same levels of economic well-being. A quick look at the data (see figures 1.2 and 1.3 in chapter 1) makes it clear that this is not the case. Growth rates of GDP per capita vary considerably between countries, and so does the level of GDP per capita. Moreover, the data suggest that there may be a geographical component involved. High- and low-growth countries are often geographically concentrated; think of south-east Asia and sub-Saharan Africa respectively. High and low levels of GDP per capita are also clearly not randomly distributed across space: one observes clusters of rich and poor countries. In this section we ask whether theories on economic growth and development have something to say on the relationship between geography and economic growth. We do not attempt a survey but simply focus on basic (and well-known) insights in order to assess the geographical relevance of growth theory.[24]

---

[24] Good books on growth are Helpman (2004) and Barro and Sala-i-Martin (2004).

2.4.1 Economic growth theory

Geography is not really relevant in neoclassical growth theory. In the short run a positive growth rate of output per capita can be achieved by means of capital accumulation or technological progress. Since capital accumulation is subject to the law of diminishing returns, however, it is only through technological progress that a positive growth rate of output per capita can be sustained in the long run. Technological progress is exogenous, such that in the end this leaves the growth of output per head unexplained. Cross-country differences in the level of output per capita are thought to be temporary. Assuming that countries have access to the same technology and are equal in all other (structural or institutional) respects, neoclassical growth theory predicts that countries will converge to the same level of output per capita in the long run. The capital stock (per capita) will be low for *initially* poor countries, which implies a high return on investment (capital accumulation), which fosters the convergence process.

There will be absolute convergence: countries end up with the same equilibrium level of output (and capital) per capita. Even though convergence may be slow, the neoclassical growth model predicts that poor countries will catch up, and that actual differences in growth rates are best thought of as reflecting this process of convergence. In such a world the spatial agglomeration of high or low (growth rates of) GDP per capita does not warrant much attention. The basic version of the neoclassical growth model has a hard time explaining the stylized facts of growth (see also chapter 10). Either convergence is extremely slow, or the theory's main prediction, absolute convergence, is flawed. There are two options to improve upon this state of affairs: (i) adapt the neoclassical growth model to allow for persistent differences, or (ii) come up with an alternative theory of economic growth.

Option (i) might include the introduction of a third factor of production, human capital, besides labor and physical capital, or the use of conditional instead of absolute convergence. This second possibility requires some explanation. Under conditional convergence, countries no longer have access to the same technology or may have different institutional characteristics. Consequently, countries need not converge to the same long-run equilibrium level of output per head. Instead, convergence is conditioned on the characteristics of a country. This allows for a (weak) link between geography and neoclassical growth theory: to the extent that the cross-country differences in technology or institutions are location-specific, geography matters. Empirical support is given by Gallup, Sachs, and Mellinger (1998) in a cross-country setting and Duncan Black and Henderson (2003) for the growth of US cities, by showing that physical geographical differences, like climate or access to the sea, have a strong impact on economic growth (see box 2.6). As with neoclassical trade theory, the role of geography in neoclassical growth theory is limited and indirect. Its impact is determined outside the model and there is no feedback from the growth variables to the location variables. Chapter 10 discusses how both first-nature geography and second-nature geography influence economic growth.

Option (ii) requires the development of an alternative theoretical model to neoclassical growth theory. Since the seminal work of Paul Romer (1986, 1990; see also Robert Lucas, 1988), this avenue of research has become known as "new growth theory." Although the models may vary considerably, two crucial (intertwined) differences from the neoclassical growth model are the attempts to endogenize economic growth and to dispense with the assumption of diminishing returns to accumulable factors (van Marrewijk, 1999). With respect to the use of scale economies, various options exist in the new growth literature. Initially, most models used pure external economies at the national or industry level, rather than internal economies at the firm level (see box 2.1). Subsequent research also used positive internal economies under imperfect competition, similar to new trade theory. Positive external economies may give rise to positive spillovers and strategic complementarity, and hence to multiple equilibria.[25]

Other possibilities also exist, such as the celebrated AK model with constant returns to capital at the economy-wide level, which implies that countries do not converge to the same long-run equilibrium. Endogenization of the growth process focuses on technological progress, a positive function of the overall stock of capital or labor, or of R&D expenditures. Let Y be output, K the stock of capital, L labor, and $A(.)$ the technology function. Consider the following production function:

$$Y = A(.)K^{1-b}L^b, \qquad 0 < b < 1 \qquad\qquad (2.2)$$

This production function looks a lot like the well-known Cobb–Douglas production function typically underlying the neoclassical growth model. In fact, if we assume that A is a constant we do have the Cobb–Douglas

---

[25] Spillovers are not the same as strategic complementarity. Positive spillovers arise if an increase in the effort of one agent positively affects the pay-off of other agents. Strategic complementarity arises if an increase in the effort of one agent increases the optimal efforts of other agents.

production function, and it can readily be seen that output per capita, Y/L, is determined by the stock of capital per worker, K/L. Growth of the latter is subject to diminishing returns (as long as $0 < b < 1$). Returning to equation (2.2), non-decreasing scale economies can be incorporated by specifying $A(.)$ as a function of the aggregate capital stock, human capital, or some dynamic "innovation" function, which captures the accumulation of aggregate knowledge in the economy. The crux of all these attempts is to ensure there are no longer diminishing returns to accumulable factors of production.

Whether the new growth theory really is different from the neoclassical growth theory is not undisputed (Solow, 1994). Our main interest here is in the possible role for geography in the new growth theory. In many versions of the new growth theory there is no such role. To allow for location to be relevant, countries must differ in some respect. Take, for example, external economies to scale. If these are the same for all countries, the economy can be described by one uniform "global" production function with increasing returns to scale. Location is not irrelevant if the spillovers associated with the external economies are somehow localized. Gene Grossman and Helpman (1991) analyze localized spillovers if the positive externalities associated with R&D or, more generally, with knowledge exist only within a certain group of countries. This model is in a number of respects very close to the core model of geographical economics (see Brakman and Garretsen, 1993: 179). The existence of localized externalities, and hence the limited geographical range of knowledge spillovers, may be due to cultural, political, and institutional differences, all of which can contribute to the localization of these external economies. They can help explain why some (groups of) countries not only have a higher growth rate and level of output per capita than others, but also why this difference might not diminish over time, making core–periphery equilibria possible.

The new growth models can thus account for the agglomeration of economic activity. The problem is how location itself is analyzed. The introduction of location in the new growth theory bears a great resemblance to the relevance of location in the neoclassical growth models that allow for conditional convergence. In both cases the role of location does not follow from the model itself, and in both cases it is stipulated, either theoretically or empirically, that a country's growth rate of technological progress depends on the location of that country. The conclusion must be that location is still not part of the analysis and that the endogenization of economic growth does not extend to the role of geography. Even though some versions of the new growth theory are in a number of respects rather similar to the geographical economics models (increasing returns to scale, imperfect competition, differentiated products, multiple equilibria), the new growth theory does not offer a theory of location.

Box 2.6 The relevance of physical geography

In their work on the geographic concentration of US industries, Glenn Ellison and Glaeser (1997, 1999) argue that this concentration may arise for two reasons, basically. The first is the existence of increasing returns technologies and other economies of scale. We might call this the role of *economics* in geography. This is what the geographical economics models are, first and foremost, about. The second reason for concentration is the existence of *natural* cost advantages that are due to differences in the actual physical geography. Ellison and Glaeser (1999: 315) conclude that about 20 percent of the observed agglomeration of US industries can be explained by variables that measure natural advantages. Similarly, Jan Haaland, Hans Kind, Karen Midelfart Knarvik, and Johan Torstensson (1999) conclude in a different context that industry concentration in Europe is significantly determined by differences in endowments across Europe. Although home market effects are even more important in explaining the geographical concentration of industry, the relevance of endowments also (indirectly) implies that physical geography may be important, since differences in endowments can be due to differences in physical geography (subsection 2.3.1).

In their study of the evolution of US cities, Black and Henderson (2003) state that the growth performance of cities may differ for two reasons: differences in physical geography and differences due to the concentration effects emphasized by geographical economics. They measure the latter by means of the market potential for each city. With respect to physical geography, they find that (370–1) "cities in warm (less heating degree days) and drier (less precipitation) climates on the coast indeed grow faster." At any rate, these studies point to the relevance of physical geography in explaining the agglomeration of economic activity. See also Diamond (1997), Daron Acemoglu, Simon Johnson, and James Robinson (2001), Sachs (2003), and Nathan Nunn and Puga (2007).

In a large cross-country study, Gallup, Sachs, and Mellinger (1998) investigate the impact of physical geography on economic growth. The starting point for their analysis is the observation that virtually all countries in the tropics are poor, whereas countries situated outside the tropics are almost invariably relatively rich (in GDP per capita). Moreover, coastal countries generally have higher incomes than countries without good access to the sea. In a number of cross-section estimations they regress economic growth upon various indicators of physical geography (controlling for the standard determinants of growth). They too find that physical geography matters – not necessarily in a direct manner (the location in the tropics is not significant but the presence of malaria very significantly lowers growth), but the significance of the location of a country vis-à-vis the sea (either by being a coastal country or a country with navigable waterways leading to the sea) gives a straightforward direct (positive) impact of physical geography on economic growth.

Box 2.6 (cont.)

Additional evidence by Mellinger, Gallup, and Sachs (2000) lends support to the idea that the physical geography is important in explaining growth and income differences across the world.

The point we want to emphasize is that physical geography matters for the location of economic activity. In the terminology used in this chapter: the first-nature aspects of location choices are important. This needs to be stressed, because geographical economics, and hence much of the remainder of this book, focuses on the second nature of location choice, thereby often assuming that space (physical geography) is homogeneous (although we discuss non-neutral space in chapter 6). These approaches are not in conflict with each other, as Gallup, Sachs, and Mellinger (1998: 132) also recognize: "The two approaches can of course be complementary: a city might emerge because of cost advantages arising from differentiated geography but continue to thrive because of agglomeration economies even when the cost advantages have disappeared. Empirical work should aim to disentangle the forces of differentiated geography and self-organizing agglomeration economies." In chapter 9, we show how the first-nature and second-nature determinants of location can be combined in one model.

2.4.2 Economic development

So far, we have used the terms "economic growth" and "economic development" interchangeably. Within economic theory, the analysis of economic development usually refers, however, to the conditions under which developing countries can achieve economic growth. This is a somewhat narrower scope than the analysis of economic growth, which should apply to all countries, but deals more with ongoing growth and less with the preconditions for growth. Nowadays, studies of economic development make extensive use of (old and new) economic growth theory. In this respect, development economics is to a large extent an application of mainstream economics to developing countries.[26] This has not always been the case. Especially in the 1950s and 1960s development economists such as Gunnar Myrdal (1957) and Albert Hirschman (1958), and others such as Perroux (1955), following Rosenstein-Rodan (1943), used an analytical framework that was very different from the neoclassical approach that is now dominant in development economics. This framework came under attack for its (alleged) lack of analytical coherence, which was not altogether surprising, because these authors, sometimes explicitly but more often

---

[26] A good example is the textbook by Pierre Agénor and Peter Montiel (1996).

implicitly, relied on external economies and imperfect competition – concepts that were not frequently invoked in mainstream economics in those days. The theories used by these development economists are interesting not only because they tried to explain the (lacking) conditions for economic growth in developing countries, but because they also had a keen eye for the geographical dimension of economic development, both within developing countries and between rich and poor countries. This explains why economic geographers to this day, when discussing economic development, still refer to the work of these "older" development economists.[27]

Again, it is not our aim to survey this field. We therefore restrict ourselves to a brief discussion of the main concepts. In the influential *big push* analysis of Rosenstein-Rodan (1943), an insufficient local market size is seen as the main cause of the underdevelopment of a region or a country. The solution to underdevelopment is to be found in a coordinated (that is, government-led) expansion of investment that enables firms to reap the benefits of (external and internal) scale economies, thus fostering industrialization of the backward region or country. An individual firm has no incentive to expand its production level because of the absence of increasing returns to scale at the firm level. The expansion of production only becomes profitable – and here external economies enter the story – if a sufficient number of other firms also expand their production (hence the term "big push"). Industrialization in the backward region or country also requires the manufacturing labor force to expand. If labor is immobile between countries, the expansion of the manufacturing labor force has to come about by drawing labor from other sectors of the economy (typically the agricultural sector), which requires a sufficiently elastic labor supply. Without a big push in investment the periphery cannot catch up with the core, so to speak.

Myrdal (1957) also describes the sustainability of core–periphery patterns of economic development (see also Thirlwall, 1991). He does not emphasize so much the conditions under which the backward country or region may start a process of economic development. Instead, he argues that, if, for whatever reason, a region or country gets a head start in terms of economic development, this lead will very likely be self-reinforcing. Myrdal introduces the concept of *circular* or *cumulative causation* to describe this process. Once a country or region takes the lead in economic development, positive

---

[27] See, for example, chapter 6 of the still widely used textbook on economic geography by Dicken and Lloyd (1990), and the discussion of the export-based multiplier in subsection 2.2.2, note 13.

external economies in this country or region will ensure that it will become more and not, as the neoclassical growth model predicts, less interesting for firms to invest and for labor to establish itself in the faster-growing region. The existence of strong *localized* spillovers leads to the establishment of a core (with the relatively larger market) and a periphery.[28]

Hirschman (1958) also focuses on the self-reinforcing nature of (differences in) economic development. His use of *backward* and *forward linkages* can be thought of as a means of illustrating how firms, by locating production in a particular region, increase the profitability of other firms that do so. In modern terminology, the ideas put forward by Hirschman have a clear flavor of increasing returns to scale. It should be noted (see, in particular, Krugman, 1995a) that the use of increasing returns to scale in the writings of Rosenstein-Rodan, Myrdal, or Hirschman is (at best) indirect, in the sense that they do not altogether analyze the relevance of scale economies for economic development themselves. This relevance is distilled from their works through the eyes of modern economic theory.[29] In fact, the difficulties of analyzing the role of increasing returns and imperfect competition ensured that the heyday of this branch of development economics was rather short-lived. The neoclassical theory of economic development with its emphasis on perfect competition and decreasing returns remained far more influential.

Nowadays, this last statement no longer holds. With the rise of the new trade theory, the new growth theory, and, of course, geographical economics, increasing returns and imperfect competition have become more of a rule than an exception in economic theorizing. When it comes to economic development, these "new" theories formalize the insights of Rosenstein-Rodan *cum suis* and give these insights a microeconomic foundation.[30] In

---

[28] The terminology suggests a resemblance with the endogenous or new growth theory. This is no coincidence, because the main ideas of this "older" literature on development economics are the same as in modern growth theory, even though these ideas are cast in different wordings.

[29] This may be true in general, but consider, for example, the following quotation from Myrdal (1957: 26–7): "The power of attraction today of a center has its origin mainly in the historical accident that something was once started there, and not in a number of other places where it could equally well or better have been started, and the start met with success. Thereafter the ever-increasing internal and external economies – interpreted in the widest sense of the word to include, for instance, a working population trained in various crafts, easy communications, the feeling of growth and elbow room and the spirit of new enterprise – fortified and sustained their continuous growth at the expense of other localities and regions where instead relative stagnation or regression became the pattern."

[30] In the case of Rosenstein-Rodan's big push theory, the best example is that of Kevin Murphy, Shleifer, and Robert Vishny (1989). They develop a model in which pecuniary external economies are generated by increasing returns to scale on the level of the firm. Krugman (1995: 8–14) uses one of the models developed by Murphy, Shleifer, and Vishny (the version in which there is a wage premium in the manufacturing sector compared to the traditional

the next chapter our in-depth discussion of the core model of geographical economics makes clear how increasing returns, imperfect competition, and, most notably, the role of location are dealt with. In chapter 10 we pick up the topic of growth and development from the perspective of geographical economics.

2.5 Conclusions

What is the main message of this chapter? Basically, that all the theoretical approaches discussed in the previous sections have something useful to say on the relationship between geography and economics, but that each approach also has its limitations. Without too much exaggeration, one can argue that in regional and urban economics there is ample room for geography or space in the analysis, but that these approaches sometimes lack the microeconomic foundation of individual behavior, and the general equilibrium structure that constitutes the backbone of mainstream economic theory nowadays. Conversely, both for the old as well as the new trade and growth theories, such a microeconomic foundation and general equilibrium structure exists, but the problem is that geography is often next to irrelevant, or, when it matters, its role is not (sufficiently) linked to the underlying behavior of economic agents. In our view, geographical economics can be looked upon as an attempt to further break down the fence between geography and economics. In doing so, it has its roots firmly in mainstream economic theory, so it is in particular an attempt to bring more geography into economics. For that reason, we prefer the term "geographical economics" to "new economic geography."

How do we proceed from here? Chapters 3 and 4 develop and discuss the core models of geographical economics. Chapters 5 and 6 review the empirical evidence with respect to geographical economics. The stylized facts are subsequently used as an input for chapters 7–11, in which various extensions of the core models are analyzed. In the final chapter of the book (chapter 12), we return to the question of whether geographical economics delivers what it promises to do – namely a better understanding of the relationships between geography and economics.

sector of the economy) to show how it captures the main insights from the aforementioned development economists.

Finally, given that von Thünen's *The Isolated State* was published in 1826, it is quite puzzling why until very recently mainstream economics more or less neglected the issue of the location of economic activity. Part of the answer must surely be (see Krugman, 1995a, and subsection 2.2.3 above) that the analysis of the location of economic activity must be grounded on increasing returns to scale and imperfect competition, and that economists have long struggled to incorporate both these elements in their models. All the same, this still cannot fully explain the neglect. Maybe Mark Blaug (1984: 630), an expert on the history of economic thought, has a point when he states:

In the final analysis, all the attempts to account for the curious disdain of location theory on the part of mainstream economists end up by invoking conservatism and blinkered thinking, which restates the puzzle instead of solving it. Perhaps, the solution of the mystery is simpler than anyone has imagined. If Ricardo had based his rent theory on locational advantages instead of fertility differences, if [von] Thünen had been a lucid instead of an obscure writer . . ., is there any reason to doubt that the whole of classical locational theory would have found a place in Marshall's *Principles* and, thereby, in the corpus of received economic doctrine?

Exercises

2.1* Assume a trade model with transportation costs but without increasing returns to scale. In fact, think of this model as a neoclassical trade model with transport costs associated with the trade of goods. Discuss the location of economic activity in such a model.

2.2* See box 2.2 about the central place theory in a Dutch polder. Why do you think it be might that the predictions of the Dutch authorities about the relative size of cities in this polder have not materialized?

2.3 We know from chapter 1 (see figures 1.2 and 1.3) that economic activity is clearly not distributed randomly across the world. How would you explain this, assuming that you can use only the neoclassical trade or growth theory for your answer?

2.4* Increasing returns to scale are an important topic in chapter 2 (see box 2.1). Below are three examples of a production structure. Explain for each example what kind of returns to scale are relevant.

(i) Assume a firm i faces the following cost function (which summarizes its production structure): $l_i = a + \beta x_i$, where l_i is the amount of labor necessary to produce output x_i and where a and β describe respectively the fixed and marginal labor input requirement.

(ii) Assume an economy has the following production function (see section 2.4): $Y = AK$. Additional question: is it to be expected that the same degree of returns to scale holds for the individual firm's i production function. If not, how can these two production functions be reconciled?

(iii) Assume the individual firm has the following production function: $y = ak^{0.3}$ with $a = K$, where K is the economy-wide capital stock.

2.5 Consider the following two quotations from the *Oxford Handbook of Economic Geography*. Explain in each instance how, in your view, these quotes relate to the location theories discussed in chapter 2:

(i) "So the tradition of international trade theory has sidestepped geographical questions – most modeling imagines a world without transport costs, let alone cities! – while that of geography has sometimes been based on what trade theorists would consider half-worked out models, and often rejected formalism altogether."

(ii) "The analytical machinery of microeconomics [plays a strong role] in Krugman's geography and his work, despite its originality, can perhaps best be seen as a continuation of the tradition of ... regional science. Better yet, we might call it a 'new' regional science."

Part II

Core models and empirical evidence

3 The core model of geographical economics

3.1 Introduction

As we noted in the preface, it was a long time ago that Ohlin (1933) observed that the fields of trade theory on the one hand and regional and urban economics on the other hand had, in principle, the same research objectives. Both research areas want to answer the questions: "Who produces what, where, and why?" Despite Ohlin's observation, each field has continued to go its own way since the nineteenth century. Chapter 2 showed that trade theory assumes that countries are dimensionless points in space. Trade theorists are mostly interested in how market structure, production techniques, and consumer behavior interact (Neary, 2004). The resulting factor and commodity prices determine the pattern of international trade flows. Location is, at best, an exogenous factor, and usually does not play a role of any significance.[1] Regional and urban economics, in contrast, takes market structure and prices as given and tries to find out which allocation of space is most efficient. The underlying behavior of consumers and producers, central in trade theory, is less important (Fujita and Thisse, 1996). Although both strands of literature produce valuable insights in their own right, trade theory and regional and urban economics are productively combined in geographical economics.

This chapter discusses and explains the core model of geographical economics, a small, general equilibrium model developed by Krugman (1991a, 1991b). As we shall see, the equilibrium equations of this model are non-linear. This means that small changes in parameters do not always

---

[1] Gravity models, discussed in subsection 1.3.2 and chapter 9, are the exception to the rule. These models are easily extended to include all kinds of transport costs. Nuno Limao and Venables (2000), for example, include trading costs related to within-country infrastructure and trading costs related to international trade into a gravity equation. See chapter 9 for a discussion.

produce the same effects; sometimes the effects are small, sometimes they are large. Translated into regional and urban economics, this means, for example, that the location decision of a single producer might not change the spatial pattern of production, but it *could* have dramatic, or "catastrophic" (to borrow a term from the chaos literature), consequences. It is possible for the location decision of a single producer to trigger a process of cumulative causation and for the spatial pattern of production to change dramatically. In addition, the model has multiple equilibria, and this characteristic is, as we have explained in chapter 2, one of the major differences with regional science or urban economics. There is no presumption on which location might become the center of production, but once a location gets a head start the process of cumulative causation starts working. What are initially small differences between locations can evolve over time into large differences in the long-run equilibrium. These and other features make models of geographical economics analytically complicated.

As a consequence, we explain the model in three steps. First, we give a simple example in section 3.2 to illustrate some important features of the core model, to which we return in the rest of this chapter. It is important to realize that it is only an example and not a model – that is, many aspects are assumed rather than derived. Second, we explain the basic structure of the core model of geographical economics in non-technical terms in section 3.3. Third, we focus on the modeling details of the core model in sections 3.4–3.7, and explain some of its interactions in sections 3.8 and 3.9. After the explanation of the model we return to our example in section 3.10.

3.2 An example of geographical economics[2]

It is possible to construct a simple example to illustrate some of the main findings of the geographical economics approach.[3] Suppose there are two regions (or countries), North and South, and two sectors of production, manufacturing and agriculture. The manufacturing industry produces varieties – that is, differentiated products – under internal economies of

---

[2] Students who do not like examples can skip this section; it is included only as an easy introduction to the model developed in this chapter.

[3] A simpler version of this example can be found in Krugman and Obstfeld (1994: 185).

Table 3.1 Geography of sales

	Sales in North	Sales in South	Total sales
All firms in North	$4+4=8$	$0+2=2$	10
All firms in South	$0+4=4$	$4+2=6$	10
25% of firms in North, 75% of firms in South	$1+4=5$	$3+2=5$	10

scale. The cost per unit of output therefore falls as a firm expands its production level. As a result, each firm produces only one variety. A firm can reside either in North or South – that is, a firm has to decide where to produce. This location decision essentially differentiates the example from new trade theory.

The total demand for each variety of manufactures in this example is exogenous. We assume that each firm sells four units to workers in the manufacturing industry and six units to farmers. Total demand for each variety is therefore ten $(6+4)$. The production of agriculture, and hence the demand it generates, is location-specific. Its spatial distribution is exogenously given; we assume that four units are sold in North and two units in South. The location of the workers in the manufacturing sector, and hence the four units they demand at that location, is not exogenous. The role of the immobile workers is important, as they ensure that there is always positive demand in *both* regions. Finally, transport costs between North and South are €1 per unit. The firms decide on their location so as to minimize transport costs.

We are now able to determine the location decision of each firm. First, we can calculate the regional sales of each firm, given the location of the other firms. In table 3.1, three (non-exhaustive) possibilities are given: all firms in North, all firms in South, and 25 percent of all firms in North and 75 percent of all firms in South. Sales in each region are equal to the sales to the workers in manufacturing plus the sales to the farmers. Take, for example, the last row in table 3.1. The firm sells five units in North, namely four to the farmers located in North plus one $(=25\% \times 4)$ unit to the manufacturing workers located in North. Similarly, the firm sells five units in South, namely two units to the farmers located in South plus three $(=75\% \times 4)$ units to the manufacturing workers located in South.

Second, using table 3.1 we can construct a decision table, by calculating transport costs as a function of the firm's location decision, given the

Table 3.2 Transport costs

	If location in North	If location in South
All firms in North	$0+2=2$ (to farmers in South)	$4+4=8$ (to workers and farmers in North)
All firms in South	$4+2=6$ (to workers and farmers in South)	$0+4=4$ (to farmers in North)
25% of firms in North 75% of firms in South	$3+2=5$ (to workers and farmers in South	$1+4=5$ (to workers and farmers in North)

location of the other firms. Suppose, for example, that all firms are located in North. Table 3.2 indicates that the transport costs for a firm locating in South will then be €8, namely €4 for sales to the farmers in North and €4 for sales to all workers in manufacturing located in North (abstracting from sales to its own workers). Similarly, if the firm locates in North, transport costs would be only €2 for sales to farmers in South. Since transport costs are minimized by locating in North if all other firms are located in North, the firm decides to also locate production in North. As table 3.2 shows (second row), a firm will locate in South if all other firms are also located there, whereas (last row) the firm is indifferent between locating in North or South (since transport costs are the same if the firm locates in either region) if 25 percent of the firms are located in North and 75 percent in South.

On the basis of this example, we can illustrate a few distinctive characteristics of the geographical economics approach. We return to each of these observations in the remainder of this chapter.

First, the concept of *cumulative causation*. If, for some reason, one location has attracted more firms than the other location, a new firm has an incentive to locate where the other firms are. Take the first row in table 3.2. If all the existing firms are located in North, the new firm should also locate there if it wishes to minimize its transport costs. Similarly, for the second row in table 3.2 the firm will locate in South.

Second, table 3.2 illustrates the existence of *multiple equilibria*. The agglomeration of all firms in either North or South is an equilibrium. We cannot determine beforehand where agglomeration will occur, however. This depends critically on the initial conditions – that is, the previous location decisions of other firms.

Third, an equilibrium might be *stable or unstable*. The bold entries in table 3.2 are both stable equilibria if a single firm decides to relocate, this decision would not influence the location decisions of the other firms. The last row in table 3.2 describes an unstable equilibrium. If a single firm decides to relocate, the new location will immediately become more attractive for all other firms. This will trigger a snowball effect: all firms will follow the pioneer. In this example, only agglomeration is a stable equilibrium.

Fourth, we note that a stable equilibrium can be *non-optimal*. If all firms are located in North, transport costs are only €2. If all firms are located in South, transport costs are €4 (see the bold entries in table 3.2). Thus, transport costs for the economy as a whole are minimized if all firms agglomerate in North, whereas agglomeration in South is still a stable equilibrium.

Fifth, the example illustrates the *interaction of agglomeration and trade flows*. With complete agglomeration – that is, all manufactures being produced in a single region – trade between regions will be of the inter-industry type (food for manufactures). In fact, this equilibrium also reflects the so-called *home market effect*; the combination of economies of scale and transport costs is responsible for the clustering of all footloose activity in a single location. Due to this combination, transport costs can be minimized. The large region ends up with a large market for manufacturing goods, which can be sold without incurring transport costs. The consequence is that this region becomes the exporter of manufactured goods; large regions tend to become exporters of those goods for which they have a large local market – hence the term, "home market effect." If the manufacturing industry is located in both regions, as described by the last rows in the tables, trade will also be of the intra-industry type. Besides trading manufactured goods for agricultural products, different varieties of the differentiated manufactured products will be traded between both regions.

The example is useful, as it illustrates some important aspects of geographical economics. An example is just an example, however, and it is not a substitute for a well-specified model. What is missing in the example?

- First of all, the interaction between transport costs, price-setting behavior, and location choice is missing. We simply assume that the demand each firm faces is given and independent of price-setting behavior and transport costs. In fact, prices are completely lacking in the example. There is no analysis of the market structure. In reality, prices, wages, and transport costs will determine the purchasing power of consumers. One might guess that this interaction drives the location decisions of consumers and producers. The next sections show that this is indeed the case.

• Furthermore, it is a partial equilibrium model, in the sense that firms do not worry about the necessary labor; wherever they decide to locate, labor availability is not the problem. It will turn out that assumptions with regard to the functioning of the labor market are important. The reader might also notice the similarity of the example and Krugman's (1980) new trade model discussed in chapter 2. In both models, scale economies and transport costs are important forces. The most important difference is that, in our example, firms can locate in either region. Consequently, the example gives rise to agglomeration, and multiple equilibria.

It is now time to move from the example to the core model, where we get back to the main insights derived from the example.

3.3 The structure of the model

This section gives a non-technical overview of the general structure of the core model of geographical economics. The nuts and bolts of the core model are laid out in Dixit and Stiglitz (1977) and Krugman (1979, 1980). These works stimulated a large body of work on monopolistic competition and international trade theory (see subsection 2.3.2, and Neary, 2004). Krugman (1991a, 1991b) extends the latter by allowing for interregional factor mobility, and this has become the core model of geographical economics.

This structure is illustrated in figure 3.1, which serves as a frame of reference throughout the remainder of this chapter. *We urge the reader to regularly consult this depiction to more easily understand the main arguments in the text.* The construction details of the model are explained in the sections to follow.

The core model identifies two regions, labeled 1 and 2. There are two sectors in the economy, the manufacturing sector and the food sector. Consumers in both regions consist of farm workers and manufacturing workers. The farm workers earn their income by working on farms in their region. The income stream of the farm workers is part of a bilateral transfer: they earn an income in exchange for their labor supply. All such bilateral transfers are indicated with double-pointed arrows in figure 3.1. The solid-pointed arrow indicates the direction of money or income flows – that is, indicates the direction of income and spending (see, however, box 3.1 on the numéraire, wages, and real wages). What the flow represents is indicated along the line connecting the arrow points. The open-pointed arrow

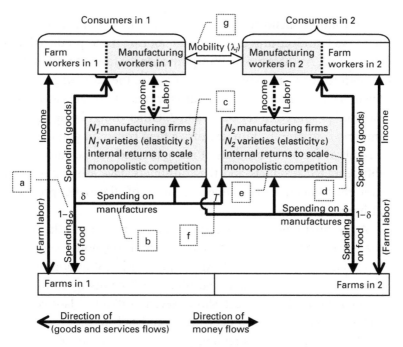

Figure 3.1   Structure of the core model of geographical economics

indicates the direction of goods or services flows. These are indicated *in parentheses* along the line connecting the arrow points. The farmers in region 1 produce food under constant returns to scale and perfect competition. They sell this food to the consumers, either in region 1 or in region 2. By assumption, there are no transport costs for food – an issue that is addressed in chapter 6.

The manufacturing sector consists of N_1 firms in region 1 and N_2 firms in region 2. Each manufacturing firm produces a differentiated product – that is, it produces a unique variety of manufactures. It uses only labor in the production process, which is characterized by internal economies of scale. This implies that the firms have monopolistic power, which they use in determining the price of their product. Furthermore, transport costs are involved in selling a manufactured good in another region. These costs do not arise if the manufactured good is sold in the region in which it is produced. As a result of the transport costs, exporting firms will charge a higher price in the foreign region than in the home region. The manufacturing workers earn their income (the manufacturing wage rate) by supplying labor to the firms in the manufacturing sector located in the home region.

Consumers spend their income on both food and manufactures. Since food is a homogeneous good they do not care if it is produced in region 1 or in region 2. As there are no transport costs for food, it fetches the same price in both regions (implying that farmers earn the same wage in both regions). Spending by consumers on manufactures has to be allocated over the many varieties produced in regions 1 and 2. Other things being equal, consuming imported varieties is more expensive than consuming domestic varieties, as a result of the transport costs of manufactured goods. Since the varieties are differentiated products and the consumers have a liking for variety, however, they will always consume some units of all varieties produced, whether at home or abroad.

A few final remarks on figure 3.1 are in order. First, the figure mentions the most important parameters to be used throughout the remainder of this book, namely ε, δ, λ_i, and T. At this point it is not important to know what these parameters are. They, and others, will be discussed in the rest of this chapter. Second, figure 3.1 shows seven "callouts," labeled a to g. These callouts refer to important construction details of the core model. They are used as a reference and a reminder in section 3.4 on the demand structure of the model (callouts a, b, and c), in section 3.5 on the supply structure of the model (callouts d and e), in section 3.6 on the role of transport costs (callout f) and in section 3.9 on the dynamics of the model (callout g). Third, and most importantly, there are shaded boxes in figure 3.1. These draw attention to the distinguishing feature of geographical economics: the mobility of factors of production (see chapter 2). The core model applies mobility only to the manufacturing sector; manufacturing workers can relocate from region 1 to region 2, or vice versa. The relocation of manufacturing firms from one region to another is the other side of the same coin, as an expansion of the manufacturing workforce in a region implies an expansion of production in the manufacturing sector. It is important to note that, in principle, the shaded boxes can disappear in a region, for example if all manufacturing workers (and thus the entire manufacturing sector) move to region 2. The non-shaded boxes, labeled "farm workers" and "farms," cannot disappear from a region. The farmers need the land for cultivation and are thus not mobile. The region, therefore, can always spend income generated by this sector. The distinction between mobile activity and immobile activity is important. For ease of reference, we have labeled these sectors "manufactures" and "food" respectively. Obviously, the immobile sector could also produce iron ore or paper, or produce a non-tradable service (housing), etc.

Box 3.1 Terminology

The terminology used in economic analysis can be confusing to the reader for a variety of reasons. Sometimes the same term has different meanings in different fields of economics. Sometimes a term can be interpreted in various ways. Sometimes the same area of research is known under a range of names. Although the terminology used in our book will, inevitably, also puzzle the reader occasionally, we would like to keep this confusion to a minimum. This box therefore briefly describes and explains our main terminology.

Agglomeration and spreading. We are interested in explaining, and describing, various forms of clustering of (economic) activity, which we refer to as "agglomeration." We use the term "spreading" to refer to the opposite of "agglomeration." Other terms used in the literature, such as "centripetal," "centrifugal," "convergent," and "divergent," will not be used in this book because they can be confusing. For example, the word "converging" can indicate either that all industry "converges" – that is, tends to locate in one region – or that all regions "converge" – that is, all industries are spread across regions.

Numéraire. The economic agents in the general equilibrium models of geographical economics do not suffer from money illusion – that is, their decisions are based on relative prices and do not depend on the absolute price level. This allows us to set the price of one of the goods in the model equal to one, and express all other prices in the model relative to the price of the numéraire good. The remainder of the book chooses food as the numéraire good, such that the price of food is always equal to one.

Wages and real wages. The core general equilibrium modeling approach used in this book chooses a numéraire good to pin down relative prices. Wages in different regions expressed in the numéraire should be referred to as "numéraire wages." Although better than the frequently used term "nominal wages" (since the monetary sector is not explicitly modeled), it is still a cumbersome term. We therefore use the shorter term "wages" whenever we refer to "numéraire wages," and explicitly use the term "real wages" when the numéraire wages are corrected for the price level to determine purchasing power.

3.4 Demand

The rest of this chapter describes and explains many details of the structure of the core model of geographical economics, as graphically summarized in figure 3.1. Whenever appropriate we refer to the callouts a–g of figure 3.1. This chapter serves a dual purpose, namely (i) giving a description and explanation of the core model that is as clear and accessible as possible, and (ii) being complete in this description, in particular by deriving all the technical details. To strike a balance between these two objectives, we have placed all the derivations in "technical note" boxes. We advise the reader to *skip all the technical notes on first reading*, in order to more easily follow the flow of the arguments. The mathematically inclined reader can then return to the technical details in the notes at a later stage.

3.4.1 Spending on food and manufactures (callout a)

As explained in section 3.3, the economy has two goods sectors, manufactures, M, and food, F. Although "manufactures" consist of many different varieties, we can define an exact price index to represent them as a group, as will be explained below. We call this price index of manufactures I. If a consumer earns an income Y (from working either in the food sector or the manufacturing sector) he or she has to decide how much of this income is spent on food and how much on manufactures. The solution to this problem depends on the preferences of the consumer, assumed to be of the Cobb–Douglas specification given in equation (3.1) for all consumers, in which F represents food consumption and M represents the consumption of manufactures:

$$U = F^{1-\delta}M^{\delta}; \quad 0 < \delta < 1 \tag{3.1}$$

Obviously, any income spent on food cannot simultaneously be spent on manufactures – that is, the consumer must satisfy the budget constraint in equation (3.2):

$$F + I \cdot M = Y \tag{3.2}$$

Note the absence of the price of food in this equation. This is a result of choosing food as the numéraire (see box 3.1), which implies that income Y is measured in terms of food. Thus, only the price index of manufactures I occurs in equation (3.2). To decide on the optimal allocation of income over the purchase of food and manufactures, the consumer now has to solve a simple optimization problem, namely maximize utility as given in equation (3.1), subject to the budget constraint of equation (3.2). The solution to this problem is given in equation (3.3), and derived in technical note 3.1.

$$F = (1 - \delta)Y; \quad IM = \delta Y \tag{3.3}$$

As equation (3.3) shows, it is optimal for the consumer to spend a fraction, $(1 - \delta)$, of income on food, and a fraction, δ, of income on manufactures. This explains callout a in figure 3.1. We henceforth refer to the parameter δ given in equation (3.1) as the fraction of income spent on manufactures.

Technical note 3.1 Derivation of equation (3.3)

To maximize equation (3.1) subject to the budget constraint (3.2), we define the Lagrangean Γ, using the multiplier κ:

$$\Gamma = F^{1-\delta}M^{\delta} + \kappa[Y - (F + IM)]$$

Differentiating Γ with respect to F and M gives the first-order conditions

$$(1 - \delta)F^{-\delta}M^{\delta} = \kappa; \quad \delta F^{1-\delta}M^{\delta-1} = \kappa I$$

Taking the ratio of the first-order conditions gives

$$\frac{\delta F^{1-\delta}M^{\delta-1}}{(1 - \delta)F^{-\delta}M^{\delta}} = \frac{\kappa I}{\kappa}; \quad \text{or} \quad IM = \frac{\delta}{1 - \delta}F$$

Substituting the latter in budget equation (3.2) gives

$$Y = F + IM = F + \frac{\delta}{1 - \delta}F; \quad \text{or} \quad F = (1 - \delta)Y$$

This indicates that the share $(1 - \delta)$ of income is spent on food, and thus the share δ on manufactures, as given in equation (3.3).

3.4.2 Spending on manufacturing varieties (callout b)

Now that we have determined in subsection 3.4.1 the share δ of income that is spent on manufactured goods, we still have to decide how this spending is allocated among the different varieties of manufactures. In essence, this is a similar problem to that in subsection 3.4.1 – that is, we have to optimally allocate spending between the consumption of a number of goods that can be consumed. This problem can be solved only if we specify how the preferences for the aggregate consumption of manufactures M depend on the consumption of particular varieties of manufactures. In this respect, the core model of geographical economics fruitfully applies a model of monopolistic competition developed in the industrial organization literature by Dixit and Stiglitz (see box 3.2). Let c_i be the level of consumption of a particular variety i of manufactures, and let N be the total number of available varieties. The Dixit–Stiglitz approach uses a constant elasticity of substitution (CES) function to construct the aggregate consumption of manufactures M as a function of the consumption c_i of the N varieties:[4]

$$M = \left(\sum_{i=1}^{N} c_i^{\rho} \right)^{1/\rho} ; \quad 0 < \rho < 1 \tag{3.4}$$

Note that the consumption of all varieties enters equation (3.4) symmetrically. This greatly simplifies the analysis in the rest of the chapter. The parameter ρ, discussed further below, represents the love-of-variety effect of consumers. If $\rho = 1$, equation (3.4) simplifies to $M = \Sigma_i c_i$ and variety as such does not matter for utility (having 100 units of one variety gives the same utility as one unit of 100 varieties). Products are then perfect substitutes (one unit less of one variety can exactly be compensated for by one unit more of another variety). We therefore need $\rho < 1$ to ensure that the product varieties are imperfect substitutes. In addition, we need $\rho > 0$ to ensure that the individual varieties are substitutes (and not complements) for each other, which enables price-setting behavior based on monopoly power (see section 3.5).[5]

It is worthwhile to dwell a little longer on the specification of (3.4). Suppose all c_i are consumed in equal quantities – that is, $c_i = c$ for all i. We can then rewrite equation (3.4) as

$$M = \left(\sum_{i=1}^{N} c^{\rho} \right)^{1/\rho} = (Nc^{\rho})^{1/\rho} = N^{1/\rho} c = N^{(1/\rho)-1}[Nc] \tag{3.4'}$$

Since $0 < \rho < 1$, the term $(1/\rho) - 1$ is larger than zero. So, from (3.4') it is immediately clear that having 100 units of one variety ($Nc = C, N = 1$), gives a consumer less utility than one unit of 100 varieties ($Nc = C, N = 100$). In many models, including many new growth models and geographical economics models, the term Nc in equation (3.4') corresponds to a claim on real resources, because Nc has actually to be produced in the first place, while the number of available varieties N represents an externality or the extent of the market. The term $N^{(1/\rho)-1}$ represents a bonus for large

---

[4] Many textbooks discuss the properties of the CES function. See also Brakman and van Marrewijk (1998), who compare it with the properties of other utility functions.

[5] One might wonder what happens if $\rho > 1$. Reducing the number of varieties increases utility in this case; 100 units of one variety is clearly better than 1 unit of 100 varieties (see also equation 3.4').

markets – hence the term "love-of-variety effect." In this sense, an increase in the extent of the market, which increases the number of varieties N the consumer can choose from, more than proportionally increases utility.

Box 3.2 Dixit–Stiglitz monopolistic competition

It has often been said that there is only one way for competition to be perfect, but many ways to be imperfect. Consequently, many competing models exist to describe imperfect competition, investigating many different cases and assumptions with respect to market behavior, the type of good, the strategic interaction between firms, preferences of consumers, etc. That was also the case with monopolistic competition (see, for example, Tirole, 1988), until Dixit and Stiglitz published an article in 1977 entitled "Monopolistic competition, and the optimum product diversity," in *The American Economic Review*, which would revolutionize model building in at least four fields of economics: trade theory, industrial organization, growth theory and geographical economics.[6]

The big step forward was to make some heroic assumptions concerning the symmetry of new varieties and the structural form, which allowed for an elegant and consistent way to model production at the firm level, benefiting from internal economies of scale in conjunction with a market structure of monopolistic competition, without getting bogged down in a taxonomy of oligopoly models. These factors are responsible for the present popularity of the Dixit–Stiglitz model. In all fields that now use the Dixit–Stiglitz formulation intensely, researchers were aware that imperfect competition was relevant as an essential feature of many empirically observed phenomena. This meant that the model was immediately accepted as the new standard for modeling monopolistic competition; its development was certainly very timely. In international trade theory, the introduction of the monopolistic competition model enabled international economists to explain and understand intra-industry trade, which until then had been empirically observed but never satisfactorily explained (Krugman, 1979, 1980). In industrial organization, it helped to get rid of many ad hoc assumptions, which hampered the development of many industrial organization models (Tirole, 1988). The Dixit–Stiglitz model was also used to explore the role of intermediate differentiated goods in international trade models. This reformulation of the standard Dixit–Stiglitz model plays an important role in the link between international trade and economic growth (see, for example, Grossman and Helpman, 1991). The model also turns out to be very useful in explaining the export FDI decision if firms are heterogeneous (see Melitz, 2003, and Helpman, Melitz, and Yeaple, 2004). Finally, the model is intensively used in geographical economics, the topic of this book.

---

[6] The paper by Michael Spence (1976) on a similar topic slightly pre-dates Dixit and Stiglitz (1977), but had considerably less influence. For an excellent discussion of Dixit–Stiglitz monopolistic competition, see Neary (2001) and Baldwin *et al.* (2003). Brakman and Ben Heijdra (2004) give a historical account on the influence of the Dixit–Stiglitz approach in economics; Dixit (2004) and Stiglitz (2004) reflect on the pros and cons of their original article.

After our brief digression on the love-of-variety effect it is time to go back to the problem at hand: how does the consumer allocate spending on manufactures over the various varieties? Let p_i be the price of variety i for $i = 1, \ldots, N$. Naturally, funds $p_i c_i$ spent on variety i cannot be spent simultaneously on variety j, as given in the budget constraint for manufactures in equation (3.5):

$$\sum_{i=1}^{N} p_i c_i = \delta Y \tag{3.5}$$

In order to derive a consumer's demand, we must now solve a somewhat more complicated optimization problem, namely the maximization of the utility derived from the consumption of manufactures given in equation (3.4), subject to the budget constraint of equation (3.5). The solution to this problem is given in equations (3.6) and (3.7), and derived in technical note 3.2.

$$c_j = p_j^{-\varepsilon} \left[I^{\varepsilon-1} \delta Y \right], \quad \text{where } I \equiv \left[\sum_{i=1}^{N} p_i^{1-\varepsilon} \right]^{1/(1-\varepsilon)} \qquad \text{for} \quad j = 1, .., N \tag{3.6}$$

$$M = \delta Y / I, \quad \text{and} \quad \varepsilon \equiv \frac{1}{1-\rho} \tag{3.7}$$

Discussion and explanation of the meaning of equations (3.6) and (3.7) are certainly warranted; we do this in the next subsection. At this point, the important thing is to emphasize that equation (3.6) gives the demand curve. We conclude this subsection simply by noting that we have derived the demand for each variety of manufactures, which explains callout b in figure 3.1.

Technical note 3.2 Derivation of equations (3.6) and (3.7)

We proceed as in technical note 3.1. To maximize equation (3.4) subject to the budget constraint (3.5), we define the Lagrangean Γ, using the multiplier κ:

$$\Gamma = \left[\sum_{i=1}^{N} c_i^{\rho} \right]^{(1/\rho)} + \kappa \left[\delta Y - \sum_{i=1}^{N} p_i c_i \right]$$

Technical note 3.2 (cont.)

Differentiating Γ with respect to c_j and equating to zero gives the first-order conditions

$$\left[\sum_{i=1}^{N} c_i^{\rho}\right]^{(1/\rho)-1} c_j^{\rho-1} = \kappa p_j, \quad \text{for} \quad j = 1,..,N$$

The next step is to take the ratio of the first-order conditions of a variety j with respect to variety 1. Note that the first term on the left-hand side cancels (as does the term κ on the right-hand side), and define $\varepsilon \equiv 1/(1-\rho)$, as discussed in the main text. Then

$$\frac{c_j^{\rho-1}}{c_1^{\rho-1}} = \frac{p_j}{p_1} \quad \text{or} \quad c_j = p_j^{-\varepsilon} p_1^{\varepsilon} c_1 \quad \text{for} \quad j = 1,..,N \tag{*}$$

Substituting these relations in the budget equation (3.5) gives

$$\sum_{j=1}^{N} p_j c_j = \sum_{j=1}^{N} p_j \left[p_j^{-\varepsilon} p_1^{\varepsilon} c_1\right] = p_1^{\varepsilon} c_1 \sum_{j=1}^{N} p_j^{1-\varepsilon} = p_1^{\varepsilon} c_1 I^{1-\varepsilon} = \delta Y, \quad c_1 = p_1^{-\varepsilon} I^{\varepsilon-1} \delta Y$$

where use has been made of the definition of I defined in equation (3.6) of the main text. This explains the demand for variety 1 as given in equation (3.6).

The demand for the other varieties is derived analogously. The question remains as to why the price index I was defined as given in equation (3.6). To answer this question we have to substitute the derived demand for all varieties in equation (3.4), and note along the way that $-\varepsilon\rho = 1 - \varepsilon$ and $1/\rho = -\varepsilon/(1-\varepsilon)$:

$$M = \left(\sum_{i=1}^{N} c_i^{\rho}\right)^{1/\rho} = \left(\sum_{i=1}^{N} \left(p_i^{-\varepsilon} I^{\varepsilon-1} \delta Y\right)^{\rho}\right)^{1/\rho} = \delta Y I^{\varepsilon-1} \left(\sum_{i=1}^{N} p_i^{-\varepsilon\rho}\right)^{1/\rho}$$

$$= \delta Y I^{\varepsilon-1} \left(\sum_{i=1}^{N} p_i^{1-\varepsilon}\right)^{-\varepsilon/(1-\varepsilon)}$$

Using the definition of the price index I from equation (3.7) simplifies this expression to

$$M = \delta Y I^{\varepsilon-1} \left(\sum_{i=1}^{N} p_i^{1-\varepsilon}\right)^{-\varepsilon/(1-\varepsilon)} = \delta Y I^{\varepsilon-1} I^{-\varepsilon} = \delta Y/I$$

This is discussed further in the main text.

3.4.3 Demand effects: income, price, elasticity ε (callout c) and the price index I

Subsection 3.4.2 derived the demand for manufacturing varieties. The demand for variety 1, for example, is given by $c_1 = p_1^{-\varepsilon}[I^{\varepsilon-1}\delta Y]$ (see equation (3.6)). This demand appears to be influenced by four things, namely (i) the income δY spent on manufactures in general, (ii) the price p_1 of good 1, (iii) some parameter ε, and (iv) the price index I. Let us go over these points in more detail.

Point (i) is straightforward. The more the consumer spends on manufactures in general, the more he/she spends on variety 1. In fact, this relationship is equiproportional: other things being equal, a 10 percent rise in spending on manufactures results in a 10 percent increase in the demand for all varieties of manufactures.

Point (ii) is also straightforward, but very important. It is straightforward in the sense that we obviously expect the demand for variety 1 to be a function of the price charged by the firm producing variety 1. It is very important in view of *how* demand for variety 1 depends on the price p_1. Note that the last part of equation (3.6) is written in square brackets. It depends on the price index for manufactures I and the income δY spent by consumers on manufactures in general. Both are macroeconomic entities that the firm producing variety 1 will take as given – that is, it will assume to have no control over these variables (see below for a further discussion). In that case, we can simplify the demand for variety 1, by defining constant$_1 \equiv [I^{\varepsilon-1}\delta Y]$ as $c_1 = $ constant$_1 p_1^{-\varepsilon}$. This in turn implies that the price elasticity of demand for variety 1 is constant and equal to the parameter $\varepsilon > 1$ (that is $-(\partial c_1/\partial p_1)(p_1/c_1) = \varepsilon$; see also footnote 7). This simple price elasticity of demand is the main advantage of the Dixit–Stiglitz approach (see box 3.2), as it greatly simplifies the price-setting behavior of monopolistically competitive firms (see section 3.5). Figure 3.2 illustrates the demand for a variety of manufactures as a function of its own price for different values of ε. Note that the demand for a variety falls much more rapidly as a result of a small price increase, say from 1 to 1.5, if the price elasticity of demand is high.

Point (iii) becomes clear after the discussion in point (ii). We have defined the parameter ε not only to simplify the notation of equation (3.6) as much as possible but also because it is an important economic parameter, as it measures the price elasticity of demand for a variety of manufactured goods. In addition, as discussed in the previous subsection, this parameter measures the elasticity of substitution between two different varieties – that

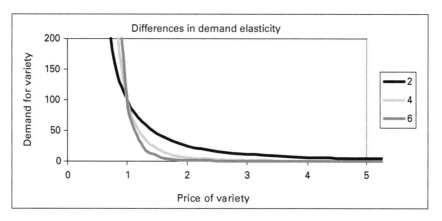

Figure 3.2   Dependence of demand for a variety of manufactures on price and ε
Note: Demand given by $c_1 = 100 \, p_1^{-\varepsilon}$; the value of ε varies (2, 4, and 6).

is, how difficult it is to substitute one variety of manufactures for another variety of manufactures.[7] Evidently, the price elasticity of demand and the elasticity of substitution are related in the Dixit–Stiglitz approach – a point that has been criticized in the literature.[8] Be that as it may, our intuitive explanations of some phenomena in the remainder of this book will sometimes be based on the price elasticity of demand interpretation of ε, and sometimes on the elasticity of substitution interpretation, using what we feel is easiest for the problem at hand.

A final remark on the parameter ε is in order. It was defined using the parameter ρ in the preference for manufacturing varieties equation (3.4) as $\varepsilon \equiv 1/(1 - \rho)$. Does this mean, then, that we do not use the parameter ρ anymore in the rest of the book? No. The reason is that we want to keep the notation as simple as possible, which sometimes requires the use of ε and sometimes requires the use of ρ. These are the only two parameters for which we will do this, referring to ε as the "elasticity of substitution," and to ρ as the "substitution parameter." It is useful to keep their relationship, illustrated in figure 3.3, in mind. This sufficiently explains callout c in figure 3.1.

[7] To prove this, you can use equation (*) in technical note 3.2, where the equation on the left can be written, for example, as $c_2/c_1 = (p_2/p_1)^{-\varepsilon}$, from which it follows immediately that $-[d(c_2/c_1)/d(p_2/p_1)][(p_2/p_1)/(c_2/c_2)] = \varepsilon$.
[8] To make things even more complicated, when combined with a simple production function of internal returns to scale, also used in geographical economics, the parameter ε can be interpreted as a measure of returns to scale. This is discussed in section 3.5. In view of the drawbacks of this interpretation, we do not use it in the rest of the book (for a discussion of this issue, see Neary, 2001).

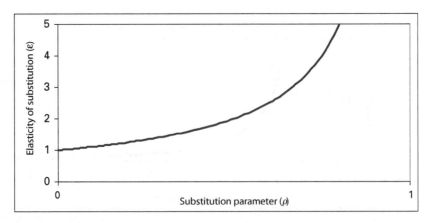

Figure 3.3   Relationship between ρ and ε

Finally, point (iv) indicates that the demand for variety 1 depends on the price index I. If the price index I increases, implying that "on average" the prices of the manufacturing varieties competing with variety 1 are rising, then the demand for variety 1 is increasing (recall that $\varepsilon - 1 > 0$). The varieties are therefore economic substitutes of one another (if the price of a particular variety increases its own demand falls and the demand for all other varieties rises).

Note that, although it may appear a bit cumbersome at first look, the price index I in equation (3.6) is defined analogously to the function in equation (3.4) specifying the preference for varieties, with $1 - \varepsilon$ in (3.6) playing the role of ρ in (3.4). In fact, if we use this information to calculate the elasticity of substitution for prices in equation (3.6) we get $1/[1 - (1 - \varepsilon)] = 1/\varepsilon$, the inverse of the elasticity of substitution for varieties. This is no coincidence, as it indicates that if the elasticity of substitution for varieties is high a small price change can have large effects, and vice versa if it is small.[9] Most importantly, however, note that the definition of the price index I implies that $M = \delta Y / I$ (see equation (3.7)). The price index I thus gives an exact representation of the utility derived from the consumption of manufactures; this utility increases if, and only if, spending on manufactures increase more rapidly than the price index I. Also note that $IM = \delta Y$ is required to justify our actions in subsection 3.4.1, where we used the price index I to derive the division of income over food consumption and labor

---

[9] Properties such as this are known under the label "duality"; see the appendix in Brakman and van Marrewijk (1998) for an overview.

consumption. Otherwise, our calculations there would not have been consistent.

We frequently use the price index I to derive real wages in the model. It is therefore worthwhile to take a closer look at the definition of consumption-based price indices (see also Obstfeld and Rogoff, 1996: 226). You may ask yourself the question "What is the minimum amount of expenditure required to buy one unit of utility?" Let I be this minimum expenditure on manufactures, such that $M=1$. Then we call I the consumption-based, or exact, price index. From this definition it follows directly from equations (3.5) and (3.7) that I is indeed such an index.[10] It is obvious that an increase in the number of varieties decreases I. We have already explained that an increase in the number of varieties more than proportionally increases the sub-utility for manufactures. This effect has a mirror image in the price index I; more varieties lower I, because it takes less expenditure for $M=1$. Furthermore, the term "I" enabled us to write the demand equations more efficiently as $c_j = p_j^{-\varepsilon}[I^{\varepsilon-1}\delta Y]$.

To conclude our discussion of the demand structure of the core model we need to make two remarks. The first is relatively short. We could use the same procedure applied in subsection 3.4.2 to derive the exact price index for the allocation over varieties to derive such a price index for the problem in subsection 3.4.1, allocating income over food and manufactures. As the reader may wish to verify, the result would be $1^{1-\delta} I^{\delta} = I^{\delta}$, in which the "1" on the left-hand side represents the price of food, which is set equal to one because it is the numéraire. Thus, the consumer's utility increases if, and only if, Y/I^{δ} rises – that is, if the income level rises more rapidly than the exact price index I^{δ}. We can thus define *real income y* as an exact representation of a consumer's preferences (see box 3.1 and section 3.8; see equation (3.8)). Similarly, if the wage rate is W, we can define the *real wage w* also using the exact price index (see again equation (3.8)). Moreover, if an individual consumer only has wage income, that is if $Y=W$, then the individual real income y is equivalent to the real wage w.

$$\text{real income:} \quad y = YI^{-\delta}; \quad \text{real wage:} \quad w = WI^{-\delta} \tag{3.8}$$

---

[10] One might wonder why this index looks so different from the familiar Paasche or Laspeyres price indices. The reason is that, for practical reasons, the weights in these indices are fixed, but in reality they are not. Consumers switch from more expensive goods to less expensive ones if relative prices change. How this substitution takes place is determined by consumer preferences. If we know these preferences, as in the model in the text, we can calculate the exact price index.

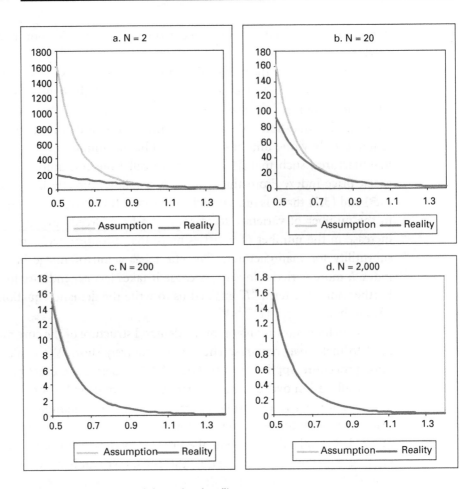

Figure 3.4 Deviation between assumed demand and reality
Note: Spending on manufactures $=100$, prices of other firms $=1$, $\varepsilon=5$.

The second remark concerns point (ii) above, wherein we argued that the (own) price elasticity of demand for the producer of variety 1 is equal to ε. Recall the specification of the demand function: $c_1=p_1^{-\varepsilon}[I^{\varepsilon-1}\delta Y]$. We argued that the term in square brackets is treated as a constant by the producer because these are macroeconomic entities. Although this is true, it overlooks a tiny detail: one of the terms in the specification of the price index of manufactures I is the price p_1. Thus, a truly rational producer would also take this miniscule effect on the aggregate price index into consideration.[11]

---

[11] In fact, using (3.6), the exact price elasticity of demand for a specific variety can be derived. Illuminating in this respect is the analysis in the neighborhood of p if $p_i=p$ for all other varieties, in which case $-(\partial c/\partial p)(p/c)$

For that reason it is often assumed that the number of varieties N produced is "large" – that is, if our producer is one of 80,000 firms we can safely ignore this effect. This is illustrated in figure 3.4, where we plot the demand curve facing the producer of a variety if he/she assumes he/she cannot influence the price index of manufactures, and the true demand taking this effect on the price index into consideration. Clearly, the assumption is a bad approximation if there are just two firms (panel a), but then nobody suggests you should use monopolistic competition in a duopoly. If there are twenty firms the approximation is already much better (panel b), if there are 200 firms the deviation is virtually undetectable (panel c), while it is unobservable if there are 2,000 firms (panel d). This suggests that we can safely ignore this detail for a reasonably large number of varieties.

3.5 Supply

3.5.1 Production structure (callout d)

We start the analysis of the supply side of the core model with a description of the production structure for food and manufactures (see also figure 3.1). Food production is characterized by constant returns to scale, and food is produced under conditions of perfect competition. Workers in this industry are assumed to be immobile. As mentioned in section 3.3, the food sector is therefore the natural candidate to be used as the numéraire. Given the total labor force L, a fraction $(1 - \gamma)$ is assumed to work in the food sector. The labor force in the manufacturing industry is therefore γL. Production in the food sector, F, equals, by choice of units, food employment:

$$F = (1 - \gamma)L; \quad 0 < \gamma < 1 \tag{3.9}$$

Since farm workers are paid the value of marginal product, this choice of units implies that the wage for the farm workers is one, because food is the numéraire.

Production in the manufacturing sector is characterized by internal economies of scale, which means that there is imperfect competition in this sector (see box 2.1). The varieties in the manufacturing industry are

---

$= [1/(1-p)][1-1/N]$. The second term on the right-hand side is inversely related to the number of varieties N, approaching one if N becomes large.

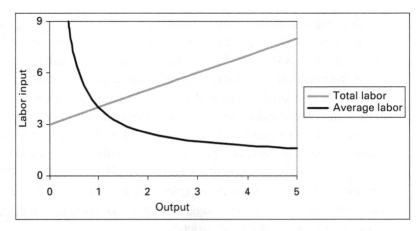

Figure 3.5   Production function for a variety of manufactures
Note: Fixed labor requirement $a = 3$, marginal labor requirement $\beta = 1$.

symmetric and are produced with the same technology. Note that even by this point we have already introduced an element of location. Internal economies of scale mean that each variety is produced by a single firm; the firm with the largest sales can always outbid a potential competitor. Once we have introduced more locations each firm has to decide where to produce. The economies of scale are modeled in the simplest way possible:

$$l_i = a + \beta x_i \tag{3.10}$$

where l_i is the amount of labor necessary to produce x_i of variety i. The coefficients a and β describe the fixed and marginal labor input requirements respectively. The fixed labor input a in (3.10) ensures that as production expands less labor is needed to produce a unit of x_i, which means that there are internal economies of scale. This is illustrated in figure 3.5, showing the total labor required to produce a certain amount of output, and the average amount of labor required to produce that amount of output. This explains callout d in figure 3.1.

3.5.2 Price setting and zero profits (callout e)

Each manufacturing firm produces a unique variety under internal returns to scale. This implies that the firm has monopoly power, which it will use to maximize its profits. We therefore have to determine the price-setting behavior of each firm. The Dixit–Stiglitz monopolistic competition model makes two assumptions in this respect. First, it is assumed that each firm takes the price-setting behavior of other firms as given – that is if firm 1 changes its price it will assume that the prices of the other $N-1$ varieties will remain the same. Second, it is assumed that the firm ignores the effect of changing its own price on the price index I of manufactures. Both assumptions seem reasonable if the number of varieties N is large, as also discussed in subsection 3.4.3. For ease of notation we drop the sub-index for the firm in this section. Note that a firm that produces x units of output using the production function in equation (3.10) will earn profits π given in equation (3.11) if the wage rate it has to pay is W.

$$\pi = px - W(a + \beta x) \tag{3.11}$$

Naturally, the firm will have to sell the units of output x it is producing – that is, these sales must be consistent with the demand for a variety of manufactures derived in section 3.4. Although this demand was derived for an arbitrary consumer, the most important feature of the demand for a variety, namely the constant price elasticity of demand ε, also holds when we combine the demand from many consumers with the same preference structure (see also exercise 3.4). If the demand x for a variety has a constant price elasticity of demand ε, the maximization of the profits given in equation (3.11) leads to a very simple optimal pricing rule, known as mark-up pricing, as given in equation (3.12) and derived in technical note 3.3:

$$p(1 - 1/\varepsilon) = \beta W \quad (or \quad p = \beta W/\rho) \tag{3.12}$$

The term "mark-up pricing" is obvious. The marginal costs of producing an extra unit of output is equal to βW, while the price p the firm charges is higher than this marginal cost. How much higher depends crucially on the price elasticity of demand. If demand is rather inelastic, say $\varepsilon = 2$, the mark-up is high (in this case 100 percent). If demand is rather elastic, say $\varepsilon = 5$, the mark-up is lower (in this case 20 percent). Note that the firm must charge a higher price than marginal cost in order to recuperate the fixed costs of labor aW. Because the price elasticity of demand ε is constant, the mark-up of the price over the marginal cost is also constant, and therefore invariant to the scale of production. Note that the price is fixed if the wage rate is fixed, as in Krugman (1980).

Technical note 3.3 Derivation of equation (3.12)

The demand x for a variety can be written as $x = \text{con} \cdot p^{-\varepsilon}$, where "con" is some constant (see the discussion in section 3.4.3, point ii). Substituting this in the profit function gives

$$\pi = \text{con} \cdot p^{1-\varepsilon} - W(a + \beta\text{con} \cdot p^{-\varepsilon})$$

Profits are now a function of the firm's price only. Differentiating with respect to the price p and equating to zero gives the first-order condition:

$$(1 - \varepsilon)\text{con} \cdot p^{-\varepsilon} + \varepsilon W\beta\text{con} \cdot p^{-\varepsilon-1} = 0$$

Canceling the term "$\text{con} \cdot p^{-\varepsilon}$" and rearranging gives equation (3.12).

Now that we have determined the optimal price a firm will charge to maximize profits we can actually calculate those profits (if we know the constant in technical note 3.3). This is where another important feature of monopolistic competition comes in. If profits are positive (sometimes referred to as excess profits) it is apparently very attractive to set up shop in the manufacturing sector. One would then expect new firms to enter the market and start to produce different varieties. This implies, of course, that the consumer will allocate his/her spending over more varieties of manufactures. Since all varieties are substitutes for one another, the entry of new firms into the manufacturing sector implies that profits for the existing firms will fall. This process of new firm entry will continue until the profits in the manufacturing sector are driven to zero. A reverse process, with firms leaving the manufacturing sector, would operate if profits were negative. Monopolistic competition in the manufacturing sector therefore imposes as an equilibrium condition that profits are zero. If we do that in equation (3.11) we can calculate the scale at which a firm producing a variety in the manufacturing sector will operate, equation (3.13), how much labor is needed to produce this amount of output, equation (3.14), and how many varieties N are produced in the economy as a function of the available labor in the manufacturing sector, equation (3.15); see technical note 3.4.

$$x = \frac{a(\varepsilon - 1)}{\beta} \tag{3.13}$$

$$l_i = a\varepsilon \tag{3.14}$$

$$N = \gamma L/l_i = \gamma L/a\varepsilon \tag{3.15}$$

Technical note 3.4 Derivation of equations (3.13) to (3.15)

Put profits in equation (3.11) equal to zero and use the pricing rule $p(1 - 1/\varepsilon) = \beta W$ from equation (3.12):

$$px - W(a + \beta x) = 0; \quad px = aW + \beta Wx; \quad \left[\frac{\varepsilon}{\varepsilon - 1}\beta W\right]x = aW + \beta Wx$$

$$\left[\frac{\varepsilon}{\varepsilon - 1} - 1\right]\beta Wx = aW; \quad x = \frac{a(\varepsilon - 1)}{\beta}$$

This explains equation (3.13). Now use the production function (3.10) to calculate the amount of labor required to produce this much output:

$$l_i = a + \beta x = a + \beta\frac{a(\varepsilon - 1)}{\beta} = a + a(\varepsilon - 1) = a\varepsilon$$

This explains equation (3.14). Finally, equation (3.15), determining the number of varieties N produced, simply follows by dividing the total number of manufacturing workers by the number of workers needed to produce one variety.

Equation (3.13), giving the scale of output for an individual firm, may seem strange at first sight. No matter what happens, the output per firm is fixed in equilibrium. The constant price elasticity of demand in conjunction with the production function is responsible for this result. It implies that the manufacturing sector as a whole expands and contracts only by producing more or fewer varieties, as the output level per variety does not change. From (3.15) we see that a larger market caused, for example, by the opening of the borders or increased international trade affects only the number of varieties. As a result of economies of scale it is not profitable to have the same variety produced by more than one firm; each firm will produce only one variety.

The question may arise as to where the economies of scale are; do they not matter anymore? There is another way of looking at the parameter ε. In equilibrium, it is also used as a measure of economies of scale. Scale economies can be measured in various ways, but one specific measure of economies of scale is this: average costs divided by marginal costs; if the marginal costs are lower than the average costs an increase in production will reduce the average costs. For the core model we can calculate this measure for the equilibrium level of production. The labor requirement is $a\varepsilon$ (see equation (3.14)), the production level is $a(\varepsilon - 1)/\beta$ (see equation (3.13)), so the average labor costs are $a\varepsilon\,/[a(\varepsilon-1)/\beta] = \beta\varepsilon/(\varepsilon-1)$. The marginal labor costs are simply β, so this measure of economies of scale reduces to average costs / marginal costs $= \varepsilon/(\varepsilon-1)$, which in equilibrium depends only on the elasticity of substitution parameter ε (note in particular that the parameters a and β of the production function do not enter). For a low value of ε this measure of scale economies is high, while for high values this measure is low. The latter means that varieties are becoming more and more perfect substitutes. In the limit, only a single variety survives. Production of this single variety takes place at the largest possible scale (all manufacturing labor is employed in producing the single variety), leaving less room for economies of scale than if ε is low, and many different varieties are produced by many different firms (see Hanoch, 1975). Recall, finally, that this measure indicates only the level of economies of scale in equilibrium. The internal economies of scale are not absent, therefore, but show up only in a rather special way in the Dixit–Stiglitz model of monopolistic competition.

3.6 Transport costs: icebergs in geography

The aim of the core model of geographical economics is to introduce geography in a non-trivial way. That is to say, the model must show how geography affects the decisions of individual consumers and producers and how these decisions in turn shape the spatial distribution of economic activity. To be able to do so, transport costs have to be introduced. Only if it is costly to move products and people over space does geography make sense in the core model.

The transport costs we introduce are special. In principle one could model a transport sector and add this to the model, but this would be very cumbersome. Every cost is also a gain for someone else, and transport costs are income for the transport sector, so one must deal with spending from this sector. In addition, the location decision of the transport sector might be different from the location decisions of the other sectors. It is for these reasons that Samuelson (1952) has introduced the concept of *iceberg* transport costs (callout f). In the context of the core model of geographical economics, iceberg transport costs imply that a fraction of the manufactured goods does not arrive at the destination when goods are shipped between regions. The fraction that does not arrive represents the cost of transportation. The core model uses T as a parameter to represent these costs, where T is defined as the number of goods that need to be shipped to ensure that one unit arrives per unit of distance. Suppose, for example, that the unit of distance is equal to the distance from Naaldwijk, in the center of the Dutch horticultural agglomeration, to Paris, and that 107 flowers are sent from Holland to France, while only 100 arrive unharmed in Paris and can be sold. Then $T = 1.07$. It is as if some goods have melted away in transit – hence the name "iceberg" costs. This way of modeling transport costs without introducing a transport sector is very attractive, because we do not have to model a separate transport sector. This implies that we do not have to deal with questions such as "Who works in this sector?" and "Where do workers in the transport sector live and spend their income?" This explains callout f in figure 3.1. Box 3.3 discusses the relevance of transports costs.

Box 3.3 The relevance of transport costs

Transport costs are essential throughout this book. Without transport costs there is no geography, and the whole exercise of transforming economic models into geographical economics models becomes pointless or very academic. Adam Smith long ago noted the importance of locations near the coast in reducing transport costs, "so, it is upon the sea-coast, and along the banks of navigable rivers, that industry of every kind naturally begins to sub-divide and improve itself, and it is frequently not till a long time after that those improvements extend themselves to the inland part of the country" (Smith, cited in Steven Radelet and Sachs, 1998).

Many measures have been constructed to measure transport cost, ranging from direct measures to travel time (see the example on Germany in chapter 5). The most straight-forward measure in international trade is the difference between the so-called c.i.f. (cost, insurance, and freight) and f.o.b. (free on board) quotations of trade. The c.i.f. quotation measures the value of imports from the point of entry, inclusive of carriage, insurance and freight. The f.o.b. quotation measures value of imports "free on board" – that is, the cost of the imports inclusive of all charges incurred in placing the merchandise on a carrier in the exporting "port." The difference between these two values is a measure of the cost of getting an item from the exporting country to the importing country, but, clearly, it underestimates the actual transport costs of international trade. Often one finds the ratio of $[(\text{c.i.f.}/\text{f.o.b.}) - 1] \times 100\%$, which represents the unit transport cost (percentage) to the f.o.b. price and provides a measure of the transport cost *rate* on imports. Different goods have different transport costs. One might expect that goods with high value added will have relatively low c.i.f./f.o.b. ratios, perishable goods probably higher ratios. David Hummels (1999b), for example, finds for the United States that the *ad valorem* freight rate is 7.6

Box 3.3 (cont.)

Table 3.3 C.i.f./f.o.b. ratios (percentages), 1965–90

Country	C.i.f./f.o.b. ratio	Country	C.i.f./f.o.b. ratio
Australia	10.3	New Zealand	11.5
Austria	4.1	Norway	2.7
Canada	2.7	Philippines	7.6
Denmark	4.5	Portugal	10.3
France	4.2	Singapore	6.1
West Germany	3.0	Spain	6.4
Greece	13.0	Sweden	3.5
Ireland	5.0	Switzerland	1.8
Italy	7.1	Thailand	11.0
Japan	9.0	United Kingdom	6.0
Netherlands	5.6	United States	4.9

Source: Radelet and Sachs (1998).

percent for food and live animals, but only 2.25 percent for machinery and transport equipment. Table 3.3 gives some indication of this transport cost measure for various countries.

The differences in shipping costs can be explained by noting that countries located further away from major markets face higher shipping costs (e.g. New Zealand), and by whether or not countries are landlocked. For example, the landlocked developing countries (not shown in the table) have on average 50 percent higher transport costs than coastal developing economies (see Radelet and Sachs, 1998). These authors also find that for developing countries a doubling of trading cost reduces economic growth by 0.5 percentage points. As argued above, these figures probably underestimate true trade costs. Hummels (1999a: 27) finds that freight rates differ substantially over exporters. *Expenditures* on freight are at "the low end of the range," however This suggests that these costs are substantial and that import choices are made to minimize transport costs. Note that products with very high transport costs are not even traded at all. Hummels (1999b) also shows that, in contrast to popular opinion, transport costs have *not* declined uniformly. His general conclusion is that, since World War II (WWII), the costs of ocean travel have increased and the costs of air transport have fallen and, furthermore, that the costs of distant travel have fallen relative to proximate transport.

For a final indication of the importance of transport costs we can compare freight costs with other trade costs. James Anderson and Eric van Wincoop (2004: 691–2) note that these other costs consist of transportation costs (not only freight costs, but also time costs), policy barriers (tariffs and non-tariff barriers), information costs, contract enforcement costs, costs associated with the use of different currencies, legal and regulatory costs, and local distribution costs (wholesale and retail). Their rough "representative" estimate for industrialized countries is that total trade costs are about 170 percent of their *ad valorem*

Box 3.3 (cont.)

tax equivalent. This number breaks down as follows: 21 percent transportation costs, 44 percent border-related trade barriers, and 55 percent retail and wholesale distribution costs $(2.7 = 1.21 \times 1.44 \times 1.55)$.

Now that we have seen that transport costs between and within countries are substantial, one might ask whether or not they matter. The answer is that they do. Limao and Venables (2000) find that transport costs are very important in the ability of countries to participate in the global economy. The tendency of trade liberalization makes transport costs as such somewhat more important than the official trade barriers, such as tariffs. Using various econometric techniques they find that the elasticity of trade with respect to transport costs is high, approximately equal to -2.5. This implies, for example, that a median land-locked country has only about 30 percent of the trade flows that a coastal country has. Being landlocked raises transport costs by around 50 percent. Moreover, Limao and Venables find that the generally poor quality of sub-Saharan African infrastructure is to a large extent responsible for the relatively low level of African trade with the rest of the world.

Finally, it must be noted that distance not only has a physical representation but also a mental element. John McCallum (1995) finds that Canadian provinces traded more than twenty times the volume of trade with each other that they traded with similar counterparts in the United States. Although the latter estimate is not undisputed (consistent estimates reduce the impact of the border by a factor of two), borders in general have a large impact on trade costs (for a discussion on border effects, see Feenstra, 2004). A recent meta-study that looks at all other studies estimating the effects of trade costs concludes that the "estimated negative impact of distance on trade rose around the middle of the [twentieth] century and has remained persistently high since then. This result holds even after controlling for many important differences in samples and methods" (Disdier and Head, 2008: 37).

Throughout the rest of the book the parameter T denotes the number of goods that need to be shipped to ensure that one unit of a variety of manufactures arrives per unit of distance, while T_{rs} is defined as the number of goods that need to be shipped from region r to ensure that one unit arrives in region s. We make the assumption that this is proportional to the distance between regions r and s. If D_{rs} denotes the distance between region r and region s (which is zero if $r = s$), we have

$$T_{rs} = T^{D_{rs}}, \text{ for } r, s = 1, 2; \quad \text{note: } T_{rs} = T_{sr}, \text{ and } T_{rr} = T^0 = 1 \qquad (3.16)$$

These definitions ease notation in the equations below and allow us to distinguish between changes in the parameter T (that is, a general change in [transport] technology applying to all regions), and changes in the "distance" D_{rs} between regions, which may result from a policy change, such as tariff changes, a cultural treaty, new infrastructure, etc. For the two-region core model discussed here, we always assume that the distance between the two regions is one. Equation (3.16), and the equations below, do not yet use this fact in order to develop a general model of multiple regions at the same time.

3.7 Multiple locations

Now that we have introduced two regions and transport costs, it becomes important to know where the economic agents are located. We therefore have to (i) specify a notation to show how labor is distributed over the two regions, and (ii) investigate what the consequences are for some of the demand and supply equations discussed in sections 3.4 and 3.5. To start with point (i), we have already introduced the parameter γ to denote the fraction of the labor force in the manufacturing sector (see section 3.5), such that $1 - \gamma$ is the fraction of labor in the food sector. We now assume that, of the laborers in the food sector, a fraction ϕ_i is located in region i, and of the laborers in the manufacturing sector a fraction λ_i is located in region i. Figure 3.6 graphically illustrates the division of labor. The boxes for the manufacturing sector are shaded, as in figure 3.1, to indicate that the size of the working population can increase or decrease, depending on the mobility of the manufacturing workforce.

Point (ii) involves more work. We will concentrate on region 1 though similar remarks hold for region 2. It is easiest to start with the producers. Since there are $\phi_1(1 - \gamma)L$ farm workers in region 1 and production is proportional to the labor input (see equation (3.6)), food production in region 1 equals $\phi_1(1 - \gamma)L$, which is equal to the income generated by the food sector in region 1 and the wage income paid to farm workers there. Following the introduction of transport costs into the model, the wage rate paid to manufacturing workers in region 1 will in general differ from the wage rate paid to manufacturing workers in region 2. We identify these with a sub-index, so W_1 is the manufacturing wage in region 1. From now on, and throughout the remainder of the book, whenever we speak of "the wage rate" we refer to the manufacturing wage rate. If we know the wage rate W_1 in region 1, we can see from equation (3.12) that the price charged in region 1 by a firm located in region 1 is equal to $\beta W_1/\rho$. The price this firm located in region 1 will charge in region 2 will be T_{12} times higher than in region 1 (in this case: $T_{12} = T^{D_{12}} = T$) as a result of the transportation costs (see also exercise 3.4). Note that this holds for all N_1 firms located in region 1. Finally,

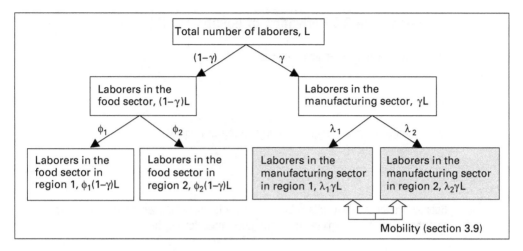

Figure 3.6   Division of labor between the regions
Notes: $\phi_1+\phi_2=1$; $\lambda_1+\lambda_2=1$.

since there are $\lambda_1\gamma L$ manufacturing workers in region 1, we can deduce from equation (3.15) the number of firms N_1 located in region 1: $N_1=\lambda_1\gamma L/a\varepsilon$. Note, in particular, that the number of firms located in region 1 is directly proportional to the number of manufacturing workers located in region 1.

We now turn to the demand side of the economy. As discussed above, the price a firm charges to a consumer for one unit of the variety it produces depends both on the location of the firm (which determines the wage rate the firm will have to pay to its workers) and on the location of the consumer (which determines whether or not the consumer will have to pay for the transport costs of the good). As a result, the price index of manufactures will differ between the two regions. Again, we identify these with a sub-index, so I_1 is the price index in region 1. Now, however, we can be more specific, since we can derive the price a firm will charge in each region, and how many firms there are in each region. All we have to do is substitute this information in equation (3.7) (see technical note 3.5):

$$I_1 = \left(\frac{\beta}{\rho}\right)\left(\frac{\gamma L}{a\varepsilon}\right)^{1/(1-\varepsilon)}\left[\lambda_1 W_1^{1-\varepsilon} + \lambda_2 T^{1-\varepsilon}W_2^{1-\varepsilon}\right]^{1/(1-\varepsilon)} \tag{3.17}$$

The impact of location on the consumption decisions of consumers in different locations on the basis of equation (3.6) requires us to know the income level of region 1. This brings us to the determination of equilibrium.

Technical note 3.5 Derivation of equation (3.17)

The number of firms in region s equals

$$\left(\frac{\lambda_s \gamma L}{\alpha \varepsilon}\right)$$

The price these firms in region s charge in region r equals

$$\left(\frac{\beta}{\rho} W_s T_{rs}\right)$$

Substituting these two results in the price index for manufactures, equation (3.6), assuming that there are $R \geq 2$ regions, gives the price index for region r:

$$I_r = \left[\sum_{s=1}^{R} \left(\frac{\lambda_s \gamma L}{\alpha \varepsilon}\right)\left(\frac{\beta}{\rho} W_s T_{rs}\right)^{1-\varepsilon}\right]^{1/(1-\varepsilon)}$$

$$= \left(\frac{\beta}{\rho}\right)\left(\frac{\gamma L}{\alpha \varepsilon}\right)^{1/(1-\varepsilon)} \left[\sum_{s=1}^{R} \lambda_s W_s^{1-\varepsilon} T_{rs}^{1-\varepsilon}\right]^{1/(1-\varepsilon)} \quad (*)$$

Equation (3.17) in the text is a special case for $R=2$ and $r=1$.

3.8 Equilibrium

Given the details of the core model of geographical economics as laid out in the previous sections, we have already explained a significant part of the structure of this model as shown by figure 3.1 in section 3.3. What needs to be done now is to establish the equilibrium relationships, which effectively will tie up all the loose ends. In particular, we have to determine the way in which the equilibrium relationships together with the shaded boxes in figure 3.1 ultimately determine the spatial distribution of economic activity. These shaded boxes (callout g in figure 3.1) refer to the mobility of manufacturing workers and firms between the two regions. As has already been explained at length in chapter 2, this mobility really sets geographical economics apart from new trade theory, upon which so much of the core model is based.

To understand the determination of equilibrium and the role of factor and firm mobility therein, we proceed in three steps. First, this section concentrates on *short-run* equilibrium relationships – that is, it gives the equilibrium analysis for an exogenously given distribution of the manufacturing labor force. It is thereby assumed that the manufacturing labor force is not mobile between regions in the short run. The spatial distribution of the manufacturing workers and firms is not yet determined by the model itself, but simply imposed upon the model. Second, the next section briefly addresses the issue of dynamics – that is, how we move through a sequence of short-run equilibria (no factor mobility) over time to a *long-run equilibrium* (with factor mobility). This is crucial for the geographical economics approach. Third, the *analysis* of both short-run and long-run equilibria turns out to be so involved that we deal with it separately in the next chapter.

3.8.1 Short-run equilibrium

This subsection summarizes the economy-wide short-run equilibrium relationships – that is, the equations for both regions in a two-region setting – and pulls together and briefly discusses the three short-run equilibrium equations for region 1. What are the short-run equilibrium relationships? As it happens, we have in fact already used a few of these without explicitly saying so. For example, we have already assumed that the labor markets clear – that is, (i) all farm workers have a job, and (ii) all manufacturing workers have a job. Point (i) has determined the production level of food in each region, in conjunction with the production function for food and perfect competition in the food sector. Point (ii) has determined the number of manufacturing varieties produced in each region, in conjunction with the production function for manufactures, the price-setting behavior of firms, and the entry or exit of firms in the manufacturing sector until profits are zero. Evidently, there are no profits for firms in the manufacturing sector (because of entry and exit), nor for the farmers (because of constant returns to scale and perfect competition). This implies that all income earned in the economy for consumers to spend derives from the wages they earn in their respective sectors.

This brings us to the next equilibrium relationship: how to determine income in each region. In view of the above, this is simple. There are $\phi_1(1-\gamma)L$ farm workers in region 1, each earning a farm wage rate of one (food is the numéraire), and there are $\lambda_1 \gamma L$ manufacturing workers in region 1, each earning a wage rate W_1. As there are no profits or other factors of production, this is the only income generated in region 1. If we let Y_i denote income generated in region i, this implies

$$Y_1 = \lambda_1 W_1 \gamma L + \phi_1 (1 - \gamma) L \tag{3.18}$$

where the first term on the right-hand side represents income for the manufacturing workers, and the second term reflects income for the farm workers.

As discussed in sections 3.6 and 3.7, the actual amount of transport costs between regions for the manufacturing sector is given by $T - 1$. Since all firms in a region face identical marginal production costs and the same constant elasticity of demand (see also below), they all charge the same price to local producers, say p_1 for region 1 producers and p_2 for region 2 producers (see also exercise 3.4). This mill price, or f.o.b. price, of a variety produced in region 1 charged to consumers in region 1 is related to the marginal production costs in region 1 through the optimal pricing condition (3.12): $p_1 = \beta W_1 / \rho$. This indicates that the f.o.b. price is directly proportional to the wage rate. The price of a variety produced in region 1 after being delivered in region 2 is $T p_1$, which is the c.i.f. price of this variety (see also box 3.3 on f.o.b. and c.i.f. prices). In addition, recall from section 3.7 that, since there are $\lambda_1 \gamma L$ manufacturing workers in region 1, it follows from equation (3.15) that the number of firms N_1 located in region 1 equals $N_1 = \lambda_1 \gamma L / \alpha \varepsilon$. That is, the number of firms located in region 1 is directly proportional to λ_1, the number of manufacturing workers located in region 1. All three aspects discussed above – namely (i) the prices of locally produced goods are directly proportional to the local wage rate, (ii) the prices charged in the other region are higher by the transport costs between regions, and (iii) the number of varieties produced in a region is directly proportional to the number of manufacturing workers in a region – are important for understanding why the price index I can have a different value in both regions. For region 1 the price index I_1 is (see technical note 3.5 for further details)

$$I_1 = \left(\frac{\beta}{\rho}\right) \left(\frac{\gamma L}{\alpha \varepsilon}\right)^{1/(1-\varepsilon)} \left[\lambda_1 W_1^{1-\varepsilon} + \lambda_2 T^{1-\varepsilon} W_2^{1-\varepsilon}\right]^{1/(1-\varepsilon)} \tag{3.19}$$

Thus, the price index in region 1 is essentially a weighted average of the price of locally produced goods and imported goods from region 2.

At this stage we notice that the only variables that are unknown in equations (3.18) and (3.19) are the wages in both regions. These wages can be derived from the equilibrium equation in the goods market: supply equals demand. We proceed as follows. First we look at demand. Demand comes from both regions. Demand in region 1 for products from region 1 is based on individual demand derived in equation (3.6), by summing the demand for all consumers in region 1. It is therefore dependent on the aggregate income Y_1 in region 1, as given in equation (3.18), the price index I_1 in region 1, as given in equation (3.19), and the price $p_1 = \beta W_1/\rho$ charged by a producer from region 1 for a locally sold variety in region 1. We simply have to substitute these three terms for the individual income, price index, and price as given in equation (3.6) to get $(\delta\beta^{-\varepsilon}\rho^{\varepsilon})Y_1 W_1^{-\varepsilon}I_1^{\varepsilon-1}$, which is the total demand in region 1 for a variety produced in region 1.

We can derive demand in region 2 for products from region 1 in a similar way, by substituting aggregate income Y_2, price index I_2, and the price $Tp_1 = T\beta W_1/\rho$ charged by a producer from region 1 for a good sold in region 2 in equation (3.6) to get $(\delta\beta^{-\varepsilon}\rho^{\varepsilon})Y_2 W_1^{-\varepsilon}T^{-\varepsilon}I_2^{\varepsilon-1}$. If there are positive transport costs, that is $T > 1$, demand in region 2 for products from region 1 is lower than without transport costs, because transport costs make them more expensive.

Total demand x_1 for a producer in region 1 is the sum of the demands discussed in the above two paragraphs – that is, the sum of demand from region 1 and demand from region 2:

$$x_1 = (\delta\beta^{-\varepsilon}\rho^{\varepsilon})\left(Y_1 W_1^{-\varepsilon}I_1^{\varepsilon-1} + Y_2 W_1^{-\varepsilon}T^{-\varepsilon}I_2^{\varepsilon-1}\right) \tag{3.20}$$

This equation simply states that total demand for a particular variety depends on income in *both* regions, transportation costs, and the price (proportional to the wage rate) relative to the price index. We can now immediately see another advantage of modeling transportation costs as melting icebergs, namely that the price elasticity of demand with respect to the f.o.b. price is constant (equal to ε).

Next we turn to supply. We have already derived the break-even level of production $x = a(\varepsilon - 1)/\beta$ for a producer of manufactures in equation (3.13). Equating this break-even production level to the total demand derived in equation (3.20) allows us to determine what the equilibrium price of a variety should be, in order to sell exactly this amount.[12] For a

---

[12] Equating total demand to supply usually results in an equilibrium market *price*. Note that, in our case, we substitute the mark-up price equation into the equilibrium equation, which results in an equilibrium *wage* instead of an equilibrium market price. This not only allows us to solve equations (3.18) and (3.19) but is also useful for modeling labor migration, which is needed to derive the long-run equilibrium.

producer in region 1 this implies $a(\varepsilon - 1)/\beta = (\delta\beta^{-\varepsilon}\rho^{\varepsilon})(Y_1 W_1^{-\varepsilon}I_1^{\varepsilon-1} +$ $Y_2 W_1^{-\varepsilon}T^{1-\varepsilon}I_2^{\varepsilon-1})$. Note the important difference with equation (3.20) for the term T on the right-hand side, namely $1-\varepsilon$ instead of $-\varepsilon$. This follows from the fact that the producer includes the amount which melts away en route from region 1 to region 2; in order to supply one unit of a variety in region 2, T units have to be shipped. Solving the above equation for the wage rate in region 1 gives

$$W_1 = \rho\beta^{-\rho}\left(\frac{\delta}{(\varepsilon-1)a}\right)^{1/\varepsilon}\left[Y_1 I_1^{\varepsilon-1} + Y_2 T^{1-\varepsilon}I_2^{\varepsilon-1}\right]^{1/\varepsilon}$$

(3.21)

Intuitively the equation makes perfect sense: wages in region 1 can be higher as this region is located close to large markets (Y_1 in region 1 with $T=1$ and Y_2 in region 2 with $T>1$) and a firm in region 1 faces less competition (recall point (iv) in subsection 3.4.3). Thus, the larger region 2 is and the smaller T is, the higher W_1 is. As we will see in chapter 5, this important consequence of the core model is used in empirical research.

Technical note 3.6 Derivation of equation (3.21)

Equation (3.6) gives the demand for an individual consumer in a region. If we replace in that equation the income level Y with the income level Y_r of region r, the price index I with the price index I_r of region r, and the price p_j of the manufactured good with the price $\beta W_s T_{rs}/\rho$ that a producer from region s will charge in region r (see section 3.7), we get the demand in region r for a product from region s:

$$\delta Y_r(\beta W_s T_{rs}/\rho)^{-\varepsilon}I_r^{\varepsilon-1} = \delta(\beta/\rho)^{-\varepsilon}Y_r W_s^{-\varepsilon}T_{rs}^{-\varepsilon}I_r^{\varepsilon-1}$$

To fulfill this consumption demand in region r, note that T_{rs} units have to be shipped and produced. To derive the total demand in all $R \geq 2$ regions for a manufactured good produced in region s, we must sum production demand over all regions – that is, sum over the index r in the above equation and multiply each entry by T_{rs} (to compensate for the part that melts during transport):

$$\delta(\beta/\rho)^{-\varepsilon}\sum_{r=1}^{R}Y_r W_s^{-\varepsilon}T_{rs}^{1-\varepsilon}I_r^{\varepsilon-1} = \delta(\beta/\rho)^{-\varepsilon}W_s^{-\varepsilon}\sum_{r=1}^{R}Y_r T_{rs}^{1-\varepsilon}I_r^{\varepsilon-1}$$

In equilibrium this total demand for a manufactured good from region s must be equal to its supply $(\varepsilon - 1)a/\beta$ (see equation (3.13)). Equalizing these two gives

$$(\varepsilon - 1)a/\beta = \delta(\beta/\rho)^{-\varepsilon}W_s^{-\varepsilon}\sum_{r=1}^{R}Y_r T_{rs}^{1-\varepsilon}I_r^{\varepsilon-1}$$

Technical note 3.6 (cont.)

which can be solved for the wage rate W_s in region s:

$$W_s = \rho \beta^{-\rho} \left(\frac{\delta}{(\varepsilon - 1)a} \right)^{1/\varepsilon} \left[\sum_{r=1}^{R} Y_r T_{rs}^{1-\varepsilon} I_r^{\varepsilon-1} \right]^{1/\varepsilon} \qquad (*)$$

Equation (3.21) in the text is a special case for $R=2$ and $r=1$.

Note that there is a close resemblance between this equation and the market potential approach, or the gravity approach discussed in chapter 2. Similarly to those approaches, the attractiveness of a region is related to the purchasing power of all regions, directed at a specific market and distance. The advantage of using a general equilibrium approach, as we do here, is that price indices play a crucial role and the income levels are endogenously determined, which is now made explicit.

Given the distribution of the manufacturing work force λ_i, we have now derived the short-run equilibrium equations for region 1. They are equations (3.18), determining income level Y_1, equation (3.19), determining price index I_1, and equation (3.21), determining the wage rate W_1. Similar equations hold for region 2, giving a total of six non-linear equations, as discussed in more detail in the next subsection, and analyzed in detail in the next chapter.

3.8.2 Long-run equilibrium

The model we have developed in this chapter is summarized in the following four equations for region 1 (similar equations hold for region 2; see below for further details):

$$Y_1 = \lambda_1 W_1 \gamma L + \phi_1 (1 - \gamma) L \tag{3.22}$$

$$I_1 = \left(\frac{\beta}{\rho} \right) \left(\frac{\gamma L}{a\varepsilon} \right)^{1/(1-\varepsilon)} \left[\sum_{s=1}^{2} \lambda_s T_{1s}^{1-\varepsilon} W_s^{1-\varepsilon} \right]^{1/(1-\varepsilon)} \tag{3.23}$$

$$W_1 = \rho \beta^{-\rho} \left(\frac{\delta}{(\varepsilon - 1)a} \right)^{1/\varepsilon} \left[\sum_{s=1}^{2} Y_s T_{s1}^{1-\varepsilon} I_s^{\varepsilon-1} \right]^{1/\varepsilon} \tag{3.24}$$

$$w_1 = W_1 I_1^{-\delta} \tag{3.25}$$

Equations (3.22) to (3.24) are the short-run equilibrium equations and equation (3.25) gives the real wage of manufacturing workers. The latter distinguishes long-run equilibria from short-run equilibria, whereby a long-run equilibrium is reached only if the *real* wages in the regions are equal ($w_1 = w_2$), which implies that there is no incentive to relocate, or if there is agglomeration in one region. In the short-run equilibrium, real wages are not necessarily the same between regions (thus creating an incentive to relocate). Note that, for both short-run and long-run equilibria, supply equals demand (markets clear). A full analysis of the difference between these equilibria is given in chapter 4, but at this stage we can already derive some interesting results.

Technical note 3.7 Normalizations

The units in which we measure variables may simplify the analysis without affecting the solution of the model (in our case: the relative position of one region versus another). The essence of these "normalizations" is that, whether you measure a football field in feet or inches, it does not change the size of the field. First (see table 3.4), we normalize the total labor supply and take $L = 1$. Suppose that your country has 300 million inhabitants then this is the unit of measurement we use (hence $L = 2$ would imply 600 million inhabitants). Second, we can choose the units in which we measure labor. Usually this is labor hours. We, however, use a unit of measurement such that the fixed labor requirement for this unit (a) equals $\lambda L / \varepsilon$. This choice of units also affects the choice of units of the marginal labour requirement. Third, we can choose a unit of measurement for output. Usually this is in kilograms, tons, or units. We choose a rather special unit such that the marginal labor requirement – in terms of the newly defined labor unit – of an additional unit of output is such that the marginal labor requirement (β) is equal to (ρ). Fourth, and finally, we assume that $\gamma = \delta$. This "normalization" does however, affect (so to speak) the size of the football field. The good news is it does so only very marginally. The reader is encouraged to reflect on these issues in exercise 3.6.

Table 3.4 Parameter normalization

$\gamma = \delta$	$L = 1$
$\beta = \rho$	$a = \gamma L / \varepsilon$

Even though it is not strictly necessary, it is convenient to simplify the equations by using some normalizations. This enables us to ignore combinations of parameters that make the expressions look more complicated than they actually are. It is convenient to use the normalizations given in table 3.4 (see the discussion in technical note 3.7). In addition, we assume that farm workers are equally divided between the two regions – that is, $\phi_1 = \phi_2 = 1/2$. Together with the normalizations, we get the simplified equilibrium equations (3.22') to (3.25').[13]

Although we have now stripped the core model of geographical economics down to its bare essentials (two regions, identical in all respects except for the manufacturing labor force, and with a suitable choice of parameters), it still does not yield easily to analysis, except in three special cases for the distribution of the manufacturing labor force. Each is discussed in turn below.

$$Y_1 = \lambda_1 \delta W_1 + (1/2)(1 - \delta); \quad Y_2 = \lambda_2 \delta W_2 + (1/2)(1 - \delta) \tag{3.22'}$$

$$I_1 = \left[\lambda_1 W_1^{1-\varepsilon} + \lambda_2 T^{1-\varepsilon} W_2^{1-\varepsilon}\right]^{1/(1-\varepsilon)}; \quad I_2 = \left[\lambda_1 T^{1-\varepsilon} W_1^{1-\varepsilon} + \lambda_2 W_2^{1-\varepsilon}\right]^{1/(1-\varepsilon)} \tag{3.23'}$$

$$W_1 = \left[Y_1 I_1^{\varepsilon-1} + Y_2 T^{1-\varepsilon} I_2^{\varepsilon-1}\right]^{1/\varepsilon}; \quad W_2 = \left[Y_1 T^{1-\varepsilon} I_1^{\varepsilon-1} + Y_2 I_2^{\varepsilon-1}\right]^{1/\varepsilon} \tag{3.24'}$$

$$w_1 = W_1 I_1^{-\delta}; \quad w_2 = W_2 I_2^{-\delta} \tag{3.25'}$$

- *Spreading of economic activity* (figure 3.7a). Suppose the two regions are identical in *all* respects – that is, the manufacturing work force is also evenly distributed $\lambda_1 = \lambda_2 = 1/2$. Naturally, we then expect the wage rates of the short-run equilibrium to be the same for the two regions. Can we explicitly calculate this wage rate? Yes, if we're clever enough.[14] One way to proceed is to guess an equilibrium wage rate, and then verify if you guessed right (a procedure we use in the next chapter as well). So, let us guess (for no particular reason, except that we turn out to be right in the end) that the equilibrium wage rates are $W_1 = W_2 = 1$. It then follows from equation (3.23') that $I_1 = (1/2)^{1/(1-\varepsilon)}[1 + T^{1-\varepsilon}]^{1/(1-\varepsilon)}$ (and similarly for I_2), while from equation (3.22') it follows that $Y_1 = 1/2$

---

[13] See van Marrewijk (2006) for a step-by-step exposition of a more general model.
[14] In chapter 4 we introduce an alternative "core" model that allows us to derive the equilibrium wage rate analytically.

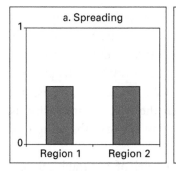
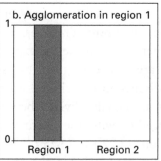
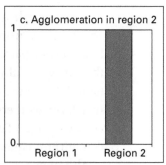

Figure 3.7   Distribution of manufacturing labor force: three examples

(and $Y_2 = 1/2$). Using these results in equation (3.24′) shows indeed that $W_1 = W_2 = 1$, so we guessed right. In this case, we can therefore analytically determine the short-run equilibrium. Note that in the spreading equilibrium all variables are the same for the two regions; therefore the real wages must be the same as well, which can be confirmed by substituting the values for the nominal wages, and the price indices in (3.25′). The spreading equilibrium is thus shown to always be a long-run equilibrium, independent of the values of the parameters.

- *Agglomeration in region 1* (figure 3.7b). Suppose now that all manufacturing activity is agglomerated in region 1 ($\lambda_1 = 1$), such that there are no manufacturing workers in region 2 ($\lambda_2 = 0$). Can we determine the short-run equilibrium? Yes. Let us guess again that $W_1 = 1$. Then, it follows from equation (3.23′) that $I_1 = 1$ (and $I_2 = T$), while from equation (3.22′) it follows that $Y_1 = (1 + \gamma)/2$ (and $Y_2 = (1 - \gamma)/2$). Using these results in equation (3.24′) does indeed show that $W_1 = 1$, so we guessed right. Again, we can analytically derive the solutions to the short-run equilibrium in this case. Note that the wage rate W_2 is not mentioned in the above discussion. Since there are no manufacturing workers in region 2, we cannot say what their wage rate is. It is instructive, however, to see what the implied wage rate will be if a firm decides to move to region 2. From (3.24′) it follows that this is

$$W_2 = \{[(1+\delta)/2]\,T^{1-\varepsilon} + [(1-\delta)/2]\,T^{\varepsilon-1}\}^{1/\varepsilon}$$

The implied real wage in region 2 can now be derived from (3.25′), $w_2^\varepsilon = [(1+\delta)/2]\,T^{1-\varepsilon-\varepsilon\delta} + [(1-\delta)/2]\,T^{\varepsilon-1-\varepsilon\delta}$. Without going into the analytical details (see chapter 4), it is easily verified that, for $T = 1$, the real wages in region 1 and 2 are both equal to one, and that, for sufficiently small values of T, $w_2 < 0$. Agglomeration in region 1 can therefore be a long-run equilibrium.

• *Agglomeration in region 2* (figure 3.7c). This is the mirror image of the second situation described above.

We have been able to derive the short- and long-run equilibria analytically for three separate cases ($\lambda_1 = 0$; $\lambda_1 = 1/2$; $\lambda_1 = 1$). Unfortunately, these are only three cases. Recall that the values can vary all the way from zero to one, so there are infinitely many other possibilities. We do not know, for example, if the three equilibria we have identified are the only long-run equilibria, or if the number of long-run equilibria depends on the value of certain parameters. We would like to draw a complete picture of all possible equilibria, long-run as well as short-run, instead of just the three possibilities depicted in figure 3.7. In order to do so we have to introduce dynamics into the model: how do we move from one equilibrium to the next one, and what economic forces determine such relocations?

3.9 A first look at dynamics

We have argued repeatedly that the introduction of a small general equilibrium model, which incorporates location, increasing returns to scale, imperfect competition, and transport costs, in conjunction with mobility for factors of production, is essentially the defining characteristic of the geographical economics approach. It implies that the shaded boxes in figures 3.1 and 3.6, illustrating the structure of the core model, can change in size over time as a result of factor mobility, which in turn implies that the short-run equilibrium changes. Since labor is the only factor of production in the core model, we must therefore address labor mobility. Some information in this respect is given in chapter 9. At this point it suffices to note that one would expect the mobile workers to react to differences in the real wage w, which adequately measures the utility level achieved, rather than the (numéraire) wage rate W. We have already determined the real wage in section 3.4 (see equation (3.8)). All we have to do now is note that these real wages may differ between regions (see equation (3.25')).

Adjustment of the short-run equilibrium over time is now simple. If the real wage for manufacturing workers is higher in region 1 than in region 2, we expect manufacturing workers to leave region 2 and settle in region 1. If the real wage is higher in region 2 than in region 1, we expect the reverse to hold.

We let the parameter η denote the speed with which manufacturing workers react to differences in the real wage, and use the simple dynamic system

$$\frac{d\lambda_1}{\lambda_1} = \eta(w_1 - \bar{w}) \tag{3.26}$$

where $\bar{w} = \lambda_1 w_1 + \lambda_2 w_2$. Note that $\bar{w}$ gives the average real wage in the economy. A similar equation holds for region 2. This essentially ad hoc dynamic specification can be grounded in evolutionary game theory (see Weibull, 1995, and box 3.4).

Box 3.4 The burden of history and the role of expectations

History can be decisive. The term "history" is used here in a very broad sense, and can imply differences in, for example, tastes, technology, or factor endowments. Past circumstances can decisively influence future outcomes. In his famous, but not undisputed, QWERTY keyboard example, Paul David (1985) argues that relatively small, and at first sight unimportant, factors can cause certain technologies to become "locked in" – that is, the initial advantage of a certain technology is almost impossible to overcome by new technologies (see also figure 2.5). His example involves the QWERTY keyboard layout of typewriters, which, once established, became impossible to substitute for other (perhaps more efficient) keyboard layouts. Another example of the same principle is the fate of competitive tape recording systems in the early days of video cassette recorders, a contest that the VHS system clearly won, even though many experts argued that other systems were technically superior.[15]

Expectations may be the most important force determining which specific long-run equilibrium gets established. Expectations become particularly important if one takes future earnings into consideration when making decisions. In the examples given above, the initial conditions determine the fate of an equilibrium; new entrants do no more than look at the present situation, and then decide what to do. In expectation-driven equilibria, the importance of future earnings is decisive. This holds, for example, for the role of computer technologies in the so-called "new economy" discussion, where network externalities are most important. The optimal choice for the adoption of a new technology depends crucially on what you expect other people will decide to use. The wider a specific technology is adopted the easier it is to exchange information with other people, and the more attractive this technology becomes. For example, if all other economists use Microsoft Word to write papers, it is easiest for you to do the same, since it makes it simpler for you to exchange information and work together. On the other hand, if all other economists use WordPerfect, it is best for you to also use WordPerfect, and similarly for Scientific Word, etc. The desirability of making a specific choice, therefore, depends on how many others make the

---

[15] For an entertaining collection of examples in which historical accident, initial conditions, and the successive arrival of newcomers in the market determine the final equilibrium, see Schelling (1978).

Box 3.4 (cont.)

same choice and increases with the number of participants. These technology-related network structures result in the possibility of multiple equilibria, in which the outcome is purely a matter of a self-fulfilling prophecy (see Krugman, 1991b: 654).

To this date little empirical research is available to determine if expectations dominate history, or vice versa. The paper by Timothy Harris and Yannis Ioannides (2000) is a first attempt in this direction. History is, in principle, a strong force, but it by no means precludes a strong role for expectations. Harris and Ionannides extend the core model by introducing housing and land explicitly. Furthermore, they assume that labor is forward-looking and that workers are able to calculate the present value of wages in a specific city. The migration decision of workers influences the prices of land and housing, and thus influences the calculation of the present values. Conclusions can be drawn only with caution, but Harris and Ioannides (11) argue that "history rules and expectations at best help history along." Baldwin (1999) shows that the standard (ad hoc) migration behavior in geographical economics is consistent with optimal behavior, subject to quadratic migration costs and static expectations. The often criticized migration equation in the core model is therefore not as primitive as sometimes believed. The relative importance of history versus expectations depends crucially on adjustment costs, and as such might turn out to be mainly an empirical matter. In Europe, migration costs are often thought to be higher than in the United States, mainly as a result of the greater differences in language, historical background, and culture.

Now that we have specified how the manufacturing work force relocates to differences in the real wage between regions, we can also note when a long-run equilibrium is reached. This occurs when one of three possibilities arises: (i) the distribution of the manufacturing work force between regions 1 and 2 is such that the real wage is equal in the two regions, not necessarily the symmetric equilibrium; (ii) all manufacturing workers are located in region 1; or (iii) all manufacturing workers are located in region 2.

Technical note 3.8 Deriving the price index effect around the spreading equilibrium

To derive the price index effect for small changes around the symmetric equilibrium, write equation (3.23') as $I_1{}^{1-\varepsilon} = [\lambda_1 W_1{}^{1-\varepsilon} + \lambda_2 T^{1-\varepsilon} W_2{}^{1-\varepsilon}]$ and totally differentiate:

$$(1-\varepsilon)I_1^{-\varepsilon}dI_1 = \overbrace{W_1^{1-\varepsilon}d\lambda_1}^{a} + \overbrace{(1-\varepsilon)\lambda_1 W_1^{-\varepsilon}dW_1}^{b} +$$

$$\underbrace{T^{1-\varepsilon}W_2^{1-\varepsilon}d\lambda_2}_{c} + \underbrace{(1-\varepsilon)\lambda_2 T^{1-\varepsilon}W_2^{-\varepsilon}dW_2}_{d} + \underbrace{(1-\varepsilon)\lambda_2 T^{-\varepsilon}W_2^{1-\varepsilon}dT}_{e} \qquad (*)$$

Technical note 3.8 (cont.)

Around the spreading equilibrium, the changes are identical but of opposite sign, so defining $dI \equiv dI_1 = -dI_2$, $dW \equiv dW_1 = -dW_2$, and $d\lambda \equiv d\lambda_1 = -d\lambda_2$ allows us to combine terms a and c and terms b and d. First collecting terms and ignoring changes in transport costs (i.e. term e is zero), subsequently evaluating at the symmetric equilibrium with $\lambda \equiv \lambda_1 = \lambda_2 = 1/2$, $W \equiv W_1 = W_2 = 1$, and $I^{1-\varepsilon} \equiv I_1^{1-\varepsilon} = I_2^{1-\varepsilon} = \lambda(1 + T^{1-\varepsilon})$, and finally dividing by the term $(1-\varepsilon)\lambda(1 + T^{1-\varepsilon})$ simplifies (*) in steps to

$$(1-\varepsilon)I^{1-\varepsilon}\frac{dI}{I} = (1-T^{1-\varepsilon})\lambda W^{1-\varepsilon}\frac{d\lambda}{\lambda} + (1-\varepsilon)(1-T^{1-\varepsilon})\lambda W^{1-\varepsilon}\frac{dW}{W}$$

$$(1-\varepsilon)\lambda(1+T^{1-\varepsilon})\frac{dI}{I} = (1-T^{1-\varepsilon})\lambda W^{1-\varepsilon}\frac{d\lambda}{\lambda} + (1-\varepsilon)(1-T^{1-\varepsilon})\lambda W^{1-\varepsilon}\frac{dW}{W}$$

$$\frac{dI}{I} = -\frac{1}{(\varepsilon-1)}\frac{(1-T^{1-\varepsilon})}{(1+T^{1-\varepsilon})}\frac{d\lambda}{\lambda} + \frac{(1-T^{1-\varepsilon})}{(1+T^{1-\varepsilon})}\frac{dW}{W}$$

Let $Z \equiv (1-T^{1-\varepsilon})/(1+T^{1-\varepsilon})$. This definition of Z can be interpreted as an index of trade costs; in the absence of transport costs (T = 1), Z is equal to zero, while Z approaches one if transport costs become arbitrarily high (T → ∞). If we denote relative changes by a tilde ($\tilde{x} \equiv dx/x$), use the index of trade costs Z, and note from the optimal price equation (3.12) that wage changes are proportional to price changes ($\tilde{p} = \tilde{W}$) and from equation (3.15) that labor force changes are proportional to changes in the number of varieties ($\tilde{\lambda} = \tilde{N}$), we can also write the last expression as $\tilde{I} = Z\tilde{p} - [Z/(\varepsilon-1)]\tilde{N}$.

What are the main economic forces that are at work in determining whether a worker relocates to another region? The model we have analyzed in this chapter is non-linear, and therefore complicated. At the symmetric equilibrium, however, we can illustrate the three main economic forces that are at work in the model. Two of these forces stimulate agglomeration: *the price index effect*, and *the home market effect*. The third force stimulates spreading: *the extent-of-competition effect*. The balance between these forces determines if it is beneficial to relocate to the other region. The analysis around the symmetric equilibrium allows for important simplifications. Define the index of trade costs $Z \equiv (1-T^{1-\varepsilon})/(1+T^{1-\varepsilon})$, which varies from zero to one as transport costs rise. We denote variables at the spreading equilibrium without a sub-index and let a tilde denote relative changes ($\tilde{x} \equiv dx/x$) in order to discuss the three forces at work.

- *The price index effect.* Technical note 3.8 shows that differentiation of the price index equation (3.23') around the spreading equilibrium leads to $\tilde{I} = Z\tilde{p} - [Z/(\varepsilon - 1)]\tilde{N}$. Assume for the moment that the supply of labor is perfectly elastic, such that from equation (3.12) we have $\tilde{W} = \tilde{p} = 0$. In that case $\tilde{I} = -[Z/(\varepsilon - 1)]\tilde{N}$, which shows that the price index falls if a location becomes larger and is able to offer more varieties. This so-called price index effect makes the larger region more attractive, because a smaller share of the varieties have to be imported at (large) transportation costs.

- *The home market effect.* Applying a similar procedure to the one used in technical note 3.8 to the wage equation (3.25′) leads to (see exercise 3.7) $\varepsilon\tilde{W} = Z\tilde{Y} + (\varepsilon - 1)Z\tilde{I}$. Substitute the total price index effect $\tilde{I} = Z\tilde{p} - [Z/(\varepsilon - 1)]\tilde{N}$ into this result, use $\tilde{W} = \tilde{p}$, and solve for the change in income to get

$$\tilde{Y} = Z\tilde{N} + \left[\frac{\varepsilon}{Z} + (1 - \varepsilon)Z\right]\tilde{W} \qquad (3.27)$$

Recall from equation (3.15) that changes in the number of varieties are proportional to changes in the labor force, such that $\tilde{N}$ can also be interpreted as such. If we again assume a perfectly elastic labor supply, $\tilde{W} = 0$ and equation (3.27) simplifies to $\tilde{Y} = Z\tilde{N}$. Since $0 \leq Z \leq 1$, this implies that the larger market has a *more* than proportional gain in the number of varieties. This so-called home market effect makes the larger region more attractive. Empirical research (see chapter 5) frequently does not assume a perfectly elastic labor supply, and therefore uses equation (3.27) in many applications. The testable implication is that in that case larger markets pay higher wages.

- *The extent-of-competition effect.* This final effect is immediately clear by studying $c_1 = (p_1^{-\varepsilon})(\delta Y_1 I_1^{\varepsilon - 1} + \delta Y_2 T^{1 - \varepsilon} I_2^{\varepsilon - 1})$. We have already established that the price index in the larger market becomes smaller. For an individual firm, given p_i, this reduces the demand as its competitive position declines.

It is the balance between these three forces that determines whether, once a firm relocates, others will follow. Box 3.5 illustrates these forces graphically.

Box 3.5 Agglomeration and spreading forces: a simple diagram

It is instructive to take a closer look at this specific example, because it can be used to illustrate the economic forces that work in the model (this example is taken from Neary, 2001). Figure 3.8 illustrates profit maximization for a single firm in the market.

Box 3.5 (cont.)

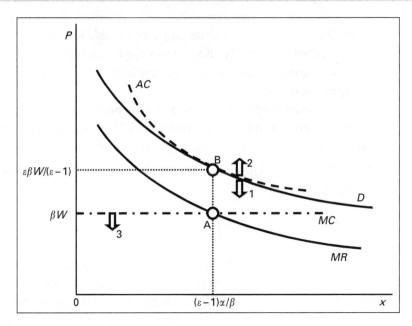

Figure 3.8   Monopolistic competition

The volume of sales is depicted along the horizontal axis, and the price along the vertical axis. The D, AC, MC, and MR lines are the demand curve, the average cost curve, the marginal cost curve, and the marginal revenue curve respectively. As always, the intersection of the MR and MC lines gives the profit-maximizing volume of sales (point A), $x = a(\varepsilon - 1)/\beta$, and the corresponding price $P = \frac{\varepsilon}{\varepsilon-1} \cdot \beta W$ (point B). In B the AC and D curves are tangent, because of the zero-profit condition. In this partial equilibrium setting it is easy to see what happens, starting from the spreading equilibrium, if one firm decides to move from region 1 to region 2. If this raises profits in region 1 the initial equilibrium was unstable and more firms will follow; if it lowers profits the initial equilibrium was stable and the firm has an incentive to return.

We can distinguish two immediate effects. The first is the extent-of-competition effect, which shifts the demand curve (indicated by arrow 1 in the figure) and the corresponding MR curve down. It follows immediately from equation (3.6), and given that an increase in the number of firms (varieties) lowers the price index, that this price index effect reduces the demand for each individual firm. This effect stimulates spreading. The second effect is that the new firm (and the corresponding labor force) raises income. This can be due either to more workers or to an increase in the demand for labor, leading to wage increases. The subsequent income increase shifts the demand curve upward; the combination of equations (3.22) and (3.24) makes this clear (indicated by arrow 2 in the figure). This effect is related to the home market effect, and stimulates agglomeration.

Box 3.5 (cont.)

A third (agglomerating) force in this example (indicated in figure 3.8 by arrow 3) is related to what we have called the price index effect. Starting from the symmetric equilibrium, if one firm decides to move to region 1 this reduces the cost of living in the larger region, making the region attractive for further migration. Migration finally stops when real wages are equalized between regions. As β is constant, this implies that in figure 3.8 the MC and AC curves shift downward, raising profitability and thus providing an extra agglomerating force (for a complete analytical analysis of all effects in figure 3.8, combined, see Neary, 2001).

3.10 Conclusions

We started our discussion of the core model of geographical economics with an example in section 3.2, and concluded with a warning: an example is just an example. We then provided a complete model that filled in the blanks of the example. We can now check if the five important characteristics of the example really are present in the more sophisticated model.

(1) *Cumulative causation.* In the example in section 3.2 it was argued that, if, for some reason, one region has attracted more manufacturing firms than the other region, a new firm has an incentive to locate where the other firms are. In the core model this is clearly visible in equation (3.20), since an increase in local income leads to a higher increase in demand than the same income increase in the other region.

(2) *Multiple equilibria.* It was pointed out in the example in section 3.2 that there may be multiple long-run equilibria; in particular, agglomeration of all firms in North, agglomeration of all firms in South, and a 1:3 distribution of firms between North and South. Similarly, in the discussion of the core model in subsection 3.8.2, three short-run equilibria were discussed, namely agglomeration in region 1, agglomeration in region 2, and spreading of manufacturing activity over the two regions. The remarks on dynamics in section 3.9 show that all three of these short-run equilibria are also long-run equilibria (see the next point).

(3) *Stable and unstable equilibria.* Although we never analyzed a dynamic system, we argued in the example in section 3.2 that there can be stable and unstable equilibria. In particular, agglomeration of firms in either North or South is a stable equilibrium, while the 1:3 distribution of

firms between North and South is an unstable equilibrium. A similar observation holds for the core model. There are, however, three important qualifications, namely (i) we specifically introduce a dynamic system in section 3.9, (ii) the analysis of this system is not easy, and is therefore postponed to chapter 4, and (iii), as we demonstrate in chapter 4, both agglomeration and/or spreading of manufacturing activity can be a stable equilibrium.

(4) *Non-optimal equilibria.* In the example in section 3.2 we saw that one long-run equilibrium might be better than another long-run equilibrium from a welfare point of view. Note that we have four different economic agents in the core model of sections 3.3 to 3.9, namely the manufacturing workers in both regions, and the farmers in both regions. This reduces to three economic agents in the long-run equilibrium, in which the real wage is the same for all manufacturing workers. Suppose we take a closer look at the agglomeration equilibria described in subsection 3.8.2. Assume for the moment that the agglomeration equilibria are stable (remember that this is analyzed in chapter 4). Some possibilities are illustrated in table 3.5, and discussed below.

In section 3.8, the farmers are divided equally between the two regions. From a welfare point of view, it then does not matter whether manufacturing is agglomerated in region 1 or in region 2. This is illustrated in the first part of table 3.5, but this observation requires some explanation. Suppose that manufacturing is agglomerated in region 1. This is good news for the farmers in region 1 (their welfare = 10 in table 3.5), because they have easy access to a large number of locally produced varieties. It is bad news for the farmers in region 2 (their welfare = 5), because they have to import all manufacturing varieties from region 1. Now suppose instead that all manufacturing is agglomerated in region 2. This time it is good news for the farmers in region 2, and bad news for the farmers in region 1. To the manufacturing workers it does not matter where they are agglomerated, as their real wage is the same (12 in table 3.5). Since total welfare is essentially the sum of the real wage of all economic agents, and the number of farmers is exactly evenly distributed between the two regions, it does not matter from a total welfare point of view whether manufacturing is agglomerated in region 1 or in region 2 (it clearly does matter for individual economic agents, notably the farmers; total welfare = 171 in either case in table 3.5).

Table 3.5 Total welfare and distribution of food production

	Agglomeration in region 1				Agglomeration in region 2		
	# labor	Welf/cap	Total		# labor	Welf/cap	Total
Even distribution of food production (50 percent in region 1)							
Farm. 1	5	10	50	Farm. 1	5	5	25
Man. 1	8	12	96	Man. 1	0	–	–
Farm. 2	5	5	25	Farm. 2	5	10	50
Man. 2	0	–	–	Man. 2	8	12	96
Total welfare			171	Total welfare			171
Uneven distribution of food production (60 percent in region 1)							
Farm. 1	6	10	60	Farm. 1	6	5	30
Man. 1	8	12	96	Man. 1	0	–	–
Farm. 2	4	5	20	Farm. 2	4	10	40
Man. 2	0	–	–	Man. 2	8	12	96
Total welfare			176	Total welfare			166

Notes: The numbers in the table are for illustrative purposes only. Farm. = farm workers, Man. = manufacturing workers, # labor = number of workers in that region, Welf/cap = welfare per capita.

A similar argument does not hold if the immobile activity – that is, food production – is unevenly distributed, as it is in the example in section 3.2. This is illustrated in the second part of table 3.5, in which 60 percent of the farmers are located in region 1, and 40 percent in region 2. Again, the agglomeration of manufacturing in region 1 is good news for the farmers in region 1, and bad news for the farmers in region 2. Once more, these roles are reversed if manufacturing agglomerates in region 2. This time, however, the agglomeration of manufacturing in region 1 is better from a total welfare point of view, simply because more farmers can then benefit, through the love-of-variety effect, from the local production of manufactures. This is analyzed in more detail in chapter 4.

(5) *Interaction of agglomeration and trade flows.* In the example in section 3.2, we noted that the so-called homemarket effect was a crucial aspect of geographical economics. Helpman and Krugman (1985: 197) observe "the tendency of increasing returns industries, other things equal, to concentrate near their larger markets and to export to smaller markets." This effect is caused by the interaction of external and internal economies of scale. Firms want to locate near demand, where they can benefit from a larger market and possible

spillovers (see arrow 2 in figure 3.8). These scale economies result in increasing-returns activities being pulled towards large markets, and the more so if these locations have good access to other markets. Because activities are attracted towards the preferred locations, (real) wages increase and labor has an incentive to migrate towards these locations, increasing the attractiveness even further. In the end, a disproportionately large share of activity ends up in these preferred locations, and this region becomes a net exporter of manufactures. Hence the name "home market effect."

It is important to see that the introduction of transportation costs is the determining factor for this effect. A comparison between Krugman (1980) and his 1979 article makes this point clear. What happens if trade is allowed between a large and small country in the absence of transport costs? One might expect a home market effect, with the larger country exporting manufactures and importing the homogeneous product. This is not the case. Free trade ensures that the prices of all varieties are equalized between countries, and in the absence of transport costs this also equalizes wages. Furthermore, production costs are not affected by the presence of other firms in the same location. The trade structure is therefore indeterminate: production of manufactures can take place anywhere; no location has a natural cost advantage over the other. With free trade, however, the total number of varieties available for consumers in each country increases. This in essence determines the gains from trade in the model. The introduction of transport costs changes this dramatically by creating the home market effect, as already shown in Krugman (1980). Concentrating the production of manufactures in the larger market makes it possible to benefit from scale economies, and at the same time economize on transport costs. This increases the real wages of manufacturing workers in the larger market, which makes this region the more attractive place to live.

Finally, we can already say something about the structure of trade between the regions by comparing the spreading equilibrium and the agglomeration equilibria with each other. Suppose, for example, that manufacturing production is agglomerated in region 1. In that case, the farmers in region 2 have to import all manufacturing varieties from region 1. Region 2 thus exports food in exchange for manufacturing varieties, an example of pure inter-industry trade – that is, trade between regions of different types of goods. In contrast, suppose that manufacturing production is spread evenly over the two regions, as is food production (the symmetric equilibrium), using the specification of section 3.8. There it is shown that $Y_1 = Y_2 = 1/2$ in this case, which implies that the demand for food in either region is equal to $(1-\delta)$ $Y_1 = (1-\delta)/2$. Since the production level of food in, for example, region 1 is equal to $\phi_1(1-\gamma)L = (1/2)(1-\delta)1 = (1-\delta)/2$ (see section 3.8), it follows that the total demand for food in region 1 is equal to the total production of food in region 1. In the spreading equilibrium, there is therefore no trade of food between the two regions. Since all consumers will spend money on all manufacturing varieties, including those produced in the other region, there will be trade in manufacturing varieties between the two regions. This is thus an example of pure intra-industry trade – that is, trade between regions of similar types of goods (importing manufacturing varieties in exchange for other manufacturing varieties).

It is now time to analyze the main implications of the core model of geographical economics more formally in the next chapter.

Exercises

3.1 From introductory microeconomics we know that the condition for profit maximization for a firm is $MC = MR$ – that, is marginal costs equal marginal revenue. Under perfect competition this condition implies that $MC = p$ – that is, marginal cost is equal to the price of a good (marginal cost pricing). Now use figure 3.8 to show that, with the average cost curve in the core model (use (3.12)), marginal cost pricing always results in a loss for the firm, implying that imperfect competition is the dominant market form.

3.2 Start again from the example in section 3.2, but now assume that each firm has the ability to open a second plant in the other region. Each firm minimizes the combined costs of setting up a second plant and transportation costs. Suppose setting up a firm costs two units. Decide where to locate given the location of the other firms.
 (i) If all other firms have a single firm in South, what is optimal for our firm?
 (ii) Suppose all firms have two plants, one in each location; what is optimal for our firm?

3.3* Suppose we start with a situation of complete agglomeration of manufacturing production in region 1 – that is, $\lambda_1 = 1$. Without calculating the equilibrium values explicitly one might suspect that $W_1 = 1$ is the equilibrium value in this case. Substituting this in the income and price equations we find

$$Y_1 = \frac{(1+\delta)}{2} \qquad Y_2 = \frac{(1-\delta)}{2} \qquad I_1 = 1 \qquad I_2 = T$$

Using these values, $W_1 = 1$ is indeed an equilibrium value for wages in region 1, as can be verified from (3.24′). Real wages also equal one in region 1. Calculate under which condition this is always a long-run equilibrium no matter how large transportation costs become.

Hint: use the expression for real wages in region 2 for this case and let T become arbitrarily large. Show that this happens only if $(\varepsilon - 1) - \varepsilon\delta < 0$.

3.4* Suppose a monopolistic producer located in region 1 can either sell in region 1 or in region 2. Let p_{11} (p_{12}) be the price charged in region 1 (respectively in region 2), and let x_{11} (x_{12}) be the demand in region 1 (respectively in region 2). Obviously, the demand functions depend on the price charged in whichever region. Production requires only labor as an input, which is paid wage rate W_1, and benefits from internal returns to scale, using a fixed labor and β variable labor. Finally, there are (iceberg) transport costs: the firm must produce Tx_{12} units to ensure x_{12} can be sold in region 2, with $T > 1$. The firm's profit π and demand functions x_{11} and x_{12} ($\varepsilon > 1$, while Y_1 and Y_2 are constants) are given below:

$$\pi = p_{11}x_{11} + p_{12}x_{12} - W_1(a + \beta x_{11} + \beta T x_{12})$$

$$x_{11} = p_{11}^{-\varepsilon} Y_1; \qquad x_{12} = p_{12}^{-\varepsilon} Y_2$$

First, give some comments on the profit function above. Second, substitute the demand functions in the profit function. Third, determine what the optimal prices p_{11} and p_{12} are – that is solve the profit maximization problem. Fourth, show that $p_{12} = Tp_{11}$ – that is, that the optimal price charged in region 2 is exactly T times higher than that charged in region 1.

3.5* In the example in section 3.2 we showed that some equilibria are better from a welfare perspective than other equilibria. Can you show this using (3.22′) to (3.25′)? Assume that the farmers are not symmetrically distributed over both regions. Suppose region 1 has one-third of all farmers and region 2 two-thirds of all farmers. Can you show that, from a welfare point of view, agglomeration in region 2 is better than agglomeration in region 1, as might be expected because region 2 potentially has the larger market?

Hint: make sure that complete agglomeration in region 1 and complete agglomeration in region 2 are both equilibria. Use the resulting equations to show that (U indicates utility)

for $\lambda_1 = 1$ we have $U_{\lambda=1} = 1 + \frac{(1-\delta)}{3} + \frac{2}{3}(1-\delta)T^{-\delta}$

and for $\lambda_1 = 0$ we have $U_{\lambda=0} = 1 + \frac{2}{3}(1-\delta) + \frac{(1-\delta)}{3}T^{-\delta}$

3.6* In technical note 3.7 we state that the normalizations we propose do not effect the outcomes of the model.

(i) Show that this is indeed the case.

(ii) We also "normalize" γ by setting it equal to δ. Is this allowed (hint: the answer is "No," but show why not)?

3.7* Technical note 3.8 derives the price index effect around the spreading equilibrium. Following a similar procedure, do the same for the home market effect by first rewriting equation (3.25'), then totally differentiating this equation, and subsequently collecting terms and evaluating at the spreading equilibrium to show that $\varepsilon \tilde{W} = Z\tilde{Y} + (\varepsilon - 1)Z\tilde{I}$.

4 Beyond the core model: solutions, simulations, and extensions

4.1 Introduction

In chapter 3 we developed and discussed the main features of the core model of geographical economics. Most importantly, the model provides a coherent framework: it is a miniature world in which the demand in one region for the manufactures of another region is not exogenously imposed but derived from the income generated in the region through production and exports. Although we set up the different aspects of the model as simple and tractable as possible, it turned out to be quite complex to study analytically.

This chapter builds on the analysis of chapter 3. First, we give a full analysis of the core model derived in chapter 3. Using simulations, we learn to understand what the long-run equilibria look like in the core model (thus endogenizing λ_r, the share of the manufacturing labor force in region r). As shown below, the so-called *break point* and *sustain point* will help us to summarize the long-run characteristics of the core model. Second, we show how these new insights regarding the core model of chapter 3 enable us to analyze some other important models in geographical economics. More specifically, we discuss three alternative models, each of which by now has also gained the reputation of being a "core" model of geographical economics.

  (i) *Intermediate goods model.* In the absence of interregional labor mobility, the main agglomeration mechanism is connection to suppliers of intermediate goods.

 (ii) *Generalized model.* Incorporating both the core model of chapter 3 and the intermediate goods model allows for a richer menu of long-run equilibria.

(iii) *Solvable model.* Identifying different factors of production in the manufacturing sector allows for explicit analytical solutions.

Section 4.2 explains in detail what computer simulations are and what they can and cannot do. Section 4.3 then shows how computer simulations can be used to better understand the core model of chapter 3, thus providing information on the determination of the long-run equilibrium. Section 4.4 then shows how shocks in a key model parameter (transport costs T) affect the long-run spatial distribution of manufacturing workers. The simulations in these sections are useful in order to get a "feel" for the workings of the core model. These intuitive findings point in the direction of two new and important concepts, which is the topic of section 4.5. Here, the analysis centers around the twin concepts of the *sustain point* (is full agglomeration sustainable?) and the *break point* (when does the spreading equilibrium become unstable?). The three alternative models (i) to (iii) mentioned above, which are all firmly rooted in the core model of chapter 3, are dealt with in sections 4.6 to 4.8 respectively. Most of the examples and simulations in this chapter focus on the case of two regions, where space itself is (deliberately) inherently neutral. Section 4.9 maintains the neutral space setting, while extending the core model to a multi-region framework in the so-called "racetrack economy." Section 4.10 concludes.

4.2 Beyond the short-run equilibrium: introducing simulations

The analytical framework of the previous chapter can be generalized to R regions using the normalizations of table 3.4 as follows:[1]

$$Y_r = \delta\lambda_r W_r + (1 - \delta)\phi_r \tag{4.1}$$

$$I_r = \left[\sum_{s=1}^{R} \lambda_s T_{rs}^{1-\varepsilon} W_s^{1-\varepsilon}\right]^{1/(1-\varepsilon)} \tag{4.2}$$

$$W_r = \left[\sum_{s=1}^{R} Y_s T_{sr}^{1-\varepsilon} I_s^{\varepsilon-1}\right]^{1/\varepsilon} \tag{4.3}$$

This set of equations for each region $r = 1, \ldots, R$ together determines income level Y_r, price index I_r, and wage rate W_r for each region r. In this short-run equilibrium, world demand for food and each variety of

---

[1] See also the (*) equations in technical notes 3.5 and 3.6.

manufactures is equal to world supply and no producer is earning excess profits. To be of any geographic interest at all, we need at least two locations ($R \geq 2$). This implies that we have to investigate at least six simultaneous, non-linear equations – a sufficiently daunting task to escape analytical tractability (although some analytical results will be derived later). How should we proceed from here?

This is the point at which we hail and glorify the benefits of the computer era, which allows us to tackle models such as the core geographical economics model by means of computer *simulations*. Five requirements must be met for these simulations to work for the core model. First, we must be clear what it is we are solving for. The short-run equilibrium determines the *endogenous* variables income Y_r, price index I_r, and wage rate W_r for each region r (and in doing so also gives us the real wages; see below). So we must find solutions to the equations above for these variables – that is determine numeric values of Y_r, I_r, and W_r for which equations (4.1) to (4.3) hold.

Second, it be must realized that the solutions for the endogenous variables depend on the values of λ_r (the distribution of the mobile labor force, which is fixed in the short run) and the values of all the *parameters* (γ, δ, ϕ_r, ε, and T; we recall that $T_{rs} = T^{D_{rs}}$ and D_{rs} is the economic distance between regions r and s, with $D_{rs} = 1$ for the case of two regions). This implies in particular that we cannot start to find solutions for the endogenous variables before specifying values for the exogenous variables and parameters. To start with the latter, table 4.1 specifies parameter values for the two-region "base scenario." Note that $\lambda_1 + \lambda_2 = 1 = \gamma L$, which gives the distribution of labor between the two regions. In the base scenario the share of income spent on manufactures (δ) is chosen fairly low at 0.4, while the substitution parameter ε, with $\varepsilon = 1/(1 - \rho)$, and the transport costs (T) are chosen fairly high, at 5 ($\rho = 0.8$) and 1.7 respectively. The rest of table 4.1 shows that the total number of laborers (L) is one, while immobile (= agricultural) production is equally large in both regions ($\phi_1 = \phi_2 = 0.5$). The latter is an important assumption, because it implies that the two regions are identical with respect to all parameters listed in table 4.1. The final parameter in table 4.1, σ, is discussed below.

Why have we chosen this set of base scenario parameters in table 4.1? To some degree, the choice is arbitrary. This holds in particular for the share of income spent on manufactures δ and the elasticity of substitution ε between manufacturing varieties. Both parameters have been chosen based on reasonable empirical estimates, to be discussed further in the

Going beyond: solutions, simulations, extensions

Table 4.1 Base scenario parameter configuration, two regions

$\delta = 0.4$	$\varepsilon = 5$	$T = 1.7$
$L = 1$	$\phi_1 = \phi_2 = 0.5$	$\sigma = 0.0001$

remainder of this book. Given the choice of δ and ε, the value of the transport costs T is chosen to demonstrate an important aspect of the core model of geographical economics as illustrated in figure 4.1 and discussed below.

Third, we must specify a *solution method*, a well-specified procedure that will lead us to solving equations (4.1) to (4.3) for numeric values of the endogenous variables, given the chosen levels of the exogenous variables and parameters. Several options are available at this point, and we use some of them in this book, but the order of equations (4.1) to (4.3) readily suggests a method, termed sequential iterations, to be used in this chapter. It works as follows for the case of two regions.

(i) Guess an initial solution for the wage rate in the two regions, say ($W_{1,0}$, $W_{2,0}$), where 0 indicates the number of the iteration (we will use $W_{1,0} = W_{2,0} = 1$).

(ii) Using ($W_{1,0}$, $W_{2,0}$) calculate the income levels ($Y_{1,0}$, $Y_{2,0}$) and price index ($I_{1,0}$, $I_{2,0}$) as implied by equations (4.1) and (4.2) respectively.

(iii) Using ($Y_{1,0}$, $Y_{2,0}$) and ($I_{1,0}$, $I_{2,0}$) as calculated in step (*ii*), determine a new possible solution for the wage rate ($W_{1,1}$, $W_{2,1}$) as implied by equation (4.3).

(iv) Repeat steps (*ii*) and (*iii*) until a solution is found.

Note that equations (4.1) to (4.3) are used repeatedly in sequence to find a solution – hence the name of the method.

Fourth, a *stopping criterion* must be specified. The above description of the solution method casually mentioned in step (*iv*) to "Repeat steps (*ii*) and (*iii*) until a solution is found," but when *is* a solution found? How close should we get to be satisfied that the numeric values we have found are indeed a solution to equations (4.1) to (4.3)? We used as a stopping criterion the condition that the relative change in the wage rate should not exceed some small value σ from one iteration to the next for all regions r – that is

$$\frac{W_{r,iteration} - W_{r,iteration-1}}{W_{r,iteration-1}} < \sigma, \text{ for all } r.$$

Table 4.1 indicates that we chose the value $\sigma = 0.0001$ for our simulations.

Fifth, and finally, we must choose a *programming language* and write a small program to actually be able to perform the above calculations. Again, several options are available, but we used Gauss™, a widely used and versatile mathematical programming language, for all our simulations. Examples of these programs can be found on the book's website.

4.3 Some first results

After explaining in some detail in section 4.2 how to perform simulations in principle, it is time to show and discuss the results of some actual simulations. It was, deliberately, *not* specified in section 4.2 what the value of the variable λ_r (the share of the mobile work force in region r) was in the two-region base scenario, although it was mentioned that such a specification is needed to perform simulations. The reason for this omission is, quite simply, that we do not want to use simulations just to find *a* solution for a given parameter setting of the model, but also to learn something about the structure of our model – notably, by investigating how the short-run equilibrium (Y_r, I_r, W_r) changes if λ_r changes as well, as we do in this section. In fact, the difference between the short run and long run equilibrium in the core model is precisely that λ_r is given in the short-run but not in the long-run. The claim to fame by geographical economics is (recall chapter 2) that the spatial distribution of economic activity is not taken as given but has to be determined by the model. This is why the understanding of the core model in the long run is so important.

Assuming that there are just two regions is particularly useful for illustrative purposes. After all, specifying λ_1 automatically implies λ_2 by using $\lambda_1 + \lambda_2 = 1$. Varying λ_1 between zero and one therefore gives a complete description of all possible distributions of the mobile workforce in a two-region setting. If we find another variable that interests us we can depict its dependence on the distribution of the mobile workforce simply in a graph. Although we are interested in various aspects of the model, we first focus attention on the real wage in region 1 relative to the real wage in region 2, as it will give us an indication of the dynamic forces operating in the model. Recall that the real wage in region r is given by

$$w_r = W_r I_r^{-\delta} \tag{4.4}$$

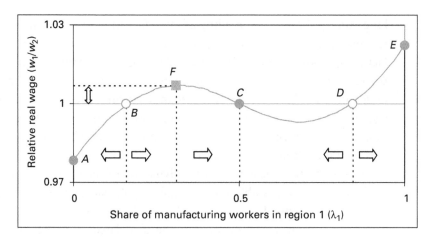

Figure 4.1   The relative real wage in region 1

which implies that, once we have found a short-run equilibrium for a particular distribution of the mobile labor force – that is, a solution to equations (4.1) to (4.3) – it is trivial to calculate the real wage in all regions using equation (4.4), and thus the relative real wage w_1/w_2.

Figure 4.1 illustrates how the relative real wage in region 1 (w_1/w_2) varies as the share of the mobile workforce in region 1 (λ_1) varies. The figure is the result of fifty-nine separate simulations in which the value of λ_1 is gradually increased from zero to one. Each time, the short-run equilibrium, the solution to equations (4.1) to (4.3), is calculated using the procedure described in section 4.2. Then the real wage in the two regions is calculated using equation (4.4), which determines w_1/w_2, and therefore one observation in figure 4.1. Figure 4.1 is very important, and we return to it time and again in subsequent chapters.

What can we learn from figure 4.1? First, recall that we argued in chapter 3 that the mobile part of the labor force, manufacturing labor, has an incentive to move to regions with a higher real wage, such that a short-run equilibrium is also a long-run equilibrium if, and only if, the real wage for the mobile workforce is the same in all regions. That is to say, a long-run equilibrium requires that the relative real wage is one as long as there are mobile laborers in both regions. It is only when a long-run equilibrium implies complete agglomeration (one region ends up with all mobile laborers, either $\lambda_1 = 1$ or $\lambda_2 = 1$) that the relative real wage is not equal to one (see points A and E).[2] In figure 4.1, the long-run equilibria B, C, and D are reached for $w_1/w_2 = 1$. Chapter 3 heuristically found two types of

---

[2] If there is complete agglomeration the relative real wage cannot actually be calculated, since there are no manufacturing workers in one of the regions. Points A and E in figure 4.1 are therefore limit values.

long-run equilibria: (i) spreading of manufacturing production over the two regions (point C in figure 4.1), and (ii) complete agglomeration of manufacturing production in either region 2 or region 1 (points A and E in figure 4.1 respectively). Figure 4.1 clearly illustrates that there is a third type of long-run equilibrium, in which manufacturing production is partially agglomerated in one of the two regions (see points B and D), leading to a total of five long-run equilibria. It would have been virtually impossible to find equilibria B and D analytically.

Second, we get a clear feel for the dynamics of the system, allowing us to distinguish between stable and unstable equilibria. Suppose, for example, that $\lambda_1 = F$ in figure 4.1. Note that the mobile workforce is larger in region 2 than in region 1. As illustrated, the associated short-run equilibrium implies $w_1/w_2 > 1$. The higher real wage in region 1 gives the mobile laborers an incentive to move from region 2 to region 1. This migration into region 1 represents an increase of λ_1 in figure 4.1. This process will continue until the spreading equilibrium at point C is reached, where the real wages are equalized. Similar reasoning, leading to the spreading equilibrium at point C, would hold for any arbitrary initial distribution of the mobile labor force strictly in between points B and D, which could therefore be called the "basin of attraction" for the spreading equilibrium. Thus, the spreading equilibrium is a stable equilibrium, in the sense that any deviation of the mobile labor force from point C within its basin of attraction will activate economic forces to bring us back to the spreading equilibrium.

Similar reasoning holds for the two complete agglomeration equilibria, points A and E, each with its own basin of attraction (from point A to point B, and from point D to point E, respectively). These stable equilibria are illustrated with closed circles in figure 4.1. In contrast, the partial agglomeration long-run equilibria, points B and D, are *un*stable, and are therefore illustrated with open circles. If, for whatever reason, we are initially at point B or D, a long-run equilibrium is reached in the sense that the real wages are equal for regions 1 and 2. Any arbitrarily small perturbation of this equilibrium will set in motion a process of adjustment, however, leading to a different (stable) long-run equilibrium. For example, a small negative disturbance of λ_1 at point B leads to complete agglomeration of manufacturing activity in region 2, while a small positive disturbance of λ_1 at point B leads to spreading of manufacturing activity.

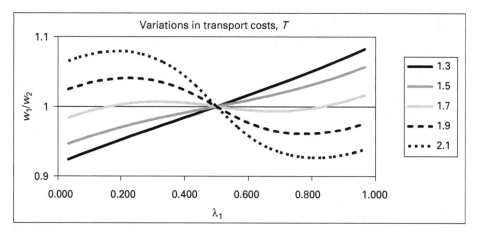

Figure 4.2   The impact of transport costs

4.4 Changes in transport costs and the introduction of the tomahawk

Transport costs are the main feature of space or geography in the core model; they are assumed to be zero within a region, but to be positive between two different regions. The term "transport costs" is a shorthand notation for many different types of obstacles to trade between locations, such as tariffs, language and culture barriers, and indeed the costs of actually getting goods or services at another location (see also box 3.1). A natural question is, therefore, what the effect of changes in transport costs are in the core model.[3] This question must be answered by repeating the simulation procedure of section 4.3 for different levels of transport costs. Figure 4.2 depicts the result of such simulations for five values of transport costs, namely $T = 1.3$, $T = 1.5$, $T = 1.7$, $T = 1.9$, and $T = 2.1$.

As figure 4.2 shows, if transport costs are large, say $T = 2.1$ or $T = 1.9$, and given the other parameters of the model (see table 4.1), the spreading equilibrium is the globally stable equilibrium. It makes intuitive sense that if manufactures are difficult to transport from one region to another the dynamics of the model lead to spreading of manufacturing activity: the

---

[3] Transport costs are obviously very important in the core model (without transport costs, there is no role for location or geography to begin with), but other parameters in the model also affect the outcomes. On the website accompanying this book, the reader can experiment with model parameters other than T.

distant provision of manufactures is too costly, and therefore they need to be provided locally. On the other hand, if transport costs are smaller, say $T = 1.3$ or $T = 1.5$, the spreading equilibrium is unstable while the agglomerating equilibria are stable, with an initial λ_1 between 0 and 0.5 as the basin of attraction for complete agglomeration in region 2, and an initial λ_1 between 0.5 and 1 as the basin of attraction for complete agglomeration in region 1. Again, this makes sense intuitively. With very low transport costs, the immobile market can be provided effectively from a distance, which therefore does not pose a strong enough force to counter the advantages of agglomeration (the home market effect). One may now start to get the feeling that the intermediate transport cost case, $T = 1.7$, in which the relative real wage crosses one in the interior three times, is special. In particular, after reading Krugman's initial paper on the core model of geographical economics, in which he concludes with respect to his version of figure 4.2 (Krugman, 1991a: 492; our notation)[4] that "it implicitly assumes that w_1/w_2 is a monotonic function . . . , or at least that it crosses one only once. In principle this need not be the case . . . I have not been able to rule this out analytically."

This immediately reveals another advantage of simulations: after only one counter-example produced by a simulation we can stop trying to rule something out analytically that cannot be ruled out. This brings us back to the question of whether the situation with intermediate transport costs, $T = 1.7$, as depicted in figure 4.1, is special or not. The answer is both "Yes" and "No," as decisively shown by Fujita, Krugman, and Venables (1999). "Yes" in the sense that it holds only for a fairly limited range of transport costs. "No" in the sense that, for any arbitrary parameter configuration as given in table 4.1, there are always a number of transport costs for which the relative real wage crosses one in the interior three times. We return to this issue in section 4.5.

It is instructive to look at the simulations and the resulting equilibria using a different illustration. In figure 4.1 we have put the relative real wage w_1/w_2 on the vertical axis and the distribution of the mobile workers λ on the horizontal axis. One could also put the share of the mobile workforce λ on the vertical axis and transportation costs T along the horizontal axis. With the help of figure 4.2 we already have some idea what such a figure would look like. Figure 4.3 depicts this case. In the literature this figure

---

[4] The analysis is performed, however, in Fujita, Krugman, and Venables (1999). See also, for instance, Baldwin *et al.* (2003: chap. 2) and Robert-Nicoud (2005) for an in-depth (and one may even say complete) analysis of the main (analytical) features of Krugman (1991a), the core model of geographical economics.

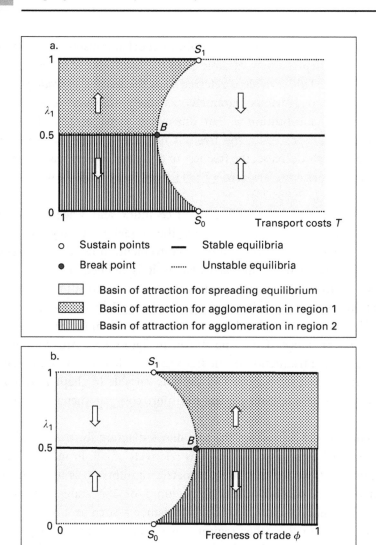

Figure 4.3   The tomahawk diagram

is known as the *tomahawk diagram*, because the combination of the solid lines looks like this type of axe (think of Winnetou in the books of Karl May). For ease of reference in later chapters, we depict two versions of the tomahawk diagram in figure 4.3. In panel a, we have transport costs T on the horizontal axis. From left to right in panel a, transport costs increase. In panel b, we depict a new variable ϕ on the horizontal axis, which is defined as $\varphi \equiv T^{1-\varepsilon}$. This variable is referred to as the *freeness of trade parameter*. It combines two previous parameters, namely transport costs T and the elasticity of substitution ε. For any given value of $\varepsilon > 1$ and infinite transport $(T=\infty)$ costs, the freeness of trade variable is zero $(\varphi=0)$. As transport costs decrease, the freeness of trade variable increases until, finally, when tranport costs are zero $(T=1)$ freeness of trade is unity $(\varphi=1$; see Baldwin *et al.*, 2003: 20).

Note that, in the equilibrium price index and wage equations (4.2) and (4.3), transport costs T enter the model invariably as $T^{1-\varepsilon}$. It is therefore straightforward, and often convenient, to use the freeness of trade variable instead of T, in particular as it is defined in a compact space (it varies from zero to one instead of from one to infinity). In terms of the tomahawk diagram in figure 4.3a, replacing T by the freeness of trade φ merely means that one ends up with a tomahawk in (φ, λ) space that is the *exact mirror image* of the one shown in figure 4.3a. Analytically, nothing changes: the introduction of the freeness of trade is just a notational matter. We introduce it here as we will use this variable in chapters to come. For now, we focus attention on the transport cost parameter T by discussing panel a.

What can we learn from the tomahawk diagram for the equilibria in the core model? First, assume that T is relatively small. From the line $T=1.3$ in figure 4.2, we see that the symmetric equilibrium is unstable, and also that complete agglomeration in region 1 or 2 is stable. Starting in the symmetric equilibrium, a small disturbance – such as a relocation of one of the firms to the other region – will lead to complete agglomeration. The area for which this holds in figure 4.3a is indicated by the two arrows that point away from the symmetric equilibrium. We can distinguish two basins of attraction, one for region 1 and one for region 2. For values of T that are small enough, these basins indicate that the larger region will attract *all* footloose labor from the other region: this is the circular causality discussed in chapters 2 and 3. The dashed line for the symmetric equilibrium indicates that it is an *un*stable equilibrium for values of T smaller than at point B.

Second, assume that T is relatively high. From the line $T=2.1$ in figure 4.2, we see that things change dramatically. Now complete agglomeration is unstable, but the symmetric equilibrium is stable, which is indicated by a solid line in figure 4.3a. This holds for values of T that are larger than S_0 or S_1. The arrows in the associated two basins of attraction now point towards the (stable) symmetric equilibrium.

Third, assume that T is larger than B, but smaller than S_0 (or S_1). From the line $T = 1.7$ in figure 4.2 we see that – besides the symmetric equilibrium and complete agglomeration – an additional long-run equilibrium arises in between complete agglomeration and the symmetric equilibrium. From figure 4.2 it is immediately clear that this is an unstable equilibrium. This equilibrium moves closer to the symmetric equilibrium if T becomes smaller in the area between B and S_0, and moves closer to complete agglomeration if T becomes larger. These unstable equilibria are indicated in figure 4.3a by the curved dashed lines that connect B to S_0 and B to S_1.

Our discussion of figure 4.3 makes the tomahawk diagram plausible. What should have become clear is that the points indicated by B, which is called the *break point*, and S_0 and S_1, which are called the *sustain points*, are rather special. In the next section we take a closer look at these two key concepts.

4.5 Sustain and break analysis

By analyzing and understanding the break and sustain points in the tomahawk diagram of figure 4.3, we can analyze how "special" the situation depicted in figure 4.1 (for $T = 1.7$), in which the relative real wage crosses one in the interior three times, really is. The simulation results shown in figure 4.2 and summarized in figure 4.3 are suggestive in this respect. It thus looks as if complete agglomeration is a stable equilibrium for small transport costs while the spreading equilibrium is stable for large transport costs. We analyze these two suggestions in this section in more detail. In doing so, we make use of and build on the analysis and terminology as initially developed in chapters 4 and 5 of Fujita, Krugman, and Venables (1999), as well as in Puga (1999). We urge the reader to become familiar with the analytical underpinnings of the break and sustain points, and thus of the tomahawk in subsection 4.5.1 below, even though this material is somewhat more advanced. Apart from the sustain and break points, this subsection also introduces two other important concepts: the *no-black-hole condition* and *path dependency*. In subsection 4.5.2 we provide a (closed-form) analytical solution for the break point.

4.5.1 Sustain and break points in the core model

Suppose that all manufacturing activity is located in region 1. Given the normalization $\phi_1 = \phi_2 = 0.5$ and the analysis in chapter 3, it is easy to verify that the solution to equations (4.1) to (4.3) if $\lambda_1 = 1$ is given by $W_1 = 1$, $Y_1 = (1 + \delta)/2$, $Y_2 = (1 - \delta)/2$, $I_1 = 1$, and $I_2 = T$. There are no manufacturing workers in region 2, so it is not really appropriate to talk of their wage W_2, but we can calculate what this wage would have been by using equation (4.3). Similarly, we can calculate the implied real wage w_2 by using equation (4.4). Noting that the real wage in region 1 (w_1) is equal to one, we see that it will be attractive for mobile workers located in region 1 to move to region 2 if the implied real wage in region 2 (w_2) is larger than one. If this is the case, complete agglomeration of manufacturing activity in region 1 is not "sustainable." Agglomeration is *not* sustainable if, and only if, equation (4.5) holds, where we use the fact that $\varepsilon = 1/(1 - \rho)$.

$$w_2^\varepsilon \equiv f(T) \equiv [(1 + \delta)/2]T^{-(\rho + \delta)\varepsilon} + [(1 - \delta)/2]T^{(\rho - \delta)\varepsilon} > 1 \qquad (4.5)$$

The value for $T (\neq 1)$ for which equation (4.5) is equal to one is the *sustain point*. It is implicitly defined by $[(1 + \delta)/2]T_S^{-(\rho + \delta)\varepsilon} + [(1 - \delta)/2]T_S^{(\rho - \delta)\varepsilon} = 1$. The function $f(T)$ is illustrated in figure 4.4 and figure A4.1 in the appendix. It shows that the real wage in region 2 is only a function of T. Note that $f(1) = 1$, which says that complete agglomeration is a long-run equilibrium in the absence of trade costs: real wages are identical in both regions and there is no incentive to relocate. But does this also hold for small trade costs? The appendix shows that $f'(1) = -\varepsilon\delta(1 + \rho) < 0$. Thus, for small transport costs (T close to 1), the function $f(T)$ will be smaller than one – that is, $w_2 < 1$. This implies that complete agglomeration of manufacturing in one region is always a sustainable equilibrium for sufficiently small transport costs, since the real wage in the periphery will be smaller than in the center.

As transport costs increase, however, the first term in equation (4.5) becomes arbitrarily small, while the second term becomes arbitrarily large if, and only if, $\rho > \delta$. We can conclude therefore that complete agglomeration of manufacturing in one region is not sustainable for sufficiently large transport costs if $\rho > \delta$. Fujita, Krugman, and Venables (1999: 58) label this the *"no-black-hole" condition*, because if this condition is not fulfilled "the forces

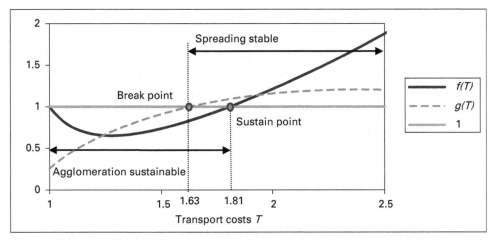

Figure 4.4   Sustain point and break point
Notes: See table 4.1 for parameter values for δ and ρ. The agglomeration equilibrium is sustainable if $f(T) < 1$ (see equation 4.5), while the spreading equilibrium is stable if $g(T) > 1$ (see equation 4.6).

working toward agglomeration would always prevail, and the economy would tend to collapse into a point." Stated differently, if the no-black-hole condition is not met, full agglomeration occurs irrespective of the level of transport costs. In chapter 5 (section 5.5), we discuss some empirical evidence about the no-black-hole condition. Figure 4.4 illustrates the above discussion if the no-black-hole condition is met. For sufficiently small transport costs, the function $f(T) < 1$ and complete agglomeration in one region is sustainable. If the transport costs exceed a critical level, labeled "sustain point" in figure 4.4, the function f $(T) > 1$ and complete agglomeration is not sustainable.

The second suggestion from figure 4.3 mentioned at the beginning of this section was that the spreading equilibrium is stable for large transport costs. So, suppose manufacturing activity is evenly spread over the two regions. It is easy to verify from equations (4.1) to (4.3) that if $\lambda_1 = \lambda_2 = 0.5$ the solution is given by $W_1 = W_2 = 1$, $Y_1 = Y_2 = 0.5$, $I_1 = I_2 = [0.5(1 + T^{1-\varepsilon})]^{1/(1-\varepsilon)}$). So, real wages are identical.[5] We want to investigate changes in this spreading equilibrium if a small (infinitesimal) number of workers are relocating from region 1 to region 2. In particular, we want to establish when this small movement results in a higher real wage for the moving workers, thus setting in motion further relocation of labor and a process of agglomeration. If so, the spreading equilibrium is unstable; if not, it is

---

[5] Note that the ratio of regional real wages is *always* equal to one in the symmetric equilibrium, irrespective of T. We are interested in whether or not the symmetric equilibrium is stable or unstable.

stable. The point where the spreading equilibrium switches from stable to unstable is labeled the "break point" by Fujita, Krugman, and Venables (1999) and Puga (1999). The technical details of this analysis are cumbersome and are relegated to the appendix. At this point it suffices to note that the spreading equilibrium is unstable – that is, $dw/d\lambda > 0$ – if, and only if, the inequality in (4.6) holds.[6] The "break point" is the borderline case for this condition, where transport costs (T_{break}) are such that the condition in equation (4.6) holds with equality.

$$g(T) \equiv \frac{1 - T^{1-\varepsilon}}{1 + T^{1-\varepsilon}} + \left[1 - \frac{\delta(1 + \rho)}{\delta^2 + \rho} \right] < 1 \qquad (4.6)$$

Note that the first term on the right-hand side of equation (4.6) is the Z term that was defined in chapter 3, and is monotonically rising (from zero to one) as transport costs T rise (from one to zero), while the second term is a constant fraction strictly in between zero and one if, and only if, $\rho > \delta$ – that is, if the no-black-hole condition is fulfilled. In that case, the function $g(T)$ is smaller than one (the spreading equilibrium is unstable) for sufficiently small transport costs (T close to one). Once transport costs exceed a certain threshold level, labeled the "break point" in figure 4.4, the function $g(T) > 1$ and the spreading equilibrium is stable. If the no-black-hole condition is not fulfilled the spreading equilibrium is unstable for *all* transport costs. The break point can be derived explicitly using equation (4.6) (see exercise 4.3).

Proposition 4.1 (Fujita, Krugman, and Venables, 1999)

Suppose the "no-black-hole" condition ($\rho > \delta$) holds in a symmetric two-region setting of the geographical economics model, then (i) complete agglomeration of manufacturing activity is not sustainable for sufficiently large transport costs T, and (ii) spreading is a stable equilibrium for sufficiently large transport costs T.

Note that the transport cost level chosen in figure 4.2 ($T = 1.7$) lies in between the break point and the sustain point of figure 4.4, such that (i) the spreading equilibrium is stable, and (ii) the agglomeration equilibria are sustainable, as illustrated in figure 4.1. How "special" is this situation

---

[6] Note that sub-indices that indicate regions are absent in the expression. We did not forget these, but around the symmetric equilibrium we can ignore all second-order effects of induced changes for the other regions. Thus we can write $dY = dY_1 = -dY_2$, and similarly for other variables. This facilitates the notation considerably. See technical note 3.8 and the appendix for a discussion.

depicted in figure 4.1, in which the relative real wage crosses one in the interior three times? Assuming that the no-black-hole condition holds, it is *not* special in the sense that, independently of the other parameters of the model, there is always a range of transport costs for which it occurs. It is special, however, in the sense that this range is relatively small.

To conclude this subsection, it is useful to point out the *hysteresis* or *path dependency* aspect of the model – that is to say, history matters. Suppose that transport costs are initially high, say $T = 2.5$ in figure 4.4. Then spreading of manufacturing activity is the only stable long-run equilibrium. Now suppose that transport costs start to fall, given that the spreading equilibrium is established, say to $T = 1.7$. This will have no impact on the equilibrium allocation of manufacturing production, since spreading remains a stable equilibrium. Only after the transport costs have fallen even further, below $T = 1.63$ in figure 4.4, will the spreading equilibrium become unstable. Any small disturbance will then result in complete agglomeration of manufacturing production in one region. It is not possible to predict beforehand which region this will be, but suppose that agglomeration takes place in region 1. Given that region 1 contains all manufacturing activity, assume now that transport costs start to rise again, perhaps because of the imposition of trade barriers, say back to $T = 1.7$. What will happen? The answer is: "Nothing!" Agglomeration of manufacturing activity remains a stable equilibrium. So, for the same level of transport costs ($T = 1.7$), the equilibrium that becomes established depends on the way this level of transport costs is reached – that is, on history. This phenomenon is called hysteresis or path dependency. Obviously, predictions of what will happen if certain parameters change are considerably harder in models characterized by path dependency.[7]

4.5.2 Solving for the break point and DIY break simulations

Figure 4.4 and equations (4.5) and (4.6), upon which this figure is based, help us to get a grip on the break and sustain points in the core model as shown in figure 4.3. All the same, given the two other model parameters (ε and δ), one would like to arrive at (simple) expressions that can be solved analytically to determine the exact values for T that correspond to the break point B and sustain points $S_0 = S_1$ in figure 4.3. Note that $\varepsilon = 1/(1-\delta)$. Without going into the actual derivations (see Puga, 1999,

---

[7] It is possible to show this mathematically, but this is not trivial (see Neary, 2001: 559–60).

Baldwin *et al.*, 2003: 31, Robert-Nicoud, 2005, Neary, 2001, and Ottaviano and Robert-Nicoud, 2006),[8] it turns out that these expressions can indeed be derived. Here, we focus on the closed-form analytical solution for the break point, because (i) such a closed-form solution is not available for the sustain point (see also Puga, 1999: 319) and (ii) the focus in applications of the core model (see chapter 6) is on the impact of a *fall* in T (moving from *right to left* in figure 4.3a).[9] More specifically, using the subscript $_{break}$ to identify the break point, this is given by

$$\varphi_{break} = T_{break}^{1-\varepsilon} = \left[\frac{(1+\delta)[\varepsilon(1+\delta)-1]}{(1-\delta)[\varepsilon(1-\delta)-1]}\right]^{(1-\varepsilon)/(\varepsilon-1)} \qquad (*)$$

To get a feel for the value of the freeness of trade or transport costs of the break point, the reader is encouraged to use the Microsoft Excel file *break* on our website, which provides solutions for different values of the parameters in the above expression. This file is also used to get a better understanding for the extensions of the core model discussed in the remainder of this chapter.

Applying the core model to, for example, the issue of economic integration, using the freeness of trade parameter φ, requires information on the location of an economy along the horizontal axis in figure 4.3b. If an economy is to the right of φ_{break} it will not experience *more* agglomeration following further economic integration, as the footloose labor and firms are already completely agglomerated. If an economy is to the left of φ_{break}, however, further economic integration potentially could have two effects: (i) no change at all (if the economy remains to the left of the break point) or (ii) a sudden, dramatic increase in agglomeration if the increase in economic integration moves the economy to the right of the break point φ_{break}. Empirical research investigating the relevance of the core model for economic integration thus has to determine the location of an economy in the tomahawk diagram. We address this question in the second part of chapter 6.

The "core" core model discussed so far uses interregional labor mobility to explain the agglomeration of economic activity, provided transport costs

---

[8] Baldwin *et al.* (2003: chap. 2) offer an excellent in-depth analysis of the core model that also shows that the value of T corresponding to the break point B is smaller than the value of T corresponding to the sustain points S_0 and S_1; see also Neary (2001).

[9] Equivalent to a move from left to right using the freeness of trade variable; see figure 4.3b.

T are small enough (or freeness of trade φ is high enough). If the degree of economic connections does not decrease in the future, full agglomeration will remain the stable outcome for ever. This is, admittedly, a rather extreme outcome (perhaps less plausible in the real world): we seldom see complete agglomeration whatever the geographical scale of analysis. At the same time, we know that in many instances interregional labor mobility is rather low within countries, or even absent between countries. The above observations raise two questions. (i) Are there alternative driving forces for the agglomeration of economic activity? (ii) Are there settings leading to less than full agglomeration? As indicated in the introduction to this chapter, the answer is "yes." Three important extensions of Krugman's (1991a) core model are discussed below.[10] The *intermediate goods* model of section 4.6 uses producer connections rather than interregional labor mobility to explain agglomeration. The *generalized model* discussed in section 4.7 incorporates the core model of chapter 3 and the intermediate goods model as special cases, giving rise to a richer menu of long-run equilibria. The *solvable model* in section 4.8 introduces different factors of production in the manufacturing sector, and along the way allows for analytical solutions of the short-run equilibrium.

4.6 Intermediate inputs without interregional labor mobility

In this section we develop a model in which intermediate inputs in the manufacturing production process open up an alternative channel for agglomeration.[11] The presence of intermediate inputs creates upstream and downstream linkages, whereby upstream sectors deliver intermediate goods used as inputs for downstream final products. The crucial simplifying assumption is that the products demanded by consumers as final goods are also used in the production process as intermediate inputs. As every consumer demands every variety (the love-of-variety effect), we also assume that each manufacturing firm uses every good as an intermediate input in its production process. Moreover, we assume (as is customary in international trade theory) that labor is mobile *between sectors* within a region, but *not between regions*. There are thus two main

[10] See Ottaviano and Thisse (2004), Baldwin *et al.* (2003), Combes, Mayer, and Thisse (2008), and Fujita and Thisse (2002: chap. 9) for excellent and in-depth coverage and surveys of the models discussed in sections 4.6 to 4.8.

[11] The model is based on Krugman and Venables (1995) and Venables (1996). Our discussion follows the exposition in Fujita, Krugman and Venables (1999: chap. 14).

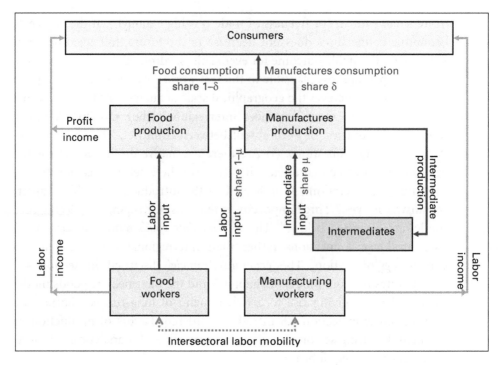

Figure 4.5   Intermediate goods model

differences with the core model of chapter 3, namely (i) there are inter-mediate goods in the production process and (ii) labor is not mobile between locations. Otherwise, the model is quite similar, as illustrated for the real aspects of the model in figure 4.5. Workers can be employed in both sectors and receive wage income in exchange for labor. This income is spent on both food and manufactures. We now turn to the model in more detail.

4.6.1 Demand

The demand side of the model is familiar. There are two sectors, a food sector (F), which is used as the numéraire, and a manufacturing sector (M). Every consumer has Cobb–Douglas preferences for determining spending on food and manufactures (Shares δ and $1-\delta$ respectively; equation 4.7) and a CES sub-utility function to determine spending on manufacturing varieties (equation 4.8). Maximizing this sub-utility function subject to the relevant income constraint (the part δY spent on manufactures) gives consumer demand for each variety j, as given in equation (4.9), where I is the price index for manufactures, $\varepsilon \equiv 1/(1-\rho)$ is the elasticity of substitution, and Y is consumer income.

$$U = M^\delta F^{(1-\delta)} \tag{4.7}$$

$$M = \left(\sum_{i=1}^{n} c_i^\rho \right)^{1/\rho} \tag{4.8}$$

$$c_j = p_j^{-\varepsilon} I^{\varepsilon-1} \delta Y; \ I = \left(\sum_i p_i^{1-\varepsilon} \right)^{1/(1-\varepsilon)} \tag{4.9}$$

So far the model is the same as before. The major difference on the demand side is that firms also use varieties from the M sector as intermediate inputs. Assuming that all varieties are necessary in the production process and that the elasticity of substitution is the same for firms as for consumers, we can use the same CES aggregator function for producers as for consumers, with the same corresponding price index I. Given that we now also have to take spending on intermediate goods into account, we can derive total demand for a variety depending on *total* spending $E = \delta Y + \mu n p x^*$, where the first term represents the share of consumer income spent on manufactures and the second term represents intermediate input demand (= the value of all varieties produced in a region, npx^*, multiplied by the share of intermediates in the production process; see below):

$$c_j = p_j^{-\varepsilon} I^{\varepsilon-1} E, \tag{4.9a}$$

As in chapter 3, the term x^* denotes the equilibrium supply of a manufacturing variety by a single firm (see below).

4.6.2 Manufacturing supply

Each firm producing variety i uses both labor and all varieties as intermediate inputs. The production process is a Cobb–Douglas composite of labor (with price W for the wage rate) and intermediates (with price index I). Total costs $C(x_i)$ are given in equation (4.10), in which the coefficients α and β are the fixed cost and marginal input requirement for the production of varieties. Maximizing profits gives the familiar mark-up pricing rule (note that marginal costs now consist of *two* elements: labor and intermediates) given in equation (4.11), which simplifies to $p_i = I^\mu W^{(1-\mu)}$ using our normalization $\beta = 1 - 1/\varepsilon$.

Note that the price index I in equation (4.9a) is now a function of I itself, because of the presence of intermediate goods. Note also that the equations reduce to those in chapter 3 if $\mu = 0$ (no intermediate inputs). Use the zero-profit condition $p_i x_i = I^\mu W_i^{(1-\mu)} (a + \beta x_i)$ and the mark-up pricing rule (4.11) to determine the break-even supply of a variety i (each produced by a single firm) in equation (4.12). Substituting this in the labor demand function, $l = a + \beta x$, gives $l = a\varepsilon$, and thus $n = \lambda L/a\varepsilon = \lambda/a\varepsilon$ for our normalizations.[12] We can use this in the expression for total expenditures E. To determine the income Y of workers, we take a closer look at the agricultural sector.

$$C(x_i) = I^\mu W_i^{(1-\mu)} (a + \beta x_i) \qquad (4.10)$$

$$p_i(1 - 1/\varepsilon) = I^\mu W^{(1-\mu)} \beta \qquad (4.11)$$

$$x_i = a/(1 - \beta) = a\varepsilon \equiv x^* \qquad (4.12)$$

4.6.3 Supply of food

The income of consumers comes from two sources, namely the wages earned in the manufacturing sector, analyzed above, and the income earned in the agricultural sector. As in chapter 3, we use food as the numéraire and assume that it is freely tradable between locations. Food production, F, depends on the amount of labor available in the agricultural sector L_F such that $F = F(L_F) = F(1 - \lambda)$. We focus on two possibilities.

- *Constant returns to scale* (CRS). $F = 1 - \lambda$. This option, in line with Krugman and Venables (1995), is analyzed in this section. A proper choice of units ensures that $W = 1$. Consequently, in the long-run equilibrium, nominal wages will be equal not only in the manufacturing and food sectors, but also between locations.
- *Decreasing returns to scale.* $F'(1 - \lambda) > 0$; $F''(1 - \lambda) < 0$. This option leads to rather different outcomes, because in the long-run equilibrium wages

---

[12] Note that the distribution of labor between the two regions is given. For two identical countries we can still use $L = 1$. Because labor is mobile between sectors we have just one parameter, λ, to describe the distribution of labor between manufactures and food.

will be equal for the two sectors within a location, but may differ between locations. Section 4.7 analyzes this case, with interregional wage differences as an additional spreading force.[13]

Consumer income equals the sum of wage income and the output in the food sector (the numéraire), so for two regions we have

$$
\begin{aligned}
Y_1 &= W_1\lambda_1 + F(1 - \lambda_1) \\
Y_2 &= W_2\lambda_2 + F(1 - \lambda_2)
\end{aligned}
\tag{4.13}
$$

Labor mobility between locations (migration) is not possible by assumption, and thus takes place only between sectors within a location. Workers in either sector living in the same location face the same price index, implying that the difference between *nominal* wages determines if a worker moves from one sector to the other:

$$
\frac{d\lambda}{\lambda} = \eta[W - F'(1 - \lambda)]
\tag{4.14}
$$

We therefore assume that the wage rate in the agricultural sector is equal to the marginal product of labor and that workers move to the sector with the higher wage rate (with speed of adjustment parameter η). If both sectors produce positive amounts, equilibrium wages are the same. If $\lambda = 1$, wages in the manufacturing sector are higher than in food. If $\lambda = 0$, wages in the manufacturing sector are smaller than in food. With constant returns to scale we must have $W = 1$ (provided $\delta < 0.5$; see below).

4.6.4 Equilibrium with transport costs

Transportation of food is free and of manufactures is costly, consisting of iceberg transport costs $T > 1$ between the two locations. Total demand for a variety is the sum of the demand from the two locations, where consumers and firms in the other location have to pay transportation costs on their imports:

$$
\begin{aligned}
x_1 &= E_1 p_1^{-\varepsilon} I_1^{\varepsilon-1} + E_2 p_1^{-\varepsilon}(T)^{-\varepsilon} I_2^{\varepsilon-1} \\
x_2 &= E_2 p_2^{-\varepsilon} I_2^{\varepsilon-1} + E_1 p_2^{-\varepsilon}(T)^{-\varepsilon} I_1^{\varepsilon-1}
\end{aligned}
\tag{4.15}
$$

---

[13] See also Puga (1999: 306–7); the importance of this becomes clear in section 4.7. One reason for assuming diminishing returns is to think of a second production factor in food production, land, that is in fixed supply and used only in food production.

We already know that the break-even supply is equal to $x_1^* = a/(1-\beta)$. Equating this to total demand gives[14]

$$a/(1-\beta) = E_1 p_1^{-\varepsilon} I_1^{\varepsilon-1} + E_2 p_1^{-\varepsilon}(T)^{1-\varepsilon} I_2^{\varepsilon-1}$$
$$a/(1-\beta) = E_2 p_2^{-\varepsilon} I_2^{\varepsilon-1} + E_1 p_2^{-\varepsilon}(T)^{-\varepsilon} I_1^{\varepsilon-1} \tag{4.16}$$

Inserting the mark-up pricing rule in (4.16) and solving for the wage rate gives the two-region wage equation in the presence of intermediate demand for varieties:[15]

$$W_1 = [(1-\beta)/a]^{1/\varepsilon(1-\mu)} I_1^{-\mu/(1-\mu)} (E_1 I_1^{\varepsilon-1} + E_2 T^{1-\varepsilon} I_2^{\varepsilon-1})^{1/\varepsilon(1-\mu)}$$
$$W_2 = [(1-\beta)/a]^{1/\varepsilon(1-\mu)} I_2^{-\mu/(1-\mu)} (E_2 I_2^{\varepsilon-1} + E_1 T^{1-\varepsilon} I_1^{\varepsilon-1})^{1/\varepsilon(1-\mu)} \tag{4.17}$$

These equations closely resemble the wage equations that we have already derived for the core model of chapter 3 (in fact, with $\mu = 0$ they are the same as wage equation (4.3)). There are also important differences. First, equation (4.17) does not use consumer income Y but total expenditures E. This indicates that demand for a variety comes not only from consumers but also from firms, which need varieties as intermediate inputs. Second, the terms $I_1^{-\mu/(1-\mu)}$ and $I_2^{-\mu/(1-\mu)}$ on the right-hand side of equation (4.17) show that the *lower* the price index the higher the break-even wage rate can be. Thus, the closer a firm is to its suppliers of intermediate products the lower its costs, and the higher the wage rate it can pay. We now have a second channel whereby the location of a firm matters. Stephen Redding and Venables (2004) call this the *supplier access* effect. In chapter 5 we analyze supplier and market access from an empirical point of view. This geographical economics model is also known as the *vertical linkages* model, as it introduces an extra agglomeration force through linkages between firms affecting production costs.

---

[14] Note that the demand from the other region is multiplied by T in order to compensate for the part that melts away during transportation.

[15] The motivation to derive a wage equation instead of a traditional equilibrium price equation is twofold. First, labor migration between regions is a function of (real) wages. Second, in empirical applications this is useful because data on regional wages are easier to obtain than regional manufacturing price data (see also chapter 5, section 5.5).

4.6.5 Simulations

As in sections 4.2 to 4.4 for the core model, we can get a grip on the workings of the model by performing simulations. Keep in mind that for the remainder of this section we assume that the production of food is characterized by constant returns to scale: $F = 1 - \lambda$. Repeating the exercise leading to the tomahawk diagram of figure 4.3 for this model results in figure 4.6. Note that we assume that δ (the share of income spent on manufactures) is smaller than 0.5.[16] This ensures that, even if *all* manufactures are produced in a single region, both regions still produce food. That, in turn, implies that the equilibrium wage rate in both regions is equal to one. If δ is larger than 0.5 and, say, all workers in region 1 produce manufactures, the remaining part of manufactures would have to be produced in region 2. In this situation, manufacturing wages in region 1 will differ from those in region 2 because interregional arbitrage through the food sector is no longer possible.

Figure 4.6 (with constant returns in food production and with $\delta < 0.5$) is qualitatively the same as figure 4.3a of the core model of chapter 3: the relation between transportation costs and long-run equilibria still looks like a tomahawk. The mechanisms behind agglomeration and spreading are different, however. Potentially, there are *four* forces at work in this model, two of which are familiar (see chapter 3 for a detailed explanation) and two of which are new.[17] The familiar forces are (i) the extent of competition effect (a higher λ results in more varieties, and thus more competition and a lower price index) and (ii) the market size effect (a higher λ increases the market for manufactures). The competition effect is a spreading force, the market size effect is an agglomerating force. The two new forces are (iii) the marginal productivity effect in the food sector (a reduction of employment in the food sector increases [for a concave production function] marginal productivity) and (iv) backward linkages (higher λ implies that firms have easy access to intermediate production of manufactures). The marginal productivity effect (not operative in this section) is a spreading force: if workers move from the food to the manufacturing sector because firms start to agglomerate in region 1, the existence of diminishing returns to food implies that wages will have to increase in

---

[16] Compare sections 14.2 and 14.3 in Fujita, Krugman, and Venables (1999) on this matter.

[17] One force disappears: the cost of living effect. Migration between regions, by assumption, is not possible. So real wage effects on migration are not relevant in this model (but they remain important for welfare).

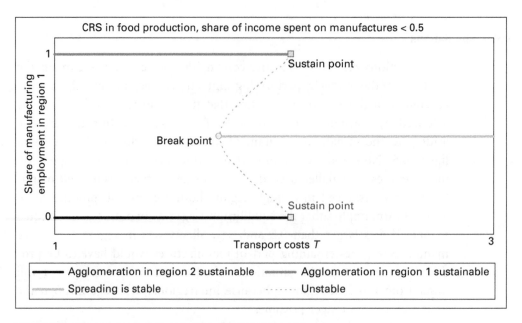

Figure 4.6   The tomahawk in the presence of intermediate products

region 1 compared to region 2 (thus creating interregional wage differences providing an incentive to move to the smaller region). The only new force in this section (backward linkages) is an agglomerating force. It is therefore, as figure 4.6 shows, not very surprising that the combination of these three forces again leads to the tomahawk diagram, in which low transport costs result in full agglomeration.

The analysis of the sustain and break points can be carried out as it was with the core model. In fact (see the *break* Excel file on the website and subsection 4.5.2), the break condition for the Krugman and Venables (1995) model is the *same* as for the core model, with δ (the share of income spent on manufactures) being replaced by μ (the share of intermediate goods in the production process; see Puga, 1999: 326, footnote 21):

$$\varphi_{break} = T_{break}^{1-\varepsilon} = \left[\frac{(1+\mu)[\varepsilon(1+\mu)-1]}{(1-\mu)[\varepsilon(1-\mu)-1]} \right]^{(1-\varepsilon)/(\varepsilon-1)} \qquad (*')$$

To round up the discussion of the Krugman and Venables (1995) model, we ask ourselves (see section 14.3 in Fujita, Krugman, and Venables, 1999) what happens under constant returns to scale if $\delta > 0.5$. The answer to this (seemingly innocuous) change is given in figure 4.7.

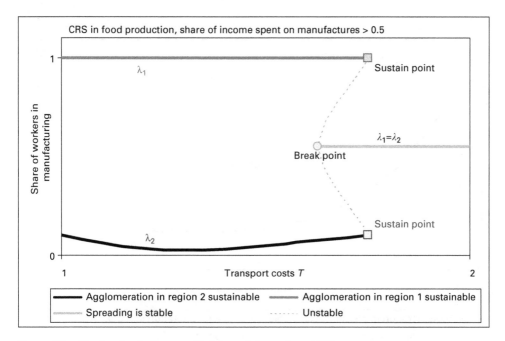

Figure 4.7   The tomahawk diagram with intermediate goods and CRS

Figure 4.7 looks rather similar to figure 4.6, but on closer inspection it is apparent that it is not exactly the same. The most visible change is the extent of specialization in manufactures in region 2. If we read along the horizontal axis from right to left in figure 4.7, we know that there is a level of transport costs for which the symmetric equilibrium is no longer stable (the break point).[18] Moving further to the left, region 1 becomes completely specialized in the production of manufactures, while some manufacturing production still takes place in region 2 (obviously, it could be the other way round: we could have swapped the region labels). From the set-up of the model we already have some information about the nominal wages. In region 2 the (nominal) wages in both sectors are equal and identical to one (labor can move freely between sectors and wages in the food sector are equal to one). In region 1, wages in the manufacturing sector are larger than or equal to one (if wages were smaller than one, workers would be better off by starting to produce food).

Moving even more to the left, a further reduction in transportation costs lowers the price index in region 1, and thus raises real wages. This decline in production costs drives up demand for labor, but labor supply is fixed by

---

[18] Note that the sustain point is to the right of the break point. In other words, agglomeration is already a stable equilibrium before symmetry becomes unstable.

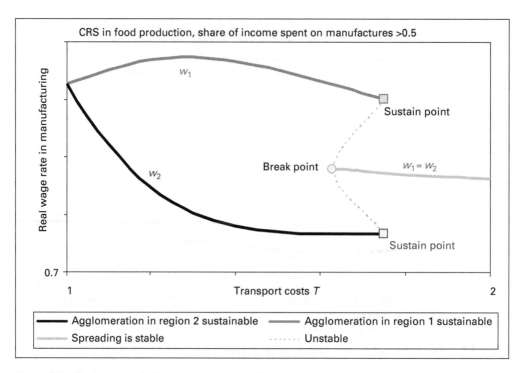

Figure 4.8   Real wages in both regions with intermediate goods and CRS

assumption. So market clearing on the labor market in region 1 results in higher wages. If transportation costs decline further, the advantage of being near consumers and producers of intermediate products becomes less important, and differences in wages become more important for production costs. This implies that the peripheral region becomes more attractive for manufacturing production as transport costs decline, which explains the curvature of λ_2 in figure 4.7. This process stimulates manufacturing production in the peripheral region and drives up real wages until they become identical in both countries. Figure 4.8 illustrates this process by drawing the *real* wages for both regions.

Based on figure 4.8, Krugman and Venables (1995) argue that the process depicted by the gradual lowering of transport costs T can be used to understand the globalization process from the late nineteenth century until the end of the twentieth century (or, in their words, "It's the history of the world, part I"). In the two-region model with the regions labeled North (let us call them the OECD countries) and South (the developing countries), high transport costs (low levels of economic integration) go along with real wage equalization. When economic integration really takes off, one region (North) becomes the core region and real wages start to differ between North and South. This is what happened during a large part of the twentieth century. With ongoing integration (think of post-1980 globalization), real wages start to converge (see also Crafts and Venables, 2003, and Baldwin, 2006).

4.7 The bell-shaped curve and a generalized model

As noted in the previous section, the intermediate goods model without interregional labor mobility may work quite differently once we replace the assumption of constant returns to scale in food production by diminishing returns to scale: $F = F(1-\lambda)$ with $F'(1-\lambda) > 0$; $F''(1-\lambda) < 0$. Once manufacturing firms start to agglomerate in a region, say region 1, the additional demand for manufacturing labor must pull workers out of the food sector in region 1. With diminishing returns for food production, having fewer workers means higher productivity and thus higher nominal wages. This creates a wage difference between the two regions (wages remain equal between sectors within a region). In terms of the four agglomeration and spreading forces discussed in section 4.6, the third force (marginal productivity effect) now becomes operative. Dropping the assumption of a perfectly elastic supply of labor adds an additional spreading force to the model.

4.7.1 Decreasing returns

Let us denote the elasticity of a region's labor supply by η. If $\eta = 0$, no intersectoral labor mobility is possible. If $\eta = \infty$, there is perfect labor mobility between sectors (infinite elasticity). In the latter case, wages in the manufacturing sector and the food sector are identical until a region becomes specialized in manufactures. If $0 < \eta < \infty$, migration from the food sector to the manufacturing sector can be consistent with a wage increase in *both* sectors. The inclusion of an upward-sloping labor supply function thus generalizes the Krugman (1991a) model (in which $\eta = 0$) and the Krugman and Venables (1995) model (in which $\eta = \infty$). Most importantly, Puga (1999) shows that for $0 < \eta < \infty$ the bang-bang long-run character of the core model disappears.[19] With an upward-sloping labor supply function,

---

[19] This version (Puga, 1999) is also provided in section 14.4 of Fujita, Krugman, and Venables (1999).

agglomeration drives up wages in the core region, which reduces the incentive for firms to agglomerate (particularly for low transport costs). Without interregional labor mobility, the long-run relationship between transport costs (economic integration) and agglomeration *might* look like figure 4.10, which has aptly been called the *bell-shaped curve* by Head and Mayer (2004a) and Ottaviano and Thisse (2004).[20]

Before we discuss the bell-shaped curve, we illustrate the workings of this model (maintaining $\delta < 0.5$) by drawing the relative wage rates of the two regions for three specific values of transport costs. Figure 4.9a ($T=1.5$) shows that, for high values of transport costs, the spreading equilibrium is stable. Figure 4.9b ($T=1.3$) shows that, for intermediate values of transport costs, the spreading equilibrium is *un*stable. Both these results are the same as those already seen. The surprise lies in figure 4.9c ($T=1.1$), which shows that, for *low* values of transport costs, the spreading equilibrium is again *stable*. Apparently, for sufficiently low transport costs the intermediate linkage advantages created by agglomeration no longer dominate the cost disadvantage (high wages), as the other region can now always be supplied at a relatively low cost.

This discussion of figure 4.9 explains the shape of the long-run equilibrium distribution curves given in figure 4.10: spreading–agglomeration–spreading. This bell-shaped curve has become popular among empirical researchers (and policy makers) because it does not predict catastrophic changes in agglomeration patterns as transportation costs fall (whereas the tomahawk diagram does). In addition, for low enough levels of transport costs, spreading forces start to dominate agglomeration forces. This is potentially good news for peripheral regions or countries, which can now benefit from ever-increasing economic integration. As before, the empirical analysis will have to determine the position of the country or region within the diagram. Now, however, we also have to determine if the bell-shaped curve is relevant or the tomahawk diagram. We address these issues in chapter 6. For a (largely non-technical) application of tomahawks and bell-shaped curves to EU regions, see Puga (2002).

Before we move to our third and final class of alternative models (solvable models) in section 4.8, two questions with respect to the bell-shaped curve warrant brief attention. First, is the intermediate goods model with

---

[20] This depends on the parameter configuration (see Puga, 1999, or Robert-Nicoud, 2005). The important distinction is whether or not low transport costs lead to agglomeration or spreading. This is depicted "smoothly" in figure 4.10, but can also come from a double tomahawk or *pitchfork* (Robert-Nicoud, 2005).

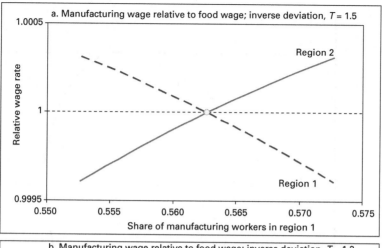

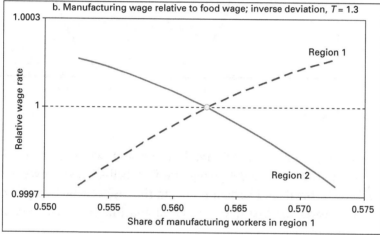

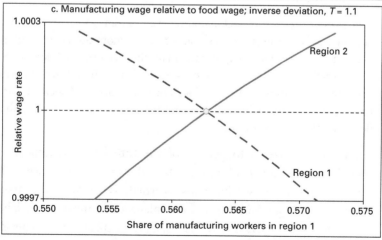

Figure 4.9   Relative wage rates; diminishing returns in food production

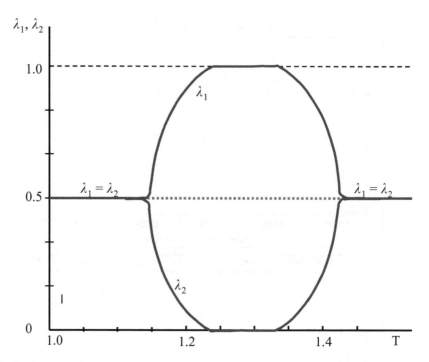

Figure 4.10   The bell-shaped curve

decreasing returns in the food sector and without interregional labor mobility the only model giving rise to a bell-shaped curve? Second, what about the break and sustain points in the case of a bell-shaped curve?

To answer the first question, Head and Mayer (2004a: 2652) argue that the core model

continues to predict full agglomeration even as transport costs become tiny. This is because the "centrifugal" forces that would promote dispersion decline with trade costs at an even more rapid rate than the "centripetal" forces that promote agglomeration. With any other congestion [spreading] force unrelated to trade costs, the equilibrium pattern of location will return to dispersion for some (low) trade costs threshold where all trade-related forces become so weak that they must dominate the congestion force.

So, when one wants to get rid of the tomahawk summarizing the core model, we need a spreading force that does not weaken when T falls. One way to do this, as we have just learned, is to drop the assumption of interregional labor mobility and to replace it by inter-sectoral labor mobility with a positive wage elasticity. As Puga (1999: 322) notes: "This is because as trade costs continue to fall, the cost saving from being able to buy intermediates locally instead of having to import them falls with trade costs, but the wage gap between regions remains."

Other mechanisms may do the trick as well. Helpman (1998) replaces the agricultural sector with a housing sector, which can give rise to a bell-shaped curve despite the fact that this model assumes interregional labor mobility. In fact, the model is the same as the core model in all other respects. Housing acts as a non-traded consumption good. With a fixed supply of housing, agglomeration goes along with rising housing prices in the larger region. The increase in housing prices acts as a spreading force, the strength of which does *not* get weaker as transports costs fall. In chapter 5 we use the Helpman model in our discussion of attempts to estimate the equilibrium wage equation.[21]

4.7.2 Generalized model

Finally, regarding the second question on the analysis of break and sustain points, we turn to Puga (1999). He has developed a general model of geographical economics, as it includes all models discussed so far (including the core model itself as a special case). In addition to the key model parameters of the core model (δ, ε, and T or $\varphi \equiv T^{1-\varepsilon}$), the generalized model allows for an upward-sloping inter-sectoral labor supply curve (parameter $\eta > 0$) as well as for intermediate inputs (parameter μ). With these five model parameters, the generalized model is essentially a marriage between the core model of chapter 3 and the intermediate input model outlined in this chapter. It is analyzed for two cases, namely (i) interregional labor mobility and (ii) interregional labor *im*mobility. This distinction is crucial, as it turns out that the model with interregional labor mobility yields a tomahawk diagram (thus showing that the core model is just one model to do so) and the model *without* interregional labor mobility gives rise to the bell-shaped curve.

The conditions for the break points in these two general models, with and without interregional labor mobility, are given below (again, similar relatively "easy" expressions are not available for the sustain points). The first break condition (for the general model with interregional labor mobility) looks familiar, because with $\mu = 0$ (no intermediate inputs) and $\eta = 0$ (no inter-sectoral labor mobility between food and manufactures) this

---

[21] For other models yielding a bell-shaped curve, see Head and Mayer (2004a: 2652–3). See box 4.1 below on other models that do not give rise to a tomahawk.

condition reduces to the one for the core model (see subsection 4.5.2):

$$\varphi_{break,\ mobility} = \left[1 + \frac{2(2\varepsilon-1)(\delta+\mu(1-\delta))}{(1-\mu)[(1-\delta)(\varepsilon(1-\delta)(1-\mu))-1] - \delta^2\eta} \right]^{(1-\varepsilon)/(\varepsilon-1)}$$

$$(*'')$$

The break condition for the bell-shaped curve of the general model without interregional labor mobility is given by the quadratic expression in the freeness of trade φ in equation $(*'' \,')$. Note from figure 4.10 that we are looking for two roots/solutions of the equation, since the bell-shaped curve has two break points: one where full spreading turns into (partial) agglomeration, and one where (partial) agglomeration turns into full spreading. The reader can again use the *break* Excel file on the website to experiment with these two break conditions. Please bear in mind that these conditions have been derived only for the case of two regions.[22]

$$a\varphi^2_{break,immobile} + b\varphi_{break,immobile} + c = 0$$
$$a \equiv [\varepsilon(1+\mu) - 1][(1+\mu)(1+\eta) + (1-\mu)\gamma]$$
$$b \equiv -2\big\{ [\varepsilon(1+\mu^2) - 1](1+\eta) - \varepsilon(1-\mu)[2(\varepsilon-1) - \gamma\mu] \big\}$$
$$c \equiv (1-\mu)[\varepsilon(1-\mu) - 1](\eta+1-\gamma)$$

$$(*'' \,')$$

To understand this quadratic equation, consult the appendix. Note the crucial importance of the assumption with regard to the production technology in the food sector (with decreasing returns to scale – that is, $F'' < 0$).

4.8 The solvable model: two factors of production in manufactures

The models discussed so far have one factor of production in the manufacturing sector. An extension of the model allowing for different production factors, such as skilled and unskilled labor, makes the model suitable for analyzing the effects of modern-day globalization, which tends to focus on this distinction. As a rather surprising bonus, it turns out that this extension simplifies matters in some respects, as it allows us to derive an explicit analytical solution for equilibrium wages. This section briefly

---

[22] Similar break conditions for n regions (with $n > 2$) exist only if one assumes that these regions are all at an equal distance (see Puga, 1999: 306, footnote 6). This is a problem if we take bell curves or tomahawks to the real world, as we will see in chapter 6, section 6.3.

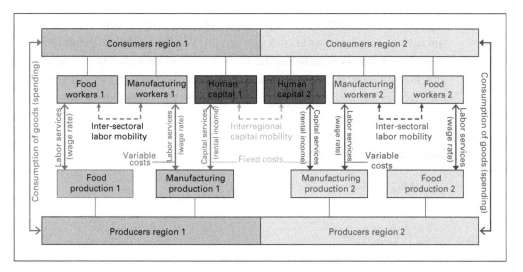

Figure 4.11 General structure of the solvable model

introduces the analytically solvable model developed independently by Forslid and Ottaviano and combined in Forslid and Ottaviano (2003).[23] The idea to use two factors of production in the manufacturing sector in the solvable model is used in later chapters as well, in particular in chapter 8 on multinationals, chapter 9 on trade, chapter 10 on growth (the Baldwin–Forslid model), and in chapter 11, in a discussion of the Baldwin–Krugman model on tax competition. It is also used in chapter 11 to discuss the role of government spending for economic policy.

The general structure of the model is illustrated in figure 4.11. Regarding the set-up of the model, we refer to the two production factors in the manufacturing sector as labor and human capital. We assume that labor is *im*mobile but that human capital is mobile between regions (there is no inter-sectoral factor mobility). In practice, it is frequently argued that labor is less mobile than human capital. It is precisely the ability to distinguish between mobile and immobile production factors in the manufacturing sector that explains why this model has become popular for policy analysis in the context of geographical economics (see Baldwin *et al.*, 2003). There are two regions ($j = 1$, 2). Each region has L_j workers and K_j human

---

[23] See also subsection 9.2.5 in Fujita and Thisse (2002) for a clear exposition of this solvable model. In general, these types of models lend themselves for policy analysis precisely because they are solvable and can be used for welfare analysis. The book by Baldwin *et al.* (2003) is an excellent source for a discussion on solvable models in geographical economics, as is Combes, Mayer, and Thisse (2008). On the website, the reader can learn more about the model from a different perspective.

capital.[24] Each agent is a worker or a capital owner, where capital can be thought of as human or knowledge capital. Workers are thus geographically immobile whereas human capital is mobile. Workers earn the wage rate W and human capital owners get a return r for their efforts. We assume that the two regions are identical with respect to the immobile factor of production: $L_1 = L_2 = 0.5$.

All agents have the same preferences, depending on the consumption of food F and manufactures M, a composite of n different varieties c_i:

$$U = M^\delta F^{(1-\delta)} \tag{4.18}$$

$$M = \left(\sum_{i=1}^{n} c_i^{(\varepsilon-1)/\varepsilon} \right)^{\varepsilon/(\varepsilon-1)} \tag{4.19}$$

where δ is the share of income spent on manufactures and ε is the elasticity of substitution between different varieties of manufactures. Utility maximization leads to the same expressions for the demand functions as derived in chapter 3.

The next step is crucial. In the manufacturing sector we assume that labor is used only in the *variable-cost* part of production β whereas human capital is used only in the *fixed part* of production a. The production of food, which is freely traded at zero transport costs, takes place under CRS and requires only workers. A suitable choice of units ensures that one unit of labor produces one unit of food. Using food as a numéraire and assuming free trade in food implies that the food price, and hence the wage rate W, can be set equal to one. This holds as long as food is produced in both countries. Standard profit maximization in the manufacturing sector leads to $p_i(1 - 1/\varepsilon) = W\beta \Rightarrow p_i = W = 1$ (using our normalization $\beta = 1 - 1/\varepsilon$). If the variety is exported, the price in the foreign market thus becomes $Tp = T$. As is shown below, the assumption that labor is also used in the variable part of manufactures production removes most of the non-linearity on the demand

---

[24] The main point here is to include a mobile and an immobile factor of production. The labeling of these two factors (unskilled versus skilled labor or labor versus capital) is not material as long as the mobile factor (be it skilled labor or capital) spends its income in the region where it is used for production. This class of solvable models (in which the mobile factor spends its income in the region where it is earned) is known as "footloose entrepreneur" (FE) models (Baldwin *et al.*, 2003: chap. 4). Solvable models in which the mobile factor repatriates its income to the region of origin are known as "footloose capital" (FC) models (Baldwin *et al.*, 2003: chap. 3; see also box 4.1 at the end of this section).

side that makes the core model of chapter 3 impossible to solve analytically. With $W = 1$ we have only to determine the return to human capital r.

Market clearing for human capital in region j allows us to determine the number of varieties produced in region j:

$$n_j = K_j/a = K_j \tag{4.20}$$

The second part of this equality follows by a choice of units such that each variety uses one unit of K ($a = 1$). Free entry and exit in the manufacturing sector ensure that total profits are zero, which – using mark-up pricing – determines the equilibrium output per firm (see equation (4.21)).[25] Using our normalization of wages, the income in region j is given in (4.22).

$$x_j = \varepsilon r_j \tag{4.21}$$

$$Y_j = r_j K_j + L_j \tag{4.22}$$

Using the "freeness of trade" parameter φ introduced above in this chapter ($\varphi \equiv T^{1-\varepsilon}$), we can write the manufacturing market-clearing conditions as

$$\varepsilon r_1 = \frac{p_1^{1-\varepsilon} \delta Y_1}{I_1^{1-\varepsilon}} + \frac{\varphi p_2^{1-\varepsilon} \delta Y_2}{I_2^{1-\varepsilon}} = \frac{\delta Y_1}{n_1 + \varphi n_2} + \frac{\varphi \delta Y_2}{\varphi n_1 + n_2} \tag{4.23}$$

$$\varepsilon r_2 = \frac{p_2^{1-\varepsilon} \delta Y_2}{I_2^{1-\varepsilon}} + \frac{\varphi p_1^{1-\varepsilon} \delta Y_1}{I_1^{1-\varepsilon}} = \frac{\delta Y_2}{n_2 + \varphi n_1} + \frac{\varphi \delta Y_1}{\varphi n_2 + n_1} \tag{4.24}$$

where $I_1 \equiv \left(p_1^{1-\varepsilon} n_1 + \varphi p_2^{1-\varepsilon} n_2 \right)^{1/(1-\varepsilon)} = (n_1 + \varphi n_2)^{1/(1-\varepsilon)}$ is the price index for manufactures in region 1 (similarly for region 2 by interchanging sub-indices 1 and 2). The left-hand sides of equations (4.23) and (4.24) give the equilibrium output per firm and the right-hand sides the associated demand.

Inspection of (4.23) and (4.24) reveals that we have a linear system of two equations and two unknowns, which can readily be solved. Using equation (4.20), (4.22), in (4.23) and (4.24), letting λ denote the share of human capital in region 1 (so $n_1 = \lambda$; $n_2 = 1 - \lambda$) finally gives

$$\frac{r_1}{r_2} = \frac{\varepsilon[2\varphi\lambda + (1-\lambda)(1+\varphi^2)] + (\varphi^2 - 1)(1-\lambda)\delta}{\varepsilon[2\varphi(1-\lambda) + \lambda(1+\varphi^2)] + (\varphi^2 - 1)\lambda\delta} \tag{4.25}$$

---

[25] Using $px - (r + \beta x) = 0$, rearranging, and using the mark-up pricing rule gives (4.21).

To round up the discussion of our model, we note that the location decision of human capital involves not only the factor rewards r_1 and r_2 but also the respective price levels. As in the core model of chapter 3, differences in real rewards determine migration flows. The incentive of human capital to relocate is therefore determined by the ratio υ:

$$
\begin{aligned}
\upsilon &= \left(\frac{r_1}{r_2}\right)\left(\frac{I_2}{I_1}\right)^\delta \\
&= \frac{\varepsilon[2\varphi\lambda + (1-\lambda)(1+\varphi^2)] + (\varphi^2-1)(1-\lambda)\delta}{\varepsilon[2\varphi(1-\lambda)+\lambda(1+\varphi^2)] + (\varphi^2-1)\lambda\delta}\left(\frac{(1-\lambda)+\varphi\lambda}{\lambda+\varphi(1-\lambda)}\right)^{\delta/(1-\varepsilon)}
\end{aligned}
$$

(4.26)

Apart from the case of complete agglomeration, human capital has no incentive to relocate if welfare is the same in the two regions ($\upsilon = 1$), while human capital moves from region 2 to region 1 if welfare is higher in region 1 ($\upsilon > 1$) and from region 1 to region 2 if welfare is lower in region 1 ($\upsilon < 1$). This completes our discussion of the set-up of the solvable model.

We can calculate the two most important "points" of this model: the break point and the sustain point. The break point can be derived from (4.26), by evaluating the derivative of (4.26) with respect to λ, at $\lambda = 0.5$. This gives $\varphi_{break} = \frac{(\varepsilon-\delta)(\varepsilon-1-\delta)}{(\varepsilon+\delta)(\varepsilon+\delta-1)}$. For values of transport costs that are smaller, the symmetric equilibrium is no longer stable, and exogenous changes in the distribution of human capital will lead to core–periphery outcomes. The core–periphery outcome cannot be sustained for transportation costs higher than the smallest root of $1 = 0.5\varphi_{sus}^{\delta/(\varepsilon-1)}\{(1+\delta/\varepsilon)\varphi_{sus} + (1-\delta/\varepsilon)/\varphi_{sus}\}$, which can be derived from (4.26) by starting from complete agglomeration, and calculating the value of transportation costs for which the real reward of human capital in the periphery becomes larger than in the core (the equation calculates the point at which the owners of human capital are indifferent and the periphery is on the brink of becoming more attractive).

Combining the information we have derived so far, we can again draw a tomahawk figure for this model. In fact, the resulting tomahawk is (qualitatively) the same as the one shown figure 4.3b in section 4.4. From this we can see therefore that, in a qualitative sense, the conclusions from the core model of chapter 3 also hold for this model (although the exact values of the sustain and break points are not the same; see Baldwin et al., 2003). Two important differences with respect to the model of chapter 3 stand out, however, in this case: we can derive explicit solutions for the rewards of the mobile factor, and the model is more attractive for cases in which the analysis with different production factors is considered to be important. It is precisely these two differences that will be useful in subsequent chapters.

4.9 The racetrack economy: many locations in neutral space in the core model

The bulk of the analysis and almost all the examples have dealt with a *two-region* model up to now. Nonetheless, the short-run equilibrium equations (4.1) to (4.3) hold generally if we identify an arbitrary number R of locations, as long as we specify the distances D_{rs} between all locations r and s, such that we can calculate $T_{rs} = T^{D_{rs}}$, and know the production level ϕ_r of the immobile activity food in each location r. In general (see our discussion of the bell-shaped curve at the end of section 4.7), it is virtually impossible to derive analytical results for a setting with an arbitrary number of locations. So, how does the core model of geographical economics behave if we apply the model to R regions instead of just two regions? This is the topic of this section, and the main vehicle for our analysis below, the so called "racetrack economy," turns out to be useful in later chapters, notably chapter 7 on cities and congestion and chapter 11 on policy (see the section on the pancake economy in chapter 11).

4.9.1 Many locations in neutral space

The main advantage of the two-region core model is that "space" is inherently (and deliberately) neutral. Neither location is preferred by construction over the other location, because the distance between the two locations is the same, and hence so are the transport costs. Any endogenous location results (agglomeration or spreading) that arise in the two-region core model are therefore a consequence of the structure of the economic interactions between agents within the model, and do not arise from some pre-imposed geographic structure favoring economic activity in a particular location.

To preserve the neutrality of space in a multi-location setting, it is useful to analyze a simple geometry, in which the locations are evenly distributed in a circle with transportation possible only along the rim of that circle. This setting has been used before, for example in economic geography or in industrial organization. In Brakman *et al.* (1996), we refer to this setting as the "equidistant circle," but Fujita, Krugman, and Venables (1999: 82–5) more aptly call it "the racetrack economy." The structure of the racetrack economy is quite simple, as illustrated in figure 4.12. The R locations are equally and sequentially spaced around the circumference of a circle, with location R next to location 1, as in a clock. The distance between any two adjacent locations is one unit, so the transport costs between adjacent locations is T. The distance between any two arbitrary locations is the length of the shortest route along the circumference of the circle. We assume the production of the immobile food activity to be evenly distributed among all locations.

Panel a of figure 4.12 illustrates the racetrack economy if there are 3 locations. The distance between all locations is one, since they are all adjacent to one another. Panel *b* illustrates the racetrack economy if there are five locations. The distance from location 1 to locations 2 and 5 is one, because these are adjacent locations, and the distance from location 1 to locations 3 and 4 is two, because it requires two steps from location 1 to reach either location. Similarly, panel c of figure 4.12 illustrates the racetrack economy if there are twelve locations, where, for example, the distance from location 1 to locations 5 and 9 is four, as both locations require four steps to be reached from location 1.

Panels d and e of figure 4.12 show a typical simulation run for the racetrack economy with twelve locations. The simulation procedure is as follows.

(1) As in the core model, we start with an initial distribution of the manufacturing labor force across the twelve locations. This distribution is chosen randomly.
(2) We determine the short-run equilibrium, given this initial distribution, using the iterative procedure described in section 4.2.
(3) We calculate the real wage in the short-run equilibrium for all twelve locations.
(4) We redistribute the manufacturing work force across the locations, moving laborers towards locations with high real wages and away from locations with low real wages; it is possible at this stage that a location stops producing manufacturing goods because there are no manufacturing workers anymore.
(5) We repeat steps 2 to 4 until a long-run equilibrium is reached in step 3 – that is, until the real wage is equal in all locations with a positive manufacturing labor force, or until all manufacturing labor is agglomerated in only one location.

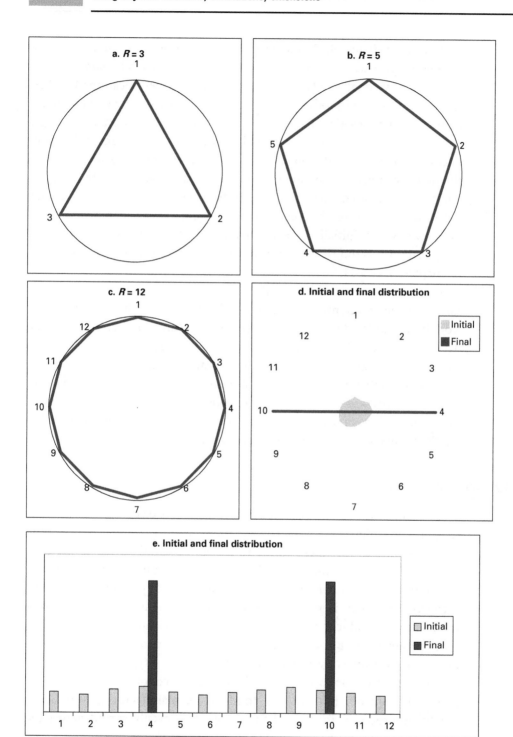

Figure 4.12 The racetrack economy
Notes: R = number of locations. Parameters for panels d and e are $\delta = 0.4$, $\varepsilon = 5$, and $T = 1.25$.

Panel d in figure 4.12 illustrates the simulation run using the same graphical approach as panels a to c. It appears that all manufacturing production eventually ends up in only two cities, namely locations 4 and 10, exactly opposite one another. Both locations produce exactly one half of the manufacturing varieties. Panel e shows the same simulation run using a column chart of the initial and final distribution of manufacturing production. Cities 4 and 10, which eventually emerge from the simulation as the only locations with manufacturing production, were already large initially, which allowed them to grow. Initial size is, however, not the only determining force for the long-run equilibrium. This is demonstrated by location 9, which initially is slightly larger than location 10, but eventually disappears as it is too close to location 10. More detailed examples are given in chapters 7 and 11.

If we repeat the simulation with the twelve-location racetrack economy for a different randomly chosen initial distribution of the manufacturing workforce, and for different parameter values, it turns out that the outcome depicted in figure 4.12 panels d and e is quite typical. Usually, all manufacturing production is eventually agglomerated in only one or two cities. If there are two cities, they are equal in size and opposite one another (though, of course, these are not always in locations 4 and 10). All other locations eventually end up producing no manufacturing goods. The next subsection briefly discusses this phenomenon and two problems associated with it.

4.9.2 Preferred frequency

Using an ingenious analysis, which is beyond the scope of this book, Fujita, Krugman, and Venables (1999: 85–94) assume that there are infinitely many locations on the racetrack economy to show that there tends to be a "preferred frequency" number of long-run equilibrium locations, depending on the structural parameters. For a large range of parameter values the preferred frequency is one, indicating that eventually all manufacturing production is produced in just one city; the monocentric equilibrium. For other parameter values the preferred frequency is two; half the manufacturing production is eventually produced in one city, the other half in another city at the opposite side of the racetrack economy. Similarly, if the preferred frequency is three, one-third of the manufacturing varieties is eventually produced in each of the three cities, evenly spread across the racetrack economy – and so on.

The preferred frequency tends to increase if (i) transport costs increase, (ii) the share of income spent on manufactures decreases, and (iii) the elasticity of substitution increases. All three results are intuitively plausible. (i) If transport costs increase, one would expect production to locate close to the market, increasing the long-run equilibrium of locations. (ii) If the share of income spent on manufactures decreases, the immobile food sector becomes economically more important, thus increasing the spreading force in the model, such that manufacturing firms locate more closely to their consumers and the number of long-run equilibrium locations increases. (iii) If the elasticity of substitution decreases, the market power of firms increases as it becomes harder to substitute one variety for another, such that the firms can get away with producing manufacturing varieties at just a few locations.

The preferred frequency analysis convincingly shows two fundamental *shortcomings* of the core model as generalized by the racetrack economy. First, the powers of agglomeration tend to be too strong – a feature that we have discussed at length in this chapter. For a large range of parameter settings only one city emerges, particularly if the share of income spent on manufactures, the mobile activity, is not too small. In this respect we are already glad when we find two cities in the long-run equilibrium of our simulations (with twelve locations), and delighted to find three cities in the final equilibrium. Most locations end up with no manufacturing activity whatsoever. The second problem is the monotone size of cities in the long-run equilibrium. This, of course, vacuously holds if we have only one city, but even if we have more than one city in the long-run equilibrium, say two or three, then those cities are exactly equal in size, and evenly distributed across the racetrack economy. This poses a problem for empirical applications, of course, say if we want to explain the rank-size distribution of India as described in chapter 1, which requires the existence of many cities of unequal size. This phenomenon is further addressed in chapter 7.

4.10 Conclusions

This chapter began with a discussion of the use of computer simulations in geographical economics: what they are, how to perform them, their advantages and their limitations. As regards the latter, even an infinite number of computer simulations cannot replace an analytical result. Nevertheless, the advantages of simulations are enormous, as they (i) allow us to do things we cannot do analytically, (ii) give a general "feel" for the model, (iii) suggest results that can be proven analytically, or (iv) disprove alleged results by producing a counter-example. We have given examples for each of these advantages for the core model of geographical economics, and in doing so introduced new concepts, such as the break and sustain points.

In the second part of chapter 4, we introduced three additional models that build on and extend the core model of chapter 3. The first model includes intermediate production and inter-sectoral labor mobility, instead of interregional labor mobility. Especially in empirical applications, in which the comparison between countries is important, this model may be attractive. It harbors the stylized facts that most commodity trade is trade in intermediate products and that labor is more mobile within countries than between countries. In addition, this model has the nice feature that decreasing returns in food production can lead to a bell-shaped curve: as trade costs fall, we see that a country goes through a spreading phase, then through an agglomeration phase, and finally through spreading again. This is qualitatively different from the tomahawk diagram summarizing the core model (which is biased towards agglomeration). The third model introduces a second production factor in the manufacturing sector. For some applications, such a model is more appealing than the core model of chapter 3, for example when analyzing the consequences of globalization for different types of workers. As a surprising bonus, the model leads to explicit solutions for factor rewards. Analytically, solvable models seem to be preferable to the core model of geographical economics of chapter 3, which requires numerical simulations. This potential advantage comes to the fore only when we focus on the case of only two regions. Once we turn to a multiple region setting and no longer get away with the assumption of neutral space, we will see that we have to rely on simulations anyway. This will be discussed in section 6.4 in chapter 6 (see also Fujita and Mori, 2005, and Behrens and Thisse, 2007).

Chapters 3 and 4 belong together and cover the basic theory of the geographical economics approach in our book. Armed with these two chapters, we can now return to the empirical examples discussed in chapter 1 and focus on the empirical relevance of geographical economics. This is the topic of chapters 5 and 6. In applications of geographical economics to specific questions or (sub-)fields, the topic of chapters 7 to

11, the models introduced in chapters 3 and 4 constitute the backbone of the analysis.

Box 4.1 For those readers who cannot get enough: more on extensions

Even though we have discussed the most important extensions of the core model of geographical economics at some length in sections 4.6 to 4.8, there is of course more that can be said about these particular extensions. In addition, there are some extensions that we have not mentioned at all so far. So, this is for those readers who would like to learn more about extensions of the core model (or, indeed, about the core model itself).

- To learn more on the core models and the three model extensions from this chapter, see in particular the books by Baldwin *et al.* (2003: chap. 2 on the core model, and other chapters on solvable models), Fujita and Thisse (2002: chap. 9), Combes, Mayer, and Thisse (2008), and Fujita, Krugman, and Venables (1999: chap. 14). Robert-Nicoud (2005) provides what is arguably the most extensive analysis, of the similarities (in terms of the underlying formal structure) between the models based on interregional labor mobility with those based on intermediate input linkages.
- Like the models discussed in this chapter, solvable models come in two basic flavors. The first flavor follows the core model – that is, models in which interregional factor mobility is included (as in the "footloose entrepreneur" model of Forslid and Ottaviano, 2003, discussed in the main text). The so-called "footloose capital" models (Baldwin *et al.*, 2003: chap. 3) also belong to this group. In the FC models, and contrary to the core model and the FE models, the income of the mobile factor is repatriated to the region of origin of the mobile factor. This greatly simplifies the analysis because much of the demand (and cost) linkages that normally characterize geographical economics do not come into play if the migration of the mobile factor does not accompany a regional shift in expenditures. The second flavor of models stems from the intermediate goods model of our section 4.6. Ottaviano and Robert-Nicoud (2006) provide a synthesis (see also Ottaviano, 2007).
- One extension that has not been mentioned until now consists of models with forward-looking expectations. Take, for instance, the core model and migration equation (4.4). In making the decision whether or not to migrate, manufacturing workers display what can be called myopic behavior. They look only at present real wages (and they ignore the migration decision made by other workers). But what about the prospects for future wages? Following Krugman (1991c), models have been developed that take the role of expectations into account and that also address the theoretical foundation of the simple migration model (4.4). On the website we provide more information on this line of work in geographical economics.
- A final extension (and here the phrase "last but not least" is appropriate) concerns those models of geographical economics that dismiss one of the central elements (or, to use the term used by Fujita, Krugman, and Venables 1999, "tricks") underlying the core

Box 4.1 (cont.)

model, the demand preference structure (Cobb–Douglas with CES sub-utility for the manufactures) based on Dixit–Stiglitz (1977), by using a quasi-linear utility function. This idea was first used by Ottaviano, Tabuchi, and Thisse (2002). It turns out that this greatly simplifies the model and leads to a rather straightforward demand structure, much like the case of the solvable model discussed in the main text above. For a good exposition of the basic quasi-linear utility model of geographical economics, see Fujita and Thisse (2002, in particular their figure 9.5). On our website we discuss the use of a quasi-linear utility function in our discussion of the solvable model by Michael Pflüger (2004). In the remainder of our book, the model of geographical economics with a quasi-linear utility function crops up in chapter 8 on multinationals, where we analyze the Baldwin and Toshihiro Okubo (2006) model.

The basic difference between Ottaviano, Tabuchi, and Thisse (2002) and Pflüger (2004) is that the former uses a quadratic quasi-linear utility function whereas the latter uses a logarithmic quasi-linear utility function (see, for a synthesis, Pflüger and Südekum, 2008). Both models assume interregional labor mobility and therefore belong to the class of "footloose entrepreneur" models and give rise to a tomahawk-like figure. The difference with the tomahawk of figure 4.3 is that, in the Ottaviano, Tabuchi, and Thisse (2002) model, the break and sustain points occur for the same value of T (or ϕ), which thus eliminates the feature of path dependency (a case such as $T = 1.7$ in figure 4.4 is not possible). Apart from the fact that the break and sustain points coincide, the resulting figure in (T, λ) space is the same as the tomahawk. In Pflüger (2004) there is a break point but no catastrophic agglomeration once spreading becomes unstable when T falls. Instead, there is a smooth, continuous increase of agglomeration until either λ_1 or λ_2 equals one. Once full agglomeration has been established (and herein lies the difference with the bell-shaped curve), full agglomeration is there to stay when T continues to fall. Instead of a tomahawk, the resulting figure looks like a pitchfork.[26]

More generally, the tomahawk turns out not to be very robust. Not only does the dismissal of the CES sub-utility function (3.4) and its replacement by a quasi-linear function do the job, but also, as we saw above in the main text in this section, the combination of no interregional labor mobility with decreasing returns to labor in agriculture (Puga, 1999) or the introduction of a housing sector (Helpman, 1998) does the trick and may yield a bell-shaped curve. The introduction of taste heterogeneity gives similar results (Tabuchi and Thisse, 2002). Finally, using the FE model, Pflüger and Jens Südekum (2007) show that, if instead of an upper-tier Cobb–Douglas utility function like equation (3.1) one uses a CES upper tier utility function, the catastrophic change from spreading to agglomeration (or vice versa) that characterizes the tomahawk ceases to exist. One gets a smooth transition from spreading to agglomeration.

[26] See footnote 20.

Appendix

The function f(T)

Following the procedure described in section 4.5, the implied wage in region 2, given complete agglomeration of manufacturing in region 1, is given by

$$W_2 = \left[\frac{1+\delta}{2} T^{1-\varepsilon} + \frac{1-\delta}{2} T^{\varepsilon-1} \right]^{1/\varepsilon} \tag{A4.1}$$

Using that to determine the implied real wage in region 2, it is convenient to note that

$$
\begin{aligned}
w_2^\varepsilon &= \frac{1+\delta}{2} T^{1-\varepsilon-\varepsilon\delta} + \frac{1-\delta}{2} T^{\varepsilon-1-\varepsilon\delta} \\
&= \frac{1+\delta}{2} T^{-(\rho+\delta)\varepsilon} + \frac{1-\delta}{2} T^{(\rho-\delta)\varepsilon} \equiv f(T)
\end{aligned}
\tag{A4.2}
$$

$$f'(T) = \varepsilon \left[-\frac{1+\delta}{2} (\rho+\delta) T^{-(\rho+\delta)\varepsilon-1} + \frac{1-\delta}{2} (\rho-\delta) T^{(\rho-\delta)\varepsilon-1} \right] \tag{A4.3}$$

$$f(1) = 1; \ f'(1) = -\varepsilon\delta(1+\rho)<0; \ \lim_{T\to\infty} f(T) = \infty \ \ iff \rho > \delta \tag{A4.4}$$

Using (A4.4), the graph of the function f(T) is sketched in figure A4.1; panel a applies if the no-black-hole condition is met ($\rho > \delta$), panel b if it is not ($\rho < \delta$). These results are used in section 4.5.

Stability of the spreading equilibrium

To analyze the break point we need to know what happens to the real wage if labor relocates to another region, making that region a little larger than the region from where labor originates. We have to analyze the change of real wages around the symmetric equilibrium. From equation (4.4) we know that we need two pieces of information: the change in the nominal wage, and the change in the price index. If we have these we can calculate the change in the real wage. If the real wage rises in the larger region, all footloose labor will follow, so the symmetric equilibrium is unstable. If the real wage falls the defecting worker will return to the original location, so the symmetric equilibrium is stable.

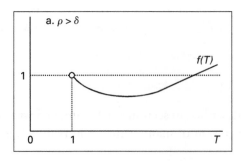

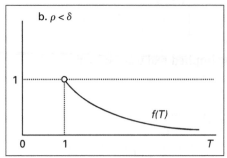

Figure A4.1 Sketch of the function $f(T)$

The spreading equilibrium is given by $\lambda \equiv \lambda_1 = \lambda_2 = 1/2$, $W \equiv W_1 = W_2 = 1$, $Y \equiv Y_1 = Y_2 = 1/2$, and $I^{1-\varepsilon} \equiv I_1^{1-\varepsilon} = I_2^{1-\varepsilon} = \lambda(1 + T^{1-\varepsilon})$. We want to investigate changes in the equilibrium if an infinitesimal number of workers are relocating from region 1 to region 2, where we will ignore all second-order effects of induced changes for the other regions. Thus we can write $dI \equiv dI_1 = -dI_2$, $dW \equiv dW_1 = -dW_2$, and $d\lambda \equiv d\lambda_1 = -d\lambda_2$, differentiate (4.1) and evaluate at the spreading equilibrium to get (4A.5).[27] Doing the same with (4.2) gives (4A.6).

$$dY = \delta d\lambda + \frac{\delta}{2} dW \tag{4A.5}$$

$$(1 - \varepsilon)\frac{dI}{I} = I^{\varepsilon-1}\left(1 - T^{1-\varepsilon}\right)\left[\frac{1 - \varepsilon}{2} dW + d\lambda\right] \tag{4A.6}$$

Define $Z \equiv (1 - T^{1-\varepsilon})/(1 + T^{1-\varepsilon})$, and note that Z is an index of trade barriers that ranges from zero when there are no transport costs ($T = 1$) to one when transport costs are prohibitive ($T \to \infty$). With this notation we

---

[27] See technical note 3.8 for some of the details.

can rewrite (4A.6) as (4A.7). Differentiating (4.3) and (4.4) and evaluating at the spreading equilibrium gives (4A.8) and (4A.9) respectively.

$$\frac{dI}{I} = \frac{2Z}{1-\varepsilon}d\lambda + ZdW \tag{4A.7}$$

$$\varepsilon dW = Z2dY + (\varepsilon - 1)Z\frac{dI}{I} \tag{4A.8}$$

$$I^\delta dw = dW - \delta\frac{dI}{I} \tag{4A.9}$$

Equations (4A.5) and (4A.7) to (4A.9) can be solved to determine the effect of a small disturbance on the real wage. Substituting (4A.5) in (4A.8) and combining with (4A.7) gives system (4A.10). Solving (4A.10) gives (4A.11).

$$\begin{bmatrix} 1 & -Z \\ Z & (\varepsilon - \delta Z)/(1-\varepsilon) \end{bmatrix}\begin{bmatrix} dI/I \\ dW \end{bmatrix} = \begin{bmatrix} 2Z/(1-\varepsilon)d\lambda \\ 2Z\delta/(1-\varepsilon)d\lambda \end{bmatrix} \tag{A4.10}$$

$$\begin{bmatrix} dI/I \\ dW \end{bmatrix} = \frac{1}{\Delta}\begin{bmatrix} (\varepsilon - \delta Z)/(1-\varepsilon) & Z \\ -Z & 1 \end{bmatrix}\begin{bmatrix} 2Z/(1-\varepsilon)d\lambda \\ 2Z\delta/(1-\varepsilon)d\lambda \end{bmatrix} \tag{A4.11}$$

where $\Delta \equiv [(1-\varepsilon)Z^2 - \delta Z + \varepsilon]/(1-\varepsilon)$. Thus

$$\frac{dI}{I} = \frac{d\lambda}{\Delta}\frac{2Z\varepsilon}{(1-\varepsilon)^2}(1-\delta Z) \quad \text{and} \quad dW = \frac{d\lambda}{\Delta}\frac{2Z}{(1-\varepsilon)}(\delta - Z).$$

These are the two pieces of information we need. Substituting these results in (4A.9) gives the change in the real wage:

$$\begin{aligned} \frac{dw}{d\lambda} &= \frac{2ZI^{-\delta}}{(\varepsilon-1)}\left[\frac{\delta(2\varepsilon - 1) - Z[\varepsilon(1+\delta^2) - 1]}{\varepsilon - \delta Z - (\varepsilon - 1)Z^2}\right] \\ &= \frac{2ZI^{-\delta}(1-\rho)}{\rho}\left[\frac{\delta(1+\rho) - Z[\delta^2 + \rho]}{1 - \delta Z(1-\rho) - \rho Z^2}\right] \end{aligned} \tag{*}$$

The spreading equilibrium is unstable if $dw/d\lambda$ is positive. The sign depends on the numerator of the expression, since the denominator is always positive. Thus, $dw/d\lambda = 0$ if, and only if, $Z = \delta(1+\rho)/(\delta^2 + \rho)$. The equilibrium is unstable if $dw/d\lambda > 0$, if $Z < \delta(1+\rho)/(\delta^2 + \rho)$, and vice versa if the spreading equilibrium is stable. Note that in equation (4.6) in the main text we add one to both sides of the equation to facilitate the comparison of the sustain and break points in figure 4.4. Moreover, in the intermediate goods model, equilibrium is determined by $[W - F'(1-\lambda)]$ (see equation 4.14). The associated stability condition is therefore ruled by the sign of $\frac{dw}{d\lambda} + F''$. Under constant returns to scale for food production $(F'' = 0)$, the condition reduces to the counterpart of (*) with a unique solution in Z. Under decreasing returns to scale for food production $(F'' < 0)$, adding (F'') to the counterpart of (*) results in a quadratic equation in Z.

Exercises

4.1 Go to the website of the book, where you will find Excel files containing the data and some of the figures used in this book. Look up the file for figure 4.2, where you will find additional information on the relationship between the relative real wage and transport costs. Make XY-scatter plots (using smoothed lines) for the transport cost ranges $T = 1.50$, 1.55, 1.60, 1.65, and 1.70 and for the ranges $T = 1.75$, 1.80, 1.85, and 1.90. Comment on your findings (in terms of stability).

4.2 The text in this chapter has not proved that the break point arises for a lower value of transport costs T than the sustain point. Convince yourself that it does, by calculating these values for a grid of admissible (ρ, δ) parameter combinations, as in figure 4.3.

4.3 Explicitly calculate the break point as a function of the transport costs T (using equation 4.6). Your answer should be $T = \left[\frac{(\rho-\delta)(1-\delta)}{(\rho+\delta)(1+\delta)}\right]^{1/(1-\varepsilon)}$.

4.4 Analyze the impact of other parameters on the sustain and break points of figures 4.2 and 4.3 by using the *break* Excel file on the website. In particular, how do these points move in figure 4.3a and 4.3b if ρ or δ is increased? Can you intuitively explain this movement?

4.5 Derive equation (4.26). Also calculate the break and the sustain points of the solvable model.

5 | Agglomeration, the home market effect, and spatial wages

5.1 Introduction

Chapter 1 of this book has presented a number of stylized facts about the clustering of economic activity to justify our inquiry into the relationships between economics and geography.[1] In chapters 2 to 4 we have mainly looked at this relationship from a theoretical point of view. In this chapter we start with a reminder that location matters. This chapter and the next focus on the *empirics* of geographical economics, in order to assess whether the spatial facts can be explained by geographical economics models as introduced in chapters 3 and 4.

We start with a brief review in section 5.2 of the main facts about the concentration and agglomeration of economic activity. This continues, and partly restates, our discussion of stylized facts of location in chapter 1. Against this background, section 5.3 answers the question of whether these facts can be reconciled with the various economic theories of location presented in chapters 2 to 4. To provide this answer, we summarize the main predictions about clustering (if any) that follow from the various theories, and conclude that the stylized facts are in accordance with multiple theories (and not only with geographical economics). This does not come as a great surprise, since many empirical studies about the concentration or the agglomeration of economic activity are, quite simply, not primarily concerned with the testing of specific theories.

In the remainder of this chapter, we analyze two implications of the geographical economics models, namely (i) the existence of the home market effect and (ii) a spatial wage structure. The home market effect

---

[1] Section 5.2 explains the distinctions between specialization, concentration, and agglomeration in connection with economic activity.

implies that, if a region displays a relatively large demand for a certain good, this increased demand will lead to a more than proportional increase in the region's production of that good. The spatial wage structure (see wage equation (4.3)) implies that wages will be higher in or near economic centers. These investigations are the first steps towards a full-fledged empirical assessment. Given the observed core–periphery patterns in real life, if both of these predictions were refuted by the data further empirical research would be rather futile.[2] In section 5.4, we look at empirical research into the home market effect. In section 5.5 we do the same for the existence of a spatial wage structure. At the end of this chapter we conclude that the empirical studies into the home market effect and the spatial wage structure, in general, confirm their relevance, but that they do not offer a complete or convincing test of the geographical economics model as such. The main reason is that both implications take the spatial distribution of economic activity as given, and in doing so are primarily concerned with what we dubbed in chapter 4 the short-run equilibrium version of geographical economics. A real test of geographical economics should also look at the empirical validity of this approach when the spatial distribution of economic activity is no longer fixed but subject to change. This is the starting point and motivation for chapter 6.

5.2 The spatial distribution of economic activity

5.2.1 Distinguishing between concentration, specialization, and agglomeration

Before we return to the empirical features of the location of economic activity it is necessary to clarify the differences between concentration, specialization, and agglomeration from an empirical point of view. We start with the distinction between concentration and agglomeration. As opposed to specialization (see below), both concentration and agglomeration refer to the question of how (some part of) economic activity, such as a specific industry or the manufacturing sector as a whole, is distributed across space.

---

[2] The reader may note that this statement does not hold at the spreading equilibrium, where all regions are of equal size. Only with size variations (some degree of agglomeration on a sectoral or regional basis) do either the home market effect or the spatial wage structure make sense. See Hanson (2000), Head and Mayer (2004a), or Overman, Redding, and Venables (2003) for in-depth surveys into the empirics of geographical economics.

Concentration and agglomeration are both concerned with the question of whether a specific part of economic activity can be found at a few locations, be it a city, a region, or a country. Even though concentration and agglomeration both deal with the location of economic activity, their focus is quite different. Following Marius Brülhart (1998: 776), concentration analyzes the location across space of a few well-defined sectors (notably industries), whereas agglomeration analyzes the location across space of a much larger part of economic activity, such as the manufacturing sector as a whole; compare, for instance, figures 5.1b and 5.1d. In the former there is concentration of the two industries (I in country A and II in country B), whereas in the latter there is agglomeration of industrial activity (nearly all industries I and II are located in country A).

The empirical analysis of the geographical concentration of industries tries to show whether or not particular industries are geographically clustered. As such, the concentration of industries need not tell us anything about the distribution of manufacturing activity overall across space – that is to say, it does not necessarily provide information on the degree of agglomeration. On the contrary, there may be geographical concentration without agglomeration. Again, to see the difference but now for regions within a single country (see figure 5.1c), suppose that country A consists of two regions, R1 and R2, and there are still two industries of equal size, I and II. Geographical concentration could imply that industry I is mainly located in region R1 of country A (whereas industry II ends up in country B). Despite the fact that, as opposed to figure 5.1b, there is now clearly also concentration at the regional level in country A, the overall distribution of manufacturing activity between the two *countries* is even. Agglomeration within a country would mean that the bulk of both industries would locate in the same country, or perhaps even within a single region of that country, as is the case in figure 5.1d. Hence, concentration and agglomeration can be two rather different things.

Of course, when in reality the majority of industries are geographically concentrated at the same *location*, this also implies a high degree of agglomeration of manufacturing activity as a whole (figure 5.1d). As a rule of thumb, it is useful to keep in mind that studies of agglomeration analyze how aggregate economic activity, often manufacturing production, is distributed across space. The empirical analysis of concentration does the same but only for a particular type of economic activity, say the production of aircraft, and then tries to show at this lower level of aggregation how the production of aircraft is distributed across space.

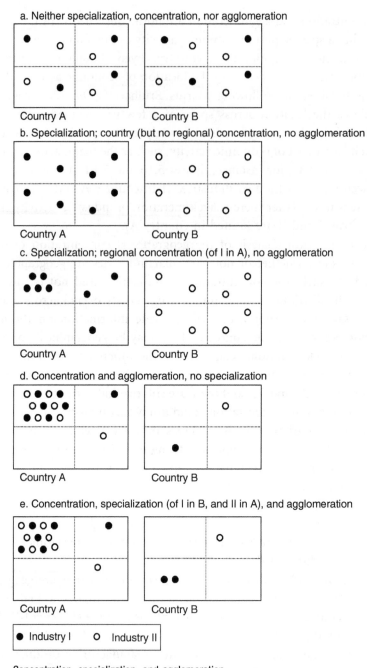

Figure 5.1   Concentration, specialization, and agglomeration

Concentration and agglomeration can be distinguished from specialization (see Hallet, 2000, Gorter, 2002, or Brakman *et al.*, 2005).[3] Specialization deals with the question of whether or not a *location's* share in, for example, the production of cars or apparel is relatively large compared to the share of other locations in the production of cars or apparel. Ever since Smith (1776) wrote about the fruits of the international division of labor, the emphasis in trade theory has been on specialization. Studies of specialization are attempts to reveal a country's or region's economic structure. Concentration in figure 5.1 reflects the regional clustering of a single industry, and agglomeration refers to the regional clustering of many industries. In figure 5.1a, countries A and B are not specialized, whereas in figure 5.1b they obviously are. In figure 5.1b, specialization coincides with no regional concentration. Actual data on specialization as such are not very useful from the perspective of geographical economics, however, since they do not necessarily tell us anything about the relative distribution of economic activity across space. Figures 5.1c and 5.1d illustrate that agglomeration, concentration, and specialization need not accompany each other. The fact that, for instance, in the European Union the Netherlands and Germany are, compared to the EU average, specialized in chemical products and machinery respectively is not conclusive evidence about either the concentration of chemical products or machinery production across the EU countries or the degree of economic agglomeration in the European Union. The Dutch specialization in chemical products might, for instance, go with France being home to a larger part of the production of chemical products (in absolute terms), which, as far as the concentration of the chemical industry is concerned, makes France more important than the Netherlands. Similarly, taken together the specialization patterns of the individual EU countries do not tell us how large each country's share is in total manufacturing production, and hence provide no conclusive information about the degree of agglomeration of manufacturing activity.

To distinguish agglomeration from concentration (a matter of degree) and specialization (a more fundamental difference) is important from a

---

[3] Although we think such a distinction can be made, this is not always deemed relevant. In addition, the term "concentration" is sometimes not used in geographical economics because it can give the false impression that one is dealing with some index measuring the share of individual firms in the production of certain goods. Statements such as "The European car industry is concentrated because the top five automobile firms have a market share exceeding X percent" are not relevant in this book, as here "concentration" has a geographical interpretation. Moreover, in contrast to Fujita and Thisse (2002: 20, note 1), we think it is useful to differentiate between the use of the terms "agglomeration" and "concentration."

theoretical point of view, as we are mostly interested in agglomeration. Geographical economics has in common with trade models that it deals with specialization and concentration, but the emphasis on agglomeration sets geographical economics apart from trade theory (see chapter 2 section 2.3), in which the concern is with specialization or concentration but not with agglomeration. Ideally, therefore, we would like to discuss empirical studies that allow for specialization, concentration, and agglomeration simultaneously. Unfortunately, the vast majority of empirical studies on trade are, first and foremost, about specialization (see Leamer and Levinsohn, 1995).

Stimulated by the new trade theory and geographical economics, there are now a number of studies dealing with geographical concentration, but there are very few studies that explicitly try to test for the only theory that strongly emphasizes the possibility of agglomeration: geographical economics. As we will see in the next section, this state of the art in empirical research is one reason why it is rather difficult to discriminate between alternative theories of location. The specialization–concentration–agglomeration distinction is important, but it should not cloud the fundamental issue that location, either because of specialization, concentration, or agglomeration, matters empirically. The next sub-section discusses the geographical unit of analysis and the type of economic activity. Box 5.1, at the end of section 5.2, gives some data and background information on the actual degree of specialization, concentration, and agglomeration for the EU countries.

5.2.2 Location matters: a reminder

At the highest level of aggregation, the supranational level, estimates of the gravity model (see equations (1.2) and (1.3)) invariably lead to the conclusion that trade is a decreasing function of the economic distance between countries and that countries predominantly trade with neighboring countries. As far as the trade pattern, and hence the degree of specialization, is concerned, the empirical evidence shows that intra-industry trade has become increasingly important in the post-war era (chapter 9). This is true not only for OECD countries but also increasingly for non-OECD countries. Within the European Union, for instance, intra-industry trade accounts for more than 60 percent of all trade. Apart from the gravity model, chapter 1 also illustrated agglomeration at the level of the world economy as a whole (see figure 1.3). The findings point to the high-income countries as the main centers of the world economy, and *within* these high-income countries three core centers are clearly discernible. These data are related to a large number of empirical studies on the (lack of) convergence of GDP per capita between countries. In general, these studies lead to two conclusions. First, for the world economy as a whole there is no (or at best a very limited) tendency towards a convergence of individual per capita income levels. This means that the income differences between core and periphery do not narrow and may very well increase further, thereby strengthening agglomeration. Second, within groupings of countries, such as the European Union, a different picture emerges. Here, convergence is taking place. For the EU countries this indicates that, say, the difference between Germany and Portugal in GDP per capita has decreased over time, hence reducing the degree of agglomeration somewhat (see box 5.1 below). See Stefano Magrini (2004) for an in-depth survey of regional convergence and the main estimation strategies involved.

Switching from the supranational level to the regional level, it remains obvious that location matters. The equivalent of the open economy gravity model for a closed economy is the market potential approach (see section 2.3). Estimates of the market potential function show that firms tend to locate in or near regions where demand is relatively high, thus fostering and reinforcing a process of agglomeration. In section 5.5, we apply the market potential function to regions in the United States and Germany. More information on agglomeration at the regional level can be found in the economic growth literature, in which the growth process is analyzed for regions instead of countries. These studies look at regions within a single country as well as at regions within a group of countries. Neven and Gouyette (1995), for instance, find evidence for convergence for a large group of EU regions in the 1960s and 1970s. This convergence process now seems to have come to a halt. The main message from these *regional* convergence studies is that there are considerable differences between regions in terms of GDP per capita, supporting the idea of an agglomeration of economic activity across space. Moreover, and in accordance with the idea of agglomeration, regions with a relatively high GDP per capita tend to be located near each other, as do regions with low levels of GDP per capita (see also Bosker, 2007, and Puga, 2002).

Empirical research in urban economics is also concerned with the *regional* level in the sense that urban areas or cities are regions in a national space. This national space as such is not considered to be very interesting, since it is taken for granted that agglomeration exists within this space. The analysis focuses on the cities themselves as the centers of economic activity (see section 2.2), without interaction between the cities and the rest of the country. The empirical question is not only how cities interact and develop over time (the fall and rise of individual cities) but also whether or not industries are concentrated in certain cities. The development of the urban system provides information on the agglomeration of cities. The main issue is (the change in) the city-size distribution, which appears to be rather stable for the industrialized countries (see, for instance, Gabaix, 1999b, or Black and Henderson, 2003, 1999b, for the United States). The city-size distribution in some Western countries displays a regularity known as the rank-size distribution, illustrated for India in chapter 1. A special case of the rank-size distribution is Zipf's Law, stating that the largest city is twice as large as the second largest city, five times as large as the fifth largest city, etc. We return to these issues in chapter 7.

The empirical evidence with respect to the geographical concentration of industries between cities leads to the conclusion that positive externalities stimulate the concentration of firms in cities. There is a lively discussion in the literature, however, about the question as to which type of positive externality is more relevant for the geographical concentration of industries across the urban landscape. Section 2.2 distinguished between *localization* and *urbanization* economies. The former applies to industry-specific external economies of scale, whereas the latter refers to inter-industry external economies of scale. Applied to cities, both types of economies of scale have recently been the topic of a considerable amount of empirical research. Depending, among other things, on the static or dynamic nature of these two economies of scale, some studies find evidence for localization economics (for example, Beardsell and Henderson, 1999), while some find that urbanization economics are more relevant (for example, the seminal study by Glaeser *et al.*, 1992, of the growth of US cities). For us, it is important that external economies of scale lead firms to locate in cities because other firms do the same. Whether or not firms in a city belong to the same industry or not is of secondary importance (yes, in the case of localization economies; no, in the case of urbanization economies) (see also Rosenthal and Strange, 2004, for a survey). We return to this topic in chapter 7.

We briefly discuss an important representative example: the seminal study by Ellison and Glaeser (1997). They have developed an index for the geographic concentration of industries, now known (surprise!) as the Ellison–Glaeser index, and study this index for the United States. The index measures the degree to which industry i is geographically concentrated (in terms of employment) in location s at time t. It corrects for the fact that, in industries consisting of only a few relatively large plants, the industry concentration index will necessarily be high.[4] The index takes on the value of zero if industry employment is not concentrated, when Ellison and Glaeser (1997: 890) argue that in this case it is *as if* "the plants in the industry [had] chosen locations by throwing darts on a map."[5]

The main empirical finding is that, at the four-digit industry level, industrial employment is indeed geographically concentrated, so the "dartboard approach" is rejected, even though for many industries the degree of concentration is rather small. Using this index, it appears that the geographical concentration is fairly stable (at the industry level, not at the plant level), and that the degree of concentration decreases slightly over time (see Dumais, Ellison, and Glaeser, 1997: 7). In our view, the results found in this and other studies using the Ellison–Glaeser index indicate clearly that the geographic concentration of industries is the rule, and not the exception (notably, China illustrates an exception, as it is "under-agglomerated"; see Fujita *et al.*, 2004: 2968). This conclusion holds not only for the United States, and Japan but also for the countries of the European Union (see Combes and Overman, 2004, for data on the European Union, Holmes and Stevens, 2004, for data on the United States, Fujita *et al.*, 2004, for data on Japan and China, and box 5.1).[6]

---

[4] Compared to simple concentration indices (see box 5.1), the Ellison–Glaeser index is quite sophisticated, as is the recent research on industry concentration by Brülhart and Traeger (2005), in which entropy indices are used to measure concentration and in which region size is controlled by land mass. Combes and Overman (2004) stress that we need selection criteria to assess the usefulness of the various indices to measure the spatial distribution of economic activity. Ideally, the statistic (index) concerned should meet the following requirements: (i) *be comparable across economic activities and spatial scales*, (ii) *take a unique value under the no-clustering benchmark*, (iii) *be amenable to the calculation of confidence intervals*, (iv) *be insensitive to changes in the industrial or regional classification*, and (v) *respond to the clustering brought by the forces stressed in the location theories*. As Combes and Overman note, there is no statistic that meets all criteria, but their "wish list" serves as a useful benchmark for the existing indices discussed in the main text and in box 5.1. The use of microdata and/or data at a very low spatial scale (microgeographic data) is probably the best answer to date to the wish list (see Duranton and Overman, 2005, 2008).

[5] The index γ (see Ellison and Glaeser, 1997: 899, or Dumais, Ellison, and Glaeser, 1997: 7) measures the degree to which industry i is geographically concentrated at time t: $\gamma_i = [G_{it}/(1-\Sigma_s s^2_{it}) - H_{it}]/(1-H_{it})$; in which G_{it} is defined as $\Sigma_s (s_{ist} - s_{st})^2$ with s_{ist} the share of industry i's employment at time t located in state s, and with s_{st} the state s's share of aggregate employment at time t. H_{it} is a Herfindahl index measuring the plant-level concentration of employment in a industry. When $\gamma_i = 0$ there are no agglomeration forces, and the location of that industry across the United States can be looked upon as being "generated by the simple dartboard model of random location choices with no natural [location] advantages or industry specific spillovers" (Ellison and Glaeser, 1997: 900). Note that γ_i has no upper limit as $0 < H_{it} < 1$. For their sample of 459 four-digit industries the mean (median) value for $\gamma_i = 0.051$ (0.026), which indicates a very skewed distribution. For 43 percent of the industries $\gamma_i < 0.02$, which is the category of not very concentrated industries, and fifty-nine industries have $\gamma_i > 0.1$, which means that these are the most geographically concentrated industries.

[6] A related topic is the clustering of firms engaging in foreign direct investment – that is, the geographical concentration of this investment. We deal with this phenomenon in chapter 8 in our analysis of multinationals.

Box 5.1 Specialization, concentration, and agglomeration in the European Union

The study by Midelfart Knarvik *et al.* (2003) provides useful and extensive information at the country level for the degree of specialization, concentration, and agglomeration for fourteen of the EU members before the accession of the new states in 2004. The study analyzes production data for fourteen EU countries and thirty-six industries from 1970 to 1997. Specialization is measured by what is called the Krugman specialization index (the index dates back to work by Edgar Hoover, 1948) – that is, for each individual EU country the index is defined as a country's share in the production of industry k minus the share of the other EU countries in the production of industry k, summed over all industries. If the Krugman specialization index is zero the country has an industrial structure that is identical to the rest of the EU: a case of non-specialization. The larger the value of the Krugman index the more this country is specialized. Figure 5.2 illustrates the Krugman specialization index for three four-year periods in the 1970s, 1980s, and 1990s. The figure clearly

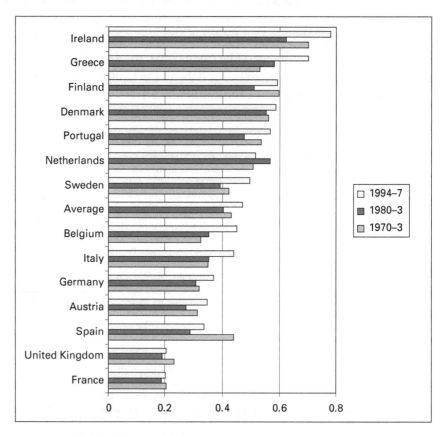

Figure 5.2   Krugman specialization index
Source: Midelfart Knarvik *et al.* (2003: 221).

Box 5.1 (cont.)

indicates that the EU countries are specialized (the indices are not zero), with France and the United Kingdom displaying an industrial production structure most similar to the EU average. As is also evident, and easy to understand, the small EU countries tend to be more specialized in their production pattern than the large EU countries.

It is apparent from figure 5.2 that the degree of specialization fell for ten and rose for four countries between the 1970s and the 1980s, leading to a decline in specialization for the European Union on average in that period. From the 1980s to the 1990s, however, there was a strong *increase* in the degree of specialization for all EU countries, particularly for Greece, Ireland, and Sweden, with the exception of the Netherlands. Midelfart-Knarvik *et al.* (2003) relate these findings to the different industry specialization patterns of EU countries. These calculations do not give any information, however, on the location of industries across the EU countries. As we saw in figure 5.1, high as well as low specialization indices may accompany either the geographic agglomeration or concentration of industries, or the absence thereof. The degree of industry concentration is measured as the relative production share across countries for a given industry: for example, the degree of concentration of the shipbuilding industry is measured by the relative share each EU country has in shipbuilding; a skewed distribution of these shares implies that shipbuilding is concentrated. In this manner one gets to know for each of the industries how its production is distributed across the EU countries. It turns out that, when all industry concentration results are grouped together, there is no clear discernible upward or downward trend in concentration from 1970 to 1997.

Overall, therefore, the degree of industry concentration in the European Union showed only a moderate increase during this period. For individual industries the results are different. Some initially concentrated industries (textiles, furniture) became more concentrated over time, whereas the reverse is true for some other initially concentrated industries (beverages, tobacco, radio and television, and communications). A similar mixed picture emerges for initially geographically dispersed industries. Notwithstanding these industrial differences, it is clear that the majority of industries are geographically concentrated in the European Union, as they are in the United States. Again, we have to be careful, as concentration is not necessarily the same as agglomeration (see figure 5.1). We can measure the degree of agglomeration by using a country's share in the total EU manufacturing activity as a proxy. This is illustrated in figure 5.3. Some spreading of manufacturing activity occurred in the period 1970–97 – that is, the three core countries (the United Kingdom, France, and Germany) lost some of their share in manufacturing activity (a fall from 63.2 percent to 59.0 percent) to the periphery of the European Union (southern EU countries, Finland, and Ireland). Overall, the degree of agglomeration seems rather stable for our group of EU countries.

To summarize, based on production data for the last three decades, the following trends arise for the manufacturing sector of the EU *countries:* (i) increased specialization, (ii) a fairly constant (overall) degree of industry concentration with large differences between individual industries, and (iii) rather stable agglomeration. If anything, we see a small decrease in the degree of agglomeration. These conclusions are subject to a number of caveats. First, they are based on very simple indices (see our discussion of Ellison and Glaeser, 1997, and Combes and Overman, 2004). Second, the use of manufacturing production data, rather than employment data or other economic activities, is important for arriving at the above conclusions, as related studies have shown. It is becoming increasingly important in connection with the European Union to include the

Box 5.1 (cont.)

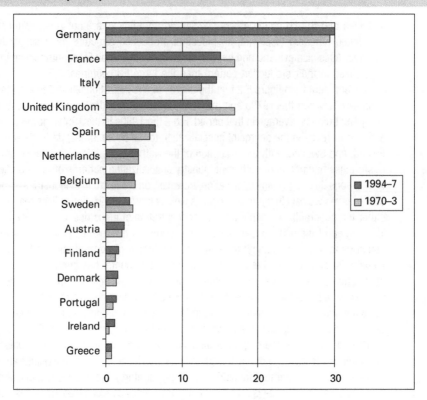

Figure 5.3 Agglomeration of manufacturing in the European Union
Source: Midelfart Knarvik *et al.* (2003: 231).

services sector in the analysis. After all, the majority of employment and value added is now in the services sector, rather than in the manufacturing sector. The consequences of this inclusion are not clear beforehand, given the difficulties with which many services are tradable. Third, in a related study and using similar indices, Martin Hallet (2000) looks at EU specialization and concentration using *regional* rather than country data. He also finds that industry concentration is fairly constant but, in contrast to Midelfart Knarvik *et al.* (2003), concludes that the EU regions became *less* specialized during the sample period 1980–95.

It appears that it can matter a great deal at which level of spatial aggregation the analysis takes place. This is a fundamental issue. Economic geographers, such as Paul Cheshire and Gianni Carbonaro (1995) and Martin (1999), emphasize that it is necessary when measuring specialization or concentration to define the geographical unit of analysis according to its economic functionality. It is by no means obvious that the EU regions or the EU countries, which are administratively, politically, and historically classified, meet this requirement. This is also why a study such as that by Brülhart and Traeger (2005) is relevant, because they develop an index for the EU regions that is not dependent on the existing administrative regional classification.

Box 5.1 (cont.)

Table 5.1 Decomposition of agglomeration for EU regions

Total value (average over period 1985–2000)	0.95
Contribution of NUTS 0 (country level)	0.30
Contribution of NUTS I	0.20
Contribution of NUTS II	0.10
Contribution of NUTS III	0.35

Notes: Agglomeration of employment for 657 NUTS III regions in nine EU countries (Denmark, France, Germany, Ireland, Italy, Luxembourg, the Netherlands, Spain, and Sweden). Agglomeration is measured using the Theil index of topographic concentration with land mass (km^2) as weights.
Sources: Brakman *et al.* (2005: 32, and appendix). Employment data – Cambridge Econometrics regional database.

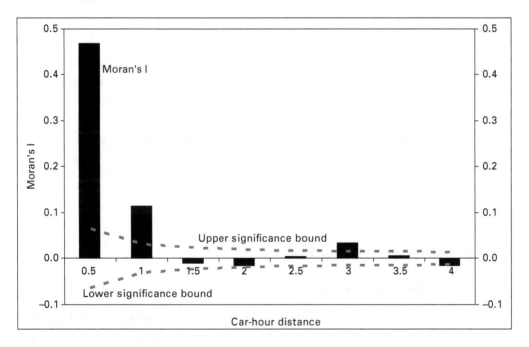

Figure 5.4   Moran's I: regions within one car-hour's distance interact with each other
Notes: The x-axis depicts the distance between regions within 0.5 hour of travel time by car, between 0.5 and 1 hour of travel time, etc.; the bars depict Moran's I, and the lines indicate the 95 percent confidence interval. Calculations for gross value added (GVA) in 2,177 NUTS III regions in 2000; GVA data are from Cambridge Econometrics.
Source: Brakman *et al.* (2005).

Box 5.1 (cont.)

The findings that concentration is constant or slightly decreasing and that specialization is falling for EU *regions* are confirmed by recent studies (see table 3.1 in Brakman *et al.*, 2005, gives a summary of the findings of more than twenty studies). More important for our present purposes is the degree of agglomeration with *regional* data for the European Union. Brakman *et al.* (2005: chap. 3) use the so-called Theil index to measure agglomeration for the period 1985–2000 at various geographical scales (NUTS 0 [= country level], I, II, and III). They find, in line with figure 5.3 above, that agglomeration (measured in terms of employment) is very stable over time. Second, as table 5.1 shows, agglomeration manifests itself most clearly at the lowest level of spatial aggregation (NUTS III). Third, when one takes the spatial ordering of regions into account (i.e. where regions are located on the map of Europe), using the so-called Moran's I statistic, it is found that spatial correlation of employment (in terms of Moran's I) is significant only between regions that are within approximately one hour's traveling time from each other (see figure 5.4).[7] This suggests that agglomeration matters most when we compare nearby or contiguous regions. In section 5.5 and chapter 6 we return to the issue of the spatial reach of agglomeration or agglomeration shadow. See Brakman *et al.* (2005).

To summarize: the facts illustrate (nothing more, but certainly nothing less) that agglomeration can be observed at various levels of aggregation, and that the geographical concentration of firms and industries is widespread. Two further questions now arise.

- First, can the facts be reconciled with economic theory at large?
- Second, if the answer to the first question is affirmative, how can we discriminate between different theories in general, and with respect to geographical economics in particular?

5.3 The facts and economic theory

5.3.1 Facts in search of a theory?

Several of the stylized facts on concentration, specialization, and agglomeration can be accounted for by various economic theories. We have already noted the presence of agglomeration at a national or regional level, and the

---

[7] Moran's I is a weighted spatial covariance and is used to detect departures from spatial randomness. One can determine whether neighboring regions are more similar/concentrated than would be expected if the distribution of – in our case – employment is random over space.

relevance of economic distance (the gravity model) and intra-industry trade for the underlying specialization pattern. The relevance of agglomeration at this level was also linked to studies of economic growth pointing to persistent differences in GDP per capita between (groups of) countries. To start with the latter, both the neoclassical and new growth theories can account for this state of affairs. From our discussion in section 2.4, this will be obvious for new growth theory. If the speed of convergence is very slow, and/or if one looks at conditional convergence instead of absolute convergence, the existence of agglomeration need not be at odds with neoclassical growth theory either. Similarly, the relevance of new trade theory as well as geographical economics in accounting for intra-industry trade is obvious, but the existence of intra-industry trade can also be explained in modern versions of the neoclassical trade model, in which technology differs between countries (see, for example, Davis, 1995).[8] Trade theory can be called upon to give a foundation not just for specialization patterns across space but also for agglomeration. This is as true for neoclassical trade theory, in which factor endowments are geographically concentrated, as it is for our geographical economics model. The basic new trade model does not have much to offer here, because it has nothing to say on the issue of *where* production will take place.

If we look at the stylized facts on agglomeration and specialization for cities, a similar conclusion emerges. Various theories can be used to explain the facts. Glaeser *et al.* (1992) try to establish empirically which type of externalities are more relevant in explaining the growth of US cities, assuming that new trade and new growth theories provide a relevant explanation. In the end, however, they conclude (1151) that the "evidence on externalities is indirect, and many of our findings can be explained by a neoclassical model in which industries grow where labor is cheap and demand is high." As for the finding that industries are geographically concentrated, Ellison and Glaeser (1997) show that their empirical results can be substantiated by the neoclassical as well as the modern theory of trade and location. In their theoretical model, concentration of industries is the result of either the natural advantages of a location (first nature) or of location spillovers (second nature). In fact, it turns out that the relationship between the levels of concentration and the industry characteristics is the same whether the concentration is the result of first-nature or second-nature causes. This implies that both neoclassical and modern theories based on

---

[8] The same is true for the gravity model; see Deardorff (1998).

increasing returns can be used as an explanation for the actual geographical concentration of industries in the United States. Ellison and Glaeser (1997: 891) conclude that "geographic concentration by itself does not imply the existence of spillovers; natural advantages have similar effects and may be important empirically."[9]

The overall conclusion is that the same empirical facts about specialization or agglomeration can be explained using different theoretical approaches. On the one hand, this is good news, because it means that the facts are not in search of a theory. On the other hand, this conclusion is not satisfactory for our present purposes, because it leaves unanswered the question as to the (relative) empirical relevance of geographical economics. This point has, of course, not gone unnoticed in the literature. Several studies have tried to test for the relevance of one or more theories of location by investigating how much of the observed specialization or agglomeration can be ascribed to each theory.

A good example is the study of the US city-size distribution by Black and Henderson (1998, 1999a), testing for the importance of actual geography (first nature) and characteristics of city neighbors (second nature) as determinants of (changes in) city size. Both forces turn out to be relevant. Guy Dumais, Ellison, and Glaeser (1997) try to show how much of the observed concentration is due to each of the three well-known Marshallian externalities (see box 2.1). They find evidence for one of these externalities – labor market pooling – and thus also indirectly find evidence for theories that rely on pecuniary external economies, such as geographical economics. This does not mean that a neoclassical foundation of the observed geographic concentration in the United States is irrelevant. On the contrary, Ellison and Glaeser (1999: 315) estimate that approximately 20 percent of this concentration can be explained by geographical advantages (endowments). In their extensive survey of the empirical evidence on agglomeration economies, Rosenthal and Strange (2004: 2167) conclude that "there is a lot that we do not know yet about agglomeration economies," but they are optimistic that the increased use of microdata sets, with data on individual firms, can help to close the gap between theory and empirics (see also chapters 2 and 7).

---

[9] Ellison and Glaeser (1999) show that natural advantages can explain a considerable part of the geographical concentration of industries in the United States. In chapter 7, and based on Duranton and Puga (2004), we argue that, at least on the theoretical front, progress is made in understanding and modeling the various spillovers that drive urban growth.

5.3.2 Geographical economics and five testable hypotheses

The various first-nature or second-nature investigations alluded to in the previous subsection do not offer a direct and conclusive test for or against a particular theory. They test for the significance of particular variables, such as endowments or economies of scale, for the location of economic activity and do not discriminate between theories. The significance of some of these explanatory variables is consistent with geographical economics, but also with other approaches. In many studies, the variables underlying the neo-classical approach as well as those that serve as proxies for the modern trade or growth theories are all empirically relevant. Such studies, therefore, do not try to test the relevance of the underlying individual theoretical approaches.

The problem is aptly summarized by Brülhart (1998: 792; see also Brül-hart, 2001), who argues that such a "regression analysis of industry con-centration suggests that all major theoretical approaches are relevant. However, they have not been used so far to assess relative merits of com-peting models across industries or countries." For the assessment of the empirical relevance of geographical economics there are two other important problems. First, proxies for market size are *not* independent variables but endogenous variables determined by the location of industries, workers, and firms in the geographical economics approach (see also Haaland *et al.*, 1999: 9, and Midelfart Knarvik *et al.*, 2002). Second, the geographical economics model is characterized by multiple equilibria. Which equilibrium gets established depends on the initial conditions, as explained in chapter 3. Without knowledge of the initial conditions it is difficult to test the model. The reason is that the core model has full agglomeration as well as spreading of economic activity as long-run equilibria. Moreover, the relationship between the key model parameters (the level of transport costs and the degree of agglomeration) is non-linear, making it difficult to use simple linear reduced-form specifications to test for the relevance of geographical economics.

So, can we devise a test for geographical economics models? In his superb but critical review of Fujita, Krugman, and Venables (1999), Neary (2001) notes that geographical economics still has to prove its "ultimate usefulness" by surviving empirical testing. Fortunately, since 2001 much empirical work has been done. In particular, the following five key features of geographical economics have been singled out for empirical research (Head and Mayer, 2004a: 2616).

- *The home market effect.* Regions with a large demand for increasing returns industries have a more than proportional share of their production and are net exporters of these goods (see subsection 2.3.2 for a discussion of the home market effect in general and equation (3.27) for the home market effect in the core model).
- *A large market potential raises local factor prices.* A large market will increase demand for local factors of production, and this raises factor rewards. From the equilibrium wage equation (3.21) we already know that regions that are surrounded by or close to regions with a high real income (indicating strong spatial demand linkages) will have higher wages.
- *A large market potential induces factor inflows.* Footloose factors of production will be attracted to those markets in which firms pay relatively high factor rewards. In our core model from chapter 3, footloose workers move to the region with the highest real wage, and, similarly, firms prefer locations with good market access.
- *Shock sensitivity.* Changes in the economic environment can (but need not!) trigger a change in the equilibrium spatial distribution of economic activity. This hypothesis goes to the heart of the idea that geographical economics models are characterized by multiple equilibria.
- *Reductions in trade costs induce agglomeration,* at least beyond a critical level of transport or trade costs. Figures 4.3 and 4.10, for example, show that for a large range of transport costs a change in these costs does not lead to a change in the equilibrium degree of agglomeration, but if a shock moves the economy beyond its break or sustain point the economy goes from spreading to agglomeration or vice versa respectively. This also implies that more economic integration (interpreted as a lowering of transport costs) should at some point lead to (more) agglomeration of the footloose activities and factors of production.

With the exception of the third of these five hypotheses, we now discuss the empirical work carried out for each hypothesis in the remainder of this chapter and in the next chapter. In doing so, we stick to the ordering of the above list.[10] We address the third hypothesis, "factor inflow," in some detail

---

[10] The reason for not discussing the "factor inflow hypothesis" here is that not much work has been done on testing this hypothesis (see Crozet, 2004, or Head and Mayer, 2004a, for good exceptions). There is not a conceptual difference with the "higher factor prices" hypothesis regarding the role of variables such as real market potential (see section 5.5). See Head and Mayer (2004a: sect 5) for an overview of empirical work on the factor inflow hypothesis, and, foreshadowing our own discussion in section 5.5 below, note how equations (11) and (14) in Head and Mayer's discussion are connected with their wage equation (6) that is central to the "higher factor prices" hypothesis of

in chapter 9 section 9.5, when we discuss labor migration. Apart from Head and Mayer (2004a), the state of the art of empirical research in geographical economics is also surveyed by Overman, Redding, and Venables (2003), Combes and Overman (2004), and Bernard Fingleton (2004). The main analytical reason for postponing the discussion of the fourth and fifth hypothesis to chapter 6 (as noted in the introduction to this chapter) is that they differ in a rather substantial way from the other hypotheses. In a nutshell, the home market and spatial wage studies that are the subject of the remainder of this chapter are based on the short-run equilibrium of geographical economics, in which the spatial differences in agglomeration are still taken as given. In the long run, as we know from chapter 4, it is the aim of geographical economics to explain these spatial differences as well. The last two hypotheses from the Head and Mayer list fall precisely into this category: what happens to the spatial distribution of economic activity itself?

5.4 In search of the home market effect

In one of the first surveys of geographical economics, Krugman (1998: 172) concludes that empirical work has "failed to offer much direct testing of the specifics of the models." This statement no longer holds, but Krugman's assertion that empirical work by Davis and Weinstein on the home market effect is an early and important exception is still correct. Their approach is now discussed at some length.

5.4.1 The home market effect: a reminder

In a series of papers, Davis and Weinstein (1996, 1997, 1999, 2001, 2003) have developed an empirical methodology that enables them "to distinguish a world in which trade arises due to increasing returns as opposed to comparative advantage" (2003: 3). Following Krugman (1980) (see section 2.3), Davis and Weinstein note that new trade models without transportation costs imply that trade leads to specialization, which is also the main implication of neoclassical trade models. With positive transportation costs,

---

section 5.5. The notion, as in Head and Mayer (2004a), that firms are attracted to (and hence "migrate" to) regions with a large demand and the idea (Crozet, 2004) that mobile workers migrate to regions with a large manufacturing production are both tested in specifications in which factor flows are (mainly) a function of (real) market potential, just as in the case of the second hypothesis dealing with factor prices as we will see in section 5.5.

however, the new trade theory allows for an empirical hypothesis that differentiates trade models based on increasing returns, including geographical economics, from their neoclassical counterpart, because it gives rise to the so-called home market effect. In chapter 2, we have already explained that this effect implies that if a country has a relatively high demand for a particular good, such as cars, it will be a net exporter of cars. More precisely, it implies that an increase in a country's demand for cars will lead to a *more than proportional* increase in that country's production of cars. In a neoclassical trade model, such an increase in home demand will at least be partly met by an increase in the foreign production of cars. The home market effect translates in Davis and Weinstein's work into the following question: *do idiosyncratic changes in demand go along with more than one-to-one changes in output?* If the answer is affirmative, this is taken as a confirmation of the geographical economics model. A negative answer would imply that either the neoclassical trade models or new trade models with zero trade costs are empirically more relevant.

The central empirical equation used by Davis and Weinstein is derived from a theoretical model in which it is assumed that comparative advantage determines trade and production at the industry level, whereas increasing returns drive within-industry specialization. In fact, they thus acknowledge that, in practice, more than one theory explains the structure of trade flows. The geographical unit of analysis is either a country or, as in Davis and Weinstein (1999), a region within a country. The following equation is estimated:[11]

$$X_{gnr} = \kappa_{gnr} + \kappa_1 \cdot SHARE_{gnr} + \kappa_2 \cdot IDIODEM_{gnr} + END + err_{gnr} \qquad (5.1)$$

where
X_{gnr} = output of good g in industry n in country r;
$SHARE_{gnr}$ = share of output of good g in industry n for country r in the total output of good g in industry n;
$IDIODEM_{gnr}$ = difference between the demand for good g of industry n in country r and the demand for good g of industry n in other countries;
END = (factor endowments for country r) × (input coefficients for good g in industry n);
err_{gnr} = error term; and
κ_{gnr} = constant.

---

[11] In the following, r is referred to as a country, but it could denote a region.

The crucial variable is $IDIODEM_{gnr}$, a mnemonic for IDIOsyncratic DEMand. This variable represents the home market effect. If every country demands the same share of good g in industry n, it will be zero. A coefficient for $IDIODEM_{gnr}$ exceeding one implies that an increase in demand for good g of industry n in country r leads to a more than proportional increase in output X_{gnr}. The inclusion of the variable $SHARE_{gnr}$ captures the tendency that, in the absence of idiosyncratic demand, each country r produces good g in industry n in the same proportion as other countries do. The fact that endowments can also determine the output X_{gnr} is the reason for the inclusion of END, ensuring that the role of neoclassical trade theory is not neglected. The home market effect is therefore verified if $\kappa_2 > 1$.[12]

5.4.2 Estimation results

Equation (5.1) is estimated for a sample of OECD countries in Davis and Weinstein (1996, 1997). In the construction of the variables, the aim is to stick as closely as possible to the theoretical model of Krugman (1980). As far as $IDIODEM$ is concerned, this means that the variable lacks some real geographical content, since it is assumed that the relative location of countries does not matter, implying that demand linkages between two neighboring countries are, a priori, not stronger than the linkages between two countries on opposite sides of our planet. This is not very realistic, and it is partly for this neglect of geography that the evidence in Davis and Weinstein (1996, 1997) with respect to the home market effect is rather mixed. For example, in Davis and Weinstein (1997) the parameter κ_2 exceeds one for only nine industries in their sample of twenty-two OECD countries and twenty-six industries.

In subsequent work on the home market effect, Davis and Weinstein (2003) use the same data set of OECD countries, but $IDIODEM$ is measured differently. They note that the structure of demand in Germany and France affects the incentives for producers locating in Belgium more strongly than the demand in Japan and Australia. We must introduce these aspects of real world geography. The latter are achieved by introducing different transport costs for each industry, which is taken into consideration in deriving the demand a producer in every country faces. This modification of $IDIODEM$

---

[12] If only factor endowments mattered for the determination of output, given the technology matrix, equation (5.1) would reduce to $X_{gnr} = END$. If $\kappa_2 < 1$ this is taken as evidence that neoclassical trade theory or new trade models are more relevant.

Table 5.2 Home market effect for Japanese regions

IDIODEM	1.416 (0.025)	0.888 (0.070)
SHARE	1.033 (0.007)	−1.7441 (0.211)
END included?	No	Yes
Observations	760	760

Notes: Standard errors in brackets. Estimation method: seemingly unrelated regressions.
Source: Davis and Weinstein (1999).

is important, because the support for the home market effect is now much more conclusive.[13]

The second strategy that is followed, and one that is pursued in Davis and Weinstein (1999), is to stick to the initial measurement of *IDIODEM* (without transport costs), but to apply equation (5.1) to *regions within a single country*, rather than between countries. A sample consisting of forty regions *r*, nineteen goods *g*, and six industry aggregates *n* is analyzed for Japan. The main results are given in table 5.2, in which the second column shows the results of the pooled regression if factor endowments (*END*) are not included. In this case κ_2 is not only significant but also larger than one, thus supporting the home market effect. Davis and Weinstein (1999: 396) interpret this result as "clearly in the range of economic geography." Things change, however, when factor endowments *END* are included; see the last column of table 5.2. The coefficient for *IDIODEM* is still significant, but now smaller than one. The second specification, therefore, does not provide support for the home market effect in the aggregate. A breakdown of the data to the goods level, however, indicates that for eight of the nineteen goods κ_2 is larger than one (at a 5 percent level of significance).

5.4.3 The home market effect and geographical economics: an assessment

The empirical work of Davis and Weinstein on the home market effect is clearly important from the perspective of geographical economics, since the

---

[13] Brülhart and Federico Trionfetti (1999) try to discriminate between new trade theory and neoclassical trade theory by testing whether or not demand for goods is *home-biased* (yes in the new trade theory, no in the neoclassical trade theory). This test (which does not require positive transportation costs) concludes (for the period 1970–85) that demand is indeed home-biased. In other words, foreign goods and home goods are not perfect substitutes. Their approach closely follows that of Davis and Weinstein. The empirical estimates of home bias in demand are found after first estimating a gravity equation. These estimates are then added to what is basically equation (5.1) as an additional explanatory variable. Interestingly, *IDIODEM* does not have much explanatory power, and the hypothesis that $\kappa_2 = 1$ cannot be rejected.

home market effect is a crucial element of the core geographical economics model. From the model in chapter 3 (see in particular section 3.10), it can be discerned that an increase in demand for manufactures in a region, which enlarges the home market for these goods, implies a more than proportional increase in manufacturing production in that region. There are two main problems that limit the usefulness of the home market effect as a test of the empirical relevance of the geographical economics model.

First, the home market effect is to be found not only in geographical economics but also in other trade models with positive transportation costs. In the discussion of the new trade theory in subsection 2.3.2 we argued that the main innovation of Krugman (1980) was the introduction of trans-portation costs together with increasing returns to scale, which lead to the home market effect.[14] Davis and Weinstein do not consider this to be a problem, because they refer to Krugman (1980) as their economic geog-raphy model, but Krugman (1980), although close, is not a geographical economics model, because regional market size – and thus demand – is exogenous. In geographical economics, market size and demand are endogenous. This endogenization of market size and demand arises because manufacturing labor (and firms) can move between regions (Krugman, 1991a, 1991b) and/or because firms require the output of other firms as intermediate input (Venables, 1996). Accordingly, in the geographical economics model the distribution of mobile endowments is not fixed, but determined by the spreading and agglomerating forces characterizing this approach.[15] This effect is only partially captured by *END* in the last column of table 5.2. The home market effect studies do not, therefore, offer a convincing or complete test for the relevance of the geographical economics literature.

A second problem with these studies is the fact that the home market effect is not very robust with respect to small changes in the assumptions. As Davis (1998) shows, the home market effect does not necessarily arise if it is

---

[14] Fujita, Krugman, and Venables (1999: 59) reach a similar conclusion: "The home market effect should apply whether or not a cumulative process of agglomeration is at work. Indeed, Krugman (1980) . . . did so in the context of a model in which relative market sizes were purely exogenous."

[15] More specifically, in their estimation of the determinants of the production of Japanese manufacturing sectors, Davis and Weinstein (1999: 396–7) include factor endowments along with the region's demand for manufactured goods. In terms of the geographical economics model this is not without problems, since both the regional demand for manufactured goods (market size) and the region's share of factor endowments (labor) are determined simultaneously. Gordon Hanson (2005), therefore argues that only truly immobile endowments (such as land) should be taken into account (see also section 5.5). In fact, this means that only first-nature determinants of location should be considered exogenous.

not just the differentiated manufacturing goods that are subject to – sufficiently high – transportation costs but also food (see also Crozet and Trionfetti, 2007). The home market effect can also disappear if we introduce more than two countries (see Behrens *et al.*, 2005). For this result to hold it is essential that countries are not at equal distance to each other. Theoretically, the assumption of equidistance allows for analytical results (Puga, 1999), but from an empirical perspective it is not realistic (in the case of two countries, distance is normalized and equidistance is not an issue). In chapter 6 section 6.3, we argue that the observation that regions or countries are not equidistant creates a serious problem for testing geographical economics.

Notwithstanding the special nature of the home market effect, it does point to another method to test for the empirical relevance of geographical economics. The extent to which an increase in a region's demand for a manufactured good translates into a (more than proportional) increase in that region's production of the good depends on the elasticity of labor supply. If labor supply is not perfectly elastic, the increased demand will lead not only to increased production but also to higher nominal wages in that region (see equation (3.27) in chapter 3 and Head and Mayer, 2006). Hence, given the (reasonable) assumption that labor supply is not perfectly elastic, it is expected that regions with a relatively high demand for manufactures also pay somewhat higher wages. This topic is addressed in the next section, in which we discuss the second of the empirical hypotheses: that a large market potential leads to higher factor prices for a region.

5.5 The spatial wage structure and real market potential

In neoclassical trade theory, there is no foundation for a spatial wage structure. The existence of economic centers can be rationalized by location-specific endowments, but this does not imply a spatial wage structure. Even with (endowment-driven) agglomeration, the main prediction of neoclassical trade theory is that trade will lead to factor price equalization. In the new trade models – without transport costs – it is true that, in autarky, wages are higher for the country with the larger labor force, but when trade opens up wages are equalized. This follows from the specialization in production of varieties of the manufactured good, such that some varieties are produced in one country and the other varieties in the other country. This rules out a spatial wage structure in new trade models, because there is no endogenous agglomeration of manufacturing production across space, and thus no possibility of a center of manufacturing production.[16] Of course, when we allow for productivity differences between countries, regions, or cities, it is perfectly possible to arrive at the conclusion that wages are higher in economic centers. In fact, much of the work in modern urban or growth economics would argue that we expect wages to be higher in economic centers because of the existence of local human capital or (pure) technological externalities that lead to productivity and wage differences across locations. Typically, however, these spillovers or externalities are confined to the location as such, and spatial interdependencies – a key ingredient of geographical economics – have no role to play (see Ciccone and Hall, 1996, Ciccone, 2002, or Combes and Overman, 2004).

Section 5.5 is organized as follows. First, we use the example of Mexico to show that wages may indeed be lower the further one moves away from economic centers (subsection 5.5.1). Second, and more in line with the equilibrium wage equation from our geographical economics model, we discuss if there is evidence to support the idea of a spatial wage structure when spatial interdependencies between regions are taken into account (subsection 5.5.2). In doing so, the well-known market potential function (Harris, 1954) that was introduced in chapter 2 (section 2.2) will be used. Next, and taking the approach of Hanson (2005) as our benchmark, we show how we can test for a spatial wage structure by making explicit use of the underlying geographical economics model (subsection 5.5.3). Finally, in subsection 5.5.4, we come up with two lines of criticism (and extensions) of the attempts to estimate the equilibrium wage equation from the geographical economics model.

5.5.1 Regional wages and the distance from the center

Hanson (1997) investigates if there is empirical evidence supporting the idea of a spatial wage structure. He analyzes what he calls "regional wage gradients" for Mexico, which serves as a good starting point for a discussion of the more encompassing, but also more complicated, analysis of regional wages in subsection 5.5.3. In the Mexico paper, Hanson starts with the observation that the agglomeration of economic activity can arise from theories other than geographical economics as well, but that this is not true for the spatial structure of regional wages that accompanies agglomeration in the geographical economics model.

---

[16] This point also holds for the Davis and Weinstein studies of the home market effect, essentially dealing with what we have defined in section 5.2 as the concentration of industries across regions/countries.

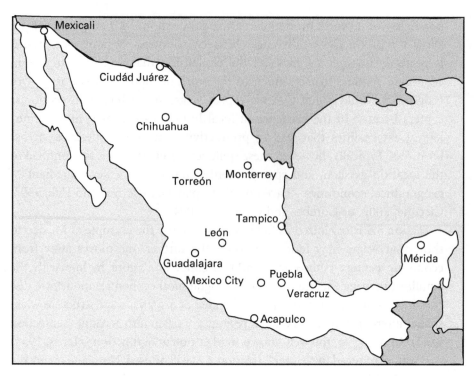

Figure 5.5   Map of Mexico

Mexico provides an interesting case because of the clear-cut changes in Mexican trade policy in the post-war period. Initially, high trade barriers and a policy of import substitution stimulated the establishment of Mexico City as the center of manufacturing production. Subsequently, a policy of trade liberalization culminating in the North American Free Trade Agreement (NAFTA) led to a gradual shift of manufacturing production from Mexico City to the US–Mexican border.[17] This shift has reinforced the considerable differences in GDP per capita between northern and southern Mexico: GDP per capita in the Chihuahua region in the north is, for instance, about three times higher than in the Veracruz region in the south (see figure 5.5). Hanson looks at regional wages in Mexico before and after

[17] See also Hanson (1996) for a discussion of US–Mexican trade on manufacturing employment in US regions in the US–Mexican border area. Krugman and Raul Livas Elizondo (1996) develop a geographical economics model in which increased trade reduces the sustainability of existing centers of production. Similarly, Alberto Ades and Glaeser (1995) present empirical evidence that shows that countries with a low degree of openness typically have a relatively high degree of agglomeration of economic activity. In chapter 7, in which we discuss the dominance of the largest or primate city in many national urban systems, we return to the case of Mexico and Mexico City.

the trade liberalization, and tests the following two hypotheses, conditional on the fact that Mexico City is the industrial center.

(1) Relative regional wages – that is, a region's wage relative to Mexico City – are lower when transport costs (the distances from Mexico City and the United States) are higher.

(2) Trade liberalization has led to a compression of regional wage differentials.

Hanson finds strong empirical support for hypothesis 1, but only weak support for hypothesis 2. The confirmation of hypothesis 1 is in line with one of the main building blocks of geographical economics, namely that regional wages are a positive function of market access (Mexico City being the main market; see figure 5.5). The opening up of trade with the United States has obviously increased market access (in terms of forward and backward linkages) for Mexican regions such as Mexicali or Ciudád Juárez that are close to the US border, but has also decreased the centrality of Mexico City in general. With respect to the latter, this should lead to an overall convergence of regional wages compared to the wages in Mexico City, but, with the exception of the US border regions in Mexico, the evidence is not very strong. The empirical specification is simple; the following equation is estimated:[18]

$$\ln(W_{it}/W_{ct}) = \kappa_0 + \kappa_1 \ln(t_{it}) + \kappa_2 \ln(tf_{it}) + err_{it} \qquad (5.2)$$

where

W_{it} = nominal wage in Mexican region i at time t;

W_{ct} = nominal wage in Mexico City at time t;

t_{it} = unit transportation costs from region i to Mexico City at time t;

tf_{it} = unit transportation costs from region i to the US market; and

err_{it} = error term.

Equation (5.2) specifies that relative regional wages fall when the distance between a region and the center increases. It is a simple reduced form of the wage equation in the core model of geographical economics, ignoring the impact of various structural parameters and of spatial demand linkages (recall wage equation 3.21), and focusing instead on the transportation costs only. Hypothesis 1 implies that both parameters κ_1 and κ_2 are negative.

---

[18] In estimates of equation (5.2), a trade policy dummy is added to distinguish between the period before and after trade liberalization. Other region-specific effects are also included (various amenities). Equation (5.2) is then estimated for the period 1965–88 on the two-digit industry level as well as on the state level. t_{it} is measured as the distance in kilometers to Mexico City and tf_{it} is measured as the distance in kilometers to the nearest US border crossing.

Hypothesis 2 implies that the parameter κ_1 decreased significantly after trade liberalization.

If demand linkages and market size are thought to be determinants of regional wage gradients, it is better to test directly for the relevance of demand for regional wages.[19] Thus, amongst others, Hanson (2005) for the United States and, extending his methodology, Brakman, Garretsen, and Marc Schramm (2004a) for Germany try to establish the relevance of demand linkages for the spatial distribution of wages across US counties and German districts respectively.[20] They specify an empirical wage equation that includes the key structural parameters of the core model of geographical economics. As an intermediate step between our Mexico case and the full-blown testing for a spatial wage structure using the underlying geographical economics model, we first show how spatial demand linkages can be introduced as a determinant of regional wages by using the "old-fashioned" market potential function.

5.5.2 Wages and the market potential function

The market potential function states that the market potential of region j is large when the firms from this region face a large demand for their goods from nearby region k (see also section 2.2). Therefore, a region's market potential depends positively on the demand coming from other regions and negatively on the distance between a region and the other regions. Suppose that we replace in the market potential function (equation (2.1)) the (rather vague) notion of the market potential MP of region j by the nominal wage W of region j, the reformulated market potential function becomes rather similar to the equilibrium wage equation from the core geographical economics model. To see this, take the normalized version of the equilibrium wage equation (4.3):

$$W_j = \left[\sum_k Y_k I_k^{\varepsilon-1} T^{D_{jk}(1-\varepsilon)} \right]^{1/\varepsilon} \tag{5.3}$$

Recall that W is the wage rate, Y is income, I is the price index, ε is the elasticity of substitution, T is the transport cost parameter, and $T_{jk} = T^{D_{jk}}$,

---

[19] In Hanson (1997) the changes in the Mexican regional wages and industry concentration are at least to some extent exogenous (due to government policy). In the geographical economics approach, however, these changes are, in principle, endogenous.

[20] See Combes and Overman (2004: subsect. 3.3.3) for an overview of other studies that apply Hanson's approach.

where D_{jk} is the distance between locations j and k. T is defined as the number of goods that have to be shipped in order to ensure that one unit arrives over one unit of distance. Given the elasticity of substitution ε, equation (5.3) immediately shows that a region's wages are higher when demand in surrounding markets (Y_k) is higher, when access to those markets is better (lower transport costs T), and when there is less competition (the competition effect, measured by the price index I_k). With the notable exception of the competition effect – measured by the price index (see below) – the wage equation is very close to the simple market potential function for wages alluded to above.

To get from equation (5.3) to a market potential function for wages that can be tested, the equation can be simplified by assuming that wages in region j depend only on a constant and income Y_k, with the impact of the latter on wages in j increasing the shorter the distance between the regions. Distance is measured relative to the economic center of a region. The resulting specification is

$$\log(W_j) = \kappa_0 + \kappa_1 \log\left(\sum_k Y_k e^{-\kappa_2 D_{jk}}\right) + err_j \tag{5.4}$$

where κ_0, κ_1, and κ_2 are parameters to be estimated. This specification is an example of a market potential function for wages, with one big difference compared to standard market potential function: W is the explanatory variable. The advantage is that it is easy to estimate, and shows if there is a spatial wage structure or not. Compared to wage equation (5.2) for the case of Mexican wages, the advantage is that spatial demand or market size linkages play an explicit role, whereas these spatial interdependencies that lie at the heart of geographical economics are clearly absent from equation (5.2).

The disadvantage of the market potential function for wages, however, is that there is not a one-to-one correspondence to the theoretical model and its structural parameters; wage equations (5.3) and (5.4) are not the same! As the reader might have noticed, (5.3) includes the price index I_k, which is absent in (5.4). This is why in the literature the terms *nominal* and *real* market potential are used; in (5.4) the *nominal* market potential (NMP) matters, whereas in the wage equation from our core model the *real* market potential (RMP) is central. The difference between the two concepts is the price index effect, $I_k^{\varepsilon-1}$. If a firm faces more competitors in region j, this will be reflected in a lower price index and a lower market share for this firm. This price index or competition effect tells us that being close to a large market also has a drawback.

Table 5.3 A spatial wage structure for Europe

	Coefficient	Standard error
κ_1	0.898	0.020
κ_2	0.013	0.001
R^2	0.61	

Notes: Ordinary least squares (OLS) estimation of equation (5.4) in first differences, constant included. Sample consists of fourteen EU countries plus regions, 1992–2000. Number of observations is 1,647. *Source:* Brakman *et al.* (2005: 40).

In recent years wage equations such as (5.4) have been estimated for various (groups of) countries and regions. By and large, they confirm that a spatial wage structure exists, but it is also concluded that the distance decay is quite strong. The latter implies that the spatial reach of demand linkages is limited, as measured by the κ_2 coefficient in (5.4). As a representative example, we briefly discuss the estimation of market potential function (5.4) for a sample of the regions of the European Union (Brakman *et al.*, 2005). Our sample includes annual observations for the EU regions at the NUTS II level (Luxembourg excluded) plus Norway, the Czech Republic, Poland, and Switzerland for the period 1992 to 2000. The wage W_j is measured as the average remuneration per employee in region j, and Y_k is measured as total gross value added in region k. As the market potential function (5.4) indicates, the parameter κ_1 captures the strength of demand linkages and parameter κ_2 shows how quickly these linkages decay over distance. When we find that both κ_1 and κ_2 are significant (and positive) we can conclude that there is a spatial wage structure. As table 5.3 shows, this turns out to be the case for our sample of EU regions. In spite of wage rigidity and national or centralized wage bargaining, the estimation results confirm the existence of a spatial wage structure for European regions.

To illustrate the importance of the estimates for κ_1 and κ_2, the following experiment was conducted: how much higher would wages in Nordrhein-Westfalen (NRW: a large German region, both in terms of area and income, that lies in the heart of Europe) be if its market size, as measured by the Y variable, were 10 percent larger than it actually is, and how much higher would wages be in surrounding regions because of this demand shock? The 10 percent demand increase in NRW combined with estimated

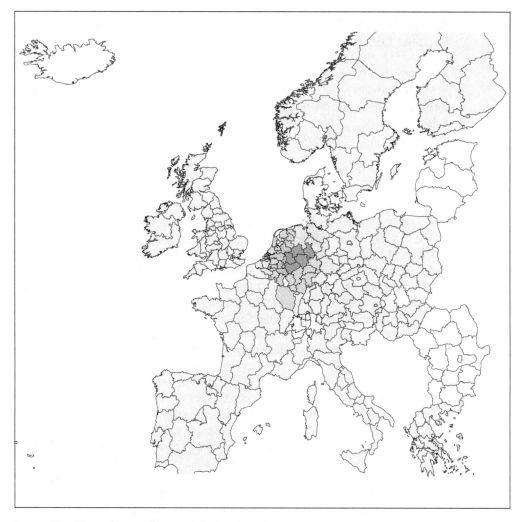

Figure 5.6   Wage effects of a demand shock
Note: The darker the shade the higher the wage response.

coefficients for κ_1 and κ_2 translate into a wage increase of 0.7 percent in the epicenter of the shock, NRW. Outside this region, however, the impact of the shock quickly decays with distance. At 100 kilometers distance from NRW only a quarter of this wage increase remains, and so the impact of the shock on wages in other regions quickly dies off the further one moves away from NRW. This finding, a strong distance decay, is in line with other market potential studies. Figure 5.6 visualizes the thought experiment; the darker the shade the higher the wage response. Clearly, only nearby regions benefit from the demand shock in NRW (the group of darkest NUTS II

Box 5.2 Border effects and mental distance: do Ossies and Wessies interact?[21]

Given the potential relevance of border effects for post-unification Germany in 1995, five years after the reunification, one might want to know if distance is less relevant *within* east or west Germany than *between* east and west Germany. In other words, is the former border between West and East Germany still discernible to the extent that it has an impact on the spatial wage structure? To answer this question, we changed equation (5.4) as follows:

$$\log(W_j) = \kappa_1 \log\left[\sum_k Y_k e^{(-\kappa_2 - \kappa_3 \varphi_{jk}) D_{jk}}\right] + \kappa_4 Dummy_{East} + \text{constant} \qquad (5.4')$$

where $\varphi_{jk} = 0$, if j and k are *both* in west Germany or *both* in east Germany; $\varphi_{jk} = 1$ otherwise.

We expect, following the studies of Charles Engel and John Rogers (1996) and McCallum (1995), κ_3 to be positive if border effects occur. As can be seen from the empirical results in column 1 of table 5.4, however, the distance parameter κ_3 is negative. Moreover, the parameters κ_2 and κ_3 cancel out if $\varphi_{jk} = 1$. What do these results with respect to the two distance parameters imply? First, κ_3 thus has the wrong sign. In this sense, no border effect is observed. Our second, and most interesting, result is that κ_2 and κ_3 cancel out when $\varphi_{jk} = 1$. This indicates that the *spatial* distribution of demand in west Germany is not relevant for the spatial wage structure in east Germany and vice versa. This result, therefore, indicates that the east–west German border still matters to the extent that there does not seem to be an effect of the localization of demand for wages across the east–west border.[22] Stated differently, for the level of east German city district wages only total west German demand matters, and the geography of this west German demand is irrelevant.

How can this finding be explained? We can only offer some suggestions here. The strong segmentation of east and west German markets could be caused by differences in firm behavior resulting from differences in management style and willingness to adjust to changes in the company environment (see Rothfels and Wölfl, 1998: 7–11). The existence of mental borders between the Ossies and the Wessies might be relevant. In this case, economic agents impose borders on themselves, for instance because they strongly identify with "their" region and are inclined to stick to this region for their economic transactions. Another possibility, which might be relevant in the initial stages of German reunification, is that agents simply lack knowledge about the other region and are therefore geographically biased when it comes to their economic transactions (see van Houtum, 1998, or Rumley and Minghi, 1991). The possible relevance of mental distance (and the norms and values that accompany them) is a reminder of the fact that economic geographers have a point when criticizing the geographical economics approach for paying too little attention to the role of (in)formal institutions in shaping spatial patterns (see Martin, 1999). We return to this issue in chapter 12.

---

[21] This box is based on Brakman, Garretsen, and Schramm (2000), in which the sample consists of the 114 city districts, excluding the country districts. Including these districts does not change the main results.

[22] This border effect is quite different from the border effect found by Engel and Rogers (1996) for the United States and Canada, where they find large variations in the movements of prices.

Box 5.2 (cont.)

Table 5.4 Estimation results: German district wages and intra-German borders

	East–west border	North–south border	North–south border (west only)
κ_1	1.579 (6.1)	0.174 (7.9)	0.193 (7.4)
κ_2	0.131 (4.4)	0.170 (3.6)	0.160 (3.7)
κ_3	−0.131 (−4.4)	0.606 (0.0)	0.422 (0.0)
κ_4	−3.702 (−6.7)	−0.234 (−4.1)	–
Constant	−14.903 (−4.7)	2.598 (12.7)	2.417 (10.0)
Adjusted R^2	0.472	0.522	0.376
Observations	114	114	88

Note: The t-statistics are in parentheses.

To check whether the third result is merely a statistical artifact, columns 2 and 3 of table 5.4 give the estimation results for different "borders." The first alternative border comes from dividing Germany as a whole into northern and southern parts (see the second column of the table). This gives us twenty-six northern and eighty-eight southern city districts. The second alternative border comes from splitting only west Germany into fifteen northern and seventy-three southern city districts (see the third column). The main point is that for these two additional borders the coefficient κ_3 becomes insignificant, such that the inclusion of those borders is immaterial to the estimation results. The only border that (still) mattered in the mid-1990s was the one between the former West Germany and East Germany.

regions). In box 5.2 the market potential function of wages is used to further illustrate the relevance of distance.

5.5.3 Spatial wages and real market potential

In this subsection, we discuss a fundamental attempt to estimate the equilibrium wage equation (5.3). In doing so, we are able to estimate the key model parameters of geographical economics. As opposed to the market potential estimates from the previous subsection, here *real* market potential matters. Before we turn to the estimation strategy and results, it is useful to remind ourselves that the equilibrium wage equation (5.3) is part of our core model from chapter 3. We also know, from chapter 4, that this model is a special case of a more general geographical economics model (Puga, 1999). The same is true for the model and the corresponding wage equation

used by Hanson (2005) in his empirical work, discussed below. Head and
Mayer (2004a: 2621–7) show clearly that an equilibrium wage equation such
as (5.3), in which regional wages are a function of real market potential,
follows only if one assumes that labor is the only primary factor in the
production process and that there are no intermediate inputs.[23] The aim is
to estimate equation (5.3).

The literature offers two estimation strategies. The first option, using a
strategy pioneered in a seminal paper by Redding and Venables (2004), is to
estimate a wage equation such as (5.3) in two steps (see also Knaap, 2006).
In the first step, a proxy for RMP is estimated using bilateral trade data and
a gravity trade equation. In the second step, the estimated RMP is inserted
into the wage equation, which is subsequently estimated. In a recent
application of this strategy, Head and Mayer (2006) analyze thirteen
industries and fifty-seven EU regions for the period 1985 to 2000 and find
clear confirmation that wages respond positively to market potential; on
average, a 10 percent increase in RMP raises wages by 1.2 percent. We
return to this strategy in chapter 9 (section 9.6), where we show how the
main vehicle for empirical research in international trade, the gravity model,
can be used to approximate real market potential.

The second option is to estimate wage equation (5.3) directly. An
advantage of this strategy is that estimates are derived for the structural
model parameters. This is the route taken by Hanson (2005). Before we turn
to the empirical results, we briefly discuss the theoretical approach in Hanson
(2005). Following Helpman (1998) and Alun Thomas (1996), the agricultural
sector of the core model of chapter 3 is replaced by a housing sector that
reflects demand for a non-tradable service in a specific region (note that food
is tradable in the core models). The motivation for this assumption is that the
core model of chapter 3 displays a bias towards monocentric equilibria: for
low enough transport costs, all manufactures end up being produced at one
location (recall the tomahawk of figure 4.3). This is clearly not in accordance
with the facts about the spatial distribution of manufacturing activity for the
United States or any other industrialized country. A local non-tradable

---

[23] Compare wage equations (6) and (9) in Head and Mayer (2004a). Equation (6) contains not only RMP but also a
term coined "supplier potential" or "supplier access" by Redding and Venables (2004) (see also section 4.7). In a
geographical economics model with intermediate inputs (hence not the Krugman, 1991a, 1991b, or the Hanson,
2005, model!), supplier access enters the wage equation (see our discussion of the Krugman and Venables, 1995,
model in chapter 4). Supplier access means that, when the price index is low (high), intermediate-input-supplying
firms are relatively close to (far from) your location of production, which strengthens (weakens) agglomeration. A
better supplier access (a lower value of *I*) lowers wage costs. This effect is stronger the larger the share of intermediate
products in production; without intermediate inputs only the real market potential term is left in the wage equation.

service provides an alternative spreading force, because, if demand for this service increases due to agglomeration, prices of these services increase too, which stimulates spreading. Moreover, for the industrialized countries agriculture provides only a weak spreading force, in contrast to the effects of prices of non-tradables, such as housing. The perfectly competitive housing sector serves as the spreading force, because housing is relatively expensive in large agglomerations where demand for housing is high. This model with a housing sector typically results in a more even distribution of manufacturing activity than the core model of chapter 3 (recall our discussion of the bell-shaped curve in section 4.7, to which, *inter alia*, the Helpman model may give rise). Fortunately, the equilibrium conditions are still very similar to the core model; in particular, the wage equation, which is central to the empirical analysis, is identical to wage equation (5.3).

The lack of reliable data on regional manufacturing price indices I_k and on the regional prices of housing P_k make an adaptation of the wage equation necessary. In order to arrive at a testable equation, the following strategy is followed. Besides the equilibrium wage equation (5.3), the equilibrium price index equation, which is identical to the price index equation (see equation (3.23) or (4.2)) from our core model and the well-known condition that regional income Y_j equals income derived from labour $(Y_j = \lambda_j L W_j)$, there are two additional equilibrium conditions (Hanson, 2005: 5):

(i) the equilibrium condition for the housing market: $P_j H_j = (1 - \delta) Y_j$; and
(ii) real wage equalization between regions: $W_j / (P_j^{1-\delta} I_j^{\delta}) = W_k / (P_k^{1-\delta} I_k^{\delta})$.

Condition (i) states that payments for housing in j equal the share of expenditures allocated to housing in j, and condition (ii) states real wage equality, implying that the economy is by definition in its long-run equilibrium. This last condition is far from innocent, and we return to it below.

To get from equation (5.3) to equation (5.5), first substitute (i) into (ii) to get rid of the housing price variable P_j, and use (ii) in (5.3) to get rid of the price index I_j. We then arrive at (in logs)

$$\log(W_j) = k_0 + \varepsilon^{-1} \log \left(\sum_k Y_k^{\varepsilon + (1-\varepsilon)/\delta} H_k^{(1-\delta)(\varepsilon-1)/\delta} W_k^{(\varepsilon-1)/\delta} T^{(1-\varepsilon)D_{jk}} \right) + err_j \qquad (5.5)$$

where k_0 is a parameter and H_k is the housing stock in region k. Note that equation (5.5) includes the three structural parameters of the core model, namely δ, ε, and T. Given the availability of US data on wages, income, the housing stock, and a proxy for distance, equation (5.5) can be estimated. The dependent variable is the wage rate measured at the US

Table 5.5 Estimation of the structural wage equation

Structural wage equation: (5.5)	1970–80	1980–90
δ	0.962 (0.015)	0.956 (0.013)
ε	7.597 (1.250)	6.562 (0.838)
$\text{Log}(T)$	1.970 (0.328)	3.219 (0.416)
Adjusted R^2	0.256	0.347
Observations	3,075	3,075
$\varepsilon/(\varepsilon-1)$	1.152	1.180
ρ	0.868	0.847

Notes: Standard errors in brackets. $\varepsilon =$ substitution elasticity, $\delta =$ share of income spent on manufactures, $T =$ transport costs. $\varepsilon/(\varepsilon - 1) = \text{mark-up}$; $\varepsilon = 1/(1-\rho)$.
Source: Hanson (2005: tab. 3).

county level.[24] The results of estimating (5.5) (in first differences and using various controls not shown here) are summarized in table 5.5 for the full sample of 3,075 US counties in the periods 1970 to 1980 and 1980 to 1990.

Note that all three structural parameters are highly significant in both estimation periods. Looking at the estimation results in table 5.5, a first (surprising) conclusion is that transportation costs seem to have increased over time, which would imply that the benefits of spatial agglomeration have increased over time. Similarly, the elasticity of substitution ε has decreased somewhat, implying that imperfect competition has become more important and mark-ups over marginal costs have increased during the period 1970 to 1990. The estimate for δ, the share of income spent on manufactures, is fairly high and constant over time (> 0.9). It implies that less than 10 percent of US personal income is spent on housing (or non-tradable goods in general), which is too low compared to actual spending on housing. Alternative specifications (see Hanson, 2005: tab. 4) lead to lower estimates of δ, but these results are not statistically superior to those shown in table 5.5 (Hanson, 2005: 19).

It can also be shown, based on the parameter values for δ and ε in table 5.5, that the degree of agglomeration of US manufacturing production depends

[24] An alternative version uses US county employment as the dependent variable. To control for correlation of the error term with the regression function, Hanson uses various checks (i.e. measuring independent variables at the state level, using time differences, and excluding the high-population counties).

on the level of transport costs. To understand this, we must return to the no-black-hole condition, discussed in chapter 4 subsection 4.5.1 for the core model, where the condition was stated as $\rho > \delta$.[25] It was argued in chapter 4 that, if the condition $\rho > \delta$ is fulfilled, the equilibrium regional distribution of economic activity depends on the level of transportation costs, whereas if this condition is not fulfilled full agglomeration (a monocentric equilibrium) is the only feasible equilibrium in the long run, such that the equilibrium spatial distribution of manufacturing activity would not depend at all on transport costs.

Based on the estimated value of δ and the implied value of ρ, it *appears* that the no-black-hole condition is violated, suggesting that the location of US manufacturing activity does not depend on the level of transportation costs. This conclusion is *not* correct, however, because the interpretation of the condition is reversed in the housing model of geographical economics estimated in equation (5.5). Why does this switching of the interpretation of the no-black-hole condition take place? The reason is that Hanson builds on the model developed by Helpman (1998), in which the agricultural sector of the core model is replaced by a housing sector. Since the agricultural good is freely traded between regions, whereas housing is a non-tradable good, the interpretation of the no-black-hole condition is reversed (see Helpman, 1998: 50–1).

To verify the strength of demand linkages across space, Hanson analyzes the spatial decay of the predicted wage changes of the estimation results reported in table 5.5. In doing so, he also compares his finding with those based on estimating a simple market potential function such as equation (5.4). For the estimation results shown in table 5.5 there is a very strong distance decay; the value for the transportation costs coefficient T is such that "changes in the market potential index affect wages only within 200 km" (Hanson, 2005: 20). For the estimation results based on his estimation of the market potential function, the spatial decay is lower (wages are affected in a range up to 400–600 kilometers), but overall the distance decay is such that, just as with the case of the EU regions in figure 5.5, the spatial reach of demand linkages as exemplified by the RMP variable in (5.3) seems rather limited.[26]

---

[25] The "no-black-hole" condition, without the label attached to it, can be found as early as Krugman (1991a: 496).

[26] The specification of the distance effect is also relevant for this conclusion; see Brakman, Garretsen, and Schramm (2006).

5.5.4 Two critical observations and extensions

The fact that we discuss Hanson (2005) in some detail reflects our view that this study and related real market potential studies constitute an important attempt to arrive at an empirical validation of the geographical economics approach regarding the hypothesis that a larger market potential raises a region's factor prices. All the same, there are a number of objections that can be raised (see also Hanson, 2005: 20–1). We single out two of these critical issues.

 (i) The relationship between the findings based on estimating the wage equation on the one hand and the underlying model on the other hand.

(ii) The use of rather strong assumptions, notably interregional real wage equalization, that may be of limited use in other cases (Europe) than the United States.

To start with the first issue, the theoretical model used by Hanson is based on Thomas (1996), who builds on the study published as Helpman (1998). A central issue in Thomas (1996) is the non-linear relationship between transport costs on the one hand and industrial agglomeration and relative wages on the other hand. This non-linearity is a hallmark of geographical economics (see chapters 3 and 4, or our discussion of Krugman and Venables (1990) in section 2.3). It implies that, as transportation costs decrease from very high to intermediate levels, the agglomeration of economic activity is strengthened and the relative wage of large regions increases. If transportation costs fall even further, from intermediate to low levels, however, firms and workers relocate to the smaller regions, the share of large regions in manufacturing production decreases, and the wage differential between large and small regions narrows. For an intermediate range of transport costs, the advantages of market proximity outweigh the disadvantages for firms and workers of the relatively large region. The advantages of market proximity arise from the backward and forward linkages that enable firms in the centers of production to pay somewhat higher wages. The disadvantages of agglomeration arise from the higher wage costs for firms and from congestion costs for workers. The latter are incorporated in Thomas (1996), and thus also in Hanson (2005), by a relatively high housing price in the center of production. At a certain point transportation costs get so low that the advantages of market proximity fall short of the disadvantages, and a relocation process starts. This is illustrated in figure 5.7 (with transportation costs falling as one moves from left to right along the horizontal axis).

Why is the theoretical possibility of a non-linear relationship, or U-shaped curve, between transportation costs and relative wages important from an

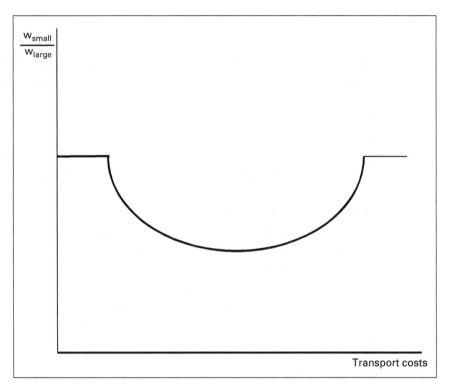

Figure 5.7   Relative real wage and transport costs

empirical point of view? Because it implies that models of geographical economics can be in accordance with the results found by Hanson (2005), as well as with a tendency towards regional wage equalization, depending on the position of the economy on the U-shaped curve. Without a hypothesis about the initial level of transport costs, it is not clear whether increasing regional wage differentials, as in the Hanson study, constitute evidence in favor of geographical economics or not. To arrive at such an hypothesis, however, we need to go back to the underlying model and stipulate what changes in key model parameters, such as the level of transportation costs, imply for the equilibrium distribution of income, wages, and prices – the endogenous variables in our model. This is precisely the topic of one of the two remaining empirical predictions to which geographical economics gives rise: that, at some critical level of transport or trade costs, a further *reduction in trade costs induces agglomeration*. This is the topic of section 6.3.

Hanson (2005) does not deal with the issues raised in figure 5.7. This may be due to his assumption of real wage equalization across regions, implying that the US economy is always in a long-run equilibrium. This is a very strong assumption, however. Without knowledge of the initial conditions of the US spatial distribution of economic activity, it is not possible to determine whether or not the observed distribution at any point in time is a long-run equilibrium. Be that as it may, it is clear that for countries other than the United States it may be more problematic to assume real wage equalization to hold. Germany, the largest European economy, is a case in point. In continental European countries such as Germany the labor market is thought to be less flexible than in the United States, which makes it more difficult to assume that real wages will always and everywhere be flexible so as to restore and maintain equilibrium. In the case of Germany, the fall of the Berlin Wall in 1989 and the formal reunification between West and East Germany in October 1990 implied a massive structural change that certainly was not accompanied by an instantaneous equilibrium of the spatial distribution of the footloose workers and firms.

The second issue mentioned at the beginning of this subsection stems from the assumption of real wage equalization that is needed for (5.5) in order to get rid of the price index I. Assuming that we do not have data on regional manufacturing prices, can we estimate (5.3) without invoking real wage equalization? Brakman, Garretsen, and Schramm (2004a) try to do so for their sample of German regions by simplifying the price index while also allowing for labor productivity differences between regions. As a benchmark, when real wage equalization is assumed to hold and the estimation strategy of Hanson (2005) discussed in the previous subsection is applied to their sample of 151 western and eastern German districts for the period 1994 to 1995, the estimated coefficients for the three key model parameters are not plausible to begin with. They end up with the following wage equation (see Brakman, Garretsen, and Schramm, 2004a, for full details):

$$\log(W_j) = \kappa_0 + \varepsilon^{-1} \log \left[\sum_{k=1}^{R} Y_k \left(T^{D_{jk}}\right)^{1-\varepsilon} I_k^{\varepsilon-1} \right] + \kappa_1 EG \tag{5.6}$$

with

$$I_j^{1-\varepsilon} = \left[\lambda_j \left(W_j \left(1+\gamma_j\right)\right)^{1-\varepsilon} + (1-\lambda_j)\left(\bar{W}_j T^{D_{j-center}}\right)^{1-\varepsilon} \right]$$

where γ_j represents the productivity gap between west Germany and district j, which is $(MPL_{west}/MPL_j) - 1$; EG is a dummy variable equal to one if j is in

Table 5.6 No real wage equalization

	Equation (5.6)
ε	3.652 (23.4)
$\mathrm{Log}(T)$	0.003 (13.7)
District-specific control variables	
EG dummy	$-0.633\ (-16.2)$
$D_{country}$	$-0.056\ (-1.4)$
Industry	1.052 (5.8)
Other services	1.983 (5.4)
High-skilled	5.456 (11.7)
Adjusted R^2	0.99

Notes: Estimation method for equation (5.6) is weighted least squares (WLS). Number of observations is 151. District-specific control variables that are not statistically significant are omitted. The t-statistics are in parentheses.

east Germany; $\bar{W}_j$ is the average wage outside district j; $D_{j\text{-}center}$ is the distance from district j to the economic center (the district of Giessen near Frankfurt); and λ_j is the district's share of manufacturing employment.

An additional advantage of equation (5.6) compared to the wage equation (5.5) is that the share of income spent on manufactures δ (which we thus found to be rather large in table 5.5 above) does not need to be estimated, and one also does not need to use the equilibrium condition for the housing market. The modeling tricks involved are beyond our present purposes, but by estimating (5.6) we want to establish the following.

- Whether, using a different version of the wage equation and a different country (Germany instead of the United States), there is evidence of a spatial wage structure, and we can therefore assess the significance of the model parameters.
- Given the key role of spatial interdependencies in geographical economics, how strong are the spatial demand linkages in terms of regional wage effects for the case of Germany?

Table 5.6 shows the estimation results for the two remaining model parameters, the substitution elasticity ε and the transport cost parameter T, and also for the various control variables that were used. As to the results for the controls: the regional wage is higher when a region is not in east Germany (EG dummy), is not a country but a city district, its sectoral employment shows more industry or services employment, and when its workers are high-skilled. The results in table 5.6 show that the transport cost parameter T is significant and has the right sign. The same holds for the substitution elasticity ε. The results support the notion that nominal wages in district j are higher if this region has better access (in terms of distance) to larger markets – that is, our alternative estimation strategy yields a spatial wage structure for Germany.

To some extent this is a surprising result. Certainly, compared to the case of the United States as reported by Hanson (2005), the German labor market is considered to be rigid, which could imply in terms of our model that, for whatever institutional reason, interregional wages are set at the same level. For a country such as Germany, one might very well expect the spatial distribution of real market potential to be reflected *not* only in spatial wage differences but (also) in the spatial distribution of quantity variables such as regional (un)employment (see also Puga, 2002: 389–90, for this assertion for Germany).[27] The proper approach to deal with the implications of wage rigidity is to incorporate the implications of wage rigidity, most notably unemployment, into the model and then to (re-)estimate the structural parameters. This is left for future research (though see Peeters and Garretsen, 2004, for a first attempt).

Returning to the estimation results in table 5.3 and following Hanson (2005), we again illustrate the strength of the interregional demand linkages that give rise to the spatial wage structure, using the following thought experiment. This experiment is similar to the NRW experiment in subsection 5.5.2. Based on the estimated coefficients in table 5.6 we derived the impact on regional wages from a 10 percent GDP increase in the city district of Munich. The localization of demand linkages turns out to be quite strong. The positive GDP shock leads to a wage increase in Munich itself of 0.8 percent, and the impact on wages in other regions decays strongly with distance. In Berlin, for instance, the impact is a mere 0.08 percent. This is in line with the findings of Hanson (2005) for the United States in the previous subsection. Figure 5.8 shows the results of our "Munich experiment" for each of the German districts. It shows clearly that the impact of the GDP shock on wages declines rapidly the further one moves away from Munich. Despite differences in the empirical specification, therefore, as well as as in the country under study, we end up with the same conclusion as in

---

[27] Interregional wage differences are not feasible, for instance, if a union ensures centralized wage setting (that is, irrespective of regional economic conditions): $W_j = W_k$ Centralized wage setting (at the industry level) is a tenet of the German labor market.

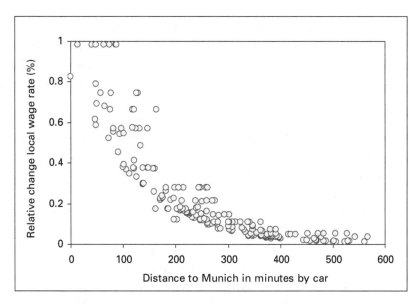

Figure 5.8   Wage growth and distance, following a 10 percent GDP rise in Munich

subsection 5.5.3 – or subsection 5.5.2, for that matter: the empirical relevance of the spatial interdependencies seems relatively limited, in the sense that the shocks of local RMP to regional wages are rather small and fade away rather quickly with increased distance.

This concludes our discussion of the second testable hypothesis to which geographical economics gives rise: a larger market potential, be it nominal or real market potential, implies higher wages. The research to which this hypothesis has given rise has been discussed extensively in section 5.5. All in all, there is evidence in favor of a spatial wage structure, but the strength or spatial reach of spatial interdependencies seems limited.

5.6 Conclusions (or why we do need chapter 6)

How can we relate the findings in the previous section about spatial wages and the role of real market potential to the other hypotheses that are on the list of testable geographical economics implications introduced at the end of section 5.3: the home market effect; factor inflows; shock sensitivity; and agglomeration induced by trade costs? We start with the home market effect, stating that an increase in a region's demand for a good will lead to a more than proportional increase of this region's production of the good. As with any shock that hits an economy, a standard question in economics is: what is adjusting, prices or quantities? In home market effect studies (see Head and Mayer, 2006), factor price equalization is always and everywhere assumed to hold, so the answer is straightforward: employment and production are doing the adjustment to the effect that real market potentials are equalized across regions. In real market potential studies such as Hanson (2005) but also Redding and Venables (2004), discussed in the previous section, it is precisely the other way around: the location of firms and workers is fixed and so is the RMP for each region, and hence factor prices (here, wages) do all the adjusting.

We know from chapters 3 and 4, however, that in geographical economics in the long run demand or income, prices, wage, production, and employment are all *endogenous!* To understand what any shock might do to the equilibrium spatial allocation of footloose economic activity (the Holy Grail in geographical economics) requires us to allow for the possibility that all these variables may change. In this respect, neither the empirical work on the home market effect nor the market potential hypothesis deal with the key question in geographical economics: what do shocks to demand or transport costs imply for the equilibrium spatial allocation of economic activity?[28] Look again at figures 4.1, 4.2, or 4.3 to see that these questions go to the heart of what geographical economics is about. Two sets of empirical questions to which these three figures, which sum up the core model, immediately give rise and that are not addressed by either home market or market potential studies are as follows.

- When hit by a shock, does a location (city, region, country) return to the initial stable equilibrium like point C in figure 4.1? If not, can we establish how large the shock must be (see the unstable equilibria or thresholds B and D) for the location to switch to a new stable equilibrium (A or E)?
- Given the key role of transportation or trade costs in geographical economics, is it possible to come up with an empirical yardstick for transportation costs and confront it with figures 4.3 or 4.10 in order to determine if changes in trade costs give rise to a change in the agglomeration pattern?

---

[28] The same applies to the factor inflow hypothesis, which was not discussed in this chapter but which will be discussed in chapter 9 section 9.5, in which the spatial allocation of economic activity is considered to be given (notably a fixed market potential) when it is investigated to ascertain whether it makes sense for a firm or worker to migrate to another region.

In the next chapter we discuss two strands of recent empirical research that try to answer these kinds of questions. First, though, we discuss the empirical research on the shock sensitivity hypothesis and then continue with research on trade-cost-induced agglomeration.

Exercises

5.1* Take the idea of a spatial wage structure as introduced in this chapter. Do you think it is possible to arrive at such a wage structure using either the neoclassical trade model or the new trade model developed by Krugman and Venables (1990) (see section 2.3 for a discussion of the latter)?

5.2* On our website you can find the results of the following experiment. Take the estimation results for the wages in German city districts based on equation (5.5). Now assume that the income in the city of Essen (one of the German city districts) is increased by 10 percent and calculate the impact of this income shock for city district wages. Explain the findings of this experiment in terms of the geographical economics model.

5.3* Suppose we apply the idea of a spatial wage structure on a global level instead of on a country level, as in this chapter. Do you think it is more difficult to find confirmation for a spatial wage structure at this higher level of aggregation? If so, why?

5.4* Take the short-run equilibrium wage equation (5.3). This equation states that low transportation costs (low T) are good for regional wages. Why does this equation not tell us what happens with regional wages when transportation costs are changed, however, such as when T is lowered?

5.5 Assume that wage equation (5.5) was estimated for the case of German districts and that the estimation results indicate that the no-black-hole condition holds. Explain what this would imply for the convergence prospects between east and west Germany.

5.6 Equation (5.1) is central to the Davis and Weinstein approach to measure the so-called home market effect. Discuss how one could amend the measurement of the "neoclassical" variable END, referring to labor endowments, in order for it *not* to be subject to the criticism that, from a geographical economics perspective, the regional allocation of endowments is part of the geographical economics model.

5.7 In practice, almost all commodities are costly to trade. The study by Davis (1998) suggests that in that case the home market effect probably vanishes. Can you find evidence that this is indeed the case?

Hint: are large countries net exporters of commodities produced under firm-specific scale economies (use intra-industry trade figures as an indication)?

5.8 As explained in chapter 3, the equilibrium wage equation of the core model is given by

$$W_j = \left[\sum_k Y_k I_k^{\varepsilon-1} T^{D_{jk}(1-\varepsilon)} \right]^{1/\varepsilon} \tag{5.7}$$

where W is the wage rate, Y is income, I is the price index, ε is the elasticity of substitution, T is the transport cost parameter, and $T_{jk} = T^{D_{jk}}$, where D_{jk} is the distance between locations j and k.

(i) Discuss the main differences between this wage equation and a simple market potential function for wages.

(ii) Explain whether or not the estimation of this wage equation can be looked upon as a test of the underlying geographical economics model.

5.9 Use the wage equation from the previous question to explain what the central message of geographical economics is.

6 Shocks, freeness of trade, and stability

6.1 Introduction

Head and Mayer (2004a: 2644; emphasis in original) argue that the empirical studies on the relevance of geographical economics of the kind that were discussed in chapter 5

all consider the impact of geographic distribution of demand as an *explanatory* variable. While this empirical approach is useful and justifiable in certain contexts, it is also problematic. The key idea of new economic geography (NEG) is that *the location of demand is jointly determined with the location of production*. In particular, the opportunity to export at low costs to immobile sources of demand allows all the mobile consumers and producers to congregate in the so-called manufacturing core. The predicted relationship between the free-ness of trade and agglomeration motivated the title of this chapter. Indeed, a large part of European academic interest in agglomeration stems from the question of whether a more united European market will lead to more spatially concentrated industry.

This quote from the chapter entitled "The empirics of agglomeration and trade" by Head and Mayer in volume IV of *The Handbook of Regional and Urban Economics* nicely illustrates what is at stake in chapter 6. We discuss empirical work that deals with one central question: what do changes in the economic environment (e.g. large exogenous shocks, demand changes, or changes in trade costs) imply for the equilibrium degree of agglomeration? This question, as the above quote suggests, goes to the heart of geographical economics. In doing so, we want to establish the empirical validity of the fourth and fifth hypotheses (shock sensitivity and trade-cost-induced agglomeration) from chapter 5's list of testable hypotheses (subsection 5.3.2).

In the next section, drawing on pioneering studies by Davis and Weinstein (2002, 2008) on Japan, we analyze whether a large, exogenous, and temporary shock, such as the destruction of Japanese and German cities during

World War II, provides a test for the shock sensitivity hypothesis of the geographical economics model. We start by asking if war-struck cities return to their initial, pre-shock equilibrium. We then proceed by asking if these war time shocks also constitute evidence of multiple equilibria. One may argue that the empirical research discussed in section 6.2 is at best only loosely connected to the models of geographical economics from chapters 3 and 4. In section 6.3 we deal with the final testable hypothesis, trade-cost-induced agglomeration. In this case, there are clear linkages with our basic theoretical models of chapters 3 and 4. When does a change in trade costs or (in the terminology of this chapter) in the *freeness of trade* lead to changes in agglomeration in the real world? We will see that is difficult to answer this question in a satisfying manner using the two-region versions of the models of chapters 3 and 4. Section 6.4 concludes our inquiry into the empirical relevance of geographical economics.

6.2 Shock sensitivity: the impact of shocks on equilibria[1]

6.2.1 City growth, the WWII shock and the return to the initial equilibrium

The core model of geographical economics is characterized by multiple equilibria, some of which are stable and some of which are unstable (see, for example, figure 4.1). To answer the question of whether a shock can move the economy out of the initial, "pre-shock" equilibrium, one ideally would like to conduct a natural experiment in which the economy under consideration is hit by a large, temporary, and exogenous shock. The shock needs to be *large* in size and scope in order to be able to be felt at all locations and to be potentially able to move the economy from one equilibrium to the next, even if it is initially in a stable equilibrium;[2] the shock needs to be *temporary* to be able to isolate the impact of the shock in question from other changes; and the shock has to be *exogenous* to ensure that causality runs from "shock to location."

---

[1] This section is based on Brakman, Garretsen, and Schramm (2004b) and Maarten Bosker, Brakman, Garretsen, and Schramm (2007a).

[2] Regarding the size of the shock: as figure 4.1 illustrates, with an initially stable equilibrium the economy may also move back to the pre-shock equilibrium. Suppose the economy finds itself in C before the shock. All a shock does is move the economy to a new stable equilibrium, *in casu* point A, if the fall in λ_1 is such that the resulting level of λ_1 is lower than that associated with point B; otherwise the economy returns to C. The unstable equilibrium B acts as a *threshold*.

Research into the impact of shocks on locations is not confined solely to geographical economics. In urban economics, one can distinguish between two basic and long-established views about the possible impact of large temporary shocks on city growth. The first view is based on the pioneering models of urban growth in the Alonso–Muth–Mills tradition, which all go back to the first "model" of urban economics by von Thünen (1826) (see chapter 2). In these models, each city has its own optimal or natural size. Following a large shock (such as a war or large-scale natural disaster), the expectation is that after some time each city will have returned to its natural size. The key to this approach is that there is a city-specific level of productivity not influenced by the shock. As a result, the shock will *not* have a permanent impact. In the second view, city productivity is a (positive) function of the city-size population, and possibly also of the interactions (spillovers) with other (nearby) cities. Changes in the level of population will change city productivity and city growth. In this case, the prediction would be that a large shock might have a lasting impact. Geographical economics is in line with this second view.

The key issue is whether one can come up with real-world examples of a large, temporary and exogenous shock that can act as a testing ground for the shock sensitivity hypothesis. In a seminal paper, Davis and Weinstein (2002) use the case of the Allied bombing of Japanese cities during World War II as an example of such a shock. As to the impact this WWII shock might have had on Japanese cities, Davis and Weinstein distinguish between three basic theoretical approaches: in their terminology, *fundamental geography, increasing returns*, and *random growth*. In the case of fundamental geography, exogenous and fixed characteristics such as access to waterways, the climate, mountains, and other fixed endowments determine city growth. This approach is in line with the first view in urban economics mentioned above. The increasing returns approach is in line with the second view, which is consistent with the geographical economics approach. The WWII shock can have a permanent effect if the shock is large enough. Finally, they introduce the random growth approach, which predicts that the evolution of city sizes by definition follows a random walk, and a large, temporary shock such as the WWII shock must have a permanent effect (see also chapter 7 on random city growth in our discussion of Zipf's law).

Brakman, Garretsen, and Schramm (2004b) apply the Davis and Weinstein (2002) approach to the case of the Allied bombing of German cities during World War II. In both studies, the question is the same: did individual cities return to their initial, pre-war growth path after the war? In terms of figure 4.1, and assuming that the initial equilibrium is at point C, the question becomes one of whether there was a return to C after WWII. If not, this would be evidence for the geographical economics approach. In subsequent work (see the next subsection), Davis and Weinstein (2008) and Bosker *et al.* (2007a) use these WWII shocks to answer a related but different question: is there evidence that city growth is characterized by multiple equilibria? In terms of figure 4.1, is there evidence, besides C, of equilibria described by points A and E (stable equilibria besides C, with B and D as unstable 'thresholds')? This would be additional evidence in favor of geographical economics.

The underlying model of city growth in the above studies is as follows. The approach is basically to test if the growth of city size (measured as a share of total population) follows a random walk. The relative city size s for each city i at time t can be represented by (in logs)

$$s_{i,t} = \Omega_i + \varepsilon_{i,t} \tag{6.1}$$

where Ω_i is the initial size of city i and $\varepsilon_{i,t}$ represents a city-specific change in size at time t. This change consists of two parts, past changes and current shocks (subscript t for time):

$$\varepsilon_{i,t+1} = \rho\varepsilon_{i,t} + v_{i,t+1} \tag{6.2}$$

where $v_{i,t+1}$ is a shock that takes place in period $t+1$. "History" (or the persistence of past shocks) is taken care of by the parameter $0 \leq \rho \leq 1$. If $\rho = 1$ all shocks are permanent and history is always important. With $\rho = 0$ the shock has no persistence at all and history does not play any role. For $0 < \rho < 1$ there is some degree of persistence, but, ultimately, the relative city size is stationary and hence any shock will dissipate over time. For some intuition with respect to the role of ρ, it is instructive to rewrite (6.1) as $s_{i,t+1} = \Omega_i + \varepsilon_{i,t+1}$. Substituting (6.2) into this rewritten equation gives $s_{i,t+1} = \Omega_i + \varepsilon_{i,t+1} = \Omega_i + \rho\varepsilon_{i,t} + v_{i,t+1}$. With $\rho = 1$ the relative city size $s_{i,t+1}$ increases with the full amount of the shock from period t such that the past will have a maximum impact on the future city size. With $\rho = 0$ a shock from period t has no impact on city size in period $t+1$. This is also known as a mean reverting process, because city size returns to its long-run expected value. With $0 < \rho < 1$ there is some degree of persistence of the shock and only a partial return to the pre-shock city size in $t+1$.

To test this model we now proceed as follows. By first-differencing (6.1) and making use of (6.2), we arrive at (6.3), which is the equation used in the empirical application:

$$s_{i,t+1} - s_{i,t} = (\rho - 1)v_{i,t} + \left(v_{i,t+1} + \rho(\rho - 1)\varepsilon_{i,t-1}\right) \tag{6.3}$$

Note that the left-hand side of (6.3) is the growth of city size. What makes the case of Japan and Germany interesting is that we can identify the WWII shock; take $(s_{i,1946} - s_{i,1939})$ as a proxy for v_{it} in the estimates.[3] The change in city size between these two dates – just before and just after the war – is assumed to have been caused by the war. The testable version of equation (6.3) becomes (in logs)[4]

$$s_{i,1946+t} - s_{i,1946} = a(s_{i,1946} - s_{i,1939}) + \beta_0 + error_i; \quad a \equiv \rho - 1 \tag{6.4}$$

If $a = 0$ (so $\rho = 1$) the war shock has a permanent effect (size is a random walk). If $a = -1$ (so $\rho = 0$) the war shock has no effect at all. If $-1 < a < 0$ (so $0 < \rho < 1$) the war shock has a temporary effect.

Before presenting the estimation results of (6.4) for Japan and Germany, we have to decide on the relevant period $1946 + t$ for the dependent variable. It should neither be too short a period (since that prevents cities from adjusting to the WWII shock) nor too long a period (because then other, more recent shocks could influence city growth). Davis and Weinstein (2002) and Brakman, Garretsen and Schramm (2004b) set the cut-off for t at eighteen years. Thus in both cases we test if the impact of WWII on city growth had vanished by the mid-1960s. Using the housing stock destruction and/or related WWII shock indicators as instruments, the estimation result of equation (6.4) is given in table 6.1.

For Japan, the estimated results strongly indicate that, eighteen years after World War II, Japanese cities had fully recovered from the WWII shock and returned to their pre-war growth path (the a coefficient does not differ significantly from -1). In terms of the model above, this suggests that WWII had no permanent effect and Japanese cities returned to their initial

---

[3] For the case of Japan, the city growth rate during WWII is the growth rate between 1940 and 1947 in Davis and Weinstein (2002).

[4] It follows from (6.3) that the shock, the growth rate between 1939 and 1946, is correlated with the error term in the estimating equation. This indicates that we have to use instruments. See, for details, Davis and Weinstein (2002) and Brakman, Garretsen and Schramm (2004b). The instruments used are city-specific variables such as the destruction of the housing stock, the number of casualties, and the amount of rubble.

Table 6.1 Do shocks matter?

Country	Dependent variable: $(s_{i,1946+t} - s_{i,1946})$
Japan: $(s_{i,1947} - s_{i,1940})$; n = 303	$a = -1.03$ (st. error 0.163); $t = 18$
West Germany: $(s_{i,1946} - s_{i,1939})$; n = 79	$a = -0.52$ (t-value 5.47); $t = 17$
East Germany: $(s_{i,1946} - s_{i,1939})$; n = 21	$a = -0.003$ (t-value 0.02); $t = 18$

Note: n = number of observations.
Sources: Davis and Weinstein (2002) and Brakman, Garretsen and Schramm (2004b).

equilibrium. According to Davis and Weinstein (2002), this finding supports the first-nature geography view of the impact of shocks on city growth.[5] The results for west German cities also indicate a tendency for the effects of the shock to be reversed, but here, as opposed to Japan, the return is only partial, which indicates that on average west German cities had not recovered fully from the WWII shock. This suggests that some cities might actually have moved to a new equilibrium growth path. Finally, the results for east German cities might lead to the conclusion that there is a permanent effect ($a = 0$). East German cities were part of the socialist German Democratic Republic (GDR), however, and in the communist planning regime that ruled the GDR people were not free to choose their location, suggesting that the GDR case is ill-suited for testing models in which economic agents are "free to choose." Box 6.1 discusses other shocks.

Box 6.1 The 9/11 attack, hurricane Katrina, and the medieval plague

Writing only a few weeks after the 9/11 terrorist attack hit New York city and destroyed the twin towers of the World Trade Center, Krugman in a column in the *New York Times* pointed out that the findings of Davis and Weinstein (2002) would imply that "if the Japanese parallel is at all relevant, the attack on New York, for all its horror, will have no effect worth mentioning on the city's long-run economic prospects."[6] Even more recently, in the wake of the destruction of the city of New Orleans by hurricane Katrina (August 2005), commentators have explicitly used the two studies discussed in the main text to ask what they imply for the future of New Orleans.[7] The crucial issue here is whether these and other historical cases can be compared with recent shocks. One difference between the WWII studies and the cases of 9/11 and Katrina is that the WWII studies concern a shock to an entire urban system, instead of a shock to a single city. Another concern is that the initial

---

[5] See also Gabaix and Ioannides (2004: 2372–3), however. They point out that the models used are partial, and do not analyze the reasons for (non-)persistence.
[6] Krugman, P. R., An injured city, *New York Times*, October 3, 2001.
[7] An example is the article by Bernasek, A., Blueprints from cities that rose from their ashes, *New York Times*, October 9, 2005.

Box 6.1 (cont.)

conditions (why did a particular city come into existence?) and government (rebuilding) policies may be hard to compare. Third, even if a city returns to its pre-shock size or if government policies try to achieve this, one could ask whether this is really welfare-enhancing. Glaeser, one of the leading urban economists, has argued *against* rebuilding New Orleans because the former inhabitants and the US economy might be better off without rebuilding.[8] Fourth, by just looking at the two studies discussed in the main text and the

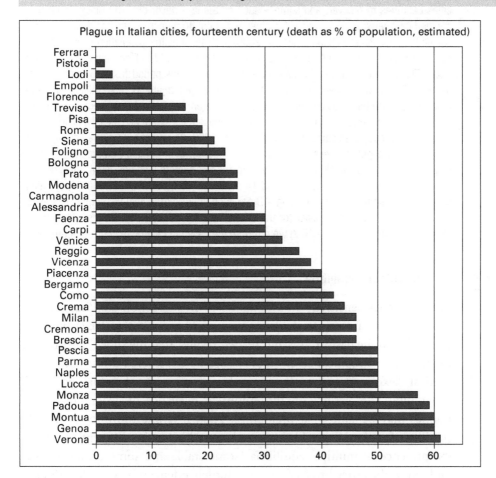

Figure 6.1   The plague and Italian cities
Source: Bosker, Brakman, Garretsen, de Jong, and Schramm (2008).

---

[8] Since you may be browsing the *New York Times* archives anyway (free access) because of the previous footnote, you may as well read the interview with Glaeser (Gartner, J., Home economics, *New York Times*, March 5, 2006) in which he discusses his research agenda and also talks about his views on the rebuilding of New Orleans. For Glaeser's view on the impact of (war) shocks on cities, see also Glaeser and Shapiro (2002).

Box 6.1 (cont.)

impact of WWII on Japanese and German cities, it is easy to forget that there also examples of more ancient shocks that clearly had a huge and long-lasting impact on city growth.

A good example of this last point is the fourteenth-century plague (the Black Death) that hit large parts of Europe, such as Italy, which had Europe's most developed urban system in those days. Figure 6.1 shows the death toll for various (northern) Italian cities as a percentage of the population. Faced with the magnitude of this "shock," it took most Italian cities centuries to recover, and some – such as Siena – never did. The Black Death that ravaged Italy between 1346 and 1353 wiped out about 40 percent of the population. Recent calculations by Paolo Malanima (1998, 2005) indicate that the population in central and northern Italy declined from an estimated 7.75 million to 4.72 million between 1300 and 1400. The urbanization rate for Italy as a whole fell in this period from 15 percent to 9 percent. By 1500 the overall population had increased again to 5.31 million and the urbanization rate had regained its 1300 level. Between 1600 and 1700 population growth stagnated again, however. A new wave of plague epidemics swept across Italy, killing more than 1 million people. In particular, the plagues of 1629–31 and of 1656–7 had detrimental effects on the population level, with an average death rate of at least 20 percent and even more in the large cities. Urban recovery from these disasters was very slow. In 1700 the urbanization rate had declined further to 14 percent, well below that of 1600. Many cities would not regain their earlier position. "There is no doubt that in Italy the consequences of the plagues were always heavier for the urban than for the rural populations" (Malanima, 1998: 99). In chapter 10 (box 10.2) we return to the case of city growth in pre-modern Italy.

6.2.2 Shocks and multiple equilibria

The two shock sensitivity studies discussed in subsection 6.2.1 suggest that urban systems are rather stable. Head and Mayer (2004a: 2662) therefore conclude, on the basis of this and related results, that the shock sensitivity in models of geographical economics should be considered a fascinating theoretical "exotica," rather than a relevant element of actual economic geography. This verdict on the empirical relevance of geographical economics may be somewhat premature. First, it is one thing to test for the stability of an initial equilibrium, and something quite different to test for the presence of multiple equilibria (some stable and some unstable). Second, given the crucial role of spatial interdependencies between locations in geographical economics models, the omission of such interdependencies in the two studies of subsection 6.2.1 is important. Third, a number of other studies on shocks suggest that these can have permanent effects (see box 6.2).

Again using the WWII shock for Japan, Davis and Weinstein (2008) develop an analytical framework to test for multiple equilibria. In doing so, they look not only at city populations but also at the economic structure of

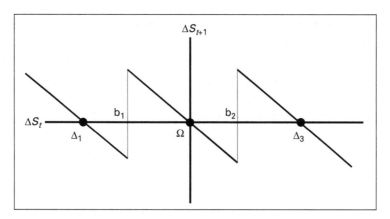

Figure 6.2   Two-period growth representation of a model with three stable equilibria

Japanese cities. Bosker *et al.* (2007a) use this framework for the WWII shock
and Germany, also taking spatial interdependencies into account. The basic
framework developed by Davis and Weinstein (2008) is summarized in
figure 6.2 (translating figure 4.1 into a dynamic framework), where ΔS_t
indicates the change in city size – or shock – in period t. The points A to E in
figure 4.1 play a similar role to, respectively, Δ_1, b_1, Ω, b_2, and Δ_3 in figure 6.2.

Figure 6.2 depicts three stable equilibria (Δ_1, Δ_3, and Ω) and two unstable
equilibria (b_1 and b_2, which act as a threshold between the stable equilibria).[9]
Given that the economy is initially in a stable equilibrium (C in figure 4.1 or
Ω in figure 6.2), a shock can in theory have two implications depending on
the size of the shock. A (small) shock around the initial stable equilibrium Ω
in period t is completely undone in the next period, $t+1$. This implies that
the slope of the solid line that passes through the origin in figure 6.2 is
exactly -1, with the solid line being depicted as $\Delta S_t = -\Delta S_{t+1}$. If the shock is
large enough to pass one of the thresholds (b_1 or b_2), however, the economy
(here, cities) moves towards another stable equilibrium with a new corresponding solid line $\Delta S_t = -\Delta S_{t+1} + constant.$[10] It is an empirical matter if
the period $t+1$ is long enough such that we really observe $\Delta S_t = -\Delta S_{t+1}$,
but from a theoretical point of view we know that at some point cities

---

[9] Note that the origin has no special meaning other than indicating the initial situation.

[10] A complication discussed in chapter 7 is that, in the real world, partial agglomeration seems to be the rule. Applied to
cities, this means that the underlying model should allow for multiple stable equilibria at which cities (agglomerations)
exist that differ in size. Our core model is not equipped to deal with this observation, since it typically allows only for
either a mono-city (full agglomeration) or equally sized cities (spreading). It is straightforward, however, to extend the
core model to include partial agglomeration as a stable equilibrium outcome (see chapter 7). For instance, by adding
an additional spreading force (congestion) to an otherwise unchanged core model of geographical economics, one can
indeed end up with alternating stable and unstable equilibria (see figure 7.6c).

must again return to a stable equilibrium (be it the initial or a new stable equilibrium) after a shock (the previous subsection used an eighteen-year period). In practice, therefore, even if the initial equilibrium is stable, the slope could be less than one (in absolute terms) if $t+1$ is too small. To facilitate comparison with the model of subsection 6.2.1, we use the symbols introduced above. Our main variable of interest is the (log-) share of city i in total population (denoted S_i; we suppress the subscript i since all cities are assumed to be alike in terms of their reaction to a particular city-specific shock of a given size; this is an important assumption, as it means that the model underlying figure 6.2 is based on the notion of a representative city).[11]

If the shock is large enough to move the city's population share outside the range $b_1 - b_2$ a new stable equilibrium will be established and the economy will move to Δ_1 or Δ_3, depending on the shock. For any new stable equilibrium, $\Delta S_t = -\Delta S_{t+1}$ must hold in a two-period setting. For the three stable equilibria shown in figure 6.2, these possibilities are indicated by the two solid lines through Δ_1 and Δ_3, both with a slope of -1. To sum up, with multiple equilibria in the two-period growth setting of figure 6.2 we have a sequence of lines with slope -1, each corresponding to a different stable equilibrium. As Davis and Weinstein (2008: 36) note:

[T]he two-period growth space thus provides a very simple contrast between a model of unique equilibrium versus one of multiple equilibria. In the case of a unique equilibrium, an observation should simply lie on a line with slope minus unity through the origin. In the case of multiple equilibria, we get a sequence of lines, all with slopes minus unity, but with different intercepts. Because in this latter case these lines have slope minus unity, the intercepts are ordered and correspond to the displacement in log-share space from the initial to the new equilibrium. These elements will be central when we turn to empirical analysis.

Imagine a scatter plot of data on city growth during WWII (S_t) and post-WWII city growth (S_{t+1}) for Japanese or German cities. Estimating equation (6.4) then simply tests whether the data points lie on a slope with -1 through the origin, in fact taking only a single equilibrium such as Ω into account, and ignores the possibility of multiple equilibria. Using the same scatter plot in terms of figure 6.2, the question now becomes whether the data are indeed best described by allowing for one or more equilibria. The question then arises of how many parallel lines with slope -1 we must use to describe the scatter plot best.

A drawback of the framework depicted by figure 6.2 is that spatial inter-dependencies are not taken into account. What happens to a particular city

---

[11] Note that the use of log-shares reformulates the model in growth rates.

following a shock can also be determined by the impact on other cities. Think, for example, of a lucky city not hit by wartime destruction surrounded by cities that have been. We would expect the destruction of these other cities to affect the lucky city as well. For that reason, Bosker *et al.* (2007a) use $\Delta S_{t+1,i} = f(\Delta S_{t,i}, \Delta S_{t,j \neq i})$, incorporating time subscript t and city subscripts i and j. Empirically, we look at the change in the size of a city i *and* changes in the size of surrounding cities j, corrected for inter-city distances between i and j.

From theory to estimates

Our starting point is equation (6.4), with some adjustments. First, assuming (for the moment) that there are indeed three stable equilibria, we have to look at three versions of this equation (one for each equilibrium). Second, we now *assume* that $a = -1$ (or $\rho = 0$). Recall that in subsection 6.2.1 our focus was on the question whether or not a was different from -1. So why do we now *assume* this to be the case? Because the need for the $a = -1$ assumption already follows from the theoretical model summarized in figure 6.2. Under the assumption that period $t+1$ in this figure is long enough for the period t shock to have dissipated, a solid line in figure 6.2 represents a stable equilibrium with slope -1 because that is what a *stable* equilibrium implies: $\Delta S_t = -\Delta S_{t+1}$. Any other assumption is difficult to reconcile with the underlying model of city growth. A third difference with the estimate of equation (6.4) is that we have to take into consideration the fact that the model places restrictions on the coefficients to be estimated. Basically, we want to arrive at the empirical equivalents of Δ_1, b_1, Ω, b_2, and Δ_3 illustrated in figure 6.2. The figure itself already suggests a specific ordering for the coefficients to be estimated (labeled δ_i in table 6.2 [where i denotes the ith equilibrium] and b_i [where i denotes the ith threshold]). If there are three equilibria, we must have the following intercept and threshold ordering condition: $\delta_1 < b_1 < 0 < b_2 < \delta_3$. Finally, since neither the number of equilibria nor the positioning of the thresholds are known beforehand (any number of equilibria is possible), the multiple equilibria version of equation (6.4) needs to determine the appropriate number of equilibria (see the website for more details).

Table 6.2 provides the estimated results for Japan and Germany. The data sets are the same as in subsection 6.2.1. The German estimate results use *spatial interdependencies* (geography) because the war shock is a function not only of a city's own destruction but also of the sum of the distance-weighted destruction of all other cities (measured as changes in the housing stock). This captures the idea that the "geography" of bombing matters. Geography also enters the post-WWII period in a simple way, as (in line

Table 6.2 Testing for multiple equilibria in city population growth

Country	Japan		Germany	
Number of equilibria	2 equilibria	3 equilibria	2 equilibria	3 equilibria
δ_1	0.0978	−0.0720	−0.193	−0.341
δ_2 (constant)	0.196	0.315	0.284	0.458
δ_3		−0.127		−0.220
b_1	−0.001	−0.056	−0.004	−0.004
b_2		0		0.017
Intercept ordering criteria	Fail	Fail	Accept	Fail
2 equilibria: $\delta_1 < b_1 < 0$				
3 equilibria: $\delta_1 < b_1 < 0 < b_2 < \delta_3$				
Number of observations	303	303	81	81

Note: Only West German cities are present in the German city sample; the dependent variable is city growth.
Sources: Japan – Davis and Weinstein (2008); Germany – Bosker *et al.* (2007a).

with a market potential function) the distance from economic centers (here, Munich) is allowed to affect a city's post-WWII growth rate.

For the case of Japan, and restricting ourselves to either two or three equilibria, the evidence does not support the hypothesis of multiple equilibria: in both estimates the intercept ordering condition is not met. Keeping in mind the results for Japan in table 6.1 from subsection 6.2.1, this outcome is not surprising, since we concluded that Japanese cities returned to the initial equilibrium after WWII (a was not significantly different from −1) and the effects of the WWII shock had completely dissipated after eighteen years. For the German case we found only a partial return, so there is a priori more scope for multiple equilibria. Table 6.2 confirms this, as we find evidence for the presence of two equilibria. There is one caveat, however: estimates for Germany without taking geography into account do *not* confirm the existence of multiple equilibria.

The evidence presented here on the impact of WWII on Japanese and German cities is mixed regarding the sensitivity of equilibria with respect to shocks. To round up our discussion on shock sensitivity, box 6.2 reviews a number of studies for different shocks and time periods. The general conclusion is that shocks can have permanent effects, thereby vindicating the relevance of a key building block of geographical economics. In addition, we find that local history, institutions, and policies are also important. Sensitivity to shocks and the underlying notion of multiple equilibria are thus not theoretical curiosa, even though it is clear that the stability or resilience of locations to shocks is greater than figure 4.1 seems to suggest.

Box 6.2 More evidence on shock sensitivity: Vietnam and the German division

Edward Miguel and Gérard Roland (2005) investigate the long-run impact of US bombing on Vietnam in the 1960s and early 1970s. Using a sample of 584 Vietnamese districts and a detailed data set on the bombing intensity, they analyze the effects of the US bombing on Vietnamese post-war development in terms of consumption, poverty, and population density. They conclude that the long-run effects of the US bombing are limited, in the sense that most districts have recovered rather quickly from the war destruction. Whether this conclusion is bad news for geographical economics is an open question (see Miguel and Roland, 2005: 6), to the extent that agglomeration effects are probably less relevant for a relatively poor country such as Vietnam (compared to Japan and Germany). Moreover, the US bombing in the Vietnam War was not targeted specifically at cities but at rural districts, which probably limited the war damage done to the economic infrastructure of Vietnam. Another feature of this shock is that in the post-war period (from 1976 onwards) the government of the centrally planned economy of Vietnam undertook major reconstruction efforts, with districts that had been more heavily bombed receiving more government investment, which helped the recovery process.

The break-up of Germany in 1949 into the Federal Republic of Germany (FRG – West Germany) and the German Democratic Republic (GDR – East Germany) and the subsequent reunification of the two Germanies in 1990 after the fall of the Berlin Wall is another example of a large, temporary (forty-one-year) shock. Redding, Daniel Sturm, and Nikolaus Wolf (2007) use this example and the shift in the location of West Germany's main airport hub from Berlin to Frankfurt am Main as a test case for multiple equilibria. The airline industry and the location of hubs fits well with the geographical economics model in the sense that it is a sector in which transport costs are (obviously) relevant, where the activity is footloose, and where scale economies are important. Before 1949 Berlin was the main hub, and after the division of Germany Frankfurt took over from Berlin. After the reunification Frankfurt remained the largest airport hub in Germany. While controlling for various other factors, Redding, Sturm, and Wolf (2007) conclude that the switch of the main airline location in Germany constitutes evidence supporting the existence of multiple equilibria.

In a related paper, Redding and Sturm (2005) use the same shock to test whether *West* German border cities (close to the FRG–GDR border) experienced a substantial decline compared to non-border cities in West Germany. Their answer is affirmative. Border cities within 75 km of the intra-German border suffered a significant decline. The authors note that there is some evidence that these cities made a recovery after reunification (when they ceased to be border cities). According to the authors, the main reason the West German border cities fell behind after 1949 is their loss of real market potential (RMP) as a result of the loss of markets in the nearby GDR. From a sample of 119 West German cities, twenty are classified as border cities. The basic empirical specification is as follows (sub-index c indicates city and sub-index t indicates time):

$$popgrowth_{c,t} = \beta\ border_c + \gamma\ border_c \times division_t + d_t + \varepsilon_{ct} \qquad (6.5)$$

Box 6.2 (cont.)

The border dummy (*border_c*) captures differences in city population growth between the two groups of west German cities before the division. The main coefficient of interest is γ, the interaction term (*border_c* × *division_t*) between the border and division dummy that "captures any systematic change in the relative growth performance of treatment and control groups of cities following German division" (Redding and Sturm, 2005: 20), where the "treatment group" are the border cities and the control group the other western German cities. The hypothesis is that γ is negative because that implies that the population growth of the border cities was lower than that of non-border cities. As Redding and Sturm show, this is indeed the case. One question that comes to mind is: which of the two shocks is the more important: WWII or the German division? Bosker *et al.* (2008) use a long time series on individual (west) German city growth, namely annual data for the period 1925 to 1999, and let the data determine where a break can be detected. It turns out that, (almost) without exception, the data indicate that the WWII shock dominated other shocks (see the website of the book for more information).

6.3 Trade costs and agglomeration: the bumpy road from theory to empirics and back

6.3.1 Where on the tomahawk diagram or bell-shaped curve are we?

The final step in analyzing the empirical relevance of geographical economics is to investigate the relation between trade costs and agglomeration (the fifth hypothesis on Head and Mayer's list of empirical propositions discussed in subsection 5.3.2). Chapter 4 has noted that the geographical economics models can be summarized in two figures. The tomahawk diagram (figure 4.3) captures models such as that of Krugman (1991a), presented in chapter 3, in which trade costs are sufficiently low at the break point to induce (complete) agglomeration from then on. The bell-shaped curve (see figure 4.10) also indicates that if trade costs fall below the break point the spreading of economic activity will turn into agglomeration. In this case, however, a further drop in trade costs will reverse the agglomeration equilibrium again to the spreading equilibrium. As explained in chapter 4, the difference between the two classes of models is determined by the assumption with respect to interregional labor mobility. In the core model of chapter 3 – leading to the tomahawk diagram – manufacturing labor can move between regions. If labor is not interregionally mobile the bell-shaped curve may appear (since higher wages act as an additional spreading force).

Notwithstanding these differences, *both* models convey the same message: in a full-fledged general equilibrium framework, agglomeration is determined by history and changes in variables and parameters (of which trade costs are the most important). As noted at the end of chapter 5, most empirical work in geographical economics is unable to deal with this aspect of geographical economics. This holds not only for the reduced-form estimates (see section 5.2) but also for the home market effect and real market potential (sections 5.4 and 5.5). In these studies, in contrast to the underlying geographical economics model, the location of important demand or supply factors is taken as *given*. Consequently, when applied to real-world problems (such as the effects of EU integration or globalization) these studies do not have much to say on the question of whether and how changes in transport costs induce agglomeration. Testing the fifth hypothesis implies an answer to the question: *where* on the Tomahawk diagram or bell-shaped curve are we? Knowing the answer to this question informs us on the interconnections between trade costs and agglomeration. In the remainder of this section we discuss possible answers to this question.

6.3.2 The freeness of trade and taking the two-region model (too) seriously

To facilitate the discussion and to ease comparison with other studies (upon which our overview is based), we focus on the freeness of trade parameter $\varphi \equiv T^{1-\varepsilon}$ introduced in chapter 4 (see also Baldwin *et al.*, 2003). Recall that $\varphi = 0$ denotes autarky and the absence of economic integration, whereas $\varphi = 1$ denotes free trade and full economic integration. Note that in the two-region models of chapters 3 and 4 (in which the distance D_{rs} between regions r and s equals one), the transport costs T and freeness of trade φ can do without the sub-indices (are not region-specific). If this assumption cannot be made (as in most empirical applications) we use $\varphi_{rs} = T_{rs}^{1-\varepsilon} = T^{D_{rs}(1-\varepsilon)}$.

At first sight, the empirical task now seems relatively straightforward. For any region pair r and s, given their distance D_{rs}, one needs to estimate T and ε (and thus the freeness of trade) and then confront this estimate with the tomahawk diagram or bell-shaped curve. Analytically, assuming for simplicity that we are interested only in an *increase* in the freeness of trade, we can thus confront the empirical value of the freeness of trade with the break points associated with the tomahawk diagram or bell-shaped curve (see subsections 4.5.2 and section 4.6 for analytical derivations in the two-region case). Let us denote the two break points for the bell-shaped curve by φ_{low}^B and φ_{high}^B and the break point for the tomahawk diagram by $\varphi_{lab\ mob}^B$ (in which *lab mob* refers to labor mobility). Substituting some reasonable values for the model parameters into the break point conditions, we can determine for the regions r and s if they are in a regime of spreading or agglomeration. Matthieu Crozet (2004) and Brakman *et al.* (2005) do this for EU regions and conclude that, typically, any pair of EU regions is (still) in the spreading range. Only when the distance between the two regions is small does the empirical value for the freeness of trade become large enough to exceed φ_{low}^B or $\varphi_{lab\ mob}^B$ for the bell-shaped curve or the tomahawk diagram respectively. Box 6.3 gives more information regarding this interesting, but ultimately problematic, experiment of forcing the analytical two-region results from chapter 4 upon a multi-region reality.

Box 6.3 Interesting but problematic: looking at a multi-region world with a two-region model

In Brakman *et al.* (2005), the freeness of trade is estimated for a sample of NUTS II regions for the period 1992 to 2000 using a wage equation similar to equation (5.5). Given some reasonable estimates on the other parameters of the break conditions (μ, η, δ, ε) for the tomahawk diagram and bell-shaped curve, we can conduct the following thought experiment in both models. From the analytical break conditions we calculate the break points φ_{low}^B, φ_{high}^B, and $\varphi_{lab\ mob}^B$. Given the values of the break points and the estimated coefficients for T and ε, we can ask what distance D_{rs} corresponds with a break point. In other words, since we know that $\varphi_{rs} = T_{rs}^{1-\varepsilon} = T^{D_{rs}(1-\varepsilon)}$, we can set the distance equal to a value of an analytical break point, given our estimates for T and ε from the wage equation.

For the EU NUTS II regions, this threshold external distance for the bell-shaped curve is 87.3 km for φ_{low}^B and 44.9 km for φ_{high}^B. This means that for any distance exceeding 87.3 km economic spreading holds. Similarly, for distances smaller than 44.9 km spreading holds again. In between these two distances we are on the (partial) agglomeration part of figure 4.10. For the tomahawk diagram, the threshold distance is 161 km. Here, the range of agglomeration forces is somewhat stronger, but still limited (the average distance between any pair of NUTS II regions is 620 km and between any pair of neighbouring NUTS II regions is 148 km). Figure 6.3 summarizes these findings. The conclusion regarding the limited spatial reach of agglomeration forces does not change when we change our benchmark parameter values. In most cases, the threshold distances beyond which agglomeration no longer holds are even *lower* than for the benchmark parameter values.

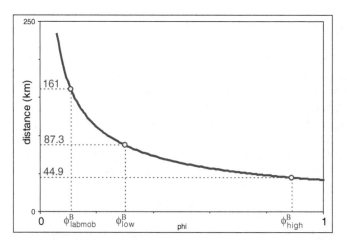

Figure 6.3   Break points and threshold distances
Notes: Benchmark parameter values for the break condition: $\mu = 0.3$, $\eta = 200$, $\delta = 0.1$, $\varepsilon = 9.53$; D_{rs} is measured in kilometers.

The line of reasoning explained in box 6.3 using empirical (gu)estimates of parameters from a multi-region world and confronting them with break points from the tomahawk diagram or bell-shaped curve derived in a two-region setting is problematic. Similar analytical solutions for break points in a multi-region setting ($n > 2$) exist only if all regions are at equal distances from each other. This assumption effectively means that the actual geography (where regions are located on a map) does not play a role, and thus that space is neutral in that sense. Any real-world application clearly violates this assumption.

How should we proceed to arrive at more conclusive evidence for our empirical hypothesis on trade-cost-induced agglomeration? There are three main options. First, we can allow for a model with non-neutral space and confront this model (and its implications regarding freeness of trade and agglomeration) with the data. It is certainly possible to incorporate non-neutral space (see box 6.4), but so far it has not been possible to derive analytical solutions for the break points of these models. Second, we can approach the confrontation between empirical and theoretical φ's using an alternative method of measurement of the freeness of trade. This is the topic of subsection 6.3.3. Again, we have to rely on the two-region analytical solutions in a multi-region setting. The third, and our preferred, option is to drop the two-region model with its analytical solutions and instead use multi-region model simulations. This is discussed in subsections 6.3.4 and 6.3.5.

Box 6.4 Introducing non-neutral space

It is a well-established stylized fact that many big cities initially evolved by having the advantage of easy access to waterways. Why have cities developed at these places? For geographers, this poses no big problem. Ports provide easy access to foreign or overseas markets. One could say that the modeling of port cities is the geographical counterpart of neoclassical trade theory based on comparative advantage (see, for example, Anas, Arnott, and Small 1998, or Fujita and Mori, 1996). Each region has a comparative advantage due to, for example, climatic conditions, natural resources, or production factors confined within the borders. Ports or transport nodes provide some locations in this setting with a "comparative advantage" in transportation. The question remains as to why port cities continue to be important, despite the fact that the transportation system has changed dramatically: waterways are now much less important than they once used to be. If comparative advantage were the major explanation for the existence of port cities, one would expect these cities to disappear, or at least become less important. Nothing of the sort has happened, however.

This requires an explanation – which can perhaps be provided by geographical economics. A good illustration is the model developed by Fujita and Mori (1996). The model itself is quite complicated, but its essence can easily be understood by analyzing figure 6.4 (the example is taken from Fujita and Mori, 1996). The assumptions are as follows. Space is definitely non-neutral. Space is linear in the sense that, in each region, activity takes place between the river and the mountain range. Space is one dimensional – homogeneous – and unbounded; as drawn here, there are two regions on each side of the river (the regions are the two stretches of land between the river and the mountain range). The quality of the land is the same everywhere and is not mobile. Non-land production factors are freely mobile. Labor is the only mobile production factor and each worker is endowed with one unit of labor. A worker can change jobs and location. In principle, regions are identical and the reasons for a cluster of activity to form are the same endogenous forces as described in chapter 3: increasing returns in production, transport costs, market size effects, and competition effects.

Suppose that, because of some initially favorable condition, somewhere a cluster of activity has already emerged – say city 1. City 1 specializes in manufacturing goods and exports manufactures in exchange for land-intensive imports from both sides of city 1. There are two natural harbors, one in b (with the economic distance from city 1 of b) and one in 2 (this is a potential city in region 2, as will become clear). The economic distance between the two regions is c. Now assume that region 1 grows. This will result in a larger city, because the agglomeration of manufactured goods production is beneficial: more varieties will be produced without having to import them from elsewhere. This creates a larger market, which stimulates even more agglomeration. As the population grows, more farmland will have to be occupied in order to support the growing city. Eventually, the development of farmland in region 2 becomes attractive if the economic distance between region 2 and the city is smaller than the distance from the "marginal" farmland in region 1 and the city – or, if l is the economic distance between the city and the marginal farmland, if $l > b + c$. New farmland in region 2 will be developed on both sides of the port in region 2. Eventually, if the population keeps growing, manufacturing products and farm products will be transported over ever-growing distances. At some point new cities will emerge if the (fixed) cost of setting up production is smaller than importing manufactured goods.

Box 6.4 (cont.)

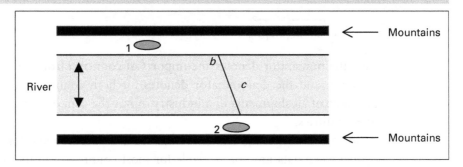

Figure 6.4 Example of non-neutral space

The potential advantage in this story of ports is obvious. What is interesting here is that new cities do not *have* to emerge at ports; self-organizing forces might also stimulate new cities in the same region. It depends on c, the position of b, transport costs in general, and all the other factors that are important in geographical economics. Ports have a natural advantage, however, because they have an extra *dimension* for trade: not just on both sides of the port but across the river as well. This is the reason why ports are also known as transport nodes in the geography literature. So, despite the favorable position of ports, non-port cities can still emerge, for example due to historical accident. Some examples are identified by Ades and Glaeser (1995), who find evidence that political factors, such as being a capital city, resulting in (244) "power [that] allows leaders to extract wealth out of the hinterland and distribute it in the capital," are exogenous forces that stimulate city growth. An example of non-neutral space is discussed in chapter 7. Some of its properties are further investigated in chapters 10 (the geography of institutions) and 11 (the pancake economy).

6.3.3 Bilateral trade and an alternative measurement of the freeness of trade[12]

To arrive at an alternative "educated guess" about the freeness of trade parameter we follow the empirical strategy of Head and Mayer (2004a). If this approach gives similar conclusions to those resulting from the method in the previous subsection, we can be more confident that the conclusions we derive are sound. The freeness of trade parameter can be approximated using bilateral trade and production data (Head and Mayer, 2004a: 2617–18). Based on Head and John Ries (2001), they define a simple estimate for the

---

[12] With some small changes, this subsection coincides with section 5 in Brakman, Garretsen and Schramm (2006).

freeness of trade that can be derived from any basic geographical economics model:[13]

$$\varphi_{trade} = \sqrt{m_{ij}m_{ji}/m_{ii}m_{jj}}$$

where the numerator denotes the imports of country i from country j and vice versa; and the denominator denotes for both country i and country j the value of all shipments of a industry minus the sum of shipments to all other countries.

The reason for using bilateral trade data at the country level is that regional trade data are not available for most countries. On the downside, we thus only have data at the country level. On the upside, we have sectoral data, so we can derive sector-specific values for φ_{trade}. If the bilateral trade between two countries is relatively important, φ_{trade} is high; if it is unimportant, φ_{trade} is low. The advantage of this estimate for the freeness of trade parameter is that it is easy to implement. Head and Mayer (2004a) calculate φ_{trade} for twenty-one industries and two country pairs (Canada/United States and France/Germany) for 1995 and then confront their implied freeness of trade parameter with the *industry-specific* break points for the freeness of trade. As discussed in chapter 4 (subsection 4.5.2 and section 4.6), Puga (1999) derives the break points for the core models of geographical economics. More specifically, Head and Mayer (2004a) confront φ_{trade} with the industry-specific break points for the bell-shaped curve only, in particular φ_{low}^{B} with the first break point, where spreading turns into partial agglomeration. Almost without exception, φ_{trade} is rather low (in the range of 0.1 to 0.2), implying that for both country pairs and most industries $\varphi_{trade} < \varphi_{low}^{B}$; in other words, most industries in this bilateral experiment are in the spreading equilibrium.

Brakman, Garretsen, and Schramm (2006) use Head and Mayer's methodology for the European Union. As well as looking at the break point $\varphi_{trade} < \varphi_{low}^{B}$ associated with the bell-shaped curve, they also look at the break point $\varphi_{lab\ mob}^{B}$ for the tomahawk diagram. In the *first experiment*, Germany is used as the benchmark country and compared with Spain, the United Kingdom, the Netherlands, and Poland. Using a similar sector classification, φ_{trade} is calculated for the four country pairs for the years

---

[13] It is straightforward to derive this expression. Note that the value of imports of i from j is $m_{ij} = n_j p_{ij} c_{ij}$, where n_j is number of commodities imported from j in region i, p_{ij} the price of commodities from j in i, and c_{ij} the demand of i for products from j. The demand for varieties follows from the bilateral demand equations. By dividing the expressions in φ_{trade} in the text, and assuming that $\varphi_{ij} = \varphi_{ji}$ and $\varphi_{ii} = \varphi_{jj} = 1$, the expression for φ_{trade} follows.

1985, 1990, 1994, and 1998. In line with the findings of Head and Mayer, the values for φ_{trade} gradually increase over time, though they remain rather low. Only for a few sectors does φ_{trade} exceed the break point φ^B_{low} or $\varphi^B_{lab\ mob}$. The sectors with agglomeration in some years are: clothing, wood, plastics and drugs, ferrous metals, and transport. The overall picture is, however, one of a "pre-agglomeration" degree of economic integration.

The *second experiment* is to compute φ_{trade} for the trade flows between the group of fifteen initial EU countries versus the group of ten accession countries (the new EU members from central and eastern Europe that joined in 2004). The parameter values needed for the derivation of these two break points are taken from Head and Mayer (2004a: appendix). For the "non-manufacturing sectors" of agriculture, energy, and services, such a theoretical benchmark was not available. For the manufacturing sectors, the conclusion is, again, that most sectors are not yet in the agglomeration regime. The exceptions (see the shaded boxes in table 6.3) are: plastics and drugs, ferrous metals, and vehicles. Even for those sectors, however, we are at the start of the upward-sloping part of the bell-shaped curve (see the respective $\varphi^B_{bell-top}$ values giving the peak of the bell curve for these sectors).[14]

The results in table 6.3 with freeness of trade estimates based on bilateral trade data at the country level are in line with the conclusions in the previous subsection based on more direct estimates of the freeness of trade. These results also suggest that the spatial reach of agglomeration forces is rather limited, such that (sectoral) economic activity is not yet concentrated in one region or only a few regions. Although supportive of our earlier findings, the analysis on which table 6.3 is based still suffers from the drawback that data derived from a multi-country world are confronted with analytical solutions for the two-country model. Using country pairs does not solve this problem because one cannot ignore the importance of other countries. This means that we really have to abandon the two-region model and its analytical results, and turn to a multi-regional model using simulations as the main tool of analysis.

6.3.4 Freeness of trade, agglomeration, and multi-region simulations: an example[15]

It is clear by now that there is no easy fix to the thorny issue of the exact relationship between freeness of trade and agglomeration in a geographical

---

[14] Here $\varphi^B_{bell-top}$ is simply taken to be the midpoint: $(\varphi^B_{low} + \varphi^B_{high})/2$.
[15] This subsection is taken from Brakman, Garretsen, and Schramm (2006: sec. 4.2).

Table 6.3 Sector-specific freeness of trade

Classification	Sector	φ_{trade}	φ^B_{low}	$\varphi^B_{lab\ mob}$
1	Agriculture	0.027	NA	NA
2	Energy	0.012	NA	NA
3	Foods, beverages, and tobacco	0.047	0.46	0.22
4	Clothing	0.1355	0.21	0.18
5	Wood	0.046	0.39	0.36
6	Paper	0.033	0.17	0.16
10/8	Plastics and drugs	0.127	0.109*	0.104
9	Petrochemicals	0.017	Symm.	0.71
11	Minerals	0.036	0.47	0.44
12	Ferrous metals	0.038	0.0**	Aggl.
13	Non-ferrous metals	0.029	0.09	0.06
14	Fabricated metals	0.050	Symm.	0.69
15/16	Machinery (and computers)	0.253	0.43	0.36
17	Electrical	0.090	0.67	0.39
19/20	Ships, railroad, and transport	0.0112	0.46	0.39
21	Vehicles	0.132	0.10***	0.08
23	Instruments	0.0155	0.57	0.45
18	Services	0.162	NA	NA

Notes: * indicates $\varphi^B_{bell-top} = 0.545$; ** $\varphi^B_{bell-top} = 0.50$; *** $\varphi^B_{bell-top} = 0.49$. 10 code 19/20 definition is based on the railroad with the lowest break point of these three sectors in Head and Mayer (2004a). NA = not available. Symm. = local stability of symmetric equilibria for all values of φ. Aggl. = only full agglomeration stable.

economics setting. We agree with Fujita and Mori (2005: 394) when they state that "in order to investigate the spatial pattern of agglomeration, the asymmetry rather than the symmetry of location space is necessary where not all other regions are neighbours of each region." This subsection illustrates what changes in the freeness of trade imply for the degree of agglomeration across the EU regions. In doing so, we use a multi-region model of geographical economics for 157 (EU NUTS II) regions. We run simulations for a set of model parameters to determine the equilibrium allocation of economic activity, measured as gross value added (the Y variable in our core model). The model is based on Krugman (1991a), the benchmark model for our book, extended to *non-neutral* space by taking the actual physical geography of Europe into account.

Non-neutral space is based on the approach by Dirk Stelder (2005) (see box 6.5). We use a grid of n locations on a three-dimensional surface. The distance between two locations is calculated as the shortest path between them, assuming that each location on the grid is connected to its direct (horizontal or vertical) neighbors with a distance of one and to its diagonal neighbours with distance $\sqrt{2}$. Non-neutral space is then introduced by making "holes" in the grid. The geographical shape of a country or a region is approximated by using a grid resolution as high as possible. The model allows for specific costs for transport across land and sea, and in hubs where (un)shipping takes place. In addition, with an extra altitude layer the grid is extended to a third dimension (height), such that the model can handle mountains too.

Box 6.5 An experiment with non-neutral space: the Stelder approach

Stelder (2005) has implemented the basic model of Krugman (1991a) on non-neutral spaces. Non-neutral space is in his case defined as a grid of n locations on a two-dimensional surface. The distance between two locations is calculated as the shortest path, on the assumption that each location on the grid is connected with its direct horizontal and vertical neighbors with distance one and with its diagonal neighbors with distance $\sqrt{2}$. To illustrate how non-neutral space can be introduced by making "holes" in a grid, take the example of a sea (see figure 6.5). Assuming no transport takes place across the sea or along the coast, transportation from A to F in the example above would follow C, D, and E with a total distance of $2 + 2\sqrt{2}$.

The model by Stelder starts with a flat initial distribution in which all locations on the grid are of equal size – an assumption that could be paraphrased as "in the beginning there

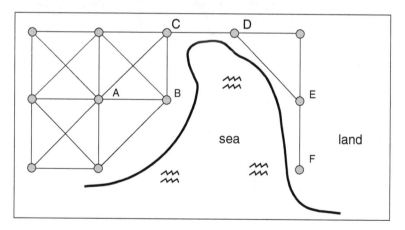

Figure 6.5   Grid of locations in geographical space

---

[16] The apparently peculiar choice of T results from a different parameterization used by Stelder, which we have respecified here using our parameterization from chapter 3.

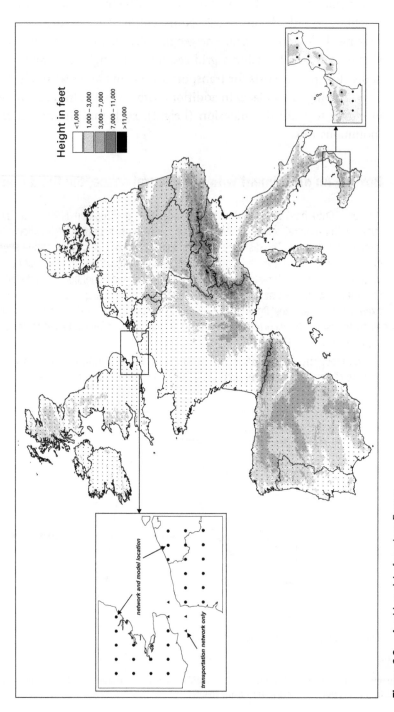

Figure 6.6 A grid model of western Europe

Box 6.5 (cont.)

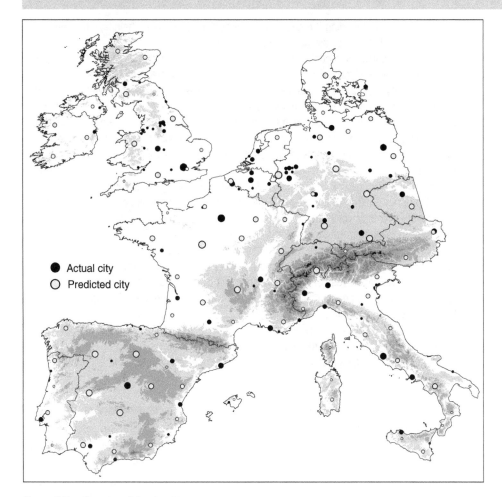

Figure 6.7   Experimental outcome

were only the little villages." The task of the model is then to calculate the equilibrium distribution of economic activity, given the assumed parameter values for the division of labor between farmers and workers, δ, the elasticity of substitution, ε, and the distance between grid points. Different parameter configurations result in long-run equilibria with highly asymmetric hierarchies of cities depending on the specific geographical shape of the economy. The geographical shape of a country is approximated by using a grid resolution as high as possible. Stelder has thus built a large geographical grid of western Europe with over 2,800 locations (see figure 6.6) in order to determine if the model can simulate Europe's actual city distribution. The inlay in figure 6.6 shows how sea transportation is

Box 6.5 (cont.)

made possible by extending the grid with some additional points in the sea, which are part of the network but do not act as potential locations for cities.

Figure 6.7 shows a model run (with $\delta = 0.5$, $\varepsilon = 5$, and $T = 1.57$) producing an equilibrium of ninety-four cities.[16] The gray dots are the simulated outcomes and the black dots the ninety-four largest actual cities in 1996. As was to be expected with a flat initial distribution, the model produces an optimal city distribution that is more evenly spread than in reality. Large agglomerations such as Paris, London, Madrid, and Rome are not correctly simulated, because population density is for historical reasons higher in the North than in the South. The model predicts too many large cities in Spain and too few cities in the United Kingdom, the Netherlands, and Belgium. The results are, nevertheless, relatively good for Germany: the Rurhgebiet, Bremen, Berlin, Frankfurt, Stuttgart, and Munich (and also Vienna) are not far from the right place. In the periphery of various countries, some cities also appear correctly, such as Lille, Rouen, Nantes, Bordeaux, and Nice in France, Lisbon and Porto in Portugal, and Seville and Malaga in Spain.

Stelder points out that these kinds of model results of course *should* be wrong. A good fit would mean the "total victory of economics over all other social sciences because then the whole historical process of city formation would be explained with the three parameters δ, ε and T." One of his goals with the model is to clarify the extent to which pure economic factors have contributed to the city formation process. The main conclusion is that even the core model can produce very differentiated city hierarchies without any theoretical extensions once it is applied to space more closely resembling geographic reality. Stelder concludes that the "geography" deserves more attention in geographical economics.

Apart from the depiction of non-neutral space, the model is similar to that of Krugman (1991a), which means that the simulation of the equilibrium allocation of economic activity hinges on three model parameters only: the share of income spent on manufactures δ, the elasticity of substitution ε, and transport cost function T_{rs}. Recall that these last two parameters constitute the freeness of trade $\varphi_{rs} = T_{rs}^{1-\varepsilon}$. The use of the actual geographical information also means that our simulations are more "realistic" than, for instance, the *racetrack* simulations (see chapter 4, where locations are not equidistant but space is neutral; locations are situated on a circle). The sample for the simulation experiment includes most EU regions.[17] Related (simulation) studies, such as those by Forslid, Haaland and Midelfart Knarvik (2002), Midelfart Knarvik, Overman, and Venables (2003), and Brülhart, Crozet and Pamina Koenig (2004), show that

---

[17] To be specific, in the multi-region simulations we used real GDP data for 157 regions in ten EU countries (Austria, Belgium, France, Germany, Ireland, Italy, the Netherlands, Portugal, Spain and the United Kingdom) and Switzerland.

agglomeration forces tend to be rather localized in Europe. The Krugman (1991a) model is useful as it has an agglomeration bias; it gives rise relatively easily to (nearly) complete agglomeration (see chapters 3 and 4).

Starting with the initial distribution of regional gross value added (the Y variable) and given estimates of T and ε, one can simulate the long-run equilibrium situation in Europe (derive an outcome in which real wages across regions are equalized). Figure 6.8 shows the outcome of some simulations. Figure 6.8a gives the initial (1992) distribution and panels b to d show the equilibrium distribution for three multi-region simulations, namely the equilibrium distribution with estimates for the freeness of trade, for lower transport costs, and for higher substitution elasticity respectively.[18] Of course, the addition of non-neutral space does not alter the simulation procedure. For a given distribution of mobile workers, the equilibrium wage equation together with the equilibrium price index equation and the income equation determine solutions for the endogenous variables Y_r, W_r, and I_r for every region r. With interregional labor mobility, a long-run equilibrium is reached if real wages ($w_r = W_r I_r^{-\delta}$) are equalized (see section 4.3).

Figure 6.8a depicts the initial (1992) distribution. Ranging from black to white, darker areas denote regions that have a larger share of gross value added. Agglomerations are found roughly along the lines of the so-called *European* or *blue banana*, ranging from London to Belgium and the south-western part of the Netherlands via west and south-west Germany to northern Italy. The central position of Paris is also noteworthy (to highlight the special position of London, each figure gives the share of London and its adjacent regions in the upper-left part of the figure). Based on the parameter estimates, figure 6.8b uses the multi-region simulation to determine the long-run equilibrium for the European regions based on our estimates of freeness of trade. Compared to the initial distribution, the region around Paris and the region around Milan are able to attract more economic activity. The same holds for other initially large regions, such as London or the southern part of western Germany. In general, when comparing panels a and b, core regions gain at the expense of nearby regions. In addition, our equilibrium simulation predicts more agglomeration than was actually observed in 1992. Even with this tendency towards agglomeration, however,

---

[18] In these three simulations, the share of income spent on manufactured goods (δ) is set at 0.3. For the regions included in our multi-region experiment, the maps show the share of the region in total gross value added. A darker (lighter) color signals a larger (smaller) share. Since we are interested in relative changes, we want to find out if a region changes "color" when we compare figures 6.8a to d.

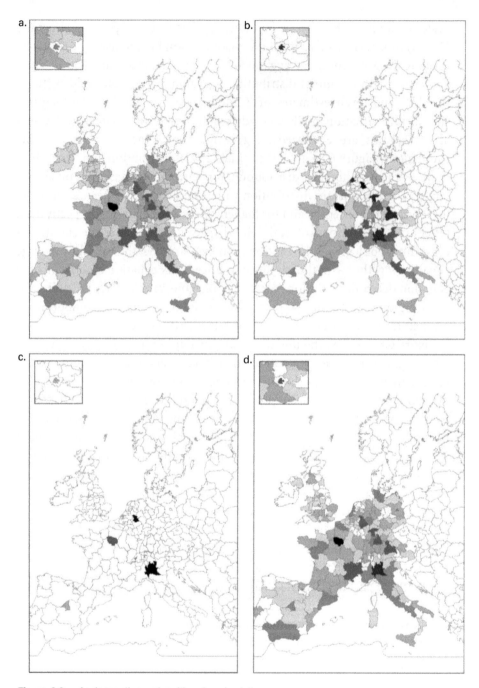

Figure 6.8   Agglomeration and multi-region simulations
Notes: Shades are quintiles, except for panel c. Panel a = intial, 1992, distribution; b = equilibrium simulation; c = equilibrium simulation with lower transportation costs; d = equilibrium simulation with higher substitution elasticity.

the long-run equilibrium in panel b has not collapsed into a strong core–periphery pattern (where one or just a few regions attract all the economic activity). Despite the above-mentioned agglomeration bias of the model, panel b still yields a considerable degree of dispersion that is qualitatively (but not quantitatively) similar to the actual spatial distribution shown in panel a.

To investigate what happens to the degree of agglomeration when the freeness of trade changes (compared to figure 6.8b), one can also simulate long-run equilibria for larger values of the freeness of trade. This is illustrated in panel c, which reinforces the above conclusions. An increase in the freeness of trade (a decrease in transport costs or the elasticity of substitution) further raises the importance of core regions at the expense of smaller regions in the vicinity. For a high level of freeness of trade, panel c shows that only five regions "survive" and attract all economic activity. These regions are London, Paris, Madrid, the Ruhrgebiet, and Lombardia. This result is in line with the underlying model, since high freeness of trade leads to complete agglomeration in a two-region setting. Similarly, when the freeness of trade falls, spreading of economic activity occurs. Panel d illustrates this by increasing the elasticity of substitution (weaker economies of scale). Compared to panels b and c, peripheral regions now have a larger share of economic activity. In fact, the resulting equilibrium is rather similar to the initial (1992) distribution depicted in panel a.

6.3.5 Where on the curves are we? A multi-region simulation answer

Section 6.3 on the last item on the list of five testable hypotheses of geographical economics asks: do changes in the freeness of trade lead to agglomeration? In answering this question we first linked the two-region models to empirical data on the freeness of trade. This attempt is flawed to the extent that it forces a two-region model (in which distance is neutral) upon a multi-region reality (in which distance is non-neutral). By giving up the analytical tractability of the two-region model and its associated break points, we can use multi-region simulations to determine what changes in trade costs imply for the equilibrium allocation of economic activity. In the previous subsection, we used the core model of this book and an example of non-neutral space to simulate the impact of changes in the freeness of trade on the equilibrium degree of agglomeration. The answer provided by figure 6.8 above is incomplete (and may be incorrect), to the extent that the Krugman (1991a) model is just a special case of a more general economics model (Puga, 1999: chap. 4) that forms the basis for our discussion of the tomahawk diagram and bell-shaped curve. By adding non-neutral space to a multi-region version of the *general* model of geographical economics (which allows for intermediate inputs and inter-sectoral labor mobility) one may find a more systematic answer to the following questions.

- What does the relationship between freeness of trade and agglomeration look like? Do the resulting curves resemble the tomahawk diagram or the bell-shaped curve in the case of interregional labor mobility and immobility respectively?
- Where are we on the multi-region equivalents of these curves?

To answer both questions, we proceed as follows (Bosker *et al.*, 2007b). First, we eliminate the assumption of equidistance and define the freeness of trade between region r and region s as

$$\varphi_{rs} = \varphi_{sr} = T_{rs}^{1-\varepsilon} = \left(TD_{rs}^{\gamma}(1 + bB_{rs})\right)^{1-\varepsilon} \text{ if } \quad r \neq s \text{ and } \varphi_{rs} = 1 \quad \text{if } r = s$$

where D_{rs} is the great circle distance between the capital city of regions r and s (γ is the distance coefficient), T is the transport cost parameter, B_{rs} is an indicator function taking the value of zero if two regions belong to the same country and one if not, and $b \geq 0$ is a parameter measuring the strength of this border effect. Specifying transport costs this way is fairly common in empirical studies (see Brakman, Garretsen and Schramm, 2006, and Redding and Venables, 2004). It captures the notion that transportation costs increase with the distance over which goods have to be shipped as well as the fact that inter-country trade is more costly than trade within a country (through tariffs or through differences in language, culture, etc).

This non-neutral space version of φ_{rs} is added to the Puga (1999) model using 194 NUTS II regions (the EU-15 countries before May 2004). By simulating the long-run equilibrium for this more general multi-region, non-neutral space model, we can answer the above two questions. Although we can analyze any parameter change, we focus our discussion on changes in transport costs T.[19] Because we are dealing with more than two regions we use the Herfindahl index (defined as $HI = \Sigma_i \lambda_i^2$) as a measure of the degree of agglomeration (λ_i denotes a region's share in the total number of firms or workers). This index varies between zero and one. The closer it is to one the more uneven the distribution of economic activity, and thus the higher the degree of agglomeration (see also chapter 10 subsection 10.5.2).

---

[19] For other parameters, see Bosker *et al.* (2007b).

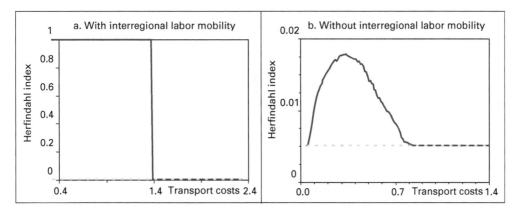

Figure 6.9   Trade costs and the long-run equilibrium when distance matters
Notes: Simulation parameters: $\mu = 0.6$, $\gamma = 0.2$, $\theta = 0.55$, $\varepsilon = 5$, b = 0, d= 0.3; for an explanation of the model parameters, see chapter 4.

Figure 6.9 shows the degree of agglomeration for a range of long-run equilbria (the long-run equilibrium is simulated for multiple values of T). Panel a is the Puga model with interregional labor mobility and panel b is the Puga model without interregional labor mobility.

Figure 6.9 shows that, in a qualitative sense, the multi-region non-neutral space model gives rise to the same conclusions as the simple two-region version of the Puga (1999) model. *With* labor mobility (panel a), spreading turns into full agglomeration once trade costs become sufficiently low. *Without* labor mobility (panel b), spreading is the long-run equilibrium for high trade costs, followed by (partial) agglomeration for intermediate trade costs, and spreading again for low trade costs. The analogy with the tomahawk diagram and the bell-shaped curve for the two-region model is clear. There is also an important difference with this model, however, as the same degree of agglomeration (the same value of the Herfindahl index) may imply a very different spatial distribution of manufacturing activity across the regions.

To answer the second question – "Where on these curves are we?" – we first note that what matters is not just distance but the interaction between the economic mass of a region and the distance to other regions as well. Accordingly, we simulate the long run equilibrium for the 194-region model not only using the aforementioned trade cost function but also based on the actual distribution of labor and land as initial conditions. The resulting long-run equilibria are shown in figure 6.10 – panel a with labor mobility, panel b without labor mobility. Though a little less clear than in figure 6.9,

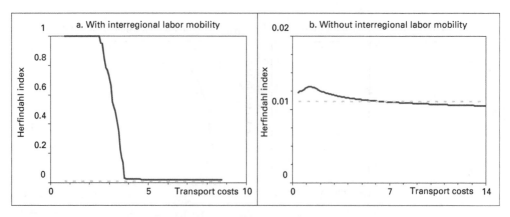

Figure 6.10 Trade costs, distance, and initial conditions
Note: The dashed line shows the value of the Herfindahl index associated with the initial distribution.

the simulations still show a clear resemblance to our tomahawk diagram and the bell-shaped curve from chapter 4.

Suppose there is interregional labor mobility (figure 6.10a). We can now give a potential answer to the million dollar question: where on the bell-shaped curve are we? Plotting the actual value of the Herfindahl index for the 194 EU regions in the figure, we see that at a certain value of the transport costs ($T = 6.183$) the Herfindahl index of the simulated long-run equilibrium is the same as the Herfindahl index of the actual distribution of manufacturing employment (the dashed line). Recall that different spatial distributions can give rise to the same Herfindahl index. With this in mind, it is even more striking to note the resemblance between the simulated long-run equilibrium distribution for this "critical" level of transport costs (figure 6.11b) and the actual distribution of manufacturing labor (figure 6.11a).[20]

This finding suggests a satisfactory answer to the question "Where on the curve are we?" Taking our pinpointed $T (= 6.181)$ seriously, and looking at figure 6.10b, we conclude that increased economic integration is likely to result in *rising* agglomeration. Only in the very distant future, when we have passed the peak of the curve in figure 6.10b, will a further increase in economic integration result in a *fall* in agglomeration. Figure 6.12, finally, shows the distribution of economic activity at the "top of the bell" (the top of the curve depicted by figure 6.10b), which resembles the so-called blue banana (described above) quite well.

---

[20] The correlation coefficient is 0.809!

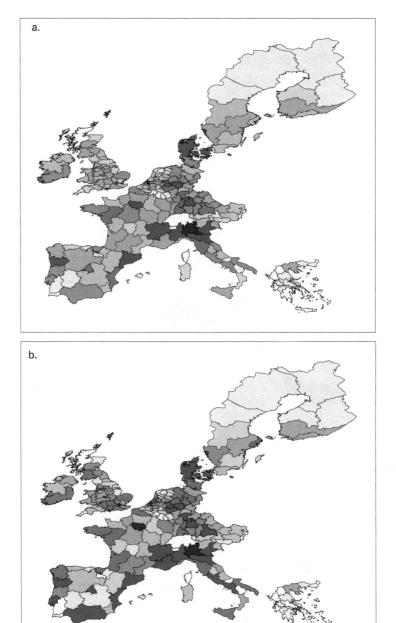

Figure 6.11 Similarity between actual distribution (a) and simulated distribution (b)

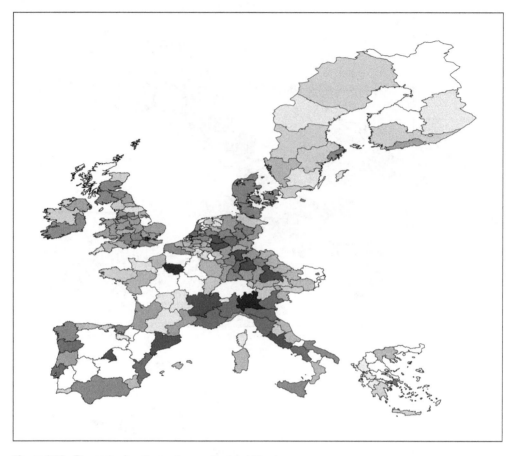

Figure 6.12 The peak of agglomeration: a simulated blue banana

6.4 Conclusions

Like the previous chapter, this chapter has analyzed the empirical relevance of geographical economics. Inspired by our findings in chapter 5, we have analyzed two hypotheses in detail. The first hypothesis is that large, temporary, exogenous shocks will lead to a shift of the long-run equilibrium. Several shock (catastrophe) studies were discussed to test the prediction that shocks (such as WWII and other disasters) will shift the economy to a new equilibrium. The empirical evidence turned out to be mixed. The second hypothesis states that at some point a reduction in trade costs will induce agglomeration. In this case, we concluded that it is actually quite difficult to test this hypothesis because of the limitations of the two-region core models when confronted with the multi-region "real world." All in all, the empirical evidence presented in chapters 5 and 6 provides considerable support for the geographical economics approach, but more empirical research is clearly needed before giving a final verdict.

Two basic problems for empirical verification of the geographical economics model are (i) many empirical studies are consistent not only with geographical economics models but also with other theories of trade and location, and (ii) attempts, such as the five hypotheses discussed in chapters 5 and 6, to focus on the relevance of geographical economics as such provide considerable empirical support, but the multi-region, non-neutral, multiple-equilibria nature of the geographical economics approach make conclusive testing very difficult. In the final chapter of this book we come back to this issue in discussing how to proceed in empirical research in/on geographical economics. Two ways to go forward are better testing (see box 8.3) and better data (see box 6.6). The former implies the use of spatial econometrics (Combes and Overman, 2004; Fingleton, 2004). The latter involves the use of micro-data to better discriminate between geographical economics and competing explanations about the spatial distribution and growth of economic activity (Duranton, 2008; Combes, Duranton, Overman, 2005). A third avenue is the improvement and extension of the theoretical models of chapters 3 and 4. Here, the question is whether and how the core model of geographical economics can be extended to deal with a number of issues regarding the location of economic activity not covered by the core models discussed so far in this book. Chapters 7 to 11 deal with extensions of the core models. The analysis in these chapters is to a considerable extent aimed at enhancing the empirical and policy relevance of geographical economics.

Box 6.6 Future direction for empirical research: micro-data

In one of the first surveys of geographical economics, Krugman (1998) argues that the approach lacks empirical backing. A similar critique was voiced by Neary (2001) in his review of the Fujita, Krugman and Venables (1999) book. The material discussed in chapters 5 and 6 shows that, since then, empirical research in geographical economics has really taken off in recent years. Nevertheless, there is room for further improvement. Here, we briefly discuss one such route: the use of micro-data (see also box 8.3 on spatial econometrics).

Typically, the research discussed in chapters 5 and 6 is based on aggregate data (city size, regional GDP, manufacturing wages for industry *x* in city *y*, etc.). Ideally, one would like to have sufficient data on the *individual* firms or workers making up a city or region,

Box 6.6 (cont.)

both varying across time and space. In other words, empirical research in geographical economics could benefit from using panel data or micro-data regarding the key variables. A good example of such an approach is provided by Combes, Duranton, and Laurent Gobillon (2008). Based on a panel with 2,664,474 observations for French workers, these authors investigate whether spatial wage disparities are the result of agglomeration effects (emphasized by geographical economics) or merely the result of sorting. More precisely, they test three competing explanations for the observed spatial wage disparities (for 341 French regions in a six-year period). The first group of explanations, of which geographical economics is part, emphasizes that spatial wage disparities are the result of positive *localized interactions* between workers. The more developed these interactions are the higher regional wages are. The benefits in terms of higher wages from these interactions may stem from market size effects (as in geographical economics) or from regional knowledge spillovers or labor market pooling (as in urban economics; see also chapter 7).

The second group of explanations points to the relevance of region-specific *fixed endowments*, or the role of first-nature geography. The labor productivity in a region, and thus wages, may simply be higher because a region has access to a navigable river, a superior climate, or high-quality public governance. The third set of explanations (which is where the use of panel data comes to the fore) states that "workers may sort across employment areas so that the measured and un-measured productive abilities of the local labor force vary. For instance, industries are not evenly distributed across areas and require different labor mixes so that we can expect a higher mean wage in areas specialized in skill-intensive industries" (Combes, Duranton, and Gobillon, 2008: 723).

The key with the *sorting argument* is that an individual worker's wage is solely a function of his/her own skill or productivity level and is *independent* of location, the local interaction with other agents, or local endowments. It is only by having access to micro-data that this sorting effect can be captured and differentiated from the interaction and endowment explanations. Combes, Duranton, and Gobillon (2008) find that sorting is quantitatively important: about 50 percent of the spatial disparities across French regions can be attributed to sorting. Local interaction of the kind emphasized by geographical and urban economics is still relevant, but the impact is much smaller when the sorting effect is taken into account. In a related study, Laura Hering and Sandra Poncet (2006) use data on *individual* wages from fifty-six Chinese cities for about 10,000 Chinese workers to estimate the wage equation central to geographical economics. They criticize the studies discussed in sections 5.4 and 5.5 because these "fail to control for cross-regional variation in skill composition. This exposes them to the risk of wrongly attributing wage disparities to economic geography explanations" (Hering and Poncet, 2006: 7). Nonetheless, after controlling for the skills effect, Hering and Poncet still find that a significant part of the variation in wages can be explained by market access!

More generally, the use of panel data allows one to control for both region- and time-fixed effects. Examples of other recent empirical studies in geographical economics that use either panel data and/or micro-data are those of Holger Breinlich (2006) for the EU regions, Bosker and Garretsen (2007b) for sub-Saharan Africa, and Mary Amiti and Lisa Cameron (2007) on Indonesia. These papers all use the equilibrium wage equation from the

Box 6.6 (cont.)

core model (4.3) as the starting point for their research. Panel data, or the use of a data set that varies both in cross-section and time-series dimension, and/or the use of individual firm data are also at the heart of those recent papers in geographical economics that look at the location behavior of multinational firms (as we will see in chapter 8 in our analysis of FDI and geographical economics); see for, instance Amiti and Beata Javorcik (2008) or Tomohiko Inui, Toshiyuki Matsuura, and Poncet (2007). In chapter 8, subsection 8.5.4, we discuss the methodology underlying these FDI papers, following Head and Mayer (2004b). In the last chapter of our book, we return to the future potential of the use of individual firm data in a discussion of Combes et al., 2008 (see box 12.4).

Exercises

6.1 Figure 6.4 suggests that port cities have a natural advantage over other cities in the sense that they have an extra "dimension" to trade, compared to "landlocked" cities. Can you find evidence that port cities are indeed on average larger than other types of cities (distinguish between landlocked cities and cities along rivers).

6.2 Suppose that, in the research on the impact of WWII bombing on German city growth (see section 6.2), the conclusion was that sixteen to seventeen years after WWII had ended German cities had returned to their initial – that is, pre-WWII – relative population size. Discuss why such a finding would not necessarily be at odds with the core model of geographical economics.

6.3 Explain in your own words while using figure 6.2 as a benchmark the key differences between the models underlying sections 6.2.1 and 6.2.2 respectively.

6.4 Apart from the impact of WWII on German and Japanese cities, this chapter also includes brief discussions of other "shock" examples (see boxes 6.1 and 6.2).
 (i) Suppose a huge storm had led to the flooding of the urban agglomeration of Rotterdam, which is partly located below sea level. How would you apply the insights from the models of section 6.2 to this case? Answer the same question if all the cities in the Dutch lowlands ("Netherlands" means "lowlands") had been affected.
 (ii) Try to think of a "shock" example yourself that is not discussed in the chapter that might be subject to the kind of analysis introduced in section

6.2 (one possible suggestion: the Irish potato famine in the mid-nine-teenth century). Try to gather some data to illustrate your case.

6.5 In chapter 3, in the discussion of the two-region core model, it was assumed that $D_{rs} = 1$. Explain why this is an innocent assumption when one is dealing with a two-region economy but not when one is dealing with an n-region economy where n is a large number.

6.6 As we will see in chapter 12, many geographers are rather critical of geographical economics. In their view, one major problem is that geographical economics – also known as new economic geography – contains too little geography. Discuss whether the arguments presented in section 6.3 of the present chapter back up the claim that geographical economics contains too little geography, or even none at all.

6.7 By sticking to the assumption of equidistance, as we did in box 6.3, one can confront the freeness of trade for any pair of real-world regions with the break points from the tomahawk or bell-curved model. On the website of our book you can find an Excel file that enables you to calculate the break points for a pair of regions r and s once you have chosen values for the key model parameters as well as for the distance between these regions, D_{rs}. On the website it is also explained what the key model parameters are. Experiment with this file and figure out whether and how the value of the break points for the freeness of trade can change when these parameters change.

6.8 Take figure 6.10b as an example and discuss why this may the best guess that geographical economics to date has to offer as to what the relationship between the freeness of trade and agglomeration – arguably the key relationship in geographical economics – may look like in reality (where "reality" in this example refers to the case of 194 NUTS II regions). In addition, discuss why in terms of future research examples such as those presented in figure 11.b are (hopefully) not the final word of geographical economics on this matter.

6.9 The central theme underlying chapters 5 and 6 is the list of testable hypotheses that comes out of geographical economics. All in all, and based on the evidence presented in these two chapters, there is some evidence supporting these hypotheses, but the evidence is mixed. Two ways to make progress and to arrive at more definite conclusions are better testing and better data. As to the former, one option is to make more use of *spatial econometrics* (see chapter 8 for more information on this topic), and, with respect to the latter, one option discussed in chapter 6 is to make more use of *microeconomic* or *panel data*. Discuss in connection with each option how best to proceed from here and why your preferred course of action would help empirical research in geographical economics forward.

Hint: search on the internet for information on recent papers by prominent researchers such as Fingleton (spatial econometrics and geographical economics) and Combes and Duranton (micro-data).

Part III

Applications and extensions

7 Cities and congestion: economies of scale, urban systems, and Zipf's law

7.1 Introduction

Typically, the long-run equilibrium allocation of footloose economic activity in the core model of geographical economics is characterized either by complete agglomeration or by spreading. Which equilibrium gets established depends critically on the initial distribution of the manufacturing labor force and a few structural parameters, notably the level of transport costs, the elasticity of substitution, and the share of income spent on manufactures. If transport costs, for example, are relatively low, the spreading equilibrium is unstable and agglomeration is the stable long-run equilibrium. Our simulations in chapter 4 with the core model of geographical economics clearly illustrate this (see figures 4.2 and 4.3). For many parameter settings the agglomeration forces are stronger than the spreading forces in the core model, which has only one spreading force: the demand for manufactured goods from the immobile labor force (the farm workers). We have also argued that the forces of agglomeration dominate in the multi-region version of the Krugman (1991a) model (the racetrack economy), such that economic activity is typically concentrated in one location, or only a few. Moreover, if the economy is concentrated in two or three locations, the distribution of economic activity is evenly spread among those locations.

These model outcomes are hard to reconcile with empirical observations. In reality we observe, at various levels of aggregation, multiple centers of economic activity that differ considerably in size (measured by the share of manufacturing production or the share of the mobile labor force). This is particularly true when we look at city sizes and city size distributions; recall the rank size distribution for India discussed in chapter 1 (figure 1.6). The core model – discussed in chapter 3 – of geographical economics has not much to say on this, and consequently it is ill-suited to deal with central topics in urban economics: the characteristics of city size distributions and the fact that for every country we observe an urban system with many cities. The balance between the agglomeration and spreading forces in the core model precludes the analysis of an urban system, because it does not allow for an outcome in which large and small centers of economic activity coexist. The perceptive reader could point out that the second core model including intermediate goods, which was developed in chapter 4, allows for large and small locations to coexist in equilibrium. For the purposes of this chapter, that model is less useful, because factor mobility is possible only between sectors and not between locations. This is a standard assumption in international trade theory, but highly unrealistic in urban economics, in which factor mobility between cities is a stylized fact.

This chapter has four main objectives.

- First, we introduce and summarize the main insights from urban economics with respect to the kind of agglomeration economies or local increasing returns to scale used to explain why cities exist. In doing so, we briefly discuss the theoretical as well as the empirical findings (section 7.2). We will see that the main focus is on individual cities and not on the interdependencies between cities. Armed with the basic insights from urban economics, we are in a position to deal with urban interdependencies or urban systems.

- Second, we compare urban economics with geographical economics (section 7.3), using a simple, non-technical, graphical representation of the core model (geographical economics in two diagrams!), as developed by Combes, Duranton, and Overman (2005).

- Third, we extend the core model of geographical economics to better accommodate the stylized facts on cities and city size distributions. As noted above, the core model has a "bang-bang" bias: either complete agglomeration occurs or there is even spreading of economic activity. In section 7.4, we show how the inclusion of an additional spreading force in the core model (congestion) changes the nature of the long-run equilibrium allocation of economic activity across space. Our discussion also serves a "didactical" purpose, as the reader will have to remind him-/herself what the basic mechanisms underlying the core model are and how they are changed by introducing congestion costs.

- Fourth, and finally, we apply our geographical economics model with congestion to an intriguing empirical regularity of city size distributions known as Zipf's law (or, in its more general form, the rank size distribution). Here we proceed in two steps. Section 7.5 first introduces and discusses the empirics of Zipf's law and the rank size distribution. Next, section 7.6 confronts Zipf's law with our congestion model and competing explanations. Section 7.7 concludes the chapter.

Box 7.1 Urbanization and congestion[1]

According to the World Bank's *World Development Indicators 2006*, 49 percent of the world's population lived in urban areas in 2004, compared to 40 percent in 1980. For the low-income countries these rates are 26 percent in 1990 and 31 percent in 2004. For the high-income countries they are 75 percent in 1990 and 78 percent in 2004. Table 7.1 lists the percentage of the urban population for all countries for which this share was at least 75 percent in 2004, except for China, which is included for comparison purposes. Table 7.1 shows that, with a few exceptions, an urbanization share of 75 percent or more is largely confined to the developed countries, Latin America, and a number of oil-exporting countries.[2]

The outcome should be interpreted with some care, because the definition of urban area differs between countries, which, for example, underestimates the degree of urbanization for China. Moreover, population size alone does not determine the economic relevance of urban agglomeration. Nevertheless, the message from these and similar data is clear and reinforces the conclusion of chapter 1: urbanization is a highly relevant phenomenon that cannot be neglected by any theory of agglomeration. It is also clear from the data that, within countries, the urban population does not live solely in a few mega-cities. The World Bank (2006) shows that, in low-income countries, 12 percent of the total population lived in urban agglomerations of more than 1 million in 2005. The same figure for the Economic Monetary Union (EMU) area is 27 percent. In 2005 a large share of the urban population lived in the largest city: 17 percent in low-income countries and 19 percent in high-income countries. A theory of urban location should therefore be able to explain the simultaneous existence of cities of varying size.

Of course, this does not mean that very large cities are not important (see box 7.4). In the twentieth century the number of mega-cities increased strongly. In 1900 only London, with a population of 6.5 million, passed the threshold of 5 million. By 2000 there were sixteen cities with a population exceeding 10 million people. Urban areas are becoming ever more important, as noted by the United Nations Population Fund (UNFPA, 2007): "In 2008, the world reaches an invisible but momentous milestone: For the first time in history, more than half its human population, 3.3 billion people, will be living in urban areas."

Congestion is a catch-all phrase for many drawbacks associated with urban agglomeration, referring to limited physical space, heavy usage of roads, communication channels, and storage facilities, limited local resources (such as water for cooling processes), and environmental pollution (which may require extra investment). The costs associated with congestion are notoriously difficult to measure. One way to quantify congestion is to focus on traffic congestion. Table 7.2 illustrates that the increase in urban agglomeration went along with an increase in the number of motor vehicles (per 1,000 people and per kilometer of road) between 1980 and 2003 for a selection of European countries. Not only has the number of motor vehicles increased but so has the number of vehicles per kilometer of road, with the

---

[1] The data in this box come from the World Bank's website at www.worldbank.org.

[2] Given the interest in China, we also include this country. The urbanization rate for China is substantially lower than for the other countries in the table. Two city states, Hong Kong and Singapore, are not included, as the urban area coincides with the country.

Box 7.1 (cont.)

Table 7.1 Urban population as percentage of total population, 2004

Argentina	90	Australia	92
Belgium	97	Brazil	84
Canada	81	China	40
Cuba	76	Czech Republic	74
Denmark	85	France	76
Gabon	84	Germany	88
Israel	92	Japan	66
Kuwait	96	Lebanon	88
Libya	87	Netherlands	80
New Zealand	86	Norway	80
Oman	78	Russia	73
Saudi Arabia	88	South Korea	81
Spain	77	Sweden	83
United Arab Emirates	85	United Kingdom	89
United States	80	Uruguay	93
Venezuela	88		

Source: World Bank (2006: tab. 3.10).

Table 7.2 Congestion: numbers of motor vehicles in selected countries, 1980 and 2003

	Vehicles per 1,000 people		Vehicles per kilometer of road	
	1980	2003	1980	2003
Belgium	349	527	28	37
Finland	288	450	18	30
France	402	596	27	40
Germany	399	578	51	206
Italy	334	610	65	73
Netherlands	343	427	–	58
Poland	86	354	10	33
Spain	239	558	120	34
United Kingdom	303	442	50	42

Source: World Bank (2006: tab. 3.12).

exception of Spain and the United Kingdom. This clearly points to an increase in congestion.[3] By and large a similar picture emerges for other countries (developed and less developed).

---

[3] As Spain illustrates, more vehicles need not necessarily imply more congestion, in terms of numbers of vehicles per kilometer of road, if more roads become available at the same time. Conversely, Poland shows that, after the communist era, road capacity has not kept pace with the strong increase of motor vehicles, leading to a tripling of the number of vehicles per kilometer of road.

Box 7.1 (cont.)

Reliable estimates of the costs of traffic congestion and other forms of congestion are hard to come by, but there is little doubt that these costs are considerable. Henderson, Zmarak Shalizi, and Venables (2000) report that, for the world as a whole, housing prices are on average more than 100 percent higher in an urban agglomeration of 5 million people compared to one of 100,000 people.

Since urbanization and congestion are two key concepts in this chapter, box 7.1 provides some background information on the relevance of both urbanization and congestion.

7.2 Agglomeration economies and cities: the view from urban economics

7.2.1 The sources of urban agglomeration economies: Marshall and beyond

In chapter 2 subsection 2.2.3, we noted that in the presence of transport (trade) costs modern economic theory relies on either non-homogeneous space or some form of increasing returns to scale to explain the basic facts of the spatial distribution of economic activity and the associated trade flows. Regarding the latter, economists have traditionally invoked the non-homogeneity of space and the resulting differences in factor endowments (the Heckscher–Ohlin–Samuelson model; see section 2.3 in chapter 2) to explain trade between countries. Within countries, however, the degree of space heterogeneity is more limited, making it harder to use this as the main explanation for trade and the concentration of economic activity in urban agglomerations. Consequently, modern urban economics turns mainly to increasing returns to scale to explain the existence of cities. It has also moved beyond the von Thünen (1826) monocentric city approach (which assumes, but does not explain, the existence of cities; see chapter 2) by providing a solid microeconomic foundation for the scale economies.

The main categorization for increasing returns to scale still dates back to Alfred Marshall, particularly in empirical research (see box 2.1). In this view, there are three main sources of economies of scale: (i) information or knowledge sharing; (ii) labor market pooling; and (iii) the sharing of (specialized) inputs. In addition to this Marshallian trilogy, the following sources of agglomeration economies are used to explain the existence of cities and their variation in size (Rosenthal and Strange, 2004: tab. 2).

- *Natural advantages*: differences in factor endowments (first-nature geography) also matter at the city level (see box 2.6).
- *Home market effects* at the industry level (see section 5.4).
- *Consumption externalities*: various city-specific amenities explain why consumers prefer to live (and work) in cities and why some cities are preferred over others (see box 7.2)
- *Rent seeking*: the empirical literature (see, for example, Ades and Glaeser, 1995, and Henderson, 2003, points out that rent-seeking behavior may lead to cities that are too large (see box 7.4 on primate cities). This is in contrast to the Marshallian trilogy and the additional sources mentioned above, which focus on the efficiency- and growth-enhancing effects of cities.

Despite numerous studies, Rosenthal and Strange (2004) conclude that there is a lot we do *not* know about the empirical relevance of the above sources of urban agglomeration economics. This is, perhaps, not surprising since (i) the spillovers/externalities cannot be observed directly and (ii) the model-based testable hypotheses in this literature are subject to observational equivalence (it is often difficult, or even impossible, to discriminate between the different sources of scale economies). Two options to deal with these problems present themselves, namely (a) the use of case studies and (b) the use of better data and testing techniques. Option (a) is preferred by most geographers, at the expense of a loss of generality. To enable option (b), therefore, urban economics is increasingly using microeconomic data sets and spatial econometrics to better distinguish between the different hypotheses on the sources of agglomeration economics. This is similar to our conclusions at the end of chapter 6 regarding the future of empirical work in geographical economics.[4]

7.2.2 The scope of urban agglomeration economies: diversity and competition

The *scope* of urban agglomeration economies refers to the extent or strength underlying economic force. We can distinguish four dimensions (Rosenthal and Strange, 2004: tab. 1).

---

[4] Duranton and Puga (2004) focus on mechanisms rather than sources. They note (2066; emphasis in original): "Consider, for instance, a model in which agglomeration facilitates the matching between firms and inputs. These inputs may be labeled workers, intermediates, or ideas. Depending on the label chosen, a matching model of urban agglomeration economies could be presented as a formalization of either one of Marshall's three basic *sources* of agglomeration economies even though it captures a single *mechanism*." They identify three basic mechanisms: sharing, matching, and learning. "Sharing" refers to indivisibilities (e.g. an opera house is economically feasible only in large cities; sharing costs). "Matching" refers to the quality of a match between worker and employer in labor market models (large cities offer a higher probability of a successful match). "Learning" refers to the need for face-to-face contact (in large cities with more contacts the quality of learning is higher). In practice, however, the distinction between sources and mechanisms is somewhat blurred, so we follow Rosenthal and Strange (2004).

(i) *Industrial scope.* What is the reach of agglomeration economies? Does it extend across all sectors within a city? The key distinction is between *localization* and *urbanization* economies (see box 2.1, and some examples of relevant studies below).

(ii) *Temporal scope.* Is there path dependency in urban growth? Do activities developed at time t extend their effect on profitability at time $t+1$?

(iii) *Geographic scope.* Is proximity (to other cities) or density (within cities) good for urban development in terms of, for instance, wage rates or the growth rate of employment? See the discussion of Antonio Ciccone (2002) and Ciccone and Robert Hall (1996) in chapter 5 section 5.5.

(iv) *Organization and business culture/competitiveness scope.* Does competition increase productivity? This issue touches upon the distinction between sector-specific and city-specific externalities (MAR and Jacobs externalities respectively; see box 2.1). In general, sectoral spillovers are important, but it is also better for sectoral growth if the size of individual establishments is smaller. This suggests that a competitive environment stimulates growth. The evidence on diversity is somewhat ambiguous. The role of organization and business culture (Florida, 2002) is discussed in box 7.2.

Box 7.2 Florida versus Glaeser: creative class and/or human capital

The current buzzword among urban policy makers is "creative class." The idea is that booming cities succeed in attracting creative people, who are the key to urban growth, by using the new information a dynamic city offers. The main force behind this idea is Richard Florida's (2002) book *The Rise of the Creative Class* (see www.creativeclass.org for Florida's website).[5] Traditionally, cities have competed with each other in attracting industrial firms. With the shift from an industrial to a service-based economy, Florida's book is a reminder that people in their dual capacity as workers and consumers are nowadays probably as important to city growth and innovation as firms are.

The connection with the urban agglomeration economies discussed in the main text is that spillovers between people (as opposed to firms and inter-firm spillovers) matter most for urban growth. This idea is not new. The long-standing human capital theory argues that a city with more human capital will grow more rapidly (with higher wages and income levels). The main current proponent of the human capital approach in urban economics is Glaeser. He argues that "creative class" is just a sexy term for human capital, and notes (2004: 3): "If Florida wants to argue that there is an effect of bohemian, creative types, over

[5] For a follow-up, see Florida (2006), *The Flight of the Creative Class.*

Box 7.2 (cont.)

and above the effect of human capital, then presumably that should show up in the data." In a study of 242 American cities, Glaeser analyzes city population growth between 1990 and 2000 using Florida's main city-specific indicators of creativity (creative employment, patents per capita, the gay and bohemian index) *as well as* a variable that measures human capital (the percentage of adults with a bachelor's degree). He finds that human capital is significant, but the Florida variables are not.

Similarly, regarding the city-specific amenities that attract creative people to a city, he argues that there is not much new in Florida's analysis, because the literature on consumption externalities in urban economics (Glaeser, Kolko, and Saiz, 2001) also shows that cities that perform well typically have various amenities attracting high-skilled people. Glaeser, Jed Kolko, and Albert Saiz (2001) argue that (large) cities have various possibilities for making themselves attractive for (high-skilled) workers by offering (i) consumption goods not available outside large cities because of scale effects (e.g. high-quality shops and theaters), (ii) historical city centers, (iii) a more diversified menu of public goods (e.g. specialized schools and hospitals), and (iv) more social interactions because of the density of population (Rosenthal and Strange, 2004: 2155). Florida's (2004: 2–3) rebuttal to this critique is that he never claimed to offer a new theory to begin with and prefers the creative class measure, which aims "to try to get what I saw as a slightly better handle on actual skills, rather than using only education-based measures to measure what people do, rather than just what their training may say about them on paper."

Based on Glaeser's back-of-the envelope American estimations, it seems that the value added of Florida's classification of jobs is limited. Research for other countries may help to determine who's right. Gerard Marlet and Clemens van Woerkens (2007) develop a more refined measure of creative jobs for Dutch cities, which is a better predictor of city employment growth than education (the percentage of residents with a bachelor's degree). Clearly, however, creativity and human capital (education) are highly correlated, as illustrated in figure 7.1 for the Netherlands. Either way, it is clear that creative/human capital is important for explaining urban growth (see Moretti, 2004, for a survey). Not only is there evidence that cities with higher levels of human capital have higher wages and income levels, there is even evidence of *divergence* as cities with initially high levels of human capital subsequently display higher growth rates of human capital (Berry and Glaeser, 2005).

This is illustrated in figure 7.2 for Germany in the period 1995 to 2003. Note that there is divergence for west german cities but not for east german cities. In the core model, there is no role for (differences in) human capital because regions do not vary in labor productivity. Instead, the fact that economic centers (cities) may have higher wages or income levels (the spatial wage structure) arises from differences in market access (see section 5.5). This lack of attention in geographical economics to human capital can be traced back to the initial focus on *pecuniary* external economies of scale, instead of on *pure* external economies of scale (as in urban economics; see section 7.3). Human capital and the resulting productivity differences between locations can, of course, be included in the geographical economics approach (see Brakman and Garretsen, 1993, and Ciccone, 2002). In a dynamic setting with Boston as a case study, Glaeser (2005) argues that cities that succeed in holding on to a critical mass of human capital in bad times manage to ride the inevitable wave of good and bad times reasonably well.

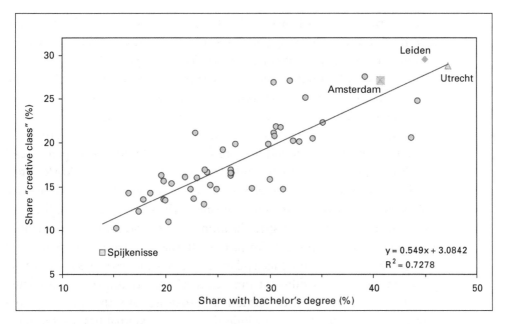

Figure 7.1   Creativity and education for largest Dutch cities, 1997
Note: The "creative class" is defined as people who are working in creative, innovative occupations.
Source: Marlet and Van Woerkens (2007).

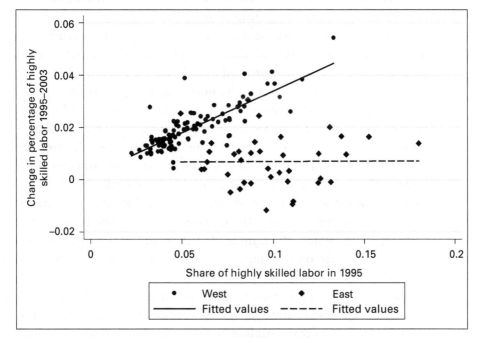

Figure 7.2   Growth of skilled labor in Germany, 1995–2003
Source: Poelhekke (2007).

It is beyond the goal of this chapter to give a survey of the empirical literature on the scope of agglomeration economies. Our focus is on some examples of *industrial scope* and *competitiveness scope* studies.

To start with localization and urbanization externalities. The distinction between urbanization and localization externalities is nowadays referred to in the literature, following Glaeser *et al.* (1992), as a distinction between so-called *Jacobs* externalities and *Marshall–Arrow–Romer* externalities. These two dynamic externalities were mentioned briefly in chapter 2, and they both refer to knowledge spillovers between firms. With MAR externalities, which feature in much of modern growth theory, knowledge spillovers occur between firms that belong to the same industry. In this case city growth is fostered by specialization, and so localization externalities are the main driving force. With Jacobs externalities, based on the work of Jane Jacobs (1969), knowledge spillovers are not industry-specific but take place among firms of different industries. Here, city growth is stimulated by diversity, and so urbanization externalities are the main driving force. Glaeser *et al.* (1992) conclude that Jacobs externalities are the most important externalities for employment growth in US cities. There is also evidence in favor of MAR externalities, however. Black and Henderson (1999a) and Mark Beardsell and Henderson (1999) find that MAR externalities are important for high-tech industries.

To measure static as well as dynamic industry-specific externalities – or, in other words, to measure localization and MAR externalities – Black and Henderson (1999a: 325–6) proceed as follows. They analyze if, for a high-tech industry located in area Z, its output at time *t* is positively affected by a current or a past increase in *either* the number of own-industry plants in area Z or by the number of *new* own-industry plants in area Z. A positive output effect of a current increase in these two determinants is taken as evidence in favor of localization externalities, whereas a similar lagged output response is evidence of MAR externalities. It turns out that both externalities matter in the high-tech industry and that MAR externalities matter in particular for non-affiliate (single-plant) high-tech firms. In other words, the output of such a firm at a particular location depends positively on the number of other high-tech firms at the same location.

It suffices for us at this point to note that the various positive externalities mentioned above all seem to matter. As Glaeser (2000: 92) puts it: "For the moment, the role of concentration and diversity does not seem to have been resolved by the literature."[6] Similarly, Duranton (2007: 38) observes that "the current consensus is that, in term of elasticities, urbanization effects are about as large as localization effects," although he also notes that "even though the elasticities are about the same, a larger size seems to be more desirable than increased specialization." A main reason for specialization to be more desirable is that city size contributes more to city productivity and wages than specialization (Ciccone, 2002; Ciccone and Hall, 1996). In the core model of geographical economics, firms group together in a city because local demand is high, and demand is high because firms have decided to produce in that city. What matters is that the positive externality is associated with the number of firms (and their workers) in the city and its surrounding cities and not with whether or not firms specialize in the production of the same type of goods. The core model is therefore a model in which, if anything, urbanization and not localization externalities are present. There is no advantage for cities in being specialized; only size as such matters.

Our brief discussion on the sources and scope of urban agglomeration economies makes it clear that the empirical research focuses on agglomeration forces. The spreading forces are not really part of the analysis. Differences between cities are therefore attributed to differences in the way the *positive* externalities influence cities. Other potential spreading forces, such as the need for city firms to serve non-city markets at positive transport costs, or congestion, are not part of this kind of empirical investigation. We think that the main reason for this neglect is the empirical focus on the determinants of the size and growth of *individual* cities, and not on the interdependencies between cities themselves and between cities and their *hinterland* (the non-urban areas). The nationwide space, which includes *both* cities and rural areas, is simply not a prime object of research in urban economics. There is, however, a well-developed literature in urban economics, based on Henderson (1974), that deals with urban systems. Here, the objective is to explain what might be gained by not looking at cities as "freely floating islands" (Fujita and Mori, 2005) without relationships with each other. The next section compares the basic urban systems model with our core model of geographical economics.

---

[6] Given our discussion in chapter 5, this should not come as much of surprise, because we concluded that the empirical evidence on spatial (here, urban) agglomeration is typically in line with multiple theories. The main problem is (Hanson, 2000) that we cannot identify the precise nature of the externalities underlying urban agglomeration; see our conclusion on observational equivalence at the start of this section.

7.3 Urban systems: urban and geographical economics in two graphs

7.3.1 The core model of urban systems

The discussion above describes a complex situation: many elements are important to explain the existence and growth of cities. It is easy to lose track of the key elements in the explanations, and how one can differentiate between different models. In an innovative paper, Combes, Duranton, and Overman, 2005 (CDO hereafter in this section for convenience), introduce a powerful graphical tool that allows us to differentiate the core model of urban systems from the core model(s) of geographical economics. The focus of the analysis is on the labor market. In particular, for both the core urban systems model (Henderson, 1974) and our core geographical economics model (Krugman, 1991a), CDO distinguish the following curves (see figures 7.3 and 7.4).

(i) The *wage curve*, which gives the wage W in a location j ($j=$ city/region/country) as a function of the size of the total local labor force N. Here, we assume that j refers to a city. The slope of the wage curve $W(N)$ may be upward- or downward-sloping, or may even be bell-shaped, depending on the precise nature of the scale economies involved. In a neoclassical model, with diminishing return to labor, the wage curve will have a negative slope. With increasing returns to scale, the curve has a positive slope. The microeconomic foundation of the direction of the slope can, for example, be explained by referring to the sharing, matching, and learning mechanisms discussed above. The larger the scope of the externalities the larger the (absolute) value of the slope.

(ii) The *cost of living curve*, which depicts how the cost of living H in city j depends on the size of the total local labor force N. Costs are defined in expenditure terms, instead of a price index. Here, too, the model specifics need to tell us for every level of N what the cost of living curve $H(N)$ looks like. In the core urban systems model, this curve has a negative slope. As we have already noted in section 2.2, in Henderson (1974) there are negative external economies of scale due to congestion/crowding costs that are a strictly positive function of the overall size of the city j, here measured by the local labor force N.

(iii) The *net wage curve* is given by the difference between the wage curve and the cost of living curve, $W(N) - H(N)$. It gives the net disposable wage for every level of the local labor force N. The shape of this curve

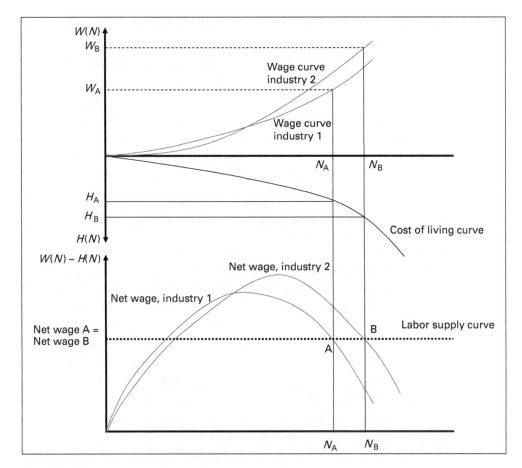

Figure 7.3   Core urban economics model

is, of course, determined by the shapes of the wage curve and the cost
of living curve.

(iv) The *labor supply curve*, finally, is a function of the net wage rate. In
the core model of urban systems, as well as in the core model of
geographical economics, labor is fully mobile between locations, and
any net wage difference between locations, however small, induces
migration. This means the labor supply curve is perfectly elastic (flat).

Equilibrium in the model is determined using figure 7.3 by the intersection of the labor supply curve and the net wage curve, where the local
labor force N is on the horizontal axis and the net wage $W(N) - H(N)$ on
the vertical axis. The intersection point gives the equilibrium city labor force
and the equilibrium net wage for city j. Based on this simple set-up, CDO
can include the main elements of the core urban systems model from

Henderson (1974) by making use of curves (i) to (iv) (see section 2.2 for the main ingredients).

In the Henderson model, external scale economies are industry-specific and thus refer to localization economies. This is in contrast to the core model of geographical economics, in which external scale economies consist of pecuniary externalities (recall figure 3.8) and the manufacturing firm's production structure is characterized by internal economies of scale (due to the fixed costs a in the cost function). Another difference with the core geographical economics model is that transport costs are absent in Henderson (1974), so market potential is not an issue. Moreover, cities do not have a hinterland other than neighboring cities. The non-urban surrounding of a city is not part of the analysis. Instead, the focus is on the forces determining the size of cities and the interactions between them. The agglomerating forces in the Henderson model imply that there are positive spillovers when a firm of a particular industry locates in a city where other firms from the *same* industry are located. In line with our discussion on the previous section, the sources for these localization economies may be Marshall's holy trinity or any other source of agglomeration economies.

The spreading force in Henderson (1974) is negative external economies of scale within the city (congestion), which is solely a function of the overall size of the city. A large city implies relatively high commuting costs and land rents, depending only on the overall size of a city. Together with the industry-specific external economies this has two important implications. First, the Henderson-type model can rationalize *systems of cities* – i.e. the existence of cities with different sizes catering to the needs of different industries. This result depends crucially on the assumption that the positive spillovers of location are industry-specific: each industry has its own optimum size. Second, this basic urban economics model provides a rationale as to why cities specialize in the production of those goods for which the economies of scale are relatively strong. It rationalizes an urban system in which cities of different sizes trade with each other. Therefore, the notion that "cities are like floating islands" (Fujita and Mori, 2005: 395) does not apply to the Henderson model, because specialization forces cities to trade with each other. Despite the inter-city trade interdependency, geography is not part of the analysis, because there are zero transport costs.

Figure 7.3 illustrates the urban economics model by depicting the *wage curve* for two industries (1 and 2). The slope of the two wage curves indicates that there are strictly positive returns to scale in both industries: wages increase when the total city labor force increases. Note that initially, for low levels of N, industry 1 has stronger increasing returns – and thus higher wages – but this is reversed for higher levels of N. Figure 7.3 also shows the *cost of living curve*, which increases when the total labor force N increases. The equilibrium is determined by equating the net wage curve $w(N) - H(N)$ with the labor supply curve (figure 7.3, bottom panel). Note that the combination of industry-specific increasing returns and a cost of living that depends only on the overall city size implies that, for an equilibrium to be stable, *each city will be fully specialized* in either industry 1 or 2. Diversification is possible only if by chance the wages in both industries are the same (this is the intersection of both curves in the top panel of figure 7.3). In all other cases, the larger industry will grow at the expense of the smaller industry, and will keep on growing until all workers are employed in that industry. Starting from the intersection, a relocation of workers from industry 2 to industry 1 makes industry 1 more attractive.

This process holds for all cities. There is a complication, however. Suppose we have two relatively large cities – the total workforce of each city is to the right of the intersection of the two curves in the top panel; will this result in two cities both specialized in industry 2? The answer is "no." If both goods are indispensable, the larger city will specialize in industry 2, because economies of scale work in favor of the larger city (or, if they are of equal size, the city that turns to industry 2 the more rapidly). This forces the other city out of industry 2 production and into industry 1 production.[7]

The cost of living increases in this example with total city population.[8] The combination of the two industry wage curves and the cost of living curve thus gives the *net wage curves*. The short-run equilibrium in the core urban system model is now determined by the intersection of each net wage curve with the *labor supply curve*, assuming perfect labor mobility between cities. As in the core geographical economics models, labor will migrate towards cities with relatively high real wages – that is, wages corrected for the cost of living. This assumption results in a horizontal labor supply curve. As figure 7.3 shows, the resulting equilibria are denoted by A and B, where the net wage is the same across cities and the city specialized in industry 1 (2) will have a population of size N_A (N_B).

---

[7] Note that full specialization requires a full model that specifies demand relations; for given initial prices, it is unlikely that complete specialization automatically implies market clearing. Prices will adjust, therefore, in order to clear markets. Although this is possible in principle we do not discuss it here, as we want only to stress different mechanisms leading to systems of cities. It is important to note that the city specializing in industry 2 always has a higher wage rate than a city specializing in industry 1 (or a combination of industry 1 and 2).

[8] Note that the cost of living depends only on city-specific variables and not on expenditures of imported commodities that include transportation costs.

Three aspects of this equilibrium are worth mentioning. First, cities specialized in a particular industry must be of the same size, as we have assumed that the cost of living curves are the same in each city, and economies of scale are industry-specific and not city-specific. Second, economies of scale are stronger in industry 2, which implies that cities specialized in industry 2 are larger than cities specialized in industry 1. Third, since cities will be fully specialized, inter-city trade will arise. Henderson (1974) thus rationalizes the existence of a system of (specialized) cities that trade with each other, driven by the tension between industry-specific returns to scale (the wage curve) and city-specific congestion (the cost of living curve). The short-run equilibrium refers to the situation in which the number of cities is fixed. For our present purposes (comparing the urban systems model with our core model of geographical economics), this will do.[9]

7.3.2 The core models of urban systems and geographical economics compared

To compare the Henderson model with Krugman (1991a), we need to squeeze the core model of chapters 3 and 4 into the diagrammatic framework of figure 7.3. As the diagram assumes that the model can be solved, we cannot use the Krugman model (see chapter 3). Instead, we can use the solvable models introduced in chapter 4 (close to the Krugman model, but with explicit solutions for the wage rates). Suppose, therefore, that there are two regions or countries (Home and Foreign) and two sectors (manufacturing, with Dixit–Stiglitz (1977) monopolistic competition, and food, with a homogeneous good produced under perfect competition). Both goods are tradable, but only the manufacturing good incurs transport or trade costs. The number of manufacturing firms (each firm producing a single manufacturing variety) is fixed. Due to the love-of-variety effect, consumers in both countries consume all available manufacturing varieties. Agricultural production is immobile, but manufacturing workers are mobile between Home and Foreign in the long run.

---

[9] Economic agents do not include the external effects of congestion into their decisions. This implies that cities tend to become too large, in the sense that points A and B in the lower panel of figure 7.3 are to the right of the maximum of the net wage curves. From a welfare point of view, city sizes that correspond to the maxima of the net wage curves are ideal. This solution would require the hand of a city developer – that is, someone with the power to create new cities. The final situation, in which the net wages in all cities are the same, and each city has its optimal size, is the long-run equilibrium (CDO, 2005: 322–3).

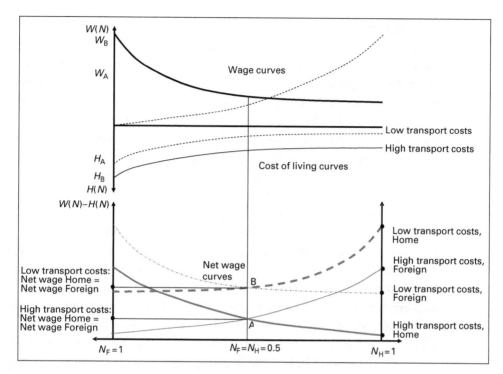

Figure 7.4   Core geographical economics model

Against this by now well-known background, the wage curve $w(N)$ for Home (similar reasoning holds for Foreign) is shown in figure 7.4. From chapters 3 and 4 we know that wages in Home depend on transport costs. Home's wages will be higher if it has a high real market potential (see equations (3.21) and (5.3)). Better market access (high Y and low T) corresponds to high market potential and thus high wages, but also to a low cost of living (a low price index). The combined effect is to produce high real wages. Home's market access gets stronger if its share of the manufacturing firms and labor force N is larger (the home market effect). Simultaneously, the price index or competition effect implies that firms can afford to pay higher wages if competition is less fierce – that is, if Home is *smaller* in terms of its share of mobile firms and workers. It is central to the geographical economics models that N is not fixed. We know from chapter 4 that migration depends on real wage differentials, which in turn depend on the level of transport costs. Figure 7.4 illustrates two cases: one for high transport costs (solid line), for which the price index or competition effect dominates, and one for low transport costs (dashed line), for which the home market effect dominates.

Similar reasoning is applied to the cost of living curve $H(N)$. In the geographical economics models, the cost of living is simply a function of the manufacturing price index (equation 3.23). Home's price index will be lower if fewer goods have to be imported from Foreign, such that the cost of living decreases when a larger part of the manufacturing firms and labor force N is located in Home. The cost of living curve therefore falls when N increases (note the difference with the Henderson model; see figure 7.3). Transport costs matter for the cost of living such that, for any given level of N, the cost of living $H(N)$ will be lower for low transport costs (see the difference between the dashed – low transport cost – and solid – high transport cost – lines in figure 7.4 regarding the cost of living).

With manufacturing labor perfectly mobile between Home and Foreign in the long run (a flat labor supply curve in Home, not drawn in the figure), figure 7.4 gives the net wages $w(N) - H(N)$ for Home (left vertical axis, thick line) and for Foreign (right vertical axis, thin line). For both countries, the lines are drawn for high transport costs – the solid lines – and for low transport costs – the dashed lines. For *low* transport costs (see chapters 3 and 4), the net wage curves for Home and Foreign ensure that the spreading equilibrium ($N_H = N_F = 0.5$, point B) is *un*stable, as any small shock in the manufacturing labor force will result in either full agglomeration in Home ($N_H = 1$) or Foreign ($N_F = 1$). For *high* transport costs (point A), the spreading equilibrium and the associated equalization of net wages between Home and Foreign will be stable. The core model of geographical economics is thus able to explain the existence of agglomeration by using market access effects (rather than pure external economies of scale, as in the urban systems model).

Note that the two models underlying figures 7.3 and 7.4 are different. Agglomeration in the urban systems model is driven by pure, local increasing returns to scale, and by pecuniary external economies in the geographical economics model. Combined with the presence of transport costs in geographical economics, and zero transport costs in the urban systems model, the two models have different implications for the wage curve (which rises if N increases in the urban systems model, but not necessarily so in the geographical economics model). Similarly, the cost of living curve $H(N)$ is increasing in N in the Henderson model and *falling* in the geographical economics model. Despite these differences, one can conclude that there is no inherent contradiction between the urban systems model and the geographical economics model. The important empirical question is which model is applicable in which situation. CDO argue that geographical economics is probably more relevant at a *larger spatial scale* (regions, countries), where market access and spatial interdependencies between locations are most important and the within-location agglomeration and dispersing forces are of secondary importance. In contrast, the urban systems model is more relevant at smaller spatial scales (cities), where local (positive and negative) externalities are most important and between-city interactions and long-distance relations are less important. In the words of Combes, Duranton, and Overman (2005: 330): "We would argue that there is no inherent contradiction between the urban systems approach and NEG [geographical economics]: the latter is trying to explain broad trends at large spatial scales while the former attempts to explain 'spikes' of economic activity." Box 7.3 discusses an attempt to discriminate between the trends of geographical economics and the "spikes" of urban economics.

The reader may wonder at this point if the geographical economics model is capable of explaining the existence of cities of different sizes in a long-run equilibrium. This was, after all, the big step with the Henderson model (see figure 7.3). Fortunately, the answer is "yes," although it requires an extension of the basic model. The remainder of this chapter provides this extension by adding congestion forces to the model. We then apply this modified framework to the stylized (but not undisputed) facts about city size distributions, known as the rank size distribution (which is equivalent to Zipf's law in a special case).

Box 7.3 Testing urban economics against geographical economics: scale matters

In chapter 5 section 5.5, we concluded that empirical research suggests that the distance decay is quite strong. The Munich experiment (figure 5.8), for instance, shows that this implies that shocks to location j affect only nearby locations. Section 7.3 argues that at higher *spatial scales* (the country level) spatial interdependencies matter a lot, whereas at lower spatial scales (the city level) these interdependencies are of second-order importance. This raises the question of which approach is empirically more relevant at intermediate spatial scales (the region level). Fingleton (2005, 2006) provides this test at the regional level for a sample of EU regions and (smaller) regions in the United Kingdom. For a sample of 186 NUTS II regions for the European Union he finds that both market potential and employment density are significant, which suggests that at somewhat larger spatial scales (EU NUTS II regions compared to the 408 smaller-scale British regions) geographical economics might be more relevant.

Fingleton (2006) estimates a wage equation for a sample of 408 regions in Great Britain, where a market potential measure is the key geographical economics variable and the density of employment (total employment per km^2) is the key urban economics variable. The control variables are technical knowledge, schooling, and commuting measures, the last of which captures the degree of regional labor efficiency. When considered in isolation, both the market potential and employment density variable are significant. As table 7.3 shows, however, the market potential variable is no longer significant when considered when the three labor

Box 7.3 (cont.)

Table 7.3 Explaining wage variations across 408 regions in Great Britain: estimated coefficients (elasticities)

	Geographical economics (GE)	Urban economics (UE)	GE and UE combined
Market potential	0.08 (2.67)	–	0.03 (0.55)
Employment density	–	0.01 (3.64)	0.01 (3.63)
Schooling	−0.001 (−1.15)	−0.001 (−1.90)	−0.001 (−1.98)
Technical knowledge	0.05 (8.96)	0.05 (9.60)	0.05 (7.49)
Commuting	0.002 (5.73)	0.0014 (16.40)	0.0017 (5.28)

Notes: For definitions of the various variables, see Fingleton (2006: 528–9). t-ratios between brackets.
Estimation method: 2SLS: 408, (UALAD) regions in Great Britain.
Source: Fingleton (2006: tabs. 1–3).

efficiency measures are included. It turns out that the commuting variable is largely responsible for this fact. Fingleton (2006: 523) therefore concludes that for the case of the 408 regions in Great Britain "it is clear that market potential alone will not explain local wage variations and that modifications allowing for labor efficiency variations are necessary."

More generally, he calls for models that combine elements of urban and geographical economics. The question of whether or not the spatial or geographical scale might matter when it comes to the empirical relevance of geographical economics is also analyzed by Anthony Briant, Combes, and Miren Lafourcade (2007) for the case of French regions. In particular, they investigate the so-called *modifiable areal unit problem*, or MAUP for short. The MAUP is relevant for geographical economics because differences in agglomeration should reflect differences in agglomeration economies and not differences in geographical units. The authors systematically investigate both parts of the MAUP. Their main conclusion is that (at least for France) the MAUP is (fortunately) of limited importance and that both the scale and shape effect are of minor importance. In line with the core of our book, they therefore (75) "urge researchers to spend their efforts on choosing the relevant specification for the question they want to tackle."

7.4 Congestion as an additional spreading force[10]

The idea that urban agglomeration, driven by positive external economies of scale, may itself give rise to external *dis*economies of scale is, of course, not new. Indeed, in sections 7.2 and 7.3 above and in chapter 2, we have already

[10] This section is based on Brakman *et al.* (1996); see also Gabaix and Ioannides (2004) for a discussion.

observed that in modern urban economics the main spreading forces are precisely external diseconomies of scale. When cities get larger they start to suffer from increasing commuting costs and higher land or housing rents (recall box 7.1). The costs involved can be quite substantial. For example, according to the US Department for Transportation, the cost of congestion for Chicago in 2003 amounted to rush-hour travelers being stuck, on average, for seven working days in traffic (fifty-eight hours), wasting thirty-four gallons of gasoline, and paying a virtual congestion tax of $976 in wasted time and fuel. Similarly, land rents also depend on the relative size of a city. In chapter 5 section 5.5, we discussed the geographical economics model used by Hanson (2005) and Helpman (1998) respectively, in which the only spreading force consists of the rising regional housing prices when more firms and workers move to the region.

External diseconomies of scale also arise from environmental pollution or limited storage facilities. We refer to all these diseconomies of scale as examples of congestion. We do not discriminate between the various forms of congestion, because our aim is to analyze the consequences of congestion, rather than its origin. The direct consequence of congestion is straightforward, since it provides an incentive for firms and mobile workers to relocate from the congested centers to the relatively uncluttered periphery. It turns out that additional spreading forces result in a system of cities. In the remainder of this chapter we therefore extend the core model of chapters 3 and 4 to allow for urban systems.

7.4.1 The modeling of congestion

In the core model, the manufacturing production function is characterized by internal increasing returns to scale. The production structure of the core model can easily be adapted to introduce congestion costs. The main idea is that the congestion costs depend on the *overall size* of the location of production. In this sense it resembles the Henderson (1974) model discussed in the previous section. The size of city r is measured by the total number of manufacturing firms N_r in that city. Congestion costs are thus not industry- or firm-specific, but solely a function of the size of the city as a whole:[11]

$$l_{ir} = N_r^{\tau/(1-\tau)}(a + \beta x_i); \qquad -1 < \tau < 1 \qquad (7.1)$$

---

[11] This specification simplifies equations (7.2) to (7.4) below considerably. Other specifications, such as the dependence of costs on the total production level in a city, are also possible. This does not alter the analysis in any

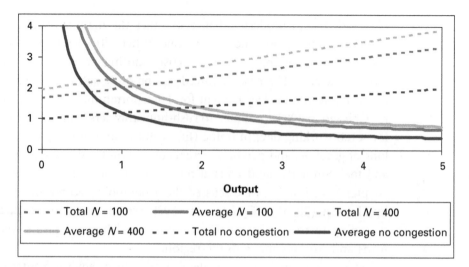

Figure 7.5   Total and average labor costs with congestion

Note: Parameter values: $a = 1$, $\beta = 0.2$; $\tau = 0.1$ for $N = 100$ and $N = 400$, $\tau = 0$ for "no congestion."

where l_{ir} is the amount of labor required in city r to produce x_i units of a variety i, and the parameter τ represents external economies of scale. There are no location-specific external economies of scale if $\tau = 0$. Equation (7.1) then reduces to the production function of the core model (see chapter 3). There are positive location-specific external economies if $-1 < \tau < 0$. Such a specification could be used to model, for example, learning-by-doing spillovers. For our present purposes, the case of negative location-specific external economies arising from congestion are relevant, in which case $0 < \tau < 1$. This is illustrated in figure 7.5.

If the parameter τ lies between zero and one, each manufacturing firm i in city r is confronted with a cost increase if other firms also decide to locate in this city. As figure 7.5 shows, a rise in the number of firms located in city r raises the fixed and marginal costs of producing in city r, and therefore the average costs of production as well. This can be compared in figure 7.5 to "no congestion," in which case $\tau = 0$ and congestion does not arise. As with any other external effect, we assume that each individual firm does not take into account that its location decision has an impact on the production functions, and thus indirectly on the decision processes, of all the other manufacturing firms. To keep the analysis tractable, this is the only

---

essential way. The main advantage of equation (7.1) is that it provides a very general specification for congestion (= negative externalities).

modification we make in the core model. We must now retrace all our steps taken in chapter 3 when deriving the short-run equilibrium of the core model to see how the introduction of congestion costs affects each step (details of this process can be found on the website, which also reproduces the normalization analysis for the core model with congestion). Equations (7.2) to (7.4) give the short-run equilibrium, incorporating the congestion modification of equation (7.1).

$$Y_r = \delta \lambda_r W_r + (1 - \delta)\phi_r \tag{7.2}$$

$$I_r = \left[\sum_{s=1}^{R} \lambda_s^{1-\tau\varepsilon} T_{rs}^{1-\varepsilon} W_s^{1-\varepsilon} \right]^{1/(1-\varepsilon)} \tag{7.3}$$

$$W_r = \lambda_r^{-\tau} \left[\sum_{s=1}^{R} Y_s T_{sr}^{1-\varepsilon} I_s^{\varepsilon-1} \right]^{1/\varepsilon} \tag{7.4}$$

When comparing this short-run equilibrium with the normalized short-run equilibrium of chapter 3 (see equations (4.1) to (4.3)), it is immediately obvious that equations (7.2) to (7.4) reduce to equations (4.1) to (4.3) if $\tau = 0$. The income equation (7.2) is not affected by the congestion parameter τ.[12] From the wage equation (7.4) it is clear that an increase of congestion in city r, resulting from an increase in the share of manufacturing workers λ_r in that city, tends to reduce the wage rate in city r, and simultaneously tends to reduce the price index in other regions (see equation (7.3)). Both forces make other cities more attractive.

Given the distribution of the manufacturing labor force across cities, which determines the number of varieties produced and hence the number of manufacturing firms in each city, equations (7.2) to (7.4) determine the short-run equilibrium. We do not use the short-run equilibrium for the congestion model. To assess the relevance of congestion for the long-run equilibrium allocation of economic activity, when the distribution of the mobile labor force is not fixed, we rely on simulations and proceed in two steps. In the first step, we illustrate the relevance of congestion in the two-city model. This allows us to compare with the simulations of chapter 4. Since it is one of the objectives of this chapter to apply the core model with congestion

---

[12] This obviously also holds for the real wage equation, not shown here.

to actual city size distributions, a two-city model will not do. In the second step, we therefore introduce many cities and congestion in the racetrack economy of the core model. Remember that, in the racetrack economy, space is neutral – that is to say, by construction no location is preferred over any other location. Any results derived in such a setting can be attributed to the workings of the model rather than the geometric construction of space. The racetrack economy with congestion will therefore be used in our attempt to give a theoretical basis for Zipf's law in section 7.6.

7.4.2 The two-city model and congestion

In the simulations of the core model with congestion, where food production is again evenly divided between the two cities, we focus on the relative real wage of city 1 compared to city 2 to determine the direction of change of the distribution of the manufacturing labor force, and thus the stability of long-run equilibria. This is identical to the approach in chapter 4 (see, for example, figure 4.1), although this time we simultaneously plot the total welfare achieved in the two cities together for each distribution of the manufacturing labor force. In other words, for each value of λ_1, the share of the manufacturing labor force in city 1, we first determine the short-run equilibrium by solving equations (7.2) to (7.4). Second, we calculate the relative real wage of city 1 and total welfare. Third, we plot the latter two variables as a function of the share of the manufacturing labor force in city 1 (see figure 7.3).

A long-run equilibrium is reached either when real wages in the two cities are equal – that is, when the relative real wage in figure 7.3 is equal to one – or when the entire manufacturing labor force is agglomerated in one city. The long-run equilibrium is stable if, going from left to right, the relative real wage cuts the "$w_1/w_2=1$ line" from above. To illustrate how the introduction of congestion alters the long-run equilibrium and its stability, we vary the transport costs T in figure 7.6, which is arranged in panels a to i for *de*creasing transport costs. Recall that we concluded in chapter 4 that the spreading equilibrium is stable for high transport costs, whereas full agglomeration in either city is stable for low transport costs (see figure 4.2). As explained at the end of chapter 4 and in the introduction of this chapter, this "bang-bang" tendency of the stable long-run equilibrium without congestion (either spreading or complete agglomeration) is not a very satisfactory outcome from an empirical point of view. As demonstrated in figure 7.6, even if we add only a small amount of congestion ($\tau = 0.01$), the possibilities for long-run equilibria change drastically.

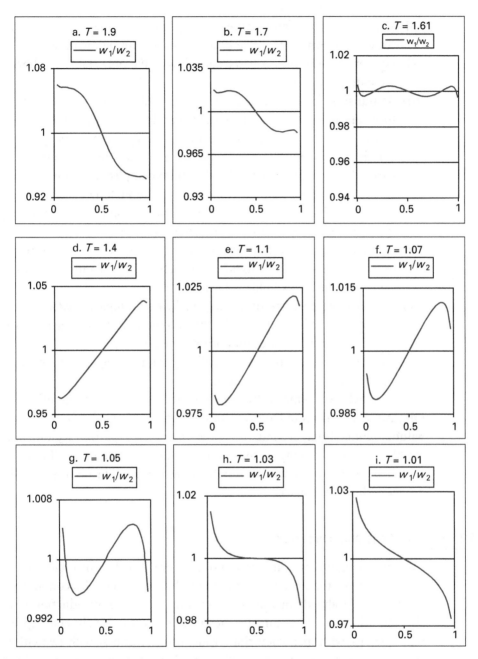

Figure 7.6   The two-region core model with congestion ($\varepsilon=5$; $\delta=0.4$; $\tau=0.01$)

Discussing the panels of figure 7.6 sequentially – that is, for gradually decreasing transport costs – five different stages can be identified.

(i) For very high transport costs, spreading is the only stable equilibrium; see panels a and b.

(ii) As transport costs decrease, spreading is still a stable equilibrium, but there are now also two other stable equilibria with *partial* agglomeration; see panel c. The introduction of congestion costs appears to enrich the possible long-run equilibrium outcomes considerably, in particular by allowing partial rather than complete agglomeration as a stable equilibrium. Also note that there are seven long-run equilibria in panel c (including complete agglomeration); going from left to right, these are alternately unstable and stable.

(iii) Complete agglomeration in either city is a stable equilibrium as transport costs continue to fall; see panels d to f. The range of transport costs for which this holds is fairly large.

(iv) As transport costs become very small, their impact relative to congestion costs is limited. Initially this implies that *partial* agglomeration in either city is a stable equilibrium; see panel g.

(v) For very low transport costs, finally, spreading is again the only stable equilibrium; see panels h and i.

Two conclusions emerge from this analysis. First, the range of possible long-run equilibrium outcomes with congestion is considerably wider than without congestion. Second, the phenomenon of partial agglomeration establishes the possibility of the simultaneous existence of small and large centers of economic activity as a stable long-run equilibrium outcome in a model with neutral space.

7.4.3 Many locations and congestion

After analyzing the two-city version of the core model with congestion, it is time to extend the analysis to the neutral-space racetrack economy with congestion. As already mentioned in chapter 4 and the introduction in this chapter, without congestion the racetrack economy usually ends up with only one city with manufacturing production, or at best with two cities of equal size, in the long-run equilibrium. Now that we have seen in the previous subsection that the two-city model with congestion allows for the viability of small economic centers of manufacturing production, we extend this analysis to a structure with many cities.

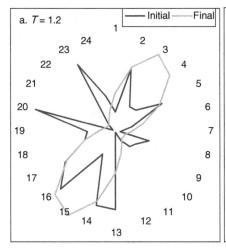

a. *T* = 1.2

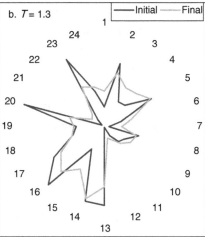

b. *T* = 1.3

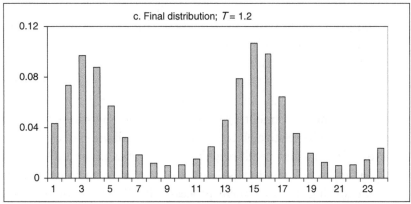

c. Final distribution; *T* = 1.2

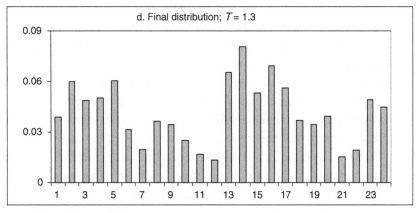

d. Final distribution; *T* = 1.3

Figure 7.7   The racetrack economy with congestion ($\varepsilon = 5$; $\delta = 0.7$; $\tau = 0.1$)

Figure 7.7 shows two simulation results of a twenty-four-city racetrack economy with congestion, one simulation with transport costs $T = 1.2$, the other with transport costs $T = 1.3$. The initial distribution of the manufacturing labor force was chosen randomly, but is the same in the two simulations. Panels a and b of Figure 7.7 show both the initial and the final (long-run equilibrium) distribution of the manufacturing labor force. The larger the distance from the center of the circle the larger the manufacturing labor force in that city is. So, for example, cities 1 and 21 are initially very small, while cities 20 and 23 are initially very large. Panels c and d of figure 7.7 just show a column chart of the final distribution of the manufacturing labor force.

Panels a and c, depicting the simulation results for transport costs $T = 1.2$, lead to the following observations. First, with congestion, many cities – not just one or two – still have manufacturing production in the long-run equilibrium. Second, these cities vary considerably in economic size, which is promising from an empirical point of view. Third, the final distribution of manufacturing production is well structured around two centers of economic activity in cities 3 and 15; see, in particular, panel c. Fourth, whether an individual city increases or decreases in economic size during the adjustment process towards the long-run equilibrium depends largely on its relative place in the initial distribution of city sizes – that is, on the size of cities in its neighborhood. Cities 20 and 23, for example, are initially very large, but isolated. Consequently, they both shrink considerably during the adjustment process. City 15, on the other hand, is initially quite small, but surrounded on both sides by large cities, namely cities 13, 14, 16, and 17. This allows city 15 to eventually become the largest city of all, even larger than cities 20 and 23 were initially. The cluster of cities 2, 3, and 4 thrives in particular because they are exactly opposite the "agglomeration shadow" imposed by the cluster surrounding city 15.

Relative to the above discussion, panels b and d for $T = 1.3$ show two additional results, namely that, depending on the parameter values, the final distribution may be much more determined by the initial distribution (see panel b), and thus be less structured (see panel d). In this sense, the importance of the initial conditions – or, in other words, the "history" – may vary. Before we turn to the empirical evidence for Zipf's law, it must be emphasized that we certainly do not want to pretend to offer a full-fledged analysis of the economics of congestion. Nonetheless, the core model with congestion does illustrate that the inclusion of an additional spreading force may give rise to many centers of economic activity that vary considerably in size, even in a setting of neutral space. This is a necessary condition for applying such a model to explain urban systems and city size distributions. This topic is addressed in section 7.6; but first we have a closer, empirical, look at city size distributions.

7.5 Zipf's law: definition, data, and estimation results

7.5.1 Urban economics and the city size distribution

In chapter 2 subsection 2.2.3, and in section 7.2 in this chapter, it became clear that any convincing story about the existence and growth of cities is based ultimately on the existence of (local) increasing returns to scale. The exact nature of the increasing returns need not concern us here (see section 7.2). In addition to increasing returns, other factors such as natural endowments (actual physical geography; see Ellison and Glaeser, 1999), political factors (see Ades and Glaeser, 1995, Henderson, 2003, and box 7.4 on primate cities), or consumption externalities (Glaeser, Kolko, and Saiz, 2001) are also thought to be relevant in determining the formation and growth of cities, but increasing returns is the dominant explanation. When it comes to the scope of urban agglomeration economies (see section 7.2), both static (e.g. localization versus urbanization economies) and dynamic externalities (so-called MAR versus Jacobs externalities and the role of competition) can be distinguished. The point to emphasize here, however, is that the literature on the sources and scope of agglomeration economies is not very useful when it comes to explaining city size distributions and stylized facts about this distribution. The reason is that this literature is concerned primarily with the size and growth of individual cities and not with the interdependencies between cities (the "cities as floating islands" metaphor), let alone with the spatial interdependencies between cities and their hinterlands, the rural areas. In geographical economics it is precisely the spatial interaction between the centers with their production (cities) and the rest of the economy that is the focal point of the analysis.

Until quite recently, it proved to be difficult to come up with a sound microeconomic foundation for systems of nationwide space, and the "old" central place theory has long remained the workhorse approach to discuss why a *system of cities* could exist and how it works (Abdel-Rahman and Anas, 2004). We have already dealt with the drawbacks of central place theory, in chapter 2. Curtis Eaton and Richard Lipsey (1982) were among the first to develop a model in which a microeconomic foundation could be given for a central place outcome. Their model verifies only that such an outcome could be an equilibrium, however. When it comes to deriving central place theory from the underlying behavior of firms and workers, Fujita, Krugman, and Venables (1999: chap. 11) show that this can be done in a geographical economics approach. As we will see in the next section, their approach suffers from the drawback that it is at odds with the observed regularities in actual city size distributions.

Black and Henderson (1999b) and Jonathan Eaton and Zvi Eckstein (1997) follow a different route when it comes to city size distributions, as they take these observed regularities as their starting point and then try to come up with a theoretical model that can deal with these facts. The facts we refer to concern the relative similarity, both across countries and across time, of city size distributions.[13] The model developed by Black and Henderson (1999b: 259) uses the well-known trade-off in urban economics (see section 7.3 on Henderson, 1974) that firms in each city face between localized economies of scale and congestion costs. They use this basic idea to show that the growth of cities (driven by this trade-off) can result in a stable city size distribution. Eaton and Eckstein (1997) develop a similar, somewhat simpler model of city growth and explicitly use their model to address the ultimate (and hotly debated) stylized fact about city distributions: the so-called Zipf's law, or the rank size rule. In section 7.6 we use Zipf's law as an empirical yardstick for the analysis of various theories (including our own congestion version of the core model) that set out to explain the facts about city size distributions. Before doing so, however, we introduce and define Zipf's law in section 7.5 and provide relevant data on this "law."

At this point, the reader may ask why, for instance, the urban economics model developed by Eaton and Eckstein (1997) does not suffice when it comes to giving a sound theoretical foundation for the stylized facts on city size distributions. The answer is that, at least from the geographical economics perspective of this book, such a theoretical foundation should use a model in which the spatial interdependencies are the heart of the analysis. As we saw in section 7.3, this is not the case in the geography-free world of urban economics.

---

[13] Of course, there are other well-established patterns with respect to urbanization, such as the observed growth in the number of and size of cities over time (Black and Henderson, 1999b: 254).

7.5.2 What is Zipf's law?

Zipf's law is a special case of the rank size distribution. How can this distribution be measured? First, as we did for India in chapter 1, collect data on the size of all cities in a particular region of the world – defined by the number of inhabitants in a city, say. Second, order these observations in decreasing size; this is their rank. Now take the natural logarithm of the rank and the size; according to the rank size distribution, this relationship should be approximately linear. In a formula:

$$log(M_j) = \log(c) - q\log(R_j) \tag{7.5}$$

where c is a constant, M_j is the size of city j (measured by its population), and R_j is the rank of city j (rank 1 for the largest city, rank 2 for the second largest city, etc.).

In empirical research q is the estimated coefficient, giving the slope of the supposedly log-linear relationship between city size and city rank. It is said that *Zipf's law holds if, and only if, $q = 1$*. If Zipf's law holds – that is, if $q = 1$ – the largest city is precisely k times as large as the kth largest city.[14] If q is smaller than one, a more even distribution of city sizes results than predicted by Zipf's law (if $q = 0$ all cities are of the same size). If q is larger than one, the large cities are larger than Zipf's law predicts, implying more urban agglomeration – that is, the largest city is more than k times as large as the kth largest city. Empirically, we have to establish if the rank size distribution holds. If it does, the question arises of whether Zipf's law holds – that is, if $q = 1$ or not.[15]

Using mostly US data, a number of authors have stressed that (i) Zipf's law holds (that is, $q = 1$) and (ii) the estimated coefficient q hardly changes

[14] Equation (7.5) is the log-linear specification of the rank size distribution as used in empirical tests. Glenn Carroll (1982) shows that the rank size distribution has been discussed prior to George Zipf (1949), notably by Felix Auerbach and Alfred Lotka. Our specification follows Zipf and notably Lotka, but many empirical studies prefer to use $log(R_j) = \log(c) - q' \log(M_j)$. To avoid confusion, all estimates for q mentioned in the text are based on equation (7.5).

[15] Zipf (1949) attempts to capture a broad range of observed social and spatial regularities by means of simple equations. His book is part of a larger tradition, sometimes referred to as the literature on gravity models, that, inspired by Newtonian physics, typically stipulates that economic or social interaction between the objects of interest is a function of the mass (economic size) of these objects weighted by their distance. These equations are not meant to explain the social or spatial phenomenon at hand. Their objective is simply, analogously to the physical sciences, to come up with an equation that describes the phenomenon. This "undeductive" approach, called *social physics* by Krugman (1995), led not only to Zipf's law but also to the gravity model and the market potential function. Zipf, a lecturer of linguistics at Harvard University, argues that the rank size distribution holds for many phenomena. A well-known example is in the use of language, wherein the expressions that are most frequently used are also the least complex. Zipf had a reputation for being eccentric. The story goes that he applauded the *Anschluss* of Austria to Nazi Germany in 1938 because the resulting city size distribution was more in line with the rank size rule!

over time (see Krugman, 1996a, 1996b, Gabaix, 1999a, 1999b, and Fujita, Krugman, and Venables, 1999: chap. 12). Indeed, when equation (7.5) is estimated, q is usually close to one when US data are used. Carroll (1982), however, surveys the empirical evidence on the rank size distribution and finds that Zipf's law does not always hold for the United States. In an influential paper on Zipf's law – or the Pareto distribution, as they call it – Kenneth Rosen and Mitchel Resnick (1980: 167) find that $q = 0.84$ for the United States, which would imply a much more even city size distribution than if Zipf's law holds. Similarly, Black and Henderson (2003: 352–4) find not only that the slope coefficient in equation (7.5) slowly increases over the course of the twentieth century for the United States, but also that this coefficient clearly is not equal to one. In fact, they find that, for the United States, $q > 1$ (around 1.17), which would imply that the US urban system is more concentrated than Zipf's Law predicts.[16]

For other countries as well a mixed picture emerges. Eaton and Eckstein (1997) find for Japan and France that Zipf's law nearly holds, and also that q has hardly changed over time. Rosen and Resnick (1980: 167), however, show that for both countries $q < 1$ (France: 0.75; Japan: 0.78). More recently, Kwok Soo (2005) and Volker Nitsch (2005) survey the available evidence and conclude that, for many countries and periods, q is significantly different from one (often it is found that $q<1$), and also that q is not constant over time.

A recent survey on many aspects of Zipf's law is provided by Gabaix and Ioannides (2004), who argue that the two most commonly used methods for estimating q (also referred to as the Pareto exponent) are the *Zipf regression* (which uses simple, OLS) and the *Hill estimator* (Hill, 1975). For large sample sizes the estimated coefficient in the Zipf regression tends with probability one to the true value. For small samples, however, the estimate is biased and inefficient. More importantly, the reported standard errors grossly underestimate the true standard errors, leading many researchers to erroneous conclusions regarding the q value. Under the null hypothesis of a perfect power law, the Hill estimator is the maximum likelihood estimator, but its properties in finite samples are also worrisome, as the bias can be very high and the computed standard errors considerably underestimate the true standard errors as a result of this bias. Various estimators have been developed to address these issues (see Gabaix and Ibragimov, 2007, for an overview). More importantly, they provide an elegant and effective solution for the estimation problems: an unbiased estimate of the coefficient is

---

[16] This is also the conclusion of Linda Dobkins and Ioannides (2000).

obtained when OLS is applied to the rank shifted by one half. In this book, we therefore apply the *Gabaix–Ibragimov* estimation method, using Marie Kratz and Sidney Resnick's (1996) asymptotic standard errors (equal to $q\sqrt{2/n}$, where q is the estimated coefficient and n is the number of observations).

If one wants to come up with a theoretical explanation for (deviations from) Zipf's law, it obviously matters a great deal whether one concludes from the available empirical evidence whether or not $q = 1$ and/or q is stable over time. Fortunately, the evidence on Zipf's law is somewhat less muddled than the previous paragraph suggests, because the differences are to a considerable extent due to differences in city definitions and sample sizes. To start with the latter, it turns out that, if the size of cities drops below a certain threshold level (which is neither constant through time nor the same for every country), there is hardly any negative correlation between size and rank left for the group of very small cities. The inclusion of very small cities makes it more likely therefore that one finds that $q < 1$. An important issue in comparing studies on Zipf's law is the choice of the sample size, therefore. Two strategies can be followed: (i) use a fixed number of cities (say the largest fifty) or (ii) define a threshold level below which cities will not be included in the sample.

In accounting for the different conclusions with respect to the size of the q coefficient, the definition of a city is also a very relevant factor. There are two main options for the empirical studies on city size distributions when it comes to the definition of a city. The first one is to confine the city to its legal boundaries, the so-called *city proper*. Hence the size of the city of New York is measured by the population of the legal or administrative entity called "New York City." The second option is to define the city as the urban agglomeration that is thought to constitute an economic unit and to disregard official city definitions. According to this definition, the city of New York consists of the urban agglomeration, including parts of New Jersey and Connecticut. As our own estimates of equation (7.5) show (see below), estimates based on the city proper usually result in a more evenly spread distribution of city sizes (a lower value for q) compared to urban agglomeration. This is to be expected, because the inclusion of suburbs favors the already relatively large cities. Rosen and Resnick (1980) use the city proper definition. Based on a sample of forty-four countries, their mean value for q is equal to 0.88, which certainly implies a relatively even city size distribution. Studies that find confirmation for Zipf's law are mostly based on the urban agglomeration definition of cities. A final issue to consider is the special role of the largest city, the so-called "primate" city. This issue is discussed in box 7.4.

Box 7.4 Primate cities

One reason why actual rank size distributions need not be in accordance with Zipf's law is the fact that the largest city, with rank 1, is much larger for many countries than predicted by Zipf's law. This holds for developed countries, such as Japan (Tokyo), France (Paris), or the United Kingdom (London), but it holds especially for many developing countries, where we can think of mega-cities such as São Paulo, Shanghai, Mexico City, Seoul, Lagos, and Cairo. To measure the relative size of the largest or *primate* city, urban as well as development economists use so-called primacy ratios, giving an indication of the dominance of the primate city in the urban system of a country. Following Rosen and Resnick (1980), we calculated the primacy ratio for fifty-six countries (see table 7.4 for a selection of countries with a primacy ratio equal to or above the sample mean of 0.5). The primacy ratio calculates the ratio of the size of the largest city to the sum of the size of the five largest cities.[17] For reasons of data availability we used city proper, rather than urban agglomeration, which underestimates the importance of the largest city.

As the results show, the primacy ratio is greater than 50 percent for quite a few countries. Analytically, the question is how the existence of the large primate city, particularly of mega-cities in developing countries, can be explained. Krugman and Livas Elizondo (1996) offer an interesting theoretical explanation from a geographical economics perspective. Their model loosely builds on the case of Mexico. As we noted in chapter 5 when discussing Hanson's (1997) work, wages in Mexico City are higher than in other Mexican regions. Why do firms want to locate in Mexico City despite the relatively high wages? According to the core model of geographical economics, it is because of the high demand for their products. In extensions, it is also because their main suppliers are located there. Similarly, the workers, and hence the demand, are located in Mexico City because the suppliers (the firms) are there. By now, all this will sound familiar. Krugman and Livas Elizondo (1996) argue that this line of reasoning depends on the assumption that Mexico is a *closed* economy. Suppose, however, that Mexican firms produce largely for the world market, buy their inputs on these markets, and that Mexican demand for goods is also directed at the world market. Suppose also that agglomeration is accompanied by high land rents in the center, which then acts as a spreading force. In that case, it no longer makes sense for Mexico City to be the center of production, or, in other words, for Mexico to have a disproportionately large primate city. One would expect a more even distribution of economic activity, with agglomeration in regions with good access to foreign markets (near the Mexican–US border or in sea harbors). Krugman and Livas Elizondo show that, as the economy in their model moves from a closed to an open economy, the initial stable equilibrium of full agglomeration at one location is replaced by spreading as the only stable equilibrium.

This suggests that increased openness of the economy goes hand in hand with a somewhat smaller size for the primate city. For Mexico this seems to be the case, since the change of a trade policy of import substitution towards trade liberalization has resulted in a decline in the relative importance of Mexico City. For a sample of eighty-five countries, Ades and Glaeser (1995) indeed find that higher levels of international trade usually imply a

---

[17] Other indicators of primacy are possible. The World Bank, for instance, gives the population in the largest city as a percentage of the *urban* population. For the group of low-income countries this percentage is twenty-seven, compared to fifteen for the EMU countries, and eight for the United States.

Box 7.4 (cont.)

Table 7.4 Primacy ratio, selected countries

France (1982)	0.529	United Kingdom (1994)	0.703
Austria (1991)	0.687	Egypt (1992)	0.499
Mexico (1990)	0.509	Chile (1995)	0.769
Peru (1991)	0.753	South Korea (1990)	0.532
Indonesia (1995)	0.523	Vietnam (1989)	0.570
Czech Republic (1994)	0.550	Hungary (1994)	0.726
Romania (1994)	0.605	Russia (1994)	0.504
Iran (1994)	0.556	Iraq (1987)	0.643
Sample mean	0.500		

Note: Year of observation between brackets.
Source: Own calculations based on UN data (www.un.org/Depts/unsd/demog//index/html).

smaller size for the primate city. There are two caveats. First, the direction of causality remains empirically unclear. The causality can also run from size to trade: "Concentration of population in a single city might give local firms a transport cost advantage over foreign suppliers and thus lower the amount of foreign trade" (Ades and Glaeser, 1995: 213). Second, the empirical results point to the relevance of political (non-economic) factors in explaining the existence of large primate cities. In particular, countries with a totalitarian regime have large primate cities. Under such a regime, and assuming that the primate city is also the political center of the country, firms and workers outside the primate city are at a disadvantage in case the political regime has large rents to dispense, and does not respect the economic or political rights of peripheral regions. It may then be cost-effective for workers and firms to ensure that they are located in the political center – that is, in the primate city. These political costs give an additional stimulus to the size of the primate city on top of the economic agglomeration forces. The relatively high primacy ratio in countries such as Iraq and Iran, or in the former communist countries in eastern Europe, are consistent with this line of reasoning.

Given these kinds of considerations, is there is an "optimal" degree of primacy, in the sense that it maximizes economic growth? Henderson, Shalizi, and Venables (2000: 22) argue that this is the case. According to them, for low-income countries ($1,100 per capita), middle-income countries ($4,900), and high-income countries ($13,400), the optimal degree of urban primacy (the percentage of the population in the largest city) is respectively 15 percent, 25 percent, and 23 percent. In section 7.2 we listed the sources of urban agglomeration economies, and we stated that rent seeking may help to explain the existence of (primate) cities. The Ades and Glaeser (1995) analysis builds precisely on the idea that rent seeking may account for the existence of urban giants that are thought of as being simply too large from an efficiency point of view. Henderson (2003) shows that primacy has a strong negative impact on economic growth.[18]

---

[18] A related but different question, and in line with the research discussed on shocks in chapter 6, is whether primacy is a stable outcome, in the sense of whether or not a given urban primacy structure is sensitive to shocks. Taking the dissolution of the Austro-Hungarian empire as an example of a large shock, Nitsch (2003) finds that the position of the primate city Vienna was not permanently affected by this shock therewith suggesting that the primacy of Vienna did not change.

Box 7.4 (cont.)

Finally, Puga (1998) develops a geographical economics model that can account for the relatively large size of primate cities in many developing countries. His model is similar to the core model but there are also some notable differences, such as the fact that labor can move between the manufacturing and agricultural sector, and the fact that the degree to which inter-sector labor migration occurs depends crucially on the elasticity of labor supply. Puga shows that, when transport costs are becoming very low and increasing returns to scale are relatively strong, an urban system with a large primate city develops. With relatively high transport costs and weaker economies of scale a more balanced urban system takes shape. According to Puga, the latter applies to nineteenth-century European urbanization, whereas the former applies to late twentieth-century urbanization in developing countries.

7.5.3 Estimating Zipf's law

We now turn to our own estimation results of equation (7.5), using the Gabaix–Ibragimov (2007) method and the Kratz–Resnick (1996) standard errors. All the data were collected from the United Nations website at www.un.org/Depts/unsd/demog/index.html. This website lists city sizes (the population measured by the number of inhabitants) for many countries around the world. Both "city proper" and "urban agglomeration" data are given, for all cities with at least 100,000 inhabitants. The rank size distribution was estimated for all countries with at least ten cities above this cut-off value. Depending on the data availability, we estimated equation (7.5) both for (i) city proper and (ii) urban agglomeration. Only forty-eight countries are included forty-two countries made it to the city proper list, twenty-two countries made it to the urban agglomeration list, and just sixteen countries appear on both lists. Table 7.5 gives the summary statistics for the q coefficient that resulted after estimating equation (7.5) for these forty-two countries (city proper) and twenty-two countries (urban agglomeration). More recent estimations and surveys of the Zipf results (see, in particular, Soo, 2005, and Nitsch, 2005, come to similar conclusions to ours, so for the sake of brevity we focus mainly on our own findings: our aim is simply to show that geographical economic models can explain the existence of systems of cities.

Table 7.5 shows that, for city proper, the mean value for q is clearly below one. As was to be expected, the mean q value for the urban agglomeration definition is larger than for city proper, namely 0.91 compared to 0.78. A simple t-test for differences in means shows that this difference is significant at the 1 percent level. For urban agglomerations we therefore find a value close to one – that is, close to Zipf's law. As indicated by the standard

Table 7.5 Summary statistics for rank size rule, q estimates

	City proper	Urban agglomeration
Mean	0.78	0.91
Standard error estimated q	0.160	0.177
Minimum q	0.48	0.59
Maximum q	1.19	1.22
Average R^2	0.95	0.95
Number of q observations	42	22
Number of q not Zipf (10% level)	19	2

Source: Authors' calculations; estimates based on Gabaix–Ibragimov (2007) method using Kratz–Resnick (1996) standard errors; table A7.1 provides country estimates.

deviations, however, there is considerable variation in the estimated coefficient. For city proper, the estimated coefficients range from a low of 0.48 to a high of 1.19. For urban agglomeration, the estimated coefficients range from a low of 0.59 to a high of 1.22. Figure 7.8, which gives the frequency distribution of the estimated coefficients, illustrates clearly that Zipf's law does not hold for many countries, irrespective of the city definition used – that is, q is often found to differ from one.[19] Most importantly, however, the average goodness of fit of the rank size distribution, as measured by the average R^2, is impressive: 95 percent of the variance in city sizes is explained, both for cities proper and for urban agglomeration (see table 7.5). In general, therefore the rank size distribution provides a good characterization of city size distributions.

Nitsch (2005) provides a meta-analysis of Zipf's law by analyzing twenty-nine studies (and in total 515 estimates of the q coefficient). With respect to our specification, equation (7.5), Nitsch finds that the estimates range from 0.5 to 2.04, with the mean (median) estimate being 0.9 (0.925). Almost two-thirds of the estimates are smaller than one, which thus suggests a more even city size distribution than predicted by Zipf's law. These results are in line with those shown in figure 7.8 for city proper. Estimates for urban agglomerations are, typically, closer to or statistically not different from one, which is also illustrated in figure 7.8. To summarize, more often than not the

---

[19] In view of the low number of observations for most countries, leading to high standard errors for the estimated coefficients, it is hard to discriminate between particular values of q. As table 7.5 indicates, Zipf's law is formally rejected for nineteen of the forty-two city proper estimates and two of the twenty-two urban agglomeration estimates. A similar test for a hypothesized value of $q = 0.8$ would be rejected only twice for city proper and twice, again, for urban agglomeration, while a similar hypothesized "far from the mean" value of $q = 1.2$ would be rejected only twenty-eight times for city proper and eight times for urban agglomeration.

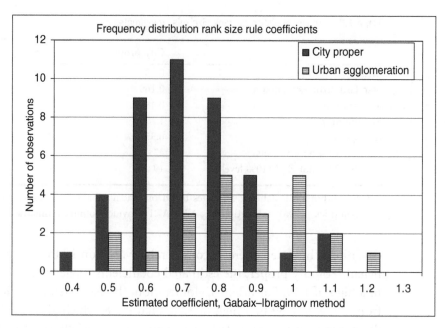

Figure 7.8   Frequency distribution of estimated q coefficients
Source: Authors's estimates; see table A7.1.

estimated coefficient q is found to be different from one. Too much attention to the value of $q = 1$ (and hence to Zipf's law) is therefore unwarranted.

This does not imply that we do not find confirmation for the rank size distribution. On the contrary, for almost every country the fit of the estimated equation is very good. The idea of a stable city size distribution across countries is no doubt confirmed by our estimations. This is illustrated in table A7.1 in the appendix to this chapter, which gives the q coefficients, the number of observations, and the R^2 for every country in our data set, both for city proper and for urban agglomerations. For the United States (on which most of the empirical research has been focused), our results are in line with Rosen and Resnick (1980) for city proper and not in line with Black and Henderson (1998) for urban agglomeration. In both these cases Zipf's law is not confirmed, whereas in our case Zipf's law is confirmed for urban agglomeration, but not for city proper. Readers interested in the individual country data, as well as full estimation results and graphical analysis for each country, are referred to the website, which also provides information on other Zipf studies and data sources.

Our country estimates for q, in line with the related studies of Soo (2005) and Nitsch (2005), point to two requirements that a theoretical explanation of the rank size distribution must meet. First, that the relationship between rank and size should be able to account for deviations from Zipf's law. This is in marked contrast with Gabaix (1999a, 1999b), Krugman (1996), and Fujita, Krugman, and Venables (1999: 216–17), who take as their starting point $q = 1$, and try to come up with a theoretical explanation of that "fact." The second, and related, requirement refers to the stability of the q coefficient over time. Our estimates, as reported in table A7.1, have little to say on this issue, because we estimated q for a single year. At most, therefore, we can discuss cross-sectional stability. Some authors put great emphasis on the fact that q hardly changes over time. Krugman (1996: 40–1), for example, concludes that "the rank size rule seems to have applied to US cities at least since 1890!" A similar observation is made by Eaton and Eckstein (1997) and Gabaix (1999a, 1999b). The idea of a constant value q over time does, of course, have different implications for a theoretical explanation than the notion, to which we adhere, that q often changes over time, as a result of structural changes in the economy. Black and Henderson (2003) present evidence for the United States that q has increased over time. In box 7.5 we show that, for Europe as a whole, the city size distribution has indeed changed over time.[20] The non-constancy of q over time implies that urban growth is not proportional (see also Parr, 1985).

7.6 Explanations for Zipf's law: the congestion model and other approaches[21]

One of the objectives of this chapter is to see whether the geographical economics approach can be used as a foundation for actual regularities in city size distributions (see section 7.1). To focus our discussion we have picked one such regularity: the rank size distribution, or Zipf's law, if $q = 1$. Since the tension between agglomerating and spreading forces is crucial in determining the spatial allocation of economic activity in geographical economics, it is clear that an attempt to explain Zipf's law based on these models must focus on this tension. In urban economics, the analytical

---

[20] A third stylized fact that a theoretical explanation for the rank size distribution should address is that the ranking of *individual* cities is not constant over time. Brakman, Garretsen, and van Marrewijk (2001: chap. 7) discuss the changes in q over time for the Netherlands. Based on a data set that spans a few hundred Italian cities for the period 1300 to 1861 (1861 was the year of Italian unification), Bosker *et al.* (2008) estimate and discuss the q coefficient and also find that q often deviates from one and is not constant over time.

[21] This section is based on Brakman *et al.* (1999).

foundation for cities and city systems (see section 7.3 and the discussion of the Henderson, 1974 model) is also based on the balance between agglomerating forces (economies of scale, such as localization economies) and spreading forces (diseconomies of scale, such as congestion costs). Both in geographical economics and in urban economics, the size of cities matters, and relative differences in city sizes must be the result of the fact that the balance between agglomerating and spreading forces differs between individual cities. In this section, we use the core model of geographical economics with congestion, as discussed in section 7.4, to explain Zipf's law.

It is clear beforehand, therefore, that we think that the tension between agglomerating and spreading forces facing each city is a useful way of thinking about city size distributions. There is, however, another route that can be taken to explain Zipf's law. This alternative route takes as its starting point the premise that the relative size of cities does *not* matter. Two main examples are the application of Simon (1955) to Zipf's law, and the use of Gibrat's law by Gabaix (1999a, 1999b) to explain Zipf's law. Before we return to the congestion model of section 7.4, we briefly discuss these two examples, mainly to bring out the differences with our explanation.[22]

7.6.1 Non-economic explanations

The basic idea of Herbert Simon (1955) is simple, the mathematics underlying the model is not.[23] Imagine a population characterized by random growth. The "newly born," who for some unexplained reason arrive in cohorts, and not one by one, may begin a new city (with probability π), or they can cling to an existing city (with probability $1-\pi$). If they cling to an existing city, the probability that they choose any particular city is proportional to the size of the population of that city. It can than be shown (provided the cohorts of newly born are neither too large nor too small) that the random growth of the population will eventually result in Zipf's law ($q = 1$). The point to emphasize is the lack of economic content in this explanation for Zipf's law, which contrasts sharply with the geographical economics approach. The size of the city, and hence the aforementioned tension between agglomerating and spreading forces, is not an issue. This also implies that changes in the rank size distribution are thought to be

---

[22] Another example is Krugman (1996a). Recent studies that build on Gabaix (1999a) are those by Juan Córdoba (2008), Jan Eeckhout (2004), Esteban Rossi-Hansberg and Mark Wright (2007), and Bosker *et al.* (2008a). For an in-depth discussion see Gabaix and Ioannides (2004).

[23] Our discussion of Simon (1955) is based on Krugman (1996a).

random. There are other difficulties; see also Fujita, Krugman, and Venables (1999: 222–3), or Gabaix (1999a: 129), who points out that "the ratio of the growth rate of the number of cities to the growth rate of the population of existing cities . . . is in reality significantly less than 1" (this ratio is assumed to be one by Simon).

Gabaix (1999a, 1999b) provides a different explanation for Zipf's law, in which the relative size of cities does not matter and the economics of city formation is not part of the explanation. He calls upon Gibrat's law, which, when applied to cities, states that the growth process of a city is independent of its size. He proves that, if every city, large or small, shares the same common mean growth rate, and if the variance of this growth rate is also the same for every city, then Zipf's law must result. Again, the point to note is that this explanation is not based on an economic model. Nevertheless, it is an interesting question as to which type of city growth model gives rise to a steady-state growth rate leading to Gibrat's law. Gabaix shows that Gibrat's law (and hence Zipf's law) results if cities are characterized either by constant returns to scale or by external economies of scale with positive and negative externalities canceling out. The latter would mean that a geographical economics model can give rise to Zipf's law only if for each city the agglomeration forces are exactly as strong as the spreading forces.[24]

There are two main problems with these explanations from the perspective of our book. First, they are not founded on a coherent framework of economic principles. Second, they do not meet the requirements for an explanation of the empirical city size distribution as formulated at the end of section 7.5, namely that the explanation must take account of the fact that q often deviates from one, and that q can change over time. Both Simon's model and the approach of Gabaix using Gibrat's law predict that

---

[24] The idea of associating Gibrat's law with the rank size distribution for city size, or also for firm size, is, as such, not new for economists (see Sutton, 1997) or geographers. As to the latter, see, for instance, the economic geography textbook by Dicken and Lloyd (1980). This association was very partial, sketchy, and incomplete at best, however, not least when it came down to using Gibrat's law to understand rank size distribution – or, more specifically, Zipf's law for cities. It is really thanks to the seminal work by Gabaix (1999b) that we now have a firm theoretical foundation for this matter. He has shown, building on Simon (1955), that a stable city size distribution according to Zipf's law in the upper tail of the distribution results naturally if the individual city growth process adheres to what is essentially Gibrat's Law of proportional effect – i.e. a city's growth rate and the variance of that growth rate are independent of the initial city size. All recent work on cities and Zipf's law (see footnote 22) builds on Gabaix (1999a, 1999b). The assumption that the variance of the growth rate is the same for every city has been criticized by Fujita, Krugman, and Venables (1999: 224), who argue that this variance must be larger for smaller, less diversified cities. Gabaix (1999b) agrees with this point, but says that this is precisely why the rank size distribution does not hold in the lower tail of the city size distribution. Dobkins and Ioannides (2001) do not find empirical support for the "uniform variance" assumption.

$q = 1$. The explanation we want to offer instead is based on the congestion model of section 7.4. In a nutshell, this explanation combines the geographical economics approach with modern urban economics, in which the spreading force arises from the congestion costs associated with urban agglomeration. This additional spreading force is important to ensure that the geographical economics approach can reasonably explain city size distributions. Fujita, Krugman, and Venables (1999: chap. 11), for example, develop an intricate urban hierarchy model – in fact, a central place model, as we have already noted in subsection 7.5.1. Simulations with this model, however, give rise to city size distributions that clearly do not match the empirical facts discussed in the previous section.[25]

As we show, this is no longer true when the balance between agglomeration and spreading forces is altered by the introduction of congestion. To illustrate the merits of the model for a discussion on city size distributions, we use the actual history of European urbanization as our benchmark (see box 7.5).

Before we turn to the case of European cites, it is important to be clear that we do not want to claim that our congestion model is the only possible economic explanation (as opposed to the Simon–Gabaix analysis) for the rank size distribution; see, for instance, the urban economics models by Black and Henderson (1999b) and Eaton and Eckstein (1997), as discussed in subsection 7.5.1, or Duranton (2006). The latter study uses an endogenous growth model in which individual cities grow or shrink following new innovations. Using French and US data, his model replicates the actual city size distributions (and the changing position of cities in these distributions) quite well. Since our book is on geographical economics, our main goal is to see if this particular economic model, our core model with congestion, is able to deal with the stylized facts about the rank size distribution.

---

[25] This is also acknowledged by Fujita, Krugman, and Venables (1999: 217; see in particular their figure 12.2). The central place model in Fujita, Krugman, and Venables (1999) is based on Fujita, Krugman, and Mori (1999). The basic idea can be understood as follows. Suppose we add to our core model of chapters 3 and 4 such that, instead of one manufacturing good (which is produced in many varieties, one variety per firm), we now have two of these manufacturing goods. Suppose also that the first manufacturing good consists of many highly differentiated varieties with a low elasticity of substitution and the second good consists of varieties that are close substitutes – i.e. have a high substitution elasticity. It can be shown that, *ceteris paribus*, the first good will be produced at a single location (the largest or central city) whereas the second good will be produced at both locations. Extending this idea to a large number of locations and a large number of manufactured goods (with a different substitution elasticity) leads to a hierarchy of locations, as in Christaller's central place theory, in which the largest or central location produces all the manufacturing goods, and the locations underneath it in the hierarchy produce only the good with the highest substitution elasticity.

Box 7.5 The rank size rule over time in Europe

Although large cities arose earliest in Africa (Memphis, Egypt) and Asia (Akkad, Lagash, and Ur in Babylonia), Europe was the earliest intensively urbanized continent. Pim Kooij (1988) distinguishes three stylized periods of urbanization in Europe, which will be used below in the main text in the simulations of the rank size distributions.

(i) *Pre-industrialization; around 1600–1850.* Characterized by high transport costs and production dominated by immobile farmers. In this period there was not really an integrated urban system. The industrialization process had yet to begin and the relatively high transport costs between cities is thought to be the main cause for the lack of an urban system.

(ii) *Industrialization; around 1850–1900.* Characterized by declining transport costs and the increasing importance of "footloose" industrial production with increasing returns to scale. In the second half of the nineteenth century an integrated urban system was formed. Two interdependent economic changes were mainly responsible for this formation. First, the development of canals, a railroad network, and, to a lesser extent, roads significantly lowered transport costs between cities, which in turn enhanced trade between cities. Second, due to the lower transport costs, the industrialization process really took off (starting in England), and cities often became more specialized, which also stimulated trade between cities.

(iii) *Post-industrialization; around 1900–present.* Characterized by the declining importance of industrial production, and the increased importance of negative externalities, such as congestion. Structural changes in the rank size distribution take decades to materialize, so it was only well into the twentieth century that the industrialized countries gradually entered the post-industrialization era. The share of the services sector in total employment becomes ever more important, at the expense of the footloose industrial sector.

Figure 7.9 provides the rank size distribution for Europe in the period 1500–1800, identifying the three largest cities and the ranking of Amsterdam in particular. The rank size distribution was relatively flat in 1500, with $q = 0.56$ and Amsterdam as a small city. There is little change in the distribution to 1600, with $q = 0.60$, although Amsterdam has become considerably more important. More substantial change occurs in the periods up to 1700 and 1800, the era leading up to the Industrial Revolution, with $q = 0.77$ and $q = 0.87$ respectively. London becomes the most important city, while Amsterdam's relative peak is reached around 1700. The city size distribution becomes more unequal, which is a process continuing up to around 1900, after which a decline in the skewness of the distrbution (lower q) takes place.

We conclude this brief discussion by noting that the industrialization period was special in its power of agglomeration, as noted by Kooij (1988: 363): "This was the era of the large cities." For all three of his stylized urbanization periods, however, the rank size distribution holds. Finally note that these three periods, in which changes in economic variables demonstrably have an impact on the rank size distribution, enable us to simulate the impact of these changes with the core model of geographical economics with congestion (see subsection 7.6.2).

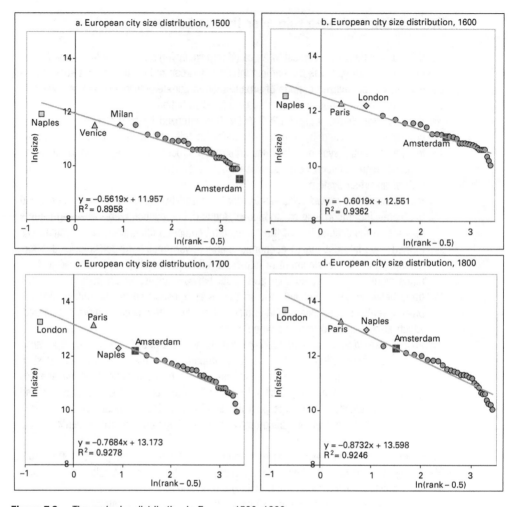

Figure 7.9   The rank size distribution in Europe, 1500–1800
Source: Authors' calculations based on de Vries (1984: 270–7), Gabaix-Ibragimov (2007).

7.6.2 Simulating Zipf using the core model with congestion

To mimic the rank size distribution using the core model with congestion, we start with twenty-four cities located on the racetrack economy. Initially, each city receives a random share of the manufacturing labor force. Furthermore, in the subsequent analysis we include only cities with a long-run manufacturing sector; pure agricultural areas are not included as they do not represent a city. In this respect, the number of cities is endogenous (but at most twenty-four). The rest of the model used to simulate the rank size

distribution is exactly the same as the model discussed in section 7.4.[26]
Based on the three stylized periods of urbanization for Europe, as discussed
in box 7.5, we now change the economic parameters in our model for each
of these three periods, which may help to explain changes in the rank size
distribution over time.

First comes the *pre-industrialization* period. The small manufacturing
sector in this period produces close substitutes, and production is dominated by immobile farmers. We simulate the small manufacturing sector by
choosing a relatively high value for the share of agricultural workers in the
total labor force $(1 - \delta = 0.5)$. The manufacturing sector is homogeneous
(i.e. it does not yet produce many varieties), represented by choosing a
relatively high value for the elasticity of substitution between varieties
$(\varepsilon = 6$; this simultaneously implies that increasing returns to scale are
relatively unimportant – see chapter 3). The low level of regional integration
(high transport costs) is described by choosing $T = 2$. Negative economies
of scale are not very important in this period, but, equally, they are not
absent (think of the disease-ridden large cities in the Middle Ages), which is
simulated by choosing a moderate value for τ: $\tau = 0.2$.

The second period is referred to as the period of *industrialization*. The
basic characteristic in this period is the spectacular decrease in transport
costs and the increasing importance of "footloose" manufacturing production with increasing returns to scale. At the same time negative externalities are not absent, but also not very important, in the sense of
preventing large cities becoming even larger. In the model we simulate these
factors by lowering transport costs to $T = 1.25$, and increasing the share of
the manufacturing labor force in total employment, to $\delta = 0.6$. The
increased importance of economies of scale and differentiated manufacturing products is represented by choosing $\varepsilon = 4$. In this period the strong
industrialization leads to the disappearance of somewhat smaller cities. This
corresponds with the idea that agglomerating forces dominate during the
era of big-city growth.

The last period is called *post-industrialization*. In this period transport
costs remain low and, as before, the manufacturing sector is characterized
by differentiated products and increasing returns to scale. The notable
difference from earlier periods is congestion, such as the growing traffic
jams, air pollution, rising land rents in larger cities, etc. Smaller cities are
less troubled by such effects and therefore have a tendency to grow more

---

[26] The specification for the production function in the simulations is $l_{ir} = aN_r^{\tau/(1-\tau)} + \beta x_i$.

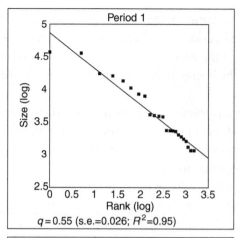

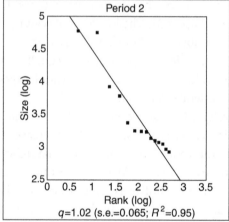

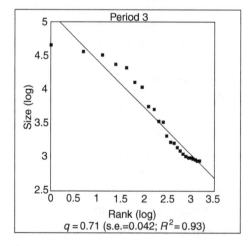

Figure 7.10 Simulating Zipf

rapidly. In the model we simulate this by increasing the congestion parameter τ to $\tau = 1/3$.

Figure 7.10 presents the simulation results for the above three periods. At least 93 percent of the variance in city size is explained by the rank size distribution. More importantly, these simulations suggest that the n-shaped pattern of q over time, identified by John Parr (1985), depends on the economic parameter changes. According to this pattern, economic development starts off with q well below one. As economic development gathers pace, q increases. When the economy matures q starts to decrease. With the congestion version of the core geographical economics model, actual rank size distributions can thus in principle be reproduced by varying those model parameters that have been identified in the literature to be relevant for understanding the changes in the size distribution of cities. However basic, this is more or less the first attempt to explicitly use a geographical economics model to study empirically testable aspects of the urban system (see Gabaix and Ioannides, 2004: 2363–4 for this assessment).[27]

7.7 Conclusions

We have investigated if and how the geographical economics approach can be applied to cities and urban systems. After a brief survey of the sources and scope of urban agglomeration economies, we used the framework of Combes, Duranton, and Overman (2005) to analyze and compare the core urban systems model and our core model of geographical economics. We concluded that the two models are not incompatible but should be looked upon as applying to different spatial scales. A key element of the urban systems model is the presence of congestion or crowding effects that are a function of the overall size of the city. This basic idea about the role of congestion was then added to our core model of geographical economics of chapter 3 to permit an application to city size distributions.

In the second part of this chapter we added an additional spreading force, congestion, to the core model of geographical economics. This extension came about by changing the production structure of the core model. The introduction of congestion as an additional spreading force served two main

---

[27] Two further questions to which figure 7.10 gives rise are these. (i) Is the rank size distribution (or Zipf) a structural outcome of the congestion model? (ii) What happens if one allows for non-neutral space (instead of our racetrack depiction of space)? See Brakman *et al.* (1999) for an answer to both questions.

aims. The first was to clarify the impact of congestion on the nature of the long-run equilibria. With congestion, the model typically results in a more even equilibrium allocation of the manufacturing labor force. Complete agglomeration is now the exception and not – as in the core model – the rule. The second aim was to apply the geographical economics model with congestion to an important topic in urban economics: the stability of city size distributions. We showed that the extended model can replicate (changes in) actual rank size distributions. This shows that geographical economics can be useful for studying urban economics, even though it is not a full-fledged model of urban economics. In fact, the usefulness of (adaptations of) the core model of geographical economics for urban economics is thought to be limited by some observers (see Henderson, 2000). We return to this topic in chapter 12.

The analysis in this chapter is also not the last word on Zipf's law, if only because our model, like all other economic explanations, merely *simulates* the rank size distribution. One obvious shortcoming of the congestion model (and the geographical economics models discussed so far) is its static nature. The question of how geographical economics can be used to analyze (urban) economic growth is dealt with in chapter 10.

Appendix

The table below summarizes the information for every country in our data set. See also the book's web site.

Table A7.1 Country overview of rank size distribution estimates

Country	City proper			Urban agglomeration		
	q	R^2	Observations	q	R^2	observations
Argentina	0.7964	0.9407	32	1.1672	0.9614	15
Australia	1.1926	0.8998	14	1.2218	0.8484	12
Bangladesh				1.0072	0.9694	18
Belarus	0.8211	0.9648	13			
Belgium	0.6187	0.9592	10	0.8302	0.9417	11
Brazil	0.7815*	0.9956	193			
Bulgaria	0.8129	0.9871	10	0.7653	0.9727	10
Canada	0.6592*	0.8913	36	1.0072	0.9655	30
Chile	0.7789	0.8608	20			

	City proper			Urban agglomeration		
Country	q	R^2	Observations	q	R^2	observations
China	0.8011*	0.8787	371			
Colombia				0.9605	0.9743	28
Congo	0.8979	0.9720	12			
Ecuador	0.9521	0.8763	10			
Egypt	1.0636	0.9649	23			
Ethiopia	0.8955	0.7863	10			
France	0.6250*	0.9759	35	0.8483	0.9658	38
Germany	0.7174*	0.9822	84			
India	0.8516*	0.9840	300	1.0009	0.9849	175
Indonesia	0.9993	0.9689	50			
Iran	0.8792	0.9865	46			
Iraq	0.7143	0.9225	18			
Israel	0.5129*	0.9594	12			
Italy				0.7945	0.9887	52
Japan	0.7234*	0.9858	217			
Kazakhstan	0.5960*	0.9397	21	0.5949*	0.9580	20
Korea	1.1126	0.9871	39			
Malaysia	0.6576	0.8438	13	0.5857	0.9693	11
Mexico	0.8257	0.9682	72			
Morocco				0.8969	0.9777	16
Netherlands	0.5767*	0.9447	21	0.6558	0.9403	21
Nigeria	0.5453*	0.9459	27			
Pakistan				1.1169	0.9676	23
Peru	0.9933	0.9266	17			
Philippines	0.6615*	0.9689	62			
Poland	0.6742*	0.9827	42			
Romania	0.6167*	0.8949	25			
Russia	0.7806*	0.9588	168	0.8134*	0.9537	104
South Africa	0.6121*	0.9399	32			
Spain	0.6789*	0.9865	55			
Sweden	0.7022	0.9483	11	0.7372	0.9539	11
Thailand				1.0845	0.8178	11
Turkey	0.9387	0.9944	47	0.8117	0.9864	38
Ukraine	0.7852	0.9473	50			
United Kingdom	0.4811*	0.9556	234			
United States	0.7245*	0.9936	209	1.0328	0.9313	115
Uzbekistan	0.7689	0.9361	15			
Venezuela	0.8253	0.9677	28	0.9925	0.9509	16
Vietnam	0.9044	0.9810	23	0.9992	0.9271	23

Note: * = significantly different from one (10% level).
Sources: Authors' calculations, Gabaix–Ibragimov estimates.

Exercises

7.1 Below we repeat the three equilibrium equations for the model with congestion (the symbols have the same meaning as in the main text).

$$Y_r = \delta \lambda_r W_r + (1 - \delta)\phi_r \tag{1}$$

$$I_r = \left[\sum_{s=1}^{R} \lambda_s^{1-\tau\varepsilon} T_{rs}^{1-\varepsilon} W_s^{1-\varepsilon} \right]^{1/(1-\varepsilon)} \tag{2}$$

$$W_r = \lambda_r^{-\tau} \left[\sum_{s=1}^{R} Y_s T_{sr}^{1-\varepsilon} I_s^{\varepsilon-1} \right]^{1/\varepsilon} \tag{3}$$

(i) Explain the differences with the model without congestion.

(ii) Assume that $0 < \tau < 1$. Explain what increased agglomeration in region r implies for wages in this region.

(iii) Why can the congestion model, as opposed to the core model, in principle be used to explain stylized facts about city size distributions?

(iv) Suppose Zipf's law holds for country X at period t and this country is hit by a large, temporary, and exogenous shock during period $t+1$. What does the geographical economics approach predict will happen to the city size distribution of this country after the shock?

7.2* Explain why equation (7.1), with τ unequal to zero, displays *external* economies of scale. Also explain why, irrespective of the value of τ, equation (7.1) is characterized by internal economies of scale as well.

7.3 One possible criticism of the application of our multiple region model with congestion costs to urban systems is that it cannot deal with the evolution of these systems in *frontier states* such as the United States. Another possible criticism is that the model of chapter 7 cannot deal with urban growth. Address both criticisms.

7.4 Go to the website for this book. Compare the rank size distributions (using the city proper definition) for developing countries with those for the developed countries, and give possible explanations for the relative difference in the importance of primate cities in these countries.

7.5* What would happen in terms of core–periphery equilibria if in equation (7.1) we chose $-1 < \tau < 0$?

7.6* Compared to the core model of chapters 3 and 4, the two-region model with congestion costs tends to favor spreading instead of complete agglomeration. The main reason why this is the case is very similar to the housing model of geographical economics due to Helpman (1998) and discussed in chapters 5 and 6. In box 7.1 some information on the difference of housing prices across city sizes was given. Explain what you expect the corresponding differences in nominal as well real wages to be between these cities.

7.7 Take the case of American cities and suppose you were asked to explain growth differences between these cities from either one of the following two classes of externalities:
• Marshallian externalities (or, in a static sense, from localization externalities); or
• Jacobs externalities (or, in a static sense, from urbanization externalities).
What kind of explanatory factors or variables would you look for (you may pick one of these two views)?
    Hint: check Glaeser *et al.* (1992) for inspiration, and in doing so also note a third class of externalities.

7.8 Use the diagrammatic representation of the core model of geographical economics (see figure 7.4) and discuss whether the congestion model of geographical economics is aptly summarized by these two graphs.

7.9 Use the diagrammatic representation of the core urban systems model of Henderson, 1974 (see figure 7.3) and discuss whether this representation of the model would have to be changed if urbanization economies were included.

7.10 Consider the following statement:

In the congestion model of chapter 7, the resulting production structure is such that both internal and external increasing returns to scale are included.

Is this statement true or false? (Right answer: go to chapter 8; wrong answer: go to jail.)

8 Agglomeration and international business

8.1 Introduction

Globalization has many faces. Perhaps the most salient feature of globalization is that it appears that the world becomes smaller as transport costs are reduced, trade barriers disappear, the exchange of information becomes less expensive, and information itself becomes an internationally traded good. According to some commentators, such as Thomas Friedman (2005), the world has even become flat. Although a more even spreading of economic activity is certainly possible, the geographical economics approach also indicates that globalization or economic integration in general may imply a spiky or lumpy world with a growing income gap between rich and poor nations, and in which, due to decreases in trade costs, center–periphery structures become the rule instead of the exception.

Among the major actors in the present era of globalization are no doubt the multinational enterprises, or multinationals for short. These firms are probably the most mobile among all firms, with sufficient "international" knowledge to seize a profitable opportunity when it presents itself. Without specific cultural ties to individual nations, they can seemingly move in and out of countries rapidly, with only economic incentives to act upon. The footloose nature of multinationals is strengthened by the fact that such firms increasingly no longer produce "under a single roof." Baldwin (2006) calls this process "the second unbundling." The first unbundling was initiated by the transportation revolution of the first Industrial Revolution (1750–1900), which made it possible to spatially separate production from consumption, thereby facilitating international specialization on an unprecedented scale. The second unbundling really took off after 1980, and spatially separates the different stages of the production process itself. Various parts of the production process can be relocated to wherever they can be carried out most productively. The main investment vehicle for multinational firms is foreign direct investment, and the decision whether or not to engage in FDI and how this interacts with agglomeration will be the main topic of this chapter.

Given the recent growth in FDI, which for some years now has outpaced the growth of international trade and GDP, one might a priori expect multinational firms to be decisive in at least some of the agglomeration and spreading trends going on today. It turns out that geographical economics provides an excellent and promising analytical framework to look at multinationals. Building on the general equilibrium models developed by Helpman and Krugman (1985) and James Markusen (2002), as well as on more recent trade theories based on the concept of heterogeneous firms, such as those of Marc Melitz (2003) and Helpman (2006), this new approach provides an improvement upon the useful, but limited, taxonomic OLI (ownership, location, internalization) framework of John Dunning, (1977, 1981) (see section 8.3).

In chapter 4 we explained how the introduction of intermediate goods can change the mechanisms leading to spreading or agglomeration. Instead of labor, firms were assumed to be mobile in the intermediate goods model of section 4.6. In this model, agglomeration can come about if workers move to other sectors; in other words, workers are immobile between regions or countries, but mobile within those regions and countries. The model does not yet incorporate the decisions of firms to set up (part of their) production in another region or country. This is the task of this chapter. In section 8.2 we present some stylized facts of multinational production. Section 8.3 discusses recent developments in explaining multinational production. Section 8.4 studies a more formal modeling approach, using the framework of geographical economics. Section 8.5 presents some (indirect) evidence on the relevance of multinationals. Finally, section 8.6 concludes.

8.2 Multinational production: stylized facts

Geography has traditionally been a very important factor in describing and explaining the behavior of multinationals, and in describing the flows of FDI. It is clear that the location choice of headquarters or production facilities, or both, is critical in describing multinational production. Firms have the ability to relocate, and therefore have to decide where to locate a particular part of the firm. Data on multinationals are notoriously difficult to obtain, not just because of the obvious availability problem but also due to conceptual difficulties. A multinational is a firm that controls, by means of ownership, productive assets in more than one country. Ownership and control may be anywhere between 0 percent and 100 percent, however. It is a matter of definition, therefore, when one speaks of "multinationals" (see Barba Navaretti and Venables, 2004: appendix A).[1] Data on FDI are systematically collected by the United Nations Conference on Trade and Development (UNCTAD) and the World Bank, thereby providing the best sources for data on FDI. They show that, since the 1980s, FDI has grown astonishingly rapidly – even more rapidly than international trade. This is illustrated in figure 8.1a.

On average, worldwide nominal GDP has grown more than 7 percent per year between 1970 and 1997. During this period international trade, measured by worldwide nominal imports, grew more than 12 percent, whereas nominal FDI grew almost 31 percent. Not only has total FDI increased, however, but the composition of FDI has changed as well, as FDI in manufacturing became less important and FDI in services became more so. Furthermore, FDI increasingly takes place in the form of cross-border mergers and acquisitions (M&As). At present, more than 75 percent of all FDI is in the form of cross-border M&As, and greenfield FDI is far less important; see figure 8.1b.

Not all types of firms seem to become a multinational. We can distinguish four characteristics. Multinationals (i) appear to be concentrated in industries that are characterized by a high ratio of R&D relative to sales, (ii) tend to have high values of intangible assets, (iii) are often associated with new or technologically advanced and differentiated products, and (iv) are often relatively old, large, and more established firms within their sector (see Markusen, 2002, or Barba Navaretti and Venables, 2004: chap. 2). More generally, see Helpman (2006) or Andrew Bernard, Bradford Jensen, Redding, and Peter Schott (2007). Within every sector, only a very small percentage of firms is active in a foreign country (either through trade or FDI).

---

[1] The International Monetary Fund (IMF) and the OECD recommend a share of 50 percent or more as a cut-off criterion for defining control. In practice, however, having less than 50 percent of the shares can also imply control if one party owns, say, 10 percent, of the shares but the rest are scattered over thousands of other shareholders. The US Bureau of Economic Analysis distinguishes majority-owned foreign subsidiaries of US parents from affiliates, which have at least 10 percent non-US ownership. Clearly, these criteria are open to discussion.

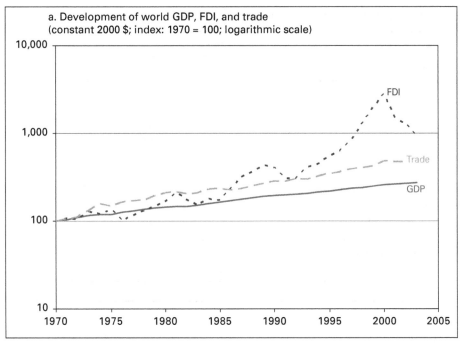

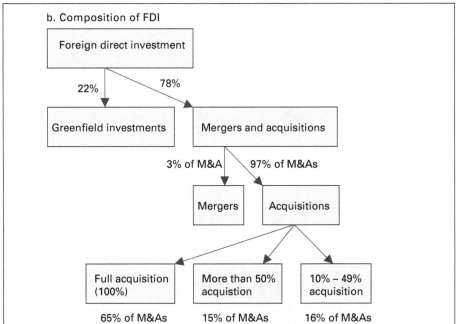

Figure 8.1   Development and composition of FDI, 1970–2005
Sources: Panel a – World Bank Development Indicators CD-ROM; panel b – van Marrewijk (2007).

Table 8.1 Distribution of FDI, by region and selected countries, 1978–2005

	Inflow			
Region	1978–80	1988–90	1998–2000	2003–5
Developed economies	79.7	82.5	77.3	59.4
European Union	39.1	40.3	46.0	40.7
Japan	0.4	0.04	0.8	0.8
United States	23.8	31.5	24.0	12.6
Developing economies	20.3	17.5	21.7	35.9
Africa	2.0	1.9	1.0	3.0
Latin America and Caribbean	13.0	5.0	9.7	11.5
Asia and Oceania	5.3	10.5	11.0	21.4
Middle East	−1.6	0.3	0.3	3.0
South, east, and south-east Asia	6.7	10.0	10.7	18.4
South-east Europe and CIS	0.02	0.02	0.9	4.7
World	100	100	100	100

	Outflow			
Region	1978–80	1988–90	1998–2000	2003–5
Developed economies	97.0	93.1	90.4	85.8
European Union	44.8	50.6	64.4	54.6
Japan	4.9	19.7	2.6	4.9
United States	39.7	13.6	15.9	15.7
Developing economies	3.0	6.9	9.4	12.3
Africa	1.0	0.4	0.2	0.2
Latin America and Caribbean	1.1	1.0	4.1	3.5
Asia and Oceania	0.9	5.6	5.1	8.6
Middle East	0.3	0.5	0.1	1.0
South, east, and south-east Asia	0.6	5.1	5.0	7.7
South-east Europe and CIS	–	0.01	0.2	1.8
World	100	100	100	100

Note: CIS is the Confederation of Independent States, the countries of the former Soviet Union.
Source: UNCTAD (2006).

Only the most productive firms engage in trade or FDI. The heterogeneity among firms is pervasive in this respect.

As shown in table 8.1, the predominant source *and* destination of FDI are the high-income developed countries. The topsection of table 8.1 gives FDI outflows and thus the source countries of FDI for the period from 1978 to

Table 8.2 Location and organization decisions

		Location decision	
		Home	Foreign
Organization decision	In-sourcing	Domestic in-sourcing	FDI
	Outsourcing	Domestic outsourcing	Foreign outsourcing (offshoring)

Note: If the firm relocates to the foreign market, we could have foreign in-sourcing.

2005, whereas the bottom half of the table does the same for FDI inflows and the destination countries of FDI. Between 1978 and 2000 the developed countries accounted for more than 90 percent of FDI outflows. The main destinations of FDI are also the advanced countries. Between 1978 and 2000 they received some 80 percent of FDI inflows. As such, these data reflect what also holds for inter- and intra-industry trade, namely that most economic interaction takes place between the developed countries (see also chapter 9). Most of these observations can be explained, of course, by the differences in economic size between developed and developing countries.

What is interesting on the basis of table 8.1 is that we can already draw some conclusions about the nature of FDI. First, the fact that most FDI flows are between developed countries already suggests that the fear that, because of FDI by domestic firms, many jobs are being "exported" to developing or low-wage countries is often an exaggeration. Second, and notwithstanding the first conclusion, although the developed countries are still the main source and destination of FDI flows, table 8.1 also reveals that between 2003 and 2005 the developing countries experienced a rapid increase in FDI inflows: from 21.7 percent in the period 1998 to 2000 to 35.9 percent. This increase suggests that, despite the first conclusion, we might expect some changes in the future distribution of FDI flows around the world. Note also that developing countries seem to be becoming more important as source countries of FDI.

What are the main decisions for a firm when it contemplates making an investment? The modern FDI literature (Bhagwati, Panagariya, and Srinivasan, 2004; Helpman, 2006) indicates that two basic decisions need to be made: the location and the organization decision. This gives us four possibilities, as table 8.2 shows. Firms can either in-source (within-firm investment) or outsource; this is the organization decision. Firms must also decide where to invest, in the home country or in a foreign country; this is the location decision.

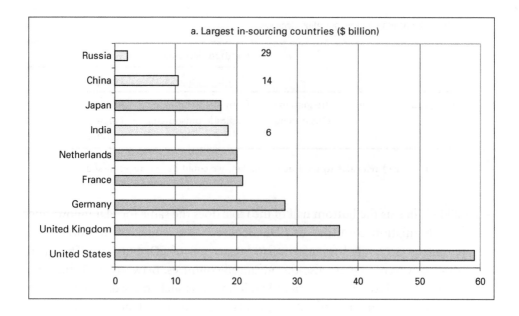

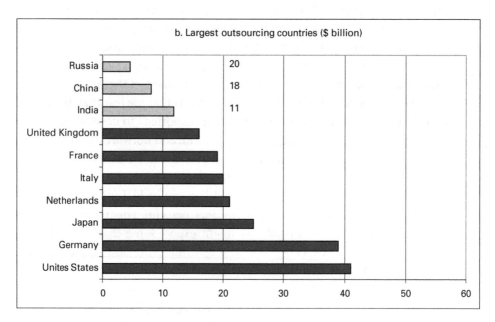

Figure 8.2   Largest in- and outsourcing countries, 2002
Source: Amiti and Wei (2005).

For our present purposes, for which we want to investigate the relationship between agglomeration and international business, we are primarily interested in the location decision (home versus foreign investment), and not in the organization decision. Table 8.2 illustrates that, besides FDI, multinationals can also invest abroad by engaging in foreign outsourcing. The conceptual difference between FDI and foreign outsourcing is that, with FDI, the investment abroad is within-firm investment: the foreign production facility is owned by the multinational. This is not the case with foreign outsourcing. In practice, the difference between FDI and foreign outsourcing is not always razor sharp (see also Amiti and Wei, 2005).

Figure 8.2 gives a ranking of the largest in- and outsourcing countries in US dollar terms. The rank numbers of relative low-wage economies – Russia, China, and India – are indicated separately in the figure. Figure 8.2 shows that the United States and the United Kingdom, and also a small country such as the Netherlands, are among the largest in- and outsourcing countries. With respect to in-sourcing (and bearing in mind the fears in OECD countries that "our" jobs are being outsourced to India and China), it is clear that emerging economies such as India and China are still less important compared to many of the most developed countries as a destination for outsourcing. Note also from panel b, however, that India and China themselves are already among the list of largest outsourcing countries. What holds for FDI also holds for in- and outsourcing; these foreign investments are not a one-way street. Countries are typically involved both as source and as destination countries.

Having established these basic facts about FDI and outsourcing, and given our focus on the location decision where by, despite their difference in terms of ownership, we broadly group FDI and outsourcing together under the heading of foreign investment, the task is in the remainder of this chapter to analyze two basic questions. First, what explains the existence of multinational production (section 8.3)? Second, how can we analyze the relationship between agglomeration (the key concept in geographical economics!) and multinational production (section 8.4)?

8.3 Explaining multinational production

The field of international economics mostly studies trade in goods, though the focus has shifted somewhat more to services recently. Indeed, the central lesson of the neoclassical workhorse model of international trade theory, the factor abundance model, suggests that trade in goods and trade in production factors are substitutes (see chapter 2).[2] In general, however, this is true only for the simple model with two countries, two factors of production, and two goods, without transport costs and with factor endowments that are not too different between countries. In most other cases, trade in goods and trade in production factors might be complements (see, for example, Wong, 1986). The implication is that, even in the neoclassical factor abundance model, it is worthwhile to look at the effects of trade in production factors, of which FDI represents a special case.

The existence of multinationals influences the behavior of variables such as the volume of trade and the share of intra-industry trade. It was not trade theory that first tried to explain the existence of multinationals, however, but the industrial organization literature. The best example of the latter is still the OLI approach of Dunning (1977, 1981). According to Dunning (1977) three conditions need to be satisfied in order for a firm to become a multinational. These three conditions are known as OLI: ownership advantage, location advantage, and internalization advantage. Ownership advantage means that a firm has a product that enjoys some market power in foreign markets; location advantage implies that a foreign location offers more profits than a home location; internalization advantage makes it more profitable for a firm to exploit the product itself than to license it to a foreign firm.

The OLI methodology has been extended in various directions, mostly concentrating on better data and more advanced tests. For good surveys, see again Markusen (2002) or Giorglo Barba Navaretti and Venables (2004). Basically, in this type of literature, variables describing existing multinationals are correlated with variables that represent the O, the L, or the I (in one form or another) of the OLI model. This method – and the same is true for the work of the highly influential business guru Michael Porter (see box 8.1) – provides a useful categorization scheme of variables and gives clues as to what set of variables best characterizes multinationals.[3] It is at best a partial equilibrium approach, which focuses on the characteristics of individual firms, or even plants, but does not explain why or how multinationals come about, or answer the question of what triggers multinational behavior in the

---

[2] With respect to capital flows, this result comes from the seminal contribution of Robert Mundell (1957).

[3] Among the frequently mentioned variables are knowledge capital, which can easily be transported or transferred, large trade barriers of one kind or another, and less expensive inputs in other countries.

first place. This is in sharp contrast with the modern theories of multi-nationals.[4]

Box 8.1 Michael Porter

The OLI literature has provided useful insights into the factors that determine the decision to become a multinational firm. In the management literature one can also find lists describing essential elements of multinationals. The management literature has seemed to develop more or less separately from the economics literature, however. The most famous example of this phenomenon is Michael Porter, the management superstar and writer of the best-selling *Competitive Advantage: Creating and Sustaining Superior Performance*. He produces impressive lists of characteristics of firms and regions, and suggests how they influence each other. The term "competitiveness" is central in his analysis. According to Porter, competitiveness is the ability to innovate and to improve processes and products. Local competition is important, and even necessary, for international success. Case study analyses serve to reinforce his point.

Multinationals can compete only when they have a strong position in their home market. Sales are most easy to multinationalize, according to Porter. R&D, on the other hand, is much harder to multinationalize. He notes that businesses are becoming more global, which introduces greater competition in each country. From his research, Porter concludes that the conditions at a company's home base are crucial for its competitiveness abroad. In particular, innovative vitality appears to be established at home. Moreover, geographical clusters of activity seem to be very important. In his *Harvard Business Review* article of 1998, he lists very familiar factors determining the success of clusters. Basically, his list comprises the forward and backward linkages already described by Marshall and the classical geographers (as has been discussed in chapters 2 and 7). He does not analyze why these clusters establish themselves or how they evolve from the characteristics he identifies. His analysis seems to give expost rationalizations of clusters. Once a cluster is successful, firms can try to establish themselves as multinationals.

Why is it that some countries are wealthier than other countries, and that some industries are more successful than other industries? According to Porter, location also matters. Not because of "location" advantages, as in the OLI literature, but because rivalry stimulates "innovation," and most competition occurs among competitors that are geographically concentrated. These clusters of excellence could be defined as a city, a region, or a continent, but nations are the most important level of aggregation. On this level, demand conditions are affected by macroeconomic policy; the dynamism of competition by national antitrust and trade policy; the level and type of skills by the national education

---

[4] A somewhat separate strand of literature stresses strategic oligopolistic interaction between firms. In such models one can show, for example, that, because of strategic interaction between firms, foreign production is the preferred option even when cost considerations might suggest that exporting is more profitable. We do not discuss this strand of literature, because it precludes agglomeration or spreading, the central topic of this book (see, for instance, Venables, 1985, or Horstman and Markusen, 1986).

Box 8.1 (cont.)

system; and the attitudes of managers, workers, and customers by a national culture. A global strategy merely supplements the competitive advantage created in the home base. National success creates the opportunity to cross borders. It is crucial that companies cling onto those virtues when they expand abroad. Going global comes from "home."

Although the elements Porter puts forward are familiar, and his analysis lists relevant factors, he does not give causal relationships between all the characteristics, nor discuss the sense in which they influence each other, the choice between exporting or going multinational, or how the difference between horizontal and vertically differentiated multinationals is established. In a sense, Porter returns to the state of affairs of the 1950s, when Myrdal was discussing issues such as cumulative causation, but was unable, at that time, to formalize his ideas into a consistent model (see also Duranton, 2007, who criticizes Porter's idea of clusters). Without some form of model, the lists that Porter produces are best seen as good starting points for further analysis, into which factors determine the "competitiveness" of firms and which factors are most relevant. In this respect (and the reader may now want to fast-forward to box 12.1), it is interesting to note that Krugman developed his core model of geographical economics (1991a) as a response to Porter's work.

8.3.1 Multinationals in trade theory

Modern theories of multinational firms try to model the behavior of firms, and identify under which circumstances they become multinational. Focusing as we do here on the *location decision*, there are basically two reasons for a firm to go multinational: one is to serve a foreign market more profitably from the foreign location, and the second is because the foreign market provides lower-cost inputs. The first reason to become multinational is associated with so-called *horizontal* multinationals. They simply duplicate their business in a foreign country, because the local provision of goods is more profitable. It usually substitutes for exports from the home country. So-called *vertical* multinationals, on the other hand, are in the business of "slicing up the value chain." The idea is that different stages of the production process can be made more cost-efficient by relocating them to a low-cost location. This type of multinational behavior is complementary to trade and usually trade-creating, because the (intermediate) products from different countries have to be shipped to other countries in order to be assembled. A brief case study was given in chapter 1, when discussing the hard disk drive industry. The distinction is not always very clear, as vertically differentiated firms might also sell to foreign markets.

The by now classic theory of vertically differentiated multinationals has been developed primarily by Helpman (1984a) and Helpman and Krugman (1985). At its most basic level, it is a general equilibrium model in which large differences in factor endowments between countries are decisive in the decision as to whether to become multinational or not. The existence of multinationals thus becomes endogenous in this model, which is basically an extended version of the factor abundance model. In Helpman and Krugman (1985) there are two sectors, food and manufactures. Food is produced using only capital and labor, which have to come from the same location, and is produced by means of a standard linear cost function. The production of differentiated manufactures requires capital and labor, but also so-called headquarter services. These (differentiated) services can be used in plants at different locations, but once specific headquarter services have been adopted they become a firm-specific asset and tied to the entrepreneurial unit or plant that uses them. Headquarter services are produced using capital and labor. The production of manufactures is characterized by increasing returns to scale. It therefore pays to concentrate the production in a single plant. As usual, all varieties have the same cost structure. The central idea is that different stages in the production process have different (production) factor intensities. For example, headquarter services are the most capital-intensive, and the production of food is the least capital-intensive. The production of manufactures, therefore, has intermediate capital intensity.

It is now easy to understand how multinationals might develop in the Helpman and Krugman (1985) model. Free trade in goods can bring about factor price equalization if factor endowments between the two countries are not too different. If this is the case, there is no incentive to form a multinational. Now suppose that factor endowments differ between the two countries in such a way that factor prices are not equalized. Then firms have an incentive to become multinational, because factor price differentials offer an opportunity to look for cost efficiency. Not surprisingly, headquarter services are located in the capital-rich country. This country therefore becomes a net exporter of headquarter (capital-intensive) services to its production location in the labor-rich country, and a net importer of labor-intensive products. Clearly, the presence of multinationals influences the structure of intra-industry trade if products of multinationals are traded, although the precise link between trade and the existence of multinationals can be quite complicated (see Helpman and Krugman, 1985: chap. 12). This specialization increases the relative demand for labor in the labor-rich country and for capital in the capital-rich country, thus increasing the probability of factor price equalization.

The Helpman and Krugman model provides a step forward compared to the more descriptive OLI models, but it seems at odds with the stylized facts of multinational production. First, the model assumes that the international trade of goods and the international trade in headquarter services are both without costs. In this model, multinationals arise in the absence of transport cost or other trade barriers, the driving force being the uneven distribution of production factors between countries. More specifically, the model assumes that splitting the production of headquarter services and the production of the final (or intermediate) good can be done at no additional costs. Most importantly, however, the model implies that no (FDI) investment takes place between similar countries (meaning similar factor endowments and thus factor price equalization). As we have seen, most international direct investment *does* take place between similar countries. Therefore, the model may provide a well-designed way of incorporating multinationals endogenously into a general equilibrium model, but it leaves a large part of these investments unexplained.[5]

Introducing trade barriers or trade costs to trade models turns out to be illuminating, and it provides a simple explanation for horizontal FDI. An exporting firm can make a decision to set up a plant in a foreign location if trade costs are high. Whether or not this is profitable depends on the balance between disintegration costs, which reflect the loss of scale economies if production no longer takes place under a single roof, and the benefits of "jumping" over trade barriers in the case of local production. The decision to locate in a foreign location depends therefore on the balance between these two forces: high trade costs stimulate horizontal foreign investment; high disintegration costs discourage such investment. This reasoning suggests that similar countries and high trade costs stimulate horizontal multinationals, the more so if these distant markets are large and the costs of disintegration are balanced by local economies of scale because of the large markets. For vertical FDI, trade costs are also important, but here high trade costs *discourage* FDI because they make it less profitable to shift part of the production to (low – (wage) cost) foreign countries if these foreign produced (intermediate) goods have to be shipped back to the home

---

[5] Venables (1999) has extended this strand of literature, stressing fragmentation and its effect on international trade in preference to agglomeration or spreading (in fact, his model assumes constant returns to scale and perfect competition).

country at high cost. Empirical research indeed shows that, by and large, the relation between trade barriers is such that if investments take place between developed countries trade costs encourage FDI (horizontal type), and if investments take place between countries with different income levels trade costs discourage FDI (vertical type) (see, for instance, Markusen, 2002: chap. 10, or Neary, 2007, 2008).

The relevance of the interplay between scale economies and trade or transport costs in modern FDI theory in determining the location decision of firms must by now sound familiar from our discussions of the models of geographical economics in the previous chapters, since it is the combination of these two factors that leads to firms concentrating their production in a few plants and not being indifferent in terms of location where to do so. With a few notable exceptions in the recent literature on FDI, however, the relation between agglomeration economies and FDI is still largely absent. In other words, geography or the economic environment in which firms operate is taken as given and not, as opposed to geographical economics, as the outcome of the investment decisions made by the individual firms. As a result, these FDI models cannot help us to begin to understand why we observe an agglomeration or clustering of (multinational) firms and of economic activity in general.

8.4 Multinationals in geographical economics

A few models have by now been developed that incorporate the potential for multinationals by using and extending the core model of geographical economics. These models allow for the endogenous formation of vertically and/or horizontally differentiated multinationals (see, for example, Karolina Ekholm and Forslid, 2001, or, for a survey, Markusen, 2002). What these studies have in common is the fact that a less simplistic notion of the firm is adapted compared to the core model. In the core model of chapter 3, the firm is essentially identical to the plant and no decisions have to be taken on the organization of the firm. A less restrictive view on the firm is the distinguishing feature of the modern literature on multinationals. How do the results of such a model compare to those of the core model with respect to agglomeration and spreading forces?

We take the study by Ekholm and Forslid (2001) as our example, because they closely follow the core model and at the same time illustrate how the existence of multinationals, both horizontally integrated and vertically integrated, changes the tendencies of agglomeration and spreading. In Ekholm and Forslid (2001), and in line with the core model, it is still assumed that all manufacturing firms are alike in terms of firm productivity; there is no room for firm heterogeneity. As we have already noted in section 8.2 in our discussion of table 8.1, however, recent research into trade and FDI has emphasized that firm heterogeneity is very prominent even between firms operating in the same sector. In box 8.2 we briefly illustrate why the introduction of firm heterogeneity may matter for the (alleged) relevance of agglomeration.

Box 8.2 Heterogeneous firms and agglomeration

In a volume published following a workshop organized to celebrate the Dixit and Stiglitz (1977) monopolistic competition revolution, Dixit (2004), Stiglitz (2004), Neary (2004), and others reflect on the current status of the Dixit–Stiglitz monopolistic competition model. One of the main criticisms of the model was the fact that firms are treated symmetrically – all firms are identical – so strategic interaction between firms is ruled out. This is a strong, and (as we have explained in chapters 3 and 4) theoretically a very useful assumption. Empirical research has indicated that firms are far from identical, however. Exporting firms turn out to be more productive and more capital-intensive and pay higher wages than firms that are not engaged in exports. Firms that are active in FDI are even more productive than exporting firms. The causality is interesting: firms are not productive because they are internationally active, but are internationally active because they are productive. The reason is that exporting and FDI are costly activities, and only productive firms can afford to be engaged in exporting or investing. By now there is a rapidly developing literature that provides empirical evidence for these productivity differences between domestic firms and firms that operate internationally as well through exporting and FDI (see, for example, Bernard et al., 2003, 2007, or Helpman, Melitz, and Yeaple, 2004).

What is the role of agglomeration advantages in models that allow for productivity differences between firms? Baldwin and Okubo (2006) answer this question. Based on Melitz (2003) and Melitz and Ottaviano (2005), they develop a model of geographical economics with heterogeneous firms. Their model therefore adds an additional complication to the basic model structure – productivity differences between firms – but, following Ottaviano, Tabuchi, and Thisse (2002), the authors also introduce a simplification, quasi-linear demand, which is convenient because one can ignore income effects in demand (recall box 4.1). The results that they derive are important. Firms that are more productive are assumed to have lower marginal costs; this is how productivity differences are modeled. The implication is that these highly productive firms are not as susceptible to the competition effect as less productive firms. Furthermore, firms line up for relocation from a small market to a large one in order of their productivity levels: the most productive firm goes first and then the less productive firms take their turn. The reason is that the

---

Box 8.2 (cont.)

most productive firms can sell more in the large market than their less productive competitors, and can thus benefit from forward and backward linkages at (early) stages of
market development that would imply a loss for the less productive competitors.

This result is a warning for empirical tests of agglomeration rents or advantages.
Without firm heterogeneity one could easily overstate the importance of agglomeration
rents, because the firms that have relocated to the larger market are also the more
productive ones. High regional productivity is not necessarily the result of being located in
an economic center, therefore; these firms are more productive irrespective of their
location. These two effects should be separated from each other. This conclusion is
essentially the same as the one we discussed in chapter 6 (see box 6.6) for the sorting or
selection effects that trouble empirical studies of labor productivity and labor migration;
recall our discussion of Combes, Duranton, and Gobillon (2008). In the concluding chapter
of our book, chapter 12, we briefly return to the selection versus agglomeration effect in a
discussion of important new research by Combes, Duranton, Gobillon, Puga, and Sébastien
Roux (2008).

We now discuss the set-up of the Ekholm and Forslid (2001) model.
Assume that there are two countries $i, j = 1, 2$. In chapter 3 the cost function
for a firm producing x_{ij} units of variety i in country j can be represented as
$W_j l_{ij} = aW_j + \beta W_j x_{ij}$ – that is, both fixed labor costs a and variable labor costs
β are incurred in the same location. From the discussion above, we know that
vertically integrated multinationals arise if factor prices differ between locations. Since the sole production factor in this framework is labor, we have only
to analyze the impact of wage differentials between locations on a firm's
location decision, provided the firms are able to split up the production
process. Now suppose that headquarter services are produced only in one
country, whereas actual production can take place either in the other country
(vertical integration) or in both countries (horizontal integration) (see below).
Typically, headquarter services are associated with R&D, financial services,
and other specialized services, such as marketing, accounting, etc., produced
and organized at a firm's headquarters. If we assume that these headquarter
services are available, without any extra cost, in the production sites, they can
be seen as goods traded at no cost. Due to the fixed-cost nature of these
services it pays to choose a single location for the headquarters of the firm. In
general, the cost function for firm i with its headquarters in country j is

$$W_j l_{ij} + W_k l_{ik} = aW_j + \beta(W_j x_{ij} + W_k x_{ik}); \quad j = 1, 2; \quad k = 1, 2 \quad (8.1)$$

where

l_{ij} = labor used by firm i in location j;

l_{ik} = labor used by firm i in location k;

x_{ij} = production level by firm i in location j; and

x_{ik} = production level of firm i in location k.

We can distinguish between three separate logical possibilities. The latter two are discussed in more detail below. To be concrete, this is illustrated in figure 8.3 for the firm producing variety "5," assuming that its headquarters are in country 1.

(i) Panel a. It is not possible to separate the production of headquarter services from the manufacture of goods in the production site – that is, both have to be produced simultaneously in the same country. This has been analyzed in the core model of chapters 3 and 4.

(ii) Panel b. It is possible to separate the production of headquarter services from the manufacture of goods in the production site. Moreover, it is possible to supervise several production locations simultaneously. The firm can thus set up production plants in both countries simultaneously, and it must choose where to set up its headquarters. This is the case of *horizontal integration*.

(iii) Panel c. It is possible to separate the production of headquarter services from the manufacture of goods in the production site. The manufacture of goods must take place at one location, however, perhaps because the headquarters can supervise only one production plant simultaneously. The firm must now choose where to set up its production plant as well as its headquarters. This is the case of *vertical integration*.

8.4.1 Horizontally integrated multinationals

We first have a look at horizontal multinationals in this model. With positive trade costs and no extra costs of setting up an extra plant in the other country, the symmetric division of production between the two countries is stable, because transport costs can be avoided by starting production in the second country. The complete agglomeration situation, in which the whole firm is located in either country 1 or country 2, can never be a stable equilibrium because a firm starting production in the periphery can capture the whole "foreign" market, as no transport costs have to be charged.

Furthermore, if all firms produce symmetrically in both regions, the price indices in both countries are identical. The location of the firm's

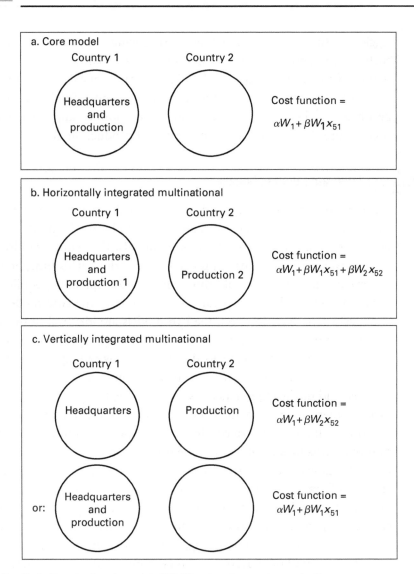

Figure 8.3   Production structure for variety "5" if headquarters are in country 1

headquarters is now straightforward; headquarter services are produced in the country with the lower wage. In this case its location is undetermined.[6] Note that this result is in contrast to the core model. For positive trade costs, the spreading of manufacturing is the only stable equilibrium.

---

[6] Once a firm chooses a site for its headquarters, the local demand for labor increases (in order to produce headquarter services) and drives up wages. Because the location of the headquarters is indeterminate and there are many firms making this decision at the same time, headquarters will be symmetrically distributed.

Agglomeration is no longer possible. Introducing extra costs into the model, such as extra costs to open a second production plant, reduces the extreme nature of this conclusion (see also Ekholm and Forslid, 2001). In general, however, agglomeration in the presence of horizontal multinationals becomes less likely. In the geographical economics approach, countries become more similar because multinational production arises.

8.4.2 Vertically integrated multinationals

Turning to vertically integrated multinationals, the firm has to choose where to locate the headquarters, and where to locate the production plant of the firm. As with horizontal multinationals, the symmetric division of firms between both regions is a possible equilibrium. This time, however, it is perhaps an unstable equilibrium. In fact, the spreading equilibrium is stable for exactly the same parameter values as in the core model of geographical economics; in effect, the two models are identical in this respect.

For parameter values for which the symmetric spreading equilibrium becomes unstable, what happens depends on how rapidly the headquarters can relocate relative to production. If the symmetric equilibrium becomes unstable and the headquarters are slow to move, first production will move to the larger region, and then the headquarters will follow, because – in contrast to the case described above – one can by assumption not avoid transport costs by locating *part* of the production unit in the other country. Here the larger market has a cost advantage, because, in the (relative) absence of transport cost, wages will be lower in the larger region. The headquarters and production will therefore eventually locate in the larger country or region, and this will eventually lead to complete agglomeration.

The analysis is more interesting, and intuitively more plausible, if the headquarters are fast movers, or if they cannot move at all, once they are established. For ease of exposition, we assume throughout the remainder of this chapter that all headquarters are located in country 1. In this case, stable equilibria in between symmetric spreading and agglomeration are possible with vertical multinationals. Note, first of all, that headquarter services have to be paid for by operating profits – that is, firms charge a higher price than marginal costs (the mark-up) to recoup the outlays for fixed costs. The basic decision problem facing a firm with its headquarters in country 1 is illustrated in figure 8.4. If the firm decides to produce in country 1, its marginal production costs are βW_1, which determines the price the firm charges, the production level at which the firm recoups its operating profits,

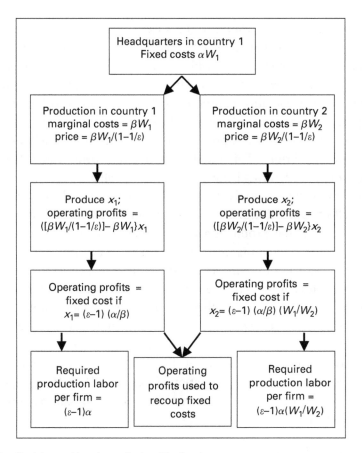

Figure 8.4   Decision problem for vertical multinationals

and the number of laborers required for this production level. Similarly, if the firm decides to produce in country 2, its marginal production costs are βW_2, which has different repercussions for the price the firm charges, the production level at which it recoups fixed costs, and the number of laborers required for this production level. Note in particular that, if the firm decides to set up a production facility in country 2, it will repatriate the operating profits ("transferring" these to country 1) to recoup the fixed costs of production. Multinationals are often criticized for this type of practice, which in this setting is entirely unwarranted.

In the short-run equilibrium the equations in figure 8.4 must hold exactly, because an individual firm should be indifferent between producing either in country 1 or in country 2, and firms producing in either country enter and exit until profits are zero. The most important thing to note is that the production level for firms producing in country 2 depends on the wage level in country 2 relative to the wage level in country 1. This obviously arises from the fact that the fixed costs from headquarter services are paid the wage rate W_1 in country 1, while the marginal costs from the production plant are paid the wage rate W_2. To be more precise, a firm producing in country 2 has an equilibrium production level equal to W_1/W_2 times that of a firm producing in country 1. Thus, if the wage rate is *higher* in country 2 than in country 1, a firm with a production plant in country 2 will produce *less* output in equilibrium. This implies, other things being equal, that a given number of manufacturing laborers in country 2 will produce a higher number of varieties locally, giving rise to a positive welfare effect through the love-of-variety effect. Other things are, moreover, not equal, but reinforce this effect. Remember that the production of headquarter services all takes place in country 1, such that all manufacturing workers in country 2 are available for production activities to reinforce the above effect of a larger locally produced number of varieties in country 2. In essence, this gives two spreading effects, which may result in partial, rather than complete, agglomeration.

Following a similar procedure to that in chapters 3 and 4, we can derive the short-run equilibrium for the model with vertical multinationals – that is, the equilibrium that arises given the distribution of the manufacturing work force. This is given in equations (8.2) to (8.5') below, imposing the normalization of chapter 4, such that these equations can be compared to equations (4.1) – (4.3).

$$\lambda_1 = N_1 + (1/\varepsilon)N_2 \tag{8.2}$$

$$\lambda_2 = (1 - 1/\varepsilon)(W_1/W_2)N_2 \tag{8.2'}$$

$$Y_r = \delta\lambda_r W_r + (1-\delta)\phi_r; \qquad r = 1,2 \tag{8.3}$$

$$I_r = \left[\sum_{s=1}^{2} N_s T_{rs}^{1-\varepsilon} W_s^{1-\varepsilon}\right]^{1/(1-\varepsilon)}; \qquad r = 1,2 \tag{8.4}$$

$$W_1 = \left[\sum_{r=1}^{2} Y_r T_{r1}^{1-\varepsilon} I_r^{\varepsilon-1}\right]^{1/\varepsilon} \tag{8.5}$$

$$W_2 = (W_2/W_1)^{1/\varepsilon}\left[\sum_{r=1}^{2} Y_r T_{r1}^{1-\varepsilon} I_r^{\varepsilon-1}\right]^{1/\varepsilon} \tag{8.5'}$$

Equations (8.2) and (8.2′) are the full employment equations for manufacturing labor in the two countries, which determines the number of varieties produced in country 1 and in country 2. In the core model of chapters 3 and 4 these two equations simplify to $\lambda_r = N_r$ for $r = 1, 2$ (and are not listed there, but simply substituted in the other equations). Since in the model with vertical multinationals all fixed labor is located in country 1 and, as discussed above, all manufacturing labor in country 2 is thus available for production activities, *ceteris paribus*, country 2 will produce more, and country 1 will produce fewer, varieties than in the core model. Equation (8.3), giving the income level in both countries, is identical to equation (4.1). Equation (8.4), giving the price index in both countries, is almost identical to equation (4.2). The only difference is that N_s replaces λ_{sr}, because equations (8.2) and (8.2′) indicate that these two variables are not (through a normalization) identical in the framework with vertical multinationals. Finally, the wage equation (8.5) is identical to (4.3) for country 1, since the equilibrium conditions for a firm producing in country 1 have not changed, as summarized in Figure 8.4. Equation (8.5′) is not identical to (4.3) for country 2, however, because the fixed costs occur in country 1, and not in country 2. Only if the wage rate in the two countries is the same is this equation identical, as is obvious from its formulation.

As argued above, we can analyze in this setting two situations, namely if the headquarters cannot move (but manufacturing labor can), and if the headquarters can be relocated quickly (as well as manufacturing labor). Both situations are illustrated simultaneously in the simulations of figure 8.5, which solves equations (8.2) to (8.5) for different distributions of the manufacturing labor force. If the headquarters cannot relocate, both the solid and the dashed lines of the short-run equilibrium hold. As always, manufacturing labor will relocate if there are real wage differences. Figure 8.5 shows that, for relatively low transport costs ($T = 1.1$) the partial agglomeration equilibrium is unstable. For somewhat higher transport costs ($T = 1.19$ and $T = 1.64$) partial agglomeration is a stable equilibrium. If the headquarters can relocate quickly, only the solid lines in figure 8.5 represent a short-run equilibrium. This holds because the firms will locate the headquarters in country 1 only if the wage rate is lower in country 1 than in country 2. Otherwise, they will quickly relocate the headquarters to the other country. We therefore have to verify whether or not $W_1 < W_2$ in the short-run equilibrium. In figure 8.5 this holds only for the solid lines, and not for the dashed lines. In any case, the results indicate again that a stable equilibrium with partial agglomeration is possible.

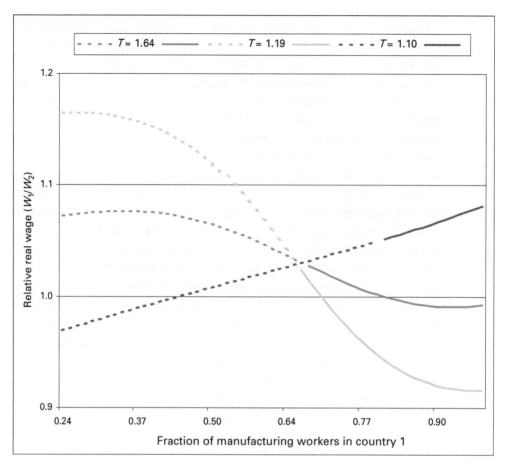

Figure 8.5   Agglomeration with vertically integrated multinationals
Notes: Parameters $\delta = 0.4$ and $\varepsilon = 5$.

In a similar model, Markusen and Venables (1998: 201) find that "multinationals tend to be found in equilibrium when firm-level scale economies and tariff/transport costs are large relative to plant-level scale economies." Among the extensions they consider are two production factors, instead of one, which facilitates the analysis of country differences. Moreover, they distinguish plant from firm economies of scale, implying that each good is produced by only one firm, but can be produced at different plants at different locations, due to the existence of transport costs. In general, they find that multinational production becomes more important as countries grow more similar in size. The analysis also implies that further (trade) liberalization shifts multinational production to the smaller and more backyard countries. Ting Gao (1999) reaches similar conclusions in an encompassing model, which allows for more elaborate demand and cost linkages between firms. Baldwin and Ottaviano (2000) show that this approach can easily be extended to create a link between trade and FDI; FDI might replace trade, but if varieties are sold to third markets it also implies trade creation instead of trade diversion.

8.5 Empirical evidence on the role of agglomeration in FDI

The literature on empirical evidence of *the determinants*[7] of multinational production is quite large (see Barba Navaretti and Venables, 2004: chap. 6, and Markusen, 2002, for surveys). We do not survey this literature, but select and discuss only those studies that can shed some light on the relevance of geographical economics – that is, the empirical relevance of agglomeration effects in understanding FDI. Until quite recently, the evidence on the relevance of agglomeration effects or of space in general for FDI was rather sketchy at best, but a number of recent empirical studies provide more direct evidence either by using spatial econometrics or by explicitly grounding their empirical work upon a geographical economics model.

8.5.1 Indirect evidence

First of all, see table 8.3; one can check whether some of the determinants of multinational behavior correspond with *some of the actual characteristics of these firms.* As mentioned earlier in this chapter, the characteristics of multinationals are that they (i) have a high ratio of R&D, (ii) employ somewhat more skilled labor, (iii) are associated with new or complex products, and (iv) have a minimum threshold size (above this threshold firm size is less important) (see Markusen, 2002). If firms with these characteristics cluster together, it suggests that the same will also hold for multinationals.

Looking at the top twenty multinationals and the sectors in which these firms are active suggests that multinationals are indeed active in sectors in which R&D and new and complex products are very important. The study

---

[7] The italics refer to the fact that there is a separate empirical literature on the consequences or effects (in terms of income or employment growth, for instance) of FDI on origin as well as destination countries. We do not deal with the literature here, but see, for instance, Barba Navaretti and Venables (2004: chap. 7 and 9).

Table 8.3 Top twenty non-financial multinationals, ranked by foreign assets, 2005

Corporation	Home economy	Industry	Assets ($ billion)		Sales ($ billion)		Employment (1,000 employees)		TNI
			Foreign	Total	Foreign	Total	Foreign	Total	
1 General Electric	United States	Electronics	413	673	60	150	155	316	50.1
2 Vodafone	United Kingdom	Telecommunications	196	220	39	52	51	62	82.4
3 General Motors	United States	Motor vehicles	175	476	65	193	194	335	42.9
4 British Petroleum	United Kingdom	Petroleum	161	207	200	254	78	96	79.4
5 Shell	United Kingdom/Netherlands	Petroleum	151	220	184	307	92	109	71.1
6 Exxon Mobil	United States	Petroleum	144	208	248	359	53	84	67.1
7 Toyota	Japan	Motor vehicles	132	244	118	186	108	286	51.6
8 Ford	United States	Motor vehicles	119	269	80	177	160	300	47.6
9 Total	France	Petroleum	108	126	133	178	64	113	72.5
10 Electricité de France	France	Electricity, gas, and water	91	202	26	64	18	162	32.4
11 France Telecom	France	Telecommunications	87	130	26	61	82	203	49.9
12 Volkswagen	Germany	Motor vehicles	83	158	86	119	166	345	57.6
13 RWE Group	Germany	Electricity, gas, and water	83	128	23	52	42	86	52.9
14 Chevron Corporation	United States	Petroleum	81	126	100	194	32	59	56.8
15 E.On	Germany	Electricity, gas, and water	81	150	29	83	46	80	48.8
16 Suez	France	Electricity, gas, and water	78	95	40	52	97	158	73.5
17 Deutsche Telecom	Germany	Telecommunications	78	151	32	74	76	244	41.8
18 Siemens	Germany	Electronics	67	104	64	96	296	461	65.3
19 Honda	Japan	Motor vehicles	67	90	70	88	126	145	80.3
20 Hutchison Whampoa	Hong Kong	Diversified	62	77	25	31	166	200	80.8

Note: TNI = transnationality index = average of (%): foreign assets/total assets, foreign sales/total sales, and foreign employment/total employment.
Source: UNCTAD (2007).

by Midelfart Knarvik *et al.* (2003), which has already been discussed in chapter 5, is particularly illuminating in this respect. Using different measures of specialization for (at least) thirteen EU countries and (at least) thirty-six industries for the period 1970 to 1997, they find evidence of increased specialization during 1994–7, which might indicate that relatively few industries become dominant in a few locations. A further regional breakdown shows that increased specialization is found either in relatively poor regions or in relatively rich regions that have undergone a major structural change – that is, become more service-oriented than manufacture-oriented (see Hallet, 2000). This evidence might reflect trade liberalization within the European Union, which allows more industry-level specialization, affecting in particular intra-industry trade.

In which industries are countries specializing, however? Midelfart Knarvik *et al.* (2003) also answer this question. Identifying industries by key characteristics, such as economies of scale, R&D intensity, skill intensity, inter-industry linkages, and technology level, they find a clear distinction between "north" and "south" Europe. The industrial structures of France, Germany, and the United Kingdom are best described by high returns to scale, high technology, and a relatively highly educated workforce. These countries are the home of industries such as motor vehicles, motorcycles, aircraft, chemicals, electric apparatus, and the petrochemical industry – industries in which multinationals are active. The industrial structure of Spain, Portugal, and Greece is characterized by low returns to scale, low technology, and less skilled labor. They are somewhat less able to attract the industries with the characteristics of the north.

Hallet (2000) also finds that the most spatially concentrated industries are to be found within manufacturing (more concentrated than GDP). Products that are not characterized by knowledge content and related factors are found all over Europe. One could call these day-to-day products, which, on account of a lack of economies of scale, do not benefit from clustering in specific regions or countries. These findings corroborate the fact that the European Union is a popular host for FDI; this holds especially for its northern part. In addition the increased specialization patterns in the European Union are consistent with the predictions of the geographical economics models that include multinationals; if multinationals are present, core–periphery patterns, or the clustering of all activity are less likely. All countries have become more specialized (increased specialization does not imply agglomeration). The broad picture within the European Union is consistent with what we expect to find on the basis of the theoretical models, but these findings only indirectly confirm the relevance of the geographical economics approach in the presence of multinationals.

8.5.2 Direct evidence I: evidence consistent with agglomeration effects

Fortunately, more direct evidence is also available. As noted by Ray Barrell and Nigel Pain (1999), obvious examples of multinationals can easily be found, such as the concentration of financial services in the city of London. Non-UK banks can better serve Europe from within when they are located in London, which provides an example of horizontal multinationals. Specialized branches of EU banks also like to have a subsidiary in London to benefit from spillovers in the City. Table 8.4 presents gross product (a value added measure) and employment for US majority-owned manufacturing foreign affiliates. As the United States is the world's largest foreign direct investor, this provides a good example.

Barrell and Pain (1999) note that these data provide some evidence for the relevance of agglomeration, since the four largest economies in Europe are also the largest destinations for US FDI. Furthermore, table 8.4 illustrates that Europe has become more important as a destination for US FDI over time. A closer look at more disaggregated data reveals that the European Union is becoming more attractive to foreign investors as a result of the ongoing process of EU integration and the associated decrease of within-EU trade costs.[8] Differences in national labor costs are important in determining the location of these investments, for which nations with relatively low labor costs are preferred. Most importantly, Barrell and Pain also find evidence for the relevance of agglomeration economies, measured by the scale of production (national to EU production) and the size of the research base (national to EU stocks of R&D). The agglomeration variables contribute significantly to the explanation for FDI.

In addition, some indication of cumulative causation is found: a 1 percent increase in the output share raises FDI by 1.7 percent, and a 1 percent increase in the relative share of R&D raises inward investment by 1.5 percent. These results are rather characteristic for this type of research (see Markusen and Maskus, 1999, Brainard, 1997, or Barba Navaretti and Venables, 2004: chap. 6). It is found that local sales of multinationals strongly depend on the

---

[8] For the period 1978–94 panel data for six countries and five sectors are used. The countries considered are France, Germany, Italy, the Netherlands, Spain, and the United Kingdom. The sectors are food and drink, metals and metal products, mechanical and electrical engineering, chemicals, and other manufacturing.

Table 8.4 Geographical distribution of the activities of US foreign affiliates, 1977–95

| Country | Gross product (percentage of total) | | | | Employment |
	1977	1982	1989	1995	1995
Europe	56.5	54.9	57.8	60.0	61.3
United Kingdom	14.9	17.3	15.9	12.2	11.6
Germany	16.8	15.3	15.0	17.2	10.8
France	8.7	7.4	6.9	8.2	6.0
Italy	3.8	3.9	4.5	4.1	3.6
Netherlands	3.1	2.6	4.5	3.7	1.8
Belgium	3.6	2.4	2.9	3.3	1.7
Ireland	0.7	1.3	2.0	3.2	1.4
Spain	2.1	1.9	3.3	2.9	2.5
Total world production	$71.6 bn	$99.8 bn	$172.0 bn	$232.8 bn	3.66 m
Share in EU	44.4	44.6	53.8	50.2	45.1

Notes: US majority-owned foreign affiliates. bn = billion; m = million.
Source: Barrell and Pain (1999).

market size of the host country and trade costs. The results also depend on the motivation behind the investments, however. If investments are made to serve the local markets, they find a positive relationship between the ratio of export to local sales and the skilled labor abundance of the parent, and a negative relationship with market size in the host country and investment costs or trade costs. If firms invest in host countries to serve third markets, high trade and investment costs stimulate firms to invest elsewhere. The bottom line of all this work is, again, that tendencies of agglomeration, if they arise, are generally smaller in the presence of multinational investment than if multinationals are absent.

In an influential study, Head, Ries, and Deborah Swenson (1995) also provide direct evidence for the relevance of agglomeration or clustering for FDI by looking at Japanese investors in the United States. They try to determine whether or not variables that are important in the geographical economics approach determine Japanese greenfield investments (new manufacturing plants) in the United States. For 225 different four-digit manufacturing industries, resulting in 751 investments, the geographical pattern of these investments is established (using investment data since 1980). The central idea is that trade theory indicates that firms in the same industry tend to cluster together in regions with adequate factor endowments, but that these location advantages (low factor prices) are enhanced through the presence of agglomeration externalities, which adds to the attractiveness of the location.

Head, Ries, and Swenson (1995) analyze the geographical difference of Japanese investments from the geographical distribution of US establishments. They hypothesize that two major explanations can be responsible for a distinctive Japanese investment pattern. Japanese firms either choose a location for specific location reasons (near a harbor, for instance) or they cluster in different regions from their US counterparts due to specific externalities that are important only for Japanese firms. Using proxies for agglomeration externalities, such as the number of US firms in the same four-digit group, the number of Japanese plants operating in the same four-digit group, the number of Japanese establishments in the same *keiretsu*,[9] and a variable measuring linkages with nearby states, it turns out that Japanese investments in the United States are significantly influenced by the previous location decisions of other Japanese firms in the same industry or keiretsu. These results do not indicate that specific location factors are not important in determining new Japanese investments, in particular since these factors might have been important in attracting the initial investments. Proximity to Japanese suppliers of intermediate products does seem important. Furthermore, the existence of technological externalities specific to Japanese firms might be important. Most of the Japanese investments in the United States are carried out by multinationals. Again, the evidence is consistent with the modern theory of multinational investments, although no clear distinction can be made between horizontal and vertical investments.

8.5.3 Direct evidence II: market potential and spatial lag in FDI

The bulk of the empirical research into the determinants of FDI focuses on a two-country setting in which only the home- and host-country variables are included and the rest of the world is not part of the analysis. This is not a big surprise, given that many empirical FDI studies are (implicitly) based on a gravity model, and such a model (see chapter 9 section 9.6) typically looks at bilateral trade or, *in casu*, FDI flows and restricts the role of geography to the distance between the home and host countries, or country-specific geography variables such as a country's climate or access to the sea. This line of empirical FDI research has provided important insights, but by

[9] A keiretsu is a conglomeration of businesses.

construction it ignores the role of agglomeration in a multi-country or multi-region perspective.

To see why agglomeration might be relevant, consider the following empirical puzzle (Neary, 2008). In recent years, and following the ongoing process of economic integration in the European Union, FDI inflows into the European Union have surged. Based on a simple two-country (home and host) FDI model and assuming that a large part of this FDI was of the horizontal, market-seeking type, this increase of FDI in the wake of *falling* trade costs cannot readily be explained. One way to reconcile FDI theory with this stylized fact is to allow for third-country effects, as in the *export platform* models of Ekholm, Forslid, and Markusen (2007). To understand the basic argument, assume that a US firm sets up an affiliate in Ireland and then uses this Irish affiliate to export its goods to the rest of the EU market. In this way, the US firm bypasses (external EU) trade costs that it would face in the case of exporting its goods from the United States to the European Union, and it benefits fully from the reduction of within-EU trade costs that accompanied EU integration. In this example it is not primarily the market size of the host country (here, Ireland) but the market size of third countries (in this case, the rest of the European Union) that is important (see, for more evidence on Ireland, Barba Navaretti and Venables, 2004: chap. 8). One simple way to capture the market size of third countries is by including a *market potential* variable (see below) as a determinant of host FDI among the set of explanatory variables in a gravity model of FDI. In chapter 5 section 5.5 we discussed the connection between geographical economics and the market potential at some length.

With respect to FDI, there are now a number of empirical papers that include third-country effects, and they find at least some confirmation that these effects are relevant. Apart from some work on the export platform case (Ekholm, Forslid, and Markusen, 2007), agglomeration effects are, for instance, a key element in the recent FDI papers by Head and Mayer (2004b), Amiti and Javorcik (2008), and Inui, Matsuura and Poncet (2007). Head and Mayer (2004b), for instance, investigate the location decisions of Japanese multinational firms across Europe. In their study, clearly grounded on a geographical economics model, agglomeration effects are captured by what is essentially a *market potential* variable that includes not only the market size (GDP) of the FDI host region but also the (distance-weighted) GDPs of other regions.

Since these recent FDI studies are based on geographical economics, we discuss them in more detail in the next and final subsection. Before we do so, however, we first want to point out that the inclusion of third-country effects points to the possible existence of spatial interdependencies in which the third-country effects are not limited to one channel (e.g. market potential) and/or a few specific (host) locations but also – possibly – to non-observed spatial interdependencies that determine the location of FDI. Here the toolkit of *spatial econometrics* can be very useful for improving our understanding of FDI patterns; see box 8.3 for some background information on spatial econometrics.

Box 8.3 Spatial econometrics and its two basic models

A promising route for future empirical research in geographical economics is to make more use of the tools of spatial econometrics (see Fingleton, 2004). Following the seminal work by Luc Anselin (1988), spatial econometrics applies and extends the toolkit of econometrics to spatial issues. In doing so, it provides an econometric foundation for some of the empirical specifications discussed in chapters 5 and 6. Spatial econometrics can thus complement geographical economics by addressing the same empirical questions from a different perspective. We give two examples to illustrate the advantages of using the tools of spatial econometrics.

First, take the attempts to test the wage equation from the core model. Basically, this equation informs us that wages in region j depend positively on the (real) income of other regions, corrected for distance. Income in the core model is simply the sum of wages, however, so, effectively, the wage equation informs us that wages in region j depend positively on other regional wages corrected for distance. In the terminology of spatial econometrics, such an equation can be estimated as a so-called *spatial lag model*, in which (as in non-spatial models with a lagged dependent variable) one seeks to establish whether there is spatial autoregression in the data. This is captured in equation (8.6) by the ρW *(wages$_i$)* term, where W is a distance matrix identifying the geographical relationships between regions, and ρ is the spatial lag coefficient to be estimated. Based on the core model, we would expect a positive spatial lag coefficient: higher wages in (nearby) region i are good news for workers in region j. Using data for Chinese cities, Hering and Poncet (2007) incorporate a spatial lag specification into a geographical economics model. In the main text of this subsection, we show the spatial lag model can also be used to understand FDI patterns.

$$wage_j = a_0 + a_1(\text{control variables}) + \rho W(wages_i) + e_j \qquad (8.6)$$

Second, we look at the *spatial error model*. By estimating equation (8.7) one tests for the significance of spatial autocorrelation. If the λ coefficient is significant, there is spatial autocorrelation, implying that a shock in city size i will have an impact on city size j. The magnitude of this impact depends on the distance between the cities i and j as measured by the distance matrix W. Equation (8.7) will be familiar from our discussion in

---

Box 8.3 (cont.)

subsection 6.3.2 (figure 6.3) for the shocks to German and Japanese cities after World War II, in particular the attempt to take geography into account in this setting. With the spatial error specification (6.7) in mind, this model allows for the possibility that "geography" matters, in the sense that city growth *i* during WW II was also determined by the degree of destruction of other cities (corrected for distance). A good example using the techniques of spatial econometrics is the study by Kristian Behrens, Cem Ertur, and Wilfried Koch (2007).[10]

$$ city\ size_j = a_0 + a_1(\text{control variables}) + e_j; \quad \text{where} \quad e_j = \lambda W\ e_i + \mu \qquad (8.7) $$

A basic spatial econometrics model that is useful for our present purposes is a model of FDI that includes a *spatial lag*. Dropping any time or region subscripts, this amounts to

$$ FDI = a_0 + a_1 X + \rho W.FDI + \varepsilon \qquad (8.8) $$

where X is the set of FDI determinants (such as the market potential variable) and the term $W.FDI$ is a spatial lag variable.

In such a spatial lag model, one seeks to establish whether there is spatial autoregression in the data (see box 8.3). This is captured in the equation above by the $\rho W.FDI$ term, where W is a distance matrix that identifies the geographical relationship among FDI host countries and ρ is the spatial lag coefficient to be estimated, which is assumed to lie between minus one and plus one. In the case of our example below, Dutch outbound FDI (that is, Dutch FDI flows to other countries), the spatial lag variable allows us to establish whether, for instance, Dutch FDI to France (the dependent variable) is affected by Dutch FDI to other host countries weighted by the distance between France and the other host countries, and this is captured by the $W.FDI$ term.

As pointed out by Bruce Blonigen, Ronald Davies, Glen Waddell, and Helen Naughton (2007) in their study of US outbound FDI, FDI theory provides clues as to the expected sign of the spatial lag coefficient. If a market potential variable is included in the set of variables X in (8.8), FDI theory makes predictions about the possible combinations of the sign of the

---

[10] Useful information (including spatial econometrics software) is provided at the home page of Anselin (http://sal. uiuc.edu/users/anselin) and the econometrics toolbox of James LeSage (www.spatial-econometrics.com).

spatial lag and market potential coefficients. Following theoretical work by, for instance, Markusen (2002), Badi Baltagi, Peter Egger, and Michael Pfaffermayr (2007) come up with four categories of FDI or multinational firm strategies: vertical FDI, horizontal FDI, export platform FDI, and complex (vertical) FDI. The first three categories should by now be familiar, and the fourth category refers to a situation in which, in a *three*-country model, a multinational firm from home country x not only has production plants in host country i but also in third country j (slicing up the value chain). Combined with the expected sign of the market potential variable (positive for export platform and/or agglomeration economies, zero otherwise), this provides testable hypotheses for the spatial lag coefficient with respect to various explanations of FDI. Note, however, that these benchmark studies contain only *aggregate* annual FDI data and thereby are the summation of all FDI decisions undertaken by all firms in a given year, neglecting the fact that these various FDI decisions may result from rather different motives. The spatial lag coefficient ρ may, for instance, not be different from zero on average, but this could simply be the result of export platform and complex vertical FDI effects canceling out.

As an illustration of an estimation of the FDI spatial lag model (8.8), we take the studies by Blonigen *et al.* (2007) and Garretsen and Jolanda Peeters (2008) for respectively US and Dutch outbound FDI as examples. In these two studies, the role of agglomeration or space is captured not only by the spatial lag variable but also by the inclusion of a market potential variable. Table 8.5 summarizes the main estimation results.

Table 8.5 shows that, while controlling for standard host-country determinants of FDI in gravity models such as population, GDP, and distance, the market potential coefficient and spatial lag coefficient are significant, vindicating the idea of third-country or agglomeration effects. Table 8.5 conveys another message as well, however, namely that, when testing for spatial interdependencies, it is very important to control for country-specific *fixed effects*. The difference between the respective columns in table 8.5 is that fixed effects are (not) controlled for in columns 2 and 4 (columns 1 and 3). As can be seen the value of the spatial lag coefficient drops considerably once country-specific fixed effects are included. For their sample of US outbound FDI, Blonigen *et al.* (2007) find that spatial or third-country effects by and large cease to be significant when fixed effects are included. This suggests that spatial effects, if at all relevant, are primarily cross-sectional, which is quite an important finding and one that

Table 8.5 US and Dutch outbound FDI and the role of agglomeration effects

	Dutch FDI	Dutch FDI	US FDI	US FDI
Population	−0.21 (−0.16)	−3.77 (0.95)***	−0.69 (0.07)***	−1.02 (0.13)***
GDP	1.14 (0.16)***	0.74 (0.16)***	1.84 (0.07)***	1.11 (0.09)***
Distance	−0.17 (0.04)***		−0.62 (0.04)***	
Market potential	−0.23 (0.09)**	4.68 (0.76)***	−0.92 (0.06)***	−0.05 (0.21)
Spatial lag coefficient p	0.44 (0.03)***	0.07 (0.02)***	0.50 (0.06)***	0.14 (0.07)*
Country-specific fixed effects?	No	Yes	No	Yes
Number of observations	378	378	551	551

Notes: All variables (expect distance) are measured for the host countries; see the respective studies for more information on the specifications used. Standard errors between parentheses. ***, **, and * denote significance at the 1 percent, 5 percent, and 10 percent levels respectively.
Sources: Blonigen *et al.* (2007) and Garretsen and Peeters (2008).

extends beyond the FDI literature as such. Or, to quote Blonigen *et al.* (2007: 1316),

[s]patial interactions are relatively stable over time. In fact there's an analogy in the international trade literature in ... that third-country interdependence in gravity model estimation delineated by Anderson and van Wincoop (2003) can be adequately accounted for a panel setting with country-level fixed effects. In our data, the inclusion of country dummies substantially eliminates the statistical and economic significance of the spatial terms.

As far as the standard FDI determinants are concerned, the results in table 8.5 are, in general, in line with the underlying theory and more significant for the fixed effects specification (note that the time-invariant distance variable drops out of the model once one controls for fixed effects). When it comes to grounding the estimation results in columns 2 and 4, the preferred spatial lag specification, on FDI theory, for the Dutch case the combination of a *positive* spatial lag coefficient with a *positive* market potential coefficient could be compatible with an FDI model of complex vertical FDI with agglomeration economies. For the US case the combination of a (weakly) significant positive spatial lag coefficient with an insignificant market potential coefficient suggests that the complex FDI model is most relevant. The main point to take away from these FDI studies is that, by allowing for third-country effects, spatial interdependencies should be taken seriously, even though a (large) part of the spatial interdependency reflects spatial heterogeneity (note the relevance of country-specific fixed effects).

8.5.4 Direct evidence III: empirical evidence grounded upon geographical economics

The *drawback* of the use of a spatial lag model, and of spatial econometrics in general, is that empirical models are often only loosely linked to economic theory. In our case, the estimated model is not derived from FDI location theory, in which spatial interdependencies have a solid microeconomic foundation. Fortunately, a number of recent empirical papers on the FDI location choice follow directly from the core model of geographical economics.

We take here the study by Head and Mayer (2004b) as our example. In this study, the location choice of 452 Japanese multinationals in the European Union is investigated for the period 1984 to 1995. More specifically, this location choice is investigated for fifty-seven host EU regions, together comprising nine European countries and for which the FDI and market potential data are industry-specific. Before we briefly discuss the main empirical results, we first deal with the theoretical set-up and the derivation of the empirical model. Head and Mayer (2004b) explicitly take the core model of geographical economics of chapter 3, the Krugman (1991a), model as their starting point. We are now familiar with the basic ingredients of this model; here the focus is on the profit equation (3.11). In the two-region model of chapter 3, the assumption that manufacturing firms make zero profits is used to derive the equilibrium wage equation (3.21). The equation for an individual manufacturing firm of the break-even level of production with its total demand yields the wage equation (recall subsection 3.8.1 and see also Head and Mayer, 2004b: 960, footnote 8). In the core model, the gross profit earned by firm i in a region j is (using the symbols from our core model of chapter 3!)

$$\pi_{ij} = (p_i - \beta W_i) T_{ij} c_{ij} = \frac{(\beta W_i T_{ij})^{1-\varepsilon}}{\varepsilon I_j} Y_j \qquad (8.9)$$

The summation of the gross profits over all destination markets or regions j ($j = 1,..R$), taking into account the fact that by definition the free ness of trade is $\varphi_{ij} = (T_{ij})^{1-\varepsilon}$, and also taking into account the fact that the establishment of a plant in region r carries a fixed cost a_r, one obtains the net profit Π_r that a firm earns by setting up its production in location r:

$$\Pi_r = \frac{\beta W_r^{1-\varepsilon}}{\varepsilon} \sum_{j=1}^{R} \varphi_{rj} \frac{Y_j}{I_j} - a_r = \frac{\beta W_r^{1-\varepsilon}}{\varepsilon} M_r - a_r$$

$$(8.10)$$

where $M_r = \sum_j \frac{\varphi_{rj} Y_j}{I_j}$

Head and Mayer (2004b) dub M_r the *Krugman market potential* and the similarity with the market potential derived in chapter 5 is obvious. When one assumes that fixed costs do not vary between locations, the location choice depends on the production costs βW_r and the market potential M_r. In regions with a high market potential, production costs (recall the spatial wage structure) will be higher too. Thus, a firm faces a trade-off, when deciding to invest, between production costs and market potential. Log-linearizing the above net profit equation (with a few simplifying assumptions) gives the main empirical vehicle for research into the location choices of firms (see also Amiti and Javorcik, 2008, Inui, Matsuura, and Poncet, 2007: equation 6; Inui, Matsuura, and Poncet take not only labor but also intermediate inputs into account).

Just as we explained at length in section 5.5 the estimation of the equilibrium wage equation, there are basically two strategies to estimate (8.10): the direct strategy (Hanson, 2005) and the indirect strategy (Redding and Venables, 2004). With the latter approach the market potential, M_r, is constructed by estimating a bilateral trade equation. In the next chapter, section 9.6, we discuss this indirect estimation strategy in more detail; here it suffices to say that M_r can be approximated. What are the main findings of Head and Mayer (2004b) as to the relevance of their main variable of interest, market potential, for the location choices by Japanese multinationals between the various EU regions? Basically, market potential (and thus agglomeration) matters: EU regions with a higher *Krugman market potential* attract more Japanese FDI. This is in line with the core model of geographical economics.

Head and Mayer (2004b: 969) also find, however, that "theory does not pay," in the sense that a simple *Harris market potential* (as introduced in subsection 2.2.2, equation (2.1)) is significant with the correct (positive) sign, and in addition that this "theory-free" market potential outperforms the Krugman market potential in terms of the quality of the fit of the estimated model and the size of the corresponding market potential coefficient. It is useful to quote Head and Mayer at some length, since their conclusions are relevant for future research into the relevance of geographical economics for FDI and the location choices made by multinational firms (2004b: 969):

We find that demand does matter for location choice. A 10% increase in our market potential term raises the chance of a region being chosen by 3% to 11%, depending on the specification. Despite the fact that we bring theory to empirical implementation in a structural way, the "correct" measure of market potential actually underperforms the a-theoretical Harris (1954) measure ... These results suggest that the downstream linkages emphasized in Krugman (1991[a]) are not the only or even the main cause of agglomeration. Future research should probably consider other reasons why firms cluster. It does not seem possible to falsify the hypothesis that observed agglomeration effects merely reflect omitted exogenous location attributes. However, a natural follow-up to this paper would be to estimate structural location models that implement the Venables (1996) setup with upstream and downstream linkages based on an input-output matrix.

8.6 Conclusions

The study of multinational firms has long been a rather descriptive one. The focus tended to be on taxonomy, classification, and empirical studies producing a large number of interesting stylized facts on multinationals, multinational behavior, and the characteristics of the source and destination countries of FDI. These facts were subsequently used to select the most relevant theoretical models. Since the 1980s theoretical models on multinationals have been developed. These explain in a consistent framework why multinationals exist, incorporating the birth and death of multinationals. These first models were constructed on the basis of extended versions of neoclassical trade theory; they may be elegant, but they are largely at odds with the stylized facts of multinationals that we have identified above. In particular, the fact that these models can explain the existence of multinationals only if relative factor endowments between countries are very different presents a problem, since FDI mostly takes place between similar countries. Moreover, a substantial share of multinationals are so-called horizontally integrated, while the extended trade models mostly emphasize the vertical nature of multinationals.

The geographical economics approach has only recently started to analyze multinational behavior. The results so far seem promising, however. Not only can the models incorporate stylized facts of multinational behavior, but they also predict how multinational behavior affects clustering or spreading. In general, agglomeration of economic activity becomes less likely if multinationals exist; that is, multinationals tend to make countries more similar. The framework discussed in section 8.4 can explain both horizontal and vertical multinationals, and is consistent with the fact that most FDI takes place between similar countries. Empirical evidence shows that the geographical economics approach is a useful addition to the empirical FDI literature, and the literature that explains the location choices of multinationals.

Exercises

8.1   Find more empirical evidence on the relevance of the separate factors in the OLI approach with respect to the explanations of multinationals; which factors are most important – those that stress the O, the L, or the I in this approach?

8.2   The neoclassical trade theory provides an explanation for the existence of (vertical) multinationals. Can you find evidence for the combination of (i) the absence of international factor price equalization and (ii) the presence of multinationals?

8.3   Apply the procedure used in chapters 3 and 4 to derive the equations that describe the short run equilibrium of (8.2) to (8.5').

8.4* Figure 8.5 suggests that, if transport cost become arbitrarily large ($T \to \infty$), the fraction of manufacturing workers in country 1 can be determined precisely; eyeballing the figure, this fraction might be in the neighborhood of two-thirds. Can you derive this fraction analytically (or approximate) and can you explain it economically?
Hint: use the fact that in the long-run equilibrium real wages are equal and then calculate λ.

8.5   The geographical economics approach stresses the importance of transportation costs. Can you find evidence that multinationals that produce commodities subject to high transportation costs are of the horizontal type?

8.6   Explain in your own words the difference in terms of the economic meaning of the spatial lag coefficient and the market potential coefficient in table 8.5

8.7   Why is it, as the book states, "obvious" that equation (8.10) is rather similar to the various market potential equations that were discussed in chapter 5 section 5.5?

9 The structure of international trade

9.1 Introduction

Until recently, the modern literature on geography and trade paid relatively little attention to the relationship between agglomerating and spreading forces on the one hand and the structure and volume of (international) trade on the other hand. International trade flows are undoubtedly determined largely by the spatial distribution of economic activity. When taking the core (symmetric) two-country model of chapter 3 as a point of departure, the predictions on the structure and size of trade flows are simple. If economic activity is evenly spread, food is not traded internationally, so there is only intra-industry trade in manufactures between the two countries. If there is complete agglomeration of manufacturing activity – the only other possible long-run outcome – there is exclusively inter-industry trade (food for manufactures) between the two countries.

Although these basic predictions are in line with empirical observations that trade is sizable between similar countries and dominated by intra-industry trade (see box 9.1, which gives some stylized facts on international trade flows), the basic framework is too extreme in its predictions and too rigid in its structure to allow for different types of international trade flows. The objective of this chapter is to demonstrate how international trade models may be combined with the geographical economics structure to allow for a diversified and rich explanation of international interactions. In doing so, it partially fills the gap in the literature observed by Ohlin in 1933, namely the need to develop a theory of location that may serve as a background for a theory of international trade (see chapter 1).

The core model of chapter 3 analyzes the forces of economic agglomeration and spreading by allowing mobile workers to migrate between regions. As we have already explained in chapter 4 in our discussion of the Krugman and Venables (1995) model, this assumption is in stark contrast with the standard procedure in international economics, one of the building blocks

Box 9.1 International trade flows

The World Trade Organization (WTO) distinguishes seven global economic regions in its *World Trade Report* (WTO, 2006), namely North America, South and Central America, Europe, the Commonwealth of Independent States, Africa, the Middle East, and Asia. As illustrated in figure 9.1, only three regions dominate international trade flows (imports and exports), namely (in declining order) Europe (about 45 percent), Asia (about 25 percent), and North America (about 18 percent). Note that in 2005 the value of exports was significantly higher than the value of imports for Asia, the Middle East, and CIS, while the reverse holds for North America. The most important entities in the three dominant regions are the United States, the member countries of the European Union (currently twenty-seven countries, but twenty-five countries in 2005), Japan, and China. Table 9.1 provides more detailed information on these countries, as well as on the source and destination of the main international trade flows. Of the $10.4 trillion merchandise trade exports, 39 percent originated in the EU countries (with 9.3 percent of world trade, Germany alone was the world's largest exporter). EU exports were substantially larger than exports from the United States (8.9 percent), China (7.5 percent), and Japan (5.8 percent).

A striking feature of table 9.1a is the enormous share of intra-EU trade flows (26.3 percent of world trade) – that is, trade going from EU countries to other EU countries. More generally, the table shows the importance of local connections; virtually all exports from "other North America" is destined for the United States and a large share of exports from Japan, China, and other Asia is destined for China, Japan, and other Asia. Table 9.1b provides the distribution of world trade if these intra-regional trade flows are not taken into consideration, diminishing the importance of Europe in global trade, but not its top position.

The intra-EU trade flows mentioned above are largely of the intra-industry type – that is, the simultaneous import *and* export of similar types of goods or services. At the theoretical level, one distinguishes between horizontal and vertical intra-industry trade, whereby the former is at the same stage of processing (product differentiation) and the latter at different stages of processing (fragmentation). At the empirical level, intra-industry trade is identified using the Grubel–Lloyd index, which is defined as

$$GL_{sec\ tor\ i} = 1 - \left(\frac{|export_{sector\ i} - import_{sec\ tor\ i}|}{export_{sector\ i} + import_{sec\ tor\ i}} \right) \tag{9.1}$$

The Grubel–Lloyd index varies between zero (indicating pure *inter*-industry trade) and one (indicating pure *intra*-industry trade). As illustrated in figure 9.2 for a selection of countries, intra-industry trade as a share of total trade is high and/or rising for most developed countries, Australia with its large availability of natural resources being a prime exception.

There are structural differences between sectors regarding the extent of intra-industry trade. To illustrate this, we use the factor intensity classification of the International Trade Center, the joint UNCTAD/WTO organization, which distinguishes between five broad factor

Box 9.1 (cont.)

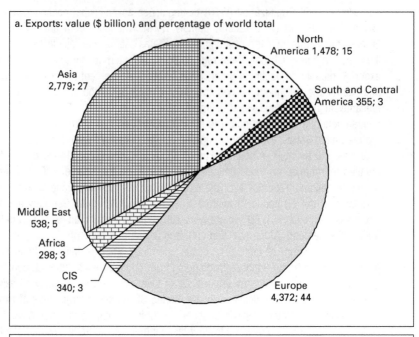

a. Exports: value ($ billion) and percentage of world total

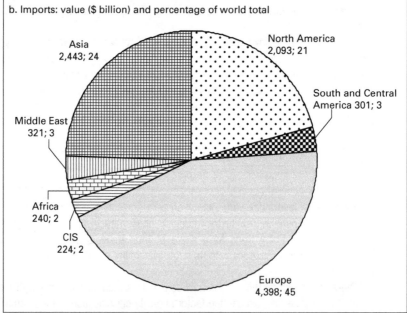

b. Imports: value ($ billion) and percentage of world total

Figure 9.1   Shares of world trade flows: merchandise trade, 2005
Source: WTO (2006).

Box 9.1 (cont.)

Table 9.1 Global distribution of merchandise trade (percentage of total), 2005

a. Inter- and intra-regional trade flows

					Destination						
Origin	USA	oNA	SCA	EU	oEU	CIS	Afr	ME	Jap	Chn	oAS	sum
USA		3.3	0.7	1.8	0.2	0.1	0.2	0.3	0.5	0.4	1.4	8.9
oNA	4.8	0.1	0.1	0.3	0.0	0.0	0.0	0.0	0.1	0.1	0.1	5.6
SCA	1.0	0.2	0.8	0.6	0.0	0.1	0.1	0.1	0.1	0.2	0.2	3.4
EU	3.0	0.5	0.5	26.3	2.6	1.0	1.0	1.1	0.5	0.6	1.8	39.0
oEU	0.3	0.1	0.0	2.4	0.2	0.1	0.1	0.1	0.1	0.0	0.2	3.6
CIS	0.2	0.0	0.1	1.4	0.4	0.6	0.0	0.1	0.1	0.2	0.2	3.2
Afr	0.5	0.1	0.1	1.2	0.1	0.0	0.3	0.1	0.1	0.2	0.2	2.7
ME	0.6	0.0	0.0	0.8	0.1	0.0	0.2	0.5	0.8	0.3	1.7	5.0
Jap	1.3	0.2	0.1	0.9	0.1	0.1	0.1	0.2		1.0	2.0	5.8
Chn	2.0	0.2	0.2	1.7	0.1	0.2	0.2	0.2	1.0		1.6	7.5
oAs	2.0	0.2	0.2	2.0	0.2	0.1	0.3	0.5	1.4	1.9	5.1	13.9
Total	15.8	4.8	3.0	39.4	3.9	2.2	2.4	3.2	4.6	4.8	14.6	

b. Interregional trade flows only

					Destination						
Origin	USA	oNA	SCA	EU	oEU	CIS	Afr	ME	Jap	Chn	oAS	sum
USA		5.1	1.1	2.8	0.3	0.1	0.2	0.5	0.8	0.6	2.2	13.8
oNA	7.4		0.2	0.4	0.0	0.0	0.0	0.0	0.1	0.1	0.2	8.6
SCA	1.5	0.3		1.0	0.1	0.1	0.1	0.1	0.2	0.3	0.3	3.9
EU	4.7	0.8	0.8		4.0	1.5	1.6	1.6	0.8	1.0	2.8	19.7
oEU	0.5	0.1	0.1	3.7		0.1	0.1	0.2	0.1	0.1	0.3	5.2
CIS	0.3	0.0	0.1	2.2	0.6		0.1	0.2	0.1	0.3	0.2	4.0
Afr	0.8	0.1	0.1	1.8	0.2	0.0		0.1	0.1	0.3	0.3	3.8
ME	1.0	0.0	0.0	1.2	0.1	0.0	0.2		1.2	0.4	2.7	6.9
Jap	2.1	0.2	0.1	1.3	0.1	0.1	0.1	0.3		1.5	3.1	8.9
Chn	3.1	0.3	0.3	2.7	0.2	0.3	0.3	0.3	1.6		2.5	11.6
oAs	3.1	0.3	0.4	3.1	0.2	0.2	0.4	0.8	2.2	2.9		13.6
Total	24.5	7.3	3.3	20.2	5.8	2.5	3.3	4.1	7.2	7.4	14.7	

Notes: USA = United States of America; oNA = other North America; SCA = South and Central America; EU = European Union; oEU = other Europe; CIS = Commonwealth of Independent States; Afr = Africa; ME = Middle East; Jap = Japan; Chn = China; oAs = other Asia, Australia, and New Zealand.

Source: Authors' calculations based on WTO (2006) and other WTO data.

Box 9.1 (cont.)

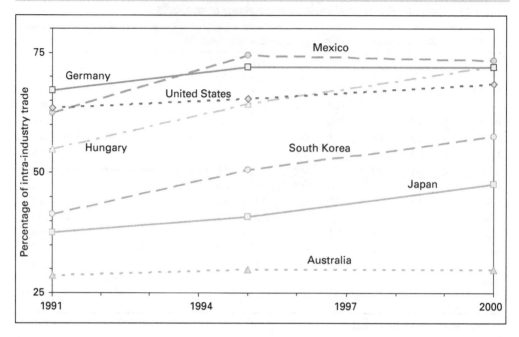

Figure 9.2   Manufacturing intra-industry trade, selected countries (percentage of total manufacturing), 1991–2000
Note: Averages are for the years 1988–91, 1992–95, and 1996–2000, located at the last contributing year.
Source: Based on OECD *Economic Outlook* no. 71, June 13, 2002, tab. VI.1: 161.

intensity categories at the three-digit level, as follows (within brackets the number of sectors belonging to the particular category).[1]

(i) *Primary products* (83); e.g. meat, dairy, cereals, fruit, coffee, minerals, and oil.
(ii) *Natural-resource-intensive products* (21); e.g. leather, wood, pig iron, and copper.
(iii) *Unskilled-labor-intensive products* (26); e.g. textiles, ships, and footwear.
(iv) *Human-capital-intensive products* (43); e.g. perfumes, cosmetics, and cars.
(v) *Technology-intensive products* (62); e.g. chemicals, electronics, tools, and aircraft.

Table 9.2 depicts the extent of intra-industry trade for these different types of sectors in China for selected years from 1980 to 2005. It shows that the level of intra-industry trade is particularly low for unskilled-labor-intensive sectors, particularly high for technology-intensive sectors, and intermediate for the other types of sectors. As countries, such as China, develop the composition of their trade flows tends to move away from primary products, initially towards unskilled-labor-intensive products, and subsequently towards technology- and human-capital-intensive products. Associated with these changes, there is a gradual increase in the extent of intra-industry trade, as illustrated for China and Taiwan one of its main intra-industry trading partners, in figure 9.3.

---

[1] See http://people.few.eur.nl/vanmarrewijk/eta for further details.

Box 9.1 (cont.)

Table 9.2 Intra-industry trade and composition of trade flows: China, 1980–2005

	Type of products				
	Primary products	Natural-resource-intensive	Unskilled-labor-intensive	Technology-intensive	Human-capital-intensive
Weighted average Grubel–Lloyd summary statistics for product type					
Average	0.27	0.38	0.16	0.56	0.36
St dev	0.11	0.07	0.04	0.04	0.08
Share of product type in total trade (per cent)					
1980	51.4	3.4	27.8	8.1	9.2
1985	49.5	2.0	33.7	7.1	7.7
1990	19.4	2.9	46.5	15.6	15.5
1995	10.1	4.0	45.4	24.9	15.6
2000	7.5	3.2	39.2	35.5	14.6
2005	4.6	3.3	28.9	47.7	15.5

Notes: Trade-weighted average Grubel–Lloyd index (three-digit level) and percentage of total trade. St dev = standard deviation.
Source: Van Marrewijk (forthcoming 2009).

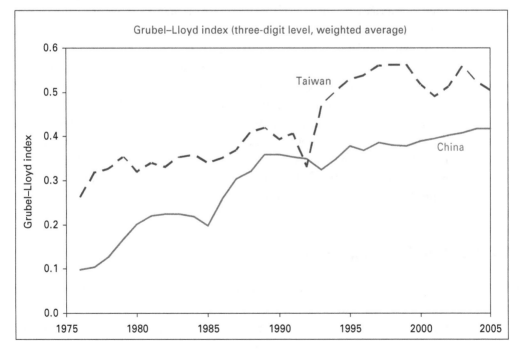

Figure 9.3   Intra-industry trade: China and Taiwan, 1976–2005

of the geographical economics literature, which assumes labor to be immobile between countries. The words "region" and "country" were used indifferently earlier in this book, which may not be quite appropriate when referring to labor mobility. In general, labor is allowed to migrate more easily between different regions in one country than between countries. Naturally, there are exceptions to this rule. In China for example, there are still severe restrictions on labor migration between Chinese cities. On the other hand, inhabitants of all nations of the European Union are allowed to migrate to any other EU nation.

To discuss the structure and size of international trade in a geographical economics setting as clearly as possible, we first assume that labor is immobile between nations. In addition, as in the core model of chapter 3, we assume that there are two countries that are symmetric in all aspects, except one. To enrich the range of possibilities we investigate two manufacturing sectors, A and B, as explained in the next section. As long as labor is not mobile between locations we assume mobility between the two sectors. We analyze this set-up by also allowing for comparative advantage, resulting from either Ricardo-style technological differences or Heckscher–Ohlin-style factor abundance. The introduction of comparative advantage makes the model different from the Krugman and Venables (1995) model of chapter 4. The comparative advantage version of the geographical economics model is the topic of the first part of chapter 9, sections 9.2 to 9.4.

The second part of chapter 9 deals with two topics: labor migration and the gravity model of international trade. In section 9.5 we briefly discuss the extent of international labor migration and show how labor migration can be used to test for the empirical relevance of geographical economics. We conclude chapter 9 with a discussion of the gravity model of international trade in section 9.6. We first show how geographical economics models, *in casu* the congestion model of chapter 7, can give rise to or mimic the gravity model. We then go on to show how the gravity model has been used in recent empirical research to estimate the equilibrium wage equation that is central to geographical economics. Section 9.7 concludes.

9.2 Two manufacturing sectors

Integrating location theory with international trade theory, which focuses on comparative advantage as a reason for two nations to trade, requires the introduction of two sectors that may benefit from differences in

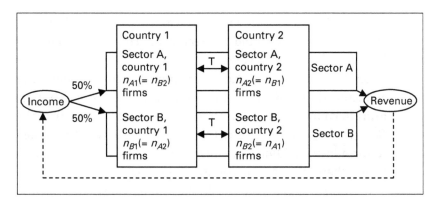

Figure 9.4   Demand and symmetry structure

comparative advantage between the two nations. For sections 9.2 to 9.4, the demand structure and notation, as well as some of its consequences, are therefore explained below, and summarized in figure 9.4. There are two manufacturing sectors, A and B, and two countries, 1 and 2. For simplicity the food sector is dropped from the analysis. The countries are identical in all aspects, except one. This ensures that the resulting equilibrium always has a mirror-image structure, which considerably simplifies the exposition. In which aspect the countries differ depends on the problem investigated. In section 9.3 they have different technologies, while in section 9.4 they have different endowments.

The demand side of the economy has the familiar nested Cobb–Douglas CES structure, ensuring that there is no consumption bias:

$$U = M_A^{1/2} M_B^{1/2} \tag{9.1}$$

$$M_A = \left(\sum_{i=1}^{n_A} c_{ai}^{\rho} \right)^{1/\rho} ; \quad M_B = \left(\sum_{i=1}^{n_B} c_{bi}^{\rho} \right)^{1/\rho} \tag{9.2}$$

where M_A is the composite index for sector A manufactures. Similarly, for sector B and M_B. Equation (9.1) indicates that 50 percent of a consumer's income is spent on sector A manufactures, and thus also 50 percent on sector B manufactures. Equation (9.2) indicates that manufacturing sector A consists of n_A different varieties. The elasticity of substitution between these varieties, important to determine the mark-up of price over marginal cost, is equal to $\varepsilon = 1/(1-\rho) > 1$. The same holds for sector B. The two sectors have the same elasticity of demand, and thus will follow the same pricing rule (see section 3.5). The symmetry structure imposed also below ensures that whatever holds for sector A in country 1 also holds for sector B in country 2, and vice versa.

Let A_2^1, be the demand facing a country 2, sector A producer in country 1, and similarly for B_1^2, etc. Moreover, let n_{A1} be the number of industry A firms in country 1, and similarly for n_{B2}, etc. By symmetry, $A_1^1 = B_2^2$, $A_2^1 = B_1^2$, $n_{A1} = n_{B2}$, $n_{A2} = n_{B1}$, etc. This implies that, if we let s denote the share of sector A firms residing in country 1 (that is, $s = n_{A1}/n_A$), then s is also equal to the share of firms in country 1 producing in sector A since $s = n_{A1}/(n_{A1} + n_{A2}) = n_{A1}/(n_{A1} + n_{B1})$. As the country 1 – sector A versus country 2 – sector B symmetry holds throughout sections 9.2 to 9.4, we henceforth focus on country 1.

9.3 Comparative advantage: David Ricardo

This section is based on the work of Luca Ricci (1997, 1999), integrating Ricardian comparative advantage and the geographical economics approach. The production function uses labor as the only input and is characterized by increasing returns to scale, ensuring that each variety is supplied by only one producer. There is, however, a technological difference between the two countries:

$$
\begin{aligned}
l_{A1i} &= a + \beta\, x_{A1i}; & l_{B1i} &= a + \bar{\beta}\, x_{B1i} \\
l_{A2i} &= a + \bar{\beta}\, x_{A2i}; & l_{B2i} &= a + \beta\, x_{B2i}; & \pi \equiv \bar{\beta}/\beta > 1
\end{aligned}
\tag{9.3}
$$

where l_{A1i} represents the amount of labor a sector A producer i in country 1 must use to produce x_{A1i} units of output, etc. Note that the marginal labor requirement is lower in country 1 for sector A, such that country 1 has a comparative (and absolute) advantage in sector A manufactures (and country 2 in sector B). The ratio of the marginal labor requirements, the variable π, measures *the extent of comparative advantage*; the larger π is the larger the technological differences between the two countries. This is summarized in figure 9.5. Transport costs between the two countries are of the iceberg type, equal to T, and are the same for sectors A and B.

As in the previous chapter, the firms in the manufacturing sector operate under a market structure of monopolistic competition. They charge a constant mark-up over marginal cost, which is the same for the two sectors since the price elasticity of demand is identical. Sector B firms in country 1

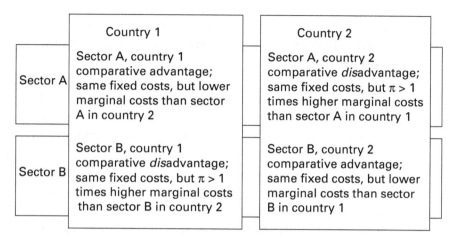

Figure 9.5   Comparative advantage structure, Ricardian model

are confronted with higher marginal costs and thus charge a higher price than sector A firms in country 1 – that is, $p_{B1}/p_{A1} = \pi$. Obviously, the price charged abroad is T times higher than the price charged at home for all firms to cover their transport costs. Firms enter and exit in each sector and country until profits are zero. This implies, as the reader may wish to verify, that a sector B producer in country 1 sells a lower quantity of goods than a sector A producer in country 1, but that the firms use the same amount of labor to produce these quantities. The number of firms active in each sector is therefore directly proportional to the number of laborers working in that sector. Moreover, the total sales revenue is the same for firms in either sector (although the distribution of foreign to domestic sales may differ; see below).

The higher productivity for sector A in country 1 than in country 2 gives firms an incentive to locate sector A production in country 1. In a standard Ricardian framework, specialization will be complete. Will the same occur in this Ricardian–geographical economics framework, or will some firms locate production in the less advantageous country? And, if so, why? The answer is, as discussed below, that both situations may occur. There may be *incomplete specialization*, in which case both countries produce goods in sectors A and B, although production by the sector with a comparative advantage will be greater than production by the sector with comparative disadvantage. The reasons are straightforward. Increasing returns to scale ensure that production is located in only one country. On the one hand, agglomeration of sector A in country 1 is promoted by the

productivity advantage. On the other hand, spreading of sector A production to country 2 is promoted by competition for segmented markets
as transport costs create a price wedge that results, through the substitution effect (see below), in higher demand for domestic goods. If there is
a balance between these two powers specialization will be incomplete.
There may be *complete specialization*, however, if the productivity
advantage dominates the spreading advantages – that is, if transport costs
are low and substitution of one variety for another is easy relative to the
productivity difference.

It can be shown (see Ricci, 1997: 55) that the share of sector A firms
residing in country 1, which is equal to the share of firms in country 1 active
in sector A (see section 9.2), if there is incomplete specialization is given by

$$s = \frac{n_{A1}}{n} = \frac{1}{2} + \frac{T^{\varepsilon-1}(\pi^{2(\varepsilon-1)} - 1)}{2[\pi^{\varepsilon-1}(1 + T^{2(\varepsilon-1)}) - T^{\varepsilon-1}(1 + \pi^{2(\varepsilon-1)})]} \equiv f(T, \varepsilon, \pi) \quad (9.4)$$

Thus, as intuitively explained above and illustrated in figure 9.6, the extent
of specialization increases if the extent of comparative advantage increases,
transport costs decrease, or the elasticity of substitution decreases. Figure
9.6 measures the extent of specialization by the share of sector A firms in
country 1 (= the share of sector B firms in country 2). The most important
influence of combining the Ricardian approach with the geographical
economics approach is the mitigation of the extent of specialization within
countries – that is, for a range of parameter values countries will only
partially, and not completely, specialize in the production of the good for
which they have a comparative advantage. Note, finally, that one of the
strong points of the Ricci (1997, 1999) Ricardian–geographical economics
approach is that it leads to a *closed-form* solution for the share of firms in
the sector with comparative advantage – that is, we can explicitly derive a
function for this share as given in equation (9.4).

Now that we have seen the impact of comparative advantage on the
distribution of manufacturing activity, we look more closely at the volume
and structure of international trade. The ratio of sales for a good produced
domestically to an imported good depends on the price ratio and the
demand elasticity. Since the wages at home and abroad are the same, as is
the mark-up, the price ratio depends on the transport costs T and the extent
of comparative advantage π only. The ratio of domestic to foreign demand

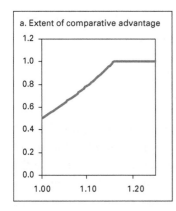 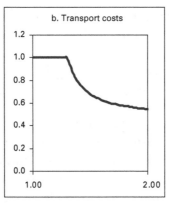 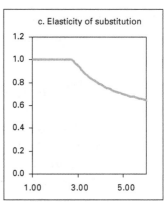

Figure 9.6   The share of sector A firms in country 1
Default parameters: $T = 1.4$, $\varepsilon = 4$, and $\pi = 1.1$.

for a good with domestic comparative advantage – that is, sector A in country 1 and sector B in country 2 – and the revenue ratio equals (see also sections 3.4 and 3.5)

$$demand = A_1^1/A_2^1 = (\pi T)^{\varepsilon}; \quad revenue = (\pi T)^{\varepsilon-1} \tag{9.5}$$

Note that both aspects, transport costs and comparative advantage, increase the demand of domestic firms relative to foreign firms as both result in a lower price for domestically produced goods. The lower foreign sales are only partially compensated for by a higher price, so the domestic to foreign revenue ratio equals $(\pi T)^{\varepsilon-1}$. Similarly, the ratio of domestic to foreign demand for a good with a domestic comparative disadvantage – that is, good B in country 1 and good A in country 2 – and the revenue ratio equals

$$demand = B_1^1/B_2^1 = (T/\pi)^{\varepsilon}; \quad revenue = (T/\pi)^{\varepsilon-1} \tag{9.6}$$

Note that this time transport costs increase and comparative disadvantage decreases the demand of domestic firms relative to foreign firms. Using equation (9.5) and the definition of s above, it follows that, of the income spent on the good with a domestic comparative advantage, the share spent on domestically produced goods dom_{A1} is

$$dom_{A1} = \frac{n_{A1}p_{A1}A_1^1}{n_{A1}p_{A1}A_1^1 + n_{A2}p_{A2}TA_2^1} = \frac{s(\pi T)^{\varepsilon-1}}{s(\pi T)^{\varepsilon-1} + (1-s)} \tag{9.7}$$

Similarly, of the good with a domestic comparative disadvantage, the share spent on domestically produced goods dom_{B1} equals

$$dom_{B1} = \frac{n_{B1} p_{B1} B_1^1}{n_{B1} p_{B1} B_1^1 + n_{B2} p_{B2} TB_2^1} = \frac{(1-s)(T/\pi)^{\varepsilon-1}}{(1-s)(T/\pi)^{\varepsilon-1} + s} \tag{9.8}$$

Knowing the distribution of domestic to foreign spending for the two sectors as given in equations (9.7) and (9.8), and keeping in mind that a half of a country's income is spent on each sector, makes it easy to calculate the share of income spent on imports (namely $[(1 - dom_{A1}) + (1 - dom_{B1})]/2$) and the extent of intra-industry trade as measured by the Grubel–Lloyd index, defined by $1 -$ |export $-$ import| / (export $+$ import), which gives $2(1 - dom_{A1})/[(1 - dom_{A1}) + (1 - dom_{B1})]$). Some shares are illustrated in figure 9.7. Panel a shows both the increasing share of firms in the sector with comparative advantage and the preference for spending on domestic goods as the extent of comparative advantage increases. Panel b shows that the degree of intra-industry trade falls from one to zero, and thus the degree of inter-industry trade rises, while the share of income spent on imports rises to 50 percent as the extent of comparative advantage rises. Again, we see a mitigation of the strong "bang-bang" results found in the standard Ricardian model. More importantly, as countries are becoming more similar – that is, as the extent of comparative advantage decreases – they are increasingly engaged in intra-industry trade, as supported by empirical evidence (recall box 9.1 at the beginning of this chapter).

9.4 Comparative advantage: factor abundance

As demonstrated in the previous section, the general implications of the Ricardian framework, focusing on technological differences between countries, can be integrated into the geographical economics approach, focusing on imperfect competition, increasing returns to scale, and forward and backward linkages, to create an intricate picture of the various powers underlying international trade flows, sometimes reinforcing one another, sometimes working in the opposite direction. This section completes the neoclassical–geographical economics marriage by integrating the factor abundance international trade theory into the geographical economics approach. To ease the exposition as much as possible we use an almost

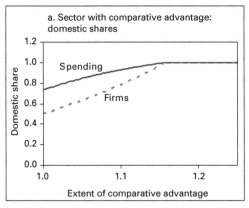
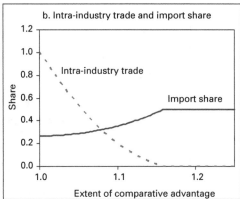

Figure 9.7   Ricardo and geographical economics ($T = 1.4$, $\varepsilon = 4$)

identical structure to that in section 9.3, again imposing "super-symmetry," and point out similarities and differences whenever appropriate.

The demand structure is explained in section 9.2. There are two countries, 1 and 2, and two sectors, A and B, each producing a variety of manufactures that are imperfect substitutes for one another. Naturally, to investigate a setting in which relative factor abundance plays a role requires the use of at least two factors of production, instead of the single factor labor used thus far. An elegant way to do this was developed by Peter Kenen (1965) and later applied by Wilfred Ethier and Henrik Horn (1984) to analyze customs unions, Brakman and van Marrewijk (1995, 1998) to analyze international transfers, and Fujita, Krugman, and Venables (1999) in a geographical economics setting.[2] The production process takes place in two stages; see figure 9.8. In the first stage, primary inputs, labeled capital K and labor L, are used to produce two sector-specific intermediate goods, D_A and D_B. In the second stage, these intermediate goods are used as inputs in the production process for varieties, as usual under internal increasing returns to scale.

Since the second-stage production process, essentially representing the geographical economics part of the model, is more familiar we start by briefly describing the second stage. As we have already analyzed technological differences in section 9.3, we assume that the production function for varieties is the same for both sectors and both countries. If D_{A1i} is the

---

[2] For related research, see Venables and Limao (2002) or Markusen and Venables (2007).

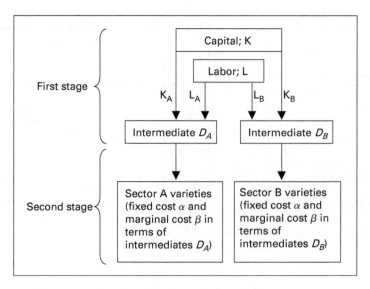

Figure 9.8   Production stages of the factor abundance model

amount of intermediate good D_A used by sector A producer i in country 1, the resulting output x_{A1i} is given by

$$D_{A1i} = a + \beta x_{A1i} \tag{9.9}$$

It is the same for D_{B2i} with respect to x_{B2i}, etc. The fixed costs a and the marginal costs β are therefore the same for both sectors in both countries when measured in terms of the intermediate goods. The rest of the second stage set-up is the same as in section 9.3. Each manufacturing firm therefore charges a constant mark-up over marginal cost ($pp_{A1} = \beta p_{DA1}$, etc.), while the entry and exit of manufacturing firms in each sector and country ensure that all varieties are produced in the same quantity, using the same amount of intermediate goods ($x = (\varepsilon - 1)a/\beta$ and $D = \varepsilon a$ respectively). Transport costs for varieties are of the iceberg type, equal to T, and the same in the two sectors.

Now we get to describing the first stage of the production process, essentially representing the factor abundance part of the model, in which the intermediate goods D_A and D_B are produced using primary inputs capital and labor under perfect competition with a standard, constant returns to scale, neoclassical Cobb–Douglas production function, which is identical in the two countries:

$$
\begin{aligned}
D_A &= [\gamma^{-\gamma}(1-\gamma)^{-(1-\gamma)}] K_A^{\gamma} L_A^{1-\gamma}; \\
D_B &= [\gamma^{-\gamma}(1-\gamma)^{-(1-\gamma)}] K_B^{1-\gamma} L_B^{\gamma}
\end{aligned}
\tag{9.10}
$$

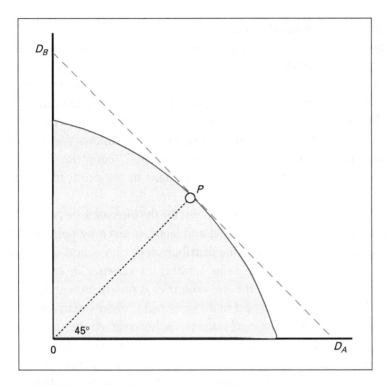

Figure 9.9   Intermediate goods transformation curve ($\gamma = 0.9$)

Note that we imposed symmetry in the production functions – that is, the capital intensity of sector A is the labor intensity of sector B and vice versa. Without loss of generality we assume $\gamma > 1/2$; in other words, sector A is relatively capital-intensive. To complete the symmetry, we assume that the total amount of capital available is equal to the total amount of labor available.

The first-stage production process for intermediate goods gives rise to a standard concave transformation curve, substituting one type of intermediate good for another. We start by analyzing a situation in which countries 1 and 2 have the same amount of labor and capital, such that they are symmetric in all respects.[3] The transformation curve is illustrated in figure 9.9. The curvature is rather strong, as we chose a high value of γ, sector A's capital share, for illustrative purposes. The large difference in capital intensity for the production of the two intermediates ensures that they are relatively difficult to substitute one for another, which results in the strong curvature. In the symmetric equilibrium the wage rate is equal to the

---

[3] Fujita, Krugman, and Venables (1999) analyze stability for this setting.

rental rate, say equal to one. Total income in each country is then equal to the sum of the available capital stock and labor stock. The cost-minimizing capital/labor intensity of production is equal to $k_A = K_A/L_A = \gamma/(1-\gamma)$ for intermediate good A and $k_B = K_B/L_B = (1-\gamma)/\gamma$ for intermediate good B. From the identity $k_A(L_A/L) + k_B(L_B/L) = K/L = 1$ it follows that $L_A/L = 1 - \gamma$ (that is, the share $1 - \gamma$ of labor is employed in sector A). From the normalization of the wage rate and rental rate it follows that the price of the intermediate goods in both sectors in both countries is equal to one, through a suitable choice of the constant in the production functions for intermediate goods.

The equilibrium production point for the intermediate goods sectors, with an equal distribution of capital and labor, is given by point P in figure 9.9. Both countries have the same distribution of capital and labor over the two sectors and produce the same number of varieties in each sector. International trade between the two countries is purely intra-industry trade. We are interested in the impact of different factor endowments on the structures and size of the international trade flows, however. At the same time, we want to preserve the mirror image structure of the model. Thus, we shift capital from country 2 to country 1 in return for an equal amount of labor from country 1 to country 2. Any adjustments in the production structure of country 1 will be mirror-mimicked in country 2. Since country 1 becomes relatively well endowed with capital, we expect country 1 to specialize (partially) in the production of the capital-intensive sector A manufactures.

There are now two ways to continue, namely the easy way and the interesting way.

The *easy way* to continue is to assume that the sector-specific intermediate goods can be costlessly transported from one country to another and that the share of total capital available in country 1 does not exceed γ, the share of capital employed in sector A in the symmetric equilibrium. Under these circumstances the original symmetric equilibrium can be replicated (this is illustrated in figure 9.11 by the production points Pr_{10} for country 1 and Pr_{20} for country 2). The shift of capital from country 2 to country 1 in return for labor from country 1 to country 2 affects the transformation curves of the two countries. Country 1's transformation curve is biased towards the production of sector A intermediate goods, which are capital-intensive, because country 1 is relatively well endowed with capital. Similarly, country 2's transformation curve is biased towards the production of sector B intermediate goods, which are labor-intensive, because country 2 is relatively well-endowed with labor. In fact, it is a well-known result from neoclassical international trade theory, partially discussed in chapter 2, that a country that increases the endowment of a factor of production, say capital, will increase the production of the capital-intensive good and reduce production of the labor-intensive good at given prices for these goods. These changes are proportional to the size of the change in the endowment – that is, we can trace out a straight line for these changes, a so-called Rybczynski line (see box 9.2), in goods space (in this case the space for intermediate goods D_A and D_B). Similar lines hold for equiproportional simultaneous changes in both endowments.

Given the prices for intermediate goods in the symmetric equilibrium, the original world production level for intermediate goods can be replicated, in essence by both countries adjusting their production of intermediate goods along the Rybczynski lines. Does this mean that the original symmetric equilibrium can be replicated? Yes, but only if the intermediate goods are costlessly tradable. In that case, country 1 would produce intermediate goods at point Pr_{10} and export intermediate good D_A in return for intermediate good D_B to reach point Pr_{11}. The same number of varieties as before would be produced in both countries, such that at the manufacturing level there would again be only intra-industry trade. This is complemented by pure inter-industry trade at the intermediate goods level to compensate for the differences in factor endowments.

Box 9.2 Factor endowments and the Rybczynski line

One of the classic results of neoclassical trade theory is the theorem developed by Tadevsz Rybczynski. If there are two final goods, say X and Y, and two factors of production, say capital K and labor L, the theorem states that, for *given* prices of the final goods X and Y, an increase in one of the factors of production, say K, leads to an increase in output of the final good using this production factor relatively intensively, and a decrease in output of the other final good. Moreover, these changes are equiproportional.

This is illustrated in figure 9.10, in which Tr_0 is the initial transformation curve, A is the initial production point, and we assume that good X uses capital K relatively intensively. If the available capital stock increases by ΔK, the transformation curve will shift out to Tr_1, somewhat more in the direction of good X, the capital-intensive good, than in the direction of good Y, as indicated by the arrow in figure 9.10. At the same final goods prices (indicated by the parallel dashed price lines) the economy will now produce at point B, increasing production of good X, the capital-intensive good, and reducing production of good Y, the labor-intensive good. Moreover, as mentioned above, the changes are equi-proportional. A second increase in capital of equal size ΔK will lead to an identical change

Box 9.2 (cont.)

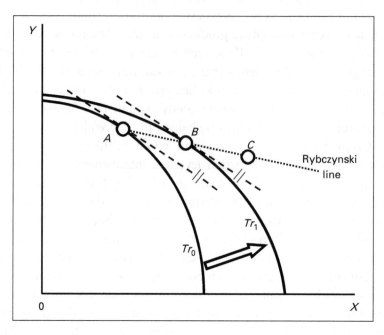

Figure 9.10 The Rybczynski line

in final goods production, from point *B* to point *C*. The line connecting all such production points is called the capital-Rybczynski line. A similar line can be derived for changes in labor.

The *interesting way* to continue can be motivated as follows. A disadvantage of the easy way described above is the assumption that intermediate goods can be traded costlessly, while final goods produced from these intermediate goods are costly to trade. Although it makes the analysis simple, this assumption, which essentially makes primary inputs costlessly tradable, is not very appealing. The remainder of this section therefore analyzes the interesting way to continue, by making the opposite assumption: that sector-specific intermediate goods cannot be traded internationally.[4]

---

[4] The arguments below are similar if intermediate goods are tradable at high costs; see also de Vaal and van den Berg (1999).

What will the production structure look like if sector-specific inter-mediate goods cannot be traded?[5] Obviously, we expect capital-rich country 1 to specialize in the production of capital-intensive sector A intermediate goods, but to what extent? A first guess might be up to production point Pr_{10} in figure 9.11, which would enable the world as a whole to produce the same number of varieties for both types of manufactures. In that case, country 1 would make a larger share of sector A manufactures and country 2 of sector B manufactures. There would be more intensive trade relations, both intra-industry and inter-industry. Since trade in manufactures is costly, however, the production points Pr_{10} and Pr_{20} cannot be an equilibrium. Indeed, the Ricci equation (9.4) in section 9.3 determining the share of sector A firms in country 1 in a Ricardian setting gives us an indication that a higher share of sector A firms in country 1 requires a higher price of sector B manufactures relative to sector A manufactures in country 1. There must therefore be a price wedge $p_{B1}/p_{A1} \equiv \pi > 1$ for final goods, which translates directly into an equal price wedge π for intermediate goods. Since at points Pr_{10} and Pr_{20} the price ratio of intermediate goods, which is equal to minus the slope of a line tangent to the transformation curve, is one, it cannot be an equilibrium point.

Now that we have established the need for a price wedge π for intermediate goods, it is immediately clear from figure 9.11 that the equilibrium pro-duction points must be something like points Pr_{11} and Pr_{21}. Obviously, the higher price for sector B intermediate goods in country 1 at point Pr_{11} implies a substitution away from the production of sector A intermediates relative to point Pr_{10}, thus reducing the size of sector A and the need for the costly transportation of manufactures. The same holds for sector B in country 2. In other words, the comparative advantage of capital-rich country 1 in the production of capital-intensive sector A intermediate goods translates into a lower price for sector A intermediate goods relative to country 2.

The analogy with the Ricardian technology-driven comparative advan-tage is almost complete if we take the price wedge π as a measure of comparative advantage. Almost, but not quite. Remember that all firms in all sectors use the same amount of intermediate goods in equilibrium. Since the price of sector B intermediate goods in country 1 is higher than the price of sector A intermediate goods, this implies that the revenue from sales for a sector B firm in country 1 must be higher than the revenue of sales from a sector A firm in country 1. One firm in sector B in country 1 therefore has a

---

[5] Note the similarity with the Krugman and Venables (1995) model discussed in chapter 4.

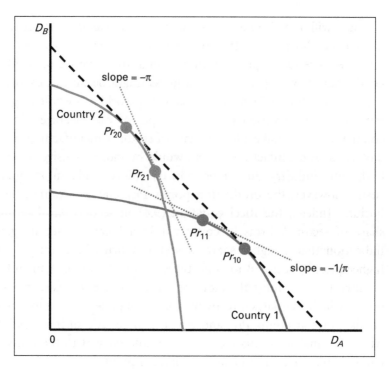

Figure 9.11 Transformation curves ($K_1/K = L_2/L = 2/3$; $\gamma = 0.9$)

higher impact on this country's income than one firm in sector A.[6] It can be shown (see van Marrewijk, 2000) that, as a result of this higher impact on a country's income the share of sector A firms residing in country 1, which is equal to the share of firms in country 1 active in sector A (see section 9.2), if there is incomplete specialization is given by

$$\frac{n_{A1}}{n} = \frac{\pi g(T, \varepsilon, \pi)}{1 + (\pi - 1)g(T, \varepsilon, \pi)}$$

$$\text{where} \quad g(T, \varepsilon, \pi) = \frac{1}{2} + \frac{T^{\varepsilon-1}(\pi^{2\varepsilon} - 1)}{2[\pi^\varepsilon(1 + T^{2(\varepsilon-1)}) - T^{\varepsilon-1}(1 + \pi^{2\varepsilon})]}$$

(9.11)

As in the Ricardian–geographical economics framework, we can thus derive a *closed-form* solution for the share of firms in the sector with comparative advantage.

As illustrated in figure 9.12, the larger impact of sector A firms for the income level in country 1 affects the extent of specialization. Panel a shows

---

[6] To be precise, $income = (n_{a1}p_{da1} + n_{b1}p_{db1})a\varepsilon = (n_{a1} + \pi n_{b1})p_{da1}a\varepsilon$.

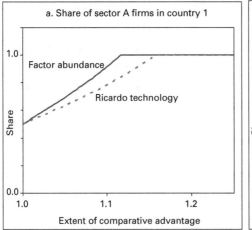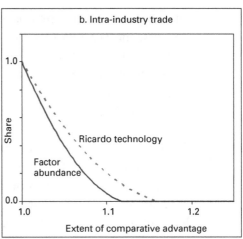

Figure 9.12 Ricardo and factor abundance ($T = 1.4$, $\varepsilon = 4$)

that the same level of specialization translates into a lower price wedge, or, alternatively, that the same level of comparative advantage as measured by the price wedge translates into a higher degree of specialization for the factor abundance model compared to the Ricardian technology model. Panel b shows that the same extent of comparative advantage leads to higher intra-industry trade flows in the Ricardian technology model than in the factor abundance model. Nonetheless, as with the Ricardian model, when comparative advantage based on factor abundance is integrated into the geographical economics model this results in higher levels of intra-industry trade between similar countries and, *ceteris paribus*, larger trade flows between dissimilar countries.

The discussion on the incorporation of comparative advantage into a geographical economics model raises the empirical question as to the relative importance of comparative advantage compared to variables such as market size, which are key to geographical economics, in explaining trade patterns and the location of firms. In chapter 5 section 5.4, in our discussion of the home market effect, we looked in some detail at the studies by Davis and Weinstein (1998, 1999). They assume that comparative advantage determines trade at higher levels of aggregation, whereas market size effects, and thereby second-nature geography, are allowed to determine finer levels of industry aggregation. Forslid, Haaland, and Midelfart Knarvik (2002) follow a different approach. In their study, sector simulations are used to show how industries (fourteen in total) across Europe react to a fall in trade or transport costs. Industries differ in terms of the strength of comparative advantage, increasing returns to scale (IRS), and intra-industry supply linkages, the last two of which can be associated with geographical economics. It turns out that a fall in trade costs has different implications for industry concentration depending on whether industries are characterized by a comparative advantage or by strong IRS and intra-industry linkages. A drop in trade costs leads to a monotonous increase of industry for comparative advantage industries, whereas the change in industry concentration for strong IRS and intra-industry linkages is highly non-linear. In particular, for the latter group of industries it is only for intermediate trade costs that falling trade costs can be associated with high and rising levels of industry concentration. Very high or very low levels of trade costs accompany lower levels of industry concentration.

Midelfart Knarvik, Overman and Venables (2001) estimate a model for fourteen EU countries and thirty-six manufacturing industries for four time periods between 1980 and 1997 in order to establish whether comparative advantage or the backward and forward linkages emphasized by geographical economics are more important for trade and the location of manufacturing industries. Their main result is that comparative advantage is important and generally more so than the geographical economics variables. Backward and, in particular, forward linkages of the kind emphasized by geographical economics are important as well, however, and their importance seems to increase over time. Since the sample period is one of increasing economic integration in Europe, this suggests that falling trade costs increase the relevance of economic geography variables.

In the empirical trade literature the measurement of comparative advantage has given rise to a large amount of research. One interesting short cut to determine a country's (sectoral) comparative advantage is to use measures of *revealed* comparative advantage; see box 9.3.

Box 9.3 Zipf's law and revealed comparative advantage

This chapter discusses two theoretical foundations for comparative advantage, namely differences in technology and differences in factor abundance. One can then empirically test the validity of these theories. Empirical trade research has also reversed the question, by first determining what a country's strong export sectors are and then subsequently trying to come up with theories that explain these observations. The most commonly used method of this so-called *revealed* comparative advantage is the index named after Bela Balassa (1965), which takes the ratio of a country's export share in a certain sector relative to that

Box 9.3 (cont.)

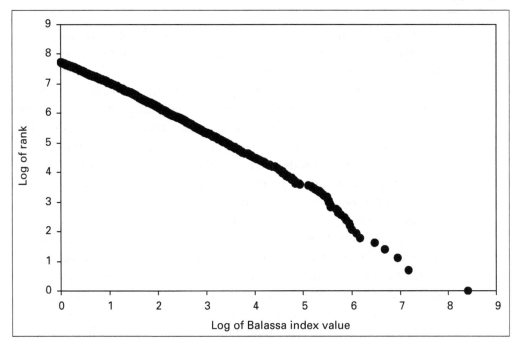

Figure 9.13   The Balassa index and the rank size rule: all countries, 1970–97
Note: The figure is based on 1 percent randomly drawn Balassa index values from the entire sample of 221,430 observations.
Source: Hinloopen and van Marrewijk (2006).

sector's export share in a group of reference countries. If the resulting Balassa index is above unity, the country is said to have a revealed comparative advantage in that sector (it is, apparently, a strong export sector).

The focus of this book is on the location of economic activity and on the interactions between these locations. In chapters 1 and 7, we have already discussed Zipf's law and the rank size rule regarding the regularity in the *distribution* of spatial activity. In chapter 1, and later in this chapter, we also discuss the gravity equation, a regularity regarding the *interaction* between locations. Recent research by Hinloopen and van Marrewijk (2006) shows that there is also an intriguing regularity regarding the combination of distribution and interaction for a country's strong export sectors as measured by the Balassa index. More specifically, by using the Gabaix–Ibragimov (2007) method discussed in chapter 7 on trade data for virtually all countries in the world in the period 1970–97, Hinloopen and van Marrewijk (2006) show that the distribution of the Balassa index follows the rank size rule. This is illustrated for all countries combined in figure 9.13. The authors also show that the estimated slope (Pareto) coefficients differ systematically between countries and sectors.

9.5 Migration

According to Krugman and Venables (1995) (recall our discussion of this important geographical economics model in chapter 4 section 4.6), a crucial difference between international economics and regional economics concerns the mobility of labor across space. As we have already noted in the introduction of the present chapter, in international economics it is often assumed that labor is not mobile between countries, whereas labor is typically assumed to be mobile between regions in regional economics. So far, we have maintained this distinction in this chapter and kept labor *immobile*. In the core model of geographical economics of chapter 3, however, labor is mobile between locations in the long run. A natural question to ask therefore, is whether and how a geographical economics model *with* labor mobility can be used for the analysis of international trade. This question is addressed in the next section, on the gravity model. In this section, we first briefly present and discuss some data to show that the international migration of labor matters. The second aim of this section, returning to the list with five empirical hypotheses in chapter 5 due to Head and Mayer (2004a), is to show how labor migration (or factor migration in general) can be used to test for the empirical relevance of geographical economics.

9.5.1 Some facts about labor migration

The process of globalization can be defined as increasing cross-country economic interdependencies through increased trade and increased factor mobility. Compared to international trade flows and capital mobility, the international mobility of labor is (still) less relevant in this process, but it is nevertheless increasingly becoming a factor to take into consideration as well. In a study for the International Labour Organization (ILO), Peter Stalker (2000) argues that, for many countries, migration, though still relatively small as a percentage of a country's total population, has been on the rise since World War II and is expected to increase further in the near future. To illustrate the phenomenon at hand, table 9.3 gives the *stock* of foreign population for selected OECD countries. The data illustrate that, as a percentage of total population countries differ with respect to foreign population. Switzerland and Japan stand out; Switzerland has a relatively large share of foreigners in the total population, and Japan a relatively small

Table 9.3 Foreign population in selected OECD countries, 1992–2001

	1992	1997	2001
Belgium	909 (7.9)	903 (8.9)	846 (8.2)
Denmark	180 (3.5)	249 (4.7)	267 (5.0)
Japan	1,282 (1.0)	1,483 (1.2)	1,778 (1.4)
Netherlands	757 (5.0)	678 (4.3)	690 (4.3)
United Kingdom	1,985 (3.5)	2,066 (3.6)	2,587 (4.4)
United States	–	25,800 (9.7)	31,811 (11.1)
Switzerland	1,214 (17.6)	1,341 (19.0)	1,419 (19.7)

Notes: Figures show stock of foreign population, in thousands, and (in brackets) the percentage of the total population. For the United States, the data relate to the foreign-born stock.
Source: OECD (2003: tab. A.1.5).

share. For the world as a whole, the total (foreign-born) migrant stock increased from 75 million to 177 million people in the period from 1965 to 2000 (Stalker, 2000: 6; OECD, 2003).

People migrate for various reasons, and to some extent migration is driven not by economic factors but, for instance, by political motives and the desire to be reunited with family members who live abroad. Having said that, a large part of migration is economically determined. The (increasing) per capita income differences between rich and poor countries (see chapter 1) are the main force behind economic migration. This helps to explain why we observe that the flow of international migration is pre-dominantly from countries with a relatively low GDP per capita to countries with a higher GDP per capita. This is important for the migration to the countries mentioned in table 9.3. Within the European Union, stimulated by the gradual abolition of legal restrictions on intra-EU labor mobility, the migration flow is from the southern periphery to the northern core of the European Union (see also subsection 9.5.2). In a similar vein, within Asia migration is from the poorer countries to nations such as South Korea or Singapore, where wages are considerably higher.

To illustrate the importance of these intra-regional migration flows: in 1995 emigration to Germany, which had by far the largest annual inflow of migrants of all EU countries, consisted of almost 90 percent of people who came from other European countries. The fact that migration flows are from low-wage countries to high-wage countries is important from

Table 9.4 Migration rates per decade (per thousand mean population), 1881–1910

	1881–90	1891–1900	1901–10
European emigration rates			
British Isles	70.2	43.8	65.3
Germany	28.7	10.1	4.5
Ireland	141.7	88.5	69.8
Italy	33.6	50.2	107.7
Norway	95.2	44.9	83.3
Portugal	38.0	50.8	56.9
Spain	36.2	43.8	56.6
Sweden	70.1	41.2	42.0
"New World" immigration rates			
Canada	78.4	48.8	167.6
United Stares	85.8	53.0	102.0

Source: O'Rourke and Williamson (1999: 122).

the perspective of geographical economics, because, in the core model, the decision for manufacturing workers to migrate is driven entirely by (real) wage differences between locations. Also relevant from a geographical economics perspective, and in line with the idea of a spatial wage structure (see chapter 5), is the fact that that migration from relatively "poor" to "rich" countries reinforces agglomeration patterns.

The experience with migration in what is sometimes called the first wave of globalization (the late nineteenth and early twentieth centuries) shows that migration flows can increase dramatically in a relatively short span of time. For migration to matter from an economic point of view it is not absolutely necessary that migration flows increase further or that the stock of migrants, as a percentage of total population, becomes larger than the stocks reported in table 9.3. Even the present migration flows can exert an influence on (marginal) wages in the rich countries, especially for low-skilled labor. The idea that the mobility of labor (similar to the trade of goods) may exert an influence on wages is of course, at home in old and new trade theories alike, and there is evidence that migration can be important for relative wages within or between countries. Kevin O'Rourke and Jeffrey Williamson (1999), for instance, show that, in the second part of the nineteenth century and the early twentieth century, not only did migration from European countries to the United States increase strongly, but also that this movement of labor exerted a significant influence on factor prices in Europe and the United States.[7] Table 9.4 illustrates for a number of European countries and two labor-receiving countries, the United States and Canada, the emigration and immigration rates for the three decades between 1880 and 1910. This era remains until today, especially for currently developed countries, the heyday of international labor mobility. To put this era of transatlantic migration into perspective: in the decade 1901–10 the share of foreign-born citizens in the United States was 14.2 percent of the total US population.

9.5.2 Migration as a testing ground for geographical economics

Many observers expect economic migration to become more important in the near future. The main reason for this forecast is that increasing wage differentials between countries are likely to increase the expected net return to migration for many people. Migration also clearly involves costs, and it can be looked upon as a risky investment. The costs of migration are often substantial, and they include not just the actual costs of moving but also the (immaterial) costs of leaving your friends and family behind and the costs of finding a job in your new country. The migration decision is also a risky one, because of the uncertainty surrounding the job and earning prospects in the new country (see Stalker, 2000: 24).[8] *Given* these costs and risks, the ever-increasing wage differentials alone will be enough to induce more migration. It is not unlikely that the costs and risks of migration will decrease in the future, however, thereby providing a further incentive for migration. Improvements in transport and communications technology may decrease the actual costs of moving, and may also make it easier for future migrants to keep themselves informed about the prospects of migrating.

The idea that labor migration is driven not just (as the core model of chapter 3 predicts) by real wage differences but also by factors such as the mobility costs and the riskiness of migration is taken up by Crozet (2004). Our discussion of the empirical relevance of geographical economics in chapters 5 and 6 was motivated by a list of five empirical hypotheses to

---

[7] In line with the factor abundance theory, this migration flow led to a rise in wage/rental ratios in Europe and a fall in wage rental ratios in the United States (in the United States the immigration of people made labor somewhat less scarce).

[8] A very simple specification that has performed well from an empirical point of view is the so-called Harris–Todaro equation, which states that migration from "poor" country i to "rich" country j will occur until $w_j(1-u_j) = w_i(1-u_i)$, where w is the wage rate and u is the unemployment rate. This equation was originally devised to explain migration from rural to urban areas within developing countries.

which geographical economics gives rise (Head and Mayer, 2004a). We discussed four of these five hypotheses in some detail in these two chapters but we skipped one hypothesis: *a large market potential induces factor inflows*. It is precisely this hypothesis that is the subject of Crozet (2004).

In the core model, with the real wage for region *s* being defined as (see equation (4.4)) $w_s = W_s I_s^{-\delta}$, manufacturing workers' migration flows will continue unless real wages are equalized. The starting point for Crozet's analysis is that the migration flow from region *s* to region *r*, mig_{sr}, is a function not only of the wages in the two regions but also of the probability of finding a job in region *r*, ε_r (this signals the riskiness of the migration decision), and the bilateral mobility or moving costs between *s* and *r*, ρ_{sr}. These mobility costs are basically taken to be increasing in the bilateral distance D_{sr} between regions *s* and *r*. Armed with this somewhat extended migration model, Crozet then confronts this migration decision rule with what is essentially the core model of geographical economics of chapter 3.[9] Somewhat simplified, the central equation of Crozet (2004) then becomes

$$mig_{sr} = \left(\frac{W_r}{W_s}\right)^A \left(\frac{L_r}{L_s}\right)^B \left(\frac{NMP_r}{NMP_s}\right)^C \frac{\varepsilon_r}{\rho_{sr}} \tag{9.12}$$

where, in addition to the variables and parameters introduced above, L_i is the size of the region (in terms of workers), W_i is the nominal wage in region *i* and NMP_i is the nominal market potential (or, more precisely, the trade-costs-weighted sums of the market size) in region *i*, and where $i = r, s$ and the positive parameters A, B, and C denote (combinations of) structural model parameters.

As we have already noted in chapter 5 section 5.3, the hypothesis that a large market potential leads to factor inflows is close to one of the other hypotheses, namely that a higher market potential accompanies higher factor prices. The latter hypothesis has been tested in section 5.5 by making use of the equilibrium wage equation (4.3) or, equivalently, (5.3) from the core model, in which nominal wages in a region are basically an increasing function of a region's real market potential. Equation (9.12) delivers a similar message. Given relative nominal wages, bilateral mobility costs and

---

[9] Although it is not quite the same as Head and Mayer (2004a: 2631), upon which our discussion of Crozet is partly based. Also note that Crozet (2004) adds a non-traded service sector to the core model.

the probability of finding a job in region r, the migration from region s to r is a function of the relative size of the hosting region L_r/L_s and the relative market potential. Similarly to the factor price hypothesis, factor flows (or migration flows) into region r are *increasing* in the relative (market) size of region r.

Crozet (2004) estimates a slightly reworked version of (9.12) for the internal bilateral regional migration flows for five EU countries (Germany, Spain, Italy, the Netherlands, and the United Kingdom) using annual data for (mostly) the early 1980s until the early 1990s. As in the studies on a spatial wage structure discussed in chapter 5, Crozet (2004: 452) concludes that "we observe here that parameters defining the market potential function are all significant. In accordance with new economic geography model's prediction, access to manufactured commodities does influence workers' mobility since it is measured by a grounded market potential function." Also in line with the findings in chapter 5 that a higher market potential raises factor prices (wages) is the fact that the extent to which a higher market potential raises factor inflows by stimulating migration is quite limited spatially. Workers' incentive to migrate from their region to a core region quickly gets very weak as the distance between their region and the core region increases. In this sense, and again in line with our conclusions at the end of chapter 5, agglomeration forces are indeed rather localized. This would mean that "labour mobility in Europe is sufficiently low to make the swift emergence of a core–periphery pattern very unlikely at the large geographical level" (Crozet, 2004: 455).

To reach this last conclusion, Crozet also makes use of the break point of the core model (see chapter 4, subsection 4.5.2) and confronts the break point condition with his estimated coefficients. In chapter 6 (see box 6.3), we have explained that such an experiment is interesting but also flawed, for it tries to force a multi-region world into the two-region model for which we can derive the break point. More interestingly for our present purposes regarding the relationship between geographical economics and international trade is the fact that Crozet's migration analysis shows that the underlying geographical economics model is quite close to the so-called *gravity equation*, the main vehicle for *empirical* research in international trade. As Crozet, puts it (2004: 445), an equation such as (9.12) above is "closely related to a simple gravity equation. Besides nominal wages and employment probability, the migration flow between two regions increases with the size of the host region and decreases with the geographic distance between the two locations." We turn now to the gravity equation.[10]

9.6 Gravity and trade

Chapter 1 has briefly discussed the empirical success of the "gravity equation" to describe international trade flows between nations; see section 1.4 on German export flows. A "demographic gravitation" model of interactions between two locations was first developed by the Princeton astronomer James Q. Stewart (1947, 1948). By analogy with the Newtonian gravity model, he finds strong correlations for traffic, migration, and communication between two places, based on the product of their population size and inversely related to their distance squared. A similar procedure was first applied to international trade between nations by Jan Tinbergen (1962). This became known as "the gravity model" in international economics (see also Linnemann 1966, for an early statement). There have been many attempts, increasingly successful and increasingly complicated, to provide a solid theoretical basis for the gravity equation based on imperfect competition and trade costs (see, for example, Anderson, 1979, Bergstrand, 1985, 1989, Harrigan, 1994, 1995, and Anderson and van Wincoop, 2004). There was a strong need for this theoretical basis in view of the empirical success of the gravity equation and its popularity in tackling difficult policy-related questions for example, see, Tinbergen, 1962, Pollins, 1989, and van Bergeijk and Oldersma, 1990.

9.6.1 Recent developments

Countries may trade with one another for various reasons. As we have seen in the first part of this chapter, there can be *comparative advantages*, based on differences in technology or in the abundance of available factors of production. There can also be *competitive advantages*, based on the competitive pressure of additional firms on the market (pro-competitive gains from trade) or extensions of the market reach of firms, leading to more varieties of final goods or increased output through production externalities

---

[10] Besides labor migration, the hypothesis that a large market potential raises factor inflows can also be investigated by looking at the interregional migration of *firms*. We have dealt with this possibility in section 8.5, where we discussed some studies (sush as Head and Mayer, 2004b) in which the FDI decision is a function of a market potential variable.

associated with intermediate goods trade. The recent analysis of the importance of multinational firms combines these insights by analyzing fragmentation of the production process, based on the various explanations for trade flows mentioned above (see, for example, Helpman and Krugman, 1985, and van Marrewijk, 2007). It turns out that one can derive the gravity equation from various economic trade theories, based both on perfect competition and on imperfect competition analyses (see the studies mentioned above). This is a big *disadvantage* for the trade economist, as it becomes difficult to falsify specific theories based on the empirical evidence (usually requiring rather subtle differences in predictions beyond the reliability scope of the data). At the same time this is a big *advantage* for empirical policy analysis, as we do not have to worry if the underlying economic structure for specific sectors is mainly one of perfect competition or imperfect competition (as both lead to similar empirical trade relations).

There are some econometric subtleties for the empirical analysis of the consequences of institutional changes on international trade flows, caused by *endogeneity bias*. Scott Baier and Jeffrey Bergstrand (2004), for example, find that the probability that two countries engage in a free trade agreement is larger (i) the larger and more similar their GDPs, (ii) the closer they are to each other, (iii) the more remote the pair of them are from the rest of the world, (iv) the wider the difference in their relative factor endowments is with respect to each other, and (v) the narrower this difference is with respect to the rest of the world. All these factors are also influential in explaining international trade flows, which has led to quite some confusion in the profession regarding the impact of institutional changes (which cannot be adequately dealt with using instrumental variables). Using an ingenious methodology based on the econometric analysis of treatment effects (see for example, Wooldridge, 2000), for all free trade agreements for a large set of (ninety-six) countries and an extended time period (1960–2000), Baier and Bergstrand (2007) are able to deal convincingly with the endogeneity problem using fixed effects and first differences in their panel data set.

Their approach is based on the influential theoretical work of Anderson and van Wincoop (2003) on the *multilateral price resistance* (MPR) terms when estimating the gravity equation and computing the impact of institutional changes. These MPR terms reflect the price indices, which by now are familiar from the core model (see, for instance, equation (3.6)). It is important to include these terms because bilateral trade flows, *ceteris paribus*, are determined not only by the bilateral price between two trading partners but also by the ratio of this price with the (aggregate) price indices. This ratio reflects the fact that a given bilateral price between two countries can have a different effect on bilateral trade between these two trading partners depending on the level of the price indices. If the "rest of the world" is far away, the high transport costs will be reflected in a high price index, and bilateral trade between the trading partners will be larger than if the "rest of the world" is nearby, in which case the relatively low transport costs will be reflected by low price indices, reducing the attractiveness of trade between the two trading partners. The disadvantage of the Anderson and van Wincoop (2003) framework is the need for custom-made, non-linear least squares in order to derive the MPR terms, such that few researchers actually perform such calculations. As noted by Robert Feenstra (2004), one can effectively overcome these problems by using region-specific fixed effects in panel data estimations.[11]

Until fairly recently, the most popular approach to estimating the gravity model using panel data was by linearizing it – that is, by taking logarithms and then estimating the log-linear model through fixed-effects ordinary least squares. The problem with this approach is that the log-linearized model is not defined for observations with zero trade flows (as is frequently the case for bilateral trade flows involving developing countries). Two common methods of handling the presence of zeros include (i) simply discarding the zeros from the sample and (ii) adding a constant factor to each observation on the dependent variable. The first approach is correct as long as the zeros are randomly distributed, which is, of course, rarely the case. The second approach leads to biased and inconsistent estimates. Better strategies are developed by Helpman, Melitz, and Yond Rubinstein (2007), who propose a theoretical model rationalizing the zero flows and suggest estimating the gravity equation with a correction for the probability of countries to trade, and by João Santos Silva and Silvana Tenreyro (2006), who suggest directly estimating the level equations using a Poisson estimate.

---

[11] If one has data for many countries over a period of time one can introduce a dummy that is specific for a country (or group of countries) that does not vary over time, or one could introduce a dummy that changes over time, but does not vary across countries (or groups of countries). Including these country or time "fixed" effects into an equation captures effects – which do not vary over time and/or countries – for which one has no data or observations. In research seminars one often gets questions such as: "Why didn't you include effect X or Y?" The estimation method of including fixed effects among the set of explanatory variables is very helpful in these cases: "I did not include X or Y explicitly, but I included country- and/or time-specific fixed effects." In this way, fixed effects act like *catch-all* effects.

9.6.2 Can geographical economics explain gravity? A simulation experiment

The geographical economics approach can provide a simple theoretical basis for the gravity equation. We could proceed in various ways, for example by identifying several regions within a country for a number of countries and assuming labor migration between different regions of one country and not between countries. As before, however, we want to keep the analysis as simple as possible. Now that we have briefly discussed the sizable migration flows between countries in section 9.5, we assume that manufacturing labor is mobile between locations. Naturally, a discussion of the gravity equation requires the analysis of many, not just two, locations. Moreover, the empirical observations in chapter 1 indicate that there must be considerable variation in the size and intensity of economic activity at these locations. Finally, we would like the gravity equation to be endogenously generated by the model, not to be pre-imposed by its geographic structure or some parameters that differ between locations. A suitable geographical economics model that fits all these requirements is the neutral-space, many-location model with negative feedbacks (congestion) developed and discussed in chapter 7. We proceed by briefly discussing some simulations with this model in relation to the gravity equation. Recall that the model has an immobile food sector and one mobile manufacturing sector, that δ is the share of income spent on manufactures, ε is the elasticity of substitution between different varieties of manufactures, and τ measures the extent of congestion costs.

The basic version of the gravity equation, which we have already discussed in chapters 1 and 2, relates the size of the international trade flows to the economic size of the two countries, and their distance is given in equation (9.13), where Tr_{ij} is the international trade flow from country i to country j, C is a constant, Y_i is the income level of the origin country, Y_j is the income level of the destination country, D_{ij} is the distance between the two countries, e_{ij} is an error term, and the parameters θ_1, θ_2, and θ_3 have to be estimated. Table 9.5 provides recent estimates of the main parameters of the basic gravity equation.

$$Tr_{ij} = CY_i^{\theta_1} Y_j^{\theta_2} D_{ij}^{\theta_3} e_{ij} \tag{9.13}$$

Using the congestion model of chapter 7 in a setting with twenty-four locations, we report four simulations, in which we change the size of the transport costs T, but not the initial distribution of the mobile labor force

Table 9.5 Empirics for the basic gravity equation

Income origin (θ_1)	0.721***
Income destination (θ_2)	0.732***
Distance (θ_3)	−0.776***

Note: ***denotes significance at the 1 percent level.
Source: Santos Silva and Tenreyro (2006: tab. 3, column PPML).

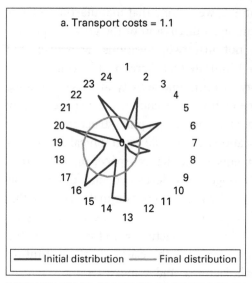

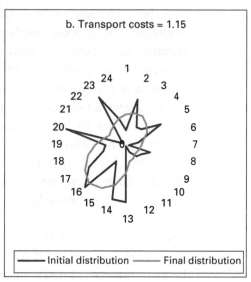

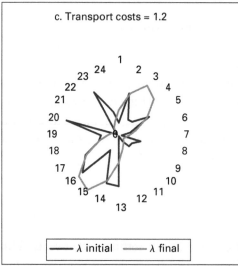

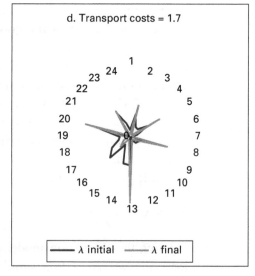

Figure 9.14 Initial and final distributions ($\delta = 0.7$; $\varepsilon = 5$; $\tau = 0.1$)

(λ initial). Naturally, the size of the transport costs has an impact on the long-run equilibrium distribution of the mobile labor force (λ final). This is illustrated in figure 9.14. Clearly, higher transport costs imply a more uneven long-run distribution of the mobile labor force, and hence of economic activity; moving from panel a to panel d the final distribution moves from almost circular to spiked.

Can the agglomerating and spreading forces that are at work in the congestion model shed some light on the underpinning of the gravity equation? To answer this question we calculate the distribution of international trade flows for the final equilibrium. This poses no problem for the manufacturing sector, of course. Since there are no trade costs involved in the food sector, these flows could in principle be from any exporting location to any importing location. To determine the food flows we therefore imposed the simple rule that each food exporting location exports food to all food-importing locations in proportion to that location's relative demand for food imports.

It is important to note that the calculation of the simulated trade flows between different locations involves detailed knowledge not only of the income levels of the locations and their geographic distance but also of wages, prices, and price indices for all locations, as well as parameters pertaining to the elasticity of substitution between different varieties, the impact of congestion, etc. This is much more detailed information than will generally be available in any database. The basic gravity equation reported above, on the other hand, uses only income levels for the various locations, as well as their geographic distance. We should actually be surprised, therefore, if the gravity equation is able to explain a fair share of the variation in the trade flows between locations. In this respect, the performance of the congestion model as given in table 9.6 is impressive: at least 67 percent of the variation of the trade flows is explained by the basic gravity equation. The estimates for the distance parameter θ_3 and the income level of the destination θ_2 are also reassuring: both are highly significant and of the correct sign. The parameter estimates for the income level of the origin is more problematic, as it has the "wrong" sign twice, both for high and low transport costs. Having shown that geographical economics (too) can be used to simulate trade flows in line with a standard gravity model, we now turn the tables and ask how the gravity model can be used to inform us about the (empirical) relevance of geographical economics.

Table 9.6 Overview of the basic gravity equation in simulations

	T = 1.1	T = 1.15	T = 1.2	T = 1.7
Income origin (θ_1)	−0.866 (−6.94)	0.840 (7.26)	0.698 (6.35)	−0.827 (−2.67)
Income destination (θ_2)	2.633 (21.11)	0.810 (7.00)	1.232 (11.19)	6.615 (21.33)
Distance (θ_3)	−1.027 (−24.81)	−2.286 (−55.34)	−2.881 (−39.23)	−7.459 (−27.14)
R^2	0.670	0.851	0.755	0.686

Note: t-values in brackets.

9.6.3. How to use the gravity model to test geographical economics

The equilibrium wage equation (see equation (4.3) or (5.3)) lies at the heart of the core model of geographical economics. As we explained in chapter 5 section 5.5, there are basically two strategies to estimate the equilibrium wage equation. The first one is based on the seminal paper of Hanson (2005) and has been discussed at length in chapter 5. This first strategy involves an attempt to *directly* estimate the wage equation (compare equations (5.3) and (5.5)). The second strategy has been pioneered by Redding and Venables (2004), and here a wage equation such as (5.3) is estimated in two steps. In the first step a proxy for real market potential (or real supplier access) is estimated using bilateral trade data and a gravity equation such as (9.12). In the second step, the estimated real market potential is then plugged into the wage equation, which is then estimated. The details of this second strategy are discussed below, because it turns out that the *gravity model* of international trade plays a crucial part in the construction of the market potential variable.

To pre-empt their main result: for a sample of (at most) 101 countries for 1996, Redding and Venables (2004) find evidence that a spatial wage structure exists, or, more precisely, that a spatial *GDP per capita* structure exists, since a lack of data on wages forces them to approximate wages by GDP per capita. While controlling for a country's resource endowments, other exogenous physical geography characteristics (such as the percentage of a country's land area in the tropics and the prevalence of malaria), and the role of institutions (the risk of expropriation, socialist rule, etc.), they find that "distance from other countries matters for GDP per capita through our measures of economic geography" (Redding and Venables, 2004: 70; see their table 3 for benchmark results). When they use as instrumental variable (IV) the geodesic distance of a country to the economic centers the United States, Belgium (representing the European Union), and Japan, the main result does not change: *countries with a larger market potential have a higher GDP per capita.* On a global level this confirms our findings from chapter 5 based on regional data regarding the empirical relevance of a spatial wage structure. In fact, when the Redding and Venables strategy itself is applied to the regional level, Breinlich (2006) finds, in a study of 193 EU regions for the period 1975–97, that a spatial income structure exists. These findings are also in line with the migration study by Crozet (2004) from the previous section.

Two questions that deserve some attention are as follows.

(i) Why go through the trouble of this indirect or two-step estimation strategy?

(ii) How does the indirect strategy work?

Starting with the first question, the indirect approach advocated by Redding and Venables (2004: 56) has the advantage that "the use of trade data reveals both observed and unobserved characteristics of market access" (where "market access" is just a different term for "market potential"). If trade data can be used to construct market potential, then the analysis of (changes in) the determinants of trade can be used to infer what (changes in) these determinants imply for market potential. With the direct Hanson (2005) strategy, we just plug in market potential as an explanatory variable in the wage equation, but we do not know how changes in other variables in turn affect the market potential, which was taken as *given* in our estimations in chapter 5.

Turning to the second question, and to learn how the *gravity model* for bilateral trade can be used to construct market access or market potential, it is useful to recall the equilibrium wage equation (4.3) (see equation (9.14)). This equation is at the heart of the empirical studies trying to establish if, as indicated by equation (9.14)), there is indeed a spatial wage structure (higher wages or GDP per capita in economic centers; see Breinlich, 2006, Brakman, Garretsen, and Schramm, 2006, Knaap, 2006, Redding and Venables, 2004, Mion, 2004, Head and Mayer, 2006, and Hanson, 2005). More precisely, equation (9.14) says that the wage level that a region s is able to pay its manufacturing workers is a function of that region's real market potential, the sum of the trade-cost-weighted market capacities.[12] Note the presence of trade costs T_{sr} in (9.14).

---

[12] The actual wage equation estimated may differ slightly from the one presented here in each particular empirical study, but the basic idea behind it is always the same – that is, with wages depending on real market access and, in a model with intermediate inputs (see equation (4.17)), the price index of manufactures. Following Breinlich (2006), we discuss the Redding and Venables (2004) strategy for the case of no intermediate inputs, which implies that we deal only with market (not supplier) access.

$$W_r = \left[\sum_{s=1}^{R} Y_s T_{rs}^{1-\varepsilon} I_s^{\varepsilon-1} \right]^{1/\varepsilon}$$ (9.14)

The connection between bilateral trade flows and market access, and hence the connection with the gravity model, now follows directly from the core model of geographical economics. To see this, we proceed in two stages. The *first stage* is to connect bilateral trade with market access. Go back to the manufacturing demand equation (3.20) or (3.6) from the core model, which gives the total demand for a manufacturing variety. Aggregating the demand from consumers in region r for all manufacturing varieties produced in region s over all firms producing in region s, n_s, gives aggregate trade equation (9.15), indicating that trade flows Tr_{sr} from country s to country r depend on the "supply capacity" of the exporting country $n_s p_s^{(1-\varepsilon)}$ (i.e. the number of firms and their price competitiveness, and the "market capacity" of the importing country r (i.e. its income level Y_r multiplied by its price index I_r [its real spending power] and the bilateral trade costs between the two countries T_{rs}).

$$Tr_{sr} = n_r p_r^{1-\varepsilon} Y_s I_s^{(\varepsilon-1)} T_{rs}^{(1-\varepsilon)}$$ (9.15)

Comparing equations (9.14) and (9.15), we note that wage rates and market potential use the *same* market capacities, weighted by bilateral trade flows. One can thus construct a measure of each country's market access using the coefficients of an empirical trade model that estimates Tr_{sr}. This is where the *second stage* (the gravity model) comes in, which is used to approximate real market access and subsequently used in the estimation of the wage equation (9.14). A gravity model consists of two sets of variables, namely (i) country-specific variables (e.g. the income levels of the importing and exporting country) and (ii) bilateral variables (e.g. the distance between the countries). Redding and Venables (2004: 60–1) estimate a gravity equation in which the country-specific characteristics are not specified as such but are captured by importer and exporter fixed effects through the use of importer and exporter dummies (recall our brief discussion on the use of fixed effects in gravity models in subsection 9.6.1). The bilateral trade costs Tr_{sr} are a function of the bilateral distance and a common border dummy. This trade cost specification differs from the one used by Hanson (2005; here, trade costs are an exponential function of distance). In the modern gravity literature (see Anderson and van Wincoop, 2004), the exact

Box 9.4 Does the specification of trade costs matter? Yes, it does![13]

Table 9.7 Trade cost functions in the empirical literature

Study and sample	Trade cost function
Direct estimation method	
Hanson (2005); US counties	$T_{ij} = \exp(\tau D_{ij})$
Brakman, Garretsen, and Schramm (2004a); German regions	$T_{ij} = \tau^{D_{ij}}$
Brakman, Garretsen, and Schramm (2006); EU regions	$T_{ij} = \tau D_{ij}^{\delta}$
Mion (2004); Italian regions	$T_{ij} = \exp(\tau D_{ij})$
Indirect estimation method	
Redding & Venables (2004); various countries	$T_{ij} = D_{ij}^{\delta} \exp(aB_{ij})$ or
	$T_{ij} = D_{ij}^{\delta} \exp(aB_{ij}) \exp(\beta_1 isl_i + \beta_2 isl_j +$
	$\beta_3 llock_i + \beta_4 llock_j + \beta_5 open_i + \beta_6 open_j)$
Knaap (2006); US states	$T_{ij} = D_{ij}^{\delta} \exp(aB_{ij})$
Breinlich (2006); EU regions	$T_{ij} = D_{ij}^{\delta} \exp\left(a_1 L_{ij} + \sum_i a_{2i} B_{ij}^i\right)$
Hering and Poncet (2006); Chinese cities	$T_{ij} = D_{ij}^{\delta} \exp(a_1 B_{ij}^f + a_2 B_{ij}^C + a_3 B_{ij}^{fC})$

Notes: D_{ij} denotes a measure of distance (usually the great circle distance, but sometimes also other measures, such as travel times); B_{ij} denotes a border dummy (either capturing the effect of two countries/regions being adjacent or the effect of crossing a national border).
Source: Bosker and Garretsen (2007a).

Table 9.7 shows, for a selection of empirical studies, that the trade or transport cost specification differs markedly in empirical research, both for the direct and indirect estimation strategies. As Anderson and van Wincoop (2004: 706) note: "A variety of ad hoc trade cost functions have been used to relate the unobservable cost to observable variables." Moreover (710): "Gravity theory has used arbitrary assumptions regarding functional form of the trade cost function, the list of variables, and regularity conditions." The (implicit) assumptions underlying the use of a trade cost function concern in particular (i) the functional form, (ii) the variables included, (iii) the regularity conditions, (iv) modeling the trade costs involved with internal trade, (v) the unobservable component of trade costs, and (vi) estimating the trade cost function's parameters (see Anderson and van Wincoop, 2004). We do not deal with these issues here, but merely wonder to what extent the conclusions on the relevance of market potential (for wages or GDP per capita) depend on the trade cost specification. Hanson (2005), for example, uses an exponential distance decay function, whereas Redding and Venables (2004) use a power function ($T_{ij} = D_{ij}^{\delta}$).

---

[13] This box is based on Bosker and Garretsen (2007a).

Box 9.4 (cont.)

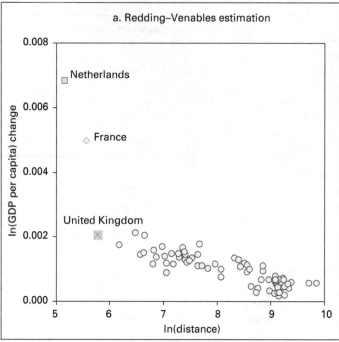

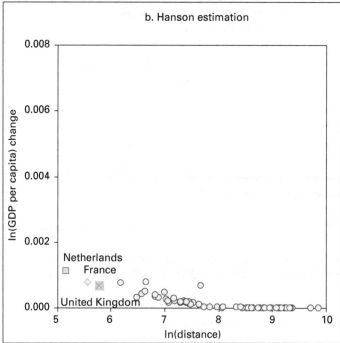

Figure 9.15 GDP per capita changes, 5 percent GDP shock in Belgium
Note: Correlation between shock and distance is −0.77 for panel a, −0.84 for panel b.
Source: Bosker and Garretsen (2007a).

Box 9.4 (cont.)

Bosker and Garretsen (2007a) estimate the equivalent of wage equation (9.14) for a sample of eighty countries in 1996 (using GDP per capita) for both the Hanson (2005) and the Redding and Venables (2004) specifications. In both cases, market potential was positive and significant. The differences between the two approaches come to the fore when the estimation results were used to conduct the following experiment. Suppose that Belgium, a country at the heart of Europe, experiences a positive 5 percent GDP shock. To what extent will this shock, given the estimation results, lead to spillovers to other countries through the market potential variable? The magnitude of this increase for a specific country depends, of course, on the strength of the spatial linkages. The lower the trade costs with Belgium the larger the impact on a country's GDP per capita. Figure 9.15 illustrates the spatial reach of the Belgian GDP shock by plotting the percentage GDP per capita change against the log of distance for the two approaches.

Using the Hanson exponential approach (panel b), the distance decay is very strong and the size of the GDP per capita changes are relatively small. In the Redding and Venables power function approach (panel a), the GDP per capita change is much larger (e.g. about *seven* times as large for the Netherlands!)[14] The effect of the income shock in the Hanson exponential distance approach also peters out quickly: there is no discernable effect any more in countries lying farther from Belgium than Egypt. In the power function approach, in contrast, Egypt still experiences a 0.1 percent increase in GDP per capita (about equal to the size of the income increase in the most heavily affected country [the Netherlands] when using the Hanson specification!).

In addition, the Redding and Venables power function specification allows contiguity to have its effect on trade costs. Consequently, the effect of the Belgian income shock is less correlated with distance and has a larger effect on its contiguous neighbors. The shock has a larger effect, for example, on Germany than on the United Kingdom (although the latter is closer to Belgium as measured by distance between capital cities). The income shock also peters out much more slowly in their approach and affects all countries in the sample in some way (Japan, with only a 0.02 percent increase in its GDP per capita, is affected the least). To conclude: trade or transport costs are a crucial element of geographical economics (without trade costs there is no role for geography). This experiment shows that the trade or transport cost specification can to a large extent determine the conclusions on the empirical relevance of market potential and the geographical reach of spatial interdependencies!

specification of trade costs is subject to close scrutiny. The reason for this attention is based on the sensitivity of the outcome regarding this specification (see box 9.4 for a further discussion).

As noted by Redding and Venables (2004: 75), one of the main disadvantages of using a gravity equation in which the country-specific features are captured by using importer and exporter fixed effects is that it does not

---

[14] Head and Mayer (2004a: 2626) note that the strong distance decay in Hanson (2005) "may be a consequence of the functional form of the distance decay function."

allow one "to quantify the effects on per capita income of particular country characteristics (for example, land locked or infrastructure), since all such effects are contained in the dummies." As a result, recommendations regarding the effect of country-specific policies aimed at increasing trade/ market access and thus GDP per capita cannot be made.[15] To illustrate the "gravity trade–market access–GDP per capita" links, Bosker and Garretsen (2007b) study sub-Saharan Africa (SSA) trade in the period 1993–2002. Employing a standard gravity model (based on GDP levels, country-specific characteristics, bilateral distance, and sharing a common border or a common language) is thus only a means to an end (to construct market access for the estimation of equation (9.14)). The advantage of this approach is that one *can* gauge the importance of changes in trade variables on market access and hence on GDP per capita. Table 9.8 shows the results of five "policy experiments," four related to conflict-ridden Sudan and one to landlocked Ethiopia.[16]

Regarding Sudan, ending the civil war in Darfur would increase market access considerably and thus raise its GDP per capita by around 11 percent (depending on the measure of market access). This illustrates the devastating impact of civil unrest on sub-Saharan African economic development in general. Similarly, hypothetically halving Sudan's distance to all its trading partners also raises market access substantially, leading to an increase in GDP per capita of about 6.5 percent. Of related interest are investments in infrastructure and the establishment of regional free trade agreements. Improving Sudan's infrastructure by one standard deviation (resulting in a quality of infrastructure comparable to Namibia!) would raise GDP per capita by about 5 percent. In contrast, forming a bilateral RFTA with South Africa would raise its GDP per capita only by 0.4 percent. The reason for this difference is the fact that improvements in infrastructure affect all trading partners alike, whereas the establishment of a bilateral RFTA affects only one trading partner. This gives a clear policy recommendation: policies aimed at improving a country's ability to trade will have a much higher pay-off when they aim at general improvements affecting as

[15] See also section 7 in Redding and Venables (2004), however.
[16] See Redding and Venables (2004: 78, tab. 8) for a similar experiment. The Bosker and Garretsen (2007b) paper is available on the website. Market access (approximated by a gravity equation) is always significant. In line with Breinlich (2006), however, the inclusion of human capital and working population density as control variables lowers the importance of market access considerably (see also Hering and Poncet, 2006, and Amiti and Cameron, 2007). If country and time fixed effects are also included the estimated market access coefficient drops further, while remaining significant.

Table 9.8 Policy experiments

Policy measure	+1 s.d. infrastructure	End to civil war	All distances halved	RFTA S. Africa	No longer landlocked
Country	Sudan	Sudan	Sudan	Sudan	Ethiopia
Increase in market access (%)	64.0	144.7	85.2	5.6	40.9
Resulting increase in GDP per capita	4.9	11.0	6.5	0.4	3.1

Notes: +1 s.d. infrastructure = one standard deviation change in infrastructure; RFTA S. Africa = regional free trade agreement with South Africa.
Source: Bosker and Garretsen (2007b).

many of the country's trading partners as possible. An example of such an experiment is shown for Ethiopia in table 9.8. When Eritrea officially became independent in 1993, Ethiopia lost its direct access to the sea. The table shows that, if this move were reversed, Ethiopia's market access would substantially improve, leading to a rise of its GDP per capita of over 3 percent.

9.7 Conclusions

This chapter has partially fulfilled Ohlin's objective of analyzing international trade flows against the background of a theory of location. For the latter we mainly used the core model of geographical economics, which, as we discussed in chapter 2, is in turn largely based on the new trade theory. We combined geographical economics with two traditional approaches in trade theory: Ricardian comparative advantage, based on differences in technology, and factor abundance theory. In both cases we derive an intricate picture of the forces underlying international trade flows, enabling us to explain both intra- and inter-industry trade flows, as well as the locational aspects of firm decisions. The geographical impact shows up in both cases through a mitigation of the effects of comparative advantage – that is, other things being equal, an increase in trade costs reduces the extent of industrial specialization within countries. This is intuitively plausible, as firms are relatively sheltered from the forces of international competition as transports costs increase, such that they benefit more strongly from the home market effect. We concluded the chapter by briefly discussing labor migration and the gravity equation of international trade, and showing the relationship with the basic geographical economics model.

Exercises

9.1 According to the cost functions given by equation (9.3), country 1 (country 2) has a comparative and absolute advantage in sector A (sector B) manufactures. Modify equation (9.3) such that country 1 has an absolute advantage in the production of both sector A and B manufactures, but still only a comparative advantage in the production of sector A manufactures.

Hint: introduce four types of β's into equation (9.3).

9.2 On the website of this book you can find a small, user-friendly "Ricardo" simulation for the model described in section 9.3. Download the simulation and start it up. Now vary the elasticity of substitution from two, three, four, through to ten, by changing the numbers in red. Describe and explain what happens if the elasticity of substitution increases to:

(i) the domestic share of the industry with comparative advantage;

(ii) the domestic share of the industry with comparative disadvantage; and

(iii) intra-industry trade and the share of GNP imported.

9.3 Download and start up the "Ricardo" simulation, but this time vary the transport costs from 1.1, 1.2, 1.3, through to two. Describe and explain what happens if the transport costs increase to:

(i) the domestic share of the industry with comparative advantage;

(ii) the domestic share of the industry with comparative disadvantage; and

(iii) intra-industry trade and the share of GNP imported.

9.4 In the core model of geographical economics there is international labor mobility. In the factor abundance model discussed in this chapter there is no labor mobility between countries. Explain why the introduction of labor mobility is at odds with the analysis underlying the factor abundance model.

Hint: remember that labor is the endowment.

9.5 On the website of this book you can find a small, user-friendly "factor abundance" simulation, comparing the models described in sections 9.3 and 9.4. Download the simulation and start it up. Now vary the elasticity of substitution from two, three, four, through to ten, by changing the numbers in red. Compare, describe, and explain what happens if the elasticity of substitution increases to:

  (i) the share of sector A firms in country 1;
 (ii) domestic spending on sector A in country 1;
(iii) the share of sector B firms in country 1;
 (iv) domestic spending on sector B in country 1;
  (v) the share of income spent on imports; and
 (vi) intra-industry trade.

9.6 Download and start up the "factor abundance" simulation, but this time vary the transport costs from 1.1, 1.2, 1.3, through to two. Compare, describe and explain what happens if the transport costs increase to:

  (i) the share of sector A firms in country 1;
 (ii) domestic spending on sector A in country 1;
(iii) the share of sector B firms in country 1;
 (iv) domestic spending on sector B in country 1;
  (v) the share of income spent on imports; and
 (vi) intra-industry trade.

9.7* According to Deardorff (1998), the gravity equation (9.12) can also be founded on neoclassical trade theory (see chapter 2 section 2.2 for this theory). Try to think of a neoclassical trade story that could result in a gravity equation and the kind of empirical results shown in table 9.8.

9.8 In the core model of geographical economics of chapter 3, manufacturing workers migrate if there are real wage differentials between regions. The speed at which they react to interregional real wage differences is given by the parameter η. A low (high) value for this parameter implies a weak (strong) reaction by manufacturing workers to real wage differences. Given the information in section 9.5, why do you think that η is low for most countries? How could the reluctance of people to migrate, even if real wage differences are significant, be modeled?

Hint: use the discussion of the Crozet (2004) model in the text.

9.9 Go back to section 5.5 and our discussion there of Hanson (2005) and the estimation of the wage equation. Discuss the main differences with the estimation strategy outlined in subsection 9.6.3.

9.10 Does the estimation of wage equation (9.14) in combination with the estimation of trade equation (9.15) offer a test of the underlying geographical economics model in your view? Answer the same question for the estimation of migration equation (9.12).

9.11* Without trade or transport costs geographical economics loses its relevance, because geography or location ceases to be an issue. In box 9.4 we argued that the specification of trade costs matters. In their important survey of gravity models and the modeling of trade costs, Anderson and van Wincoop (2004) discuss various ways to assess the usefulness of trade cost functions. Use their survey (and the list i–vi mentioned in box 9.4) to assess the trade cost functions that have been used in geographical economics (see table 9.7).

10 Dynamics, growth, and geography

10.1 Introduction

So far we have not paid much attention in this book to the role of dynamics in geographical economics. Instead, we have focused attention on the relationship between a long-run equilibrium and the structural parameters, given an initial distribution of labor and production. We argued, in chapter 3, that the novelty of the core model of geographical economics is the *endogenous* determination of market size, fostered by the migration of mobile workers to regions with higher real wages. The dynamics underlying the adjustment path – that is, how we evolve over time (see our remarks below on "time") from an initial distribution to a final distribution, and the intricacies of economic growth and development – have been virtually absent from the analysis so far. This chapter partially fills this void. In doing so, we distinguish between three types of dynamics, increasing in complexity and in real-world importance:

  (i) adjustment dynamics;
  (ii) simulation dynamics; and
  (iii) growth and development

  (i) *Adjustment dynamics.* This type of dynamics analyzes the adjustment path over time, from an initial distribution of manufacturing production between regions to a final long-run equilibrium, by showing the sequence of short-run equilibria leading to the long-run equilibrium. The driving force behind this adjustment process in the core model of geographical economics is, therefore, the migration decisions of individuals moving towards regions with higher real wages, the differences arising from the tensions between the home market effect and the price index effect in this sequence of short-run equilibria. Adjustment dynamics are discussed in section 10.2. The reader should realize that the time dimension in that section (and in section 10.5) is "simulation time," in which ten simulation reallocations might represent an actual time frame of six months, or three weeks, or some other "real" time frame, divided into ten steps.

(ii) *Simulation dynamics.* At various parts in this book we give interpretations of models of the "suppose" type, such as "Suppose the economy is initially in a long-run spreading equilibrium and the transport costs T gradually decrease over time." The story continues to discuss what may happen in the model to the distribution of manufacturing activity as the transport costs fall. In essence, we then invoke an exogenous fall in a structural parameter to discuss how the model may be useful in explaining the evolution of some phenomenon over time. So far we have done this almost always without explicitly performing and showing such simulations (chapter 7 provides some exceptions). We label this type of reasoning "simulation dynamics" and discuss it in sections 10.4 and 10.5.

(iii) *Growth and development.* The most important, but also the most complex, type of dynamics is the investigation and modeling of "real" economic growth. In terms of the geographical economics models, this implies not only modeling the forces giving rise to the agglomeration or spreading of economic activity, as we have done so far, but also modeling traditional and novel forces explaining the increase in economic prosperity over time. This increase may result from rising production levels or the invention and availability of new goods and services, requiring, for example, investment in capital goods or research and development. Properly modeling economic growth therefore requires analyzing the investment decisions of economic agents, and hence introducing (some form of) capital as a production factor and the use of intertemporal optimization. To extend our geographical economics model in this direction is far from easy, but, fortunately, important breakthroughs in the agglomeration and growth literature have been made in, recent years (see Baldwin and Martin, 2004, for an excellent survey). An in-depth analysis of these issues is beyond the scope of this book, but the important assumptions and insights, as well as an example based on Baldwin and Forslid (2000b), are discussed in section 10.6.

In section 10.7 we continue the analysis of the relationship between agglomeration and growth – or more accurately, between geography and development – by showcasing recent research on the so called "deep" determinants of economic development and the relevance of both first- and second- nature geography. In addition to the aforementioned sections, we also provide stylized facts of economic growth (section 10.3), as a prelude to the discussion on simulation dynamics and economic growth in sections 10.4 to 10.7. Section 10.8 concludes.

10.2 Adjustment dynamics

It is time to pay some explicit attention to the adjustment paths from an initial distribution of the manufacturing labor force to a final distribution as represented by a long-run equilibrium. To focus the analysis in this section, we analyze adjustment paths using the two-region base scenario of the core model, also used in chapter 4, in which the elasticity of substitution $\varepsilon = 5$, the share of income spent on manufactures $\delta = 0.4$, and the transport costs $T = 1.7$. As a reminder, the short-run equilibrium real wage of region 1 relative to region 2 for all distributions of the manufacturing work force is reproduced here as figure 10.1a (see also figure 4.1). In the interior, a long-run equilibrium is reached if the relative real wage is one. As the reader may recall, this setting gave rise to five possible long-run equilibria: three stable equilibria (spreading [point B], agglomeration in region 1 [point A], or agglomeration in region 2 [point E]), and two unstable equilibria (in this particular case, if the share of the manufacturing work force in region 1 is roughly 16 percent [point B] or 84 percent [point D]).

The remainder of this section addresses two main issues. First, in subsection 10.2.1, we briefly describe the "regular" adjustment of the economy over time. The term "regular" conveys the idea that this type of adjustment occurs most frequently in the simulations of the various geographical economics models. Second, in subsection 10.2.2, we draw attention to some "special" cases that may arise in an adjustment process. As suggested, these special cases occur rarely, but the reader should be conscious of the fact that they may arise when performing simulation exercises.

10.2.1 Regular adjustment

Before we can analyze the adjustment path of the economy over "time" we must choose an initial distribution. This choice is largely arbitrary, as long as it is not a long-run equilibrium. For this section, we choose an initial distribution in the "basin of attraction" of the spreading equilibrium, with 30 percent of the manufacturing work force in region 1, as illustrated by the square in figure 10.1a. The reader may recall the adjustment equation of the manufacturing workforce, based on migration decisions, invoked in chapter 3 (see equation 3.26) in which laborers move gradually to the region with the highest real wage:

$$\frac{d\lambda_1}{\lambda_1} = \eta(w_1 - \bar{w}); \quad \text{where} \quad \bar{w} = \lambda_1 w_1 + \lambda_2 w_2 \tag{10.1}$$

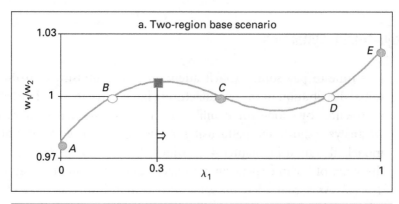

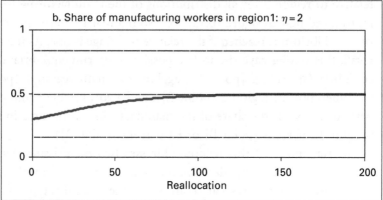

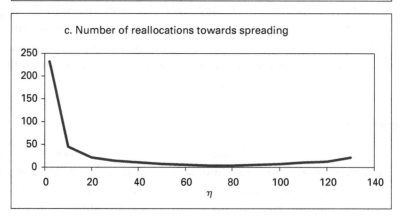

Figure 10.1 Regular adjustment dynamics

In this differential specification, starting from an initial distribution with
30 percent of the manufacturing workforce in region 1, manufacturing
workers would gradually migrate from region 2 to region 1, as indicated by
the arrow in figure 10.1a, until the stable long-run spreading equilibrium is

reached in which 50 percent of the manufacturing work force is located in region 1. The swiftness of this migration process depends on the speed of adjustment parameter η (see equation (10.1)), which is the focus of analysis in this section. It is important to realize, however, that, in the simulations of the geographical economics models, differential equation (10.1) is approximated by equation (10.2), where a subscript t denotes the number of the reallocation:

$$\begin{bmatrix} \lambda_{1,t+1} \\ \lambda_{2,t+1} \end{bmatrix} = \begin{bmatrix} \lambda_{1,t} \\ \lambda_{2,t} \end{bmatrix} + \eta \begin{bmatrix} (w_{1,t} - \bar{w}_t)\lambda_{1,t} \\ (w_{2,t} - \bar{w}_t)\lambda_{2,t} \end{bmatrix} \tag{10.2}$$

For most simulations reported in this book, we chose a relatively low speed of adjustment parameter, namely $\eta = 2$. For this setting, figure 10.1b depicts the adjustment of the economy over time, with time measured in terms of the number of reallocations – i.e. the number of times λ is adjusted before a long-run equilibrium is reached. The thin horizontal lines in figure 10.1b, and in similar figures to follow, depict the interior long-run equilibria of the economy, in accordance with points B, C, and D in figure 10.1a. As illustrated, the share of manufacturing workers in region 1 rises slowly (from 30 percent to 50 percent) until the long-run spreading equilibrium is reached. If the speed of adjustment $\eta = 2$, this occurs after 233 reallocations.[1]

Increasing the speed of adjustment η, first to ten and then by increments of ten, shows that the adjustment process illustrated in figure 10.1b holds for a large range of adjustment speeds.[2] The most important difference, as would seem obvious, is that the long-run spreading equilibrium is reached using fewer reallocations if the speed of adjustment increases. As illustrated in figure 10.1c, this reasoning holds only up to a certain point, in this case until the speed of adjustment $\eta = 80$ (with only three reallocations). For even higher speeds of adjustment, there is some "overshooting" of the long-run spreading equilibrium – that is, at some point a reallocation increases the manufacturing workforce in region 1 above 50 percent, necessitating a reduction to reach the long-run spreading equilibrium. This overshooting then leads to a gradual rise in the number of reallocations, as illustrated in figure 10.1c.

---

[1] The number of reallocations is actually the number reported minus one and depends not only on the speed of adjustment parameter η but also on the tightness of the stopping criterion as measured by the parameter σ and discussed in section 4.2: $\frac{W_{r,iteration} - W_{r,iteration-1}}{W_{r,iteration-1}} < \sigma$. In this case $\sigma = 0.00001$.

[2] Details of these simulations are available on the website.

Figure 10.1c shows clearly why it is tempting for researchers to increase the speed of adjustment η when performing simulations of geographical economics models: the end result is the same (the economy converges towards the long-run spreading equilibrium), while the number of reallocations (and thus the computing time involved) reduces drastically. The next subsection illustrates, however, that there are also serious, and perhaps unexpected, costs associated with increasing the speed of adjustment. (Nevertheless, we must admit that some of the issues and problems explained in the next subsection can in principle also arise if a low speed of adjustment is chosen, although usually in a less extreme form, as is illustrated by the discussion of the so called "pancake" economy in chapter 11 section 11.4).

10.2.2 Special adjustment dynamics

When performing computer simulations, one should be aware in general of some special cases that may arise while the economy is adjusting from one short-run equilibrium to another short-run equilibrium on its path towards a long-run equilibrium. We focus our attention on three issues, all of which can be clearly illustrated and understood using the two-region core model example, namely:

(i) the dynamic path of the economy may converge to "cycles";
(ii) the dynamic path of the economy may lead to an unstable equilibrium; or
(iii) the dynamic path of the economy may not lead to the "nearest" stable equilibrium.

For the first issue, that of the dynamic path of the economy converging to "cycles," figure 10.2a shows the adjustment of the economy over time for the first 1,000 reallocations if the speed of adjustment $\eta = 200$. The figure appears not to be very clear, or at least does not give a clear picture of the adjustment process, since there is one thick line around 0.5. Panel b, therefore, enlarges a small detail of panel a. As is evident from the enlargement here, showing reallocations up to 130, the dynamic path of the economy is zigzagging around the stable spreading equilibrium (in this case for a manufacturing workforce in region 1 of roughly 36 percent and 64 percent). The specified dynamics imply that the economy will continue to do so for ever.

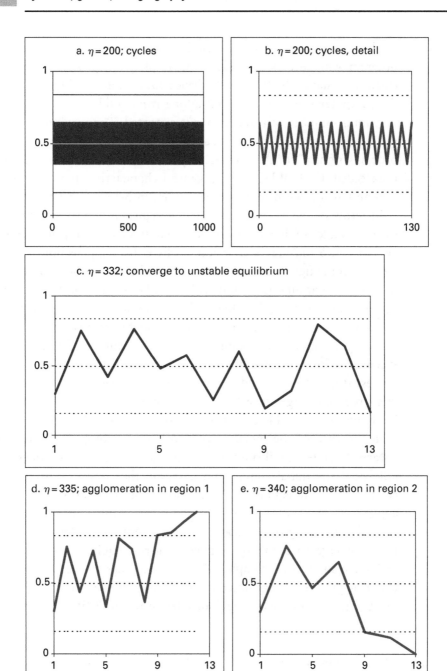

Figure 10.2 Special adjustment dynamics
Notes: Along vertical axis, λ; horizontal axis, number of reallocations.

This process is called a two-period "cycle."[3] By implication, the computer program will never stop, unless you unplug the power supply or, as is customary, have a built-in safety device. Our built-in safety device specifies the computer program to stop if a long-run equilibrium is reached or if a maximum number of reallocations is exceeded. The maximum number of reallocations we used was 1,000, after which we have labeled the adjustment process "infinity" for the two-region program on our website if this number is exceeded. Cyclical behavior in general characterizes the dynamics of the economy if the speed of adjustment η lies in between 140 and 331.[4]

In terms of the second issue, at first sight, an adjustment path leading to an unstable equilibrium seems like a contradiction. In principle it should be, but figure 10.2c gives an example where this happens nonetheless. As is clear from the figure, at this high speed of adjustment the economy appears to be moving around randomly within the boundaries of the unstable long-run equilibria (the dashed lines). Then, "by accident," the economy hits the unstable long-run equilibrium with roughly 16 percent of the manufacturing workforce in region 1 on the thirteenth reallocation. Thus, as specified, a long-run equilibrium is reached and the dynamic adjustment process stops.[5] One should therefore be aware that, if the dynamic adjustment path converges to a long-run equilibrium, this does not necessarily imply that it is a stable equilibrium, although it usually does.

In the case of the dynamic path of the economy not leading to the "nearest" stable equilibrium, the term "nearest" should be interpreted as follows: if the initial equilibrium is within the "basin of attraction" of a certain long-run equilibrium, this does not necessarily imply that the adjustment process leads the economy towards this long-run equilibrium. Instead, depending on the speed of adjustment parameter η, the economy may converge to a different stable long-run equilibrium. Figures 10.2d and 10.2e show two examples of this phenomenon, one in which manufacturing production agglomerates in region 1 (if $\eta = 335$) and one in which manufacturing production agglomerates in region 2 (if $\eta = 340$).

[3] The reader might notice the similarity of (10.1) to the famous logistic equation in chaos theory. Indeed, as noted by Martin Currie and Lagrid Kubin (2006), one should be careful with adjustment processes, as they can easily lead towards "chaotic" behaviour. Note, for example, the similarity between our figure 10.2 and figure 6.17 – and related figures – in Shone (1997).
[4] We say "in general" because there are cases in which the long-run spreading equilibrium is reached "by accident," for example if $\eta = 280$ or $\eta = 300$. This phenomenon is similar to case (ii) described in this subsection.
[5] Because of the stopping criterion, discussed in section 4.2, the adjustment process stops whenever the allocation is within a small neighborhood around the unstable long-run equilibrium.

There are two general remarks to make. First, the special adjustment cases illustrated above may be relatively clear to understand and easy to avoid in the two-region example, but they are less easy to understand and less easy to avoid in a more general setting, with many locations, complicated transport structures, congestion costs, and the need to distinguish between different industrial sectors with intermediate deliveries, in particular because it is then very hard to identify the long-run equilibria. Second, it is clear from the discussions and examples above that the "special" adjustment phenomena arise more easily if the speed of adjustment η is high. We can be confident that it is, in general, less likely for such special cases to occur if the speed of adjustment is not so high, which seems to be more in line with the gradual processes empirically observed for migration decisions, which are not taken lightly. It is nevertheless important to be aware of the possibilities that may arise, as these may also arise for moderate speeds of adjustment. An example of this is given in the pancake model of chapter 11. Moreover, high speeds of adjustment may be relevant in a different economic setting, for example when examining adjustment processes in financial markets.

Now that we have seen in more detail the adjustment processes that may arise while the economy is moving from an initial distribution to a long-run distribution of manufacturing activity, it is almost time to take the next steps and analyze simulation dynamics and economic growth. We deal first with simulation dynamics. The aim of simulation dynamics is to show the most important model implications of parameter changes. That is, it tries to understand a model by telling a story. Before you can do this, however, you must know which "dynamic" story to tell. The next section therefore briefly discusses some important facts about economic growth.

10.3 Some stylized facts of economic growth

The field of economic growth basically deals with two questions. First, why do countries grow over time? Second, why do some countries grow more rapidly than others? These questions are interesting, because, as discussed in chapter 2, within a neoclassical growth framework, diminishing returns to capital ensure that "poor" countries grow more rapidly than "rich" countries. In the extreme case, similar countries should tend to have the same income per capita in the long run. In the absence of technological progress, income per capita should eventually not grow at all. Neither is the case in practice, however.

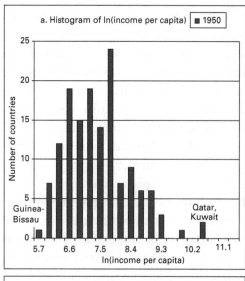

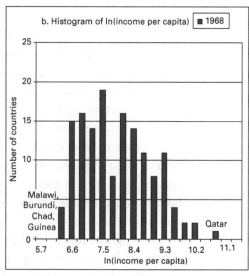

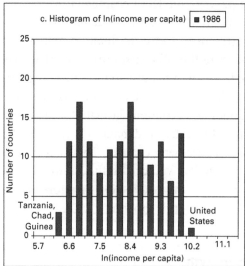

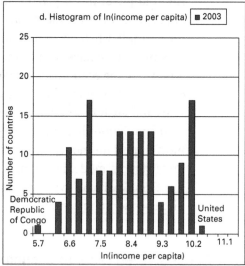

Figure 10.3   Histogram of per capita income, selected years 1950–2003
Source: Brakman and van Marrewijk (2008).

Figure 10.3 presents income per capita data for the world. It illustrates the distribution of income per capita for a selection of years (equally spaced across time) in the period 1950–2003 by providing a histogram with the natural logarithm of income per capita on the horizontal axis (to limit the range) and the number of countries within a certain range on the vertical axis. In 1950, for example, one country (Guinea-Bissau) has ln(income per capita) below 5.7 (= income level of $300) whereas seven countries are in

Table 10.1 GDP per capita (annual average compound growth rate, %)

	1820–70	1870–1913	1913–50	1950–75	1975–2003	1820–2003
Western Europe	1.0	1.3	0.8	3.8	2.0	1.5
Western offshoots	1.4	1.8	1.6	2.2	2.0	1.7
Eastern Europe	0.6	1.4	0.6	3.8	0.7	1.2
Former Soviet Union	0.6	1.1	1.8	3.1	−0.5	1.1
Latin America	0.0	1.9	1.8	2.6	0.7	1.2
East Asia	−0.1	0.8	−0.2	2.0	1.4	0.6
West Asia	0.4	0.8	1.5	4.5	0.4	1.3
Africa	0.4	0.6	0.9	1.9	0.3	0.7
World	0.5	1.3	0.9	2.7	1.7	1.3

Source: Brakman and van Marrewijk (2008), based on www.ggdc.net/maddison (version August 2007); see this website for details on country groupings.

the range between 5.7 and 6.0, and so on. The panels of Figure 10.3 show a gradual movement from the left to the right, indicating increasing income per capita levels for most countries. Note that we discuss absolute income changes, not relative positions. Clearly, as noted above, there is considerable variation in income per capita. It is hard to determine any trends in the panels of the figure by visual inspection, although comparing the first panel (with most of the mass on the left-hand side) with the last panel (in which the mass is more evenly distributed) seems to suggest an increase (rather than a decrease) in income dispersion. Most countries, therefore, do not stay in the same place as far as absolute income per capita is concerned. More importantly, income dispersion has increased between 1950 and 2003.

Table 10.1 shows the differences in economic growth rates for groups of countries rather than individual countries, indicating, for example, that the "Western offshoots" (the United States, Canada, Australia, and New Zealand) grew substantially more rapidly on a per capita basis than the world average in the periods 1820–70 and 1870–1913. The opposite direction of aggregation is also interesting, as the above country-level analysis may obscure important economic developments at lower levels of aggregation, specifically within-country developments. Most regional convergence analysis focuses on regions within a specific country or within a coherent group of countries. Robert Barro and Xavier Sala-i-Martin (2004), for example, analyze convergence between US states, Japanese prefectures, and European regions. These studies usually find some evidence of income convergence at the regional level. There are, however, two important caveats.

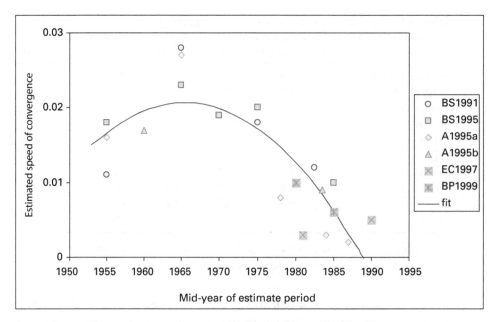

Figure 10.4 Regional convergence in the European Union: speed of convergence estimates, 1955–90
Source: Brakman and van Marrewijk (2008).

First, restricting the analysis to regions within a country or a coherent group of countries is not representative of regional income trends in general. This is similar to the *biased sample* problem at the country level. When William Baumol (1986) analyzes convergence from 1870 to 1979 by investigating sixteen industrialized countries he finds strong evidence for income convergence. As pointed out by Bradford DeLong (1988), however, Baumol's country sample is biased, as he focuses on sixteen countries with high income levels in 1979. This is an example of biased sample selection: the sixteen countries that have a high income in 1979 were special – according to some criterion – in 1870 (what criterion is another matter). The evidence for country-level income convergence tends to disappear when an unbiased country sample is taken.

Second, the degree of regional income convergence, as measured by the estimated speed of convergence, tends to *decrease* over time. This observation holds for the states of the United States, the prefectures in Japan, *and* the regions in the European Union. It is illustrated in figure 10.4 for regional income convergence in the European Union using the Ron Martin (2001) data. As explained below, appreciating this tendency towards an absence of regional income convergence in the European Union is crucial for understanding recent developments in EU regional income distribution.

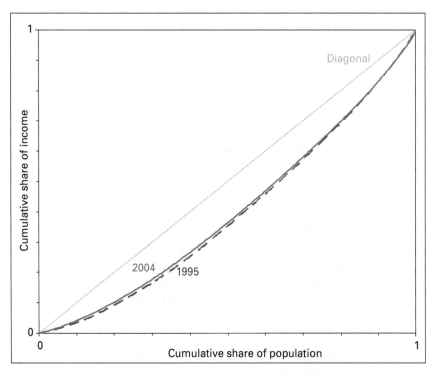

Figure 10.5   Regional income inequality in the European Union: Lorenz curves, 1995 and 2004
Source: Brakman and van Marrewijk (2008).

The European Union identifies "regions" at three different levels, referred to as NUTS regions. The twenty-seven EU countries consist of ninety-five NUTS1 regions, 268 NUTS2 regions, and 1,284 NUTS3 regions. Focusing on the NUTS2 level (which is probably most readily comparable between countries), we collected income and population data for 257 regions, to construct Lorenz curves and calculate Gini coefficients in the period 1995–2004.[6] Figure 10.5 provides the Lorenz curves for 1995 and 2004, the most *un*equal and the most *equal* regional EU income distribution in this period respectively. The figure suggests that this distribution is becoming a little more equal. Indeed, the average Gini coefficient for the EU regions in this

---

[6] We excluded the regions in Romania and Malta, and two Spanish regions, for lack of data availability. The Lorenz curve draws the   percentage of total income earned against the cumulative share of income earners, lined up according to their income per capita. If the curve is below the diagonal, as in figure 10.5, it indicates that, for example, the first 10 percent of income earners earn less than 10 percent of world income. The Gini coefficient calculates the area between the diagonal and the Lorenz curve, and is a measure of income inequality: the larger the Gini coefficient the larger the area between the two curves, and the bigger the income inequality.

period is 0.2075, varying from a high of 0.2145 in 1995 to a low of 0.1979 in 2004. This slight trend, however, still obscures within-country effects. Looking at regions instead of countries still assumes that, within a region, income per capita is the same, which is not the case.

Measurements of within-country or -region income inequality is not trivial, as not all countries have household surveys to provide the necessary data, and, even if they do, do not necessarily use the same definitions of income (see Milanovic, 2006a, 2006b). In general, the following picture emerges. There is consensus in the literature that the between-country inequality has decreased recently, and also that the between-country differences account for about 70 percent of global inequality and the within-country inequality for some 30 percent (Sala-i-Martin, 2006). There is no clear consensus, however, on developments with respect to within-country inequality, which seems to be more volatile than the between-country developments. Still, we give an indication of the within-country/-region income inequality using the Theil index.[7] An advantage of the (non-negative) Theil index (in which zero indicates complete income equality) is that it *can* be decomposed into different components, and the within-country/-region income inequality can be calculated without detailed census information.[8] Sala-i-Martin (2006: 388), for example, uses this to decompose global income inequality to within-country and between-country inequality:

The "within-country" component is the amount of inequality that would exist in the world if all countries had the same income per capita . . . The "across-country" component is the amount of inequality that would exist in the world if all citizens within each country had the same level of income, but there were differences in per capita incomes across countries.

Noting that global income inequality as measured by the Theil index has fallen in the period 1970–2000, he then uses the decomposition to show that the *within*-country component has become *more important* over time.

A similar decomposition for EU regional income inequality as measured using the Theil index, which (like the Gini coefficient) has fallen in the period 1995–2004, reveals, similarly, that the regional income inequality *between* EU countries has *fallen,* whereas regional income inequality *within* EU countries has *increased* (see figure 10.6). As such, it continues a trend noted by Juan Duro (2001) using data for 1982–95. As also pointed out by

---

[7] The Theil index is an alternative to the Gini coefficient for measuring income inequality.

[8] A decomposition is not possible with the Gini coefficient (see, for example, Milanovic, 2006a, 2006b).

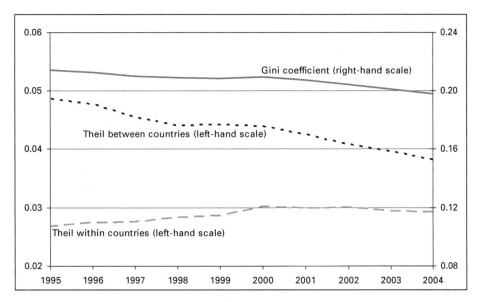

Figure 10.6 Regional income inequality in the European Union: Theil index and Gini coefficient, 1995–2004
Source: Brakman and van Marrewijk (2008).

Puga (2002), and discussed by him in a geographical economics/new economic geography framework, regional inequality (in terms of income and unemployment) within EU countries has increased recently, not decreased. In this context, Puga highlights the importance of increased inequality in terms of economic accessibility among EU regions (absolute gains for most regions, but proportionately larger gains for the core regions).

The impression we give is that, to some extent, current developments in the world economy are "business as usual"; countries grow, some rapidly, some slowly. We have not paid any attention, however, to the question of whether the leading positions of some countries in the world economy might be challenged in the future, or whether these positions are stable over time. It is instructive to take a somewhat longer historical look; if we consider only the last twenty-five years or so, no leapfrogging takes place. We can express the extent of a country's lead or lag as a country's income per capita as a percentage of the world average income per capita in the year under consideration. As an added bonus, this provides us with additional information on economic growth and the degree of income convergence or divergence, as discussed below.

For twenty-eight individual (current) countries from all continents we have fairly reliable population and income data for the last 2,000 years (Maddison, 2007), namely two countries in Africa, three in the Americas,

Table 10.2 Individual countries and regions

Twenty-eight individual countries

Australia	Greece	Norway
Austria	India	Portugal
Belgium	Iran	Spain
Canada	Iraq	Sweden
China	Italy	Switzerland
Denmark	Japan	Turkey
Egypt	Mexico	United Kingdom
Finland	Morocco	United States
France	Netherlands	
Germany	New Zealand	

Seven regions – groups of countries (number of countries)

Eastern Europe (12)	Other east Asia (42)	Other west Asia (12)
Former Soviet Union (15)	Other Latin America (46)	Other western Europe (15)
Other Africa (55)		

Note: See Brakman and van Marrewijk (2008) for details, of regional groupings

six in Asia, fifteen in Europe, Australia, and New Zealand. Together, these twenty-eight countries (with about 3.7 billion inhabitants in 2007) represent about 82 per cent of the world population in the year 1, gradually declining to about 56 per cent of the world total in 2003. Although detailed information for the remaining 197 countries in the world is not available for the entire period, it is possible to construct seven different regions – groups of countries for which fairly reliable aggregate population and income data are available for the last 2,000 years (see table 10.2 for an overview). Taken together, this provides us with thirty-five observations (twenty-eight countries plus seven regions) on the distribution of population and income across the world in the last two millennia.

Figure 10.7 depicts the respective leaders and laggards over time in terms of income per capita. In the year 1 Italy (Rome) was the leader, with an income level about 73 percent higher than the world average. The leading position had been taken over by Iran and Iraq (44 percent above the average) by 1000, before being regained by Italy (Venice, Florence) by 1500 (94 percent above the average). The Dutch trading power gained prominence from 1600 to about 1820, with a relative income peak in 1700 (246 percent above average). Since then the lead has switched frequently, going first to the United Kingdom, then to Australia, followed by the United

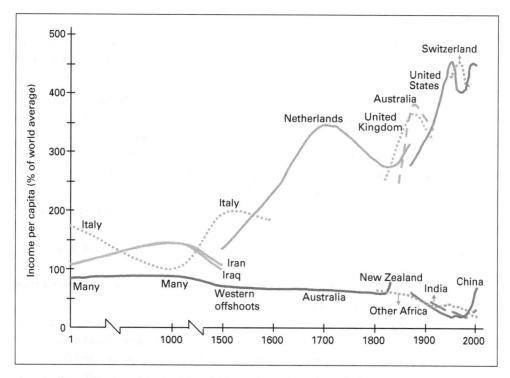

Figure 10.7 Leaders and laggards in the world economy, 1–2003
Note: Western offshoots = Canada, the United States, Australia, and New Zealand.
Source: Brakman and van Marrewijk (2008).

States, Switzerland, and again the United States. The highest relative peak (374 percent above average) was reached in 1999. It is clear not only that the leadership changes from one country to another over time but also that (despite prolonged periods of decline) the relative income position of the leader tends to increase over time.

Many countries qualified for the top "lagging" position in the year 1, including all of the Americas, Australia, Japan, and what is now the former Soviet Union; their income level lagged about 14 percent behind the world average. Most of these countries (with the exception of Japan) were still lagging behind in 1000 (11 percent below the average). In 1500 and 1600 only what Maddison labels the "Western offshoots" (Canada, the United States, Australia, and New Zealand) still qualify for the top lagging positions (about 30 percent below average), from which the United States and Canada escape after 1600, Australia after 1700, and New Zealand only after 1820. Note the remarkable increase in prosperity for these countries, as both

Australia and the United States become the world leader relatively shortly afterwards. Africa (excluding Egypt and Morocco) becomes the laggard in 1870 (45 percent below average), a position to which it returned in 1990 (up to 80 percent below average in 2003).[9] For most of the rest of the twentieth century India and China (the currently feared top globalization countries from an OECD perspective) took turns in being the world's laggard. It is again clear that there is leapfrogging (the top laggard position changes regularly) and that the relative income position of the laggard tends to decrease over time. Furthermore, figure 10.7 suggests that long periods of stagnation can be followed by periods of rapid growth.

We can summarize the most important facts on economic growth as follows.

(i) For almost all countries, there is an ever-increasing level of income per capita.

(ii) Differences in economic growth rates between countries/regions may persist for a long time.

(iii) Long periods of stagnation can be followed by long periods of growth.

(iv) There are frequent changes in economic ranking, known as leapfrogging.

To some extent these observations are consistent with the stylized facts from the static geographical economics models: spatial income differences can persist for long periods of time, and leapfrogging is possible. It is time to see how some of these observations can be explained. This provides the main motivation for the remainder of this chapter.

10.4 Explaining the facts: endogenous growth and geographical economics

Two different fields of economics can play a role in understanding the empirical observations summarized at the end of section 10.3, namely (endogenous) growth models and the (essentially static!) geographical economics models that have been introduced before in this book. We argue below that the former is especially useful for understanding facts (i) and (ii), while the latter is potentially useful for understanding facts (iii) and (iv). The usefulness of geographical economics is further illustrated in section 10.5 by means of a simulation experiment. In doing so, the

---

[9] The figure ignores developments in Iraq since 1991, which reached the all-time low laggard position (84.2 percent below average) in 2003.

limitations of the previously introduced geographical economics models (namely that they are static) also come to the fore. We then subsequently argue in section 10.6 that a marriage between modern growth theory with geographical economics is warranted to really come to terms with the four stylized facts above.

10.4.1 Endogenous growth

Our discussion on the usefulness of the endogenous growth for explaining fact (i) will be brief. Some more details are given in chapter 2, and good surveys are given in Barro and Sala-i-Martin (2004: chap. 11) and Helpman (2004). The essence of this literature is quite simple. The aim is to construct models capable of explaining facts (i) and (ii) – that is, persistent increases in income per capita and persistent differences in economic growth rates. Essentially, this is done as follows. Take the standard neoclassical production function $Y = Af(K, L)$, in which production (income) Y rises if the variable A (total factor productivity) rises, or if the available inputs capital K or labor L rise. In the endogenous growth models, the variable A is some function of other economic factors – for example, capital K with technological spillovers, or research and development expenditures, or some kind of Schumpeterian innovation process. Consequently, instead of decreasing returns to capital, the model now has constant or increasing returns, which enables the economy to grow for ever. This explains fact (i): ever-increasing income levels per capita.

Most endogenous growth models analyze a closed economy. If the structural influence on the variable A is then different in one country from another country, this can vacuously explain fact (ii): long-lasting differences in economic growth rates. The analysis is more interesting, and more challenging, in an open economy setting, as pioneered by Grossman and Helpman (1991).[10] Their aim is to discover along which channels international trade effects long-run innovation and growth. This depends fundamentally on what is assumed with respect to knowledge spillovers and the extent to which countries differ in factor endowments. The opening of trade might stimulate or reduce growth. If knowledge spillovers are geographically localized in specific countries, the smaller country might find that fierce competition from abroad can reduce the returns on investment in

---

[10] See Rivera-Batiz and Romer (1991) for the initial endogenous growth models in an open economy.

knowledge, which in turn might reduce the growth rate. Alternatively, if a country is relatively well endowed with unskilled labor, it might specialize in traditional sectors rather than the R&D sector, which also reduces the growth rate. To the extent that the structural influences on the variable A are localized in an international setting, fact (ii) may still hold – that is, there may be long-lasting differences in economic growth. Facts (iii) (periods of stagnation and rapid growth) and (iv) (leapfrogging) cannot be explained in endogenous growth models, since these models focus strongly on, and are even constructed to lead to, balanced growth equilibria.

10.4.2 Static geographical economics and the use of simulation dynamics

The geographical economics approach cannot contribute to explaining facts (i) (rising income levels) and (ii) (persistent growth differences), simply because there is no mechanism in the models discussed so far through which there is an increase in production levels or investment in R&D leading to the invention and development of new manufacturing varieties. The models discussed so far are essentially static and deal with the (re-) allocation across space of economic activity. Fortunately, however, facts (iii) and (iv) naturally arise even within this kind of geographical economics framework, as indicated below.

In chapter 4 section 4.6 we provided a lengthy discussion of the Krugman and Venables (1995) model: a two-country model in which there is no labor mobility between countries and in which the use of intermediate inputs acts as an additional agglomeration force. Labor combined with intermediate inputs produces the final product, which can be used for consumption and the intermediate product. The central questions in this particular set-up are: what determines the allocation of manufacturing industry over the two countries and what determines the allocation of the labor force over potential activities? If, for some reason, one country has a larger market for intermediate products, this will be an attractive place for other firms because all varieties are available without transport cost, which also lowers the cost of producing a final product.

Starting from an initially very high level of transport costs, Krugman and Venables (1995) discuss what happens in this model if transport costs start to fall, taking this description as representative of actual developments in the world economy (the paper was initially titled "The history of the world, part I"). Essentially, they interpret the workings of the model as if it describes what happens if an exogenous parameter falls over time. Note, however, that we labeled this type of practice "simulation dynamics" in section 10.1. In any case, and sticking to the interpretation of Krugman and Venables, the sequence of events is as follows. Initially, manufacturing production is spread evenly over the two countries. As transport costs start to fall, the world spontaneously divides itself into a core–periphery pattern. If the manufacturing sector is large enough this will also result in different real wages between the two countries (different income per capita levels). Eventually, as transport costs continue to fall, the core–periphery pattern disappears again. The appearance and the disappearance of the core–periphery pattern both are in accordance with fact (iii) (periods of stagnation and rapid economic growth).

Puga and Venables (1996) extend the Krugman and Venables (1995) model, not only by assuming three instead of two countries, but also by analyzing how industrialization spreads from country to country.[11] They assume that some exogenous force increases the size of the industrial sector in one of the countries relative to agriculture (which makes their analysis "simulation dynamics" in our terminology). Since it is assumed that the income elasticity of consumer demand for manufactures exceeds one, this increases demand for manufactures relative to agriculture, which leads to wage increases. Starting with the situation in which industry is agglomerated in country 1, this implies that wages become higher, but it is still profitable for firms to agglomerate because they benefit from inter-firm relationships. As wages increase further, at some point it becomes beneficial to relocate to a low-wage country. The process then repeats itself, and might finally result in waves of industrialization.[12] This phenomenon of a sequence of industrialization and the descriptions given in Puga and Venables (1996) are in accordance with fact (iv) (leapfrogging).

---

[11] For a similar extension and an attempt to explain "the history of the world economy" since the Industrial Revolution in the nineteenth century, see Crafts and Venables (2003); see also Baldwin's comment on this particular attempt (Baldwin, 2003).

[12] The resemblance to Murphy, Shleifer, and Vishny (1989) is not coincidental. In this model, firms are also characterized by increasing returns to scale, and, furthermore, pecuniary externalities are important. The central question here is, whether a country that finds itself in an "underdevelopment trap" or has become a periphery can do something to industrialize itself. The answer, basically, is "yes": coordinated investments and adopting the increasing returns technologies simultaneously may tilt the balance, because each firm creates income and a market for all other firms. Without such coordinated action the investments might very well turn out to be unprofitable, and the country could stay for ever in an underdevelopment trap. The analysis does not deal with the question of how the core–periphery pattern itself came into existence, however: it is a closed-economy exercise, and therefore provides no more than a starting point for the questions we are dealing with in this chapter. Moreover, the model does not provide a description of the stylized facts of growth; the underdevelopment trap does not necessarily come before the development path.

The seminal paper by Redding and Venables (2004) (see chapter 9) gives some evidence as to the relevance of this use of the geographical economics approach to "explain" (changes in) economic development across countries. Essentially, they estimate the equilibrium wage equation (4.17), in which real market access and supplier access are approximated by estimating a gravity trade model and in which, instead of wages, GDP per capita is the dependent variable. The empirical implications are that the distance of countries from the markets in which they sell and the distance to countries that supply intermediates are crucial determinants for explaining cross-country income differentials. The further away final markets and suppliers of the intermediate products are the lower the income levels in the countries concerned.

Redding and Venables (2004) give a simple example to illustrate the potential impact of transport costs in such a model. If the prices of all goods are set on the world market and transport costs are borne by the producing country, and if intermediates account for 50 percent of the total value, the effects of small changes in transport costs turn out to be quite large. Transport costs of 10 percent on both final products and intermediate products reduce the value added by 30 percent. Transportation costs of 20 percent reduce value added by 60 percent. This example makes it intuitively clear why Redding and Venables are able to explain more than 70 percent of cross-country variation in income per capita. The latter ("What happens if transport costs are such and such . . .") is another example of what we have dubbed "simulation dynamics."

This section has briefly described how the modern growth literature is useful for understanding empirical facts (i) and (ii) identified in section 10.3, while the geographical economics models are useful for understanding facts (iii) and (iv) (by using simulation dynamics). It would be nice to have the best of both worlds by merging the endogenous growth approach and the geographical economics approach. We return to this issue in section 10.6 below. First, however, and before we can continue the analysis of economic growth in that section, we must explain in somewhat more detail what simulation dynamics entail.

10.5 Simulation dynamics: an experiment with the reduction of transport costs

As we have already explained in the introduction to this chapter, many insightful interpretations of the geographical economics models are of the

"Suppose ..." type, in which the reader is "talked through" what might happen if some important parameter in the model is changing. Following Krugman and Venables (1995), Fujita, Krugman, and Venables (1999) refer to such thought experiments as a "history of the world," which seems a bit presumptuous (see also Neary, 2001). We prefer to call these experiments "simulation dynamics." A fall over time of the transport cost parameter T has been particularly popular in such thought experiments, as in Krugman and Venables, 1995 (and see figure 4.2) for a first example in our book, but the same principle of course also applies for changes in other parameters, such as the share of income spent on manufactures or the degree of congestion, or a simultaneous change in more than one parameter (see, for example, chapter 7).

10.5.1 Structure of the simulation dynamics experiment

Two general observations on simulations dynamics can be made. First, they are almost always literally thought experiments – that is, the model simulations underlying the discussions in the text are not actually performed.[13] In some cases this is understandable, for example if the author wants to emphasize the arbitrariness of a certain outcome in a situation with multiple long-run equilibria. Second, the great majority of discussions on simulation dynamics restrict their attention to a two-region or two-country setting. In contrast, and keeping the lessons of section 6.4 in mind, this section discusses a series of simulation dynamics in a multi-region setting.

For the remainder of this section we use the twelve-region (neutral-space) racetrack economy model. To allow for the simultaneous existence of economic centers of different size and to avoid bang-bang (corner) solutions (see van Marrewijk and Verbeek, 1993), we use the model with congestion costs that was introduced in chapter 7. This model has an additional advantage, in that it does not require small perturbations of manufacturing activity around a long-run equilibrium to set the dynamic process in motion. Thus, once we have chosen an initial distribution of manufacturing activity between the twelve regions, the entire simulation dynamics experiment is determined, as explained below.

In the discussion we focus attention on the impact of a fall in transport costs T that is gradual but nonetheless provides a shock to the system. The other parameters of the model remain fixed. We have chosen empirically

---

[13] If simulations are undertaken, they are not reported.

reasonable estimates. More specifically, the elasticity of substitution $\varepsilon = 5$, the share of income spent on manufactures $\delta = 0.6$, the speed of adjustment parameter η, (discussed in section 10.2) $= 2$, and congestion costs are modest at $\tau = 0.05$. The experiment runs as follows.

(i) We set the transport costs at a very high level, namely $T = 3$.

(ii) We randomly select an initial distribution of manufacturing production across the twelve regions.

(iii) Since the initial distribution is not a long-run equilibrium, manufacturing workers migrate to regions with higher real wages until a long-run equilibrium is reached (as discussed in section 10.2).

(iv) Given the long-run equilibrium established in step (iii), we now give a shock to the system by lowering the transport costs from $T = 3$ to $T = 2.9$.

(v) The distribution of manufacturing activity over the twelve regions, which was a long-run equilibrium in step (iii), will, in general, no longer be an equilibrium after the change in transport costs in step (iv). This sets in motion a new process of labor migration to regions with higher real wages until a new long-run equilibrium is reached for the new level of transport costs (similar to step (iii)).

(vi) We continue to shock the system along the lines of steps (iv) and (v) by progressively lowering transport cost to $T = 2.8$, $T = 2.7$, etc.

10.5.2 Measuring agglomeration: the Herfindahl index

The fact that we analyze a twelve-region setting has the advantage that it allows for a much richer structure and more surprising economic interactions than the usual two-region setting. The disadvantage, however, is that it is more difficult to succinctly present and interpret the results of the simulations. The phenomenon we have been interested in throughout this book is the degree of agglomeration of economic activity. Part of the discussion that follows therefore concentrates on this degree of agglomeration. To do so, we report a widely used empirical measure of industry concentration that is also used for policy purposes: the Herfindahl index.

This index, originated by Orris Herfindahl (1950), is defined simply as the sum of the squared shares of manufacturing in each region (or of a firm in industry output). Thus, for example, if there are three regions and all manufacturing is located in one region, the Herfindahl index is $1^2 + 0^2 + 0^2 = 1$; if manufacturing activity is equally divided between two of the three regions, the index is $0.5^2 + 0.5^2 + 0^2 = 0.5$; if the manufacturing

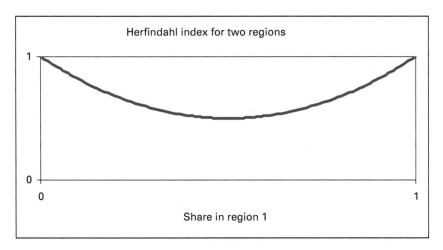

Figure 10.8 Distribution of manufacturing and the Herfindahl index

activity is equally divided between all three regions, the index is $0.33^2 +$ $0.33^2 + 0.33^2 = 0.33$; etc. In general, therefore, the Herfindahl index is lower if manufacturing activity is more equally spread over the regions, and higher if economic activity is more agglomerated. It can therefore be used as a measure of agglomeration. The index is illustrated for all possible divisions of manufacturing activity in a two-region setting in figure 10.8. Some of the shortcomings of the Herfindahl index as a measure of agglomeration are illustrated in subsection 10.5.3.

10.5.3 Discussion of the results of the experiment

During the simulation experiment explained in subsection 10.5.1, manu-facturing activity is reallocated precisely 800 times between the twelve regions. This subsection briefly describes the most interesting and remarkable aspects of the simulation dynamics; more complete details can be found on the website. Figure 10.9 gives an overview of the evolution of the extent of agglomeration, as measured by the Herfindahl index, during the reallocation process as the transports costs fall. Each time the line in figure 10.9 changes shade there has been an exogenous fall in transport costs. There does not appear to be much change in economic structure in the initial phase of the experiment – say roughly up to reallocation number 130. Further reductions in transport costs then start to set in motion a long process of increasing agglomeration of economic activity, reaching a peak at about 0.46 roughly from reallocations 480 to 580. As transportation costs

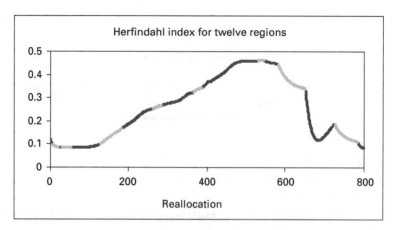

Figure 10.9 Evolution of agglomeration: the Herfindahl index

continue to fall the agglomeration of economic activity starts to decrease again. There seems to be a slight revival during the transition process, roughly from reallocations 650 to 730, which is discussed below. Eventually, as transport costs continue to fall (in the end $T = 1.01$) manufacturing activity is fairly equally spread over the twelve regions.

Table 10.3 gives an overview of the number of reallocation steps after each exogenous reduction in transport costs, as well as the Herfindahl index once the long-run equilibrium is reached. Thus, for example, if $T = 3$ there are four reallocations from the random initial distribution until the long-run equilibrium is reached (when the Herfindahl index $= 0.102$). If T then falls to 2.9, eighteen reallocations are required to reach a new long-run equilibrium (when the Herfindahl index $= 0.085$), etc.

In the initial phase, when transport costs are very high and manufacturing activity is relatively evenly spread, reductions in transport costs have very limited effects (roughly the range from $T = 3.0$ to $T = 2.2$). This is illustrated by the small number of reallocations after a fall in transport costs that is needed to reach a new long-run equilibrium (sometimes only one, two, or three reallocations; in one case no reallocation is required). In this phase the Herfindahl index is about 0.083, virtually equal to the theoretical minimum if manufacturing activity is perfectly evenly spread over the twelve regions.[14]

The first long adjustment process occurs when transport costs fall from 2.2 to 2.1, and seventy-four reallocations are needed. This reallocation

---

[14] We are grateful to Wilfrid W. Csaplar for pointing out an error in an earlier version of this section.

Table 10.3 Overview of reallocations and the Herfindahl index

$T =$	Number of reallocations	Herfindahl index	$T =$	Number of reallocations	Herfindahl index
3.0	4	0.102	2.9	18	0.085
2.8	7	0.084	2.7	16	0.083
2.6	1	0.083	2.5	2	0.083
2.4	1	0.083	2.3	0	0.083
2.2	3	0.083	2.1	74	0.098
2.0	58	0.168	1.9	77	0.252
1.8	23	0.266	1.7	80	0.323
1.6	22	0.343	1.5	144	0.460
1.4	14	0.462	1.3	36	0.448
1.2	70	0.342	1.1	75	0.189
1.05	58	0.111	1.01	16	0.085

Note: Total $= 800$.

process has only a limited impact on the Herfindahl index, however which rises from 0.083 to 0.098. As shown in figure 10.10a, the stability of the Herfindahl index is deceptive, because in the course of this long reallocation process the distribution of manufacturing activity becomes "spiked," rather than almost equally distributed. The "spiked-ness" continues for a long time as transport costs continue to fall, becoming even more pronounced along the way (see panels b to e: if $T = 2$ we have five spikes (at locations 1, 3, 6, 8, and 11), if $T = 1.9$ we have four spikes (the spike at location 1 disappears), if $T = 1.7$ we have three spikes (the spike at location 8 disappears), and if $T = 1.5$ we have two spikes (the spike at location 3 disappears). The adjustment processes in this phase are usually quite lengthy. If transport costs fall from 1.6 to 1.5, for example, the number of spikes reduces from three to two, which requires 144 reallocations of manufacturing activity. As transport costs become quite small, at $T = 1.1$, the spikes disappear and a lop sided distribution emerges in which region 9 (halfway in between the previously largest manufacturing centers of regions 6 and 11) attracts most manufacturing activity (see figure 10.10f). Finally, the lopsidedness disappears altogether if transport costs become very small, resulting in an almost even distribution of manufacturing activity (not illustrated).

The evolution of manufacturing activity during the simulation is shown in figure 10.11 for a selection of regions (3, 6, and 9). Again, as in figure 10.9, a change in the shade of a line in figure 10.11 indicates an exogenous change in the transport costs, which sets in motion a new adjustment process to reach a

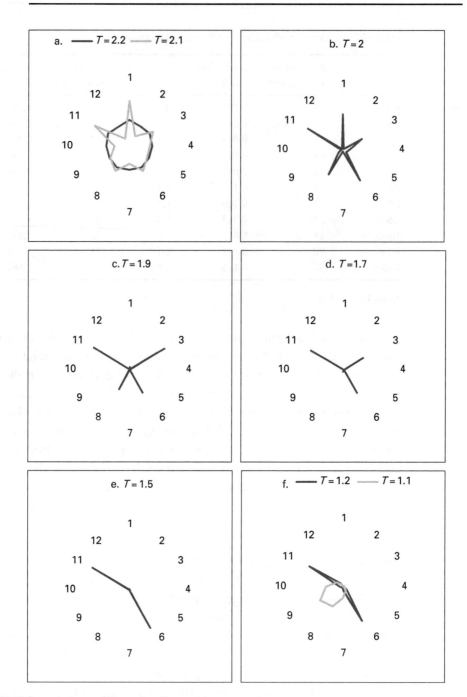

Figure 10.10 Several phases of the reallocation process

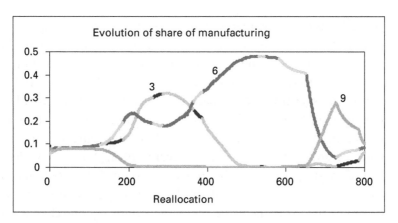

Figure 10.11 Dynamics of regional size: regions 3, 6, and 9

new long-run equilibrium. Figure 10.11 dramatically illustrates the leapfrog-ging phenomenon. Let us look at the dynamics of these regions in more detail.

(i) There is an initial phase, in which all regions are roughly equal in size.

(ii) Then the process of agglomeration starts. Region 6 rapidly attracts a substantial amount of manufacturing activity, while region 3 increases in size more slowly. In contrast, manufacturing activity in region 9 disappears quite quickly.

(iii) There is an intermediate phase, in which the size of region 6 falls and region 3 takes over as the largest region.

(iv) The further reduction in transport costs causes a long, gradual decline of manufacturing activity in region 3, and a simultaneous long-lasting rise of production in region 6, which for some time attracts almost a half of all manufacturing activity.

(v) When transport costs become very low, economic production in region 6 falls dramatically in a short period of time. Simultaneously, production in region 9 rapidly increases to a peak of almost 30 percent of total production. This is remarkable, in view of the fact that pro-duction in region 9 virtually disappeared when the process of agglomeration started.

(vi) Eventually, manufacturing production in all three regions is approxi-mately of the same size when transport costs are virtually absent.

We discussed the general practice on what we have dubbed simulation dynamics in section 10.4. In this section we have actually performed and discussed in detail a particular simulation dynamics experiment, namely gradually but in a manner so as to generate shock reducing transportation costs in the twelve-region racetrack economy with congestion. The experiment substantiated and enriched the practice of simulation dynamics (compare with the discussion of the Krugman and Venables, 1995, model in the previous section). We indeed saw that, as transport costs fell from an initially high level, the distribution of manufacturing activity was agglomerating in ever fewer and larger manufacturing centers. Only as transport costs became very small did the degree of agglomeration decrease and manufacturing production become more evenly distributed. In addition, we have seen many examples of the leapfrogging phenomenon. During the course of the experiment the economic size of regions changed drastically (and sometimes rapidly), with different regions being the largest manufacturing center at different phases (see figure 10.10). This important empirical stylized fact of economic growth, as discussed in section 10.3, cannot be explained using either neoclassical or endogenous growth theories, but is more readily understood in a geographical economics framework.

The simulation dynamics discussed in this section do not allow for an increase in the number of varieties produced, however, or for an increase in output per capita (as explained by endogenous growth theories), which is another important empirical fact discussed in section 10.3. That is to say, the model underlying the simulation experiment is a static one, and this also holds for the other models of geographical economics as introduced in chapters 3 to 9. It is therefore time to see if we can integrate the two approaches.

10.6 Agglomeration and economic growth

10.6.1 Main ingredients

The early literature on agglomeration and growth combines the insights of the endogenous growth literature with those of geographical economics (see Martin and Ottaviano, 1999, and Baldwin, Martin, and Ottaviano, 2001; for a survey, see Baldwin and Martin, 2004). All the elements of the core model are present, but the main difference is that the focus is on (the growth) of capital, and its mobility. This is crucial because growth – in essence – is caused by the accumulation of (a form of) capital. Furthermore, if (knowledge) spillovers are localized, the agglomeration of firms can stimulate growth in the core region. The process of cumulative causation can be enhanced in such a growth model. Interestingly, Baldwin, Martin, and Ottaviano (2001) already show that an adapted version of this model can explain four well-known stages in economic development following the Industrial Revolution: (i) the industrialization of the core, (ii) the subsequent growth take-off, (iii) global income divergence, and (iv) rapid trade expansion.

Baldwin and Martin (2004: 2673) start their survey of the agglomeration and growth literature by observing that agglomeration and growth are inextricably linked, since "agglomeration can be thought of as the territorial counterpart of economic growth." Models incorporating both are characterized by (i) the introduction of capital as a production factor and (ii) the assumptions made about the interregional mobility of capital and the degree of knowledge spillovers. The assumptions regarding capital mobility are crucial. In the absence of capital mobility, the resulting model is (still) rather similar in its main conclusions to, for instance, the core model of chapter 3: catastrophic agglomeration (recall the tomahawk) is still an outcome of a growth model without capital mobility. We already know that the introduction of capital into geographical economics is straightforward; in our discussion of the solvable model in chapter 4 (section 4.8), we introduced capital by differentiating factor input between the fixed costs parameter, α, from the variable cost parameter, β, in the manufacturing production function.

This is not sufficient in a full-fledged growth model, however, since we also need capital growth so as to make economic growth possible. To do this (see equation (10.3) below), a capital-producing sector is introduced. In a two-region setting, the production of K can take place in both regions, and if K production is allowed to differ between regions the assumptions made with respect to capital mobility and knowledge dispersion will be crucial. With *global* knowledge spillovers and perfect capital mobility, the location or geography of K production does not matter. With *localized* knowledge spillovers, it may matter a great deal where K production takes place. In this latter case, geography (location) can have an impact on growth, whereas this is not possible with global knowledge spillovers. Depending on the assumptions made with respect to capital mobility and knowledge spillovers, Baldwin and Martin (2004) show (and summarize) whether and how the findings about agglomeration and growth can differ. In the next subsection we take a particular example of an "agglomeration and growth" model to illustrate the working of such a model and to compare it to the (static) core model of geographical economics.

10.6.2 Agglomeration and growth in the Baldwin–Forslid model

Baldwin and Forslid (2000b) provide an endogenous economic growth version of the core model of geographical economics, not least because they include labor mobility between regions. It combines the structure of the core model with a dynamic framework of intertemporal optimization to explain increases in output per capita. The Baldwin–Forslid model thus gives an explanation of the interaction between economic integration, for example through a fall in transport costs, the location of manufacturing activity, and economic growth. The model incorporates the fact that economic growth affects location and location affects economic growth. More precisely, the technical externalities or knowledge spillovers that are the driving force behind endogenous growth theories are related to the distribution of manufacturing activity across space. The empirical study of Eaton and Samuel Kortum (1996), for example, shows that knowledge creation at a distance gives rise to lower knowledge spillovers than locally produced knowledge (see also Coe and Helpman, 1995, and Coe, Helpman, and Hoffmaister, 1997).

It is important to realize that trade in goods and services is only one aspect of international beneficial exchange. Trade in ideas is equally, if not more, important. Sharing knowledge internationally, about businesses, cultures, technology, etc., through personal and business travel, cross-border mergers and acquisitions, and the like, has reduced the localization of commercially relevant knowledge, such as product and process innovation. Many governments stimulate knowledge flows to peripheral regions, setting up universities or high-technology industrial parks. These changes, in turn, have an impact on the interaction between economic growth and localization, as we will see below. This section first presents the basic structure of the Baldwin–Forslid model and then discusses its main findings. The reason for focusing on this particular model (out of many other possible candidates; see Baldwin and Martin, 2004) is that its basic structure is very close to the core model of geographical economics of chapter 3 that constitutes the benchmark model for our book.[15]

To see that the basic structure of the Baldwin–Forslid model is identical to the two-region core model of chapter 3, we note that there is an even distribution of immobile food production in two regions, on which $1 - \delta$ of income is spent, as well as the production of many different varieties of

---

[15] See Baldwin and Martin (2004: 2702–3) for their discussion of this model, and compare their figure 9 with figure 10.12 below.

manufactures, with an elasticity of substitution ε. Manufacturing production may relocate if workers decide to move to a region with a higher real wage. To allow for economic growth in the model we must explicitly model the time structure, and explain the driving force behind economic growth. To start with the latter, producing a manufacturing variety requires a one-time fixed cost of one unit of capital K, as well as the traditional variable costs in terms of labor (see van Marrewijk, Stibora, and Viaene, 1994, for an identical structure). Capital K can be viewed as either human capital, knowledge capital, or physical capital (see Baldwin and Martin, 2004, and van Marrewijk, 1999, for more discussion), but within this framework it is probably best seen as new knowledge embedded in a manufacturing facility that is immobile across regions. The cost function is therefore given by $R + W\beta x_i$, where R is the rental rate of capital, W is the wage rate, β is the unit labor requirement, and x_i is the output of variety i.

Box 10.1 Discounting the future

Consumers care not only about current consumption levels but also about future consumption levels. This is important to determine their savings decisions – that is, the supply of funds that can be used by firms to finance their investment decisions. To reflect the preference for current consumption by consumers, and take uncertainty about future developments into account, economic growth models assume that consumers discount future consumption using the discount rate $\theta > 0$. Consumption t periods from now is then "discounted" by the factor $[1/(1+\theta)]^t$.

Suppose we take into consideration only three periods, rather than the infinite number of periods in equation (10.4) below, in which the contemporaneous utility derived from consumption is ten in each period. Total utility derived from this consumption pattern if the discount rate $\theta = 0.1$ is then

$$\left(\frac{1}{1.1}\right)^0 10 + \left(\frac{1}{1.1}\right)^1 10 + \left(\frac{1}{1.1}\right)^2 10 = 10 + 9.09 + 8.26 = 27.35$$

The weight given today for the utility derived from consumption two periods from today is therefore only 8.26, rather than ten. This effect is stronger if the discount rate rises. For example, if $\theta = 0.2$

$$\left(\frac{1}{1.2}\right)^0 10 + \left(\frac{1}{1.2}\right)^1 10 + \left(\frac{1}{1.2}\right)^2 10 = 10 + 8.33 + 6.94 = 25.27$$

which shows that consumption two periods from now is given a weight of only 6.94, rather than ten. These examples show that savings today, which is equivalent to forgone consumption today, require a higher return in the future to make up for this forgone consumption if the discount rate is high.

The capital needed for the production of manufactures must in turn be manufactured in the investment good (or innovation) sector *In*, which produces under perfect competition using only labor as an input. One unit of capital is made using α_I units of labor. Individual firms in the investment goods sector view α_I as a parameter. The investment goods sector benefits from technological externalities (knowledge spillovers), however: as output rises, the unit labor requirement for the investment goods sector falls (see Lucas, 1988, Romer, 1990, or Grossman and Helpman, 1991). This fall in the unit labor requirement is necessary within the model for long-run economic growth to occur; without it, output per capita would ultimately reach an upper limit. As suggested by the empirical work of Eaton and Kortum (1996), the distribution of manufacturing activity will affect the degree of knowledge spillovers. In particular, firms will benefit more from locally accumulated knowledge than from knowledge accumulated in the other region.

The production function is

$$Q_K = \frac{L_I}{a_I}; \qquad a_I = \frac{1}{K_{-1} + \kappa K_{-1}^*}; \qquad 0 \leq \kappa \leq 1 \tag{10.3}$$

where Q_K is the flow of new capital, L_I is employment in the investment sector, K is the stock of knowledge, κ is a parameter, an asterisk denotes the other region, and the subscript -1 indicates a one-time lag. Note that this specification implies knowledge spillovers with a one-period lag, leading to a gradual fall in the unit labor requirement a_I. The term κ measures the degree of knowledge spillovers – that is, the extent to which knowledge accumulated in the other region contributes to this region's stock of knowledge. If $\kappa = 0$, knowledge is generated only locally; any knowledge generated in the other region does not contribute at all to this region's stock of knowledge. Similarly, if $\kappa = 1$, knowledge is a global phenomenon; any knowledge generated in the other region leads to an identical increase in this region's stock of knowledge. Baldwin and Forslid assume, for analytic convenience, that capital depreciates in one period (suggesting that one period stands for roughly ten years).

Analyzing economic growth also requires intertemporal preferences. Consumers care not only about current consumption levels of food and manufactures but also about future consumption levels. To reflect their preference for current consumption and their uncertainty about future developments, consumers discount future consumption using the discount rate $\theta > 0$ (see box 10.1). Preferences U are given by

$$U = \sum_{t=0}^{\infty} \left(\frac{1}{1+\theta}\right)^t \left[\ln\left(F_t^{1-\delta} M_t^{\delta}\right)\right]; \qquad M_t = \left(\sum_{i=1}^{N_t} c_{it}^{\rho}\right)^{1/\rho} \qquad (10.4)$$

where the subscript t is a time index and all other variables are as defined in chapter 3. The specification of utility derived from contemporaneous consumption is therefore identical to that in chapter 3. This is crucial for the demand functions, implying that the price elasticity of demand for a variety of manufactures is again $\varepsilon \equiv 1/(1-\rho) > 1$. Consequently, the producer of a particular manufacturing variety applies the same optimal pricing rule as in the core model.

Labor migration between the two-region model arises from differences in real wages. To allow for forward-looking behavior in this economic growth model, rather than the static expectations of the core model, the wage pressure is related to the log difference between the present values of the real wages in regions 1 and 2. Manufacturing workers therefore take (expected) future developments in the real wages into account in the migration decision (see also box 3.4).

10.6.3 Discussion of the main results

A complete analysis and derivation of the main results of the Baldwin–Forslid model described in the previous subsection is beyond the scope of this book, as it requires knowledge on intertemporal optimization techniques. Fortunately, the three main conclusions of their approach, as discussed below, can be readily understood without going into the technical details.

First conclusion

Baldwin and Forslid show that there are only three possible stable long-run equilibria in which the distribution of the manufacturing work force remains stable over time: (i) complete agglomeration in region 1, (ii) complete agglomeration in region 2, or (iii) an even spreading of manufacturing activity between the two regions.[16] These three long-run equilibria

---

[16] There may be other interior long-run equilibria, but they are always unstable.

are identical to those of the core model. The main difference, of course, is that, in this economic growth version of the model, firms keep investing in knowledge and keep inventing new varieties of manufactures indefinitely. The ceaseless increase in the number of varieties raises contemporaneous utility without bound through the love-of-variety effect.

Second conclusion

Baldwin and Forslid analyze the stability properties of the steady-state equilibria using the freeness of trade index $\varphi = T^{1-\varepsilon}$ (see chapter 4). Recall that this index ranges from zero to one and rises as transport costs T fall or the elasticity of substitution ε falls.

The stability properties of the steady-state equilibria hinge crucially upon the size of two parameters: the freeness of trade parameter as defined above, and the degree of knowledge spillover parameter κ as used in equation (10.3). Both parameters may vary from zero to one, such that we can summarize the stability properties in a compact space, as given in figure 10.12. The plane in figure 10.12 is subdivided into three different areas: (i) an area in which spreading is a stable equilibrium and agglomeration is not; (ii) an area in which agglomeration is a stable equilibrium and spreading is not; and (iii) an area in which both agglomeration and spreading are stable equilibria. If we fix the degree of knowledge spillovers, for example by analyzing the horizontal solid line in the figure, we see a perfect correspondence between the stability properties of the Baldwin–Forslid model and the core model. As transport costs fall over time (following the arrows on the horizontal line), initially spreading is the only stable equilibrium, then agglomeration and spreading are both stable equilibria, and finally only agglomeration is a stable equilibrium. It is most reassuring that the simple dynamics of the core model can be reproduced in this more sophisticated dynamic framework.

In addition, figure 10.12 shows that Baldwin and Forslid have enriched our insights into the dynamic interaction between location and economic growth by incorporating the degree of between-location knowledge spillovers. The European Union, for example, is much more closely integrated economically now than it was forty years ago. This arises not only from a reduction in trade costs, as measured by the transport costs parameter T, but also from improved information transmissions across borders. Think of the increased traveling possibilities, watching foreign television channels, increased foreign direct investment, improved communication possibilities, the rise in intra-European mergers and acquisitions, and the funds spend on fostering intra-European knowledge exchanges. Arguably, then, the degree of knowledge

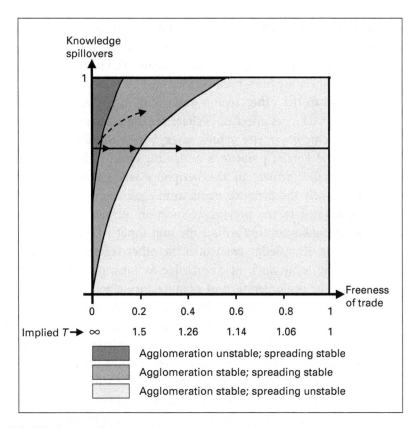

Figure 10.12 Stability in the Baldwin–Forslid economic growth model

spillovers between locations κ has also increased across time. Rather than the horizontal movement over time illustrated by the solid line in figure 10.12, which brings us quite rapidly into the area in which only agglomeration is a stable equilibrium, we have been witnessing a simultaneous rise in knowledge spillovers and a reduction in transport costs – that is, a movement as illustrated by the dashed line in the figure. Evidently, this keeps the economy much longer in the area in which both the agglomeration and the spreading of manufacturing activity are stable equilibria, implying that it is less likely that economic integration leads to complete agglomeration. This may be one of the reasons we did not find much evidence in chapter 5 on increasing agglomeration within the European Union.

Third conclusion

In the welfare analysis of the core model of geographical economics (see chapter 4), we concluded that the agglomeration of manufacturing activity benefits the manufacturing workers and the farmers in the region in which agglomeration occurs as a result of the local provision of all manufacturing varieties (such that transport costs are avoided). On the other hand, farmers in the periphery are hurt, because they have to import all the manufacturing varieties from the other region and incur high transport costs (see also chapter 11). The net effect on welfare for the economy as a whole depends on the specific parameter values, as explained and illustrated in chapter 4. Baldwin and Forslid point to a mitigating effect in their economic growth model for the farmers in the periphery when economic agglomeration occurs, namely the dynamic gains from agglomeration.

As explained in the previous subsection, economic growth arises from knowledge spillovers that reduce the unit input requirement for the investment sector. Knowledge created in the other region contributes only partially to the local stock of knowledge as measured by the parameter κ, however. The agglomeration of manufacturing activity in only one region implies that all knowledge is locally generated, which therefore increases the growth rate of the economy. Farmers in the periphery therefore face a static welfare loss (they have to import all varieties of manufactures) and a dynamic welfare gain (the number of varieties increases more rapidly if manufacturing activity agglomerates; this benefits them as consumers through the love-of-variety effect). Baldwin and Forslid also show (for some parameter values) that the dynamic welfare gain only mitigates and does not reverse the static welfare loss.[17] Again, it is reassuring to see that the conclusions derived in the core model are reproduced in the dynamic Baldwin–Forslid model.

The question therefore arises, can extensions of the Baldwin-Forslid model explain the four empirical facts (rising income levels, lasting differences in growth rates, periods of stagnation followed by rapid growth, and leapfrogging) mentioned at the end of section 10.3? Perhaps, but it is still too early to give a final verdict on the potential of the dynamic geographical economics literature. Also, as we have emphasized in subsection 10.6.1, the conclusions in these truly dynamic models as to the implications for agglomeration and growth are quite sensitive to the assumptions with respect to capital mobility and knowledge spillovers. Finally, as with all endogenous growth models, one can ask the question as to whether models such as that of Baldwin and Forslid (2000b) really address the fundamental

[17] In the area in which the dynamic gain is larger than the welfare loss, the spreading equilibrium is unstable.

causes or determinants of (differences in) economic growth and prosperity. It is to this topic that we turn next.

10.7 Geography and institutions as deep determinants of economic development

In principle, a dynamic geographical economics model such as the Baldwin–Forslid model can explain our four stylized facts of economic growth. According to some authors, however, the problem with such explanations is that it reveals only the *proximate* causes of economic growth. If GDP per capita differs between countries because of differences in localized knowledge creation, human capital formation, or, more generally, in factor productivity, this begs the question of why countries differ with respect to these determinants of growth. To explain income differences, we therefore need to understand the *ultimate* or fundamental determinants of economic growth.

In the recent empirical literature on the allegedly fundamental causes of income or growth differences, three *deep* determinants have in particular been emphasized: (i) institutions, (ii) first-nature geography, and (iii) economic integration or openness. The main conclusion in the literature is that institutions have a strong and direct impact on GDP per capita, that first-nature geography is at best only of indirect importance to explain income differences (via its impact on institutions), and that economic integration, when set against institutions and geography, does not have a significant impact on income. This consensus view is best exemplified by the seminal paper by Dani Rodrik, Arvind Subramanian, and Francesco Trebbi (2004), who conclude that *institutions rule*. They find a strong positive relationship between institutional quality and GDP per capita. For similar conclusions, see Rodrik (2003), Easterly and Levine (2003), and Acemoglu, Johnson and Robinson (2001). In this section we first briefly discuss why institutions should matter to begin with, and then address the question of whether the relevance of geography is perhaps too easily discarded in this literature.

10.7.1 The correlation between institutions and income levels

Why would institutions matter? Basically, because the protection of property rights, an effective judicial system, a certain amount of mutual trust between citizens, and the like are all crucial conditions for a market

Table 10.4 Correlation coefficients between institutions and GDP per capita

Variable	a	b	c	d	e	f
a. GDP per capita	1.00					
b. Growth rate	0.65	1.00				
c. Growth volatility	−0.53	−0.36	1.00			
d. Overall governance measure	0.86	0.59	−0.61	1.00		
e. Property rights	0.76	0.54	−0.62	0.79	1.00	
f. Constraint on power of executive	0.72	0.45	−0.64	0.73	0.63	1.00

Notes: All correlations are significant at 5 per cent level. Real GDP per capita in dollars in 1995. Growth rate = average annual growth rate of real GDP per capita for 1960–98. Growth volatility = standard deviation of annual growth of real GDP per capita for 1960–98.
Source: IMF (2003: 98).

economy to function at all. If institutions do their job properly they reduce transactions costs, and this is welfare-enhancing. The relevance of institutions for economic development is not just a hot topic among researchers, but every modern policy institution emphasizes the importance of good institutions for economic development (see IMF, 2003, or World Bank, 2002). Table 10.4 illustrates, for three institutional measures, the correlation with economic performance for a large sample of countries. The table suggests that better governance, better protection of property rights, and more constraints on the power of the executive all accompany higher GDP per capita, a higher growth rate, and less growth volatility (for details on measuring institutional variables, see IMF, 2003).

Correlation is not causality, however: does a higher growth rate imply better institutions or vice versa? To establish whether the latter is the case, the recent literature referred to above tries to extract the exogenous component of the institutional variables from the data by instrumenting institutions so as to ensure that a positive correlation between institutions and GDP per capita can be interpreted as a causal relationship, meaning that better institutions lead to higher GDP per capita (see Acemoglu, Johnson, and Robinson, 2001, Hall and Jones, 1999, and Frankel and Romer, 1999).[18]

---

[18] How to arrive at the exogenous component of institutions? Acemoglu, Johnson, and Robinson (2001) argue that the mortality rate of colonial settlers provides a means to extract the exogenous component from institutions. These mortality rates can be taken as given or exogenous, certainly to the extent that the current level of income per capita in country X cannot be a determinant of the mortality rate in X as it was colonized in 1600 or whatever distant year in the past. The idea is that these mortality rates in turn did have a lasting impact on the type of institutions that were introduced by the colonizers. High mortality rates meant that the colonizing powers did not invest much in

The methodology used and the conclusions reached by Rodrik Subramanian, and Trebbi (2004) and others have not remained unchallenged, however. Sachs (2003), for instance, strongly disputes the alleged irrelevance of physical or first-nature geography, and argues that alternative measures of geography (such as tropical disease indicators) show that geography is as important as institutions. Glaeser, Rafael La Porta, Florencio Lopez-de-Silanes, and Shleifer (2004) argue that institutions are poorly measured and identified in the new growth empirics. Once this is acknowledged, other and more standard determinants (notably human capital; recall box 7.2) are far more important in explaining differences in economic prosperity. As to the conclusion that economic integration or openness is not important, Francisco Alcalá and Ciccone (2004), for instance, use alternative measures of openness and then show that openness is significant in explaining cross-country differences in productivity.[19]

From the perspective of our book, however, the new or deep growth empirics can be criticized for a different, and perhaps even more fundamental, reason. Following the distinction introduced in chapter 2, the literature looks only at the role of first-nature or absolute geography (e.g. looking at the impact of variables such as distance from the equator, the climate, or the disease environment) in explaining cross-country income differences. *Second-nature* geography does *not* play a part at all. As a result, the relative geography of a country – i.e. the location of a country vis-à-vis other countries (in our view also clearly a deep determinant) – is not regarded as an issue. This neglect, in fact, holds not only for economic interdependencies but also for other variables, such as political and institutional interdependencies, that may be affected by neighboring countries. So, for the income of country *j* only the geography in terms of its own climate or its access to the sea is thought to be important; whether or not this country is surrounded by countries with a high income level and/or good institutions, or is located near large markets and/or main suppliers, is

setting up good institutions themselves, whereas the opposite is the case with low mortality rates. Finally, moreover, there is the fact that institutions are strongly path-dependent or determined by history. By first regressing the quality of institutions on these exogenous mortality rates and other exogenous variables for each country, and by subsequently using the part of institutional variation that is explained by these exogenous variables as the main independent variable in a regression with income per capita as the dependent variable, one hopes to establish whether the correlation message from table 10.4 is also one of causation: that better institutions lead to higher GDP per capita.

[19] Another critique, (that by Raghuram Rajan and Luigi Zingales, 2006), examines whether institutions are "deep" determinants at all.

considered to be of no importance. It goes without saying that this neglect of spatial interdependencies flies in the face of geographical economics.

10.7.2 The geography of institutions

From the core model of geographical economics, and also from its empirical applications (see chapter 5), we know that spatial income interdependencies are important. In the debate on the fundamental causes of growth and the importance of institutions, the question as to whether spatial interdependencies in institutions matter would be foremost. In other words, does the *geography of institutions* matter?

Several authors have discussed channels through which the institutional set-up in neighboring countries may be of importance. William Easterly and Ross Levine (1998) show that the poor economic performance of one country (as a result of, for instance, bad policy) negatively affects income levels in its neighboring countries. Ades and Hak Chua (1997) provide evidence that instability in neighboring countries (measured by the number of revolutions and coups) has a negative effect on the economic performance of a country itself. Regional instability disrupts trade, especially for landlocked countries that are dependent on trade routes (access to the sea) through neighboring territory. It also results in increased military expenditures to prevent conflicts spreading and/or to deter potential future military aggression from unstable neighbors (thereby crowding out productive investment by the government). In a similar vein, James Murdoch and Todd Sandler (2002) argue that civil war in neighboring countries disrupts economic activity at home. Finally, Beth Simmons and Zachary Elkins (2004) show that countries copy (avoid) policies from other (neighboring) countries that have been proven (un)successful, or that countries are forced to adopt similar policies to stay economically competitive or in order to comply with regional or global pressures. For a sample of 147 countries and with institutions being measured by the *rule of law* variable (Kaufman, Kraay, and Mastruzi, 2005) and with contiguity being used to define a country's neighbors, figure 10.13 shows the correlation between a country's own institutions and those of its neighbors.

Figure 10.13 shows the relationship between a country's own and its neighbors' institutions (the pairwise correlation is 0.73). Countries below (above) the thick 45° line are countries with better (worse) own institutions than those of their average neighbor. It turns out that Hong Kong (the Philippines) has the best (worst) institutions relative to its neighbors, followed by

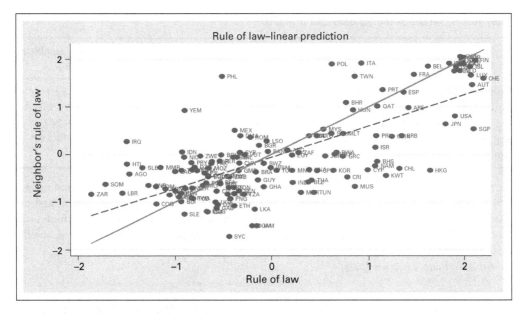

Figure 10.13 Scatterplot of own and neighboring institutions

Notes: The institutional measure, *rule of law* in 2000, ranges from −2.50 (worst) to +2.50 (best). The 'neighboring' institutions are based on contiguity spatial weights. The simple correlation is 0.73. (p-value = 0.00; dotted line). The thick line is the 45° line (147 countries).

Kuwait and Chile (Yemen and Iraq). In absolute terms the Seychelles (followed by the Dominican Republic, Jamaica, and Sierra Leone) have the worst neighbors in terms of institutions, whereas the Democratic Republic of Congo has the worst own institutions (followed by Somalia, Liberia, and Iraq).

10.7.3 The geography of institutions and/or the geography of markets?

When estimating the impact of own and neighboring institutions on GDP per capita (with the percentage of population speaking a European language as the instrument for institutions; Hall and Jones, 1999), it turns out that neighboring institutions do matter. This result is robust to various checks (sample size, various controls, definition of neighbor, etc.). Better own and neighboring institutions both increase a country's GDP per capita; first-nature geography does not matter. From the perspective of our book, however, it might be argued that the real importance in terms of including second-nature geography is not so much spatial institutions but spatial income. That, at least, is what the core model of geographical economics shows! As a first pass, table 10.5 therefore includes nominal market potential or nominal market access (MA) among the set of explanatory

Table 10.5 Market access and the geography of institutions

	Baseline	Market access	MA + neighbor institutions
Geography (distance to equator)	−2.45 (−2.13)		−0.62 (−0.60)
Institutions (rule of law)	0.92 (2.75)		0.90 (4.55)
Neighboring institutions (rule of law)	0.75 (2.69)	0.84 (5.38)	0.54 (2.87)
Market access			−0.41 (−1.97)
Number of observations	147	147	147

Notes: Dependent variable = log GDP per capita, 1995 (t-value). The estimates are two-stage least squares (2SLS) regressions with the first-stage instruments: speaking a European language, geography, and the distances to New York, Brussels, and Tokyo. Similar conclusions hold if regional dummies (Africa, Latin America, and south-east Asia) and other geography measures (being landlocked, being an island, and the area) are included.
Source: Bosker and Garretsen (2008).

variables, which is measured as $A_j = \sum_i GDP_i/D_{ij}$, with D_{ij} being the great circle distance between the capital cities of countries i and j. This measure of market access is a simple market potential function. The study by Redding and Venables (2004) (see subsection 9.6.2), using far more sophisticated market access measures, invariably finds that market access is important for explaining cross-country differences in GDP per capita: better market access implies higher GDP per capita. This finding also holds when they control for the role of institutions.

Column 1 in table 10.5 shows the baseline results, with only own and neighboring institutions and first-nature geography as explanatory variables. Column 2 illustrates that, when looked at in isolation, market access has the expected significant positive effect on GDP per capita. Following Redding and Venables (2004), MA is instrumented by the log distance to three economic centers (New York, Brussels, and Tokyo). When we subsequently add own-country institutions and neighboring institutions, MA has the wrong sign. More importantly, the addition of the market access variable does not alter our main finding that institutions matter and that neighboring institutions play a role. After controlling for regional and other fixed-geography effects, for which the landlocked dummy is significant, (spatial) institutions remain significant and market access becomes insignificant (not shown). As to the question of why these findings differ from those of Redding and Venables (2004), a number of possibilities arise. They do not instrument institutions, but instead just look at own-country institutions, and their country sample is somewhat smaller (101 countries, excluding a number of [African] countries with bad institutions). Moreover, the focus of their analysis is different. Even though they report estimation results for the specification with our simple market access variable and institutions, the bulk of their paper and estimation results deals with market access measures that are more sophisticated and better grounded in geographical economics (see section 5.5).

An interesting question for future research is to investigate which kinds of spatial interdependencies matter most in explaining income differences between countries. The main conclusion for now is that existing models of economic growth, including dynamic geographical models such as the Baldwin–Forslid model, can be criticized for not dealing with the deep determinants of growth. At the same time, recent attempts to include these deep determinants and the role of institutions by and large ignore the possible relevance of spatial interdependencies. The way forward is to come up with models and estimations that allow for spatial interdependencies to matter at both the theoretical level (as in figure 10.12) and the empirical level (as in table 10.5). In doing so, it would probably also pay to make more (and better) use of economic history to better understand the relationship between growth on the one hand and first- and second-nature geography on the other hand (see box 10.2). The reason for turning to economic history is that the literature on the deep determinants of economic development (and this is in line with geographical economics at large) suggests that economic development is probably strongly history- or path-dependent.

Box 10.2 A historical look: bad and old geography

A closer historical look at the importance of geography for the growth of countries and cities reveals that geography is important, but not always in the way one expects. Nunn and Puga (2007), for instance, argue that *bad* (first-nature) geography can also have a favorable effect on GDP per capita. For Africa, they show that the ruggedness of the terrain has an indirect positive effect on GDP per capita, whereas the direct effect is negative. A more rugged terrain makes the agricultural use of land more difficult, makes building more expensive, and in general increases the costs of doing economic transactions. Indeed, for all countries an increase in ruggedness or "bad geography" has this direct negative effect on income levels. The main conclusion of their analysis is that "in Africa, additional to this negative direct effect, ruggedness may also have had a positive indirect effect on economic outcomes, by allowing areas to escape from the slave trades and their negative consequences" (Nunn and Puga, 2007: 2).

Box 10.2 (cont.)

Table 10.6 Estimates for Italian city growth, 1300–1861

	Combined		Separate	
Geography				
Seaport	0.316	[0.016]	0.250	[0.046]
Roman road	0.070	[0.287]	0.036	[0.571]
Hub	0.339	[0.063]	0.277	[0.047]
Navigable waterway	0.388	[0.008]	0.433	[0.003]
Mountains	−0.087	[0.116]	−0.091	[0.098]
Urban potential	0.015	[0.815]	−0.042	[0.566]
Institutions				
Capital	0.702	[0.000]		
North			0.535	[0.000]
South			1.575	[0.001]
R^2	0.50		0.57	
Number of observations	623		623	

Notes: Dependent variable = log of city size, 1995 [p-value]. Cut-off city size is 10,000 inhabitants. Time fixed effects and north–south controls are not reported. *Source:* Bosker *et al.* (2008).

The basic idea here is that ruggedness offered protection to those areas in Africa that were raided by slave traders in the era of the slave trade (1400–1900). It turns out that, for African countries (and for African countries alone!), ruggedness has the predicted positive effect. This study is important for two reasons. First, and keeping the discussion in the main text of section 10.7 in mind, it helps to differentiate between the direct and indirect impact of (first-nature) geography on GDP per capita, which is extremely important given the unsettled debate between the researchers (e.g. Sachs) who argue that the impact must be a significant direct one and the researchers (e.g. Rodrik) who argue that the impact of geography is at best an indirect one. Second, the innovative paper by Nunn and Puga (2007) reminds us that bad geography is not always and everywhere bad for economic outcomes.

Reliable historical data on growth at the country or regional level are hard to come by, certainly if one takes a really long-term view. One reason is that in the Middle Ages, or even before that period, our present-day countries often just did not exist. Data on cities are more useful, since they go back many centuries. For an historical look at the role of geography and other "deep" determinants (e.g. institutions) on economic prosperity, therefore, a number of recent papers have turned to the analysis of city growth. The papers that include measures of first-nature as well as second-nature geography are particularly interesting. One finding seems to be that the results on the importance of geography are more robust for first-nature geography. Based on a data set from Malanima (1998, 2005), Bosker, Brakman, Garretsen, Herman de Jong, and Schramm (2008) analyze urban growth

Box 10.2 (cont.)

in Italy (one of the earliest urbanized countries in the world) for the period 1300–1861. First-nature geography variables (e.g. if the city was a seaport, located near or at a Roman road, or had access to a navigable waterway) are significant in explaining urban growth; see table 10.6.

The geographical divide between the north and south of Italy is also an important determinant of city growth. Second-nature geography (here measured by a simple *urban potential function* – that is, essentially a market potential with population size replacing GDP) is, however, never significant! One reason might be that in the days before our modern economy (let us say before the nineteenth century) an integrated urban system in which locations (Italian cities) were really connected did not yet exist. Table 10.6 also shows that institutions (here, whether a city was a capital city) are important (see the website for the complete version of this paper). More research, as to the relative importance of "old" first- versus second-nature geography for urban growth, is warranted, as the results in Bosker, Buringh, and Luiten Van Zanden (2008) illustrate. Using a data set that covers (almost) all cities in western Europe and, exceptionally, (the Muslim world of) north Africa and the Middle East for the period 800–1800, they find that second-nature geography (again measured by an urban potential variable) is significant.

10.8 Conclusions

We have identified three rather different types of dynamics, dubbed adjustment dynamics, simulation dynamics, and economic growth. Adjustment dynamics analyzes the reallocation processes within a geographical economics model that brings us from an initial distribution to a long-run equilibrium. This process is usually quite smooth, but the reader should be aware of some special cases that may arise during the adjustment process, in particular for high speeds of adjustment (cycles, movement to a non-stable equilibrium, and movement away from the nearest stable equilibrium).

Simulation dynamics involves the discussion and interpretation of a model based on a series of exogenous changes in some parameter. Before you can perform such an exercise, you have to know which story to tell. We therefore had a brief look at some stylized facts of economic growth and development, and focused attention on four stylized facts: (i) rising income levels, (ii) lasting differences in growth rates, (iii) periods of stagnation followed by rapid growth, and (iv) leapfrogging. We argued that the (endogenous) growth literature can help us to understand the first two facts, while geographical economics can help us to understand the latter two facts,

Applications and extensions

in particular by using simulation dynamics. We discussed this claim at length in an experiment based on a twelve-region version of the racetrack economy with congestion.

The most complex type of dynamics is the analysis of economic growth, which requires the modeling of traditional and novel forces explaining the increase in economic prosperity over time, whether resulting from rising production levels or from the invention and availability of new goods and services based on investment in capital goods or research and development. This can only satisfactorily be modeled in a framework of intertemporal optimization, which makes the technical analysis more complex, certainly in a model with multiple long-run equilibria. To this end, we briefly discussed the "agglomeration and growth" class of models within geographical economics, and in particular the Baldwin–Forslid model, a merger of the core model of geographical economics with an endogenous growth model. Fortunately, and most reassuringly, the main conclusions derived in this framework are consistent with our findings in the core model, particularly with respect to the stability and welfare analysis. It justifies the short cuts we have been taking in other chapters of this book.

The Baldwin–Forslid model gives us also some new insights, for example into the importance of interregional knowledge spillovers, and into the distinction between static and dynamic welfare effects. All the same, as is to be expected from any model, however elaborate it may be, this model also has its shortcomings. We zeroed in on the argument that this model, like all modern growth models, has been criticized for focusing only on the proximate causes of growth at the expense of the so-called deep determinants of economic development: institutions and geography.

Exercises

10.1 Economists often use the idea of instantaneous price adjustment, meaning that, after a shock has occurred, prices adjust so rapidly that everybody and everything in the economy remains in equilibrium. In the model of geographical economics, however, this is not the case for labor (see equations (10.1) and (10.2)). Discuss why a very swift reallocation of labor across regions may not necessarily be a good thing. Also (*), what is the (implicit) assumption in the models of geographical economics in this book about the adjustment behavior of manufacturing firms?

10.2 In chapter 5 subsection 5.2.2 it was argued that, in terms of GDP per capita, convergence has taken place in the post-war period in the countries of the European Union: for example, Portugal has caught up with Germany. Use the endogenous growth theory to explain this.

10.3 At the end of section 10.3 four stylized facts about economic growth were formulated. Discuss how these four facts can in principle be explained by the Baldwin–Forslid model of economic growth and location.

10.4 Worldwide, there has been a clear reduction in transport costs associated with international trade in recent decades (think of the WTO-inspired reduction in tariffs, the decline in the costs of communication, etc.). Despite this reduction, there has not been a clear convergence in GDP per capita at the global level. Use figure 10.12 and equation (10.3) to explain why this might be the case.

10.5 Section 10.5 of chapter 10 deals with so-called simulation dynamics. Suppose that globalization (defined as ever-decreasing transport costs) ultimately results in a truly global economy; what does this mean for the degree of economic agglomeration?
    Hint: use figure 10.9.

10.6 Figure 10.7 shows some examples of "leapfrogging" (the United States versus Australia around 1900). How can this phenomenon be explained in a geographical economics model?
    Hint: look at figure 10.9.

10.7 The freeness of trade index is defined as $\varphi = T^{1-\varepsilon}$. The index depends on two parameters, T and ε (both of which are larger than or equal to one). Using a spreadsheet program (such as Excel), make graphs of the evolution of φ as a function of T for different values of ε and, similarly, make graphs of the evolution of φ as a function of ε for different values of T. Comment on your findings.

Part IV

Policy and evaluation

11 The policy implications of geographical economics

11.1 Introduction

So far we have paid little attention to the policy implications (if any) that arise from geographical economics. Can geographical economics be used for policy analysis? This chapter addresses this important question. Two opposing views on the usefulness of geographical economics for policy purposes come to the fore. According to the first view (see Baldwin *et al.*, 2003, and Ottaviano, 2003), it is useful to take the core models literally regarding the main policy implications they show. The idea is that, by sticking to the simple models of chapters 3 and 4, the policy differences between geographical economics and other approaches are most clearly visible. The dangers of taking the core models too seriously for policy purposes have, however, been emphasized by both economists (Neary, 2001) and geographers (Martin, 1999). While not neglecting this second view (see also chapter 12), we mainly follow the first view and try to draw out the policy implications from the core models, if only because these models are by now familiar to the reader.

This chapter is organized as follows. In the next section (based largely on Ottaviano, 2003), we briefly discuss the general policy implications of the core model of geographical economics. We single out three policy issues:

  (i) government taxation and spending;
 (ii) changing the infrastructure and transport costs; and
(iii) the welfare implications.

In section 11.3 regional policy in the form of tax competition is discussed. Section 11.4 provides a simple policy experiment dubbed "building a bridge" in the multi-region congestion model of chapter 7. This serves as an example of how infrastructure policies might affect agglomeration. Section 11.5 discusses welfare implications and applies these insights to the policy experiment of building a bridge between two locations. Section 11.6 concludes this chapter.

11.2 Six basic policy implications of the core model[1]

11.2.1 The lip service paid to geographical economics in policy discussions

When geographical economics is mentioned in policy discussions it is mostly when the consequences of large-scale economic integration are at stake. A prime example is the process of economic integration in the European Union: think of the discussions on the consequences of Economic and Monetary Union (EMU) in the 1990s or, more recently, on the extension of the European Union with the new member states from central and eastern Europe. Right from the start, geographical economics was used heavily in these discussions.[2] This does not come as a surprise, as one of the main questions in the discussions is if, and how, the process of economic integration would change the spatial distribution of economic activity across the European Union. This question lies at the very heart of geographical economics.

In terms of the core model of geographical economics, the above question reduces to the question: what happens if transport costs fall, or, equivalently, if the freeness of trade increases? Who will benefit, the core or the periphery? In chapter 5 (see box 5.1) we argued that economic integration in the European Union has coincided with some lowering of the degree of agglomeration at the country level. Erstwhile peripheral countries, such as Ireland, Portugal, and Spain, have seen their share of overall manufacturing activity increase, while the opposite has happened in core countries such as France and the United Kingdom. With respect to economic integration in Europe, geographical economics has often been used to argue that we might see an *in*crease in the degree of agglomeration of manufacturing production and more industry concentration in the future, however. This is then

---

[1] Our discussion of the six policy implications in this section is based on Ottaviano (2003), who in turn summarizes the main findings of Baldwin *et al.* (2003). The latter is to date the standard reference when it comes to analyzing and modeling public policies in models of geographical economics.

[2] In a way, the idea that the analysis of core–periphery patterns is important for economic integration in the European Union even pre-dates the geographical economics approach, because the study by Krugman and Venables (1990), a crucial forerunner of the approach (as discussed in chapter 2), was explicitly aimed at analyzing the core–periphery implications of EU integration. Moreover, Krugman's 1991 book *Geography and Trade* already mentions the potential relevance of geographical economics to the analysis of the feasibility of EMU in Europe.

thought to undermine the monetary union, the existence of a single currency in the EU countries that make up Euroland, because it implies more country-specific economic shocks.[3] Suppose that all manufacturing activity ends up in the core countries Germany, France, and the United Kingdom, but also that the automobile industry ends up in Germany and the fashion industry in France (on a European scale, an example of agglomeration and specialization). The monetary union is then prone to economic shocks for the core countries but not the periphery, which has only agricultural/services production. Within the core countries, Germany and France, economic development might diverge if, for instance, the automobile industry is booming while the fashion industry is in recession.

The use of geographical economics in actual policy discussions is indirect, however, since the policy issue itself (e.g. EU integration), the policy makers (e.g. European and national governments), and the policy instruments (e.g. taxes, subsidies, interest rates) are typically *not* analyzed within the context of a model of geographical economics. In these policy discussions there are many references to Krugman (1991a), but the policy issue at hand is mostly not analyzed by means of a geographical economics model. To fill this gap, the recent literature on the policy implications of geographical economics proceeds in two steps (Baldwin *et al.*, 2003). First, and without necessarily referring to any specific policy question, the (qualitative) policy implications of the core model are drawn out. This is the topic of the remainder of this section. Second, and with these general policy implications in mind, one can analyze specific policy questions using a geographical economics model. This will be done in sections 11.3 to 11.5.

11.2.2 Six basic policy implications and the tomahawk diagram

Following Ottaviano (2003: 669–72), we can illustrate the basic policy implications of the core model of geographical economics by using the tomahawk diagram (recall figure 4.3b) as a benchmark. For convenience, the tomahawk diagram, with the freeness of trade φ along the horizontal axis, is replicated as figure 11.1. Ottaviano (2003) argues that the core model gives rise to the following six general policy implications:

- regional side effects;
- trade interaction effects;

---

[3] Good early examples of this use of geographical economics in the EMU discussions are Krugman (1993a) and, from the side of geography, Martin (2001).

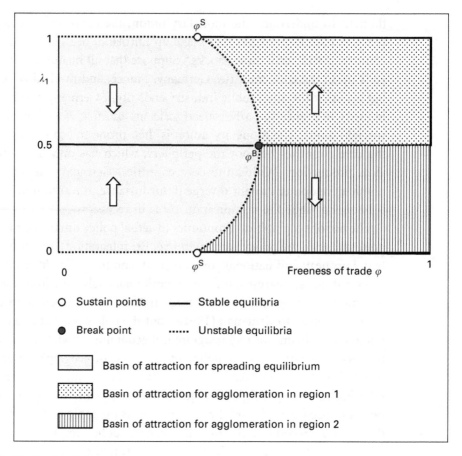

φ^S

λ_1

φ^B

φ^S

Freeness of trade φ

○ Sustain points   — Stable equilibria

● Break point   ...... Unstable equilibria

▭ Basin of attraction for spreading equilibrium

▦ Basin of attraction for agglomeration in region 1

▥ Basin of attraction for agglomeration in region 2

Figure 11.1 The tomahawk diagram

- lock-in effects;
- selection effects;
- coordination effects; and
- threshold effects

We briefly discuss these effects in turn, but focus on the threshold effects, because they nicely sum up the basic policy message of geographical economics, and also because they are used in the remainder of this chapter.

To start with the *regional side effects*, the policy implication here is merely that all kinds of allegedly "non-regional" policies can have consequences for the regional or spatial allocation of economic activity. For instance, trade liberalization, competition policy, and (interregional) income redistribution are typically not aimed at the location decisions of footloose economic agents, but all of them can, in principle, affect core–periphery patterns. We know from the core models of chapters 3 and 4 that any policy-induced change in the key model parameters may *potentially* affect the equilibrium spatial allocation of economic activity. We say "potentially" because whether the equilibrium actually is affected depends critically on if and how the policy measure changes the balance between agglomeration and spreading forces.

The policy implication of *trade interaction effects* focuses on the fact that the effect of any policy intervention on the spatial allocation of economic activity depends on the (initial) level of trade or economic integration. Any given policy intervention that brings an economy beyond the sustain or break points could have a large impact.

The third policy implication, *lock-in effects*, can best be illustrated by using the tomahawk diagram (see figure 11.1). The central idea is that temporary policies can have permanent effects on the equilibrium spatial allocation of the footloose economic activity. Suppose that we start to the right of both the sustain point φ^S and the break point φ^B in figure 11.1 and that all footloose economic activity happens to be agglomerated in region 1, $\lambda_1 = 1$. Now suppose that the peripheral region, region 2, introduces a subsidy to footloose firms and workers that succeeds in convincing all footloose agents to migrate from region 1 to region 2. The lock-in (or hysteresis) effect now refers to the fact that, once the footloose agents have all moved to region 2, this region may withdraw or stop its subsidy because, for the same (unchanged) level of freeness of trade, complete agglomeration in region 2 is also a stable long-run equilibrium, and without the subsidy no footloose agent has an incentive to move back to region 1; temporary policies (the subsidy) can have lasting effects.

To illustrate the fourth basic policy implication, *selection effects*, figure 11.1 is again useful. Suppose initially that the spreading equilibrium is stable and that the actual freeness of trade is lower than φ^B. If the actual freeness of trade increases such that $\varphi > \varphi^B$, we see in the figure that all footloose agents will either end up in region 1 or 2. As long as the two regions are identical however, the outcome is undetermined. In this situation any policy intervention, however small, that gives one of the two regions an advantage will be enough to secure that all footloose agents end up in that region. Policy acts as a selection device between spatial equilibria.

The policy implication of *coordination effects* refers to the way that policy makers can influence the expectations of individuals as to where all other agents will locate. This is important if multiple equilibria are possible. In terms of figure 11.1, if the actual freeness of trade is such that $\varphi^S < \varphi < \varphi^B$, spreading and agglomeration are both stable equilibria. Policy makers can determine which equilibrium gets established, such as, for instance, full agglomeration in region 1, if they succeed in convincing (some of) the footloose agents that region 1 is the preferred location by offering a subsidy if they move to region 1. This policy will lead to self-enforcing agglomeration (as long as agents expect the government to pay the subsidy and act accordingly; ironically, the policy might work without the government actually handing out any subsidy as long as the expectations of economic agents are affected by the government!).

The final policy implication of Ottavano's list deals with *threshold effects* and these, arguably, are the most important of all (Baldwin *et al.*, 2003: 228–30). Policy measures will have an affect on the equilibrium spatial distribution of footloose economic activity only if these measures attain a certain critical mass. An increase in the degree of economic integration or, in modeling terms, an increase in the freeness of trade (see figure 11.1) can have either no or a huge impact. What happens depends crucially on the initial level of freeness of trade and on the gap between the initial level of freeness of trade and the break or sustain point. The possibility of a non-linear impact of policy measures means that it can be misleading to use the standard approach to policy analysis, which analyzes the impact of *marginal* policy changes under the assumption that the impact of policies on the economy is continuous. In terms of figure 11.1, with $\varphi < \varphi^B$, policy interventions, however large, that will not succeed in ensuring $\varphi > \varphi^B$ will not have an effect on agglomeration. At the same time, if φ is initially smaller but very close to φ^B, the threshold effect implies that a very minor policy intervention that just about increases φ beyond φ^B may do the job.

The reason for the threshold effect is that, even though initially there exists a high degree of flexibility as to location, once these choices have been made the spatial pattern turns out to be rigid. This threshold or non-linear property visualized by the tomahawk diagram implies that "marginal policy changes are completely ineffective until the cumulated change remains a certain threshold. After the threshold is crossed, the impact is catastrophic" (Ottaviano, 2003: 670). The advantages of a chosen location have a tendency to reinforce themselves, and the choice of location will be reconsidered only if policy interventions acquire sufficient mass to offset the (accumulated) benefits of agglomeration, the so-called *agglomeration rent* (see section 11.3). Stated differently, the threshold effect in geographical economics can be traced back to the "putty-clay" character of geography in these models (Fujita and Thisse, 2002). In the introduction to chapter 6, and following

Head and Mayer (2004a), we have already noted that in empirical research it is problematic to test for the relevance of geographical economics by imposing a linear relationship between, *in casu*, trade costs and the degree of agglomeration. The same conclusion is reached when it comes to the policy implication of the threshold effect (Baldwin *et al.*, 2003: 229).

11.2.3 Taking the core model too seriously?

Apart from the threshold effect, there are therefore five other policy implications that present an alternative view on the impact of policy on the economy. Considered separately these implications are not always unique to geographical economics, but taken together they offer, at least in a qualitative sense, an idea as to how geographical economics can be useful for policy analyses. The use of figure 11.1 as a benchmark does not imply that these implications are specific to the Krugman (1991a) model or other models that also give rise to the tomahawk diagram. The six implications apply to all core models of geographical economics, subject, of course, to the necessary qualifications. The model, which may, for instance, give rise to a bell-shaped curve instead of a tomahawk diagram (see chapter 4), shows that the above policy implications need to be qualified in the sense that the threshold effect suggests that spreading will turn into full agglomeration and vice versa in a catastrophic manner, whereas in the bell-shaped curve models a more gradual change from spreading to agglomeration and vice versa occurs.

More fundamentally, applying geographical economics to a specific policy question, the core model underlying the tomahawk diagram is too abstract and too simple. This is why Neary (2001) points out that one should be very careful in using geographical economics for actual policy analyses. This reservation is also due to the fact that (i) core regions are always better off than peripheral regions in the core model and (ii) the core models suggest that policy makers can pick the equilibrium they prefer. The presence of multiple equilibria indeed suggests that policy makers can try to pick a "better" equilibrium. This supposes that equilibria can be ranked from a welfare perspective and that policy makers know how to move the economy from one equilibrium to another.

In practice, these requirements are beyond the knowledge and possibilities of policy makers. As Neary (2001: 27) puts it:

It is tempting to suggest a role for government in "picking equilibria." This in turn may encourage a new sub-field of "strategic location policy," which ... has produced much interesting theory but no simple robust rules to guide policy making.

All these are temptations to be resisted, since they take too literally the neat structure of the [geographical economics] model, and ignore the econometric difficulties in estimating the non-linear, non-monotonic relation it predicts.[4]

We quote Neary here at some length because his skepticism is important when geographical economics is applied to more specific policy issues. At the same time (see notably Baldwin *et al.*, 2003: 277), Neary's criticism applies to the earlier geographical economics models discussed in chapters 3 and 4. More recent models try to include a more "realistic" depiction of policy making.[5]

Armed with the basic policy implications of geographical economics, and also with some reservations as to their usefulness, we are now in a position to deal with three policy issues (for a more extensive list of examples we refer to Baldwin *et al.*, 2003):

(i) government taxation and spending;
(ii) changing the infrastructure and transport costs; and
(iii) the welfare implications.

In the next three sections we address each of these issues in turn.

11.3 Agglomeration rents, public policy, and policy competition

11.3.1 Corporate income taxation and the race to the bottom: the standard view

In recent years capital has become increasingly mobile internationally: most of the remaining capital controls and restrictions on, for instance, the activities of multinational firms have been removed by now, and as a result FDI flows have increased strongly (see chapter 8). One side effect of the increased international capital mobility is that it provides opportunities for multinational firms to minimize or even avoid paying corporate income taxes. In this setting, many people fear that globalization, and in particular increased capital mobility, forces national governments to decrease the tax burden on the most mobile production factor, capital. In doing so, tax competition between governments is intensified. This may result in a "race to the bottom" in corporate income taxes. Some critics even go a step

---

[4] This is probably also the reason why Fujita, Krugman, and Venables (1999: 349) are reluctant to discuss policy implications.

[5] See Neary's (2006) review of Baldwin *et al.* (2003) as to whether he has changed his opinion on this matter (the answer seems to be affirmative).

further and conclude that, ultimately, the redistributive function of the welfare state is threatened by footloose capital (Sinn, 2003).

These concerns are fueled, at least to some extent, by the actual development of the most obvious and readily available measure of corporate income taxes, the *statutory* tax rate. In recent years almost every OECD country has reduced its statutory tax rates. Not only statutory tax rates but also *effective* corporate taxes have decreased in a period when, as illustrated below, the restrictions on capital mobility (here, on inward FDI) have clearly decreased too. As a consequence, many policy makers see the drop in corporate tax rates as a direct consequence of the increased financial integration. Figure 11.2a gives, for a sample of nineteen OECD countries for the period 1981–2000, the effective average corporate income tax rate and the corresponding standard deviation, whereas figure 11.2b shows for each of the countries concerned the change in the so-called Golub index (named after its inventor), an index that measures the statutory barriers on inward FDI (a *higher* score on this index means more restrictions). It is clear that the effective average tax rate fell in this period while at the same time the restrictions on FDI inflows also decreased sharply. We also know from chapter 8 that during this period international capital mobility, measured by FDI flows, increased markedly.

The public's fears about the negative effects of increased capital mobility on the supply of taxation capital and the provision of public expenditures can indeed be given a theoretical foundation. Using the *standard tax competition literature*, it is quite easy to show that an increase in capital mobility could go along with a decrease of the corporate income or capital tax rate and an under-provision of public goods.[6] Assume a two-country model with two factors of production (capital and labor), in which labor is immobile but capital is mobile between the two countries. Production takes place under perfect competition and constant returns to scale. Firm output can be traded freely – that is, there are no trade costs – thereby ensuring perfect goods market integration. It is also assumed that the government provides a public good, which is financed with a source-based tax on capital. Given symmetry in every other respect (e.g. technology, preferences, country size), it can be shown that any increase in the degree of economic integration, which coincides in this model with an increase in the degree of capital mobility, will imply a lower tax rate in both countries.

---

[6] The seminal contribution here is the model by George Zodrow and Peter Mieszkowski (1986); see also the survey paper by John Wilson (1999).

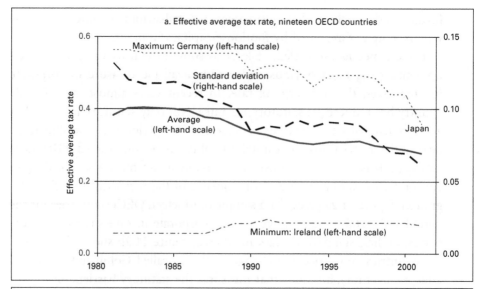

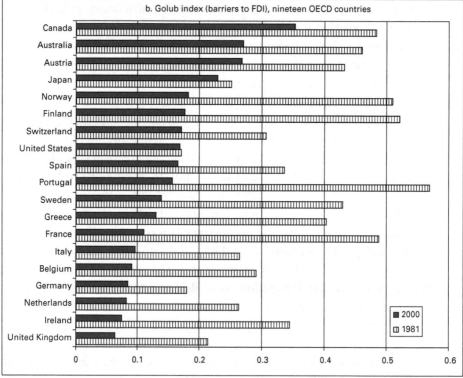

Figure 11.2   Effective average tax rate and Golub index, 1981–2000
Source: Based on Garretsen and Peeters (2007).

For a summary of this standard view, see also figure 11.3 in the next subsection. Not only does the equilibrium tax rate set by the government fall when capital mobility increases, the resulting equilibrium tax rate is also lower than the socially optimal tax rate. The gap between these two tax rates widens as the degree of international capital mobility increases. This last result vindicates those who argue that increased factor (here, capital) mobility leads to a race to the bottom.

The race to the bottom is certainly not an inevitable outcome, however. For instance, if one allows for tax policy coordination, it is no longer clear why increased capital mobility needs to accompany lower tax rates. In addition, when using tax revenues to provide for public goods that benefit the mobile production factor, Baldwin and Forslid (2002) show that increased factor mobility will not lead to a race to the bottom. Also, when the tax rates on (mobile) capital and (immobile) labor are allowed to differ, the race to the bottom result is no longer inevitable, since governments, when confronted with an increase in capital mobility, may simply decide to shift the tax burden to labor. Another reason why increased capital mobility does not need to have a negative effect on the capital tax rate is to be found in the ownership of firms. If the firms located in a particular country are allowed to be owned by domestic as well as foreign owners, it is no longer obvious that increased capital mobility leads to lower tax rates. In fact, increased foreign ownership per se provides countries with the incentive to *increase* tax rates, as it introduces the possibility of tax exportation (see Huizinga and Nicodème, 2003).

The introduction of other asymmetries leads to similar qualifications. Notably, and most importantly for our present purposes, when the two countries differ in size (for instance in terms of their GDP or population) it can be shown that the *larger* country will have a *higher* equilibrium tax rate. In the standard tax competition literature (see Bucovetsky, 1991), this size effect results from the fact that a large country suffers somewhat less when it has a higher tax rate in terms of capital outflows than a small country. For any given capital flow between a large country and a small one, the introduction of a tax rate differential has a larger impact on the smaller country. More fundamentally, asymmetries between countries need not necessarily be the result of exogenous differences in country size, as is the case in the standard tax competition literature, but may very well be the endogenous outcome of the location choices of the mobile factors of production. This is, of course, the main contribution from the geographical economics literature. How geographical economics differs from the standard view is the topic of the next section.

11.3.2 Corporate income taxation and the race to the bottom: agglomeration rents

The key difference between geographical economics and the standard, neoclassical view on the taxation of mobile factors of production is that, in geographical economics, factor rewards for the mobile factors of production are higher in the "center" compared to the "periphery." This means that, by being located in the core region, the mobile factors of production receive an *agglomeration rent*. Such rents are absent in the standard, neoclassical tax competition models. Referring back to the tomahawk diagram (figure 11.1), it can be shown that in the core model the agglomeration rent is strictly positive whenever the freeness of trade φ is such that $\varphi^S < \varphi < 1$.[7] For higher trade costs, $\varphi \leq \varphi^S$, agglomeration is not a long-run stable outcome and agglomeration rents are zero or even negative. Similarly, whenever $\varphi = 1$ ($T = 1$), so when trade costs are zero we know (see chapter 3) that agglomeration is not a stable equilibrium either, and consequently the agglomeration rent is zero. Hence, for intermediate levels of freeness of trade, when agglomeration is a stable long-run equilibrium, agglomeration rents will be positive.

The presence of agglomeration rents has important implications for the relationship between capital mobility and capital tax rates. With a positive agglomeration rent and perfect capital mobility, the core country – that is, the country in which (most) capital is located – can have higher tax rates than the peripheral country, as long as the agglomeration rent exceeds the tax differential. Attempts by the peripheral country to lure capital away from the core country by decreasing its tax rate will not lead to a relocation of capital as long as the tax gap falls short of the agglomeration rent. Starting from complete agglomeration, Baldwin and Krugman (2004) show in a two-country geographical economics model that, even with full capital mobility, a race to the bottom will not materialize.[8] The assumption of agglomeration is important, because it ensures that the agglomeration rent is positive.

The model used in Baldwin and Krugman (2004) is a two-region (North and South) model with two factors of production, labor L and human capital K. The model is basically the Forslid–Ottaviano model introduced

---

[7] See chapter 15 in Baldwin *et al.* (2003), especially figure 15.3 (page 375).
[8] This observation was made previously by Kind, Midelfart Knarvik, and Guttorm Schjelderup (2000), Rodney Ludema and Ian Wooton (2000) and Fredrik Andersson and Forslid (2003). See also Baldwin and Forslid (2002) and Brakman, Garretsen and van Marrewijk (2008).

and analyzed in chapter 4 section 4.8. Both factors of production are necessary to produce a variety of the manufacturing good, which requires one unit of K and a_x units of labor per unit produced. The cost function for a manufacturing firm i is then $r + Wa_x x_i$, where r is the wage for human capital and W is the wage for labor. Apart from this production structure, the model is essentially the same as the core model albeit with one more exception: labor is assumed to be immobile between countries; only capital can move between North and South. Capital moves to the region with the highest real wage *after tax.*

Let s_k be the share of capital in North. Given the set-up of the model, the resulting equilibria are well known and not surprising against the background of the core model: (i) $s_k = 1$, (ii) $s_k = 0$, or (iii) $0 < s_k < 1$. Depending on the level of freeness of trade, these equilibria are either stable or unstable. Assume now that the freeness of trade is neither very low nor very high, such that $s_k = 1$ is a stable long-run equilibrium Also assume that the economy finds itself in this equilibrium, with all human capital and all manufacturing production in North. We know from chapter 4 that, in this case, real wages for the mobile factor of production – here, human capital K – will be higher in North. This creates the *agglomeration rent* for human capital. It is immediately clear that capital will not move from North to South as long as this agglomeration rent is positive. Hence, if North taxes human capital it has to make sure that the tax rate is set at such a level that capital does not migrate. If this condition is fulfilled, the tax rate in North can be higher than the tax rate in South. There is thus no need for tax harmonization. In this case, South need not bother to try to attract capital, and its tax rate will depend only on "domestic" considerations. Crucial for the "no tax harmonization" result is that capital is fully agglomerated in North and that the level of economic integration (that is, the level of freeness of trade) is such that agglomeration is a stable equilibrium.

To underline the importance of the assumption of complete agglomeration, and as an attempt to synthesize the geographical economics and the standard view, figure 11.3 depicts three cases: (i) the geographical economics case with intermediate trade costs (dashed line); (ii) the geographical economics case with very high (or zero) trade costs (solid line); and (iii) the standard tax competition view (dash-dot line).

As figure 11.3 indicates, the corporate tax rate in North exceeds the corresponding tax rate in South: $t^N - t^S > 0$. The model of Baldwin and Krugman (2004) deals with case (i). Here, the spreading equilibrium (point C) is unstable and all footloose firms end up in North (point D), firms located

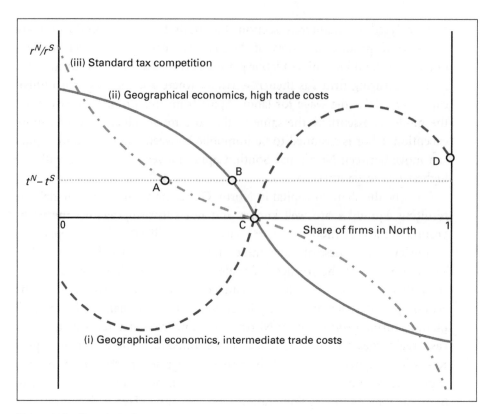

Figure 11.3 The wiggle diagram
Source: Baldwin *et al.* (2003: 372).

in North with equilibrium real human wages in North being higher than in South: $r^N/r^S > 1$. As long as the tax differential $(t^N - t^S)$ falls short of the real human wage differential, firms in North reap an agglomeration rent. This implies that the North can continue to have a higher tax rate than South. In the standard tax competition literature (case (iii): dash-dot line), and without a tax differential, the stable equilibrium is the spreading equilibrium C. Now, the introduction of the positive tax differential between North and South leads to some relocation of human capital from North to South. In figure 11.3, this relocation continues until point A is reached and the higher real wage in North precisely offsets the higher tax rate in North. If transport costs are not in the intermediate range (case (ii): solid line), the geographical economics model leads to the same conclusion as the standard tax competition model: a country with a higher tax rate (*in casu*, North) will lose (some of its) mobile capital (here, relocation occurs from the initial spreading equilibrium towards South until point B is reached).

Which of these three cases is the most relevant one is an empirical issue; see box 11.1 for an attempt to gauge the relevance of capital mobility as well as agglomeration effects on corporate income taxes.

The model by Baldwin and Krugman (2004) demonstrates how geographical economics can be used in a *direct manner* (because the policy question is explicitly modeled) to address a specific policy issue. There is also a problem, however, with the use of such a model for policy applications, related to the welfare implications of agglomeration. In the core model of chapters 3 and 4, as well as in the Baldwin and Krugman model, the mobile factors of production are always better off with full agglomeration because this maximizes their real income. Given the bias in most geographical economics models towards agglomeration, this has a strong policy implication that "tempts" regional policy makers to try to make sure that the mobile workers agglomerate in their region. This is precisely what drives the behavior of the policy maker in North in Baldwin and Krugman (2004), which leads us back to the criticism by Neary (2001), as discussed in subsection 11.2.3.

Box 11.1 Corporate income taxes, capital mobility and agglomeration

Ultimately, the question of how relevant agglomeration effects are when it comes to the impact of capital mobility on corporate income tax rates is an empirical issue. Signe Krogstrup (2004) and Garretsen and Peeters (2007) address this matter. The latter study estimates for nineteen countries in the period 1981–2000 a model in which the effective average corporate tax rate is the dependent variable, along with a set of control variables. Capital mobility (measured by FDI flows) and a market potential variable (capturing agglomeration effects) are the main explanatory variables. The agglomeration effect is captured by a simple market potential function, as introduced in chapter 5: $MP_i = \sum_j GDP_j / D_{ij}^\gamma$, where i and j are country indices, D_{ij} is the great circle distance (in kilometers) between countries i and j, and γ is the distance decay parameter (corrections for the internal distance of country i are included too). Table 11.1 shows the estimation results for three versions of this specification of the market potential function (the first three columns) by respectively setting the distance decay parameter γ to 1, 0.5, and 2.

Since causality between FDI and the tax rates may run both ways, the FDI variable is instrumented with the Golub index (figure 11.2) that measures the formal restrictions on (inward) FDI flows. The control variables are as follows.
• SIZE: the GDP of country i as a share of total GDP in the sample.
• NEIGHBOR: the average statutory corporate tax rate in all other countries.
• LEFT: leftist party Cabinet portfolios as percentage of all Cabinet portfolios.
• GOVINV: fixed government investment as a percentage of total disbursements.

Box 11.1 (cont.)

Table 11.1 Corporate income tax rates and agglomeration

	MP- $\gamma = 1$	MP- $\gamma = 0.5$	MP- $\gamma = 2$	MP trade costs
Constant	0.024 (0.326)	−1.153 (−3.875)***	−0.308 (−3.837)***	0.0279 (0.376)
FDIFLOWS	−0.360 (−4.909)***	−0.521 (−4.395)***	−0.320 (−5.063)***	−0.351 (−4.911)***
LEFT	0.045 (3.012)***	0.043 (2.512)**	0.024 (1.870)*	0.045 (3.060)***
NEIGHBOR	0.392 (2.922)***	1.755 (5.467)***	0.787 (6.862)***	0.383 (2.867)***
GOVINV	0.010 (2.266)**	0.012 (2.338)**	0.007 (1.895)*	0.010 (2.296)**
SIZE	1.854 (2.802)***	2.530 (3.096)***	2.845 (4.320)***	1.834 (2.814)***
MARKET POTENTIAL (MP)	0.002 (2.174)**	0.002 (3.903)***	4.585 (5.194)***	0.002 (2.051)**
Adjusted R^2	0.651	0.536	0.717	0.659
Number of observations	306	306	306	306

Notes: Dependent variable = effective average tax rate (taken from Devereux, Griffith, and Klemm, 2002). 2SLS estimation; t-values in brackets; fixed effects are included (but not shown). Instruments: Golub index and independent variables listed in table (except FDI variable); unbalanced panel. Adjusted sample period: 1982–99. ***, **, and * denote significance at the 1 percent, 5 percent, and 10 percent levels respectively.

Source: Garretsen and Peeters (2007).

From the core model of geographical economics, we know that the market potential term consists not only of income Y (here, GDP) and distance variable D_{ij} (normalized in the two-region model) but also of the price index I and the transport or trade costs T (or freeness of trade $\varphi \equiv T^{1-\varepsilon}$), (see section 5.5). To capture transport or trade costs and to include this in an alternative specification of the market potential function in the estimations, trade costs are included via the so-called c.i.f./f.o.b. ratios (see also box 3.3 for measurements of these ratios). These ratios may be imperfect but they are still useful measures of trade costs, and figure 11.4 shows that, for the sample under consideration, the average c.i.f./f.o.b. ratio has fallen (as well as the standard deviation), which indicates a decrease of trade costs (see also Hummels, 2007, for a similar finding).

The market potential specification adjusted for trade costs is also used in the estimations (column 4 of table 11.1). Focusing on capital mobility (FDIFLOWS) and agglomeration (MARKETPOTENTIAL), the main conclusions are as follows. First, an increase in capital mobility (here, an increase in FDI flows) exerts a significant downward pressure on corporate income tax rates. This finding supports the tax competition view. Second, agglomeration matters too. An increase in market potential exerts a positive impact on corporate tax rates. Therefore, even though an increase in capital mobility means lower tax rates across the board, core countries (that is, countries with a large MP) will on average have a higher tax rate which is in line with the "agglomeration rent" view of geographical economics outlined in the main text (the estimation results for the SIZE variable also suggest this to be the case). Since causality between FDI and corporate tax rates runs both

Box 11.1 (cont.)

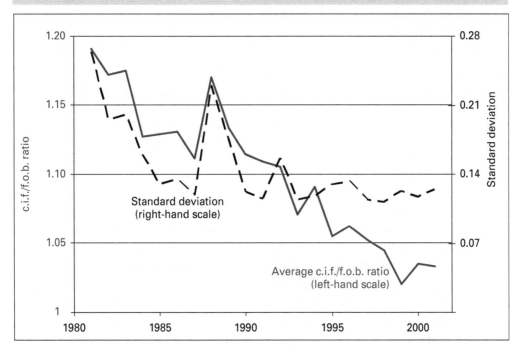

Figure 11.4 C.i.f./f.o.b. ratios: averages and standard deviations for nineteen OECD countries, 1981–2001
Source: Garretsen and Peeters (2007).

ways and it is well established that FDI is negatively influenced by an increase in corporate income tax rates, a follow-up to the research summarized in table 11.1 is to find out whether and how agglomeration and location effects matter for the determination of FDI when corporate income tax rates are also taken into account. In chapter 8 we have discussed an example of such a follow-up.

11.3.3 Government spending

Although the contribution by Baldwin and Krugman (2004) challenges the standard views about the race to the bottom, their treatment of the government sector is rather one-sided. It emphasizes taxes, not government spending, let alone the possible productive effects of public expenditures on the economy, whereby, as is the case in practice, government expenditures are also an instrument of locational competition between governments in their attempt to attract or to keep hold of mobile production factors.

Table 11.2 Preferred locations in north-west Europe

Niedersachsen (Germany)	Close to Hanover
Nordrhein Westfalen (Germany)	Enough space; good accessibility
Saarland (Germany)	Near highways leading to Ruhrgebiet; subsides to start businesses; enough space; low land prices
Picardie (France)	Near Paris (airport); good accessibility; low land prices
Champagne (France)	Good infrastructure; has always had a strong position (path dependency)
Netherlands	Good accessibility; near airport (Schiphol); good infrastructure (connections to Germany)

Source: Ministry of Economic Affairs (1999: 36).

Furthermore, as we saw above, Baldwin and Krugman concentrate on the agglomeration equilibrium and then analyze the relationship between the agglomeration rent and the tax gap between core and periphery.

When the effects of agglomeration are thought to be important, tax and spending policies represent two opposing forces. All other things being the same, higher taxes stimulate spreading, even though the existence of an agglomeration rent may prevent the spreading from actually taking place. Similarly, an increase in public spending stimulates agglomeration if this spending enhances the attractiveness of the location for the mobile factors of production. All things are not the same however, in the sense that higher taxes typically also imply higher public spending, and vice versa. The extent to which a larger government sector (meaning higher public spending and taxes) really leads to better-quality infrastructure for a country is an issue that has troubled policy makers for a long time. To illustrate the potential relevance of broadening the scope of government policy beyond mere taxation in order to understand the location choices of footloose agents, table 11.2 gives the results of a benchmarking study by the Dutch Ministry of Economic Affairs into important location characteristics for large firms in north-west Europe.

Table 11.2 indicates that the attractiveness is to some extent thought to be the result of (past) regional public spending. The table lists just a few reasons why some regions are preferred locations, but it does suggest that location decisions can be affected by regional government spending and not just by the levels of taxation. This last point also comes across from an UNCTAD survey on location and foreign direct investment (UNCTAD, 1996). Large companies such as Samsung and Daimler-Chrysler stated that, apart from taxes and subsidies, the social and economic infrastructure (transport networks) are key determinants for their location decisions.

What is stressed in the remainder of this section is the role of national government spending for firms' location choices in a model of geographical economics. Another important example of government spending concerns international government transfers, as in the case of development aid, for which the taxation takes place in a different country from those in which the spending takes place. Box 11.2 briefly discusses the consequences of these between-country transfers, such as development aid, from a geographical economics perspective.

Box 11.2 Transfers and agglomeration

The theory of international transfers or development aid has a long and interesting history. Without doubt, the most famous discussion on this topic was the exchange in *The Economic Journal* between John Maynard Keynes and Ohlin in 1929. Much earlier, however, other well-known economists, such as David Hume, Smith, Ricardo, and John Stuart Mill, had already discussed the effects of international transfers. The early debates mostly revolved around war reparation payments, in which the analysis of terms-of-trade effects or exchange rate effects dominated (see Brakman and van Marrewijk, 1998, 2007). After the Keynes–Ohlin debate the focus of the modern literature on transfers soon moved to the welfare effects of transfers, which is also more relevant in the context of development aid. An interesting complication in this literature is the possibility of so-called transfer paradoxes – in which the donor gains and/or the recipient loses from the transfer.[9] These transfer paradoxes can easily arise in the contest of three or more countries, and in quite normal circumstances.

In a simple two-country context, the consequences are straightforward from a geographical economics perspective. Extending the Krugman (1991a) core model with the possibility of development aid (only two equations need to be changed: add aid to the income of the recipient, and subtract it from the income of the donor), Brakman, Garretsen, and van Marrewijk (2007) show that the effects of a small transfer on the spreading equilibrium are temporary if the spreading equilibrium is locally stable (i.e. stopping the flow of foreign aid returns the economy to its original position). These effects are permanent if the spreading equilibrium is locally unstable (i.e. stopping the flow of foreign aid does not return the economy to its original position). Thus, the consequences of transfers such as foreign aid are fundamentally different depending on the level of integration between donor and recipient. If economic integration is high – that is, if the level of transportation costs is low – aid can have dramatic, lasting effects on the distribution of economic activity. On the other hand, if the level of economic integration is low – that is, transport costs are high – the effects of foreign aid are temporary and the distribution of economic activity is affected only as long as the foreign aid flow continues. Similarly, starting from complete agglomeration, aid either has no lasting effect whatsoever, or a catastrophic effect beyond the sustain point.

---

[9] Transfer paradoxes date back to Wassily Leontief (1936), who raised the possibility of transfer paradoxes by means of an example.

Box 11.2 (cont.)

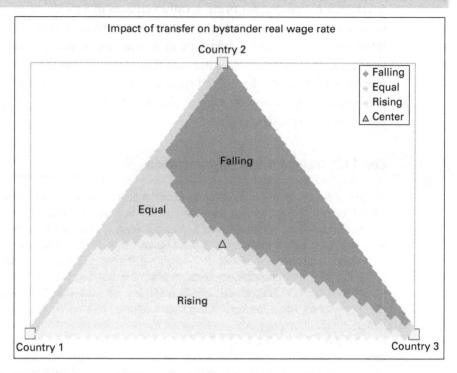

Figure 11.5 Change in real wage rate of bystander (intermediate transport costs)

The presence of a *third* country or bystander does not change these observations if the countries are of a similar size. In an asymmetric setting, however, we can show that the effects for a bystander can be influential in a geographical economics model, although transfer paradoxes do not occur. This is illustrated in figure 11.5, which shows the effects of a *discrete* transfer from country 1 to country 2 on the real wage rate of the bystander – country 3 – as a function of the distribution of the mobile labor force. Figure 11.5 is a two-dimensional representation of the three-country model in a unit simplex. If one gets closer to one of the corners, this means that the country in question produces a larger share of total manufacturing output. We can distinguish three different areas in figure 11.5: an area in which the real wage increases; an area in which it remains the same; and an area in which it decreases. Figure 11.5 illustrates, therefore, that the effects of the transfer depend on the initial distribution of the footloose workers.

To analyze the role of national government spending, we can use the same model that underlies the Baldwin and Krugman (2004) analysis, the Forslid–Ottaviano model of chapter 4 (section 4.8), to include a non-trivial role for government spending and then establish what the implications are.

Here we focus on the differences between the model with government spending as compared to the model without government spending.[10] Firms in the manufacturing sector use labor and human capital to produce a variety of manufactures under increasing returns to scale. The fixed-cost component represents the knowledge-intensive part of the manufacturing production process, such as R&D, marketing, and management. Both the fixed- and variable-cost components of production depend upon the quality of the infrastructure, education level, judicial system, police services, etc. All of these are related to the level of government spending Z_j. The reduction in costs is measured by the efficiency function $f_j(Z_j)$ with $f_j(0) = 1, f_j' \leq 0$. This distinguishes the model from Andersson and Forslid (2003) and Baldwin and Krugman (2004). Let r_j again be the return to human capital in region j, then the costs of producing $\times$ units of a manufacturing variety in region j are equal to

$$f_j(Z_j)\left[r_j + [(\sigma - 1)/\sigma]x\right] \tag{11.1}$$

The production of public goods requires human capital only under constant returns to scale. This is the second extension: it is assumed that the production of public goods takes up net resources. It captures the idea that government production competes with private production and relates to the discussion about the optimal size of the government sector. Market clearing for human capital in region j allows the determination of the number of varieties produced in region j:

$$n_j = (K_j - Z_j)/f_j(Z_j) \tag{11.2}$$

Equation (11.2) reflects the fact that the private and public sector compete with each other on the labor market. Equilibrium in the public sector requires that public spending be fully paid by taxes:

$$r_j Z_j = t_j Y_j \tag{11.3}$$

where t_j is the uniform income tax rate that applies to both labor and human capital. Given the sectoral distribution of human capital and the return to human capital, choosing a level of public goods determines the tax rate and vice versa. In addition, it is assumed that human capital employed in the public sector earns the same return as in the private sector. This

---

[10] For the complete model, see section 4.8 and Brakman, Garretsen, and van Marrewijk (2008).

reflects the notion that the public sector has to pay competing wages in order to attract human capital.

To round up the discussion of the model extensions as compared to the solvable Forslid–Ottaviano model of chapter 4, note that the location decision of human capital involves not only the factor rewards r_1 and r_2 and the respective price levels but also the tax rates and, in addition to Baldwin and Krugman (2004), *the provision of public services*. The incentive of human capital to relocate is therefore determined by the ratio ρ of indirect utilities (or *welfare*):

$$\rho = \left(\frac{(1-t_1)r_1}{(1-t_2)r_2}\right)\left(\frac{P_2}{P_1}\right)^{\delta} \tag{11.4}$$

Apart from the case of complete agglomeration, human capital has no incentive to relocate if welfare is the same in the two regions ($\rho=1$), while human capital moves from region 2 to region 1 if welfare is higher in region 1 ($\rho>1$) and from region 1 to region 2 if welfare is lower in region 1 ($\rho<1$).

Against this background, the key question is whether and how the introduction of government spending influences the central relationship in geographical economics: the relationship between the freeness of trade and the degree of agglomeration. We illustrate this for the case of the spreading equilibrium: what happens to the stability of the spreading equilbrium when we allow for public goods? In particular, we want to know if agglomeration becomes more likely or not. To simplify matters, let's assume that

(i) the two regions have a constant and given level of public goods $Z_1 = Z_2 = Zi$ and

(ii) the influence of government spending on the cost of production in the two regions are identical: $f_1 = f_2 = f$.

With these assumptions, it can be shown that over a wide range of parameter values the introduction of public goods into the model usually leads to a fall in the freeness of trade break point φ^B, tending to reduce the stability of the spreading equilibrium, as illustrated in figure 11.6. That is, with government spending fulfilling the role outlined above, agglomeration becomes more likely. The key parameters here are the substitution elasticity ε and the share of income spent on manufactures δ_i as the reader may recall from chapter 4, these are the two parameters that make up the no-black-hole condition.

For Europe, for example, this suggests that incorporating the impact of the provision of public goods on the stability of the economic process, the process of continued economic integration (EU enlargement), which increases

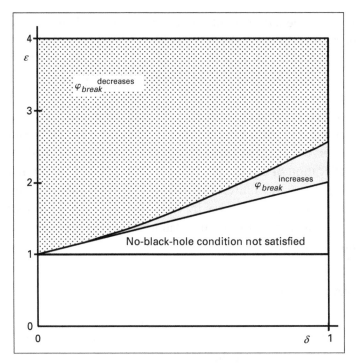

Figure 11.6   Marginal impact of introducing public goods on break point
Source: Brakman, Garretsen, and van Marrewijk (2008).

the freeness of trade parameter φ, is more likely to lead to instability in the spreading equilibrium, or, equivalently, more likely to result in core–periphery outcomes. The reason is that the additional provision of public goods represents a negative externality, as it reduces the number of available varieties; this in turn implies that, for lower values of the freeness of trade index, the incentive to move to a (marginal) larger region (more varieties) is reached sooner than without public goods.

11.4 Building a bridge: a simple policy experiment in non-neutral space

Time and again throughout our book, we have analyzed what happens to the spatial distribution of economic activity when transport costs change. We know that the conclusions as to what happens depend critically on a number of factors, such as (i) the initial level of transport costs, (ii) the underlying model of geographical economics (the tomahawk diagram or bell-shaped curve discussion), (iii) the specification of the transport cost function and the modeling of the infrastructure, and (iv) the definition of transport costs, in particular whether or not these costs include tariffs and other trade restrictions as well. Transport costs change not only when the transport technology changes but also when trade policy induces a change in trade restrictions.

When it comes to a discussion of the policy implications of geographical economics, therefore, it is also important to deal with the question of how policy interventions that somehow alter transport costs might change the spatial allocation of economic activity. In this section, we conduct our own simple experiment to address this issue. For a more elaborate treatment, the reader is referred to the survey by Puga (2002) or, again, to Baldwin *et al.* (2003), who in a more formal and elaborate manner try to answer the same fundamental questions.

11.4.1 The pancake economy

We adapt the racetrack economy that was introduced in chapter 4 to demonstrate the effects of a simple policy-inspired and highly stylized experiment. The model to be used in this section is the core model with congestion, as was discussed at length in chapter 7. The example that constitutes the topic of this section not only serves to illustrate some of the policy implications, it also provides an example of non-neutral space. In addition, the appendix to this chapter again gives the reader the opportunity to study some of the basics of the core model, the backbone of our book.

Suppose that we take the circle of the racetrack economy as introduced in section 4.9, say with twelve cities, and flatten this circle to the "pancake" shape illustrated in figure 11.7.[11] Assume, moreover, that the manufacturing workforce and farm workers are uniformly distributed between the twelve cities, each city thus hosting and producing one-twelfth of the economy's total. As we know from chapters 3 and 4, such a symmetric structure implies that this initial distribution represents a long-run equilibrium, which Fujita, Krugman, and Venables (1999) call the "flat earth" equilibrium. We now analyze the consequences of disturbing this long-run flat earth equilibrium as a result of an active policy intervention involving two of the twelve cities. Throughout the remainder of this section we refer to it as an infrastructure project, namely building a bridge (though it could as easily have been a road

---

[11] Some people might argue that it now in fact looks more like a racetrack than it did beforehand. See tables A11.1 to A11.4 in the appendix for the distance matrices related to the cases depicted in figure 11.7.

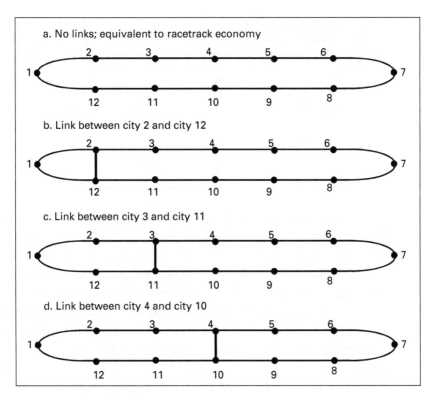

Figure 11.7 The pancake economy

or a tunnel), which directly connects the two cities and thus reduces the distance between them. The policy project can also be interpreted as a reduction in distance between the two cities as a result of closer cooperation, however, resulting say, from economic integration or monetary unification. Building a bridge between two cities in the pancake economy implies that space can no longer be considered to be neutral, as opposed to the racetrack economy of chapter 4.

We analyze three possible infrastructure projects, namely
- building a bridge between cities 2 and 12 (illustrated in figure 11.7b);
- building a bridge between cities 3 and 11 (illustrated in figure 11.7c); and
- building a bridge between cities 4 and 10 (illustrated in figure 11.7d).

In all cases, it is assumed that the link between the two cities reduces the distance between those two cities to one unit. In principle, there could be five "vertical" bridges (in addition to the three mentioned above, one could also envisage a bridge between cities 6 and 8 [though this is analytically equivalent to a bridge between cities 2 and 12] or between cities 5 and 9 [though this is analytically equivalent to a bridge between cities 3 and 11]).

Table 11.3 Average distance, pancake economy

City	No links	Link 2–12	Link 3–11	Link 4–10
1	3	3.00	3.00	3.00
2	3	2.58	2.67	2.75
3	3	2.67	2.08	2.33
4	3	2.75	2.33	1.92
5	3	2.83	2.58	2.33
6	3	2.92	2.83	2.75
Average	3	2.79	2.58	2.51

The cities not directly linked by the vertical bridge may or may not benefit from the bridge in terms of reducing the distance to other cities. In particular, cities 1 and 7 never benefit in this sense from any of the possible bridges. The other cities do benefit, either directly or indirectly. For example, the bridge between cities 3 and 11 illustrated in panel c reduces the distance not only between these two cities themselves (which falls from four units to one), but also between cities 3 and 11 and some other cities, as well as reducing the distance between some of the other cities. An example of the former is the distance between cities 3 and 10 (which falls from five units to two), and an example of the latter is the distance between cities 4 and 12 (which falls from four units to three). Table 11.3 gives an overview of the impact, in terms of the average distance to other cities (including the city itself), for all cities when there are no bridges, and for the three different bridges mentioned above. In our set-up it suffices to analyze only these six cities.[12] As is intuitively obvious, the bridge between cities 4 and 10 leads to a larger reduction in average distance than the bridge between cities 3 and 11, or 2 and 12. Similarly, the greatest reduction in average distance arises of course, for the linked cities themselves. Tables A11.1 to A11.4 in the appendix give more detailed information.

11.4.2 Bridges and the equilibrium spatial distribution

To analyze the general impact of the infrastructure projects on the distribution of manufacturing activity in our pancake economy, we calculate the long-run equilibrium for each of the three bridges, starting from a uniform initial distribution. For our base scenario we chose the following parameter

[12] By construction, the impact on average distance for cities 2 and 12, 3 and 11, 4 and 10, 5 and 9, and 6 and 8 are identical, while there is no impact for cities 1 and 7. It therefore suffices to list just the first six cities.

Table 11.4 Distribution of manufacturing workers

City	Link 2–12	Link 3–11	Link 4–10
1	8.2	4.1	2.7
2	**16.4**	7.0	3.8
3	10.3	**20.7**	8.5
4	7.1	9.8	**22.8**
5	5.4	5.3	8.5
6	4.6	3.5	3.8
7	4.3	3.0	2.7

Notes: All figures are percentages. The impact on cities 8, 9, 10, 11, and 12 is identical to the impact on cities 6, 5, 4, 3, and 2 respectively.

values: the share of income spent on manufacturing, δ is equal to 0.6, the elasticity of substitution ε is five, the transport costs parameter T is 1.2, and the congestion parameter τ is equal to 0.1. It is important to note that, in the absence of a bridge, the flat earth equilibrium is a stable equilibrium for the base scenario parameter setting. We have therefore essentially stacked the deck *against* economic agglomeration.[13] Nonetheless, as is clear from table 11.4 and illustrated in figure 11.8 (with the share of manufacturing activity λ_i on the vertical axis), building bridges in the pancake economy has a large impact on the distribution of manufacturing production, and leads to considerable agglomeration of economic activity (see especially the bold entries in table 11.4).

The reduction of transport costs that results from the building of a bridge benefits the cities that undertake such a project by enabling them to attract a large share of manufacturing production. The rationale behind this phenomenon is straightforward. If manufacturing activity is evenly distributed, the workers in the two cities at each end of the bridge have the highest real wage as they have to pay lower transport costs. This attracts other manufacturing workers into the linked cities, which on the one hand reinforces the process and on the other hand leads to more congestion and makes demand in the more remote markets more attractive. These forces are balanced in the long-run equilibrium. In general, the impact of building the bridge, an obvious example of non-neutral space, is remarkably high. Even the link "on the edge" between cities 2 and 12 leads to a doubling of manufacturing activity in cities 2 and 12.

[13] In fact, we have stacked the deck rather strongly. Even the simulations with an initial distribution far away from the uniform distribution lead to the flat earth equilibrium in the absence of links.

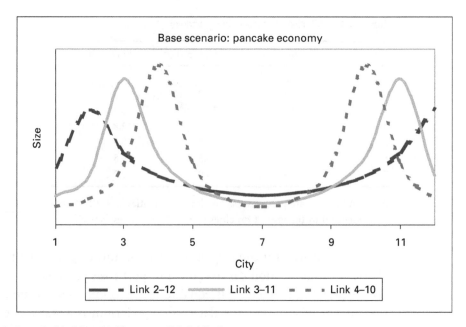

Figure 11.8 Impact of building a bridge on spatial distribution

In the appendix to this chapter, we analyze the impact of parameter changes on the equilibrium distribution of economic activity for the case of building a bridge between cities 4 and 10. We urge the reader to have a look at this appendix, if only *to test* the *intuition* developed for the geographical economics approach during the study of this book. See box 11.3 for a discussion of the most important parameter, transport costs *T*.

Box 11.3 Changing transport costs with a bridge between cities 4 and 10

We have, of course, already become used to the fact that the impact of transport costs on the resulting long-run equilibrium is non-monotonic. This holds in particular if we allow for negative feedbacks such as congestion (see, for example, figure 7.6). A similar observation holds in this case, when we analyze the impact of building a bridge between cities 4 and 10 in our pancake economy, as illustrated in figure 11.9 for cities 1 to 4.

Let us look first at the two extreme cases, namely (i) very large and (ii) very low transport costs. If the transport costs become very large (in figure 11.9 this is the case if *T* is close to two), the impact of building a bridge is minimal. City 4 becomes some-what larger, but the possibilities for welfare improvement are limited because of the high transport costs – that is, each city is almost autarkic. As a result, the linked cities are able to attract only a little extra manufacturing production. If, however, transport costs become very low – that is to say, when *T* gets very close to one – the impact of building a bridge is

Box 11.3 (cont.)

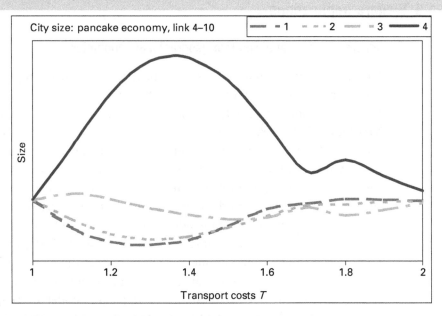

Figure 11.9   Impact of transport costs: bridge between cities 4 and 10

again minimal. In the absence of any transport costs, that is if $T=1$, there is no impact of building a bridge because trade in manufactures is costless. This reasoning extends to the situation of low transport costs – that is, it holds in the neighborhood of $T=1$. As illustrated in figure 11.9, however, this neighborhood is very small. Even for very modest transport costs, say $T=1.05$, the impact of building a bridge is already substantial. In this sense, the neighborhood of low transport costs appears to be smaller than the neighborhood of large transport costs.

For intermediate values of transport costs, the impact of building a bridge is substantial There are two local maxima, namely for low to intermediate values (around $T=1.35$) and for high to intermediate values (around $T=1.8$). The impact is largest for low to intermediate values. More specifically, cities 4 and 10 combined will attract more than 50 percent of total manufacturing activity if transport costs are between $T=1.25$ and $T=1.45$. The peak for high to intermediate transport costs is much smaller (cities 4 and 10 combined attract almost 28 percent of total manufacturing activity). The contrast between the two peaks is fascinating. For high to intermediate transport costs (around $T=1.8$), when trade is difficult, cities 4 and 10 grow only at the expense of their immediate neighbors (cities 3 and 5 and 9 and 11). There is virtually no impact on the cities that are far away (cities 1, 2, 6, 7, 8, and 12), which, as a result of high transport costs, mostly trade amongst themselves. In contrast, for low to intermediate transport costs, say in the range $T=1.1$ to $T=1.5$, when trade of manufacturing goods is much easier, cities 4 and 10 grow mostly at the expense of the cities that are far away (cities 1, 2, 6, 7, 8, and 12). In this case, the opportunities for trade are easier, which allows the manufacturing producers in the central cities 4 and 10 to serve the remote markets in the cities further away.

11.5 Welfare implications

11.5.1 Introducing welfare analysis into geographical economics

So far, very little attention has been paid to the welfare implications of policy changes or other changes that affect the equilibrium spatial distribution of economic activity. In their seminal book, Fujita, Krugman, and Venables (1999) (deliberately) shy away from welfare analysis, but nevertheless (348–9) consider it an important topic for further research for geographical economics. A main reason for this reluctance to deal with welfare implications is probably the belief that the core models are too simplistic and/or too biased towards agglomeration as the preferred equilibrium to warrant an attempt to address the welfare implications. In fact, in section 11.2 of the present chapter we have used Neary (2001) to make this point. Nevertheless, and without wishing to neglect these reservations, it is our judgment that a chapter on policy implications ought to include a section on the welfare implications of the core model of geographical economics. In doing so, we first lay out the simplest way conceivable that a welfare analysis can be introduced, and then apply these insights to our bridge experiment in the pancake economy of the previous section. In this way, we hope to give the reader some idea of how the normative implications of the core model might be addressed.

Taking the two-region core model of chapter 3 – that is, the Krugman (1991a) model – as our benchmark, it is obvious that different allocations of manufacturing activity will have different welfare implications for different sets of people. Given transport costs T, it is, for example, clear that the mobile workforce will generate a higher welfare level in the complete agglomeration equilibrium than in the spreading equilibrium, since in the latter these workers have to import part of their consumption of manufactures from the other region. It is also obvious that the immobile workforce in region 2, given complete agglomeration in region 1, is worse off compared to the spreading equilibrium, as these workers will have to import all their manufactures from the other region. It is impossible to argue *ex ante* which effect is more important, so somehow we have to *weigh* the importance of various groups, using their size as weight.

Recall that in the core model there are two types of agents within each region in the core model, namely the share λ_i of all manufacturing workers and the share ϕ_i of all farm workers. Since there are γL manufacturing workers in total and $(1-\gamma)L$ farm workers, we concluded in equation (3.18) that total income in region i is equal to $Y_i = \lambda_i W_i \gamma L + \phi_i (1-\gamma)L$, because manufacturing workers in region i earn wage W_i and farm workers earn wage 1. To determine the welfare level for both types of workers, we have to correct for the price level I_i in region i. In this chapter, we focus attention on total welfare. To determine this, let $y_i \equiv Y_i I_i^{-\delta}$ be the real income in region i, and note that total welfare is simply given by

$$welfare = \sum_{i=1}^{R} y_i \tag{11.5}$$

In addition, for different groups in the economy we can easily calculate welfare consequences by simply adding the real wages of that particular group. With this welfare measurement instrument we can now return to our pancake economy of the previous section.

11.5.2 Welfare implications of a bridge in the pancake economy

To round up our bridge experiment, we now get to the reasons for building a bridge in terms of the welfare implications using the welfare criterion that was introduced in the previous subsection. After all, building a bridge is costly, so the authorities must have a good reason to start and complete such a project. Although one can think of various reasons for building a bridge, we concentrate in this subsection on the welfare implications of building a bridge, with a city's welfare being given by its real income, and total welfare is the summation of the real income across the twelve cities.

The basic effect of building a bridge is, of course, the reduction of the distance between cities, either directly or indirectly, as shown in section 11.4. Here we are more interested in the long-run welfare implications of building a bridge – that is to say, in the welfare implications *once we allow for manufacturing workers to migrate* in response to the building of the bridge. As is clear from the above description, and the uneven distribution of the reduction in average distance over the cities, inhabitants in different cities enjoy different welfare effects from the completion of the bridge. The inhabitants of the linked cities initially enjoy the largest welfare gain. This sets in motion a process of migration that, as we have seen in the previous section, leads to substantial economic agglomeration in the linked cities. This second-round effect – the migration process – thus also influences the distribution of welfare gains. In general, the cities that grow in size enjoy a

Table 11.5 Overview of welfare effects: long-run equilibrium

	Link 2–12	Link 3–11	Link 4–10
Average change in real income (%)	0.9	1.9	2.2
Average change in real farm income (%)	−0.3	0.2	0.2
Average change in real manufacturing income (%)	1.6	2.8	3.5

positive welfare effect in the second stage as they can purchase a larger number of manufacturing varieties locally. As we will see below, the second-round effect can dominate the first-round effect.

There are, essentially, thirteen different economic agents in the long-run equilibrium, namely the farm workers in the twelve cities and the manufacturing workers. Since the manufacturing workers will migrate to other cities until their real wage is equalized, the long-run welfare impact of building a bridge is the same for all manufacturing workers. Table 11.5 summarizes the average long-run welfare effects of building a bridge – that is, for the economy as a whole – for the average farm worker, and for a manufacturing worker. For the economy as a whole the average welfare effect is always positive, although the economy will obviously benefit more from a more centrally placed bridge, linking cities 4 and 10, than from a more peripherally placed bridge, linking cities 2 and 12. This reasoning holds more strongly for the manufacturing workers: they benefit more than the economy on average, and the extent of their welfare increase is greater the more centrally the bridge is located.

The welfare picture is not so positive for the average farm worker. In particular, if the bridge is peripherally placed, linking cities 2 and 12, the average farm worker enjoys a reduction in real income of 0.3 percent, as a large share of manufacturing activity is moved to peripherally placed cities, requiring the average farm worker to pay substantial transport costs. Even if the bridge is more centrally placed, linking cities 3 and 11, or cities 4 and 10, the average farm worker enjoys only a small gain (0.2 percent) in real income. The calculation of averages can be deceptive, however, which is clearly the case here. As is illustrated in figure 11.10, the information in table 11.5 on the welfare of the average farm worker is a poor indicator of what happens to a particular farm worker.

The welfare increase for the farm workers in the linked cities is always positive, and much greater than the average increase for the manufacturing workers (up to an 8.1 percent improvement for the farm workers in cities

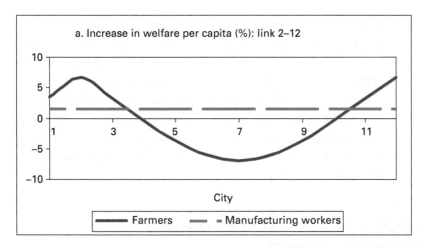

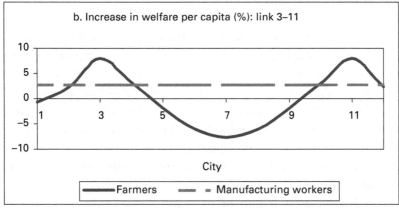

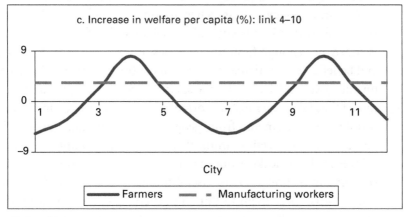

Figure 11.10 Real income and welfare changes

4 and 10 when there is a bridge between these cities). In contrast, the welfare impact for the farm workers in the cities far away from the linked cities is always negative, and substantially so (up to − 6.9 percent for the farm workers in city 7 if there is a bridge between cities 2 and 12).

What are the main lessons of this policy and simulation example? First, it shows that policy experiments, however simple, can be performed with straightforward applications of the core model. Second, it demonstrates that even a simple policy experiment with a simple model can have quite complex implications.

11.6 Conclusions about the policy relevance of geographical economics

In this chapter we have, *inter alia*, analyzed a policy experiment in non-neutral space, the building of a "bridge" in the pancake economy. In this sense, we have given in to the temptation mentioned by Neary (2001), because the "bridge" example shows in a simple and general manner how the introduction of non-neutral space, created by policy intervention, affects the equilibrium outcome and welfare. We have also discussed other more general (section 11.2) and more specific (section 11.3) policy implications of geographical economics, but the conclusions with respect to the bridge experiment apply to these other examples as well. Two questions come to mind.

First, does this kind of simulation experiment have any relevance for "real-world" policy issues? When it comes to policy applications, simulations with such a highly stylized model are only of limited relevance. There is clearly not enough flesh on the bones of the core model to tackle the costs and benefits of a particular plan to build a bridge. Obviously, when deciding on the costs and benefits of a specific issue, one first has to construct a model that takes the most important aspects of this issue into consideration, possibly using elements from geographical economics models. In a qualitative sense, we certainly think that simulation examples, such as building bridges in the pancake economy or the analysis of government taxation and spending in section 11.3, are useful thought experiments for policy makers. They at least force them to think in general equilibrium terms about policy proposals and their geographical (non-linear or lumpy) implications. A major lesson for policy makers is that the core and the periphery are mutually dependent on each other's existence, and cannot be dealt with separately, although this is often done.

Suppose, for example, and returning once more to our simple bridge example, that the European Commission has a large sum of money at its disposal with which it could either finance a bridge between Denmark and Sweden (e.g. the new bridge across the Öresund) or a "bridge" between the United Kingdom and France (e.g. the Channel tunnel between Calais and Dover). In a multi-country instead of a multi-city setting, our pancake economy can be thought of as representing the European Union "lying on its back" with Norway as country 1 and Spain as country 7 (recall figure 11.7 for the depiction of the pancake economy). A bridge across the Öresund could then be thought of as a bridge between countries 2 and 12, and the Channel tunnel as linking countries 4 and 10. Our simulations show that the European Commission, in deciding which of the two projects it wants to carry out, must take into account not only the net benefits of the bridge for the two adjacent countries but also the benefits for the other EU countries. This would mean that, other things being equal, the financing of the Channel tunnel would be a better idea than the bridge across the Öresund to connect Denmark and Sweden.

The second, more general, question that comes to mind at the end of this chapter is whether the current state of affairs in geographical economics permits substantial policy analysis at all. Is it possible to go beyond the simple simulations discussed above? In this respect, we have seen that progress *has* been made in recent years, and we refer again to the book by Baldwin *et al.* (2003), in which policy is an integral part of the models. This is, no doubt, an improvement upon the exogenous role of policy in our bridge example and the indirect use of geographical economics in most actual policy discussions, but it remains to be seen if models such as the "tax competition" model of section 11.3 are able to become workhorse models for policy makers. This brings us, finally, to the overall assessment of geographical economics: when all is said and done, what is the value added of geographical economics? It is to this topic that we now turn in the final chapter of the book.

Appendix

Effects of parameter changes with a bridge between cities 4 and 10

In this appendix we illustrate the impact of changes for important model parameters on the ability of linked cities to attract more manufacturing activity. For ease of exposition we concentrate on building a bridge between cities 4 and 10. We investigate, in turn, the impact of changes in the share of income spent on manufactures δ, the elasticity of substitution parameter ρ, the congestion cost parameter τ, and the speed of adjustment η. The first three parameters, together with the transport parameter that has already been discussed in box 11.3, determine the long-run equilibrium and these parameters cannot be "eliminated" by normalization. The last parameter, η, determines the responsiveness of manufacturing workers to real wage differences between cities.

Before turning to the answers below to see what happens when the parameters are changed, the reader might first want to come up with an answer him-/herself, as the previous discussions about the impact of parameter changes in chapters 4 to 10, plus of course box 11.3 on the impact of changing T, provide important information as to what expect when δ, ρ, τ, or η are changed.

- An increase in the share of income spent on manufactures δ implies that the mobile economic activity becomes more important and the immobile economic activity becomes less important. We therefore expect that an increase in δ will make building a bridge more attractive by allowing a larger agglomeration of economic activity in the linked cities. This is indeed what happens, as illustrated in figure A11.1a, in which we note that the size of city 4 increases as δ becomes larger.
- An increase in the elasticity of substitution parameter ρ implies that it becomes easier for the consumer to substitute between different varieties of manufactures. This essentially reduces the impact of transport costs on welfare (real wages), such that we expect that an increase in ρ reduces the impact of building a bridge. This is confirmed in figure A11.1b, in which the size of city 4 falls as ρ becomes larger – that is, as it becomes easier to substitute between different varieties.
- If the congestion costs measured by the parameter τ increase, economic agglomeration of manufacturing activity becomes less attractive as it leads to high congestion costs. The attractiveness of building a bridge therefore reduces as congestion costs increase, by reducing the extent of economic agglomeration. This is illustrated in figure A11.1c, in which the size of city 4 falls as τ becomes larger.
- The final parameter to look at is the speed of adjustment η. As has already been discussed in chapter 10, depending on the speed of adjustment of

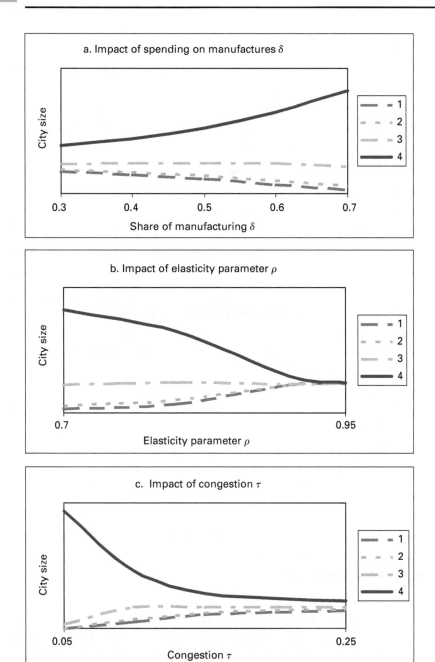

Figure A11.1 Impact of some parameters: bridge between cities 4 and 10

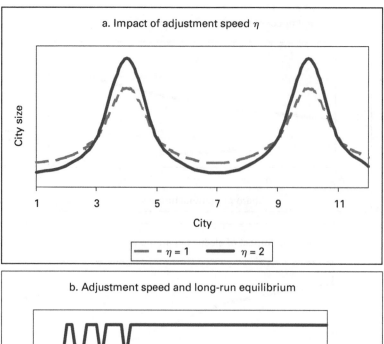

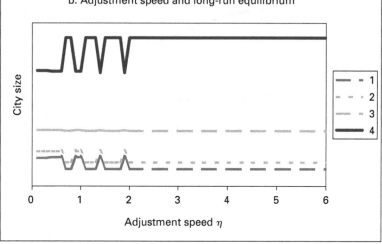

Figure A11.2 Impact of adjustment speed

manufacturing labor – that is, the speed of migration flows – the economy may end up in a different (stable) long-run equilibrium. In chapter 10 this was illustrated for very high speeds of adjustment; here we illustrate two relatively low speeds of adjustment ($\eta = 1$ and $\eta = 2$); see figure A11.2a. It appears that, cities 4 and 10 are able to attract more manufacturing activity in the base scenario (when $\eta = 2$) than if the speed of adjustment is $\eta = 1$. Figure A11.2b shows the long-run equilibrium to which the economy converges for a large range of adjustment speeds (η ranges from 0.1 to six in subsequent steps of 0.1). It shows clearly that the economy converges to one of only two possible long-run equilibria, namely the two illustrated in figure A11.2a.[14] For all adjustment speeds above two the economy converges to the equilibrium illustrated in the base scenario of figure A11.2a. For all adjustment speeds below 0.6 the economy converges to the other long-run equilibrium, with somewhat less economic agglomeration, as illustrated in figure A11.2a. In the range between 0.6 and two the long-run equilibrium to which the economy converges is very sensitive with respect to the speed of adjustment η, as illustrated by the comb-like part in figure A11.2b.

Distance matrices related to the cases depicted in figure 11.7

Table A11.1 Distances: pancake economy, no links

	1	2	3	4	5	6	7	8	9	10	11	12
1	0	1	2	3	4	5	6	5	4	3	2	1
2	1	0	1	2	3	4	5	6	5	4	3	2
3	2	1	0	1	2	3	4	5	6	5	4	3
4	3	2	1	0	1	2	3	4	5	6	5	4
5	4	3	2	1	0	1	2	3	4	5	6	5
6	5	4	3	2	1	0	1	2	3	4	5	6
7	6	5	4	3	2	1	0	1	2	3	4	5
8	5	6	5	4	3	2	1	0	1	2	3	4
9	4	5	6	5	4	3	2	1	0	1	2	3
10	3	4	5	6	5	4	3	2	1	0	1	2
11	2	3	4	5	6	5	4	3	2	1	0	1
12	1	2	3	4	5	6	5	4	3	2	1	0

---

[14] This does *not* imply that these are the only two long-run equilibria.

A11.2 Distances: pancake economy, link between cities 2 and 12

	1	2	3	4	5	6	7	8	9	10	11	12
1	0	1	2	3	4	5	6	5	4	3	2	1
2	1	0	1	2	3	4	5	5	4	3	2	1
3	2	1	0	1	2	3	4	5	5	4	3	2
4	3	2	1	0	1	2	3	4	5	5	4	3
5	4	3	2	1	0	1	2	3	4	5	5	4
6	5	4	3	2	1	0	1	2	3	4	5	5
7	6	5	4	3	2	1	0	1	2	3	4	5
8	5	5	5	4	3	2	1	0	1	2	3	4
9	4	4	5	5	4	3	2	1	0	1	2	3
10	3	3	4	5	5	4	3	2	1	0	1	2
11	2	2	3	4	5	5	4	3	2	1	0	1
12	1	1	2	3	4	5	5	4	3	2	1	0

Note: Shaded cells indicate the deviation of distances in the racetrack economy

Table A11.3 Distances: pancake economy, link between cities 3 and 11

	1	2	3	4	5	6	7	8	9	10	11	12
1	0	1	2	3	4	5	6	5	4	3	2	1
2	1	0	1	2	3	4	5	5	4	3	2	2
3	2	1	0	1	2	3	4	4	3	2	1	2
4	3	2	1	0	1	2	3	4	4	3	2	3
5	4	3	2	1	0	1	2	3	4	4	3	4
6	5	4	3	2	1	0	1	2	3	4	4	5
7	6	5	4	3	2	1	0	1	2	3	4	5
8	5	5	4	4	3	2	1	0	1	2	3	4
9	4	4	3	4	4	3	2	1	0	1	2	3
10	3	3	2	3	4	4	3	2	1	0	1	2
11	2	2	1	2	3	4	4	3	2	1	0	1
12	1	2	2	3	4	5	5	4	3	2	1	0

Note: Shaded cells indicate the deviation of distances in the racetrack economy

The policy implications of geographical economics

Table A11.4 Distances: pancake economy, link between cities 4 and 10

	1	2	3	4	5	6	7	8	9	10	11	12
1	0	1	2	3	4	5	6	5	4	3	2	1
2	1	0	1	2	3	4	5	5	4	3	3	2
3	2	1	0	1	2	3	4	4	3	2	3	3
4	3	2	1	0	1	2	3	3	2	1	2	3
5	4	3	2	1	0	1	2	3	3	2	3	4
6	5	4	3	2	1	0	1	2	3	3	4	5
7	6	5	4	3	2	1	0	1	2	3	4	5
8	5	5	4	3	3	2	1	0	1	2	3	4
9	4	4	3	2	3	3	2	1	0	1	2	3
10	3	3	2	1	2	3	3	2	1	0	1	2
11	2	3	3	2	3	4	4	3	2	1	0	1
12	1	2	3	3	4	5	5	4	3	2	1	0

Note: Shaded cells indicate the deviation of distances in the racetrack economy

Exercises

11.1 In section 11.2 six basic policy implications of geographical economics were briefly discussed. Consider the following two statements about these implications.
  (i) The threshold effect refers to the possibility of a sudden or catastrophic change in the equilibrium allocation of economic activity across space.
  (ii) The lock-in effect does not occur in the case of a bell-shaped curve (as shown by figure 4.10).
     Are these statements true or false, and why?

11.2 From chapter 11 we know that some economists are rather reluctant to use geographical economics for policy analysis, but (and anticipating chapter 12) why do you think geographers object to the use of geographical economics for policy purposes?

11.3 Use the analysis of agglomeration rents in section 11.3 and the so-called wiggle diagram (figure 11.3) to discuss the prospects for a future race to the bottom in the European Union in terms of corporate income taxation when economic integration continues to deepen.

11.4 Why (and as opposed to the racetrack economy of chapter 4) is space non-neutral in the pancake economy?

11.5 To determine welfare we let $y_i \equiv Y_i I_i^{-\delta}$ be the real income in region i and then define total welfare for this region as

$$welfare = \sum_{i=1}^{R} y_i$$

(i) Why is this definition of welfare too simple from the perspective of section 11.3?

(ii) "According to this definition of welfare, the welfare for mobile workers must always be the same in geographical economics." Discuss the validity of this statement.

12 Criticism and the value added of geographical economics

12.1 Introduction

The core model of geographical economics has been introduced, explained, and extended in chapters 3 and 4 of this book. In our analysis of various applications in chapters 5 to 11, we have typically investigated relatively small modifications of the core model, notably only those affecting the cost function and thus the production structure of the core model. This has been done on purpose: not just for didactic reasons (each time returning to the familiar ground of the core model), but also to demonstrate that (seemingly) small changes in the core model can drastically increase its applicability and have interesting and sometimes far-reaching consequences. In our discussions of these adaptations of the core model one important question has been unduly neglected, however: what on balance are the strong and weak points of geographical economics? What is the verdict on geographical economics after its introduction in 1991?

The closing chapter of this book therefore deals with the *criticism* and *value added* of geographical economics. This is, inevitably, a subjective undertaking, but it gives us the opportunity to express our own views on the advantages and disadvantages of geographical economics. We are now in a position to evaluate the contribution of geographical economics to understanding the location of economic activity. We start with some of the main criticisms in section 12.2, and then react to these criticisms in the next section. In doing so, we clarify our own position. Section 12.4 concludes this chapter, and our book, and also makes some predictions regarding the future of geographical economics.

12.2 Criticism of geographical economics

In chapter 2, the role of geography in various location theories that pre-date but nevertheless foreshadow geographical economics has been extensively discussed. It is precisely from these fields that the strongest criticism against the geographical economics approach has been raised. To a large extent, these criticisms boil down to the observation that geographical economics (or new economic geography) is either (i) not new, (ii) not about geography, (iii) constitutes bad economics, or (iv) is not relevant for practical purposes. In some cases, all four charges have been raised against geographical economics!

As noted throughout this book, geographical economics can be seen as an attempt to answer Ohlin's call for a unification of *international* and *regional economics* (Ohlin, 1933). It is clear that Krugman, the main founding father of geographical economics, sees it this way (Krugman, 1995a, 1995b, 1999). He has an international economics background, however, while most doubts about the usefulness of geographical economics have been raised from other quarters: regional and urban economics, and, most strongly, from economic geography. In this section we therefore present the critical reflections on geographical economics of some leading scholars from regional and urban economics, and international economics, followed by a somewhat lengthier assessment from economic geographers.[1]

12.2.1 Comments from regional and urban economics

As has been made clear in chapter 2, there is a substantial group of researchers within the sub-field of regional economics (or regional science) who, at least since Isard (1956, 1960), have continued to build on the work of the pioneers of modern location theory such as Christaller, Weber, Lösch, and, from a growth perspective, Perroux by formalizing and extending the initial insights on the location of economic activity. Regional economics relies heavily upon the neoclassical framework that the economic geographers reject (see subsection 12.2.3 for more on this). In terms of the basic analytical apparatus, regional economics has therefore much in common with geographical economics. We conclude in chapter 2, based on Ottaviano and Thisse (2004), that there is also much overlap in content between regional and geographical economics.

Notwithstanding these similarities, some regional economists have been rather critical of geographical economics. In his review of the seminal book

---

[1] There are two reasons for dwelling a bit longer on economic geography and its relationship with geographical economics. The first is that we have not said much about economic geography in chapter 2 in our discussion of location theories. The second reason is that economic geographers in particular have been engaged in the debate about geographical economics.

by Fujita, Krugman, and Venables (1999), Nijkamp (2000), a leading regional economist, lists the following five complaints. In his view, geographical economics and the aforementioned book in particular

(i) neglect the work done by forerunners;

(ii) have too narrow a view of geography through their reliance on iceberg transport costs, neglecting psychological transport costs or mental distance;

(iii) pay no attention to spatial competition among firms, since there is no well-developed theory of the firm within geographical economics;

(iv) give scant attention to the role of institutions; and

(v) rely too much on numerical simulations, resulting in a lack of quantitative and empirical research.

Whether these criticisms are valid is addressed in the next section, but it is already noteworthy that the first, second, and fourth issues are also frequently mentioned by economic geographers in their assessment of "Krugman-style" economic geography. In a similar vein, urban economists who have criticized geographical economics have also pointed to the lack of empirical support, the overly simple depiction of (urban) geography, and the excessively strong reliance on simulations. In his criticism of the core model of geographical economics, Henderson (2000), for instance, concludes that for these reasons the core model, the Krugman (1991a) model, is not suited for research within urban economics. From chapter 7, however, we know that there are certainly similarities between the two core models of geographical and urban economics, the Krugman (1991a) and Henderson (1974) models respectively.

In addition, and this also holds for modern, "post-1991," regional economics, it is our view that the differences between regional and urban economics on the one hand and geographical economics on the other hand are narrowing. In his review of the fourth volume of *The Handbook of Regional and Urban Economics*, Arnott (2006) notes that, from the point of view of urban economics, geographical economics can be criticized for its reliance on simulations and specific functional forms and its lack of welfare analysis. He also notes, however, that urban and geographical economics are both relevant, and that it very much depends on the geographical scale or resolution as to which type of model or explanation is to be preferred. This is in line with our comparison of Henderson (1974) and Krugman (1991a) in chapter 7, where we state that geographical economics or models of agglomeration in general are more relevant at a larger spatial scale.

12.2.2 Comments from international economics

What about the position of international economics, the other half involved in the merger between regional and international economics as prophesized by Ohlin (1933)? One of the main themes in chapter 2 is that the core model of geographical economics is to a large extent an extension of the new trade model developed by Krugman (1979, 1980), as illustrated by Krugman himself (see box 12.1).

Box 12.1 The $100 bill on the sidewalk between 1980 and 1991

In chapter 2 of our book we come to the conclusion that the core model of geographical economics by Krugman (1991a) is very similar to the new trade model of Krugman (1980), except for one crucial difference: the *endogenization of regional market size* that is the direct result of interregional factor mobility in Krugman (1991a). In the core model, the mobility of manufacturing workers implies that each region's market size, as well as the regional distribution of manufacturing firms and labor, is no longer given. This has been emphasized before. On the continuity of the Krugman (1980) and Krugman (1991) approaches, it is illuminating to quote Krugman himself (1999: 6):

It is obvious – in retrospect – that something special happens when factor mobility interacts with increasing returns... This observation is, as I suggested, obvious in retrospect; but it certainly took me a while to see it. Why exactly I spent a decade between showing how the interaction of transport costs and increasing returns at the level of the plant could lead to the "home market effect" (Krugman, 1980) and realizing that the techniques developed there led naturally to simple models of regional divergence (Krugman, 1991) remains a mystery to me. The only good news was that nobody else picked up that $100 bill lying on the sidewalk in the interim.

With the benefit of hindsight, it seems that the decision to add factor mobility to the Krugman (1980) model has really paid off in academic terms. At the time of writing this chapter, Krugman's most cited paper is "Increasing returns and economic geography" (1991a), which is cited far more often than "Scale economies, product differentiation, and the pattern of trade" (1980): according to Google's Scholar search engine, Krugman (1991a) was cited 2,829 times relative to 1,102 citations for Krugman (1980).[2]

When asked by us, Krugman wrote the following about the origins of the core geographical economics model of Krugman (1991a):

Michael Porter had given me a manuscript copy of his book on *The Competitive Advantage of Nations*, probably late 1989. I was much taken by the stuff on clusters, and started trying to make a model – I was on a lecture tour, I recall, and worked on it evenings, I started out with complicated models with intermediate goods and all that, but after a few days I realized that these weren't necessary ingredients, that my home market stuff basically provides the necessary. I got stumped for a while by the analytics, and tried numerical examples on a spreadsheet to figure them out. It all came together in a hotel in Honolulu...

---

[2] We used http://scholar.google.nl on January 7, 2008. On that day Krugman's 1991 book *Geography and Trade* headed the list of his citations, with 3,572; *The Spatial Economy*, by Fujita, Krugman, and Venables (1999), had "only" 1,720 citations.

Trade economists have also made this point, and in fact we have used Head and Mayer (2004a) in chapter 2 to substantiate this claim. It is therefore no coincidence that, in their advanced textbook on trade theory, Jagdish Bhagwati, Arvind Panagariya, and T. N. Srinivasan (1998: 187–92) discuss both the Krugman (1980) new trade model and the Krugman (1991a) model in the same section on economic geography. In his influential graduate textbook on international trade, Feenstra (2004) discusses Fujita, Krugman, and Venables (1999) in the context of monopolistic competition as it is used by international economists.[3] In addition, Neary (2001), in his review of Fujita, Krugman, and Venables (1999), leaves no doubt as to the fact that geographical economics is first and foremost, firmly based in (new) trade theory. In Neary's (2001) view, "In stressing the relevance to regional issues of models derived from trade theory, Krugman has not so much created a new sub-field as extended the applicability of an old one."

In addition to questioning the antecedents of geographical economics, Neary (2001) criticizes the contents of geographical economics as well. Since in his view geographical economics is analytically rather similar to the existing and well-established new trade models from international economics, it is perhaps not surprising that his overall verdict is far more positive compared to that of regional or urban economists. Nonetheless, he singles out the following weak points:

(i) a lack of analysis of individual firms; there is no strategic interaction between firms;

(ii) the depiction of geography is too simple; here the use of iceberg transport costs is criticized, as well as the depiction of space as (mostly) being one-dimensional;

(iii) the reliance on specific functional forms and numerical simulations; the effect is that welfare and policy analysis are nearly absent; and

(iv) a lack (until recently) of a strong body of empirical evidence to back up the theoretical work.

In his review of another seminal book on geographical economics (Baldwin et al., 2003), and despite an overall favorable assessment, Neary (2006: 506–7) arrives at a similar conclusion regarding the "weak points" of geographical economics:

In conclusion, an overall assessment of this book is hard to separate from one's views about the new economic geography as a whole. While I find much to admire

---

[3] Furthermore, Feenstra (2004) discusses Redding and Venables (2004) not as a test of geographical economics but as an application of the gravity model.

in this literature, I have some residual worries. One, discussed in Neary (2001), is the universal assumption of monopolistic competition, including in particular an infinitely elastic supply of ex ante identical firms. For many policy issues, such as competition policy, which is mentioned briefly in the concluding chapter, oligopolistic models with some limitations on entry seem more appropriate. Another worry is that, while path dependence seems self-evidently a feature of the world, it does not follow that it must be a property of our models. From Kaldor's 1940 model of the trade cycle onwards, economists have been fascinated by the potential for "captivatingly complex behavior" (p. 27) of models with multiple equilibria. But simpler explanations of empirical phenomena are often available, and by Occam's Razor they will usually be preferred. Moreover, taking models of multiple equilibria to data is a serious challenge. Recent works by Davis and Weinstein (2002) and Redding and Sturm (2005), among others, make an interesting start in this direction, but to date they do not provide persuasive evidence that multiple equilibria arising from agglomeration-related pecuniary externalities are pervasive.

It is clear that the points raised by Neary (2001, 2006) have a lot in common with the comments made by regional and urban economists. Again, the question arises as to whether these critical remarks are (still) valid.

12.2.3 Comments from economic geography

In chapter 2 section 2.2 we briefly survey the role of geography in urban and regional economics, and in passing also mention economic geography, whose scholars have been particularly critical of the main features of geographical economics. The critique from economic geography falls into one of two categories. Many economic geographers go for an outright rejection of geographical economics (or even economics in general) as a starting point for carrying out research. There is also, however, a group of economic geographers who, despite their criticism of Krugman *cum suis*, take geographical economics (and economics) seriously and are interested in a discussion with geographical economists.

Ron Martin is a prime example of this second category of economic geographers. Martin (1999) argues that geographical economics must more than anything else be seen as a belated attempt to cast the old insights of Christaller and Lösch into a general equilibrium framework, in which the interdependent decisions of profit-maximizing firms and utility-maximizing consumers are explicitly modeled. Martin (1999) has two main (related) objections against geographical economics (see also Dymski, 1998, Martin and Sunley, 1996, 2006, Martin, 2008, Clark, 1998, Marchioni, 2004, and

Scott, 2004, 2006, for examples of similar observations).[4] First, economic geography has moved on since the days of Christaller and Lösch, mainly because of the limitations associated with the work of these and other "old" economic geographers. It is beyond the scope of this book to discuss modern economic geography (see the references in the introduction to chapter 2), however, but the main criticism of this earlier work is that, ultimately, it is merely an exercise in geometry (see our figure 2.3 on the central place theory as a prime example) and contains too little real-world economic geography. This weakness of the Christaller-style economic geography is addressed in more recent work in economic geography. In the appendix to this chapter (based on Martin, 2008), the main ingredients of geographical economics and economic geography proper are briefly summarized and compared.

Second, the general equilibrium framework and the deductive theorizing upon which geographical economics is based are thought to be ill suited to deal with the analysis of economic geography proper. This framework is thought to be *un*able to deal with the role of institutions, uncertainty, and the resulting non-optimizing behavior of agents, all of which are argued to be decisive for the location of economic activity in the real world by modern economic geographers. To put it more bluntly, the complaint is that the new economic geography is neither new (but merely a restatement of outdated earlier insights of economic geographers) nor economic geography (since there is no place for real-world geography). Given this position, it is hardly a surprise that most economic geographers think that geographical economics cannot be applied to policy issues, because in their view spatial policy making is far too complicated for the models of geographical economics.

This is why Michael Storper (2003: 81) refers to economists as "the kings and queens of generality," whereas economic geographers are "the kings and queens of specificity and particularity." This is reflected in the regional science of the 1950s and 1960s, which was at best characterized by increasingly complex statistics. All this empirical knowledge was very much in search of a theory; and this, of course, was the great contribution of Paul Krugman, who provided such a theory. For geographers, some of the theoretical simplifications were simply unacceptable, however, because they do not reflect (Storper, 2003: 81) "the soft side of things, the more complex behavioural patterns, relational issues and all that." Economic geographers

---

[4] See also the various contributions by economic geographers to *The Oxford Handbook of Economic Geography* (Clark, Feldman, and Gertler, 2000).

point not only to the limitations of the analytical framework but also to the alleged oversimplification in geographical economics in, for instance, not discriminating between various levels of spatial aggregation. Indeed, in the previous chapters the location index *r* has interchangeably represented a city, a region, or a country.

Despite being highly critical, Martin (1999) clearly takes geographical economics (and economics in general) seriously. This also holds for geographers such as Allen Scott, Storper, Andrés Rodriguez-Posé, Ron Boschma and Koen Frenken (see Boschma and Frenken, 2006, for a useful categorization of economic geography *versus* geographical economics). For these geographers, the adjective "economic" in economic geography signals that economics should be an important component of economic geography. There are many economic geographers who have turned away from economics as a pillar on which research in social or human geography should rest, however. Formal (deductive) modeling and empirical testing have definitely become "no-go areas" for a large number of geographers, and they are replaced by discourse analysis and case studies. This plea for a cultural turn in economic geography is by no means the only recent call for a change in economic geography. In his critical assessment of the state of the art in economic geography, Overman (2004: 501), a leading geographical economist himself, notes that one can observe a range of (possible) turns in economic geography. Apart from the cultural turn, there are calls for a relational turn, a quantitative turn, a holistic turn, or an about-turn, the latter implying an engagement with mainstream economics.[5]

The field of economic geography is thus far from unified, and there is much internal debate and disagreement (see Amin and Thrift, 2000, and the reaction by Martin and Sunley, 2001 and Scott, 2004, 2006). For a fruitful debate between (geographical) economists and (economic) geographers, some minimum requirements have to be fulfilled (see box 12.2). First, both "camps" have to have at least a basic understanding of each other's work and to show a willingness to study what the other side has to say (so one at least knows what to disagree with!). While this requirement is not met by most geographers, in our experience, it is certainly not met by almost all geographical economists, who simply neglect what's going on in economic geography (see below for some exceptions). Second, there has to be some

---

[5] As *The Byrds* once famously sang, "To everything (Turn, turn, turn), There is a season (Turn, turn, turn)," and it is against these various turns in economic geography that the title of the influential paper by Martin (1999), "The new 'geographical turn' in economics," in which geographical economics is critically assessed, should be understood.

Box 12.2 Are *Homo economicus* and *Homo geographicus* two different species?

In an interesting paper on the (non-)debate between economists and geographers from an anthropological angle, Duranton and Rodriguez-Posé (2005) ask the question as to whether *Homo economicus* and *Homo geographicus* are really that different. Their conclusion is that there are considerable differences in terms of both style and content, but that, nevertheless, a (renewed) debate between geographical economists and economic geographers might be beneficial for all parties concerned. Duranton (a geographical economist) and Rodriguez-Posé (an economic geographer) note the following barriers to a more fruitful communication.

- (Geographical) economists and (economic) geographers ignore each other's publications. This is evident from the lack of citations on work done by economic geographers in leading geographical economics journals, and vice versa (the only recent exception being the discussion by prominent geographers of Krugman, 1991a, and Fujita, Krugman, and Venables, 1999).
- Economists and geographers do not go to the same conferences, and when they do there is a culture shock with respect to presentation and discussion style.
- The research methods often differ so markedly that communication becomes rather difficult.
- There is in many cases an unwillingness to take each other's work seriously.

These are not minor obstacles, to say the least. Duranton and Rodriguez-Posé see a number of ways for a debate to be (re-)launched, however. In their view, a key word here is *compromise*. Only if both "parties" are willing to compromise (more) on what constitutes acceptable research and on the use of concepts (more or less fixed in economics and changeable and rather fluid in geography) will such a debate be feasible. Duranton and Rodriguez-Posé (2005: 1704–5) conclude their analysis by stating that, "despite their differences in methods, terminology, and organization, geographical economists and economic geographers . . . share a common genetic code that makes them more similar to one another than each species is willing to admit. They can try to grow apart, but their instinct always brings them back to their original shared set of research questions and interests."

middle ground or overlap that might enable a useful exchange of opinions, or that even allows for mutual research or new research initiatives. Examples of the former are scarce but there are notable exceptions, such as the studies by Edward Leamer and Storper (2001) and Storper and Venables (2004). Regarding the dangers of the status quo on the non-debate between (geographical) economists and (economic) geographers, it is useful to quote geographer Scott (2006: 106–7).[6]

[6] The quote is from his review of volume IV of *The Handbook of Regional and Urban Economics*, a book that, according to Scott (2006: 104), "geographers will neglect at their peril."

In any case, the ill-considered advice put forth recently by some geographers, to the effect that all attempts at intellectual exchange with the economics confraternity should now be more or less brought to an end, strikes me as being only a recipe for self-marginalization. In spite of the important ideological, political, and scientific differences between the two camps, geographers will profit significantly from continued critical engagement with the often insightful and original research of economists. There may even be some possibility – dare I say it? – of using any such engagement as an opportunity for recovering some of the discipline's lost quantitative and analytical skills. If economists, for their part, continue to proceed as though geographers do not exist, then that presumably is their problem, though in view of their own peculiar form of self-marginalization in the contemporary social sciences, it is probably one they will not recognize.

The inclusion of the above quotation in the present book signals that the authors, all born and bred mainstream economists, think that Scott's call for more engagement has to be taken seriously by economists and geographers alike. It is also worth noting that Ron Martin (2008), writing (almost) two decades after the inception of geographical economics and one decade after his critique of geographical economics (Martin, 1999), concludes that there is value in interaction for both economic geographers and geographical economists. As Martin (2008) argues (note: NEG = new economic geography = geographical economics; PEG = proper economic geography; see also the appendix):

For their part, NEG theorists would benefit from engaging in dialogue with the arguments concerning the causal explanations of spatial agglomeration – and regionally uneven development more generally – found in the empirically grounded, "appreciative" theory of economic geographers. The empirically-orientated work found in PEG – on real world agglomerations, clusters, cities and the like – addresses a whole range of explanatory factors, and conceptual ideas not found in NEG, and NEG theorists need to get much closer to the "appreciative-theoretic" stories and local empirical models found in some quarters of PEG ... Getting closer to the "appreciative" theories of economic geographers would not only encourage NEG theorists to take such factors more seriously – if only in stylised form – but would also compel them to give explicit consideration to the interpretative structures behind their models. But at the same time, economic geographers need to be more amenable to learning from NEG. Economic geographers may well be disinclined to take the formal models of NEG seriously. But NEG formal theory can be of help in thinking through appreciative theory: it can identify gaps in PEG explanations, and can lead to consideration of mechanisms and factors downplayed in the latter. Thus (as Overman [2004] points out) NEG theorists could encourage economic geographers to pay much greater attention to the role of market forces, prices and other basic economic processes that seem to have but disappeared from the appreciative-theoretic work in PEG. Further, NEG models and methodology could be useful in working through the logical implications of local explanations developed by geographers. In these ways, the model solutions produced in NEG could provide a useful stimulus to appreciative theory in PEG, though this will only happen if the formal models of NEG are recognised by economic geographers as representing an accurate version of their beliefs, and if, at the same time, the logic of NEG models is understandable by economic geographers.

A good example of a new research initiative that starts from the common ground between modern geography and economics is the recent establishment of the so-called evolutionary economic geography (EEG) approach (Boschma and Frenken, 2006). In this, insights from evolutionary and geographical economics are combined to develop an interesting new approach in economic geography that is positioned halfway between geographical economics and the more institutional approaches that currently dominate the field of economic geography. Though EEG is still a work in progress and far from unified (assuming the latter to be necessary, see Boschma and Martin, 2007, on the EEG research agenda), it is interesting to see how some of the proposed models overlap with or stem from the same "core material" as some of the research on geographical economics that has been discussed in previous chapters.[7]

Two interesting examples are the papers by Frenken and Boschma (2007) and Christopher Fowler (2007). The first builds directly on the work on stochastic growth by Simon (1955) discussed in chapter 7 in relation to Zipf's law. The authors reformulate Simon's model so as to understand industry and city growth. Their major change compared to the Simon model is that they replace the exogenous arrival of new agents (firms) with a model of product innovation that stipulates how firms enter or exit an industry and how firms grow as a result. Despite a clear overlap in terms of models used and the papers referred to, the differences with the core models

---

[7] See also the special issue of *The Journal of Economic Geography* (volume 7, September 2007) edited by Boschma and Martin on evolutionary economic geography. On a more general level, and despite the differences in analytical approaches, evolutionary economic geography and geographical economics both start from the same fundamental question that one way or the other characterizes (and essentially unites) all spatial or location theories. This key question is *how to deal with both the stability (persistence) of and change (evolution) in spatial outcomes over time*. To answer this question, both approaches rely on similar terms and concepts, such as path dependence, even though the meaning of path dependence varies markedly across the spectrum of location theories (Martin and Sunley, 2006). The "fundamental spatial question" can indeed be framed in terms of paths, however: how to reconcile the persistence of paths with the change of paths? Whatever their analytical and methodological differences, both geographical economics and evolutionary economic geography take this key question as a starting point; compare, for instance, Fujita and Thisse (2002) and Boschma and Martin (2007).

of geographical economics are also clear to see. Key elements of geo-graphical economics are not part of their model, such as market structure, the demand side (or the interdependency between supply and demand), transport or trade costs, and factor mobility, to name the most important "missing" elements when one looks at the Frenken–Boschma model through the eyes of geographical economics.

The second example, Fowler (2007), is linked to geographical economics, as it takes the core model of chapter 3 and its parameter configuration to simulate the long-run equilibrium from chapter 4 (section 4.2) as its benchmark. By starting essentially with equations (4.1) to (4.3) – that is, the short-run equilibrium version of the core model – Fowler then adds so-called "agent-based simulations," in which, in contrast to the way a long-run equilibrium is reached in the core model, agents (firms, workers) have to decide individually where to locate. The reason put forward for turning to these agent-based simulations is that this opens up the possibility of analyzing out-of-equilibrium behavior, which is a hallmark of evolutionary economic(s) (geography). In geographical economics, given its foundation in neoclassical economics, only states of equilibria are analyzed. The attempt by Fowler (2007) to adapt the geographical economics model in such a way as to allow for disequilibrium behavior is interesting, but it is also flawed, since one cannot on the one hand call for or use out-of-equilibrium simulations while at the same time sticking to equilibrium(!) conditions (4.1) to (4.3), which presuppose goods and labor market equilibrium (see also Fowler, 2007: 277, on this issue).

12.3 An evaluation of the critique

So, are the critical remarks with respect to geographical economics listed in the previous section valid? Our answer is threefold: (i) *yes*, (ii) *no longer so, and* (iii) *no*.

(i) The "yes" answer. It is true that the state of the art in geographical economics implies that many models are short on analytical solutions, which hampers empirical and policy analysis. This does not mean that there are no analytical solutions but, rather (as we have highlighted throughout the book), that solvable models and important analytical conditions, such as those for the break and sustain points in chapter 4, are typically available only for the case of the two-region model. It is the case, of course, that numerical solutions are part and parcel of the geographical economics approach, and, given the lack of analytical results for the n-region (non-convex) world in which we live, it will remain important to use and build numerically computable models (see also Fujita and Mori, 2005, and Behrens and Thisse, 2007). In addition, the criticism that the core model of geographical economics, like new trade theory, relies heavily on specific functional forms and specific assumptions, such as Dixit–Stiglitz monopolistic competition and iceberg transport costs, is no doubt also valid, even though we now know that it is possible to relax or change these assumptions without undermining the main insights.

Similarly, a racetrack (or pancake) depiction of space, such as the one we came up with in the previous chapter, is indeed very simple and hard to swallow for anyone who believes that Copernicus was right and that the believers in the "flat earth" were wrong.[8] With regard to the handling of geography, the idea that geography matters only because a proportion of manufactured goods melt away during transport from one location to another is surely too stringent; the transport sector itself can have an influence on spatial developments, because in reality this sector is not a neutral bystander (it uses up scarce resources, and has to spend income somewhere), and also to the extent that geography has a sociological and psychological component (see the opening page of chapter 1). This last remark also refers to the criticisms of the neoclassical model of individual behavior underlying geographical economics and its neglect of institutions that are needed to understand how the coordination of economic activity across space comes about. Finally, it cannot be denied that geographical economics at times leads to theoretical and empirical conclusions that appear not to be new.

(ii) The "no longer so" answer. The critical remarks are not inappropriate, but in our view it is evident that they paint too dark a picture of geographical economics, for two main reasons. First – and this is the "no longer so" part of our answer – geographical economics has clearly moved on after the development of the core model by Krugman (1991a). Chapters 5 to 11 of this book give many examples of extensions of the core models of chapters 3 and 4, as well as of recent policy and empirical applications. Second, and more importantly, one's assessment of geographical economics depends very much on what the aim of geographical economics is considered to be, or what the proper framework is within which to analyze the

---

[8] An important advantage of the neutral-space racetrack economy, already mentioned, is the fact that the agglomeration outcome cannot be the result of a pre-imposed geographic structure. As to the flatness of the world, see box 12.3.

location of economic activity. On that point, we answer below with a resounding "no" on the validity of the critique.

Most scholars who criticize the geographical economics approach cannot resist giving in to the temptation to use the core model of geographical economics as a scapegoat. Many of the comments made by economic geographers, regional and urban economists, and international economists focus attention too strongly on the shortcomings of the core model. Recent developments in geographical economics have dealt effectively with a number of criticisms. We have given a host of examples in the previous chapters. Recall, for instance, the discussion of Baldwin *et al.* (2003) on the use of geographical economics for policy questions in the previous chapter. Similarly, as we discussed at length in chapter 4, the Krugman (1991a) model has been turned inside out and has been changed in a number of important (and, at times, solvable) ways. There has also been clear progress on the empirical front, as we saw in chapters 5 and 6.[9] In addition, the introduction of (housing) services (chapter 5), intermediate goods and non-neutral space (chapters 4 and 6), congestion (chapter 7), the fragmentation of production and FDI (chapter 8), international trade and agglomeration (chapter 9), and the ability to analyze dynamics with the inclusion of first-nature geography and institutions (chapter 10) has also addressed some of the other criticisms. Last but not least, the simplicity of the core model is intentionally so; Krugman's goal was to develop the most simple model in which core–periphery patterns arise endogenously.[10]

Another way to illustrate our "no longer so" answer is by pointing out that, like most new theories, geographical economics has initially focused on the bare essentials of the new approach and that, subsequently, various refinements and extensions have been added. This is a normal procedure not just in economic theorizing but in scientific development at large. To quote Krugman (2000: 59):

We might note in particular that the new economic geography, like the old trade theory, suffers to some extent from the temptation to focus on what is easiest to

---

[9] In his review of the fourth volume of *The Handbook of Regional and Urban Economics*, Lucas (2006) rightly stresses that, in spatial economics, theorizing as well as empirical research are both stimulated by the fact that, perhaps more so than in other fields, its "practioners are not apologetic about using the data of ordinary experience" (112). A prime example of this is perhaps the use of maps, of which Lucas goes on to note: "Is anyone drawn to spatial economics who did not grow up poring over maps?"

[10] Note that this is also the best riposte to all those who object to the habit of formalization in economics: if one is unable to understand a problem in the simplified world of mathematics, one can forget about saying anything useful about the same problem in the complex real world.

model rather on what is probably most important in practice ... Still, there are good reasons why mainstream economics does place a high value on being able to produce tightly specified models – if only to provide the backdrop for less tight, more empirically motivated study. And the new economic geography, while it may be past its first rush of enthusiasm, has ended the long silence of mainstream economics on the whole question of where economic activity takes place and why; now that the conversation [with geographers] has begun, it is sure to continue.

(iii) The "no" answer. We now come to the third part of our answer about the validity of the criticisms, and it is here that we arrive at the two most important contributions of geographical economics. As already argued in chapter 2, the real novelty of geographical economics is not so much to be found in its research topic but, instead, in the way it tackles the relationships between economics and geography. True in spirit to Ohlin (1933), geographical economics has succeeded in lowering the fences between international economics on the one hand and regional and urban economics on the other hand. By using highly stylized models, which no doubt neglect a lot of specifics about urban/regional/international phenomena, geographical economics is able to show that, quite often, the same mechanisms are at work at different levels of spatial aggregation. The idea that at least to some extent the same underlying economic forces are relevant for explaining the spatial organization of cities, the interaction between regions within a nation, and the uneven distribution of GDP between countries is very important. In order to lay the foundations for such a unified approach, there is a price to be paid in terms of the neglect of institutional and geographical details, as the aforementioned criticisms make clear. This is a price well worth paying, though, certainly in view of our optimism that a number of these voids have already been filled or will be so in future research, as geographical economics – or, perhaps more accurately, the rediscovery of the importance of space by mainstream economics – is here to stay.

The second major contribution of geographical economics is that the clustering of economic activity, which can be observed at various levels of aggregation, is not taken for granted. By this we mean that, in contrast to the "older" location theories, geographical economics does *not* assume beforehand what has to be explained (Ottaviano and Thisse, 2004). It is crucial to see that geographical economics is, above all, an attempt to bridge the gap between economics and geography *from the perspective of mainstream economic theory*. The clustering of economic activity is inextricably linked to the existence of increasing returns to scale and trade costs

(Fujita and Thisse, 2002). It is shown how in such a world the decisions of individual economic agents may give rise to clustering or agglomeration. By explicitly modeling the choices of firms, consumers, and workers in a general equilibrium framework, within a market structure of imperfect competition, geographical economics is the *only* field of economics that provides a consistent general equilibrium framework for the spatial distribution of economic activity.

Of course, the importance one attaches to such a foundation depends crucially on the question of whether one thinks the deductive reasoning that is central to neoclassical or mainstream economics provides a good place to start the inquiry into the relationships between economics and geography. We think it is. Not only because a well-developed alternative is to date simply lacking in economics, but also because the meta-approach of geographical economics towards the *why, who,* and *where* of the location of economic activity offers additional insights compared to approaches that focus only on cities, regions, trade, or growth (see also box 12.3).

Box 12.3 Fuzzy concepts: flatness and clusters

At the time of the writing of this chapter, the book *The World is Flat* by Friedman (2005) was still riding high on most best-seller lists around the world. This book is about the "flattening" impact that twenty-first-century globalization will have on the world economy. It is in particular concerned with the question of what this "flattening," spurred on by lower communication costs, implies for highly developed economies such as the United States. Even though Friedman lists ten "flatteners" that have caused the world economy to change rapidly since 2000, it is not always clear what "flat" means. Our quotation marks signal this ambiguity. In many instances, "flat" just seems to be a sexy word for "change."

Whatever the precise meaning of "flat," the book has certainly made an impact.[11] Friedman's blockbuster proves to be an important reference for many policy makers and politicians when it comes to discussing the effects of globalization. From the point of view of geographical economics, economic geography, or any other location theory, the book also raises an interesting question. For one thing, the phrase "the world is flat" has a clear geographical connotation. In a lengthy and highly readable review of the book, Leamer (2007), the trade economist, tries to make sense of the "flat" metaphor from the point of view of economic theory.[12] Interestingly, by explicitly referring to Krugman (1991a),

---

[11] We carried out a search on Google on January 7, 2008. We recorded 860,000 hits for this book (search term: Friedman World Is Flat), compared to 37,500 hits for the *Spatial Economy* by Fujita, Krugman, and Venables (1999).

[12] Note that Friedman's book has also had quite an impact in academia: we recorded 938 citations in Google scholar. Compare to 1,859 citations for Fujita, Krugman, and Venables (1999), 381 for Baldwin *et al.* (2003), 345 for Fujita and Thisse (2002), and 181 for the first edition of this book (March 10, 2008).

Box 12.3 (cont.)

Leamer turns also to geographical economics to make sense of the flatness idea. He observes (87–8; emphasis in original) that "flatness doesn't create a relationship-free equilibrium; it merely changes the geography of relationships...The what-if question that economic geographers ask is *not*: 'What if the world were flat instead of spherical or bumpy?' Their what-if question is: 'What if transportation costs were low instead of high?' The answer to such a question is: '*It depends.*' It depends on the power of the agglomeration externalities, and the costs of delivery and distribution of consumers and their preferences across space." Once our book has been read, Leamer's view on flatness hopefully rings a bell![13]

More generally, geographical economics and the underlying analytical framework may be useful for more than just making sense of ill-defined, catch-all concepts, such as "flatness" in the case of Friedman's book. They may also help to clarify the use of other concepts, such as clustering or path dependence, that all too easily remain rather *fuzzy* without an explicit model (which partly helps to explain their appeal). Maybe (see box 12.1) Krugman indeed came up with his core model of geographical economics after reading Porter in an attempt to be more precise as to Porter's emphasis on *clusters*. The advantage of the modeling approach used in geographical economics is that it forces one to be explicit on what is meant by the various variables and how the interdependencies and resulting constraints shape the economy under consideration (Overman, 2004; Krugman, 1998). The observation that all too often the study of spatial phenomena in the social sciences is plagued by rather loose concepts is not confined to geographical economists; see also, for instance, the critical assessments by geographers such as Ron Martin and Peter Sunley (2003, 2006), Örjan Sjöberg and Fredrik Sjöholm (2002), and Ann Markusen (2003) of such "fuzzy" concepts as clusters, path dependency, or the region as an economic agent.

In a policy paper aptly called California dreamin': the feeble case for cluster policies, Duranton (2007) examines the case for cluster policies.[14] Armed with Porter's work on clusters and with the example of California's Silicon Valley in their mind, policy makers try to stimulate or even "build" clusters of economic development within their territory in an attempt to foster economic development. In line with Martin and Sunley (2003), Duranton (2007) finds the concept of clusters rather vague. In his view, though, the real problem with the cluster idea is not at the conceptual level: "Instead, the problem with cluster policy literature is one of a well-articulated theory: what is the 'problem' that cluster initiatives are

---

[13] For an in-depth analysis of and reaction to Friedman's *The World Is Flat* by scholars from international economics, urban economics, economic geography, economic history, political science, and sociology, see the *Cambridge Journal of the Regions, Economy, and Society* (CJRES), November 2008, volume 1, issue 3. Glancing at the titles of the various papers in the CJRES issue, one immediately suspects that the contributing authors all argue that the world is not flat at all; see www.oxfordjournals.org/our_journals/cjres/about.html. See also the website of our book for more material that tries to test Friedman's main flatness claims and for some of the papers (Brakman and van Marrewijk, 2008) included in this special issue of the CJRES.

[14] Recall also box 8.1, in which we listed the main ingredients of Porter's analysis in our discussion of FDI and multinationals.

Box 12.3 (cont.)

trying to fix" (3). In his opinion, such a theory of clusters should have an underlying structure that consists of three elements: (i) *a spatial structure* (geography should matter somehow because of land or transport or trade costs); (ii) *a production structure* (which includes some form of local increasing returns for firms to benefit from "clustering"); and (iii) *assumptions about the spatial mobility of goods and factors of production* (can goods and/or capital and labor "move" between or within locations?).

In Duranton's attempt to make sense of Porter's cluster framework, the combination of elements (i) to (iii) gives rise to the basic model (or, more accurately, basic diagrams) of urban systems that we have discussed in chapter 7 (the diagrammatic representation of Henderson, 1974, by Combes, Duranton, and Overman, 2005). The point to emphasize here is that allegedly fuzzy spatial concepts (such as clusters) not only call for a clear definition but also require a spatial "model" that in formal/diagrammatic/verbal or other terms has to include the basic ingredients (i) to (iii) as its backbone. Clearly, the spatial structure (i) to (iii) lies at the heart of the core model of geographical economics. The combination of transport costs (external and internal), increasing returns to scale, and the interregional mobility of manufacturing firms and workers is what makes the Krugman (1991a) model tick.

To sum up, despite some well-argued and valid criticisms, the value added of geographical economics is self-evidently positive in our view. Not only because it gives a sound theoretical foundation for a fruitful combination of sub-fields within economics, but also because in doing so it points out the similarities in these approaches and the common economic forces underlying various empirical phenomena at different levels of aggregation. When it comes to the value added of geographical economics for the field of economic geography, we maintain that the generalizations offered by geographical economics are at least a useful benchmark for the more place- and space-specific contextualizations offered by geographers (see box 12.3).[15] The final question to address in this book is what the future of geographical economics looks like.

12.4 Growing up: where will geographical economics go from here?

It is, of course, very difficult to predict what geographical economics will look like in, say, ten or twenty years from now. At the end of the book, we

---

[15] And, vice versa, see Martin (2008): economists should acknowledge that these contextualizations are also useful for the further development of the theory and empirics of geographical economics.

can only offer some tentative suggestions as to the directions for future research, thereby offering the following "predictions."

Not "one size fits all"...

Given that the core model of geographical economics is in many ways too simplified, one feasible line of future research is to combine the basic elements and insights of the core model with well-established causes and determinants of trade and location from international and regional economics. With respect to *trade theory*, one can think of models in which, alongside the interaction between factor mobility, increasing returns, and transport costs that is central to geographical economics, there is also a role for more "classical" determinants of trade, such as factor endowments or productivity. Indeed, we have already discussed some simple examples of this possibility in chapter 9. Moreover, it seems a safe bet to assume that there will be more research in international economics on the incorporation of agglomeration effects into trade and FDI models of firm heterogeneity along the lines of Baldwin and Okubo (2006). It also seems reasonable to expect that the main elements of geographical economics will merge with existing models of endogenous growth, simply because of the clear kinship between geographical economics and models of economic growth as summarized in Grossman and Helpman (1991) (see Baldwin and Martin, 2004). Such a development would provide a larger role for geography in economic *growth theory*, while, at the same time (see chapter 10 of this book), it would also give an opportunity to go beyond the simple simulation dynamics that characterizes the bulk of geographical economics at present.

Similarly, we think that, despite the criticisms raised in *regional* as well as *urban economics* against geographical economics, there will be more interaction between these respective fields in the near future, with more attention being paid to the question as to which agglomeration mechanisms are relevant for different spatial scales. There is mutual self-interest in taking better notice of each other's work, and hence we forecast more attempts to try to incorporate elements of geographical economics into these two other fields, and vice versa. In urban economics it seems more than likely that the basic elements of geographical economics, notably the (Dixit–Stiglitz) model of imperfect competition and the inclusion of trade costs between cities, will be integrated with existing models of systems of cities (Henderson, 2000). Given the similarities in the analytical toolkit between urban economics and geographical economics, we predict that the difference between these two fields will become blurred (see also Combes, Duranton, and Overman, 2005). This will probably also occur because, for various applications, geographical economics needs a richer menu of agglomerating and spreading forces, such that variables such as congestion/commuting costs or land use, which have long been emphasized by urban economists, receive more attention (see also Fujita, Krugman, and Venables, 1999: 346). In addition, with respect to the mechanisms behind local increasing returns, we think that geographical economics could learn from modern urban economics (see Duranton and Puga, 2004, for a survey of the micro-foundations for these mechanisms). Moreover, the theory of the firm is rather ill-developed in geographical economics (Neary, 2001, 2006). When it comes to urban systems and the establishment of new cities, modern urban economics, with its emphasis on the land development market, can also be important in our view.

There are also signs that part of modern *economic geography* is taking geographical economics seriously. To some extent this is out of dissatisfaction with the descriptive modes of analysis that are currently dominant in economic geography. The recent literature on evolutionary economic geography provides a good example of research that, though quite different from the models of geographical economics in our book, is nevertheless in some ways a direct consequence of the rise of geographical economics.

Spatial data and techniques and the comeback of simulations

Empirical research in geographical economics to date does not offer much in the way of direct testing of geographical economics against other location theories, and it also has little to say as yet on the role of institutions, or, more generally, on the relevance of "softer" location factors in the determination of location decisions. We think that this will change, also in view of the ongoing empirical work within geographical economics itself. At any rate, with the increasing availability of micro-data sets and the increased use of spatial econometrics (recall the concluding section of chapter 6), empirical research that is directly or indirectly based on geographical economics will probably be at the forefront of research in geographical economics in the coming years; see box 12.4 for an example of the kind of research we have in mind.

At the theoretical front, it seems time to move away from the two-region models that have dominated geographical economics ever since Krugman (1991a). With analytical results or solvable models for multi-region models

Box 12.4 The way forward: agglomeration versus selection and the use of micro-data

The key message of the models of geographical economics that have been discussed in our book is that agglomerations are characterized by higher wages, higher productivity, and/or a higher growth rate. The empirical evidence suggests that this is the case at all geographical scales (city, region, country). In geographical economics, but also in urban economics (see chapter 7), the explanation for this *agglomeration bonus* is the existence of various positive localized externalities, which make firms and workers more productive in larger locations. Thus it is the spatial concentration of firms and workers that creates the agglomeration benefits. The empirical evidence also suggests that this bonus is *caused* by the positive agglomeration externalities or economies of scale. As we have already mentioned in chapters 6 and 8, however, the modern literature on firm or worker heterogeneity shows that the observed agglomeration bonus may simply be the result of a *selection effect*. Firms are on average more productive in larger markets merely because only the more productive firms survive in larger markets. If this is the case, the higher productivity of firms in larger or more centrally located regions is *not* caused by the alleged positive agglomeration economies but is, instead, the result of a selection process.

To test the agglomeration bonus explanation against the competing selection explanation, the models and empirical work discussed in the previous chapters are not sufficient, for two reasons. First, the core models do not include the possibility of firm or worker heterogeneity to begin with. The way forward here would be to build theoretical models that allow for both agglomeration and selection effects. Building on Melitz (2003) and Melitz and Ottaviano (2005), Baldwin and Okubo (2006), for instance, show how the geographical economics model can be extended to include selection effects (see chapter 8, box 8.1). Second, testing these competing explanations requires the use of micro-data, but the existing empirical work in geographical (and urban) economics is based on data that are typically not firm- or worker-specific. Ideally, one would like to tackle the agglomeration versus selection issue by developing a theoretical model that allows for both explanations and then testing such a model. This is precisely what the recent paper by Combes *et al.* (2008) does. In our view, it is a safe bet to predict that their paper will turn out be a good example of the direction that research in geographical economics will take in the second decade of the twenty-first century.

On the theoretical side, Combes *et al.* (2008) generalize and extend the model by Melitz and Ottaviano (2005) by, *inter alia*, including agglomeration forces alongside the selection effects of the Melitz–Ottaviano model, in which low-productivity firms cannot survive in a large market because of the stiffer competition that exists in larger markets. Specifically, in large markets a firm's mark-up of price over marginal cost will be lower because of the stiffer competition, thereby forcing low-productivity (high-marginal-cost) firms to exit. With respect to agglomeration forces, large regions or markets give rise to agglomeration economies because each worker becomes more productive when the size of the population of workers in this region increases. The local *interaction* of workers gives rise to agglomeration economies, and hence to a higher productivity level per worker. This productivity effect is stronger when the number of workers is larger. Therefore, the

Box 12.4 (cont.)

Table 12.1 Agglomeration versus selection in France

Sector	Agglomeration effect A	Specialization effect S	R^2	Number of observations
Food, beverages, and tobacco	−0.11	0.02	0.50	25,853
Clothing and leather	0.39	−0.10	0.87	5,964
Publishing and printing	0.27	−0.01	0.97	10,493
Pharmaceutical products	0.35	−0.01	0.91	1,831
Domestic equipment	0.20	−0.01	0.99	6,880
Motor vehicles	0.31	−0.09	0.80	1,816
Ships, locomotives, and rolling stock	0.34	0.03	0.97	1,143
Machinery and equipment	0.40	−0.02	0.90	16,332
Electric and electronic equipment	0.22	−0.00	0.98	7,735
Textiles	0.16	0.00	0.96	3,718
Wood, pulp, and paper	0.18	0.00	0.99	5,985
Chemicals	0.26	−0.01	0.98	6,987
Basic metals and fabricated metal products	0.12	0.01	0.97	15,161
Electric and electronic components	0.10	0.02	0.96	3,337
Construction	0.28	−0.01	0.91	78,511
Vehicle sale and maintenance	0.22	−0.00	0.96	32,052
Wholesale and commission trade	0.30	−0.02	0.98	70,242
Transportation	0.26	−0.01	0.86	39,948
Consultancy and assistance activities	0.36	−0.01	0.99	56,129
Average	0.26	−0.01	0.92	

Source: Combes et al. (2008).

agglomeration effect, just like the selection effect, predicts that large regions will have, on average, higher productivity.

On the empirical side, Combes et al. (2008) use a very detailed panel data set of French firms (1.15 million companies for the period 1994–2002!) that covers (almost) all firms in the country. The main empirical prediction from their underlying model is that, even though both the agglomeration effect and the selection effect predict that average productivity will be higher in large markets, the (log-)productivity distribution will be different in both cases when comparing larger and smaller markets. In particular, "stronger selection effects in larger markets should lead to an increased left-truncation of the distribution of firm

Box 12.4 (cont.)

log-productivities whereas stronger agglomeration effects should lead to a rightwards shift of the distribution of firm log-productivities" (Combes *et al.* 2008: 1). The empirical work then basically exploits this difference in the predicted firm productivity distribution across large and small French locations between the agglomeration and selection effects. Total factor productivity is computed at the establishment level for each firm at the two-digit industry level for every large and small location (metropolitan areas with more and fewer than 200,000 people respectively).

The econometric specification is such that, instead of specifying the underlying productivity distribution, Combes *et al.* directly estimate the "left-truncation" effect associated with the selection effect as well as the "rightwards shift" effect associated with the agglomeration effect. More specifically, and with i (j) denoting large (small) locations, the parameters to be estimated are S and A (see table 12.1), where S captures the selection effect and A captures the agglomeration effect as a difference in the shift between large and small locations i and j in the following way:

$$S \equiv \frac{S_i - S_j}{1 - S_j} \ and \ A \equiv A_i - A_j \qquad (12.1)$$

This in turn gives rise to the following predictions:
- the strength of the selection effect is invariant to location size: $S = 0$;
- the selection effect is stronger in large locations: $S > 0$;
- the strength of the agglomeration effect is invariant to location size: $A = 0$; and
- again, the selection effect is stronger in large locations: $A > 0$.

Given the theoretical predictions regarding the A and S coefficients, it is clear that the estimation results suggest that, typically, $A > 0$ and $S \approx 0$. This would imply that productivity differences between French metropolitan areas are primarily the result of the agglomeration effect. This is not to say that selection effects are not important, but only that the strength of this effect does not depend on the location size. As to the quantitative importance of the A effect, Combes *et al.* (2008: 18) note:

[A] back-of-the-envelope calculation suggest that the average value of A we find (0.26) corresponds to a productivity increase across the board (after accounting for selection) of roughly 4% for a doubling of city size, which is in line with what is found using very different methods in the agglomeration literature (Rosenthal and Strange, 2004; Combes et al. 2007). Our model showed that the extent to which agglomeration economies varied across locations of different size was closely related to the extent to which interactions are local or global (national in our [French] case). Our results would be consistent with a situation where interactions are quite local, which matches the empirical literature looking at spatial decay of different types of agglomeration economies (Rosenthal and Strange, 2004).

This last observation on the limited spatial reach of agglomeration economies is in line with our conclusions about the empirical evidence on geographical economics (see chapter 5). The main conclusion to take away from this important research is that agglomeration effects are important in the case of France. It appears therefore, that in this line of research as well, which is based on richer models and better data, agglomeration does seem to matter.

in short supply in the foreseeable future, a shift from two-region models to multi-region ones implies a return to the use of simulations. These simulations and the techniques involved are expected to become more precise in line with increasing computer power and better simulation software, and this may also open up the possibility of agent-based simulations and, consequently, the out-of-equilibrium analyses advocated by evolutionary economic geographers (Fowler, 2007).

More conversation with the "others" – wishful thinking?

The launching of a major new journal in 2001, the *Journal of Economic Geography*, which has an editorial board firmly rooted in economic geography, urban economics, *and* geographical economics, was an encouraging sign of more cooperation, or, at least, of more conversation. In a way, the journal can be seen as a field experiment: can geographers and economists start to communicate or collaborate? At the time of writing this chapter (early 2008) the journal has been around for seven years, and in many ways it is a resounding success (e.g. in terms of impact and citation scores, and the fact that leading authors have published their work in this journal). At the same time, cross-referencing between "economics" and "geography" papers is still not widespread, to put it mildly. This certainly holds for actual cooperation, but, as Duranton and Storper (2006) note in a special issue of the journal on the theme of "agglomeration and growth," when such an exchange of ideas and cooperation does take place it turns out to be very stimulating.

A prerequisite for a useful conversation is that the various "camps" take each other seriously. In academic terms, this means that they at least take notice of each other's work. The evidence suggests (Duranton and Rodriguez-Posé, 2005) that this is not the case for the bulk of economists and geographers, and anecdotal evidence also suggests that the interest is somewhat one-sided: leading geographers seem to be more aware of the work going on in (geographical) economics than vice versa. To take just one example, the list of references given by Martin (2008), without a doubt a leading economic geographer, contains at least as many references to economists as to geographers, but one is hard pressed to find papers by top-notch geographical, urban, or regional economists that display similar awareness of the "others" (the few exceptions have already been mentioned in this chapter).

The end of geographical economics as a separate sub-field within economics?

What many of the above examples regarding directions for future research have in common is that they point to research in geographical economics along the lines of "general to specific" – from the highly abstract and simple core model of chapters 3 and 4 to models that are more or less geared towards a specific research question. Such a trend would not be surprising, because that is what often happens when a research field matures. Accordingly, here is another prediction. In geographical economics, researchers will increasingly adapt the model to the locational issue at hand and adjust the set of agglomerating and spreading forces to suit. Now that the basics of geographical economics are well known, one can therefore also expect more empirical research and policy applications.[16] In this respect, there is a similarity with new growth theory, in which, after the theoretical developments in the second half of the 1980s, the emphasis in the following years was focused on empirical research. More empirical research will probably also mean that more attention will be paid to policy issues in the years to come.

Finally, is it realistic to expect that geographical economics will really become established as a field of its own? This is an open question. If, as we believe, integration with other fields within international and regional economics is on the research agenda it might very well be that the label "geographical economics" (or "new economic geography") becomes less fashionable. This does not really matter. What matters is the economic content of geographical economics. In this regard we are optimistic about its contribution in the long run. Geographical economics will have a lasting impact on trade and growth theory, translating into increased attention to geography in these theories. Similarly, insights from geographical economics will also become part of the core literature for the various branches of regional economics. In this respect, Ohlin (1933) can be satisfied: geographical economics is the most fruitful and promising attempt thus far to marry international and regional economics together.

---

[16] For the core model of geographical economics, this feeling of "completion" is also due to the fact that its basic structure and the nature of the resulting equilibria can be understood as much via analytical reasoning as by numerical solutions. See in particular Baldwin *et al.* (2003: chap. 1), Neary (2001), and Robert-Nicoud (2005).

Appendix

NEG pegged: geographical economics and economic geography compared

In his critical assessment of both geographical economics and economic geography, Martin (2008) comes up with a highly stylized, but useful and concise comparison of the main ingredients of (using his acronyms) NEG and PEG. NEG, as we have seen, stands for new economic geography and thus for geographical economics, whereas PEG stands for proper economic geography. Keeping in mind that any summary of these two approaches in a single table is a short cut and inevitably leaves out many subtleties, the NEG–PEG comparison in table A12.1 captures many of the major ingredients involved, and it also restates some of the criticisms raised against geographical economics as discussed in section 12.2.

In a nutshell, and at the risk of oversimplification, table A12.1 drives home the point that, in their search for spatial explanations, geographical economists tend to generalize and economic geographers tend to contextualize. Ideally, one would probably like a theory of the economic landscape to do both, but (Martin, 2008) "the options, it would seem, are that we must either downplay the locally-specific quantity of economic life, or limit our scope to generalize across space. Of course, to state the explanatory challenge in such stark oppositional terms is far too simplistic. Nevertheless, NEG can be seen as occupying a position towards the first extreme, and PEG a position nearer the second." Table A12.1 illustrates this tension between generalized and locally specific explanations of the economic landscape. For more reading on proper economic geography or modern economic geography, see the references in subsection 12.2.3 and the textbooks mentioned in the introduction of chapter 2.

Exercises

12.1 As we know from chapter 11, and also from the present chapter, Neary (2001) provides a very good but also rather critical review of Fujita, Krugman, and Venables (1999), to date still the most important

Table A12.1 NEG and PEG compared

	"New economic geography" (NEG)	"Proper economic geography" (PEG)
Key aim	Construction of general equilibrium model ("universal grammar") of spatial economic agglomeration, applicable at various spatial scales and various types of agglomeration.	To identify both possible general causal mechanisms and spatially specific processes and factors in explaining the genesis and development of particular spatial agglomerations and clusters.
Theoretical framework and causal mechanisms	Extension of mainstream (production function and utility function) theory to incorporate increasing returns, imperfect competition, transport costs, and location theory. Agglomeration driven purely by economic logic.	Eclectic and "appreciative," drawing on neo-Marshallian localization economies, social network theory, cultural theory, institutional economics, and evolutionary economics.
Form of economic space	Flat ontology. Economic landscape as absolute space, pre-given, and typically idealized and geometric.	Structured ontology. Space as not only absolute but also relative and relational, and multi-scalar; socially and historically produced.
Epistemology	Deductivist, axiomatic, abstract theorizing. Theory as models. Analytical solutions as explanation.	Realistic and pragmatic. Theory as explanation of process. General concepts used to frame explanations of specific cases.
Methodology	Formal mathematical model building. Numerical simulations dominate over empirical testing.	Discursive, empirically grounded, intensive, and often local-case-study- and actor-network-orientated.
Institutions and social context	Either ignored, or reduced to (subsumed under) "initial conditions" and parameter settings of models.	Considered central, and basic to understanding formation and reproduction of specific spatial agglomerations.
Role of history	Recognized as important, but treated in terms of "ad hoc dynamics" and the "starting conditions" of the model, and possibility of multiple equilibria acknowledged.	Increasingly recognized as important; economic landscape regarded as inherently evolutionary, path-dependent, and adaptive.

Source: Martin (2008).

book on geographical economics. Go to our website and read Neary (2006), which is his review of Baldwin *et al.* (2003). Compare Neary's 2006 review with the summary of his views in the present chapter, and assess whether or not research in geographical economics is making progress.

12.2* After reading box 12.2, can you imagine why Duranton and Rodriguez-Posé (2005) refer to (geographical) economists as *lions* and to (economic) geographers as *butterflies*?

12.3 Go to www.metacritic.com (a website for reviews of books, music, etc.) and check for the reviews of *The World Is Flat* by Friedman. Try to come up with examples from these reviews (mainly from newspapers and magazines) that are linked to the arguments raised by Leamer (2007) against Friedman's book.

12.4 Write a (very short – one-page) essay in which you set out your views regarding the future developments of geographical economics.

References

Abdel-Rahman, H. M., and A. Anas (2004), Theories of systems of cities, in J. V. Henderson and J.-F. Thisse (eds.), *The Handbook of Regional and Urban Economics*, vol. IV, *Cities and Geography*, Amsterdam: North Holland, 2293–340.

Acemoglu, D., S. Johnson, and J. A. Robinson (2001), The colonial origins of comparative development: an empirical investigation, *American Economic Review*, 91: 1369–401.

Ades, A., and H. B. Chua (1997), Thy neighbor's curse: regional instability and economic growth, *Journal of Economic Growth*, 2: 279–304.

Ades, A., and E. L. Glaeser (1995), Trade and circuses: explaining urban giants, *Quarterly Journal of Economics*, 110: 195–228.

Agénor, P. R., and P. J. Montiel (1996), *Development Macroeconomics*, Princeton NJ: Princeton University Press.

Alcalá, F., and A. Ciccone (2004), Trade and productivity, *Quarterly Journal of Economics*, 119: 613–46.

Alonso, W. (1964), *Location and Land Use*, Cambridge, MA: Harvard University Press.

Amin, A., and N. Thrift (2000), What kind of economic theory for what kind of economic geography?, *Antipode*, 32: 4–9.

Amiti, M., and L. Cameron (2007), Economic geography and wages, *Review of Economics and Statistics*, 89: 15–29.

Amiti, M., and B. S. Javorcik (2008), Trade costs and location of foreign firms in China, *Journal of Development Economics*, 85: 129–49.

Amiti, M., and S.-J. Wei (2005), Fear of service outsourcing: is it justified?, *Economic Policy*, 20: 308–47.

Anas, A., R. Arnott, and K. A. Small (1998), Urban spatial structure, *Journal of Economic Literature*, 36: 1426–64.

Anderson, J. E. (1979), A theoretical foundation for the gravity equation, *American Economic Review*, 69: 106–16.

Anderson, J. E., and E. van Wincoop (2003), Gravity with gravitas: a solution to the border puzzle, *American Economic Review*, 93: 170–92.

(2004), Trade costs, *Journal of Economics Literature*, 42: 691–751.

Andersson, F., and R. Forslid (2003), Tax competition and economic geography, *Journal of Public Economic Theory*, 5: 279–303.

Anselin, L. (1988), *Spatial Econometrics: Methods and Models*, Boston: Kluwer Academic.

Armstrong, H., and J. Taylor (2000), *Regional Economics and Policy*, 3rd ed., Oxford: Basil Blackwell.

Arnott, R. (2006), *Handbook of Regional and Urban Economics*, vol. 4: a retrospective, *Journal of Economic Geography*, 6: 100–4.

Baier, S. L., and J. H. Bergstrand (2004), Economic determinants of free trade agreements, *Journal of International Economics*, 64: 29–63.

(2007), Do free trade agreements actually increase members' international trade?, *Journal of International Economics*, 71: 72–95.

Bairoch, P. (1988), *Cities and Economic Development: from the Dawn of History to the Present*, Chicago: University of Chicago Press.

Balassa, B. (1965), Trade liberalization and "revealed" comparative advantage, *Manchester School of Economic and Social Studies* 33: 92–123.

Baldwin, R. E. (1999), *The Core–Periphery Model with Forward-looking Expectations*, Working Paper no. 6921, National Bureau of Economic Research, Cambridge, MA.

(2003), Comment on Crafts and Venables, in M. D. Bordo, A. M. Taylor, and J. G. Williamson (eds.), *Globalization in Historical Perspective*, Chicago: University of Chicago Press, 364–9.

(2006), *Globalisation: The Great Unbundling(s)*, Geneva: Graduate Institute of International Studies.

Baldwin, R. E., and R. Forslid (2000), The core–periphery model and endogenous growth: stabilizing and destabilizing integration, *Economica*, 67: 307–24.

(2002), *Tax Competition and the Nature of Capital*, Discussion Paper no. 3607, Centre for Economic Policy Research, London.

Baldwin, R. E., R. Forslid, P. Martin, G. I. P. Ottaviano, and F. Robert-Nicoud (2003), *Economic Geography and Public Policy*, Princeton, NJ: Princeton University Press.

Baldwin, R. E., and P. R. Krugman (2004), Agglomeration, integration and tax harmonization, *European Economic Review*, 48: 1–23.

Baldwin, R. E., and P. Martin (2004), Agglomeration and regional growth, in V. Henderson and J.-F. Thisse (eds.), *The Handbook of Regional and Urban Economics*, vol. IV, *Cities and Geography*, Amsterdam: North-Holland, 2671–712.

Baldwin, R. E., P. Martin, and G. I. P. Ottaviano (2001), Global income divergence, trade and industrialization: the geography of growth take-offs, *Journal of Economic Growth*, 6: 5–37.

Baldwin, R. E., and T. Okubo (2006), Heterogeneous firms, agglomeration and economic geography: spatial selection and sorting, *Journal of Economic Geography*, 6: 323–46.

Baldwin, R. E., and G. I. P. Ottaviano (2000), Multiproduct multinationals and reciprocal FDI dumping, mimeo, Graduate Institute of International Studies, Geneva.

Baltagi, B. H., P. Egger, and M. Pfaffermayr (2007), Estimating models of complex FDI: are there third-country effects?, *Journal of Econometrics*, 140: 260–81.

Barba Navaretti, G., and A. J. Venables (2004), *Multinational Firms in the World Economy*, Princeton, NJ: Princeton University Press.

Barrell, R., and N. Pain (1999), Domestic institutions, agglomerations and foreign direct investment in Europe, *European Economic Review*, 43: 925–34.

Barro, R., and X. Sala-i-Martin (2004), *Economic Growth*, 2nd ed., Cambridge, MA: MIT Press.

Baumol, W. (1986), Productivity growth, convergence, and welfare, *American Economic Review*, 76: 1072–85.

Beardsell, M., and J. V. Henderson (1999), Spatial evolution of the computer industry in the USA, *European Economic Review*, 43: 431–57.

Becker, R., and J. V. Henderson (2000), Intra-industry specialization and urban development, in J. M. Huriot and J. F. Thisse (eds.), *The Economics of Cities: Theoretical Perspectives*, Cambridge: Cambridge University Press, 138–66.

Behrens, K., C. Ertur, and W. Koch (2007), *'Dual' Gravity: Using Spatial Econometrics to Control for Multilateral Resistance*, Discussion Paper no. 2007/59, Center for Operations Research and Econometrics, Catholic University of Louvain, Belgium.

Behrens, K., A. R. Lamorgese, G. I. P. Ottaviano, T. Tabuchi (2005), *Testing the "Home Market Effect" in a Multi-country World: A Theory-based Approach*, Working Paper no. 561, Economic Research Department, Bank of Italy, Rome.

Behrens, K., and J. F. Thisse (2007), Regional economics: a new economic geography perspective, *Regional Science and Urban Economics*, 37: 457–65.

Bergstrand, J. H. (1985), The gravity equation in international trade: some microeconomic foundations and empirical evidence, *Review of Economics and Statistics*, 67: 474–81.

(1989), The generalized gravity equation, monopolistic competition, and factor-proportions theory in international trade, *Review of Economics and Statistics*, 71: 143–53.

Bernard, A. B., J. Eaton, J. B. Jensen, and S. S. Kostum (2003), Plants and productivity in international trade, *American Economic Review*, 93: 1268–90.

Bernard, A. B., J. B. Jensen, S. J. Redding, and P. Schott (2007), Firms in international trade, *Journal of Economic Perspectives*, 21: 105–30.

Berry, C., and E. L. Glaeser (2005), The divergence of human capital levels across cities, *Papers in Regional Science*, 84: 407–44.

Bhagwati, J. N., A. Panagariya, and T. N. Srinivasan (1998), *Lectures on International Trade*, 2nd ed., Cambridge, MA: MIT Press.

(2004), The muddles over outsourcing, *Journal of Economic Perspectives*, 18: 93–114.

Black, D., and J. V. Henderson (1998), *Urban Evolution in the USA*, Working Paper no. 98-21, Brown University, Providence, RI.

(1999a), Spatial evolution of population and industry in the United States, *American Economic Review, Papers and Proceedings*, 89: 321–7.

(1999b), A theory of urban growth, *Journal of Political Economy*, 107: 252–84.

(2003), Urban evolution in the USA, *Journal of Economic Geography*, 3: 343–72.

Blaug, M. (1984), *Economic Theory in Retrospect*, Cambridge: Cambridge University Press.

Blonigen, B. A., R. B. Davies, G. R. Waddell, and H. T. Naughton (2007), FDI in space: spatial autoregressive relationships in foreign direct investment, *European Economic Review*, 51: 1303–25.

Boschma, R., and K. Frenken (2006), Why is economic geography not an evolutionary science? Towards an evolutionary economic geography, *Journal of Economic Geography*, 6: 273–302.

Boschma, R., and R. Martin (2007), Constructing an evolutionary economic geography, *Journal of Economic Geography*, 7: 537–48.

Bosker, E. M. (2007), Growth, agglomeration and convergence: a space-time analysis for European regions, *Spatial Economic Analysis*, 2: 91–100.

Bosker, E. M., S. Brakman, H. Garretsen, H. de Jong, and M. Schramm (2008), Ports, plagues, and politics: explaining Italian city growth 1300–1861, *European Review of Economic History*, 12: 97–131.

Bosker, E. M., S. Brakman, H. Garretsen, and M. Schramm (2007a), Looking for multiple equilibria when geography matters: German city growth and the WWII shock, *Journal of Urban Economics*, 61: 152–69.

(2007b), *Adding Geography to the New Economic Geography*, Working Paper no. 2038, Center for Economic Studies/ifo Institute for Economic Research, Munich.

(2008), A century of shocks: the evolution of the German city size distribution 1925–1999, *Regional Science and Urban Economics*, 38: 330–47.

Bosker, E. M., E. Buringh, and J. L. van Zanden (2008), *From Baghdad to London: The Dynamics of Urban Growth in Europe and the Arab World, 800–1800*, Discussion Paper no. 6833, Centre for Economic Policy Research, London.

Bosker, E. M., and H. Garretsen (2006), *Economic Development and the Geography of Institutions*, Working Paper no. 1769, Center for Economic Studies/ifo Institute for Economic Research, Munich [forthcoming *Journal of Economic Geography*].

(2007a), *Trade Costs, Market Access and Economic Geography: Why the Empirical Specification of Trade Costs Matters*, Working Paper no. 2071, Center for Economic Studies/ifo Institute for Economic Research, Munich.

(2007b), *Economic Geography and Economic Development in Sub-Saharan Africa*, working paper, Utrecht University.

Brainard, S. L. (1997), An empirical assessment of the proximity – concentration trade-off between multinational sales and trade, *American Economic Review*, 87: 520–44.

Brakman, S., and H. Garretsen (1993), The relevance of initial conditions for the German unification, *Kyklos*, 46: 163–81.

(2008), *Foreign Direct Investment and the Multinational Enterprise*, Cambridge, MA: MIT Press.

Brakman, S., H. Garretsen, R. Gigengack, C. van Marrewijk, and R. Wagenvoort (1996), Negative feedbacks in the economy and industrial location, *Journal of Regional Science*, 36: 631–52.

Brakman, S., H. Garretsen, J. Gorter, A. van der Horst, and M. Schramm (2005), *New Economic Geography, Empirics and Regional Policy*, The Hague: Netherlands Bureau for Economic Policy Analysis.

Brakman, S., H. Garretsen, and M. Schramm (2000), *The empirical relevance of the new economic geography: testing for a spatial wage structure in Germany*, mimeo, University of Nijmegen/University of Groningen.

(2004a), The spatial distribution of wages: estimating the Helpman – Hanson model for Germany, *Journal of Regional Science*, 44: 437–66.

(2004b), The strategic bombing of German cities during WWII and its impact on city growth, *Journal of Economic Geography*, 4: 201–18.

(2006), Putting new economic geography to the test: freeness of trade and agglomeration in the EU regions, *Regional Science and Urban Economics*, 36: 613–36.

Brakman, S., H. Garretsen, and C. van Marrewijk (2001), *An Introduction to Geographical Economics*, Cambridge: Cambridge University Press.

(2007), Agglomeration and aid, in S. Lahiri (ed.), *Theory and Practice of Foreign Aid*, vol. I, Amsterdam: Elsevier, 31–53.

(2008), Agglomeration and government spending, in S. Brakman and H. Garretsen (eds.), *Foreign Direct Investment and the Multinational Enterprise*, Cambridge, MA: MIT Press, 89–116.

Brakman, S., H. Garretsen, C. van Marrewijk, and M. van den Berg (1999), The return of Zipf; towards a further understanding of the rank-size curve, *Journal of Regional Science*, 39: 183–215.

Brakman, S., and B. J. Heijdra (eds.) (2004), *The Monopolistic Competition Revolution in Retrospect*, Cambridge: Cambridge University Press.

Brakman, S., and C. van Marrewijk (1995), Transfers, returns to scale, tied aid and monopolistic competition, *Journal of Development Economics*, 47: 333–54.

(1998), *The Economics of International Transfers*, Cambridge: Cambridge University Press.

(2007), Transfers, non-traded goods, and unemployment: an analysis of the Keynes–Ohlin debate, *History of Political Economy*, 39: 121–43.

(2008), It's a big world after all: on the economic impact of location and distance, *Cambridge Journal of the Regions, Economy and Society*, 1: 411–37.

Breinlich, H. (2006), The spatial income structure in the European Union: what role for economic geography?, *Journal of Economic Geography*, 6: 593–617.

Briant, A., P.-P. Combes, and M. Lafourcade (2007), Does the size and shape of geographical units jeopardize economic geography estimations?, mimeo, University of Aix-Marseille (available at www.vcharite.univ-mrs.fr/pp/combes/).

Brülhart, M. (1998), Economic geography, industry, location and trade: the evidence, *World Economy*, 21: 775–801.

(2001), Evolving geographical concentration of European manufacturing industries, *Welwirtschaftliches Archiv*, 137: 215–43.

Brülhart, M., M. Crozet, and P. Koenig (2004), Enlargement and the EU periphery: the impact of changing market potential, *World Economy*, 27: 853–75.

Brülhart, M., and R. Traeger (2005), An account of geographic concentration patterns in Europe, *Regional Science and Urban Economics*, 35: 597–624.

Brülhart, M., and F. Trionfetti (1999), Home-biased demand and international specialisation: a test of trade theories, mimeo, Centre for Economic Performance, London School of Economics, London.

Bucovetsky, S. (1991), Asymmetric tax competition, *Journal of Urban Economics*, 30: 167–81.

Carroll, G. (1982), National city-size distributions: what do we know after 67 years of research?, *Progress in Human Geography*, 6: 1–43.

Cheshire, P. C., and G. Carbonaro (1995), Convergence–divergence in regional growth rates: an empty black box?, in H. Armstrong and R. Vickerman (eds.), *Convergence and Divergence among European Regions*, London: Pion, 89–111.

Christaller, W. (1933), *Central Places in Southern Germany* (trans. C. W. Baskin), London: Prentice Hall.

Ciccone, A. (2002), Agglomeration effects in Europe, *European Economic Review*, 46: 213–37.

Ciccone, A., and R. E. Hall (1996), Productivity and the density of economic activity, *American Economic Review*, 86: 54–70.

Clark, G. L. (1998), Stylized facts and close dialogue: methodology in economic geography, *Annals of the Association of American Geographers*, 88: 73–87.

Clark, G. L., M. P. Feldman, and M. S. Gertler (eds.) (2000), *The Oxford Handbook of Economic Geography*, Oxford: Oxford University Press.

Coe, D. T., and E. Helpman (1995), International R&D spillovers, *European Economic Review*, 39: 859–87.

Coe, D.T., E. Helpman, and A.W. Hoffmaister (1997), North–South R&D spillovers, *Economic Journal*, 107: 134–49.

Combes, P.-P., G. Duranton, and L. Gobillon (2008), Spatial wage disparities:
sorting matters!, *Journal of Urban Economics* 63: 723–42.

Combes, P.-P., G. Duranton, L. Gobillon, D. Puga, and S. Roux (2008), The
productivity advantages of large markets: distinguishing agglomeration from
firm selection, mimeo, Groupement de Recherche en Economic Quantitative
d'Aix Marseille.

Combes, P.-P., G. Duranton, L. Gobillon, and S. Roux (2007), Estimating
agglomeration effects: does playing with different instruments give a consistent
tune?, mimeo, University of Toronto.

Combes, P.-P., G. Duranton, and H. Overman (2005), Agglomeration and the
adjustment of the spatial economy, *Papers in Regional Science*, 84: 311–49.

Combes, P.-P., T. Mayer, and J.-F. Thisse (2006), *Economic Geography* [in French],
Paris: Economica.

(2008), *Economic Geography*, Princeton, NJ: Princeton University Press.

Combes, P.-P., and H.G. Overman (2004), The spatial distribution of economic
activities in the EU, in J.V. Henderson and J.-F. Thisse (eds.), *The Handbook
of Regional and Urban Economics* vol. IV, *Cities and Geography*, Amsterdam:
North-Holland, 2845–911.

Copus, A.K. (1999), *A New Peripherality Index for the NUTS III Regions of the
European Union*, ERDF Study no. 98/00/27/130, Brussels: European Commission, Directorate General for Regional Policy.

Córdoba, J.-C. (2008), On the distribution of city sizes, *Journal of Urban Economics*,
63: 177–97.

Courant, P.N., and A.V. Deardorff (1992), International trade with lumpy countries, *Journal of Political Economy*, 100: 198–210.

Crafts, N.F.R., and A.J. Venables (2003), Globalization in history: a geographical
perspective, in M.D. Bordo, A.M. Taylor, and J.G. Williamson (eds.), *Globalization in Historical Perspective*, Chicago: University of Chicago Press, 323–64.

Crozet, M. (2004), Do migrants follow market potentials? An estimation of a new
economic geography model, *Journal of Economic Geography*, 4: 439–58.

Crozet, M., and F. Trionfetti (2007), *Trade Costs and the Home Market Effect*,
Working Paper no. 2007–05, CEPII Research Center, Paris.

Currie, M., and I. Kubin (2006), Chaos in the core–periphery model, *Journal of
Economic Behavior and Organization*, 60: 252–75.

David, P. (1985), Clio and the econometrics of QWERTY, *American Economic
Review, Papers and Proceedings*, 75: 332–7.

Davis, D.R. (1995), Intra-industry trade: a Hechscher–Ohlin–Ricardo approach,
Journal of International Economics, 39: 201–26.

(1998), The home market, trade and industrial structure, *American Economic
Review*, 88: 1264–77.

Davis, D.R., and D.E. Weinstein (1996), Does economic geography matter for
international specialization?, mimeo, Harvard University, Cambridge, MA.

(1998) *Market Access, Economic Geography and Comparative Advantage: An
Empirical Assessment*, Discussion Paper no. 1850, Harvard Institute of Economic
Research, Harvard University, Cambridge, MA.

(1999), Economic geography and regional production structure: an empirical
investigation, *European Economic Review*, 43: 379–407.

(2001), An account of global factor trade, *American Economic Review*, 91: 1423–53.

(2002), Bones, bombs and breakpoints: the geography of economic activity, *American Economic Review*, 92: 1269–89.

(2003), Market access, economic geography and comparative advantage: an empirical assessment, *Journal of International Economics*, 59: 1–23.

(2008), A search for multiple equilibria in urban industrial structure, *Journal of Regional Science*, 48: 29–65.

De Vaal, A., and M. van den Berg (1999), Producer services, economic geography and service tradability, *Journal of Regional Science*, 39: 539–72.

Deardorff, A. V. (1998), Determinants of bilateral trade: does gravity work in a neoclassical world?, in J. A. Frankel (ed.), *The Regionalization of the World Economy*, Chicago: University of Chicago Press, 7–32.

DeLong, J. B. (1988), Productivity growth, convergence, and welfare: comment, *American Economic Review*, 78: 1138–54.

Devereux, M., R. Griffith, and A. Klemm (2002), Corporate income tax reforms and international tax competition, *Economic Policy*, 35: 449–96.

Diamond, J. (1997), *Guns, Germs, and Steel: The Fates of Human Societies*, New York: W. W. Norton.

Dicken, P., and P. E. Lloyd (1980), *Location in Space*, New York: Harper & Row.

Disdier, A.-C., and K. Head (2008), The puzzling persistence of the distance effect on bilateral trade, *Review of Economics and Statistics*, 90: 37–41.

Dixit, A. (2004), Some reflections on theories and applications of monopolistic competition, in S. Brakman and B. Heijdra (eds.), *The Monopolistic Competition Revolution in Retrospect*, Cambridge: Cambridge University Press, 123–33.

Dixit, A., and V. Norman (1980), *Theory of International Trade*, Cambridge: Cambridge University Press.

Dixit, A., and J. E. Stiglitz (1977), Monopolistic competition and optimal product diversity, *American Economic Review*, 67: 297–308.

Dobkins, L. H., and Y. M. Ioannides (2000), Dynamic evolution of US city size distributions, in J.-M. Huriot and J.-F. Thisse (eds.), *The Economics of Cities*, Cambridge: Cambridge University Press, 217–60.

(2001), Spatial interactions among US cities, *Regional Science and Urban Economics*, 31: 701–31.

Dumais, G., G. Ellison, and E. L. Glaeser (1997), *Geographic Concentration as a Dynamic Process*, Working Paper no. 6270, National Bureau of Economic Research, Cambridge, MA.

Dunning, J. H. (1977), Trade, location of economic activity and the MNE: a search for an eclectic approach, in B. Ohlin, P. O. Hesselborn, and P. M. Wijkman (eds.), *The International Allocation of Economic Activity*, London: Macmillan, 395–418.

(1981), *International Production and the Multinational Enterprise*, London: Allen & Unwin.

Duranton, G. (2006), Some foundations for Zipf's law: product proliferation and local spillovers, *Regional Science and Urban Economics*, 36: 543–63.

(2007), California dreamin': the feeble case for cluster policies, mimeo, University of Toronto (available at http://individual.utoronto.ca/gilles/research.html).

(2008), Spatial economics, in S. N. Durlauf and L. E. Blume (eds.), *New Palgrave Dictionary of Economics*, (2nd ed.), New York: Palgrave Macmillan, S1–S10.

Duranton, G., and H. G. Overman (2005), Testing or localization using micro-geographic data, *Review of Economic Studies*, 72: 1077–106.

(2008), Exploring the detailed location patterns of UK manufacturing industries using microgeographic data, *Journal of Regional Science*, 48: 213–43.

Duranton, G., and D. Puga (2004), Micro-foundations of urban agglomeration economies, in J. V. Henderson and J.-F. Thisse (eds.), *The Handbook of Regional and Urban Economics* vol. IV *Cities and Geography*, Amsterdam: North-Holland, 2063–118.

Duranton, G., and A. Rodriguez-Posé (2005), When economists and geographers collide, or the tale of the lions and the butterflies, *Environment and Planning, A*, 37: 1695–705.

Duranton, G., and M. Storper (2006), Agglomeration and growth: a dialogue between economists and geographers, *Journal of Economic Geography*, 6: 1–7.

Duro, J. A. (2001), *Regional Income Inequalities in Europe: An Updated Measurement and Some Decomposition Results*, working paper, Institut d'Anàlisi Econòmica, Barcelona.

Dymski, G. (1998), On Paul Krugman's model of economic geography, *Geoforum*, 27: 439–52.

Easterly, W., and R. Levine (1998), Trouble with the neighbours: Africa's problem, Africa's opportunity, *Journal of African Economics*, 7: 120–42.

(2003), Tropics, germs, and crops: how endowments influence economic development, *Journal of Monetary Economics*, 50: 3–40.

Eaton, B. C., and R. G. Lipsey (1982), An economic theory of central places, *Economic Journal*, 92: 56–72.

Eaton, J., and Z. Eckstein (1997), Cities and growth: theory and evidence from France and Japan, *Regional Science and Urban Economics*, 27: 443–74.

Eaton, J., and S. Kortum (1996), Trade in ideas patenting and productivity in the OECD, *Journal of International Economics*, 40: 251–78.

Eeckhout, J. (2004), Gibrat's law for all cities, *American Economic Review*, 94: 1429–51.

Ekholm, K., and R. Forslid (2001), Trade and location with horizontal and vertical multi-region firms, *Scandinavian Journal of Economics*, 103: 101–18.

Ekholm, K., R. Forslid, and J. R. Markusen (2007), Export-platform foreign direct investment, *Journal of the European Economic Association*, 5: 776–95.

Ellison, G., and E. L. Glaeser (1997), Geographic concentration in US manufacturing industries: a dartboard approach, *Journal of Political Economy*, 105: 889–927.

(1999), The geographic concentration of industry: does natural advantage explain agglomeration?, *American Economic Review, Papers and Proceedings*, 89: 311–16.

Engel, C., and J. H. Rogers (1996), How wide is the border?, *American Economic Review*, 86: 1112–25.

Ethier, W. J., and H. Horn (1984), A new look at economic integration, in H. Kierzkowski (ed.), *Monopolistic Competition and International Trade*, Oxford: Clarendon Press, 207–29.

Feenstra, R. C. (2004), *Advanced International Trade: Theory and Evidence*, Princeton, NJ: Princeton University Press.

Fingleton, B. (2004), Some alternative geo-economics for Europe's regions, *Journal of Economic Geography*, 4: 389–420.

(2005), Beyond neoclassical orthodoxy: a view based on the new economic geography and UK regional wage data, *Papers in Regional Science*, 84: 351–75.

(2006), The new economic geography versus urban economics: an evaluation using local wage rates in Great Britain, *Oxford Economic Papers*, 58: 501–30.

Florida, R. (2002), *The Rise of the Creative Class ... and How It's Transforming Work, Leisure, Community, and Everyday Life*, New York: Basic Books.

(2004), Reaction to Glaeser's review of *The Rise of the Creative Class*, see www.creativeclass.com.

(2006), *The Flight of the Creative Class*, New York: Basic Books.

Forslid, R., J. I. Haaland, and K. H. Midelfart Knarvik (2002), A U-shaped Europe? A simulation study of industrial location, *Journal of International Economics*, 57: 273–97.

Forslid, R., and G. I. P. Ottaviano (2003), An analytically solvable core–periphery model, *Journal of Economic Geography*, 3: 229–40.

Fowler, C. S. (2007), Taking geographical economics out of equilibrium: implications for theory and policy, *Journal of Economic Geography*, 7: 265–84.

Frankel, J. A., and D. Romer (1999), Does trade cause growth?, *American Economic Review*, 89: 379–99.

Frenken, K., and R. A. Boschma (2007), A theoretical framework for evolutionary economic geography: industrial dynamics and urban growth as a branching process, *Journal of Economic Geography*, 7: 635–49.

Friedman, T. (2005), *The World Is Flat*, London: Allen Lane.

Fujita, M. (1989), *Urban Economic Theory: Land Use and City Size*, Cambridge: Cambridge University Press.

Fujita, M., P. R. Krugman, and T. Mori (1999), On the evolution of hierarchial urban systems, *European Economic Review*, 43: 209–53.

Fujita, M., P. R. Krugman, and A. J. Venables (1999), *The Spatial Economy; Cities, Regions, and International Trade*, Cambridge, MA: MIT Press.

Fujita, M., and T. Mori (1996), The role of ports in the making of major cities: self-agglomeration and the hub effect, *Journal of Development Economics*, 49: 93–120.

(2005), Frontiers of the new economic geography, *Papers in Regional Science*, 84: 377–407.

Fujita, M., T. Mori, J. V. Henderson, and Y. Kanemoto (2004), Spatial distribution of economic activities in Japan and China, in J. V. Henderson and J.-F. Thisse (eds.), *The Handbook of Regional and Urban Economics*, vol. IV, *Cities and Geography*, Amsterdam: North-Holland, 2911–80.

Fujita, M., and J.-F. Thisse (1996), Economics of Agglomeration, *Journal of the Japanese and International Economies*, 10: 339–78.

(2000), The formation of economic agglomerations: old problems and new perspectives, in J.-M. Huriot and J.-F. Thisse (eds.), *Economics of Cities: Theoretical Perspectives*, Cambridge: Cambridge University Press, 3–73 [extended version of Fujita and Thisse, 1996].

(2002), *Economics of Agglomeration: Cities, Regions, and International Trade*, Cambridge, MA: MIT Press.

Gabaix, X. (1999a), Zipf's law and the growth of cities, *American Economic Review, Papers and Proceedings*, 89: 129–32.

(1999b), Zipf's Law for cities: an explanation, *Quarterly Journal of Economics*, 114: 739–66.

Gabaix, X., and R. Ibragimov (2007), *Rank-1/2: A Simple Way to Improve the OLS Estimation of Tail Exponents*, Technical Working Paper no. 342, National Bureau of Economic Research, Cambridge, MA.

Gabaix, X., and Y. M. Ioannides (2004), The evolution of city size distributions, in J. V. Henderson and J.-F. Thisse (eds.), *The Handbook of Urban and Regional Economics*, vol. IV, *Cities and Geography*, Amsterdam: North-Holland, 2341–80.

Gallup, J. L., J. D. Sachs, and A. D. Mellinger (1998), *Geography and Economic Development*, Working Paper no. 6849, National Bureau of Economic Research, Cambridge, MA.

Gao, T. (1999), Economic geography and the department of vertical multinational production, *Journal of International Economics*, 48: 301–20.

Garretsen, H., and J. Peeters (2007), Capital mobility, agglomeration and corporate tax rates: is the race to the bottom for real?, *CESifo Economic Studies*, 53: 263–94.

(2008), *FDI and the Relevance of Spatial Linkages: Do Third-country Effects Matter for Dutch FDI?*, *CESifo*, Working Paper, no. 2191, Center for Economic Studies/ifo Insitute for Economic Research, Munich [forthcoming *Review of World Economics*].

Glaeser, E. L. (2000), The new economics of urban and regional growth, in G. L. Clark, M. P. Feldman, and M. S. Gertler (eds.), *The Oxford Handbook of Economic Geography*, Oxford: Oxford University Press, 83–99.

(2004), Book review of Richard Florida's "The Rise of the Creative Class," mimeo, Harvard University, Cambridge, MA (available at www.economics.harvard.edu/faculty/glaeser/files/Review_Florida.pdf).

(2005), Reinventing Boston 1630–2003, *Journal of Economic Geography*, 5: 119–53.

(2007), The economic approach to cities, mimeo, Department of Economics, Harvard University, Cambridge, MA.

Glaeser, E. L., H. D. Kallal, J. Scheinkman, and A. Schleifer (1992), Growth in cities, *Journal of Political Economy*, 100: 1126–52.

Glaeser, E. L., and J. E. Kohlhase (2004), Cities, regions and the decline of transport costs, *Papers in Regional Science*, 83: 197–228.

Glaeser, E. L., J. Kolko, and A. Saiz (2001), Consumer city, *Journal of Economic Geography*, 1: 27–50.

Glaeser, E. L., R. La Porta, F. Lopez-de-Silanes, and A. Shleifer (2004), Do institutions cause growth?, *Journal of Economic Growth*, 9: 271–303.

Glaeser, E. L., and J. M. Shapiro (2002), Cities and warfare, *Journal of Urban Economics*, 51: 205–24.

Gorter, J. (2002), The economic geography of Europe, *CPB Report*, 2002/4: 22–8.

Gourevitch, P., R. Bohn, and D. McKendrick (2000), Globalization of production: insights from the hard disk drive industry, *World Development*, 28: 301–17.

Grossman, G. M., and E. Helpman (1991), *Innovation and Growth in the Global Economy*, Cambridge, MA: MIT Press.

Haaland, J. I., H. J. Kind, K. H. Midelfart Knarvik, and J. Torstensson (1999), *What Determines the Economic Geography of Europe?*, Discussion Paper no. 2072, Centre for Economic Policy Research, London.

Hall, R., and C. I. Jones (1999), Why do some countries produce so much more output per worker than others?, *Quarterly Journal of Economics*, 114: 83–116.

Hallet, M. (2000), *Regional Specialisation and Concentration in the EU*, Economic Paper no. 141, European Commission, Brussels.

Hanoch, G. (1975), The elasticity of scale and the shapes of average costs, *American Economic Review*, 65: 492–7.

Hanson, G. H. (1996), Economic integration, intra-industry trade, and frontier regions, *European Economic Review*, 40: 941–9.

(1997), Increasing returns, trade and the regional structure of wages, *Economic Journal*, 107: 113–33.

(2000), *Scale Economies and the Geographic Concentration of Industry*, Working Paper no. 8013, National Bureau of Economic Research, Cambridge MA.

(2005), Market potential, increasing returns, and geographic concentration, *Journal of International Economics*, 67: 1–24.

Harrigan, J. (1994), Scale economies and the volume of trade, *Review of Economics and Statistics*, 76: 321–8.

(1995), Factor endowments and the international location of production, *Journal of International Economics*, 39: 123–41.

Harris, C. (1954), The market as a factor in the localization of industry in the United States, *Annals of the Association of American Geographers*, 64: 315–48.

Harris, T. F., and Y. M. Ioannides (2000), *History versus Expectations: An Empirical Investigation*, Discussion Paper no. 2000–14, Department of Economics, Tufts University, Medford, MA.

Head, K., and T. Mayer (2004a), The empirics of agglomeration and trade, in J. V. Henderson and J.-F. Thisse (eds.), *The Handbook of Regional and Urban Economics*, vol. IV, *Cities and Geography*, Amsterdam: North Holland, 2609–65.

(2004b), Market potential and the location of Japanese investment in the European Union, *Review of Economics and Statistics*, 86: 959–72.

(2006), Regional wage and employment responses to market potential in the EU, *Regional Science and Urban Economics*, 36: 573–94.

Head, K., and J. Ries (2001), Increasing returns versus national product differentiation as an explanation for the pattern of US–Canada trade, *American Economic Review*, 91: 858–76.

Head, K., J. Ries, and D. Swenson (1995), Agglomeration benefits and location choice: evidence from Japanese manufacturing investments in the United States, *Journal of International Economics*, 38: 223–47.

Helpman, E. (1984a), A simple theory of international trade with multinational corporations, *Journal of Political Economy*, 92: 451–71.

(1984b), Increasing returns, imperfect markets and trade theory, in R. W. Jones and P. B. Kenen (eds.), *Handbook of International Economics*, vol. I, Amsterdam: North-Holland, 325–65.

(1998), The size of regions, in D. Pines, E. Sadka, and I. Zilcha (eds.), *Topics in Public Economics*, Cambridge: Cambridge University Press, 33–54.

(2004), *The Mystery of Economic Growth*, Cambridge, MA: Belknap Press.

(2006), Trade, FDI and the organization of firms, *Journal of Economic Literature*, 44: 589–630.

Helpman, E., and P. R. Krugman (1985), *Market Structure and Foreign Trade*, Cambridge, MA: MIT Press.

Helpman, E., M. J. Melitz, and Y. Rubinstein (2007), *Estimating Trade Flows: Trading Partners and Trading Volumes*, Working Paper no. 12927, National Bureau of Economic Research, Cambridge MA.

Helpman, E., M. J. Melitz, and S. Yeaple (2004), Exports versus FDI with heterogeneous firms, *American Economic Review*, 94: 300–16.

Henderson, J. V. (1974), The sizes and types of cities, *American Economic Review*,
64: 640–56.

   (1977), *Economic Theory and the Cities*, New York: Academic Press.

   (1988), *Urban Development: Theory, Fact and Illusion*, Oxford: Oxford University
Press.

   (2000), The monopolistic competition model in urban economic geography,
paper presented at the seminar "The Monopolistic Competition Revolution
after 25 Years," University of Groningen, October 30.

   (2003), The urbanization process and economic growth: the so-what question,
Journal of Economic Growth, 8: 47–71.

Henderson, J. V., A. Kuncoro, and M. Turner (1995), Industrial development in
cities, *Journal of Political Economy*, 103: 1067–85.

Henderson, J. V., Z. Shalizi, and A. J. Venables (2000), Geography and development,
mimeo, London School of Economics.

   (2001), Geography and development, *Journal of Economic Geography*, 1: 81–105.

Henderson, J. V., and J.-F. Thisse (2004), *The Handbook of Regional and Urban
Economics*, vol. IV, *Cities and Geography*, Amsterdam: North-Holland.

Herfindahl, O. C. (1950), *Concentration in the steel industry*, unpublished PhD.
dissertation, Columbia University, NY.

Hering, S., and L. Poncet (2006), *Market Access Impact on Individual Wages: Evidence from China*, Working Paper no. 2006–23, Centre d'Etudes Prospectives
et d'Informations Internationales, Paris [forthcoming *Review of Economics and
Statistics*].

   (2007), Economic geography, spatial dependence and income inequality in
China, mimeo, University of Paris I.

Hill, B. M. (1975), A simple approach to inference about the tail of a distribution,
Annals of Statistics, 3: 1163–74.

Hinloopen, J., and C. van Marrewijk (2005), Locating economic concentration, in
S. Brakman and H. Garretsen (eds.), *Location and Competition*, London:
Routledge, 1–31.

   (2006), *Comparative Advantage, the Rank-size Rule, and Zipf's Law*, Discussion
Paper no. 06-100/1, Tinbergen Institute, Amsterdam.

Hirschman, A. (1958), *Strategy of Economic Development*, New Haven, CT: Yale
University Press.

Holmes, T. J. (1999), Scale of local production and city size, *American Economic
Review, Papers and Proceedings*, 89: 317–20.

Holmes, T. J., and J. J. Stevens (2004), Spatial distribution of economic activities in
North America, in J. V. Henderson and J.-F. Thisse (eds.), *The Handbook of
Regional and Urban Economics*, vol. IV, *Cities and Geography*, Amsterdam:
North-Holland, 2797–844.

Hoover, E. M. (1948), *The Location of Economic Activity*, New York: McGraw.

Horstman, I. J., and J. R. Markusen (1986), Up the average cost curve: inefficient
entry and the new protectionism, *Journal of International Economics*, 20:
225–48.

Huizinga, H., and G. Nicodème (2003), *Foreign Ownership and Corporate Income
Taxation: An Empirical Evaluation*, Discussion Paper no. 3952, Centre for
Economic Policy Research, London.

Hummels, D. (1999a), Towards a geography of trade costs, mimeo, University of Chicago.

(1999b), Have international transportation costs declined?, mimeo, University of Chicago.

Huriot, J.-M., and J.-F. Thisse (2000), *The Economics of Cities: Theoretical Perspectives*, Cambridge: Cambridge University Press.

IMF (2003), *World Economic Outlook, April 2003: Growth and Institutions*, Washington, DC: International Monetary Fund.

Inui, T., T. Matsuura, and S. Poncet (2007), The location of Japanese MNCs affiliates: agglomeration, spillovers and firm heterogeneity, mimeo, Paris University 1.

Isard, W. (1956), *Location and Space Economy*, Cambridge, MA: MIT Press.

(1960), *Methods of Regional Analysis*, Cambridge MA: MIT Press.

Jacobs, J. (1969), *The Economy of Cities*, New York: Vintage.

Kaldor, N. (1940), A model of the trade cycle, *Economic Journal*, 50: 78–92.

Kaufman, D., A. Kraay, and M. Mastruzi (2005), *Governance Matters V: Governance Indicators for 1996–2005*, Washington, DC: World Bank.

Kenen, P. B. (1965), Nature, capital, and trade, *Journal of Political Economy*, 73: 437–60.

Kind, H., K. H. Midelfart Knarvik, and G. Schjelderup (2000), Competing for capital in a "lumpy" world, *Journal of Public Economics*, 78: 253–74.

Knaap, T., (2006), Trade, location, and wages in the United States, *Regional Science and Urban Economics*, 36: 595–612.

Kooij, P. (1988), Peripheral cities and their regions in the Dutch urban system until 1900, *Journal of Economic History*, 48: 357–71.

Koopmans, T. C. (1957), *Three Essays on the State of Economic Science*, New York: McGraw-Hill.

Kratz, M., and S. I. Resnick (1996), The QQ-estimator and heavy tails, *Communications in Statistics: Stochastic Models*, 12: 699–724.

Krogstrup, S. (2004), *Are Corporate Tax Burdens Racing to the Bottom in the European Union?* Working Paper no. 04-04, Economic Policy Research Unit University of 'Copenhagen.

Krugman, P. R. (1979), Increasing returns, monopolistic competition, and international trade, *Journal of International Economics*, 9: 469–79.

(1980), Scale economies, product differentiation, and the pattern of trade, *American Economic Review*, 70: 950–9.

(1991a), Increasing returns and economic geography, *Journal of Political Economy*, 99: 483–99.

(1991b), *Geography and Trade*, Cambridge, MA: MIT Press.

(1991c), History versus expectations, *Quarterly Journal of Economics*, 106: 651–67.

(1993a), Lessons from Massachusetts for EMU, in F. Torres and F. Giavazzi (eds.), *Adjustment and Growth in the European Monetary Union*, Cambridge: Cambridge University Press 241–69.

(1993b), On the number and location of cities, *European Economic Review*, 37: 293–8.

(1995a), *Development, Geography and Economic Theory*, Cambridge, MA: MIT Press.

(1995b), Increasing returns, imperfect competition and the positive theory of international trade, in G. M. Grossman and K. Rogoff (eds.), *Handbook of International Economics*, vol. III, Amsterdam: Elsevier, 1243–77.

(1996a), *The Self-organizing Economy*, Oxford: Basil Blackwell.

(1996b), Confronting the mystery of urban hierarchy, *Journal of the Japanese and International Economies*, 10: 399–418.

(1998), Space: the final frontier, *Journal of Economic Perspectives*, 12: 161–74.

(1999), Was it all in Ohlin?, mimeo, Massachusetts Institute of Technology, Cambridge, MA (available at http://web.mit.edu/krugman/www.ohlin.html).

(2000), Where in the world is the new economic geography?, in G. L. Clark, M. Feldman, and M. Gertler (eds.), *The Oxford Handbook of Economic Geography*, Oxford: Oxford University Press, 49–60.

Krugman, P. R., and R. Livas Elizondo (1996), Trade policy and Third World metropolis, *Journal of Development Economics*, 49: 137–50.

Krugman, P. R., and M. Obstfeld (1994), *International Economics: Theory and Policy*, 3rd ed., Glasgow: HarperCollins.

(2000), *International Economics: Theory and Policy*, 5th edn., Upper Saddle River, NJ: Addison-Wesley.

Krugman, P. R., and A. J. Venables (1990), Integration and the competitiveness of peripheral industry, in C. Bliss and J. Braga de Macedo (eds.), *Unity with Diversity in the European Economy*, Cambridge: Cambridge University Press, 56–75.

(1995), Globalization and the inequality of nations, *Quarterly Journal of Economics*, 110: 857–80.

Launhardt, W. (1885), *Mathematische Begründung der Volkswirtschaftslehre*, Leipzig: Teubner.

Leamer, E. E. (2007), A flat world, a level playing field, a small world after all, or none of the above: a review of Thomas L. Friedman's *The World Is Flat*, *Journal of Economic Literature*, 45: 83–126.

Leamer, E. E., and J. Levinsohn (1995), International trade theory: the evidence, in G. M. Grossman and K. Rogoff (eds.), *Handbook of International Economics*, vol. III, Amsterdam: North-Holland, 269–87.

Leamer, E. E., and M. Storper (2001), *The Geography of the Internet Age*, Working Paper no. 8450, National Bureau of Economic Research, Cambridge, MA.

Leontief, W. (1936), A note on the pure theory of transfers, in *Explorations in Economics: Notes and Essays Contributed in Honor of F. W. Taussig*, New York: McGraw-Hill, 84–92.

Limao, N., and A. J. Venables (2000), Infrastructure, geographical disadvantage and transport costs, mimeo, World Bank, Washington, DC.

Linnemann, H. (1966), *An Econometric Study of International Trade Flows*, Amsterdam: North-Holland.

Lösch, A. (1940), *The Economics of Location* (trans. W. H. Woglom and W. F. Stolper), New Haven, CT: Yale University Press.

Lucas, R. E. (1988), On the mechanisms of economic development, *Journal of Monetary Economics*, 22: 3–42.

(2006), *Handbook of Regional and Urban Economics*, vol. 4: theory and observation, *Journal of Economic Geography*, 6: 110–12.

Ludema, R., and I. Wooton (2000), Economic geography and the fiscal effects of regional integration, *Journal of International Economics*, 52: 331–57.

Maddison, A. (2003), *The World Economy: Historical Statistics*, Paris: Organisation for Economic Co-operation and Development.

(2007), *Contours of the World Economy 1–2030 AD: Essays in Macroeconomic History*, Oxford: Oxford University Press.

Magrini, S. (2004), Spatial distribution of economic activities in North America, in J. V. Henderson and J.-F. Thisse (eds.), *The Handbook of Regional and Urban Economics*, vol. IV, *Cities and Geography*, Amsterdam: North-Holland, 2741–96.

Malanima, P. (1998), Italian cities 1300–1800: a quantitative approach, *Rivista di Storia Economica*, 14: 91–126.

(2005), Urbanisation and the Italian economy during the last millennium, *European Review of Economic History*, 9: 97–122.

Marchioni, C. (2004), Geographical economics versus economic geography: towards a clarification of the dispute, *Environment and Planning, A*, 36: 1737–53.

Markusen, A. (2003), Fuzzy concepts, scanty evidence, policy distance: the case for rigour and policy relevance in critical regional studies, *Regional Studies*, 37: 701–19.

Markusen, J. R. (2002), *Multinational Firms and the Theory of International Trade*, Cambridge, MA: MIT Press.

Markusen, J. R., and K. E. Maskus (1999), *Multinational Firms: Reconciling Theory and Evidence*, Working Paper no. 7163, National Bureau of Economic Research, Cambridge, MA.

Markusen, J. R., and A. J. Venables (1998), Multinational firms and the new trade theory, *Journal of International Economics*, 46: 183–203.

(2007), Interacting factor endowments and trade costs; a multi-country, multi-good approach to trade theory, *Journal of International Economics*, 73: 333–54.

Marlet, G. A., and C. M. van Woerkens (2007), The Dutch creative class and how it fosters urban employment growth, *Urban Studies*, 44: 2605–26.

Martin, P., and G. I. P. Ottaviano (1999), Growing locations in a model of endogenous growth, *European Economic Review*, 43: 281–302.

Martin, R. (1999), The new "geographical turn" in economics: some critical reflections, *Cambridge Journal of Economics*, 23: 65–91.

(2001), EMU versus the regions? Regional convergence and divergence in Euroland, *Journal of Economic Geography*, 1: 51–80.

(2008), The "New Economic Geography": credible models of the economic landscape?, in R. Lee, A. Leyshon, L. McDowell and P. Sunley (eds.), *A Compendium of Economic Geography*, London: Sage.

Martin, R., and P. Sunley (1996), Paul Krugman's geographical economics and its implications for regional development theory: a critical assessment, *Economic Geography*, 72: 259–92.

(2001), Rethinking the "economic" in economic geography: broadening our vision or losing our focus?, *Antipode*, 33: 148–61.

(2003), Deconstructing clusters: chaotic concept or policy panacea, *Journal of Economic Geography*, 3: 5–35.

(2006), Path dependence and regional economic evolution, *Journal of Economic Geography*, 6: 395–437.

McCallum, J. (1995), National borders matter: Canada–US regional trade patterns, *American Economic Review*, 85: 615–23.

McCann, P. (2002), *Urban and Regional Economics*, Oxford: Oxford University Press.

Melitz, M. J. (2003), The impact of trade on intra-industry reallocation and aggregate industry productivity, *Econometrica*, 71: 1695–725.

Melitz, M. J., and G. I. P. Ottaviano (2005), *Market Size, Trade and Productivity*, Working Paper no. 11393, National Bureau of Economic Research, Cambridge, MA.

Mellinger, A. D., J. D. Sachs, and J. L. Gallup (2000), Climate, coastal proximity and development, in G. L. Clark, M. P. Feldman, and M. S. Gertler (eds.), *The Oxford Handbook of Economic Geography*, Oxford: Oxford University Press, 169–94.

Midelfart Knarvik, K. H., H. G. Overman, S. J. Redding, and A. J. Venables (2000), *The Location of European Industry*, Economic Paper no. 142, European Commission, Brussels.

(2002), Integration and industrial specialisation in the European Union, *Revue Economiques*, 53: 469–81.

(2003), The location of European industry, in A. Dierx, F. Ilzkovitz, and K. Sekkat (eds.), *European Integration and the Functioning of Product Markets*, Cheltenham: Edward Elgar, Chap. 5.

Midelfart Knarvik, K. H., H. G Overman, and A. J. Venables (2001), Comparative advantage and economic geography: estimating the determinants of industrial location in the EU, mimeo, London School of Economics/University of Oxford.

(2003), Monetary union and the economic geography of Europe, *Journal of Common Market Studies*, 41: 847–68.

Miguel, E., and G. Roland (2005), The long run impact of bombing Vietnam, mimeo, University of California, Berkeley (available at http://elsa.berkeley.edu/~emiguel/research2.shtml).

Milanovic, B. (2006a), Economic integration and income convergence: not such a strong link?, *Review of Economics and Statistics*, 88: 659–70.

(2006b), *Global Income Inequality: What It Is and Why It Matters*, Policy Research Working Paper no. 3865, World Bank, Washington, DC.

Mills, E. S. (1967), An aggregate model of resource allocation in a metropolitan area, *American Economic Review*, 57: 197–210.

Ministry of Economic Affairs (1999), *Location Patterns of Leading Companies in North-west Europe*, The Hague: Ministry of Economic Affairs.

Mion, G. (2004), Spatial externalities and empirical analysis: the case of Italy, *Journal of Urban Economics*, 56: 97–118.

Moretti, E. (2004), Human capital externalities in cities, in J. V. Henderson and J. -F. Thisse (eds.), *The Handbook of Regional and Urban Economics*, vol. IV, *Cities and Geography*, Amsterdam: North-Holland, 2243–92.

Mulligan, G. F. (1984), Agglomeration and central place theory: a review of the literature, *International Regional Science Review*, 9: 1–42.

Mundell, R. A. (1957), International trade and factor mobility, *American Economic Review*, 47: 321–35.

Murdoch, J. C., and T. Sandler (2002), Economic growth, civil wars and spatial spillovers, *Journal of Conflict Resolution*, 46: 91–110.

Murphy, K. M., A. Shleifer, and R. W. Vishny (1989), Industrialization and the big push, *Journal of Political Economy*, 97: 1003–26.

Muth, R. (1969), *Cities and Housing*, Chicago: University of Chicago Press.

Myrdal, G. (1957), *Economic Theory and Underdeveloped Regions*, London: Duckworth.

Neary, J. P. (2001), Of hype and hyperbolas: introducing the new economic geography, *Journal of Economic Literature*, 39: 536–61.

(2004), Monopolistic competition and international trade theory, in S. Brakman and B. J. Heijdra (eds.), *The Monopolistic Competition Revolution in Retrospect*, Cambridge: Cambridge University Press, 159–84.

(2006), Review of *Economic Geography and Public Policy*, *Journal of International Economics*, 70: 503–7.

(2007), Cross-border mergers as instruments of comparative advantage, *Review of Economic Studies*, 74: 1229–57.

(2008), Trade costs and foreign direct investment, in S. Brakman and H. Garretsen (eds.), *Foreign Direct Investment and the Multinational Enterprise*, Cambridge, MA: MIT Press, 13–38.

Neven, D., and C. Gouyette (1995), Regional convergence in the European community, *Journal of Common Market Studies*, 33: 47–65.

Nijkamp, P. (2000), Review of *The Spatial Economy: Cities, Regions and International Trade*, *Economic Journal*, 111: F166.

Nijkamp, P., and E. S. Mills (eds.) (1986), *The Handbook of Regional and Urban Economics*, vol. I, *Regional Economics*, Amsterdam: North-Holland.

Nitsch, V. (2003), Does history matter for urban primacy? The case of Vienna, *Regional Science and Urban Economics*, 33: 401–18.

(2005), Zipf zipped, *Journal of Urban Economics*, 57: 86–100.

Nunn, N., and D. Puga (2007), *Ruggedness: The Blessing of Bad Geography in Africa*, Discussion Paper no. 6253, Centre for Economic Policy Research, London.

Obstfeld, M., and K. Rogoff (1996), *Foundations of International Macroeconomics*, Cambridge, MA: MIT Press.

OECD (2003), *Trends in International Migration*, Paris: Organisation for Economic Co-operation and Development.

Ohlin, B. (1933), *Interregional and International Trade*, Cambridge, MA: Harvard University Press.

O'Rourke, K., and J. Williamson (1999), *Globalization and History*, Cambridge, MA: MIT Press.

Ottaviano, G. I. P. (2003), Regional policy in the global economy: insights from the New Economic Geography, *Regional Studies*, 37: 665–73.

(2007), Models of "new economic geography": factor mobility vs. vertical linkages, in B. Fingleton (ed.), *New Directions in Economic Geography*, Cheltenham: Edward Elgar, 53–69.

Ottaviano, G. I. P., and D. Puga (1997), *Agglomeration in the Global Economy: A Survey of the "New Economic Geography,"* Discussion Paper no. 356, Centre for Economic Policy Research, London.

Ottaviano, G. I. P., and F. Robert-Nicoud (2006), The "genome" of NEG models with vertical linkages: a positive and normative synthesis, *Journal of Economic Geography*, 6: 113–39.

Ottaviano, G. I.P., T. Tabuchi, and J.-F. Thisse (2002), Agglomeration and trade revisited, *International Economic Review*, 43: 409–35.

Ottaviano, G. I. P., and J.-F. Thisse (2004), Agglomeration and economic geography, in J. V. Henderson and J.-F. Thisse (eds.), *The Handbook of Regional and Urban Economics*, vol. IV, *Cities and Geography*, Amsterdam: North-Holland, 2563–608.

Overman, H. G. (2004), Can we learn anything from economic geography proper?, *Journal of Economic Geography*, 4: 501–16.

Overman, H. G., S. J. Redding, and A. J. Venables (2003), The economic geography of trade, production and income: a survey of the empirics, in J. Harrigan and K. Choi (eds.), *Handbook of International Trade*, London: Blackwell, 353–87.

Parr, J. B. (1985), A note on the size distribution of cities over time, *Journal of Urban Economics*, 18: 199–212.

Peck, J. (2000), Doing regulation, in G. L. Clark, M. P. Feldman, and M. S. Gertler (eds.), *The Oxford Handbook of Economic Geography*, Oxford: Oxford University Press, 61–83.

Peeters, J. J. W., and H. Garretsen (2004), Globalisation, wages and unemployment: an economic geography perspective, in S. Brakman and B. Heijdra (eds.), *The Monopolistic Competition Revolution in Retrospect*, Cambridge: Cambridge University Press, 236–61.

Perroux, F. (1955), Note sur la notion de pole de croissance, *Economique Appliquée*, 7: 307–20.

Pflüger, M. (2004), A simple, analytically solvable, Chamberlinian agglomeration model, *Regional Science and Urban Economics*, 34: 565–73.

Pflüger, M., and J. Südekum (2007), *On Pitchforks and Tomahawks*, Discussion Paper no. 3258, Institute for the Study of Labor, Bonn.

(2008), A synthesis of footloose-entrepreneur new economic geography models: when is agglomeration smooth and easily reversible?, *Journal of Economic Geography*, 8: 39–54.

Poelhekke, S. (2007), *The Effect of Skills on Employment Growth: Adjusting Bias and Weak IVs with New Evidence from German Metropolitan Areas*, working paper, European University Institute, Florence.

Pollins, B. M. (1989), Conflict, cooperation, and commerce: the effects of international political interactions on bilateral trade flows, *American Journal of Political Science*, 33: 737–61.

Porter, M. E. (1985), *Competitive Advantage: Creating and Sustaining Superior Performance*, New York: Free Press.

(1990), *The Competitive Advantage of Nations*, New York: Free Press.

(1998), Clusters and the new economics of competition, *Harvard Business Review*, 76: 77–90.

Pred, A. (1966), *The Spatial Dynamics of US Urban-Industrial Growth*, Cambridge, MA: MIT Press.

Puga, D. (1998), Urbanization patterns: European versus less developed countries, *Journal of Regional Science*, 38: 231–52.

(1999), The rise and fall of regional inequalities, *European Economic Review*, 43: 303–34.

(2002), European regional policy in light of recent location theories, *Journal of Economic Geography*, 2: 372–406.

Puga, D., and A. J. Venables (1996), The spread of industry: spatial agglomeration in economic development, *Journal of the Japanese and International Economies*, 10: 440–64.

Radelet, S., and J. Sachs (1998), Shipping costs, manufactured exports, and economic growth, mimeo, Harvard University, Cambridge, MA.

Rajan, R. G., and L. Zingales (2006), *The Persistence of Underdevelopment: Institutions, Human Capital or Constituencies*, Working Paper no. 12093, National Bureau of Economic Research, Cambridge, MA.

Redding, S. J., and D. M. Sturm (2005), *Costs of Remoteness: Evidence from German Division and Reunification*, Discussion Paper no. 5015, Centre for Economic Policy Research, London. Forthcoming, *American Economic Review*.

Redding, S. J., D. M. Sturm, and N. Wolf (2007), *History and Industry Location: Evidence from German Airports*, Discussion Paper no. 6345, Centre for Economic Policy Research, London.

Redding, S. J., and A. J. Venables (2004), Economic geography and international inequality, *Journal of International Economics*, 62: 53–82.

Ricci, L. A. (1997), A Ricardian model of new trade and location theory, *Journal of Economic Integration*, 12: 47–61.

(1999), Economic geography and comparative advantage: agglomeration versus specialization, *European Economic Review*, 43: 357–77.

Rivera-Batiz, L., and P. Romer (1991), Economic integration and endogenous growth, *Quarterly Journal of Economics*, 106: 531–55.

Robert-Nicoud, F. (2005), The structure of simple new economic geography models (or, on identical twins), *Journal of Economic Geography*, 5: 201–34.

Rodrik, D. (ed.) (2003), *In Search of Prosperity: Analytic Narratives on Economic Growth*, Princeton, NJ: Princeton University Press.

Rodrik, D., A. Subramanian, and F. Trebbi (2004), Institutions rule: the primacy of institutions and integration in economic development. *Journal of Economic Growth*, 9: 131–65.

Romer, P. M. (1986), Increasing returns and long-run growth, *Journal of Political Economy*, 94: 1002–37.

(1990), Endogenous technological change, *Journal of Political Economy*, 98, part 2: S71–S101.

Rosen, K. T., and M. Resnick (1980), The size distribution of cities: an examination of the Pareto law and privacy, *Journal of Urban Economics*, 8: 165–86.

Rosenstein-Rodan, P. (1943), Problems of industrialization in eastern and south-eastern europe, *Economic Journal*, 53: 202–11.

Rosenthal, S. S., and W.C. Strange (2004), Evidence on the nature and sources of agglomeration economies, in J. V. Henderson and J.-F. Thisse (eds.), *The Handbook of Regional and Urban Economics*, vol. IV, *Cities and Geography*, Amsterdam: North-Holland, 2119–72.

Rossi-Hansberg, E., and M. L. J. Wright (2007), Urban structure and economic growth, *Review of Economic Studies*, 74: 597–624.

Rothfels, J., and A. Wölfl (1998), Determinanten der Produktivitätslücke in Ostdeutschland: Ergebnisse einer Tagung am IWH, *Wirtschaft im Wandel*, 1/1998: 3–11.

Rumley, D., and J. V. Minghi (1991), *The Geography of Border Landscapes*, London: Routledge.

Sachs, J. D. (2003), *Institutions Don't Rule: Direct Effects of Geography on Per Capita Income*, Working Paper no. 9490, National Bureau of Economic Research, Cambridge, MA.

Sala-i-Martin, X. (2006), The world distribution of income: falling poverty and ... convergence, period, *Quarterly Journal of Economics*, 121: 351–97.

Santos Silva, J. M. C., and S. Tenreyro (2006), The log of gravity, *Review of Economics and Statistics*, 88: 641–58.

Samuelson, P. A. (1952), The transfer problem and transport costs: the terms of trade when impediments are absent, *Economic Journal*, 62: 278–304.

Schelling, T. C. (1978), *Micromotives and Macrobehavior*, New York: W. W. Norton.

Scitovsky, T. (1954), Two concepts of external economies, *Journal of Political Economy*, 62: 143–51.

Scott, A. J. (2000), Economic geography: the great half-century, in G. L. Clark, M. P. Feldman, and M. S. Gertler (eds.), *The Oxford Handbook of Economic Geography*, Oxford: Oxford University Press, 18–49.

(2004), A perspective of economic geography, *Journal of Economic Geography*, 5: 479–99.

(2006), *Handbook of Regional and Urban Economics*, vol 4: a view from geography, *Journal of Economic Geography*, 6: 104–7.

Shone, R. (1997), *Economic Dynamics*, Cambridge: Cambridge University Press.

Simmons, B. A., and Z. Elkins (2004), The globalization of liberalization: policy diffusion in the international political economy, *American Political Science Review*, 98: 171–89.

Simon, H. (1955), On a class of skew distribution functions, *Biometrika*, 42: 425–40.

Sinn, H. W. (2003), *The New Systems Competition*, Oxford: Basil Blackwell.

Sjöberg, Ö., and F. Sjöholm (2002), Common ground? Prospects for integrating the economic geography of geographers and economists, *Environment and Planning*, A, 34: 467–86.

Smith, A. (1776), *An Inquiry into the Nature and Causes of the Wealth of Nations*, London: Strahan and Cadell.

Solow, R. M. (1994), Perspectives on growth theory, *Journal of Economic Perspectives*, 8: 45–54.

Soo, K. T. (2005), Zipf's law for cities: a cross-country investigation, *Regional Science and Urban Economics*, 35: 239–63.

Spence, A. M. (1976), Product selection, fixed costs and monopolistic competition, *Review of Economic Studies*, 43: 217–35.

Stalker, P. (2000), *Workers without Frontiers: The Impact of Globalization on International Migration*, Geneva: International Labour Organization.

Starrett, D. (1978), Market allocation of location choice in a model with free mobility, *Journal of Economic Theory*, 17: 21–37.

Stelder, D. (2005), A geographical agglomeration model for Europe, *Journal of Regional Science*, 45: 657–79.

Stewart, J. Q. (1947), Suggested principles of "social physics," *Science*, 106: 179–80.

(1948), Demographic gravitation: evidence and applications, *Sociometry*, 11: 31–58.

Stiglitz, J. E. (2004), Reflections on the state of the theory of monopolistic competition, in S. Brakman and B. Heijdra (eds.), *The Monopolistic Competition Revolution in Retrospect*, Cambridge: Cambridge University Press, 134–48.

Storper, M. (1997), *The Regional World: Territorial Development in a Global Economy*, New York: Guilford Press.

(2003), *Institutions, Incentives and Communication in Economic Geography*, Heidelberg: Franz Steiner Verlag.

Storper, M., and A. J. Venables (2004) Buzz: face-to-face contact and the urban economy, *Journal of Economic Geography*, 4: 351–70.

Sutton, J. (1997), Gibrat's legacy, *Journal of Economic Literature*, 45: 40–59.

Tabuchi, T. (1998), Urban agglomeration and dispersion: a synthesis of Alonso and Krugman, *Regional Science and Urban Economics*, 44: 333–51.

Tabuchi, T. and J.-F. Thisse (2002), Taste heterogeneity, labor mobility and economic geography, *Journal of Development Economics*, 69: 155–77.

Thirlwall, T. (1991), *Growth and Development, with Special Reference to Developing Countries*, London: Macmillan.

Thomas, A. (1996), Increasing returns, congestion costs and the geographic concentration of firms, mimeo, International Monetary Fund, Washington, DC.

Tinbergen, J. (1962), *Shaping the World Economy*, New York: Twentieth Century Fund.

Tirole, J. (1988), *The Theory of Industrial Organization*, Cambridge, MA: MIT Press.

UNCTAD (1996), *Incentives and Foreign Direct Investment*, Geneva: United Nations Conference on Trade and Development.

(2006), *World Investment Report 2006*, Geneva: United Nations Conference on Trade and Development.

UNFPA (2007), *State of World Population 2007*, New York: United Nations Population Fund.

Van Bergeijk, P. A. G., and H. Oldersma (1990), Détente, market-oriented reform and German unification: potential consequences for the world trade system, *Kyklos*, 43: 599–609.

Van Houtum, H. (1998), The development of cross-border economic relations, PhD thesis, Tilburg University, Tilburg.

Van Marrewijk, C. (1999), Capital accumulation, learning and endogenous growth, *Oxford Economic Papers*, 51: 453–75.

(2000), Factor abundance and geographical economics, mimeo, Erasmus University, Rotterdam.

(2006), Geographical economics model with congestion, in N. Schuh and P. Schuster (eds.), *New Regional Economics in Central European Economies: The Future of CENTROPE*, Vienna: Oesterreichische Nationalbank, 17–35.

(2007), *International Economics: Theory, Application and Policy*, Oxford: Oxford University Press.

(forthcoming 2009), Intra-industry trade, in: K. A. Reinert and R. S. Rajan (eds.), *The Princeton Encyclopedia of the World Economy*, Princeton, NJ: Princeton University Press.

Van Marrewijk, C., J. Stibora, and J.-M. Viaene (1994), *Capital Goods and Baumol's Law*, Discussion Paper no. 94-42, Tinbergen Institute, Amsterdam.

Van Marrewijk, C., and J. Verbeek (1993), Sector-specific capital, "bang-bang" investment and the Filippov solution, *Journal of Economics*, 57: 131–46.

Venables, A. J. (1985), Trade and trade policy with imperfect competition: the case of identical products and free entry, *Journal of International Economics*, 19: 1–20.

(1996), Equilibrium locations of vertically linked industries, *International Economic Review*, 37: 341–59.

(1998), Localization of industry and trade performance, *Oxford Review of Economic Policy*, 12: 52–60.

(1999), Fragmentation and multinational production, *European Economic Review*, 43: 935–45.

Venables, A. J., and N. Limao (2002), Geographical disadvantage: a Heckscher–Ohlin–von-Thünen model of international specialisation, *Journal of International Economics*, 58: 239–63.

Von Thünen, J. H. (1826), *Der Isolierte Staat in Beziehung auf Landwirtschaft und Nationalökonomie*, Hamburg: Perthes.

Weber, A. (1909), *Über den Standort der Industrien*, Tübingen: JCB Mohr.

Weibull, J. W. (1995), *Evolutionary Game Theory*, Cambridge, MA: MIT Press.

Wilson, J. (1999), Theories of tax competition, *National Tax Journal*, 52: 263–304.

Wong, K. Y. (1986), Are international trade and factor mobility substitutes?, *Journal of International Economics*, 20: 25–44.

Wooldridge, J. M. (2000), *Introductory Econometrics*, Cincinnati: South-Western College Publishing.

World Bank (2002), *Globalization, Growth and Poverty: Building an Inclusive World Economy*, Oxford: Oxford University Press.

(2006), *World Development Indicators 2006*, Washington, DC: World Bank.

WTO (2006), *World Trade Report*, Geneva: World Trade Organization.

Zipf, G. K. (1949), *Human Behavior and the Principle of Least Effort*, New York: Addison-Wesley.

Zodrow, G. R., and P. Mieszkowski (1986), Pigou, Tiebout, property taxation, and the underprovision of local public goods, *Journal of Urban Economics*, 19: 356–70.

Index

Lightning Source UK Ltd.
Milton Keynes UK
UKHW05f0815070218
317498UK00006B/61/P